D1294312

497609

Poets of Great Britain and Ireland, 1945
PSCR PN451.+D52v.27

3 1797 10005 2624

Dictionary of Literary Biography • Volume Twenty-seven

Poets of Great Britain and Ireland, 1945-1960

NO LONGER

PROPERTY OF

HAVERFORD COLLEGE

Dictionary of Literary Biography

1: *The American Renaissance in New England*, edited by Joel Myerson (1978)
2: *American Novelists Since World War II*, edited by Jeffrey Helterman and Richard Layman (1978)
3: *Antebellum Writers in New York and the South*, edited by Joel Myerson (1979)
4: *American Writers in Paris, 1920-1939*, edited by Karen Lane Rood (1980)
5: *American Poets Since World War II*, 2 parts, edited by Donald J. Greiner (1980)
6: *American Novelists Since World War II*, Second Series, edited by James E. Kibler, Jr. (1980)
7: *Twentieth-Century American Dramatists*, 2 parts, edited by John MacNicholas (1981)
8: *Twentieth-Century American Science-Fiction Writers*, 2 parts, edited by David Cowart and Thomas L. Wymer (1981)
9: *American Novelists, 1910-1945*, 3 parts, edited by James J. Martine (1981)
10: *Modern British Dramatists, 1900-1945*, 2 parts, edited by Stanley Weintraub (1982)
11: *American Humorists, 1800-1950*, 2 parts, edited by Stanley Trachtenberg (1982)
12: *American Realists and Naturalists*, edited by Donald Pizer and Earl N. Harbert (1982)
13: *British Dramatists Since World War II*, 2 parts, edited by Stanley Weintraub (1982)
14: *British Novelists Since 1960*, 2 parts, edited by Jay L. Halio (1983)
15: *British Novelists, 1930-1959*, 2 parts, edited by Bernard Oldsey (1983)
16: *The Beats: Literary Bohemians in Postwar America*, 2 parts, edited by Ann Charters (1983)
17: *Twentieth-Century American Historians*, edited by Clyde N. Wilson (1983)
18: *Victorian Novelists After 1885*, edited by Ira B. Nadel and William E. Fredeman (1983)
19: *British Poets, 1880-1914*, edited by Donald E. Stanford (1983)
20: *British Poets, 1914-1945*, edited by Donald E. Stanford (1983)
21: *Victorian Novelists Before 1885*, edited by Ira B. Nadel and William E. Fredeman (1983)
22: *American Writers for Children, 1900-1960*, edited by John Cech (1983)
23: *American Newspaper Journalists, 1873-1900*, edited by Perry J. Ashley (1983)
24: *American Colonial Writers, 1606-1734*, edited by Emory Elliott (1984)
25: *American Newspaper Journalists, 1901-1925*, edited by Perry J. Ashley (1984)
26: *American Screenwriters*, edited by Robert E. Morsberger, Stephen O. Lesser, and Randall Clark (1984)
27: *Poets of Great Britain and Ireland, 1945-1960*, edited by Vincent B. Sherry, Jr. (1984)

Documentary Series:
1: *Sherwood Anderson, Willa Cather, John Dos Passos, Theodore Dreiser, F. Scott Fitzgerald, Ernest Hemingway, Sinclair Lewis*, edited by Margaret A. Van Antwerp (1982)
2: *James Gould Cozzens, James T. Farrell, William Faulkner, John O'Hara, John Steinbeck, Thomas Wolfe, Richard Wright*, edited by Margaret A. Van Antwerp (1982)
3: *Saul Bellow, Jack Kerouac, Norman Mailer, Vladimir Nabokov, John Updike, Kurt Vonnegut*, edited by Mary Bruccoli (1983)
4: *Tennessee Williams*, edited by Margaret A. Van Antwerp and Sally Johns (1984)

Yearbooks:
1980, edited by Karen L. Rood, Jean W. Ross, and Richard Ziegfeld (1981)
1981, edited by Karen L. Rood, Jean W. Ross, and Richard Ziegfeld (1982)
1982, edited by Richard Ziegfeld; associate editors: Jean W. Ross and Lynne C. Zeigler (1983)
1983, edited by Mary Bruccoli and Jean W. Ross; associate editor: Richard Ziegfeld (1984)

Dictionary of Literary Biography • Volume Twenty-seven

Poets of Great Britain and Ireland, 1945-1960

Edited by
Vincent B. Sherry, Jr.
Villanova University

A Bruccoli Clark Book
Gale Research Company • Book Tower • Detroit, Michigan 48226

Advisory Board for
DICTIONARY OF LITERARY BIOGRAPHY

Louis S. Auchincloss
John Baker
D. Philip Baker
A. Walton Litz, Jr.
Peter S. Prescott
Lola L. Szladits
William Targ

Matthew J. Bruccoli and Richard Layman, *Editorial Directors*
C. E. Frazer Clark, Jr., *Managing Editor*

Manufactured by Edwards Brothers, Inc.
Ann Arbor, Michigan
Printed in the United States of America

Copyright © 1984
GALE RESEARCH COMPANY

Library of Congress Cataloging in Publication Data
Main entry under title:

Poets of Great Britain and Ireland, 1945-1960.

(Dictionary of literary biography; v. 27)
"A Bruccoli Clark book."
Includes index.
1. English poetry—20th century—History and criticism. 2. English poetry—20th century—Bio-bibliography. 3. Poets, English—20th century—Biography. I. Sherry, Vincent B. II. Series.
PR610.P56   1984   821'.914[B]   84-5994
ISBN 0-8103-1705-2

For Hiroko

497609

Contents

Contents

Plan of the Series

. . . Almost the most prodigious asset of a country, and perhaps its most precious possession, is its native literary product—when that product is fine and noble and enduring.

Mark Twain*

The advisory board, the editors, and the publisher of the *Dictionary of Literary Biography* are joined in endorsing Mark Twain's declaration. The literature of a nation provides an inexhaustible resource of permanent worth. It is our expectation that this endeavor will make literature and its creators better understood and more accessible to students and the literate public, while satisfying the standards of teachers and scholars.

To meet these requirements, *literary biography* has been construed in terms of the author's achievement. The most important thing about a writer is his writing. Accordingly, the entries in *DLB* are career biographies, tracing the development of the author's canon and the evolution of his reputation.

The publication plan for *DLB* resulted from two years of preparation. The project was proposed to Bruccoli Clark by Frederick G. Ruffner, president of the Gale Research Company, in November 1975. After specimen entries were prepared and typeset, an advisory board was formed to refine the entry format and develop the series rationale. In meetings held during 1976, the publisher, series editors, and advisory board approved the scheme for a comprehensive biographical dictionary of persons who contributed to North American literature. Editorial work on the first volume began in January 1977, and it was published in 1978.

In order to make *DLB* more than a reference tool and to compile volumes that individually have claim to status as literary history, it was decided to organize volumes by topic or period or genre. Each of these freestanding volumes provides a biographical-bibliographical guide and overview for a particular area of literature. We are convinced that this organization—as opposed to a single alphabet method—constitutes a valuable innovation in the presentation of reference material. The volume plan necessarily requires many decisions for the

placement and treatment of authors who might properly be included in two or three volumes. In some instances a major figure will be included in separate volumes, but with different entries emphasizing the aspect of his career appropriate to each volume. Ernest Hemingway, for example, is represented in *American Writers in Paris, 1920-1939* by an entry focusing on his expatriate apprenticeship; he is also in *American Novelists, 1910-1945* with an entry surveying his entire career. Each volume includes a cumulative index of subject authors. The final *DLB* volume will be a comprehensive index to the entire series.

With volume ten in 1982 it was decided to enlarge the scope of *DLB* beyond the literature of the United States. By the end of 1983 twelve volumes treating British literature had been published, and volumes for Commonwealth and Modern European literature were in progress. The series has been further augmented by the *DLB Yearbooks* (since 1981) which update published entries and add new entries to keep the *DLB* current with contemporary activity. There have also been occasional *DLB Documentary Series* volumes which provide biographical and critical background source materials for figures whose work is judged to have particular interest for students. One of these companion volumes is entirely devoted to Tennessee Williams.

The purpose of *DLB* is not only to provide reliable information in a convenient format but also to place the figures in the larger perspective of literary history and to offer appraisals of their accomplishments by qualified scholars.

We define literature as the *intellectual commerce of a nation*: not merely as belles lettres, but as that ample and complex process by which ideas are generated, shaped, and transmitted. *DLB* entries are not limited to "creative writers" but extend to other figures who in this time and in this way influenced the mind of the people. Thus the series encompasses historians, journalists, publishers, and screenwriters. By this means readers of *DLB* may be aided to perceive literature not as cult scripture in the keeping of cultural high priests, but as at the center of a nation's life.

DLB includes the major writers appropriate to each volume and those standing in the ranks immediately behind them. Scholarly and critical counsel has been sought in deciding which minor figures to include and how full their entries should be.

*From an unpublished section of Mark Twain's autobiography, copyright © by the Mark Twain Company.

Wherever possible, useful references will be made to figures who do not warrant separate entries.

Each *DLB* volume has a volume editor responsible for planning the volume, selecting the figures for inclusion, and assigning the entries. Volume editors are also responsible for preparing, where appropriate, appendices surveying the major periodicals and literary and intellectual movements for their volumes, as well as lists of further readings. Work on the series as a whole is coordinated at the Bruccoli Clark editorial center in Columbia, South Carolina, where the editorial staff is responsible for the accuracy of the published volumes.

One feature that distinguishes *DLB* is the illustration policy—its concern with the iconography of literature. Just as an author is influenced by his surroundings, so is the reader's understanding of the author enhanced by a knowledge of his environment. Therefore *DLB* volumes include not only drawings, paintings, and photographs of authors, often depicting them at various stages in their careers, but also illustrations of their families and places where they lived. Title pages are regularly reproduced in facsimile along with dust jackets for modern authors. The dust jackets are a special fea-ture of *DLB* because they often document better than anything else the way in which an author's work was launched in its own time. Specimens of the writers' manuscripts are included when feasible.

A supplement to *DLB*—tentatively titled *A Guide, Chronology, and Glossary for American Literature*—will outline the history of literature in North America and trace the influences that shaped it. This volume will provide a framework for the study of American literature by means of chronological tables, literary affiliation charts, glossarial entries, and concise surveys of the major movements. It has been planned to stand on its own as a vade mecum, providing a ready-reference guide to the study of American literature as well as a companion to the *DLB* volumes for American literature.

Samuel Johnson rightly decreed that "The chief glory of every people arises from its authors." The purpose of the *Dictionary of Literary Biography* is to compile literary history in the surest way available to us—by accurate and comprehensive treatment of the lives and work of those who contributed to it.

The *DLB* Advisory Board

Foreword

The fifteen years following World War II is now an identifiable period in the history of modern British poetry. At its center is the group of poets known as The Movement, which emerged in the mid-1950s. Conservative and formalist in practice, neoclassical in outlook, these poets were reacting against the romantic writers of the "New Apocalypse" in the 1940s, while their normative attitudes created the opposition of the Mavericks in the 1950s. All three groups produced anthologies with polemical prefaces, which express, all in all, the concerns recurring to many of the poets who found these years a first flourishing period. Thus the 1940s and 1950s reveal a lively variety of tastes and allegiances among poets. In an important sense, too, the war preceded and provided for these literary groupings.

Writing in the face of global ideological war, poets of the New Apocalypse shunned the political commentary of many 1930s writers. Assaulted by the physical experience of war, seeking to reach an equal level of emotionally and sensually charged awareness, they exaggerated the mannerisms of earlier romantics such as Dylan Thomas. Thus G. S. Fraser insisted, in his introduction to *The White Horseman: prose and verse of the new apocalypse* (1941), that the poet was no ideologue but an imaginative mythmaker. To fulfill this role, the poet should shift his source of energy and force a tap into the subconscious mind. Unlike some surrealists of the 1920s, however, Fraser stressed the need to control the arbitrary imagery of the dream flow through intellect and will. Will can allow rhetoric to do the work of the imagination, Yeats had cautioned, and most verse of the New Apocalypse seems even more forced than obscure. Norman MacCaig and Vernon Scannell would later repudiate the poetry they wrote under this influence, while Edwin Morgan soon parodied the practices he had followed. Nonetheless, the New Apocalypse remained an influential force, continuing to generate discipleship and reaction into the 1950s.

This reaction found its chief expression in the introduction to Robert Conquest's anthology of Movement poets, *New Lines* (1956), including work by Conquest, Kingsley Amis, Donald Davie, D. J. Enright, Thom Gunn, John Holloway, Elizabeth Jennings, Philip Larkin, and John Wain. The most typical and obvious sign of Conquest's reactionary

stance is his tendency, in assessing the common qualities of his writers, to define by negatives. Thus the poets shared "a negative determination to avoid bad principles." Such principles were notions related to "great systems of theoretical constructs" and "unconscious commands," terms hinting at the political and literary excesses of the 1940s. Along the same lines, Kingsley Amis, writing a Fabian tract on romanticism, would associate the ideological extremism of the recent war with the emotional and imaginative excesses of romanticism, which could lead one, he suggested, to believe in causes that are not one's own, that are not subject to the approval of the individual's reason.

If poets in The Movement were cynical, in Conquest's words, about the "collapse of public taste" in the previous decade, they were also attempting to regenerate the sensibility. A new humanism stressed the value of individual intelligence, the power of reason to check and guide the emotions, the use of traditional forms as a means of control. Paradoxically, though, control most became a problem when there was too little to be controlled. A certain hollowness, a drably mechanical quality, lingers in some poets' attempts to revive traditional verse forms. Davie most frequently attained the intelligent lucidity and classical economy the others sought. His literary criticism, moreover, most notably his *Purity of Diction in English Verse* (1952) and *Articulate Energy: An Enquiry into the Syntax of English Poetry* (1955), served as a touchstone for most poets in The Movement. Davie rejected the work of most modernists, who had dislocated syntax to accommodate their hard images and imaginative leaps, and reclaimed a conventional prose syntax for rational statements in verse. This emphasis moved, in practice, in two directions, toward two models. The native, plain speech of Thomas Hardy appealed to Davie and Larkin as an idiom for clear discourse. Wain, and Davie occasionally, handled a more sententious kind of statement, the witty celebrations of William Empson, but other poets found it easier to imitate Empson's stylistic mannerisms than to capture his elusive intelligence.

That a number of poets in The Movement were also novelists helps to explain their capacity for anecdotal narrative, their attention to concrete setting and realistic characters, and their aptitude for social observation in verse. Thus Amis could write poetic miniatures of social comedies such as *Lucky Jim*. Enright found scenes for many poems among the working classes, whom he described sometimes in comic but never in patronizing tones. Larkin's much-anthologized "Mr. Bleaney" typifies The Movement poet's observation of character from the outside, through the details of Bleaney's room, while his "Church-going" expresses the empiricist's skepticism about matters of religion and myth. This element of imaginative shyness in some Movement poetry, however, became a target for critics. The *TLS* reviewer of *New Lines* disliked the "fear of the irrational," a sensibility at odds with "the deepest springs of poetry."

This critic seems to have reacted to the categorical principles of the introduction, not to actual poems. In fact, the backgrounds and tastes of the poets were more pluralistic, their practices more varied, than is commonly recognized even now. Larkin, after all, had passed through a Yeatsian phase in the years of the New Apocalypse. Wain was capable of admiring Dylan Thomas's *Collected Poems* even while he deplored the excesses of romanticism. Elizabeth Jennings, who shared the other poets' dislike for mystification, could preserve a deep religiousness in her poems. Thom Gunn, as the poet most conspicuously different from others in the group, also shows the range of variation within its central concerns. The emphasis on control through poetic form and wit reaches a kind of savage intensity in some of his early poems, and reveals a disturbing parallel in the experience of power through psychological domination. Other poets were sometimes critical, moreover, of those central values of restraint, reason, and form. Davie's "Limited Achievement," for example, might be read as a critique of restrained poetry in particular, programmatic confinement in general.

More eclectic than narrowly programmatic, The Movement could have included a number of other poets not featured in Conquest's anthology. These writers seemed to be extending, in various ways, the general reaction against the excesses of the 1940s. Thus Charles Causley progressed through the 1950s to the tightly formal structures of his mature work; he emphasized increasingly the value of graceful simplicity, while the essential conservatism of The Movement shows in his restoration of the ballad form. Similarly, C. H. Sisson apprenticed himself to the classical authors he was translating, attempting to develop for his own poetry a manner of elegant plainness. Anne Ridler evolved a metaphysical style whose forceful clarity seems related not so much to seventeenth-century models as

to the standards of The Movement. Thomas Kinsella committed himself to the forming and ordering power of verse, and so moved into alignment with poets who were, as the *TLS* reviewer of *New Lines* had put it, "makers rather than bards." Similarly, in the face of religious divisions in Northern Ireland, John Hewitt resembles Movement poets in preferring individual reason over group compulsions, and expresses his medial stance in politics through deliberated, thoughtful cadences. The most striking case of a poet developing in step with The Movement, and with literary history, is Norman MaçCaig, who appeared in *The White Horseman*, then abjured those surrealistic excesses and engaged in his "long haul to lucidity" through the 1950s and 1960s.

Reaction against The Movement came so quickly—*Mavericks* (1957), edited by Dannie Abse and Howard Sergeant—that it seemed merely a reflex action, venting resentment at exclusion rather than expressing a considered poetic stance. But Abse, exchanging letters with Sergeant to introduce their collection, goes beyond cynicism; he sustains a coherent argument for specific qualities in poetry. While he does not deny the importance of discipline and form and stylistic finish, he questions the neat formulas of Movement poets, and challenges a flat, empirical, merely referential character in their language. Not a tool of reference, the poetic word might be a unit of resonance; not a window on a world that is already there, but a medium for conjuring what is possible to imagination. He aimed thus at recovering that "mysterious, permanent element in poetry that irradiates and moves us and endures down the centuries"—phrases that hint at his link with the romantic and apocalyptic poets of the previous decade.

Since a school of mavericks is a contradiction in terms, these writers might be expected to vary considerably in practice from Abse's precepts. Nonetheless, the most important poets in the collection conformed in different ways to his principles. Abse's own poems could open easily, empirically, then reverse their perspectives, provide surprises that evoke the mystery behind the matter. Jon Silkin cultivated the oracular voice of the prophet, and joined the vatic privilege, at various levels of effectiveness, with urgently personal and political concerns. Michael Hamburger's early work reveals some parallels with Yeats, whose aesthetic ideals and symbolist principles help to produce a poetry of formal perfection and mysterious power.

Other poets, likewise opposed to the apparent clarities of The Movement, used symbolist techniques and mythic or religious subjects. John

Heath-Stubbs, who was associated with the romantics in the 1940s, developed Celtic and Mediterranean myths as poetic material, and absorbed some of the techniques of French symbolism through his translations. Norse myths joined with Catholicism to provide the imaginative medium for George Mackay Brown, an isolated and rather eccentric figure, who sought to recover in verse the enchantment of ancient legends. More facile, the early poetry of James Kirkup indulged in automatic writing to release the mythic and archetypal patterns of the imagination, though, like MacCaig, he tempered the excesses in late volumes. *Patmos and Other Poems* (1955) linked Robin Skelton to the apocalyptic prophet John of Patmos, and to the New Apocalyptic writers of the 1940s, while a Jungian influence led him to the subconscious in search of archetypal configurations. Thomas Blackburn's poetry could move through Yeatsian incantations toward a type of visionary religious experience, while his incipient madness gives the verse its peculiar intensity. Jack Clemo's physical handicaps largely confined his awareness to his native landscapes of Cornwall and the religious indoctrination from his mother, but his symbolist techniques and Calvinist preoccupations joined him with these other poets in the 1950s.

Variously regional and Celtic in their affinities, a number of poets ranged far from the central, normative, up-to-date, "BBC" tones of The Movement. Local, ancient, rooted, the culture of the south Cumberland coast provided much of the substance of Norman Nicholson's poetry, while his verse dramas display patterns of primitive ritual still limned in the folk life. R. S. Thomas, finest of the Welsh poets, focuses in detail on the landscapes, customs, and peculiar temperaments of his rural parishioners. Unsentimental, unidealized in view, Thomas's poems show, in their strong accentual beat and shapely cadences, a quality of tough, proud craftsmanship, characteristic of the countryman. Roland Mathias has used the cultural history of Wales imaginatively as a poet, and promoted it as an editor, while Leslie Norris and John Ormond have followed in the tradition of Welsh lyricism. Hugh MacDiarmid's earlier achievements with the Scots dialect helped Tom Scott and Sydney Goodsir Smith to reclaim it for their poetry. The musical density of Scots, the knotty particularity of

its words, seemed to limit its scope, however, to lyric and descriptive verse.

A separate line of dissent from The Movement appears in the work of Edwin Morgan: experiments with open form, combining the projective verse of the American Black Mountain poets with concrete and phonic poetry. Morgan's pyrotechnical flair also harkened back to the modernists, who provided a point of reference for poets at odds with the conservative mainstream. Thus Christopher Logue followed the lead of Pound in his creative remakings of classical literature, while his resistance to established tastes led him into the counterculture of pop poetry, play- and poster-poems in the 1960s.

Many poets included in this volume of the *Dictionary of Literary Biography* continued to refine their practices in subsequent decades, and some would significantly alter their styles. Nonetheless, the historical situation and critical debates of the 1940s and 1950s shaped alternatives for developing talents, and so exerted a formative influence on many careers. The most important force, The Movement, helped to launch at least three of the major poets in the period: Davie, Gunn, and Larkin. Kinsella is also a superior talent, while the achievements of Hamburger, Silkin, and R. S. Thomas will probably gain greater recognition. It is fair to say, however, that few poets dealt directly and intelligently with the chief historical influence on them, the atrocities of World War II. (Henry Reed's verse is a notable exception.) The approach of the New Apocalypse to war was obviously compulsive and sensationalist, but the attitudes and practices of The Movement remained defensive and reactionary. Keith Douglas, killed late in the war, had written poems penetrating to the intellectual and emotional paradoxes of combat. Largely disregarded for his imaginative daring by Movement poets in the 1950s, he would draw the admiration of such poets as Geoffrey Hill, Ted Hughes, and Charles Tomlinson, who began publishing in that decade, but who belong temperamentally to the next generation. Continuing to develop at odds with the standards of The Movement, these and other poets were also responding to new pressures, and will be included in the forthcoming *DLB* volume *Poets of Great Britain and Ireland Since 1960*.

–Vincent B. Sherry, Jr.

Acknowledgments

This book was produced by BC Research. Karen L. Rood, senior editor for the *Dictionary of Literary Biography* series, was the in-house editor.

The production manager is Lynne C. Zeigler. Art supervisor is Claudia Ericson. Copyediting supervisor is Joycelyn R. Smith. Typesetting supervisor is Laura Ingram. The production staff includes Mary Betts, Rowena Betts, Patricia Coate, Lynn Felder, Kathleen M. Flanagan, Joyce Fowler, Patricia C. Sharpe, and Meredith Walker. Jean W. Ross is permissions editor. Joseph Caldwell, photography editor, did the photographic copy work for the volume.

Helpful advice has been given by Neil Brennan, John Matthias, John Press, James K. Robinson, and Donald Stanford. Virginia Bondurant and Joan McLaughlin, secretaries in the English Department at Villanova University, have performed a number of essential tasks. Mark Niemeyer and Irja Uotila, research assistants, worked with Helen Kerrigan and other staff members in the Falvey Library at Villanova to help secure research materials.

Walter W. Ross did the library research with the assistance of the staff at the Thomas Cooper Library of the University of South Carolina: Lynn Barron, Sue Collins, Michael Freeman, Gary Geer, Alexander M. Gilchrist, Jens Holley, David Lincove, Marcia Martin, Roger Mortimer, Harriet B. Oglesbee, Jean Rhyne, Karen Rissling, Paula Swope, and Ellen Tillett.

Anthony Rota of Bertram Rota, Ltd., was especially helpful in providing illustrations for this volume.

Poets of Great Britain and Ireland, 1945-1960

Dictionary of Literary Biography

Dannie Abse
(22 September 1923-   )

Daniel Hoffman
University of Pennsylvania

SELECTED BOOKS: *After Every Green Thing* (London: Hutchinson, 1948);

Walking Under Water (London: Hutchinson, 1952);

Ash on a Young Man's Sleeve (London: Hutchinson, 1954; New York: Criterion, 1954);

Some Corner of an English Field (London: Hutchinson, 1956; New York: Criterion, 1956);

Fire in Heaven (London: Hutchinson, 1956);

Tenants of the House (London: Hutchinson, 1957; New York: Criterion, 1958);

The Eccentric (London: Evans, 1961);

Poems, Golders Green (London: Hutchinson, 1962);

Dannie Abse (London: Vista Books, 1963);

Three Questor Plays (Lowestoft, Suffolk: Scorpion Press, 1967)—includes *House of Cowards, Gone*, and *In the Cage*;

Medicine on Trial (London: Aldus, 1968; New York: Crown, 1969);

A Small Desperation (London: Hutchinson, 1968);

Demo (Frensham, Surrey: Sceptre Press, 1969);

O Jones, O Jones (London: Hutchinson, 1970);

Selected Poems (London: Hutchinson, 1970; New York: Oxford University Press, 1970);

The Dogs of Pavlov (London: Vallentine, Mitchell, 1973);

Funland and Other Poems (London: Hutchinson, 1973; New York: Oxford University Press, 1973);

A Poet in the Family (London: Hutchinson, 1974);

Collected Poems 1948-1976 (London: Hutchinson, 1977; Pittsburgh: University of Pittsburgh Press, 1977);

Pythagoras (London: Hutchinson, 1979);

Way Out in the Centre (London: Hutchinson, 1981);

Miscellany One (Bridgend, Mid Glamorgan: Poetry Wales Press, 1981);

A Strong Dose of Myself (London: Hutchinson, 1982);

One-Legged on Ice (Athens: University of Georgia Press, 1983).

OTHER: *Mavericks*, edited by Abse and Howard

Sergeant (London: Editions Poetry & Poverty, 1957);

Modern European Verse, edited by Abse (London: Vista Books, 1964);

Corgi Modern Poets in Focus, volumes 1, 3, and 5, edited by Abse (London: Corgi, 1971, 1971, 1973);

Poetry Dimension 2-7, edited by Abse (London: Robson, 1974-1980);

My Medical School, edited by Abse (London: Robson, 1978).

"Way out in the center," the title of his 1981 volume of poems, is how Dannie Abse situates his own work in relation to that of his contemporaries. In a series of six annual anthologies of poetry and criticism (*Poetry Dimension 2-7*, 1974-1980) he has acknowledged by the catholicity of his taste the "variousness and lucidity" of British poetry. On a map of the territory that ranges from the romantic primitivism of Ted Hughes to the modernist sophistication of Charles Tomlinson, from the chthonic depths of Geoffrey Hill to the plangent ironies of Philip Larkin, Dannie Abse occupies an identifiable place, at once in the central British tradition of poetry as a social act of communication and yet "way out" at a distance from the work of his principal fellow poets. Introducing his *Collected Poems* (1977), he says that his ambition is "to write poems which appear translucent but are in fact deceptions. I would have a reader enter them, be deceived he could see through them like sea-water, and be puzzled when he can not quite touch the bottom." Further, he would "wish to look upon the world with the eyes of a perpetual convalescent." Among his abiding themes is the relationship, in art and in belief, between truth and illusion; and as for being "a perpetual convalescent," the phrase implies Abse's openness to experience, his humanistic optimism. For this "convalescent" is in fact a medical doctor whose experience of life, sickness, and death informs his poetry. He well knows the limits of the doctor's art; yet "convalescence" suggests the possibility of recovery from the ills of life. For Abse such recovery, such redemptive knowledge, comes from the poet's insight into what the doctor cannot see. The claims and attitudes to experience of the physician and those of the poet are among the dichotomies whose tensions give Abse's work its interest and its power.

Abse was born to Kate Shepherd and Rudolf Abse on 22 September 1923 in Cardiff, Wales. His father part owned and operated several motion-picture theaters in the Welsh valleys. Abse attended St. Illtyd's College, Cardiff (1935-1941; matriculation, 1940), and the University of South Wales and Monmouthshire (1941-1942). He received his medical training at King's College, London (1942-1944), and Westminster Hospital (1944-1947 and 1949-1950), and is a Member of the Royal College of Surgeons and a Licentiate of the Royal College of Physicians.

During postwar service as a squadron leader in the R.A.F. (1951-1955), Dr. Abse was posted to a military chest clinic near Middlesex Hospital in London. He has remained on its staff as a civilian chest specialist. He married Joan Mercer in 1951; they have three children and live in the London suburb of Golders Green. Abse's first book of verse, *After Every Green Thing* (1948), appeared when he was twenty-five and in medical school. Since then he has published eleven volumes of poems, three novels, and eight plays. Along the way he also edited a little magazine, and wrote a survey of British medicine (*Medicine on Trial*, 1968), an autobiography (*A Poet in the Family*, 1974), and a collection of essays (*A Strong Dose of Myself*, 1982). He was given the Charles Henry Foyle New Play Award in 1960 for *House of Cowards* (published in *Three Questor Plays*, 1967) and received a Welsh Council Award in 1971. Abse is a Fellow of the Royal Society of Literature. In 1973-1974 he was Poet in Residence at Princeton University, and he frequently visits the United States.

Although Abse's parents were financially insecure in the 1930s, one brother and several relatives went on to become physicians, and his other brother, Leo, became a prominent Labour M.P. "There were few poetry books in the house," but young Abse "was exposed to the adult dialogue of the thirties . . . between Sigmund Freud and Karl Marx," as "interpreted and argued by my two elder brothers." Abse was attracted to John Lehmann and Stephen Spender's anthology, *Poems for Spain* (1939), where he first found "poets whose adult moral concerns and protestations engaged my own wrath and imagination. Their voices had a passionate immediacy and their language was fresh, of the twentieth century." Abse's own writings are consistently focused on "moral concerns." From 1949 to 1954 he edited a desultory little magazine entitled *Poetry and Poverty*. His play *The Dogs of Pavlov*, based upon experiments by the psychologist Stanley Milgram, explores "how men would obey commands that were in strong conflict with their conscience," and thus grapples with what Hannah Arendt, referring to the Holocaust, called "the banality of evil." Abse's poems, though not usually political, address responsibility to others and to oneself. The subtitle of Joan Abse's biography, *John Ruskin*, can as well apply to her husband: *The Passionate Moralist.*

Publishing his *Collected Poems* in 1977, Abse reached no farther back 'Ian 1948; nothing appears from his first book, which he has dismissed as "apprentice work," in the vein of "the then fashionable neo-romantic school," with diction "too florid and approximate," "themes too arcane, too private," and the "unpremeditated influences . . . of Dylan Thomas and Rainer Maria Rilke." In *Walking Under Water* (1952) Abse moved away from such joint-stock lyricism toward a more individual diction, attempting in time to avoid both the stridency of political verse ("A voice shouting . . . becomes the raised voice of anonymous humanity") and the opposite anonymity of "pure song" that "has no particular voice in it." "In the 1950s, I still wished to tell it slant and tell it eloquently . . . not conversationally, flatly, but with my voice not too far away from song." At this time Abse identified the Dionysian element in poetry—his own, and poetry generally—with the romanticism he was soon to modify.

The principal movement of British poetry in the 1950s was the one which modestly accepted the designation The Movement, defined by Robert Conquest in his introduction to the anthology *New Lines* in 1956. Here nine disparate poets (among them Philip Larkin, Donald Davie, D. J. Enright, Thom Gunn, and John Wain) were said to share a common aesthetic, free from the arbitrary claims of "great systems," "theoretical constructs," and "unconscious commands." Tied down by neither "mystical" nor "logical compulsions," this new British poetry, "like modern philosophy—is empirical in its attitude." A quarter-century later this aesthetic looks like merely a continuation of the commonsensical English lyrical tradition of Hardy and Graves, but at the time *New Lines* stirred up considerable controversy, in which Dannie Abse played a part. Together with Howard Sergeant, Abse mounted a rival anthology, *Mavericks* (1957), protesting that The Movement poets "distrust the image and seem to fear primary Dionysian excitement," as though "afraid of the mystery conversing with the mystery." Accordingly Abse and Sergeant present their rival nine (including Michael Hamburger, Jon Silkin, Vernon Scannell, South African poet David Wright, and Abse). Neither the Mavericks nor The Movement was really a movement, each of the poets going his own way subsequently. But *New Lines* did dramatize the repudiation by some of Britain's leading poets of the grandiloquence of wartime poetry and the rhetorical indulgences of Edith Sitwell and Dylan Thomas, and so reflected their sense of the shrunken possibilities of life in postwar Britain. For Abse, however, the Dionysian element of poetry, as of life, resists the drabness of the quotidian. His own poetry would continue to seek it, though the tone, the style in which he expressed "the mystery conversing with the mystery," would soon become less rhetorical, more a conversational voice of unmistakable individuality.

That Abse was torn between the Dionysian and the drab quotidian is inferable from *Tenants of the House* (1957), with its title's allusion to the "dry thoughts in a dry season" of T. S. Eliot's "Gerontion." In "Poem of celebration" Abse writes, "This world confirms my senses. / / Swaying and drunk with seeing / the near magnificence of things, / I cry out a doxology," a passage he might have written ten years later but for that last word, and goes on to affirm,

> How else may I give thanks, give praise,
> but to trap a visible poem
> in the invisible cage and leave it there?
> Look. I'm back again to where you are.
> I came through a hole in the air.

At this time, as he recalls, he devised "markedly rhythmical structures which progressed as an allegorical or symbolic narrative." These "parable poems" include two of his most successful on overtly political themes: "New Babylons" deals with the pressures of conformity, while "Emperors of the island" is a "political parable" on the lust for power. The parable structure is universalized in "The race," an allegory in which Past, Present, and Future contend in a fated confusion of identities. The balladlike couplets of "The trial" trace the permutations of guilt and identity, the fate of the man whose self is his mask: "I must seek my own face, find my own grave." The theme is explored in "Leaving Cardiff," as the poet, departing from his boyhood home, muses, "Not for one second, I know, / can I be the same man twice." It is elaborated in "Duality"—"Now, now, I hang these masks on the wall. / Oh Christ, take one and leave me all / lest four tears from two eyes fall."

In *Poems, Golders Green* (1962), Abse's individual style becomes clearer, as do the sources and ramifications of his dualities. In "Return to Cardiff," the journey "seemed less a return than a raid / on mislaid identities." One, or rather two, of these identities may be inferred from the title of this volume. *Poems, Golders Green* is a virtual oxymoron, proposing that poems can be found in, or made from, this Jewish suburb, a community at once a part of London and so unlike the rest of England that it has no pub. The English poet returning to Cardiff finds his mislaid identity as a Welshman; the British poet is also a Jew.

The principal poem in his earlier work expressing his Jewish identity had appeared in *Walking Under Water* as "Song," retitled "Song for Dov Shamir" in Abse's *Collected Poems*. This poem, written after the establishment of Israel in 1948, had originally been published as a translation from the Hebrew of an invented Israeli poet. Abse included it among some poems he sent to T. S. Eliot at that time, and "Eliot, who did not know about my Dov Shamir impersonation," advised "that I should do more Dov Shamir translations because they were better than my own work!" Now, more than a dozen years later, having sloughed off the singing voice of "Song for Dov Shamir," Abse treats his dual identities without impersonation. In "After the release of Ezra Pound" Abse explores the difficulty of forgiving Pound, who "did not hear the raw Jewish cry, / the populations committed to the dark." In "Red Balloon," Abse presents a narrative in which the simple, balladlike quatrains present a surreal image of a red balloon—"It was my shame, it was my joy" that "sailed across the startled town," making "the girls of Cardiff sigh," "but to no one dare I show it now / however long they swear their love."

> "It's a Jew's balloon," my best friend cried,
> "stained with our dear Lord's blood."
> "That I'm a Jew is true," I said,
> said I, "that cannot be denied."

The "best friend" cries, "Your red balloon's a Jew's balloon, / let's get it circumcised," but the balloon resists the "dirty knives" with which the boys lunge at it; so they turn upon him and beat him up. This fable invokes by allusion the ball thrown, with such dire results, in the traditional ballad "Sir Hugh, or The Jew's Daughter," based on the putative ritual murder of Hugh of Lincolnshire in the year 1255 (the motif recurs in the tale of Chaucer's Prioress). The dream of the boy in Abse's "Red balloon" recalls the whole, complex history of the Jews in England.

Other poems in *Poems, Golders Green* turn from the fabulous to the quotidian. In "Public library" and "The shunters" the diminished possibilities of contemporary life are traced in such images as "bed-sitting rooms," "rainy, dejected railway stations," "the tired afternoon drizzle" in which the smoke of "proletarian" engines "fades into industrial England" and their "hurt, plaintive whistles . . . punctuate / the night, a despair beyond language." Yet England's other face, the pastoral, is evoked in "Summer's Sunday song," if only later to be disowned.

In "Odd" Abse's dichotomies are still more clearly limned. This poem proclaims the poet's divided nature, half as family man and householder in a respectable suburb with lawn and rose bushes, where

> Sodium lamp-posts, at night, hose
> empty roads
> with gold that treacles over pavement trees.
> . . . .
> If a light should fly on in an upstairs room
> odds on two someones are going to sleep.

But when "From the sensible wastes of Golders Green / I journey to Soho where a job owns me" (the job is his post as a chest physician at the clinic), "the dark is shabby with paste electric / of peeporamas, brothels, clubs, and pubs," and here, if a light shows in an upstairs room, "odds on two someones are going to bed." In Golders Green "I want to scream" and thus "by the neighbours, am considered odd." But he reacts to Soho with the same impulse and is considered odd by his friends there, too. The poet is odd man out—or rather, in, for his involved detachment makes possible his participation in experience. The job that "owns" him is dual, as his life is: in his job as poet, he will make poems from Golders Green and from Soho, from the dualities of London and Cardiff, being British and a Jew, being a bourgeois family man and a bohemian, a believer and a skeptic, a man of imagination and a man of reason, a doctor and a poet. Indeed, the tensions between imagination and reason's skepticism striate Abse's work throughout.

At this point, in "The water diviner," he deals with reordering and the regenerative power of imagination (which of course subsumes religious faith). "Late, I have come to a parched land / doubting my gift, if gift I have," says his water diviner. He tries "To hold back chaos," to transform "clay, fire, or cloud, / so that the aged gods might dance"; perhaps he had better "have built, plain brick on brick, / a water tower." And yet,

> sometimes hearing water trickle,
> sometimes not, I, by doubting first,
> believe; believing, doubt.

At the same time, in "The magician," Abse explores art in relation to illusion—"Offstage, the Great Illusionist owns bad teeth, / cheats at cards, beats his second wife, is lewd," but with the aid of "unseen wires, luminous paint," he is "Transformed by glamorous paraphernalia" and

> Sometimes, something he cannot understand
> happens—atavistic powers stray unleashed,
> a raving voice he hardly thought to hear,
> the ventriloquist's dummy out of hand.

Yet the great Illusionist had better not believe in his own magic, for offstage he reverts to the fallible man he was at the start, "an obsessional liar, petty thief." This ambiguous image of the artist-illusionist will be extended in Abse's later work. Meanwhile, the poet's skepticism is more than balanced by the affirmation of "The grand view":

> There are moments when a man must praise
> the astonishment of being alive.
> when small mirrors of reality blaze
> into miracles; and there's One always
> who, by never departing, almost arrives.

The title of Abse's next volume of poems, *A Small Desperation* (1968), hints at a diminution of scale, a commitment only to personal emotion, which at the same time embodies the Weltanschauung of Britain after the loss of its power and empire. The book opens with "From a suburban window": "Such afternoon glooms . . . / such negatives of a featureless day . . . / unemployed sadness loiters here." In the desolation "six mourners appear": "They use this grey inch of eternity, / and the afternoon, so praised, grows distinct." This book appeared after the death of Abse's father, a loss which colors the poet's usually sanguine tone.

Two poems help to define his place relative to the pastoral tradition of British poetry. In "As I was saying" he assures a woman who had upbraided him for not writing nature poems that "Yes, madam, as a poet I *do* take myself seriously," but he declines to "mug up anew / the pleasant names" of British wildflowers, or "compete with those nature poets you advance . . . few as calm as their words: / Wordsworth, Barnes, sad John Clare who ate grass." And in "Not Adlestrop" Abse writes a riposte to Edward Thomas's bucolic "Adlestrop," finding his epiphany at this railway stop not in the twittering of birds but in an exchange of looks with "a very, *very* pretty girl" leaning out of a departing train.

The theme of his Jewish identity recurs in "A night out," in which the poet and his wife see, in a new film from Poland, "images of Auschwitz almost authentic"; "Resenting it, we forgot the barbed wire / was but a prop and could not scratch an eye." Watching, they "munched milk chocolate" as "trusting children, no older than our own . . . without fuss" enter the gas chambers "whilst smoke, black and curly, oozed from the chimneys." The enormity of "the human obscenity" can scarcely be taken in; at home, reassured by "the au pair girl from Germany" that their children are well, the parents console each other and reassert their own life force as they "in the dark, in the marital bed, made love."

In this volume a new theme emerges as Abse deals with those feelings mysterious in their genesis, quiddities of emotion experienced in sense impressions, importunate images. "I am searching for something forgotten," he writes in "Olfactory pursuits," finding a "bitter or candied scent" like "a signpost pointing backwards / on which is writ no place and no distance." Experience is fragmented, "a few stones instead of a wall, / . . . broken stones instead of a house. / Hopelessly, with odours I conjoin." He writes another poem ("Halls") instigated by the "sweet biscuity smell" of "Arcane, unparaphrasable halls." The sight of sheds evokes in him an image of inarticulate suffering, "long sheds where a man could only howl"; as in a dream "the sheds disappeared, / . . . until the moon, as pale as pain, holed in a cloud." These private associations of the ineffable, the inarticulate, are summoned in "Hunt the thimble" ("Hush now. You cannot describe it . . . "), which concludes with "old men in hospital dying," "the darkness inside a dead man's mouth." Not even these images embody what it is that "You cannot describe."

In another half-dozen or more poems Abse draws more directly than hitherto upon his experience as a medical doctor. "Pathology of colours" identifies the shades of suffering flesh, for he has seen the rose hue of a tumor, the "red-blue tinged with hirsute mauve / in the plum-skin face of a suicide."

> So in the simple blessing of a rainbow,
> in the bevelled edge of a sunlit mirror,
> I have seen, visible, Death's artifact
> like a soldier's ribbon on a tunic tacked.

Such mortal knowledge qualifies aesthetic assumptions; experience requires a moral response, as Abse makes clear in "Not beautiful." This poem

Ted Hughes, Dannie Abse, and Israeli poet Yehuda Amichai outside the Mosque of Omar in Jerusalem during a 1971 reading tour of Israel (Jeremy Robson)

takes issue with a "saintly" person whose "vocation" was to "find the beautiful" in such scenes as "raw and raving voices" after "all hiroshimas," in "live skeletons of the Camp, . . . in war, in famine. . . ." But Abse concludes,

>   One sees the good point, of course, and may
> admire it;
>   but, sometimes, I think that to curse is
> more sacred
>   than to pretend by affirming.
> And offend.

Such suffering is made personal as Abse watches his aged father's last illness; though himself a physician, he is impotent to assuage the inevitable:

>   "To hasten night would be humane,"
>   I, a doctor, beg a doctor,
>   for still the darkness will not come—
>   his sunset slow, his first star pain.

There is no help. "Here comes the night with all its stars, / bright butchers' hooks for man and meat." At the last, "like a child I question why / night without stars, then night without end." The helplessness of doctoring the dying, the impenetrable mystery of death are limned in another poem, "Give me your hands."

But his medical practice puts the physician-poet in touch with ineffable joy as well as suffering. In "The smile was" it is the smile—"No man can paint it"—of the mother of a newborn babe affirming life, affirming joy, that is the "one thing I waited for always":

>   the smile the smile
>   always the same
>   an uncaging
>   a freedom.

Funland and Other Poems (1973) contains Abse's strongest work thus far. "I start with the visible / and am startled by the visible," he writes on the opening page in a poem ("Mysteries") in which the wakened speaker does not know the identity of his dreaming self, yet respects what he does not know, for "a vision dies from being too long stared at." This theme is elaborated in "Forgotten." The power of art to "summon back the dead" is touchingly affirmed in "Three street musicians," with "the old-time sound, old obstinate sounds, / such as they achingly render and suspend,"

> And, as breadcrumbs thrown
> on the ground charm sparrows down
> from nowhere,
> now, suddenly, there are too many ghosts
> about.

This artist theme recurs in "The bereaved," in which twelve women mourn one whose voice had once "been so thrilling." "Off and on TV / he was charming, . . . / . . . He was their pinup." But suddenly the pop star has "Twelve women pulling him . . . screaming, / kicking, scratching, pulling at him . . . / he was being smothered, / bitten by women's teeth. . . ." After these maenads have rent their Orpheus, "the women stood back silent, / most of them already smoking / and the others lighting up."

The two figures of power and vision on whom Abse's imagination broods are the artist-poet and the doctor. In *Funland* they are presented with increasing authority. Perhaps the most powerful of his poems on medical themes is "In the theatre," a chilling description of a botched brain surgery performed in 1938 and witnessed by the poet's brother, Dr. Wilfred Abse. In those days the surgeon had to probe manually to find the tumor, "the fingers . . . rash as a blind man's, inside his soft brain." An hour later, "the growth / still undiscovered, ticking its own wild time," the surgeon "desperate,"

> Then, suddenly, the cracked record in
> the brain,
> a ventriloquist voice that cried, "You sod,
> leave my soul alone, leave my soul alone," —
> the patient's dummy lips moving to
> that refrain,
> . . . .
> that voice so arctic and that cry so odd
> had nowhere else to go—till the antique
> gramophone wound down and the words
> began
> to blur and slow, ". . . leave . . . my . . .
> soul . . . alone . . ."
> to cease·at last when something other died.
> And silence matched the silence under snow.

The "ventriloquist voice" recalls the "raving voice"

of "the ventriloquist's dummy out of hand" in "The magician," where it spoke with "atavistic powers" the illusionist "cannot understand." Here the dummy's voice seems to come from an "antique gramophone," a mechanism which runs down "to cease at last when something other died"—something other, that is, than the body. The long vowel in *soul* is echoed by the thirteen other O-sounds in the stanza.

In the poem "The case," the physician is shown as sometimes a mere technician, not a humane healer. "The tall doctor my colleague," tells the speaker of the "sedimentation rates, white cell counts, / haemoglobin content," of his patient's blood, but when asked "What's his name?" this colleague "knew the man's heart but not the man." In "Miracles" the need for belief is explored in a colloquy between a priest and a physician. The priest "dreamed he quit his church," then had a midnight vision of "a rainbow in a black sky." The doctor reassures him that such "conjunctions," though odd, are common and "are no more incredible than God." "A Doctor must believe / in miracles, but I, a priest, dare not," said "my incurable cancer patient, / the priest."

"Funland," a nine-part sequence, presents a madhouse-world populated by Fat Blondie, Mr. Poet, Pythagoras, a few other patients, and the Superintendent. This last, "a cautious man . . . is drawing the plans of the void / working out its classical proportions." The void of course resists such classicism; for instance, Pythagoras "wanted to found / a Society not a Religion," and since a Society "has to be exclusive . . . someone must be banished." The lunatic fantasy takes on political overtones, soon developed and mythologized:

> Who's next for the icepick?
>
> Already the severed head of Pythagoras
> transforms the flagpole
> into a singularly
> long white neck.
>
> It has become a god that cannot see
> how the sun drips its solutions
> on dumpy snowacres.

The broken rhythms and fragmentary images are new in Abse's work and contribute to the dissolution of consciousness and the contemporary despair that comprise the themes of "Funland." "The more we know / the more we journey into ignorance." Mr. Poet's poster invites the reader to "HEAR THE

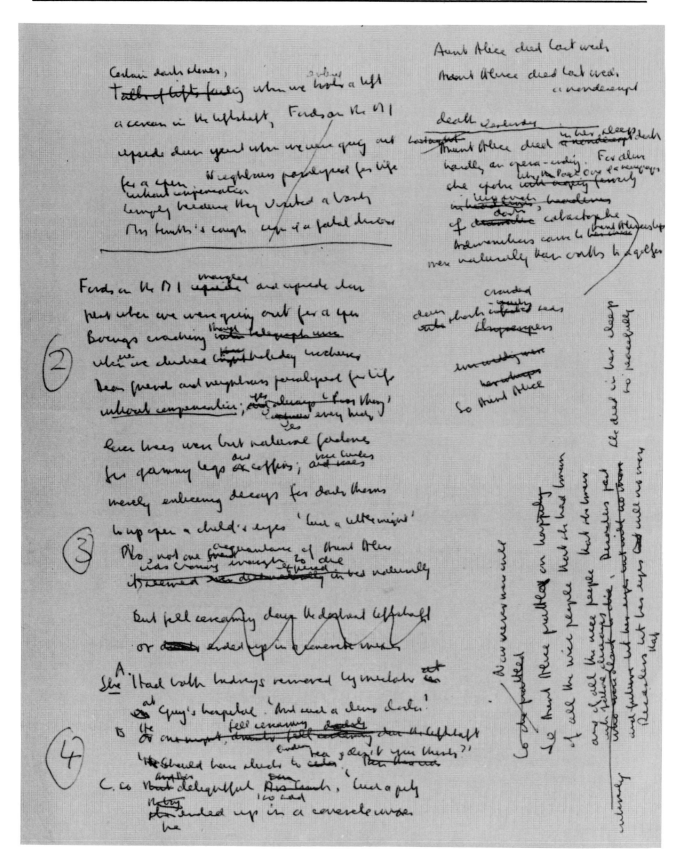

Both sides of a worksheet for an early draft of "Death of Aunt Alice" (the author)

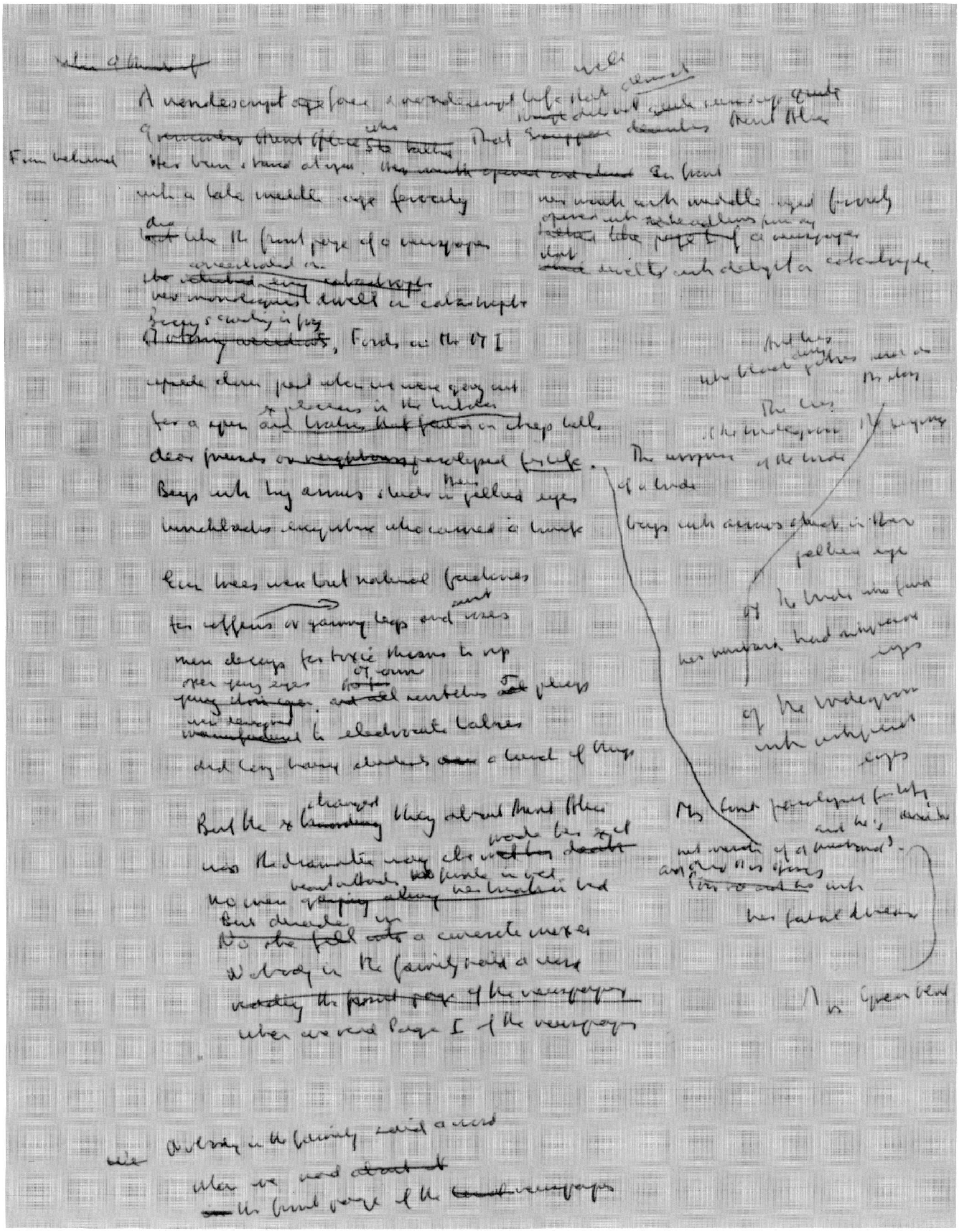

VOICES ENTANGLED" in "THE THORN-BUSH," "MERLIN'S / MESMER'S / ALL THE UNSTABLE MAGICIANS"—

Not me I said thank you no
I'm a rational man touch wood
Mesmer is dead these many years
and his purple cloak in rags.

In time Abse came to see that he could more fully realize the dramatic possibilities of his materials, the contrasting and conflicting claims and powers of "the contemporary white cloak of medicine and the old purple cloak of charismatic Mesmer," as he suggests in the introduction to his play *Pythagoras* (1979). Here the political-mythical implications of "Funland" are replaced by the dramatized confrontation between Pythagoras, who before his commitment to The Cedars was a stage illusionist (like the subject of the early poem "The magician"), and Dr. Aquillus, a "rational man" who feels no urge to "touch wood." The most successful of Abse's plays, *Pythagoras* embodies the fullest exploration in his work of his characteristic tensions between imagination and rationalism, between the life of feeling and the reductiveness of a skeptical empiricism.

Abse's two subsequent collections are the "New Poems 1973-1976" in *Collected Poems* and *Way Out in the Centre* (1981). The "New Poems" include several sketches of family members and two more notable poems, "The weeping" and "The stethoscope." In "The weeping" the speaker thinks "how sleep is a going into exile"; awaking, he is aware of his doubled identity, reiterating this constant theme. In "The stethoscope" the physician muses that "Through it," in pregnant women's wombs, "I have heard the sound of creation / and, in a dead man's chest, the silence / before creation began." Should he "pray therefore? . . . Mimic priest or rabbi. . . ? / Never! Yet I could praise it"—"I should / by doing so celebrate my own ears" and "the wind / travelling from where it began." Abse again affirms his distrust of religiosity, his compassionate humanism.

In *Way Out in the Centre* several poems further explore his consciousness as a medical practitioner. In "A winter visit," his mother, now ninety, "like the sybil says, 'I would die' "; and though he would cry, he "must not . . . for I inhabit a white coat . . . and am not qualified to weep." In "The doctor" he must give what "the patient expects," "the unjudged lie: 'Your symptoms are familiar / and benign'— someone . . . to transform tremblings, gigantic

unease, / by naming like a pet some small disease. . . ." "X-ray" again broods on his mother's last illness—Abse, the physician, in his "white sleeve," holds "your X-ray to the glowing screen. My eyes look / but don't want to. . . ." In "Lunch and afterwards," learning from a pathologist that "After death, of all soft tissues the brain's / the first to vanish, the uterus the last," he replies by describing "silhouettes/hunched in a field . . ./feasting, preoccupied. . . . / Partial to women they've stripped women bare / and left behind only the taboo food, / the uterus, inside the skeleton." The pathologist "wiped his mouth . . . / picked shredded meat from his canines, / said, 'You're a peculiar fellow, Abse.' " This dream of ritual cannibalism is followed by a soliloquy in which the doctor shares several of the irrational perceptions and extrarational intimations of his character Pythagoras.

Exploring the irrational, in "Variations" Abse ventures into neoprimitivism. "The bad boy of the North-West coast" is a version of an American Indian song of sexual prowess; and "The young man and the lion" is based upon a prose fable from W. H. Bleek and L. C. Lloyd's *Bushman Folklore* (1911). Abse had first published in *Poetry and Poverty 5* (1953) this legend of a lion who could not die until it had eaten the man whose tears it had drunk. As Abse says in "One Sunday afternoon," "I am / less rational, more alone, since in my book / *not* seeing is believing."

The title of his book is taken from "A note to Donald Davie in Tennessee," a poem which may well allude to Davie's essay about Basil Bunting, "English and American in *Briggflats*," which Abse included in *Poetry Dimension: Best of the Poetry Year 6* (1979). In this polemical essay Davie maintains that the true direction for English poetry is that pointed by Bunting and the Objectivist movement, a poetry more concerned with the relation of the poet to his subject than with that between the poet and his readers. Abse finds his friend Davie's advice decidedly eccentric, saying "Still poets / jog eagerly, each molehill mistaken / for Parnassus" and asking "But where's the avant-garde when the procession / runs continuously in a closed circle?" He concludes,

I too am a reluctant puritan, feel uneasy
sometimes as if I travelled without ticket.
Yet here I am in England way out
                in the centre.

As is by now evident, Abse is "way out" among English poets as a Welshman, a Jew, a Dionysian, a physician. These sides of his identity isolate him so that he feels he "travelled without ticket." Yet he is at the same time "here . . . in England . . . in the centre," because his work is rooted in the central English tradition of intimate address to a reader, more concerned to communicate through shared conventions of rhetoric and syntax than to substitute idiosyncratic inventions. Abse's reluctant Puritanism, too, is an attitude shared with English poetry and British culture generally. This is by no means to suggest that Abse's work is merely conventional, for, as he implies, it maintains its distance from and extends the conventions that it uses. If his style is conversational, his rhythms those of English speech, the fingering of the language as well as the humane and compassionate point of view in Abse's poems is unmistakable. Dannie Abse is a poet whose range of experience is wide, whose tone—at once intimate and unselfconscious—is inimitably his own; who, when he is not speaking to us directly, lets us overhear him musing on "the irreducible strangeness of things / and the random purposes of dreams." His poems do not shrink from grappling with the most pressing questions of identity and of existence.

Interviews:

Interview with Abse, *Jewish Quarterly* (London), 11 (Winter 1963-1964): 3-11;

Interview with Abse, *Manchester Daily Guardian*, 31 January 1978, p. 6;

Interview with Abse, *Times* (London), 28 February 1983, p. 13b.

References:

William F. Claire, ed., *Literature and Medicine*, special Abse issue, no. 3 (1984);

Joseph Cohen, ed., *The Poetry of Danny Abse* (London: Robson, 1983);

Tony Curtis, *Dannie Abse* (Cardiff: University of Wales Press, forthcoming 1984);

Roland Mathias, "The Poetry of Dannie Abse," *Anglo-Welsh Review*, 16 (Winter 1967): 84-98;

John Pikoulis, "Predicaments of Otherness," *Poetry Wales*, 13 (Autumn 1977): 10-17;

David Punter, "Varieties of Defiance," *Straight Lines*, no. 2 (University of East Anglia, 1979): 33-35;

Jeremy Robson, "Dannie Abse," in *Corgi Modern Poets in Focus 4*, edited by Robson (London: Corgi, 1971), pp. 30-35;

Howard Sergeant, "The Poetry of Dannie Abse," *Books and Bookman*, 22 (July 1977): 35-36;

John Tripp, "Dannie Abse Revisited," *Poetry Wales*, 13 (Autumn 1977): 18-31.

Papers:

Several of Dannie Abse's manuscripts are in the National Library of Wales.

Kingsley Amis

(16 April 1922-   )

Neil Brennan
Villanova University

See also the Amis entry in *DLB 15, British Novelists, 1930-1959*.

SELECTED BOOKS: *Bright November* (London: Fortune Press, 1947);

A Frame of Mind (Reading: Art School of the University of Reading, 1953);

Lucky Jim (London: Gollancz, 1954; Garden City: Doubleday, 1954);

[Poems] Fantasy Poets, no. 22 (Oxford: Fantasy Press, 1954);

That Uncertain Feeling (London: Gollancz, 1955; New York: Harcourt, Brace, 1956);

A Case of Samples: Poems 1946-1956 (London: Gollancz, 1956; New York: Harcourt, Brace, 1957);

Socialism and the Intellectuals (London: Fabian Society, 1957);

I Like It Here (London: Gollancz, 1958; New York: Harcourt, Brace, 1958);

New Maps of Hell: A Survey of Science Fiction (New York: Harcourt, Brace & World, 1960; London: Gollancz, 1961);

Take a Girl Like You (London: Gollancz, 1960; New

BBC Hulton, Evening Standard *Collection*

Kingsley Amis

York: Harcourt, Brace & World, 1961);

My Enemy's Enemy (London: Gollancz, 1962; New York: Harcourt, Brace & World, 1963);

The Evans Country (Oxford: Fantasy Press, 1962);

One Fat Englishman (London: Gollancz, 1963; New York: Harcourt, Brace & World, 1964);

The James Bond Dossier (London: Cape, 1965; New York: New American Library, 1965);

The Egyptologists, by Amis and Robert Conquest (London: Cape, 1965; New York: Random House, 1966);

The Book of Bond, Or Every Man His Own 007, as William Tanner (London: Cape, 1965; New York: Viking, 1965);

The Anti-Death League (London: Cape, 1966; New York: Harcourt, Brace & World, 1966);

A Look Round the Estate: Poems 1957-1967 (London: Cape, 1967; New York: Harcourt, Brace & World, 1968);

Colonel Sun, as Robert Markham (London: Cape,

1968; New York: Harper & Row, 1968);

Lucky Jim's Politics (London: Conservative Political Centre, 1968);

I Want It Now (London: Cape, 1968; New York: Harcourt, Brace & World, 1969);

The Green Man (London: Cape, 1969; New York: Harcourt, Brace & World, 1969);

What Became of Jane Austen? and Other Questions (London: Cape, 1970; New York: Harcourt Brace Jovanovich, 1971);

Girl, 20 (London: Cape, 1971; New York: Harcourt Brace Jovanovich, 1972);

On Drink (London: Cape, 1972; New York: Harcourt Brace Jovanovich, 1973);

The Riverside Villas Murder (London: Cape, 1973; New York: Harcourt Brace Jovanovich, 1973);

Ending Up (London: Cape, 1974; New York: Harcourt Brace Jovanovich, 1974);

Rudyard Kipling and His World (London: Thames &

Hudson, 1975; New York: Scribners, 1975);

The Alteration (London: Cape, 1976; New York: Viking, 1977);

Jake's Thing (London: Hutchinson, 1978; New York: Viking, 1979);

Collected Poems 1944-1979 (London: Hutchinson, 1979; New York: Viking, 1980);

Russian Hide and Seek (London: Hutchinson, 1980).

OTHER: Martin Starkie and Roy Macnab, eds., *Oxford Poetry 1948*, includes poems by Amis (Oxford: Blackwell, 1948);

Oxford Poetry 1949, edited by Amis and James Michie, with a foreword and "Backgrounds" by Amis (Oxford: Blackwell, 1949);

D. J. Enright, ed., *Poets of the 1950's*, includes an introduction and poems by Amis (Tokyo: Kenkyusha, 1955);

Robert Conquest, ed., *New Lines* (London: Macmillan, 1956; New York: St. Martin's, 1957);

"Communication and the Victorian Poet," in *British Victorian Literature*, edited by S. K. Kumar (New York: New York University Press, 1969);

The New Oxford Book of Light Verse, edited, with an introduction, by Amis (Oxford: Oxford University Press, 1978); republished as *The Oxford Book of Light Verse* (New York: Oxford University Press, 1978).

PERIODICAL PUBLICATIONS: "A True Poet," review of *Song of the Year's Turning*, by R. S. Thomas, *Spectator*, 196 (13 January 1956): 56;

"Why You Won't Sell Me the Bright Lights . . . ," *Evening Standard* (London), 5 January 1958;

"Robert Graves: A Great Poet in an Island Paradise," *Show*, 2 (December 1962): 78-81;

"Death of a Poet" [on C. Day Lewis], *Observer*, 28 May 1972, p. 9;

"Why Poetry?," *Observer*, 30 September 1973, pp. 39-40;

"After Ralph Hodgson," in "Weekend Competition . . . No.2567," *New Statesman*, 97 (15 June 1979): 890.

"Crisp, witty, sardonic. . . ." That is one way to introduce Kingsley Amis, the way one editor, Edward Lucie-Smith, took in 1970. Amis's wit began to delight the world in 1954 when his first novel, *Lucky Jim*, appeared. In verse it had begun to delight his friends two decades before. The first of his poems to be published—"Prelude," in a 1938 issue of the City of London School magazine—Amis dismisses

now as "a kind of suburbanite's *Waste Land* tizzied up with bits of Wilde." The tizzying up would seem to point to his earlier discovery at school "that to be liked you needed pre-eminently to be able to raise a laugh occasionally. . . ."—a feat Amis has been accomplishing ever since, in verse and prose. By 1957 he was considered by several critics one of the best of the younger British poets.

Born in 1922 near Clapham Common in South London, the son of William Robert Amis, a senior export clerk for Coleman's Mustard, and Rosa Annie Lucas Amis, Kingsley Amis defines his upbringing as Nonconformist (Baptist) and middle class. Yet, he recalls in "A Memoir of My Father," churchgoing or "Chapel, as such, was a thing of the past by the time I was old enough to care about such matters. Reacting against his upbringing . . . my father had turned his back on any form of worship and, I suspect, on the Christian faith as well." Christian morals he nevertheless retained and insisted upon, and his son could react—with only partial success—against them. The incongruities of human nature (a staple theme of the poems to come) appear in his father's despair about his son's shortcomings: "he . . . put them down to my complete lack of religion." They quarreled about politics and art: "He wanted me to like Gilbert and Sullivan and took me to *The Pirates of Penzance* and *The Yeoman of the Guard*; I meanly exaggerated their boredom." Once at least his father took him to cricket at Lord's, the Yankee Stadium of British cricket, and met his son's rare enthusiasm by offering to arrange coaching in cricket for him—but his son claimed to be "working too hard for exams" to take such lessons. In a contrite elegy, "In Memoriam W. R. A. (*ob. 18th April 1963*)," Amis describes an experience of that year, batting for "The Gentlemen of Cambridge," and scanning the stadium for his father in vain:

> I'm sorry you had to die
> To make me sorry
> You're not here now.

When Amis's father resolved that his son would have "a better chance than he . . . he succeeded at considerable financial cost." The best school he could afford in the early 1930s was local Norbury College, a secondary school where Amis wrote his first poems, one of them, as assigned, "a ninety-nine line poem, in blank verse, about the miracle of St. Sophia." A scholarship (and his continuing status as an only child) enabled him to move up to the City of London School, which he was later to characterize as "excellent." Daily from 1935 until 1939 he commuted, as his father did, to the center of London, but to an island of reading, art, and talk within school bounds. This idyll fractured under the impact of World War II. The school was evacuated from the city to share facilities in Wiltshire with the "gentlemen scholars" of posh Marlborough College: "The unlooked-for descent of six or seven hundred London day-boys, many of them noisy and taterdemalion, was no gift from the gods, but after a time some host-like gestures . . . might reasonably have been expected. None were made to my knowledge in the five terms I was at school in Marlborough." Snobbery experienced at an elite public school might have made another man radical—or reactionary—and without doubt it colored the rest of Amis's career, but in no simple way. His poem "Masters" (first collected in *A Frame of Mind*, 1953), for instance, holds in classic equipoise the presumptions of aristocracy:

> That horse whose rider fears to jump will fall,
> Riflemen miss if orders sound unsure:
> They only are secure who seem secure;
>   Who lose their voice, lose all.

That truth once admitted, the poem moves to its obverse, that to be loved one must be known, "and we are known / Only as we are weak." The arrogant, needed by society and rewarded, are viewed ultimately with compassion:

> By yielding mastery the will is freed,
> For it is by surrender that we live,
> And we are taken if we wish to give,
>   Are needed if we need.

Insistence on the complexities of responsibility and power later marked both his position paper on the left, *Socialism and the Intellectuals* (1957), and his essay "Lucky Jim Turns Right" (written in 1967).

A scholarship to St. John's College, Oxford, led Amis to his first contact with a first-rate contemporary poet in April 1941 (according to Amis). As Philip Larkin recalls in the preface to *Jill,* he and a friend met "a fair-haired young man" coming down a staircase of his Oxford college. The friend aimed a hand like a pistol, coughed "to signify a shot," and "The young man's reaction was immediate. Clutching his chest in a rictus of agony, he threw one arm up against the archway and began slowly crumpling downwards, fingers scoring the

stonework. . . . I stood silent. For the first time I felt myself in the presence of a talent greater than my own." The friendship that blossomed was not interrupted totally even when Amis was called up as a lieutenant in the Royal Corps of Signals. A physical impediment kept Larkin out of the services; he remained at Oxford, and Amis visited him when stationed nearby.

The earliest poems Amis collected date from 1943 and deal with army experiences. "Radar" begins ostensibly as a hymn of praise for the British inventors of radar—"Kolster and Dunmore made a remarkable valve" that made radio direction finding possible. The ironic quatrain that ends the poem alludes indirectly to the suffering brought about on the enemy side by improved air defenses:

> On the enemy side stood aerials like the bereaved
> Who mask their essence with respectable sound;
> And Kolster and Dunmore heard their interference,
> It was dismissed by them as a stray effect.

The poem compares in ironic tone with Thomas Hardy's "The Convergence of the Twain." "O Captain, My Captain!" protests conventionally, in conventional quatrains, the army's apparent hostility to beauty:

> If you ever stood still for a moment to listen
> To music, or turn your head into the rain,
> Or look at a beautiful face seen in a crowd,
> Then stop it; you must never do that again.

"Aviator's Hymn" reveals traces of Dylan Thomas—"the hot blood lashes seed / Unsilting channels in the absent shell"—that Amis was soon to sweep out with the broom of clarity. "Belgian Winter," more ambitious, places the winter of 1944-1945 in historical perspective:

> From my window stretches the earth,
>   containing wrecks:
> The burrowing tank, the flat grave, the
> Lorry with underside showing, like a
>   dead rabbit.
> . . . .
> Behind is the city, a garnished London,
>   a Paris
> That has no idea how to live, of
>   Chirico squares;
> A feast of enemies, the stranger entertained
> With opera and lesbian exhibitions.

Such chic allusions, although precise enough, to the haunted cityscapes of de Chirico, were to be combed ruthlessly out of his later verse by Oxford and Oxford friends. The influence of W. H. Auden on Amis's imagery is both perceptible and more long lasting.

Demobilization led to one of the most revealing poems in Amis's first book, *Bright November* (1947): "Release," which is also the longest and the poem that gives the volume its title. Its speaker finds November 1945 bright and himself "once more faced with a beginning," as the "scaffoldings of war are dismantled":

> But when I saw them going I was kind
> And shook their hand, forgetting
>   to remember
> The sage brutality, the shrewd blind eye.
> . . . .
> Now all day I can only quote myself
> And am duller than I thought I was.

The colloquial touch, the casual self-deprecation, and the subterranean moral concerns all indicate that Amis was beginning to emerge from the shells of other poets.

W. H. Auden has been called the first English major to become a major English poet—not a very startling paradox in retrospect, for English as a discipline was a twentieth-century innovation—but at Oxford twenty years after Auden, Amis "read English" with a quite different reaction to the "discipline" of studying Anglo-Saxon. Auden radiated enthusiasm; Amis hostility. The 1947 version of his poem "Beowulf" bristles from epigraph to final parenthesis. One can well imagine Professor J. R. R. Tolkien ending a lecture with a long section of Beowulf in Old English, closing his text and sighing, "There is not much poetry in the world like this" (the epigraph, attributed to Tolkien). In the 1940s many an undergraduate must have mumbled "Thank God!," and as Amis says:

> So, bored with dragons, he lay down to sleep.
> . . . .
> The peerless prince had taken his last bribe
> (Zupitza's reading); useless now the byrnie.
>
> Consider now what this king had not done:
> Never was human, never lay with women
> (Weak conjugation), never saw quite straight
> Children of men or the bright bowl of heaven.

This early version of "Beowulf" concludes angrily: "But what have we to learn in following / His tedious journey to his ancestors / (An instance of Old English harking-back)?" Amis's attitude later mellowed. The revised "Beowulf" (published in *A Case of Samples*, 1956) omits the ambiguous quotation from Tolkien, omits the pedantic allusions to scholars Thorkelin and Zupitza, drops the juvenile equation of humanness and sexuality (while neatly retaining the double entendre), and intensifies the Anglo-Saxon texture:

> Grendel's dam was his only sort of woman
> (Weak conjugation). After they were gone
> How could he stand the bench-din,
>   the yelp-word?

It concludes with a protest, not that Old English is studied at Oxford, but that it is studied in a boring way: "Must we then reproduce his paradigms, / Trace out his rambling regress to his forebears / (An instance of Old English harking-back)?"

More significant than Oxford dons in Amis's growth as a poet were classmates and friends: John Wain and Philip Larkin in particular. As Blake Morrison has remarked, "the role played by these 'original readers' or mentors" is one Amis himself emphasizes in his scholarly article "Communication and the Victorian Poet" (1969). In the first of four poems that Amis contributed to *Oxford Poetry 1948* the speaker imagines the future, a change of scene, and other

>   men and women
> Not to be guessed at now, whose lives my life
> Must learn to touch and, being changed,
>   to change.

Amis wrought change in his friends. Even in his first year, Larkin recalls, Amis became "editor of the University Labour Club Bulletin and in this capacity printed one of my poems." And his friends changed him; as Larkin explains, "This is not to say that Kingsley dominated us. Indeed, to some extent he suffered the familiar humorist's fate of being unable to get anyone to take him seriously at all." Still, in matters of politics, jazz, and poetics he held authority, and when he and James Michie came to edit *Oxford Poetry 1949*, the mass of Oxford poets, who had not bothered to read Auden yet, found themselves scorned in Amis's foreword: "The typical furniture of the mass of the poems [submitted but rejected] was not, as we soon came to wish it would be, the telegraph-pole and the rifle, but the amethyst and the syrup; the typical subject not the rehearsed response, but the beautiful rapture; the typical rhyme not of 'lackey' and 'lucky,' but of 'bliss' and 'kiss.' All the efforts of the poets of the 'thirties had failed to throw the Georgian lumber out of the window." The best of the poets selected "show an eagerness to explore the possibilities of language . . . that can be traced to the innovations of Auden." On the other hand, "the few poems traceable to Dylan Thomas, none of which are printed here, seem to indicate . . . a harmful influence."

Amis thus defines the qualities essential to good poetry as three: a sharp eye on the up-to-date ("the telegraph-pole and the rifle"), the satiric ear for "the rehearsed response," and a crafty hand for the innovative technique here represented by his reference to pararhyme or double consonance in " 'lackey' and 'lucky.' " Reading one another's poems and criticizing them helped form a congruent standard that scorned first of all the lazy, a fact sometimes neglected. The group surrounding Amis and Larkin, which a decade later many perceived as the nucleus of The Movement, revered craftsmanship, technique, and art. That they ridiculed the pretentiousness of much "art appreciation" and most cultural display tended to obscure their essentially serious concerns with both art and culture. Amis was to dedicate his first novel, *Lucky Jim*, simply "To Philip Larkin"; the *"il miglior fabbro"* in Eliot's dedication of *The Waste Land* to Ezra Pound has to be inferred. The three, never-republished poems entitled "Backgrounds" that Amis contributed to *Oxford Poetry 1949* might be seen as finger exercises for the development of the fabricator's hand. Quarter rhymes, terminal consonance, and an apposite off-accent rhyme mark the first:

> The pond held goldfish that had pleased
> > her once,
> But now the unflowering lilies, the
> > useless leaves
> Split and half-waterlogged, carried a sense
> Of a distress outside her mind, of griefs
> Enacted like the figures of a dance.
> . . . .
> Left on a railway platform, she resents
> The lack of proper setting for her tears
> . . . .
> Instead of trees to moan for her, she hears
> Indifferent engines ruining her silence.

The ruined mood finds, in the "ruined" meter of the last line and the thwarted expectation of pure rhyme, a fine technical onomatopoeia.

Amis stayed on for a year and a half of graduate work after receiving his B.A. at Oxford in 1948, apparently with some disappointment. (A

copy of his rejected dissertation on Victorian poetry, annotated by his tutor Lord David Cecil, is to be found in the Humanities Research Center at the University of Texas.) The time had come to get a job. In *Bright November*, after "Our Country / an eighth poem for Elisabeth" comes "Poem for Hilary," and in 1948 he married Hilary Ann Bardwell. The following year he left Oxford to accept an assistant lectureship in the department of English at University College in Swansea, Wales, where he was to remain for twelve years. Here he completed his first published novel, *Lucky Jim*, and wrote the second, *That Uncertain Feeling* (1955), dedicated to his wife, and a third, *I Like It Here* (1958), dedicated to their three children, Philip, Martin, and Sally.

Fame followed the success of his novels. Mislabeled an Angry Young Man, the Lucky Jim image plastered over his own, he became a man in demand, or worse, a poet sought by the spotlight. London beckoned, and the poet declined. "Why You Won't Sell Me the Bright Lights, No, Not Even Now I've Hit the Jackpot" is no doubt a title supplied by the editors of the *Evening Standard* in 1958, but the sentiments are genuine enough: "Here in Swansea I conduct myself in a quiet, orderly manner . . . lecturing in English. This is all right actually. Few of my colleagues are barbarians in wire-rimmed glasses . . . fewer still are tremulous, Greek-quoting ninnies. . . . Unless you are very lazy, or appear before him wearing a bow-tie, the Welsh student will not molest you. . . ." Having spent a few weeks as a minor celebrity in London, he rejects it: "Besides its horrible effect on you, London literary society . . . can be fairly horrible in its own right. I know some writers, of course, who are as nice as any insurance salesman or club steward you could meet, and witty too. A literary party, though, can be a jungle of marauding egos." Like Larkin and Wain, he seemed "a determined provincial," but reconciled, as he put it, to doing "my stuff as husband and father" also; it might seem that Amis was a poet in decline.

His output of poetry did diminish, but his next volume of verse, *A Frame of Mind* (1953), revealed a marked growth in quality. Most often republished of the new poems in this volume is probably "Something Nasty in the Bookshop" (later retitled "A Bookshop Idyll"). The speaker, browsing in an idle hour, takes a poetry anthology off the shelf and finds a moral in its table of contents, as he looks at the titles of poems by male and female poets:

> Like all strangers, they divide by sex:
> *Landscape near Parma*

Interests a man, so does *The Double Vortex*,
    So does *Rilke and Buddha*.

"I travel you see," "I think" and "I can read"
    These titles seem to say. . . .

This masculine ego is discountenanced by the heart-exposing titles of the poems by women: "*I Remember You, Love is my Creed, Poem for J*," and, the speaker decides, "Women are really much nicer than men:/No wonder we like them." The poem could have concluded there, with the speaker having found "something nasty in the bookshop," his machismo deflated. What makes it a better poem is the concluding quatrain, with its wry reflection that men should feel as women do but be unable to expose themselves:

    Deciding this, we can forget those times
        We sat up half the night
    Chock-full of love, crammed with bright
                thoughts, names, rhymes:
        And couldn't write.

Overpacked line three followed by caved-in line four shows Amis's developing skill in merging form and content; the counterreflection on female openness and male inhibition, deepening thought.

"Romanticism in a political context I would define as an irrational capacity to become inflamed by interests and causes that are not one's own," Amis was to write in Fabian Tract 304, *Socialism and the Intellectuals* (1957). "Against Romanticism" is his poetic rejection of the mood, deprecating the frame of mind that is perennially

    Raging to discard real time and place,
    Raging to build a better time and place
    Than the ones which give prophecy
                its field.

Seeing himself trapped in an era incurably romantic, Amis turns Audenesque:

    Let the sky be clean of officious birds
    Punctiliously flying on the left;
    Let there be a path leading out of sight
    And at its other end a temperate zone:
    Woods devoid of beasts, roads that please
                the foot.

The simplistic world view of that archromantic Shelley and his "Ode to the West Wind" are mocked by Amis's "Ode to the East-North-East-by-East Wind." Amis begins with ironic praise:

    We know, of course, you blow the
                windmills round,
        And that's a splendid thing to do;
    Sometimes you pump up water from
                the ground
        Why, darling, that's just fine of you!

But the poem concludes less critical of the wind ("But what's the point of you?") than of romantic poets:

    Poetic egotists make you their theme,
        Finding in you their hatred for
    A world that will not mirror their desire.
    Silly yourself, you flatter and inspire
        Some of the silliest of us.
            And is that worth the fuss?

The poems in *A Frame of Mind* helped launch The Movement. In 1956 Robert Conquest in his anthology *New Lines* brought together publicly for the first time the works of the poets who had influenced one another at Oxford in the 1940s: Amis, Larkin, Wain, Elizabeth Jennings, and others. All have regarded the subsequent publicity as a mixed blessing. In 1956, before *New Lines* was published, Amis wrote: "When so much criticism of modern verse takes the form of erection or sapping of generalisation and category, the poet who is indifferent to poetic schools is apt to get left out of account. None of the posher reviewers is going to hang round his neck a garland labelled 'Significant Trend' . . . although it may be true that such garlands often turn into millstones." Amis about the same time presented in the introduction to D. J. Enright's anthology *Poets of the 1950's* (1955) a more analytic view of the trend, seeing only two things that the members of the group had in common: "a desire to be lucid if nothing else, and a liking for strict and fairly simple verse forms." Looking back on the 1950s, John Wain agreed: "For years it was a journalistic habit to speak of 'Amis-Wain,' as people spoke in the thirties of 'Auden-Spender-MacNeice.' In both cases, it was excusable up to a point." That point was the point of conflation: misreading Amis's poems to fit them into a thesis valid enough for Larkin's, making generalizations about Wain's sense of comedy valid only for Amis's satiric verse. What they agreed about was a sense of form, with freedom to make use either of "modern experimental" or traditional forms, a desire for clarity, and an abhorrence of certain subject matter. As Amis wrote in his introduction to *Poets of the 1950's*:

"no one wants any more poems on the grander themes for a few years, but at the same time nobody wants any more poems about philosophers or paintings or novelists or art galleries or mythology or foreign cities or other poems."

Surveying the poetic world in the mid-1950s, Amis was not merely negative, of course. The poets of The Movement shared a keener sense of duty to one's audience, as well as one's art. Before beginning a new poem, Amis wrote, "I ask myself: Is this idea likely to interest anyone besides myself? and try to forget about it if the answer seems to be No; and—if I do go ahead with the poem—I try to work it into a verse form I haven't used before, or at any rate not recently."

Development keeps Amis's best work above the category of light verse, as his next volume, *A Case of Samples* (1956), showed. Poem after poem begins with a comic view of the world, only to shock the reader with serious reflection. The poem that gives the volume its title, "A Song of Experience," is typical; as if the sexual experience of the commercial traveler were to end as it begins with a smutty laugh:

> A quiet start: the tavern, our small party,
> A dark-eyed traveller drinking on his own;
> We asked him over when the talk
>   turned hearty,
> And let him tell of women he had known.
>
> He tried all colours, white and black
>   and coffee;
> Though quite a few were chary, more
>   were bold;
> Some took it like the host, some like a toffee;
> The two or three who wept were
>   soon consoled.

The sadness of Don Juanism—or sexual experience as an end in itself—slips in as if another comic anecdote:

> For seven long years his fancies
>   were tormented
> By one he often wheedled, but in vain;
> At last, oh Christ in heaven, she consented,
> And the next day he journeyed on again.

Yet after the salesman has "drained his liquor" and "paid his score," even he, rootless, lonely, is viewed with compassion:

> I saw him, brisk in May, in Juliet's weather,
> Hitch up the trousers of his long-tailed suit,

> Polish his windscreen with a chamois-leather,
> And stow his case of samples in the boot.

The car's trunk may hold the samples of whatever it is he sells; nothing can buy back the possibilities of a life with meaning he has squandered. To him "Nausicaa and Circe were the same," even Juliet another one-night stand.

A Case of Samples is subtitled *Poems 1946-1956*, and it includes two of the poems from *Bright November* and fifteen (of the eighteen) from *A Frame of Mind*, affording reviewers the opportunity to take stock of Amis as a poet. Resisting a tendency to dismiss him as merely a comic poet, the reviewer for the *Times Literary Supplement* warned that "Mr. Amis may make a great show of nonchalance in taking aim, but one can scarcely dismiss the gesture as being made in anything else but deadly earnest." This reviewer added, "Indeed, one's only reproach is that he seems to be in danger of taking too seriously his refusal to take certain things seriously: to refuse to be gulled by certain postures can itself become a posture." A. Alvarez in the *Observer* traced Amis's light satiric line through Chesterton and Mark Twain in *Huckleberry Finn* back to Matthew Prior and John Skelton. Seeing that a half-dozen of the twenty-eight previously uncollected poems were in what looked like terza rima, Hilary Corke, not alone, rashly dismissed Amis as a member of the "*terza rima* post-Empsonian school." Actually only one, "The Triumph of Life," is in straight terza rima form; the others are in unlinked tercets or experimental variations (such as the *AAB CCD EEB FFD* linkage of "A Pill for the Impressionable"). Robert Conquest argued that the contrary was true, that not a poem bore traces of Empson-Thomas obscurantism, that all were exploratory, not of the self but of the human condition. The highest praise came from the United States, where William Van O'Connor, in an authoritative article on "The New University Wits" (*Kenyon Review*, Winter 1958) quoted in full one now well-known poem from *A Case of Samples*, "The Last War," and concluded that Amis is "possibly the best poet of the group."

After time out to write what is often regarded as the most witty and profound book on science fiction yet to appear, *New Maps of Hell* (1960), Amis explored new territory in putting together a coherent sequence of poems about Wales, *The Evans Country* (1962). The volume is "Dedicated to the Patrons and Staff of the Newton Inn, Mumbles, Swansea," and in that, or in similar public houses in Wales, Amis may have begun his observations for Dai Evans—a character lecherous and nonchalant enough to have been found in Dylan Thomas's *Under Milkwood*, but sly, brash and greedy too, a complex prowler of a territory somewhat like Willie Loman's, but in Glamorgan, the county in South Wales. Like Willie in hearty optimism, he differs in living only in the present: no ear for the sounds at his back, an eye only for the skirt immediately ahead.

The poems all have real or imaginary Welsh place names as titles, although only one, "Welch Ferry, West Side" (originally entitled "The Influence of Natural Objects"), is at all topographical. Leaving a woman to recompose herself in the back seat of his 1960 Humber, Dai steps out on the dark hillside furze and is surprised as the smog below lifts from oil tankers and steelworks:

> and more stars
> Than he knew what to do with filled the sky,
> And a lighted lighthouse, civic centre, quay.
> . . . .
> "Looks beautiful tonight," he muttered,
> Then raised his voice: "Eurwen get
> moving do,
> You think I want to hang around here
> all night?"

No two place names and no two titles are the same, and the woman is always a new one: only the tacky environment remains. "Pendydd" is a mock aubade, for dawn has come and gone and so has Miss Protheroe, to work, and Evans is reflecting:

> Love is like butter, Evans mused, and stuck
> The last pat on his toast. Breakfast in bed
> At the Red Dragon
> . . . .
> . . . encouraged thought
> And so did the try-asking-me-then look
> The bird who fetched the food had
> given him.
> . . . .
> . . . Better than guns
> He thought, ringing the bell for more
> of both.

Several of the poems are witty about the problems of the voyeur ("Llansili Beach" and "St Asaph's"), but given the voyeur's dream, to be judge at a beauty contest (to pick "Miss Glamorgan / [West] 1963"), Dai Evans, in "Maunders," has to choose. A fellow judge, Mrs. Pugh, has insisted

> "Miss Clydach just won't do;
> And as for, well, her figure,

> It's too . . . too much on view."
> . . . .
> Dai's seen in Clydach's hip-swing
> Rich bosom and mean face,
> Two threats: his own destruction
> By passion's fell embrace
> Or else (a bit more likely)
> Not getting to first base.

Being practical, Dai sides with Mrs. Pugh, "votes against Miss Clydach," and proposes to Mrs. Pugh that they "Pop up the Newlands Inn, / And strengthen our acquaintance / Over a spot of gin?" No mere satiric look at Welsh hypocrisy, *The Evans Country* gives us a sardonic vision of human nature.

Chaucer's "Miller's Tale" is updated in "Aberdarcy the Chaucer Road," where Evans is trapped by his timetable:

> 6:30. Balls to where. In like a whippet;
> A fearsome thrash with Mrs No-holds-barred
> (Whose husband's in his surgery till seven);
> Back at the wheel 6:50, breathing hard.

Even at his father's funeral in "Fforestfawr," he is eager for the mourners to depart for he has a telephone call to make:

> "Hallo, pet. Alone? Good, It's me.
> Ah now, who did you think it was?
> Well, come down the Bush and find out.
> You'll know me easy, because
> I'm wearing a black tie, love."

Dai Evans might have joined Gulliver—or Leopold Bloom—as a limited man in whom we see humanity, but even as the Evans poems were coming into focus, Amis was lured by the offer of a fellowship at Peterhouse College, Cambridge, to move up in the academic world, away from the Evans country.

It was the summer of 1961. What he had disliked about Oxford—dons twittering of Chaucer as "a perpetual fountain of good sense" and of Milton's "organ music," the feeling that culture was an upper-class property—he hoped had been driven out of Cambridge by F. R. Leavis and "a couple of Labour governments." Although Peterhouse itself proved "an oasis of good nature and common sense," donnish gossip from the university at large labeled him a pornographer and he found "undergraduate Cambridge . . . still the resort of the upper classes." After two years he left the academic life and, except for a semester as a visiting lecturer at Vanderbilt University in Tennessee (1967-1968), has not returned.

It was a period of personal unrest. Hilary Amis went to the United States and into business on her own (later, in response to criticisms in the *New Statesman* that she had called her Ann Arbor enterprise "Lucky Jim's Fish and Chips," she responded: "Kingsley doesn't mind, so why should you?"). His fifth novel, *One Fat Englishman* (1963), was dedicated "To Jane"; the following year James Douglas-Henry sued his wife Elizabeth Jane for divorce; and in 1965 Amis and novelist Elizabeth Jane Howard were married. In 1980 a second split occurred — "the happiness went out of their marriage," as one gossip columnist put it after an interview with Elizabeth Jane Howard. The poems of these years do not, however, reflect the upheavals in Amis's personal life. They remain nonconfessional, "classic and austere."

The next collection, *A Look Round the Estate: Poems 1957-1967* (1967), adds about twenty poems to those of *The Evans Country*, and not one could be labeled confessional.

> By bluster, graft, and doing people down,
> Sam Baines got rich, but, mellowing at last,
> Felt that by giving something to the town
> He might repair the evils of his past.

In this quartet of quatrains, "A Tribute to the Founder," Amis, with terse wit, takes Sam from remorse to the endowment of a university to teach the young nobler values. Instead the dons refine Sam's:

> Graft is refined among the tea and scones,
> Bluster (new style) invokes the public good,
> And doing-down gets done in pious tones
> Sam often tried to learn, but never could.

Of most interest technically is "The Voice of Authority," a play upon the drill sergeant's game "O'Grady says." The monotony of drill is captured by a variation on the sestina pattern: no rhyme, but three end words, each repeated in the same order seven times. In counterpoint, the tricky game of surprises and the staccato voice of authority echo in the clipped tercet form and the ever-varying stop points of the caesuras:

> Do this. Don't move. O'Grady says do this,
> You get a move on, see, do what I say.
> Look lively when I say O'Grady says.

Two final poems of the 1957-1967 group are especially excellent: "Science Fiction" and "After Goliath." The first is notable for its analysis of the popularity of a genre that is, after all, only fantasy:

> What makes us rove that starlit corridor
> May be the impulse to meet face to face
> Our vice and folly shaped into a thing
> And so at last ourselves . . .
> . . . .
> In him, perhaps, we see the general ogre
> Who rode our ancestors to nightmare,
> And in his habitat their maps of hell.

But science itself promises "new maps of hell" with threat of "nightmares worse than theirs."

"After Goliath," in quick, overriding couplets, is technically as well as thematically remarkable. It sees the Old Testament battle from David's Monday-morning point of view — "The champion laid out cold / Before half the programmes were sold." As David scans those cheering his victory, he turns grim at the sight of

> Academics, actors who lecture,
> Apostles of architecture
> . . . .
> Angst-pushers, adherents of Zen.

The applause of this circle of critics charts a new philistia:

> even the straightest
> Of issues looks pretty oblique
> When a movement turns into a clique.

Shocked, he realizes the hardest battle is yet to be

> fought in the mind
> For faith that his quarrel was just,
> That the right man lay in the dust.

Critics generally liked *A Look Round the Estate*, though, as always, some, like Ian Hamilton, misread Amis's poems as merely "amusing [and] self-centered," and others observed that his colloquial language was dating, however much in the 1950s it had been what Julian Symons called "a useful corrective to Dylanesque rhetoric." Most, like the *Sunday Times* reviewer, found the collection, if "sometimes savage, always utterly readable, witty, cerebral," marking an advance in what Roy Fuller called "ethical acuteness and insight into behavior."

Eleven years elapsed before Amis's next volume of poetry appeared, and so varied were his experiments in fiction in the interim — *Colonel Sun* (1968), a spy novel in the James Bond tradition, written under the pseudonym Robert Markham; a ghost story, *The Green Man* (1969); two mainstream novels, *I Want It Now* (1968) and *Jake's Thing* (1978); a spoof on the detective novel, *The Riverside Villas Murder* (1973); a novel sounding the interface of classical music and rock, *Girl, 20* (1971); and a science-fiction novel, *The Alteration* (1976)—none would have been amazed had the later works in *Collected Poems 1944-1979* revealed some stagnation. The opening poem, "South," (reflecting perhaps his months in Tennessee in the winter of 1967-1968) might seem symptomatic. The ten pages of worksheets, or early versions of the poem, published in *Malahat Review* (October 1969), are prefaced with the remark that "to take a poem through as many versions as I did with *South* has always turned out to mean, for me, that I started with the wrong form." The form he ends with is syllogistic: nature gave the American Southern states Edenic charm, the possibility of utopia; but Southern whites are rancorous ("If they try it I'll shoot me a coon"); therefore,

> in the South, nothing now or ever.
> For black and white, no future.
> None. Not here.

This sentiment is not one to which Martin Luther King, or anyone who knows the South well would have subscribed, and history since has not been kind to it.

Happily other new poems are quite up to the standard set by *A Look Round the Estate*. One of the finest is Amis's first to be explicitly on the idea of death, an address in an antimetaphysical mood to a dying man:

> Look thy last on all things shitty
>   While thou'rt at it: soccer stars,
> Soccer crowds, bedizened bushheads
>   Jerking over their guitars
> ....
> High-rise blocks and action paintings,
>   Sculptures made from wire and lead:
> Each of them a sight more lovely
>   Than the screens around your bed.

The wry twist of the last lines might have pleased Pope.

Despite witty poems such as "Report" in the science-fiction vein and "Crisis Song" in the political, the mood of the best poems seems elegiac. "Their Oxford," its title recalling the bitter affection of George Orwell's "Their England," depicts a stroll through Oxford a decade before 1984, with stinging images of changed hotel and pub. The speaker

is brought to remember his disapproval of "their Oxford" of the 1940s and to realize sardonically that "their Oxford" of the 1970s is even more alien.

> In my day there were giants on the scene,
> Men big enough to be worth laughing at:
> Coghill and Bowra, Lewis and Tolkien.
> Lost confidence and envy finished that.
> ....
> Do costly girls still throng the
>   chequered lawn,
> All bosom and bright hair, as they did then,
> And laugh and dance and chatter until dawn
> With peacock-minded, donkey-voiced
>   young men?

But the bitterness is muted by nostalgia:

> Where once a line of college barges lay,
> Haunt of the rich (comparatively) few,
> A single hulk welters and rots away;
> So goes the Oxford that I hardly knew.

Writer of a monthly review of jazz for the *Observer* during the 1950s, Amis fuses his later resentment of rock music and anguish for what it replaced in his finest elegy yet, "Farewell Blues." Appropriately, satire is packed into each verse, emotion left for the refrain: "For Louis Armstrong, Mildred Bailey . . . lie in Brunswick / churchyard now." The genius of jazz improvisations extended

> Far beyond what feeling, reason, even
>   mother wit allow,
> While Muggsy Spanier . . . Sterling Bose and
>   Henry Allen lie
>   in Decca churchyard now.

> What replaced them no one asked for, but it
>   turned up anyhow
> And Coleman Hawkins . . . Bessie Smith and
>   Pee Wee Russell lie
>   in Okeh churchyard now.

Three record-company vaults entomb the masters of jazz. "Dead's the note we loved that swelled within us . . . / Simple joy and simple sadness thrashing the astounded air. . . ." Jazz has had few better requiems.

In 1979 the *New Statesman* offered prizes for "additions" "to Kingsley Amis's *Collected Poems*" and then asked Amis to judge. The results were witty, amusing, and informative:

> The losers separated themselves at a glance;
> couldn't rhyme or scan, you see.

1.

To reach the centre you turn left, not right,

And drive halfway to Abingdon before

You start to double back past building-site,

Road-works, ex-pickle factory, chain store,   2.

2. By

~~Past~~ uncouth alleys to ~~hotel~~ the old hotel,   1

Now newly faced. THere, t

~~With its new facing~~ Thirty years ago,

They tried their gravelled best to do you well;

~~Now a coach-load of Dutchmen fills the bar~~

~~The food fell flat, floors creaked, service was slow,~~

~~But parents dined with~~

~~But parents~~

~~They tried their gravelled best to do you well;~~

Floors creaked, the food was flat, the waiters slow,

3.

But parents and fiancées ~~fitted in~~ drawled at ease

Here, mad old ladies gibbered   freely on,

Dour scholars, ~~flushed with~~ taking their degrees,   warmed by *!*

Were safe with sherry, ~~and~~ a queerish don   *while*

Could lush up his star pupil. Here, today,

Floors creak, the waiters stroll, the food is ~~nice glazed~~ *looks* ~~nice~~

You have to do yourself well as you may   *fine*

In the dim bar

At first. (you) do yourself well as you may

4.   ~~*no one stays here twice*~~

Could lush up his star pupil. Here, to-day,

Floors creak, the food is glazed, the waiters skive;

You have to do yourself well as you may

In the dining bar, where fifty Swedes arrive   2

A minute before you; and businessmen

Though dressed like   *call for Highland malt*

In a footballer's accents.

Page from a working typescript for "Their Oxford" (the author)

First prize went to Stanley Sharpless—"for the only one I'm cross about not having written myself"— and last to Robert Markham (Amis himself) for "After Ralph Hodgson"—a critique of "trendy little tarts . . . / and little Lefty farts."

Reviewers of Amis's *Collected Poems* either deplored the fact that Amis had still not developed a spiritual dimension—a large request perhaps to make of a satiric poet—or agreed with Clive James that "Only the fact that he is so marvellously readable can now stop Kingsley Amis from being placed in the front rank of contemporary poets."

Amis has not found his characteristic form, however, and it seems at the moment likely that he will not, that he will appear in history among the minor classics of English poetry—with Lovelace and Suckling, Prior and Landor, Clough and Muir—remembered for no great work, but respected forever for a dozen perfect, if perfectly minor, poems. Still, Amis has not yet written his last poem.

Bibliographies:

Jack Benoit Gohn, *Kingsley Amis: A Checklist* (Kent, Ohio: Kent State University Press, 1976);

Dale Salwak, *Kingsley Amis: A Reference Guide* (Boston: G. K. Hall, 1978).

References:

Philip Gardner, *Kingsley Amis* (Boston: Twayne, 1981);

Philip Larkin, Introduction to *Jill: A Novel*, revised edition (New York: St. Martin's Press, 1964);

Blake Morrison, *The Movement: English Poetry and Fiction of the 1950s* (Oxford: Oxford University Press, 1980);

William Van O'Connor, *The New University Wits and the End of Modernism* (Carbondale: Southern Illinois University Press, 1963);

John Press, *Rule and Energy: British Poetry Since the Second World War* (Oxford: Oxford University Press, 1963);

J. D. Scott, "In the Movement," *Spectator*, 193 (1 October 1954): 399-400;

Anthony Thwaite, *Contemporary British Poetry: An Introduction* (London: Heinemann, 1959);

"Too Late the Mavericks," *Times Literary Supplement*, 8 March 1957, pp. 137-138;

John Wain, *Sprightly Running* (London: Macmillan, 1962);

Alan Watkins, *Brief Lives* (London: Hamilton, 1982).

Papers:

Some of Amis's papers are at the Humanities Research Center, University of Texas, Austin.

Thomas Blackburn
(10 February 1916-13 August 1977)

William B. Worthen
University of Texas at Austin

SELECTED BOOKS: *The Outer Darkness* (Aldington, Kent: Hand & Flower Press, 1951);

The Holy Stone (Aldington, Kent: Hand & Flower Press, 1954);

In the Fire (London: Putnam's, 1956);

The Next Word (London: Putnam's, 1958);

A Smell of Burning (London: Putnam's, 1961; New York: Morrow, 1962);

The Price of an Eye (London: Longmans, 1961; New York: Morrow, 1961);

A Breathing Space (London: Putnam's, 1964; Philadelphia: Dufour, 1964);

The Judas Tree, music by Peter Dickinson (London: Novello, 1965);

Robert Browning (London: Eyre & Spottiswoode, 1967; Totowa, N.J.: Rowman & Littlefield, 1974);

A Clip of Steel (London: MacGibbon & Kee, 1969);

Thomas Blackburn and John Heath-Stubbs: Poems (London: Longmans, 1969);

The Feast of the Wolf (London: MacGibbon & Kee, 1971);

The Fourth Man (London: MacGibbon & Kee, 1971);

The Devil's Kitchen (London: Chatto & Windus, 1975);

Selected Poems (London: Hutchinson, 1975);

Post Mortem (Liverpool: Rondo, 1977);

Thomas Blackburn (courtesy of Mrs. Margaret Blackburn)

Bread for the Winter Birds (London: Hutchinson, 1980).

OTHER: *Middle School Book of Verse,* edited by Blackburn (London: Harrap, 1955);
45 to 60: An Anthology of English Poetry 1945-60, edited by Blackburn (London: Putnam's, 1960);
Presenting Poetry: A Handbook for English Teachers, edited by Blackburn (London: Methuen, 1966);
A Gift of Tongues: A Selection from the Work of Fourteen 20th Century Poets, edited by Blackburn (London: Nelson, 1967);
"Hospital for Defectives" and "Felo de Se," in *The Oxford Book of Twentieth-Century English Verse,* edited by Philip Larkin (London: Oxford University Press, 1973), pp. 484-486.

PERIODICAL PUBLICATIONS: "Inroads on Dying," *Light* (Winter 1974): 183-188;
"End-Stopped Poets," *Temenos,* no. 2 (1982).

Thomas Blackburn's poetry is the poetry of trauma. Haunted by the demons of his childhood and racked by depression, Blackburn used poetry to probe his painful inner world, questioning the difficulty of faith, his problematic sexuality, and the mysterious inspiration offered by nature. Sometimes maudlin, Blackburn typically undertakes a tough-minded self-scrutiny, controlled through a fine command of traditional verse forms. In his later volumes, Blackburn increasingly abandons religious abstractions and turns to a more personal and unorthodox exploration of the spirit and of the eternal life beyond death. He is now best remembered for two early poems that appear in Philip Larkin's *The Oxford Book of Twentieth-Century English Verse* (1973), "Hospital for Defectives" and "Felo de Se."

The roots of Blackburn's poetry lie in his painful and turbulent childhood. In *A Clip of Steel* (1969)—a lightly fictionalized autobiography—Blackburn details the spiritual and psychological crises of his youth. Blackburn was born in Hensingham, Cumberland, to Charles Eliel and Adelaide Fenwick Blackburn. As a child he was thoroughly tyrannized by his father, a stern Anglican priest of Mauritian descent. Obsessed both by his own guilty sexuality and by the fear that his English ancestors may have bred with island natives, the elder Blackburn persistently tormented his son, scouring his face with peroxide to lighten his complexion and relentlessly chastising him for suspected erotic fantasies (the "clip" of the title is a device that Blackburn's father procured to prevent nocturnal ejaculations). In later life, Blackburn struggled to overcome the psychological damage inflicted by his father's abuse and by his mother's impulsive affection, confronting his past both in psychotherapy and in several autobiographical poems.

After study at Bromsgrove, a minor public school, Blackburn crammed privately and went up to Selwyn College, Cambridge, in the Michaelmas term of 1934. His stint at Cambridge was a mixture of tedium and anarchy. On the verge of his first nervous breakdown, Blackburn sought relief in alcohol and began the drinking binges that would continue throughout his life. Although listed as a candidate for the Law Tripos of May 1935, Blackburn had already collapsed and withdrawn from the university. He was treated briefly at Brooklands, a sanatorium for wealthy addicts and alcoholics, and then began a more successful psychoanalysis. While in therapy, Blackburn read D. H. Lawrence, Freud, and Jung, who catalyzed his ingrained fascination with myth, the psyche, and the spirit. As he suggests in *A Clip of Steel,* he began to see the dynamics of his own mind as the source both of his affliction and of his art: "For some years I lived in that shadowy no-man's land which, if you find your way out of it, is the birthplace of myth, poetry, legend, symbol, but whose permanent residents are insane." In 1937 he transferred to Durham University, taking a literature B.A. in

1940, and an M.A. in absentia in 1950. In 1941 or 1942, Blackburn married a severely disturbed young woman—the nymphomaniac mentioned in *A Clip of Steel*—who was later hospitalized herself. The violent marriage had lasted only six months, after which Blackburn's parents intervened to arrange a divorce. During World War II, Blackburn was invalided from service in the Merchant Navy and served in the Fire Force in Ilford, Essex, through 1945. In the late 1940s he began to have poems published in periodicals, visited Wales and Europe, and took up the two avocations that figure prominently in his poetry, mountain climbing and spiritualism. He married his second wife, the abstract painter Rosalie de Meric, in 1945; their daughter, now free-lance journalist Julia Blackburn Bonger, was born in 1948. Blackburn taught English and religion at the King's School in Kent from 1945 to 1947, and then took a position at the Marylebone Grammar School, London, where he remained until 1960.

Blackburn's battles with faith and sexuality form the core of his first two volumes, *The Outer Darkness* (1951) and *The Holy Stone* (1954). The opening poem of *The Outer Darkness,* "The End of an Age," declares Blackburn's despair at the modern age's loss of faith; the poem, which depicts the saints and martyrs of the Christian tradition as swept from the stage of the world, introduces several other poems on explicitly Christian themes and occasions—"The King and His Saints," "Good Friday," an Eliotic "Pentecost," "Lazarus," "The Path," and "Dives." "The Outer Darkness" reinforces this common thread, envisioning the soul's flight to the dark limits of faith. The conflict between spiritual and carnal love is less compellingly dramatized in "The Beast." A steamy beauty-and-the-beast narrative, "The Beast" quickly degenerates into a manic portrayal of the leering bestiality of lust. "The Beast" is an odd companion to Blackburn's restrained meditative verse, and the tonal inconsistency of *The Outer Darkness* pervades Blackburn's writing as a whole; indeed, this lurid beast resurfaces in Blackburn's later novel, *The Feast of the Wolf* (1971), shouldering aside an otherwise urbane portrait of university life. Blackburn's use of folktale in "The Beast" is complemented, however, by his fusion of personal autobiography and mythic archetype in several more successful poems. In "Oedipus," for instance, Blackburn explores his response to his mother's impulsive love through the Oedipus myth and invokes both classical and Freudian associations. Moreover, the closing lines of the poem ("I see beyond all words his future

shape, / Its feet upon the carcass of the ape / And round its mighty head prophetic birds") clearly recall the rhythm and imagery of Yeats's "The Second Coming." Blackburn's early poetry is suffused by Yeatsian cadences, imagery, and themes. In "The Dancing Masters," for example, Blackburn glances obliquely at the singing masters of "Sailing to Byzantium." At best Blackburn reharmonizes Yeats's music, training a Yeatsian "high talk"— without Yeats's irony—on his own abiding themes of guilt and repentance. Finally, though, the sustaining impulse of *The Outer Darkness* is neither the imitation of Yeats, the mythic vision of "Oedipus," the gloomy gothic of "The Beast," nor the devotional verse of "Good Friday." While there is an autobiographical dimension to the entire volume, Blackburn's strongest poetry is forecast in poems such as "Scenes from Childhood," where he directly recounts his personal struggles with his family, with sex, with morality, and with madness.

In 1954 the BBC Third Programme broadcast "A Place of Meeting," a short verse play which, retitled "The Holy Stone," closes Blackburn's second volume of poems. While several poems in *The Holy Stone* lack the pressure of the best poems in his first collection, Blackburn's technical resources and poetic voice are markedly more certain. In "Pasiphae," for example, Blackburn reconsiders the monstrous union of the carnal and the spiritual that he treats so hysterically in "The Beast." Here, though, the mythic frame of the poem and its obvious indebtedness to Yeats's "Leda and the Swan" provide the conceptual structure and rhetorical distance that Blackburn needs to phrase this personal concern with a more general resonance. "Intimations" suggests Blackburn's growing admiration for Wordsworth, whose poetry becomes a guiding touchstone. In "The Holy Stone," Blackburn again resorts to a Yeatsian mode— symbolic verse drama. The play represents the natural and supernatural worlds vying for the soul of the hero, the murderer Adam Aramain.

Blackburn achieves his mature voice in his next two volumes, *In the Fire* (1956) and *The Next Word* (1958). *In the Fire* develops Blackburn's central themes and subjects: flesh and spirit in "Eros and Agape," myth in "Orpheus and Eurydice," and family turmoil in "Family History." But Blackburn also turns his attention to more immediate questions of social morality, dedicating "The Clockwork" to students executed by the Nazis during the war. In *The Next Word,* Blackburn completes his mastery of strict verse forms in poems such as "Ballad of the Last Night." More than earlier volumes, *The Next Word* addresses the contemporary scene, layering the tensions of modern marriage, for instance, with mythic and folkloric analogues in "The Lucky Marriage," and imaging the German concentration camps in "The School of Babylon." Instead of retelling family history, in *The Next Word* Blackburn explores the evil influence of his childhood on his adult life; as he remarks in "Othello's Dream," "To murder love was my heritage." And in "Hospital for Defectives" Blackburn finds a public voice for a private tragedy, when a visit to a mental hospital provokes a meditation on the inscrutable order of providence.

Blackburn's career as an educator also crested in the early 1960s. He spent 1956-1958 as Gregory Poetry Fellow at Leeds University and then returned briefly to his position at Marylebone. In 1960 he was appointed lecturer in English at the College of St. Mark and St. John, a Church of England teacher's college attached to London University. He was quickly promoted to senior lecturer in 1962 and to principal lecturer and department head in 1963. At "Marjohns," Blackburn taught the general B.A. course in literature, literature courses for teacher-certification candidates, and courses on teaching methods. A dedicated teacher, Blackburn edited several classroom anthologies of poetry, notably *Presenting Poetry* (1966), a handbook sponsored by the London University Institute of Education; he also served as examiner for the Central School of Drama from 1962 to 1970. In 1964 he joined the Royal Society of Literature.

Blackburn won the Guinness Poetry Prize in 1960 for "Sediment," a moving account of his father's old age included in his next volume, *A Smell of Burning* (1961). Like "Sediment," the sharpest poems in this volume arise from immediate occasions. In "Felo de Se," Blackburn records his desperate reaction to the attempted suicide of his onetime lover, Patricia Beer: "The blue stone I recall on her left hand; / Just what it means I do not understand." Again, though, Blackburn's taste remains inconsistent, whether reaching for wit in "Bombs" ("With something not unlike aplomb; / It's nice to think one has the Bomb!") or for irony in "Memento Mori" ("Cyanide, Monoxide, Zyklon B, / 'Any man's death diminishes me.' "). In both poetry and fiction, Blackburn's irony is too easy; his tone is more assured when he speaks sympathetically about his daily experience. The nervous tension of "From the Park" ("I must go down into the dark / Benches and twittering trees / Of the man-handling park, / The blank uncertainties / Where my reason ends, and catch / At the flare mere blackness gives / Af-

ter a scraping match") marks the direction of Blackburn's best later work. Even the childhood scenes of "A Smell of Burning" and "Another Old Snapshot" seem less immediately rendered than in earlier poems about childhood. Overall, Blackburn seems to be taking stock in *A Smell of Burning,* and fittingly he reprints four poems in the boldly mythic mode that he increasingly disregards — "Cnossos," "Oedipus," "A Child," and "Pasiphae." *A Smell of Burning* recalls past attitudes, problems, and styles, while charting the more intimate terrain of Blackburn's later poetry.

Blackburn also undertook two book-length studies in the 1960s, *The Price of an Eye* (1961), a survey of modern poets, and *Robert Browning* (1967), an examination of Browning's unorthodox religious poetry. In *The Price of an Eye,* Blackburn formulates his poetic creed, arguing that poetry should fuse the "two worlds" of our perception, the objective material world and the subjective inner world of faith and suffering. Since great poetry, in Blackburn's view, always attempts to resolve this dialectic, it transcends issues that are simply individual or local; great poetry is concerned with the eternal, with the unconscious dynamics of the psyche and the spirit. The "poetic image acts as a bridge between this inner world and that of our external environment, and through it some unrealised truth about ourselves is able to shoulder up from its shadowy hinterland into our waking consciousness. It is this intrusion into the well-lit, orderly circle of our daily awareness of some new statement from the unlit depths of ourselves, which can make the images of poetry and myth disturbing and at times frightening." Blackburn's vision of poetry as a spiritual medium informs the poetic lineage he adopts in *The Price of an Eye.* For Blackburn, Donne, Blake, Wordsworth, Yeats, Eliot, and the Larkin of "Church Going" perform poetry's spiritual mission, and so transcend the more limited aims of poets such as Pound, who are too exclusively interested in technique, and of those such as Auden, who are sadly immersed in the narrower claims of politics and society.

Blackburn confirms this creed in *A Breathing Space* (1964). "Teaching Wordsworth" declares Blackburn's allegiance to the Wordsworthian power immanent in nature, the "something far more deeply interfused" that sustains his own bleak efforts in the Wordsworthian mode in poems such as "Trewarmett." Blackburn explores the irrational flux of the psyche in "An Encounter," where a chance meeting with his deranged first wife prompts a reflection on his own sanity and identity.

Surprisingly, though, the volume is marred by a series of bitter poems written in reaction to his divorce from Rosalie de Meric (the "Decree Absolute," discussed in one of the poems, was granted in February 1963). Again, the irony of poems such as "A Small, Keen Wind" seems flaccid: "My wife, for six months now in sinister / Tones, has muttered incessantly about divorce, / And, since of the woman I'm fond, this dark chatter / Is painful as well as a bit monotonous." Nor is the volume entirely salvaged by the visionary poems such as "Schiara" that frame Blackburn's belief in a natural, redeeming "catharsis of thunder." Set in the Italian Dolomites, "Schiara" and "San Lorenzo" also record a personal change of heart; Blackburn visited the Dolomites with Margaret Gerardis (née McGuire), whom he married in March 1963.

Returning to London, Blackburn collaborated on a different venture, *The Judas Tree,* a musical drama about Judas Iscariot written with his "Marjohns" colleague, composer Peter Dickinson. *The Judas Tree* drew national attention to its premiere at the college on 27 May 1965, and it played subsequently at the Southwark Cathedral, at the Liverpool Cathedral, at the Edinburgh Festival, and in Washington, D.C.

The early 1970s witnessed a renewed burst of activity, with the publication of *A Clip of Steel* in 1969, and of his novel, *The Feast of the Wolf,* and a collection of poems, *The Fourth Man,* in 1971. The novel's hero, Simon Armstrong, a poet teaching at a small London college, has written a book on Tennyson and edited a poetry handbook. He is obsessed by an especially infernal hallucination: the forces of evil gather themselves into the tormenting and erotic image of an all-consuming vampire, Legion. In the course of the novel, Legion demonically possesses Simon in the form of an upwelling fear that his lover Stella may be bisexual and nearly drives him to murder her. In agonies of guilt, Simon flees Stella and undertakes an extraordinarily dangerous midwinter climb on a Welsh mountainside. His foot slips, and he plunges to his death, finally free of his personal torment. Although its satire on university life is occasionally witty, this melodramatic tale is deeply flawed by haphazard plotting, by undigested autobiography, and by the hero's self-absorbed fear of a predatory female sexuality. The poems in *The Fourth Man* are linked to the novel in several ways. One of them, "Aberdeen," is presented as having been written by Armstrong on a lecture tour of Scotland. "Aberdeen" aside, the verse of *The Fourth Man* is generally more idiomatic than Blackburn's earlier verse, and poems such as "A Signpost to

Dachau" and "Mental Ward" typify the broader range of subject and tone of Blackburn's last poems. Despite the long-winded abstractions of "The Fourth Man," Blackburn continues to refine his special meditative strengths in this transitional volume; as he suggests in "Homage to Shelley," "It was the narrowness that made him free."

The removal of the College of St. Mark and St. John from Chelsea to Plymouth in 1973 effectively ended Blackburn's tenure there. Like many of his colleagues he chose to remain in London, and in September 1973 he was appointed lecturer at Whitelands College, Putney, also part of the London University Institute for Education. During his two and one-half years at Whitelands, Blackburn's mental and physical health deteriorated sharply, and he met his teaching and administrative duties only infrequently. Blackburn's hellish depressions increased in number and intensity during these years; he was intermittently hospitalized, drank heavily, took antidepressants by the handful, and finally underwent Jungian analysis on a Royal Literary Fund subsidy. After several disputes with the Whitelands administration over his teaching performance, Blackburn retired in February 1976 to his cottage in Snowdonia, Wales, where he continued to write until his sudden death in August 1977. He is buried in Llanfrothen, and his tombstone bears an inscription from the poem "An Epitaph": "I wait for birth again, now dying / Has opened its door and let me enter."

Despite the ravages of his last years, Blackburn nonetheless published his *Selected Poems* (1975), a fully representative sampling from *The Next Word* onward, and a new collection, *Post Mortem* (1977). In an essay entitled "Inroads on Dying" (*Light,* 1974), Blackburn described the visionary experiences that inform the values of his last poems: "What is nearest to eternity are the intense moments of living whether in creation, love, relationship, mountains, thought, or contemplation, where you are almost (you will never have it entirely here) at one with your activity." *Post Mortem* is tightly focused on these intense moments, on dying, and on the life of the spirit after death. The volume opens, though, with a bitter yet admiring poem addressed to painter Francis Bacon. In earlier years, their friendship had drawn Blackburn and Bacon into a homoerotic affair, and Bacon's sexuality is central to the poem (and to the unflattering portrait of him in *The Feast of the Wolf*): "And marvel at you, very rich and famous, / Still crucified by what takes place in a bed, / And uttering, with superb technique, pretentious / Platitudes of rut, that you have said and said." When he writes about the more recent catastrophes of his life, as he does in "Alone," "New Year's Eve," and "Fracture," Blackburn strikes a more accommodating posture. As he suggests in "Ego," "The later themes of work and sex are well charted"; the contemplation of death "is the theme I cannot but have / Till the dissipation of my body and my grave."

In many respects, Blackburn's posthumous *Bread for the Winter Birds* (1980), like Yeats's *Last Poems,* contains his most vigorous and colloquial verse. In her foreword, Margaret Blackburn recounts his last days in their Welsh cottage, describing his work, his premonitions of death, and the apparently premeditated overdose of the antidepressant parastelin that killed him. Although poems such as "Alcohol" remind us of his tenuous psychological stability, others such as "William Wordsworth," fittingly written in the shadow of Snowdon, suggest Blackburn's faith in his eventual redemption by the saving presence of nature. Not that this faith is easily or unambiguously achieved; as he admits in "Crag of Craving," he cannot finally give a "name" to the "other / Uncircumscribed quality, / To which you and I will come." Throughout this posthumous volume Blackburn's tone is lighter, less affected by bitterness, and unstained by irony; his observation of nature is clear and minute; his verse structure is unintrusive. In view of his mental suffering, the calm of many of the poems in *Bread for the Winter Birds* is hard-won. Indeed, as he remarks of his parents in "Ash Tree," by forgiving the ghosts of his past life, he may finally have been able to forgive himself.

The vicissitudes of Blackburn's life are fully contemplated in his poetry. In both his life and his art, Blackburn rarely could sustain the emotional balance that typifies his best poems. The body of his work is technically proficient and honestly records the movements of an individual, often troubled, eccentric, and occasionally visionary mind. Before his death, Blackburn was writing an autobiographical sequel to *A Clip of Steel*, concerned in part with his life at Whitelands; one copy of the manuscript is in the archives of Hutchinson and Company, and another is in the possession of his daughter. More recently, several of Blackburn's unpublished poems have appeared in literary periodicals, and a second posthumous volume may be forthcoming. Apart from reviews, the secondary literature on Blackburn is slight. Although it covers only the early work, John Press's discussion of Blackburn in *Rule and Energy: Trends in British Poetry Since the Second World War* remains the most incisive and sympathetic study. Blackburn's reputation as a writer has been eclipsed by those of several of his friends — John Heath-Stubbs, George Barker, and R. S. Thomas — and by that of his estranged younger brother, the novelist John Blackburn. At this time, the place of Blackburn's poetry in the postwar canon is uncertain. An accomplished minor poet, Blackburn has attracted a devoted group of admirers, particularly for his spiritual and meditative verse. His posthumous poems may well renew a more general interest in his poetry.

Reference:

John Press, *Rule and Energy: Trends in British Poetry Since the Second World War* (Oxford: Oxford University Press, 1963), pp. 150-158.

George Mackay Brown
(17 October 1921-   )

Joseph Reino
Villanova University

See also the Brown entry in *DLB 14, British Novelists Since 1960*.

SELECTED BOOKS: *The Storm and Other Poems* (Kirkwall: Orkney Press, 1954);

Loaves and Fishes (London: Hogarth Press, 1959);

The Year of the Whale (London: Chatto & Windus / Hogarth Press, 1965);

A Calendar of Love and Other Stories (London: Hogarth Press, 1967; New York: Harcourt, Brace & World, 1968);

Twelve Poems (Belfast: Queen's University Festival Publications, 1968);

A Time to Keep (London: Hogarth Press, 1969; New York: Harcourt, Brace & World, 1970);

An Orkney Tapestry (London: Gollancz, 1969);

A Spell for Green Corn (London: Hogarth Press, 1970);

Lifeboat and Other Poems (Bow, Crediton, U.K.: Richard Gilbertson, 1971);

Fishermen with Ploughs: A Poem Cycle (London: Hogarth Press, 1971);

Poems New and Selected (London: Hogarth Press, 1971; enlarged edition, New York: Harcourt Brace Jovanovich, 1973); enlarged as *Selected Poems* (London: Hogarth Press, 1977);

Greenvoe (London: Hogarth Press, 1972; New York: Harcourt Brace Jovanovich, 1972);

Penguin Modern Poets 21, by Brown, Norman MacCaig, and Iain Crichton Smith (Harmondsworth: Penguin, 1972);

Magnus (London: Hogarth Press, 1973);

Hawkfall and Other Stories (London: Hogarth Press, 1974);

The Two Fiddlers: Tales from Orkney (London: Chatto & Windus, 1974);

Letters from Hamnavoe (Edinburgh: Gordon Wright, 1975);

Edwin Muir: A Brief Memoir (West Linton: Castlelaw Press, 1975);

The Sun's Net (London: Hogarth Press, 1976);

Winterfold (London: Chatto & Windus / Hogarth Press, 1976);

Pictures in the Cave (London: Chatto & Windus, 1977);

George Mackay Brown

Witch and Other Stories (London: Longman, 1977);

Under Brinkie's Brae (Edinburgh: Gordon Wright, 1979);

Six Lives of Fankle the Cat (London: Chatto & Windus, 1980);

Portrait of Orkney, text by Brown, photographs by Werner Forman (London: Hogarth Press, 1981);

Andrina and Other Stories (London: Hogarth Press, 1983).

PERIODICAL PUBLICATION: "Writer's Shop," *Chapman*, 4 (Summer 1976): 23-24.

George Mackay Brown is not only a poet but also an acknowledged novelist and a sensitive writer of short stories and plays. His successes in poetry and the prose narrative are considerable, and the really surprising thing about him is not so much his extensive talents, but rather that he is not more widely known as one of Britain's outstanding contemporary authors. Unfortunately, he has a somewhat retiring disposition and is not given to advancing his accomplishments. In fact, he behaves as if genuinely astonished that attention is accorded to anything he has written.

Two aspects of Brown's personal convictions are important to keep in mind: his rejection of nineteenth- and twentieth-century concepts of progress and his personal belief that Scotland (as he phrases it in his prologue to *The Storm and Other Poems*, 1954) is a "Knox-ruined nation," that is destroyed by the Calvinist reformer John Knox. Perhaps as a consequence of his shyness and not exactly popular convictions, it is not unusual to find him unrepresented in most anthologies of modern poetry. Not unexpectedly, he is sometimes accused of being "negative" or "anti-modern," but often enough, as in Vernon Young's evaluation, Brown is praised as the "most wizard shape to appear in British poetry since Dylan Thomas," who is "giving back to poetry much of its ancient courtesy," commemorating "human mischief," and casting "spells about our ears." Young extolls "The Condemned Well" (in *The Year of the Whale*, 1965) as a "cantata of his skills, a work I have promptly added to my select anthology of great poems about the finite world."

Brown was born on 17 October 1921 in Stromness, a small fishing and shipbuilding seaport town of about fifteen hundred residents on the southwest coast of the island of Orkney. Stromness is located about twenty miles from one of the chief medieval monuments of pre-Protestant Scotland, St. Magnus Cathedral. Brown refers to his place of birth and sixty-year residence by its original name, Hamnavoe (Icelandic for "haven-bay"), poeticizing the legends, myths, sagas, archaeological sites, and historical as well as contemporary residents not only of this native seaport town but just as often of the entire Orkney archipelago. He is virtually a twentieth-century poet laureate of these northern islands. The Old Norse name for Stromness appears in the title of his volume of collected newspaper commentaries on specifically Orkneyian and generally Scottish matters, *Letters from Hamnavoe* (1975), and in such poems as "The Twelve Piers of Hamnavoe," "Hamnavoe Market," and "Hamnavoe."

In "Hamnavoe," the harbor of the town is imaginatively transformed into something approximating William Butler Yeats's mythical city of Byzantium: "Herring boats, / Puffing red sails, the tillers / Of cold horizons, leaned / Down the gull-gaunt tide // And threw dark nets on sudden silver harvests." But whereas in "Sailing to Byzantium" Yeats leaves his native land to voyage back in Mediterranean history to an imaginary and mystical "Byzantium," Brown by contrast remains in the seedtown of his birth, reconceiving it as the medieval Hamnavoe in order to combat what he consistently regards as the "greyness of contemporary life."

His father, John Brown, whose job as postman is the subject of the poem "Hamnavoe" ("My father passed with his penny letters / Through closes opening and shutting like legends"), was born in 1875 and was married in 1910 to Mhairi Sheena Mackay, the nineteen-year-old daughter of a crofter-fisherman of Strathy, Sutherland, and a native speaker of Gaelic. Brown characterizes his father as a "great egalitarian," a Labour-party man who loved hymns and music-hall ballads. His mother he remembers as having the "sweetest nature of any person I have known," even with money worries and precarious health. She "always sang as she went about her housework" in a "kind of low happy monotone." The family consisted of four boys and a girl, with George the youngest.

Except for his manifest talent for writing, Brown was not an especially good student in his young years. He first began to suspect that he had some ability as a writer when, at the age of seven or eight, he was required to produce compositions in standard one of the Stromness Academy. He always found "to his astonishment" that he had composed the best essays on such topics as "A day in the life of a beachcomber," "The last day of the holidays," or "A night out of doors"—subjects resembling those of his later published poetry. He was "astonished" at his early abilities "because in all the other subjects I was only average or below average," poor at drawing, geography, and arithmetic—astonished, too, because the "phrases, sentences and paragraphs came so easily," and "anything so effortless must have small value." His English teacher consistently attributed young George's excellent compositions to the "reading of good books." Though the budding author was to be eventually influenced by the works of Thomas Mann, E. M. Forster, Bertolt Brecht, T. S. Eliot, Gerard Manley Hopkins, and inevitably Keats and Yeats, the only literature he read as a boy were "stories . . . out of *The Wizard* and *The Rover*, magazines that all boys read in those days." As a matter of fact, the boy who wrote such promising compositions for his schoolteacher did not really like books.

Brown had to make several attempts at the examinations for the Higher Leaving Certificate before it was finally granted in 1940. His graduation occurred shortly after the outbreak of World War II and coincided precisely with the capitulation of France in June 1940. For Brown, unfortunately, his graduation was immediately followed by an attack of tuberculosis that forced him into the sanatorium in Kirkwall for the first of several periods of extended treatment and convalescence. For many years afterward, Brown's physicians would not allow him to work "except at light things like local reporting." He was thus compelled to live on national assistance, a kind of survival he found tiresome and humiliating. As attested to by the few letters he has allowed to be published, he sometimes yielded to despondency and tended to become gradually more introspective and introverted—qualities that were to manifest themselves in his published work, especially his poetry, wherein (as in "Poet") his "cold stare / Returned to its true task," the "interrogation of silence"; or (as in "Dream of Winter") his sensitivities so delicately refined themselves that there "dinned" into his inner ear the "spider's fatal purring and the gray / Trumpeting of old mammoths locked in ice."

Entrapped in the consequences of his physical disabilities, he responded eagerly to the suggestion, in 1951, of Alex Doloughan, Orkney's director of Further Education, that he enroll in a residential adult-education college in Dalkeith, a small town to the north of Edinburgh. Acting on this suggestion proved a major turning point in his life, for the warden of the newly reopened college, Newbattle Abbey, proved to be the Scottish poet and fellow Orkneyman Edwin Muir, an excellent teacher who was eager to encourage creative work in his students. The year at Newbattle beginning in October 1951 Brown now remembers as the "happiest" in an otherwise not entirely happy life. Muir recommended one of Brown's poems, "The Exile," to the *New Statesman* (where it was published on 5 April 1952) and eventually composed a brief but enthusiastic introduction to Brown's privately printed first collection of fourteen poems, *The Storm and Other Poems* (1954).

In this introduction, Muir describes himself as a "great admirer" of Brown's poetry and praises Brown for a "great gift of imagination and the gift of words: the poet's endowment." "Dream of Winter," "Saint Magnus in Egilshay," and "Gregory Hero" (all subsequently republished in *Loaves and Fishes*, 1959) are what Muir considers "beautiful and original poems, with a strangeness and a magic rare anywhere in literature today." When Muir had first read these and other poems, what struck him was their "fresh and spontaneous quality." Upon re-reading them, Muir was "impressed as well by something which I can only call *grace*. . . . that breathes warmth into beauty and tenderness into comedy"—a "crowning gift, for without it beauty would be cold, and comedy would be heartless." As a fellow Orkneyman, Muir was "proud of this book celebrating life, and proud, above all, that it [the Orkney community] had produced a young poet of such gifts."

On 5 December 1957, Brown received an important communication from Muir commenting at length on a typescript of Brown's poems. Muir was "greatly impressed" and praised the poet for writing better and better. In particular Muir extolled "That Night in Troy" for its "imagination and language"; noted the "dark splendor" of "The Shining One"; and observed that he liked "as much as ever after the last reading," the two poems "Thorfinn" and "Hamnavoe." The only inadequacies he pointed to were in "The Eve of the Corn God," characterized as "cold, abstract and theoretical compared with the others," the poem apparently on a theme that had "not inflamed the imagination."

In the same December letter, Muir again urged Brown to publish, going so far as to suggest that he himself might send the poems to Hogarth Press. Without Brown's knowledge Muir sent the typescript on 6 March 1958 to Norah Smallwood at Hogarth, who accepted the poems immediately. Brown subsequently recorded that "I was surprised one day in 1958, staying in digs in Marchmount Crescent [Edinburgh] to get a letter from Hogarth Press saying that they'd like to publish a book of my poems." *Loaves and Fishes* (1959) was Brown's formal introduction to the poetry-reading public of Britain. This relationship with Hogarth Press was to prove most advantageous, and the title (deriving from the gospel account of miraculous feeding of the five thousand in the desert) was more than a little prophetic. This initial commercial publication, despite the reluctance of the author, was to multiply into at least seventeen additional Hogarth volumes of poetry, short stories, novels, and children's stories.

Despite the scriptural allusion in the title of *Loaves and Fishes*, not much contained therein expresses the kind of faith and hope one might normally expect of Christian poetry. Almost everything is imbued with a meandering melancholy that ultimately derives from such Anglo-Saxon poems as "The Wanderer," "The Seafarer," "Wulf and Eadwacer," and "Deor's Lament" (this last a poem that Brown translates into modern English in *Winterfold*, 1976). Often the main character in a little dramatic vignette (always a male: a Thorfinn, a "grey-eyed sober boy," a "shining one," a "winterman," a "Gregory hero," an unidentified "he") wanders through a hostile landscape—not to a resurrection, a forgiveness, or the blessed sight of a Holy Grail, but toward a rather meaningless annihilation. This "sea-change" is often wrought by the obsessive claws of crabs and lobsters: for example, "sail to the lobsters in a storm and drown," "to their peril they [the lobsters] eat man fodder," "down the throat of crabs . . . in a core of shells," "A penitential wail / For the blue lobster . . . flashed." In "Thorfinn," who derives from the historically important Thorfinn of the Old Icelandic *Orkneyinga Saga*, the divine act of creation is rendered thus: "God puts in their beautiful claws / Sweet algae and tiny glimmering fish / The dropping surfeits of the rich Atlantic. . . ."

Loaves and Fishes consists of twenty-five poems of varying lengths and patterns, arranged in three groups, called respectively "The Drowning Wave," "Crofts Along the Shore," and "The Redeeming Wave." Adjectives in the titles of the first and last sections ("Drowning" and "Redeeming") reveal a good deal about Brown's symbolic patterns. The "waves" themselves (usually filled with literal or figurative crabs and lobsters) are the destructive forces in life or nature that cannot be resisted—Brown's negative evaluation of the philosophy of naturalism. For the Trojans in "That Night in Troy," the "wave" is the inevitable fire destruction of their city. For the despairing and dying traveler in "The Masque of Bread," it is the ominous answerless figures at the "fragrant doorpost" of the "Angel with a sword / Or Grinning Rags." The unidentified man in "The Shining Ones" falters between what is behind him ("the night . . . a funnel of darkness, roaring with stars") and what is ahead of him on the purgatorial hill ("silent watchers / Out of the dawn lifted their swords"). Brown's formula is a seemingly simple one, but highly personal in its spiritual implications: the "drowning" waves of nature are destructive, while the "redeeming" waves of Christianity are only darkly purifying.

In *Loaves and Fishes*, perhaps only "St. Magnus on Egilsay" can be called a thoroughly Christian poem, yet even here ominous images of crabs and lobsters (metamorphosed into ploughs, harrows, and scythes) haunt the poem, turning it into a Christian version of "Thorfinn"—as "red ploughs cleave their snow and curve for ever / Across the April hill." Brown's interest in the twelfth-century Orkneyian martyr Magnus Erlendsson, Earl of Orkney, derives from his reading of several chapters in the *Orkneyinga Saga*. Brown's poem is based on the presumed location of the martyrdom of St. Magnus, the "cold hill" on the northern island of Egilsay, that "locked thighs of stone against / The ardent ploughs" (a reference to the martyr's practice of plunging himself into icy water to preserve himself against sexual temptation)—the "cold hill," where he bowed his "blank head," offered "innocent vein," and the "red wave" of martyrdom "broke." The place of martyrdom is marked by St. Magnus Kirk on the island of Egilsay. Reference in T. S. Eliot's *The Waste Land* (1922) to the "inexplicable splendor of Ionian white and gold" (also associated with "fishmen") of Sir Christopher Wren's Magnus Martyr in London was not without its influence upon George Mackay Brown. But while Eliot's line draws attention to artistic splendors, Brown (as Eliot himself was to do later in life) attempts to commit himself to more essential Christian implications.

During the preparation and publication of *Loaves and Fishes*, Brown was at Edinburgh University, having entered in 1956, and in 1960 graduated with a second-class honors degree in English literature. Almost immediately he experienced another attack of tuberculosis, though less severe than preceding attacks in 1941 and 1953, and recuperated at Tor-Na-Dee Sanatorium in Aberdeen. Upon recovery, he applied to do postgraduate work on Gerard Manley Hopkins at Edinburgh University, where he remained from 1962 to 1964. Brown had entered the Catholic Church in 1961, a fact that may have informed his choice of the convert-priest Hopkins as his subject. Considering such poems as "St. Magnus at Egilsay" and his consistent distaste for the Protestant Reformation, especially the drab Presbyterian sermons and services (during which, as a boy, both he and his father "ate sweets"), the conversion was not entirely unexpected. His attraction to Catholicism began in his midteens, and he characterizes himself as always "intrigued by the majesty and mystery" of the Catholic faith, the "long history of the church . . . enriched by all that poetry and music, art and architecture, could give; and still apparently as strong as ever in our gray twentieth century."

In 1965 Hogarth Press and Chatto and Windus jointly published *The Year of the Whale*. Consisting of twenty-five poems on topics similar to those of the preceding Hogarth volume, the collection has been criticized for its morbid and monotonous tendencies. The cause of Brown's depressions may derive from the insecurities of his conversion to a religion that was the historical antithesis of Scotland's traditional and more "patriotic" Calvinism; and the overlay of an ancient Catholicism of crosses and contradictions upon a traditionally hell-haunted Presbyterianism may have been more than Brown's personality could bear. Additionally, the debilitating illness that periodically afflicted him, confining him to endless months of inactivity, also took its inevitable psychological toll. But whatever the cause, the 1965 collection must be considered less effective than the incisive and imaginative vignettes of the earlier *Loaves and Fishes* (which are equally death-obsessed).

Because of the consistently high quality of his poetic language, it is difficult to fault Brown on specific poems, or even on individual lines and images. Something always strikes and catches fire in his poetry, as in "Old Fisherman with Guitar," where a sad tune becomes a "gentle wing the west had thrown / Against his breakwater wall with salt savage lament"; and manly hands that guide a melody through the strings of a guitar are hands that once "cut from the net / The strong / Crab-eaten corpse of Jock washed from a boat / One old winter, and gathered the mouth of Thora to his mouth." Despite the vibrant language that Brown can produce almost at will, the main problem with this second major volume is technical—a monotonous regularity and sameness of design. The fifty-two-line litany "Our Lady of the Waves" (one of the earliest of several such religious lyrics that Brown produced) seems to have encouraged litanylike patterns that prevail throughout *The Year of the Whale*. In successive stanzas, the mother of Jesus is invoked as "Blessed Lady." "Holy Mother," "Sweet Virgin," and "Queen of Heaven," and parallelisms and subject-predicate arrangements abound: "We have done three things. / We have bent hooks. / We have patched a sail. / We have sharpened knives."

Consequently, the reader becomes tired of such poems as "Hamnavoe Market," in which each of seven three-line stanzas is devoted to an otherwise unknown and unidentified person; or "The Abbot," in which seven unknown "brothers" are presented in seven stanzas; or "Shipwreck," in which five sailors are given five lines each; or "Weather Bestiary," in which aspects of the weather are catalogued in childlike metaphors. In his essay "Writer's Shop," Brown recalls that he "hated arithmetic in school, and later geometry and trigonometry, but later these disciplines taught me to reverence form—the beauty and mystery and inevitability of numbers." These hated mathematical forms "proved useful" when Brown turned to the numbers of poetry; and, coupled with the mystically repetitive litanies of his newly adopted Catholicism, they emerged with a vengeance in *The Year of the Whale*. Significantly, Brown believes it "important to stress . . . early impulses because they set the rhythm and tone of one's whole life," and he regards the biography of an artist as a "pattern of those [youthful] moments, that, once realised, appear and re-appear over and over again in his work."

Of the poems that follow such boxed-in patterns, "The Funeral of Ally Flett" is one of the most imaginative. Here too, six of seven stanzas begin with "because" (the other with a similar "although"), and each of the eight-line stanzas is dedicated to some aspect of Ally Flett's life, his drinking and sexuality in the opening stanzas, or grief and futility of his passing ("One skipper . . . bowed his head"; "The preacher spoke the holy word"; "Old Betsy came with bitter cries"; "Tammas brought his Swedish fiddle"). What saves the poem from the monotony of the other litanylike poems is the complicated rhyme structure, and interesting and unusual line arrangements.

Two poems in *The Year of the Whale* are notable for historical reasons. One of these is "The Seven Houses," composed in memory of the assassination of John F. Kennedy on 22 November 1963. Like the incremental repetitions of other poems, stanzas are structured on repeated lines, words, and images. The beginning of each stanza indicates that someone is at a door ("Man, you are at the first door," for example), and final lines identify Brown's version of Shakespeare's seven stages of man as a house: that is, "House of the Womb," "House of Birth," "House of Corn and Grape," and so on. A woman, or women, appears in every stanza, except the sixth which concerns the politics of the presidency itself. One of the few criticisms that Edwin Muir ever directed at Brown was that occasionally a poem would turn out "cold, abstract and theoretical," and this criticism applies perfectly to "The Seven Houses." It is more an exercise in rhetoric than a lament for an assassinated president. The only attractive parts of the poem are the central portions of each stanza, where something in Kennedy's life is wrapped in a symbol. Thus, Rose Kennedy's pregnancy becomes "nine candles" whereby "with reptile and fish and beast / You dance in silence." The third stanza ("House of Man") projects three women (like three Eves) standing at a symbolic "bare bitter bloody tree" that is "loaded with apples." The poem imposes upon the reader the necessary burden of puzzling out obscure relationships between poetic symbol ("seven stars," "seven bright drops," "seventy thousand ordered days," "disordered dangerous board") and the personal and political life of Kennedy.

By contrast, the second important historical poem, "*Culloden*: The Last Battle," is more effective in creating the air of sorrow and frustration that Brown must have been trying for in the Kennedy poem. It commemorates the defeat of "Bonnie Prince Charlie," the Scottish pretender, by the Duke of Cumberland on 16 April 1746. This phase of the struggle for Scotland began on 3 August 1745, when the pretender landed in the Hebrides, and extended through a series of temporary Stuart triumphs only to end in disaster at Culloden, when approximately one thousand Highlanders were killed and many hundreds taken prisoner and summarily executed by the victorious English forces. The English soldier in the poem has "eyes . . . hard as ice," his "Saxon bayonet / Bright as a wolf's tooth." In Brown's poem the Englishman is killed. The Scottish companions of the Drumnakeil man, who is narrator, are either killed in battle ("Donald gave a cry / Like a wounded stag") or die in the retreat ("Alastair died in the straw"). With "three wounds . . . heavy and round" (most likely symbolizing male genitals), the Drumnakeil speaker returns to his woman Morag, who (like the classical Penelope or the one of the three Fates) has been weaving "plaid." In a typical turn of phrase, it is she, Morag, who "Weaving . . . sings of the beauty of defeat." The subject of Culloden comes up again in "The Escape of the Hart" (*Winterfold*) and "Prince in the Heather" (*Poems New and Selected*, 1971), this second poem imaginatively composed by "The bard Alasdair MacNiall . . . the day after the true prince left Scotland for France, 1746."

In 1965, the year of the publication of *The Year of the Whale*, Brown received an Arts Council grant for poetry. Later a Society of Authors Travel Award opened up an opportunity for the Orkney-bound Brown to visit Ireland in 1968. His well-received second volume of short stories, *A Time to Keep* (1969), earned him a Scottish Arts Council Literature prize, and for the title story he was given a Katherine Mansfield Menton Short Story prize, a triennial French-English award offered by the vil-

lage of Menton, France, and administered by the P.E.N. Club of Great Britain. One of his most distinguished nonliterary awards was the widely conferred Order of the British Empire in 1974.

Fishermen with Ploughs (1971), subtitled *A Poem Cycle*, is Brown's most impressive poetic effort, a sequence of obscurely connected lyrics based on island "history" as the author reconceives it. The sequence extends from approximately the ninth century, with the arrival of the Norsemen in the Rackwick valley of the island of Hoy (directly south of Brown's native Orkney), to its progress- and Protestant-ruined condition in the twentieth century. As a matter of fact, Brown offers his readers two versions of the same materials: a melancholy, impressionistic prose piece called "Rackwick" in *An Orkney Tapestry* (1969), and an in-depth poetic analysis of similar historical and social matters in the quasiepic poem cycle *Fishermen with Ploughs*, both spawned by the accidental drowning in the summer of 1952 of two brothers who had been playing on a raft in the Rackwick valley—the only young people left in the valley among their elders.

The poetic cycle is divided into six uneven sections entitled "Dragon and Dove," "Our Lady," "Hall and Kirk," "Foldings," "The Stone Hawk," and "The Return of the Women." The first few poems are gathered together under the symbols of dragon and dove—the dragon (as in the book of *Revelation*) representing "starvation, pestilence and turbulent neighbors"; the dove (as in the stories of Noah and the Gospels) representing the ship of salvation, the promise of peaceful coexistence, and the love union of the Holy Trinity. There are five main characters: an unnamed blind helmsman of the "ship called Dove," who utters several prophetical poems to the fishermen-turned-farmers; Thorkeld, the old pagan chieftain, who must endure the "horn" and "hoofbeat" of enemies and the cruel burning of his tribal town and build that "vibrant cluster" of ship ribs called *Dove*; Njal, his son and chieftain after his death, who must preside over the new agricultural community and, through anguish, learn that "Lust, bread kissed, becomes love"; Norn, the wife of the harried Thorkeld, who like "all women" is "glad . . . at a man's stillness," in this instance, the death of her husband, whose body has been "charted with twelve wounds"; and Gudrun, who is a "sweet grain jar" to Njal her husband, but who realizes that women are "A crude workaday winter vessel," whose "first honey is soon drunk," and is thereafter used by men for all "oil and salt and brine."

The Nordic alliterative and kenning-clipped

manner of part one is contrasted with the far less oracular style of part two, "Our Lady." The life of the new crofters (who by now have ceased being craftmakers) is compared to the fourteen stations of the cross, and twelve women (like twelve apostles) can "light their lamps now," and cease being, as Gudrun asserted in an earlier poem of the cyle, "thrown on a devious wheel" of sexual misfortune. Thus, croft women, fishermen, shepherds, tinkers, washerwomen, and death watchers offer a litany—gentle and touching—to the Virgin Mary, praying in an ancient repetitive manner before "The Statue in the Hills." But the idyllic life proves abrasive, and like Old Testament Hebrews wandering for forty years in the desert ("they are tired of salt beef"), they yearn for delicacies that deteriorate the spirit of heroic sacrifice and patient endurance: "Their loins are restless. / The oarsmen like olives. / They gulp that French wine like ale."

Section three, "Hall and Kirk," spans the period from the Calvinizing of Scotland in the sixteenth century to the Napoleonic era of the nineteenth. As Brown explains in *An Orkney Tapestry*, by the nineteenth century everything had utterly changed. The chief, who in spite of everything had once been the peoples' protector, was now a stranger and an extortioner. The religion that had sweetened their labors and sufferings had turned to a creed of terror and hellfire. Our Lady of Furrows on the side of the hill remained, but she had to be visited secretly and at night. According to Brown's reading of these events "Their green peace was broken." As a consequence, there followed the burning of witches ("Witch"), a yielding to the "black music" of Calvinism ("A Reel of Seven Fishermen"), cruel taxations ("Taxman"), and "sometimes, the horsemen would carry off a young man" of the Rackwick valley "for His Majesty's ships of war" against the French (especially Napoleon), and "leave a guinea on the table, bounty money"—a family tragedy explored in depth in "Buonaparte, the Laird, and the Volunteers."

The fourth and fifth sections, "Foldings" and "The Stone Hawk," are by far the most expansive parts of the Fishermen sequence. The eighteen poems of "Foldings" represent the 1800s, that is the Victorian Age, when the Orcadians were presumably made literate and secure with such enlightened legislation as the Scottish Education Act of 1872 and the Crofters' Act of 1886. Despite these and other social "advances," much of the people's efforts is spent in "Peat Cutting" to supply heat for homes, calling up ghosts of the dead men of Hoy as in "New Year Stories," driving old horses back to their patch

of clover as in "A Warped Boat," or never saying a word to one another as in "Twins." The final poem, "Ploughman and Whales," has a farmer, amid the frustrations of field ploughing, hearing a "low thunder" and seeing "whales / On trek from ocean to ocean."

In the nineteen extraordinary poems of the fifth part, "The Stone Hawk" (the nineteen standing for the present century as the 1900s), Brown presses the thesis that—to use the words of his preface to the volume—"perhaps . . . the quality of life grows poorer as Progress multiplies its gifts on a simple community." His position against progress is not absolutist or dogmatic, as the "perhaps" clearly indicates, but more like the bird of prey in the "Laird's Falcon" that drift[s] like a still question over / The fecund quarterings of the field." All too often, Brown seems to argue, progress increases the productivity of some areas of the earth while at the same time through excessive waste, careless judgments, and industrial poisonings decreases the productivity of other lands and even the life-filled oceans themselves.

Whales, for example, though abundant in early poems, become fewer and fewer as the poetic cycle progresses toward the "enlightenment" of the present century, and are seen only in quick glances and occasional metaphors. Also, the "Beachcomber" finds only a "boot," a "spar of timber," a "half can of Swedish spirits," and, not infrequently, "nothing." "Haddock Fishermen" probe the "emptiness" of the sea with their honey-dripping oars and taut lines (as if the sea were an infertile woman) to catch only "twelve cold mouths" of fish that "scream without sound." Progress is somehow remotely responsible even for the drowning of the two boys in 1952, "dark angels" Brown calls them, and imaginatively resurrects them in the poem "Drowning Brothers." Like the children in the opening chapter of Virginia Woolf's *The Waves* (1931), the spirits of these young boys speak to one another with such metaphoric intensity ("The burn is a fish in a net of fences," "The silver tongue yearns on and out," "Heather to cornstalk to seaweed he burbles gossip") that a reader can have no way of knowing, from the poem alone, whether the boys are real or carefully carved voices of the imagination. In the last line, the boys are, in fact, called "statues"; and in the slow elegiac tone of "Drowning Brothers," they become like the figure of drowned Edward King in Milton's stately "Lycidas"—in Brown's words, "half marble and half flesh."

In a comment quoted in Alan Bold's monograph, Brown observed, "I'm much better at stories than poetry: more original, fresh—there's more of myself in my imaginative prose." Although many of the lyrics in *Fishermen with Ploughs* are beautiful (though bold and sometimes bleak), Brown felt the medium of poetry inadequate for a full statement of his feelings against materialist progress and the consequent abandonment of the Rackwick valley. In the sixth and last section, "The Return of the Women," he shifts to whole pages of prose, not a surprising development considering the attention that his prose was receiving at this point in his career.

"The Return of the Women" is a three-part arrangement of monologues, influenced by the narrative techniques of Virginia Woolf's *The Waves* and William Faulkner's *As I Lay Dying* (1930). Each block of prose is spoken by one of seven women, who, along with six silent men with whom six of them are paired, have escaped some technological devastation, identified only as the "Black Flame." As the unlucky thirteen voyage to the once-abandoned haven, Rackwick, the sea scene resembles the return of Odysseus to Ithaca, or more deliberately, the crossing of the infernal Styx by the souls of the pagan abandoned. In their individual monologues, both during the voyage, and after landing in part two, and the eventual harvest of corn in part three, the women gradually expose the true characters of their mates, who, despite the heroic ring of some of their names (such as Siegfried and David) prove rather inadequate. Surprisingly, however, the weakest of all, John the science student, shows the greatest courage by not uttering a single cry despite forty-five lashings by the cruel skipper-dictator ("patriarch, law-giver, priest, keeper of seed, measurer of the west, laird") for having accidentally broken the blade of a scythe.

Beginning in 1967 (only four years prior to publication of *Fishermen with Ploughs*) and continuing thereafter for approximately eleven years, Brown produced four volumes of short stories (*A Calendar of Love and Other Stories*, 1967; *A Time to Keep*, 1969; *Hawkfall and Other Stories*, 1974; and *The Sun's Net*, 1976), two novels (*Greenvoe*, 1972, and *Magnus*, 1973), two volumes of children's tales (*The Two Fiddlers: Tales from Orkney*, 1974, and *Pictures in the Cave*, 1977), and a set of imaginative essays (*An Orkney Tapestry*, 1969).

In addition to *Fishermen with Ploughs*, the year 1971 also saw the publication of *Poems New and Selected*, containing fifteen poems from *Loaves and Fishes*, twenty-one from *The Year of the Whale*, and about a dozen new poems. In 1973 Harcourt Brace Jovanovich published an enlarged American edition of these selected poems, thereby introducing

Brown's poetry, otherwise generally unknown to the American poetry-reading public. With eleven new poems from *Fishermen with Ploughs*, an expanded edition was published by Hogarth Press in 1977 under the title *Selected Poems*. The year before Chatto and Windus and Hogarth Press jointly published *Winterfold* (1976), with a five-part poem to Mary and Joseph in Bethlehem ("Winterfold"), and nine variations on one of Brown's favorite themes ("Stations of the Cross")—a devotional volume that surfaces as a kind of Catholic postcript to the despair and disillusionment of the apocalyptic *Fishermen with Ploughs*.

Brown's otherwise conspicuous Catholicism plays a negligible role, curiously, in the final female "resolutions" of *Fishermen with Ploughs*. Catholic ritual and prayer practices so often noted in commentaries on Brown's work, and apparently so significantly placed in the "Our Lady" section of the sequence ("Stations of the Cross" and "Statue in the Hills"), are reduced to a mere memory of Our Lady Star of the Sea in a school chapel. What looks like a statue of the Virgin turns out to be only a stone ("It was indeed only a stone that the sea had washed"). It remains for *Winterfold* to attempt some sort of aesthetic and / or spiritual regeneration. Brown does this by making the Bethlehem story (in the title poem "Winterfold") and the "Nine Variations" on the Stations of the Cross the beginning and the end of the volume. The Bethlehem sequence of five poems is not only a retelling of the gospel incidents already exploited in "The Heavenly Stones" (*Loaves and Fishes*) and the "Midwinter Music" section of *An Orkney Tapestry*, but one of the segments, "The Golden Door," is a reworking of major themes in the unsatisfactory Kennedy assassination poem, "The Seven Houses." According to Brown's personal aesthetic, as expressed in the foreword to *Winterfold*: "An imperfect poem goes on seeking the silence."

This constant "interrogation of silence"—the artist's true task as phrased in "The Poet" (*The Year of the Whale*)—is what motivates the constant repetition of the Stations of the Cross poem "From Stone to Thorn," which reappears as the first of the "Nine Variations" (Brown expresses his apologies in the foreword). It can also be found in the "Rackwick" section of *An Orkney Tapestry*, and in such out-of-the-way places as the autobiographical essay, "Writer's Shop," in *Chapman* magazine, where he speaks of it as a "key poem for anyone who is interested in my writing." The "Nine Variations" are inventive, innovative, and even spiritually uplifting for those who have similar religious orientations. "Pilate," the second set of fourteen "stations" (each station a separate line or set of lines), is Pilate's version of the events to which he is a central witness. The third set is a series of haikulike poems on "The Lesser Mysteries of Art." The fourth set, influenced by Wallace Stevens's "Thirteen Ways of Looking at a Blackbird" and Gerard Manley Hopkins's "Windhover," views the stations from the vantage point of a hawk. The fifth to ninth sets are treated with varying emphases: "Potter and Jar," "The Stone Cross," "Sea Village," "Creator," "Kingdom of Dust," "Carpenter."

One of the most interesting aspects of these nine variations, actually little dramatic or figurative vignettes, is that they can be read "cruciform," that is both downward from the first line to the last and crosswise from, say, the fourth station of the first poem through the fourth stations of all the others. The cumulative effect of reading the poem both downward and crosswise is startling. For example, the "stripping" (the tenth station) in one poem is "rags of flesh about the bone," in another "flake of feather and slivers of bone," and yet another: "He suffered himself to become, on a hill, / Starker than seed or star."

In the twenty-nine poems of *Winterfold*, Brown exploits his usual Orcadian preoccupations: the martyrdom of St. Magnus ("April the Sixteenth"), the *Orkneyinga Saga* ("Norse Lyrics of Rognvald Kolson"), and the "selkie-seal" legends of the Orkneys ("The Desertion of the Women and Seals"). Brown apologizes for the free renderings of the original Old Icelandic poems of Earl Rognvald, calling them "imitations," a term derived from that composite genre, the imitation-translations of Robert Lowell, and explains that "what I have tried to do is preserve some of the gaiety, savagery, piety of the originals." Except for purists, however, these reservations are hardly necessary, for the eight lyrics of the historical Rognvald sequence ("The Accomplishments of an Earl," "Merchant Ship," "The Westray Monks," "A Shipwreck in Shetland," "Love Songs to the Lady Ermengarde of Narbonne," "In Praise of Audun," "Jerusalem," and "A Mass at Sea") are quite pleasing. The "Crusader" section of *An Orkney Tapestry* describes Rognvald, who for Brown is both "Earl and Saint," as "nephew to the martyred Magnus" and the "most attractive person in the saga of the Orkney," who made a "penitential voyage to the Holy Land" as "one way of redeeming" the "murder, piracy, rape, war, sacrilege" perpetrated by the Norsemen. The "Crusader" chapter also contains additional poems interspersed with the prose. The three harp songs, "Vikings," that immediately follow the Rognvald poems in *Winterfold* ("Bjorn the Shetlander," "The

New Skipper," and "A Battle in Ulster") continue the Viking theme, though without Catholic connotations—a pattern of poem arrangement that reveals much about Brown's alternating, and perhaps even coexisting, spirituality and secularism. In general, however, *Winterfold*, published when Brown was fifty-five, is quieter, subdued, more resolved, and perhaps even more resigned, than his earlier crab- and lobster-eaten obsessions, the *Sturm und Drang* of earlier and more youthful poetry.

The bulk of Brown's poetic output is contained in *Loaves and Fishes, The Year of the Whale, Fishermen with Ploughs*, and *Winterfold*, plus the new poems in *Poems New and Selected*. The poems of the smaller volumes—*The Storm and Other Poems, Twelve Poems* (1968), and *Lifeboat and Other Poems* (1971)—are, with trifling exceptions, mostly republished in the larger collections. Critical reaction has, on occasion, been negative. Louis Coxe, reviewing *Poems New and Selected* in the *New Republic* (6 October 1973), commented that the poems are "repetitious and derivative in a way that deprive them of true meaning"—although Coxe made an occasional exception for a poem that he found "wholly authentic and right." More often, however, critics have been inclined to the view expressed by Rowe Portis in *Library Journal* (July 1973) that Brown is "one of the best writers currently producing in English" and that the "poetry is mature, adept, haunting," and "splendid mingling of myth and reality."

In a penetrating essay in *Poetry Nation* (1974), Douglas Dunn observed that even "when excessive alliteration and heavy rhythm . . . seem to intrude on the contemporary veracity of his observations, it is like an unconscious recall of the past making itself felt." Quite perceptively, Dunn noted that the "anxious feeling in Brown's poems for the unknowable scale of time, and the existence of mysterious dimensions" is one "explanation for the bardic styles he sometimes uses." Commenting on his use of border ballads and Icelandic sagas, Brown considers these "seminal stories" things "conceived in simplicity" that "grow surrounded by silences"— silences that are eventually transmuted into poetry. "To utter a name or a word," Brown explains, is "to set the whole web trembling" and "be caught up" in the "beautiful dance of fruition."

Reference:
Alan Bold, *George Mackay Brown* (Edinburgh: Oliver & Boyd, 1978).

Charles Causley
(24 August 1917-   )

Dana Gioia

SELECTED BOOKS: *Runaway* (London: Curwen, 1936);

The Conquering Hero (London: Curwen, 1937; New York: Schirmer, 1937);

Benedict (London: Muller, 1938);

How Pleasant to Know Mrs. Lear: A Victorian Comedy (London: Muller, 1948);

Hands to Dance (London: Carroll & Nicholson, 1951); revised and enlarged as *Hands to Dance and Skylark* (London: Robson, 1979);

Farewell, Aggie Weston (Aldington, Kent: Hand & Flower Press, 1951);

Survivor's Leave (Aldington, Kent: Hand & Flower Press, 1953);

Union Street: Poems (London: Hart-Davis, 1957; Boston: Houghton Mifflin, 1958);

Johnny Alleluia: Poems (London: Hart-Davis, 1961);

Underneath the Water (London: Macmillan, 1968);

Figure of 8: Narrative Poems (London: Macmillan, 1969);

Figgie Hobbin: Poems for Children (London: Macmillan, 1970; New York: Walker, 1973);

The Tail of the Trinosaur (Leicester: Brockhampton Press, 1972);

As I Went Down Zig Zag (London & New York: Warne, 1974);

Collected Poems, 1951-1975 (London: Macmillan, 1975; Boston: Godine, 1975);

The Hill of the Fairy Calf (London: Hodder & Stoughton, 1976);

The Gift of a Lamb (London: Robson, 1978);

The Ballad of Aucassin and Nicolette (Middlesex: Kestrel, 1981).

OTHER: *Dawn and Dusk: Poems of Our Time*, edited by Causley (Leicester: Brockhampton Press, 1962; New York: Watts, 1963);

Rising Early: Story Poems and Ballads of the 20th Century, edited by Causley (Leicester: Brockhampton Press, 1964); republished as *Modern Ballads and Story Poems* (New York: Watts, 1965);

The Puffin Book of Magic Verse, edited by Causley (Harmondsworth: Penguin, 1974);

Hamdija Demirovic, *Twenty-five Poems*, translated by Causley (Richmond: Keepsake Press, 1980);

The Sun, Rising: Christian Verse, edited by Causley (Harmondsworth: Penguin, 1982).

PERIODICAL PUBLICATION: "Charles Causley Writes . . . ," *Poetry Book Society Bulletin*, no. 56 (Spring 1968): 1-2.

Charles Causley has stood apart from the mainstream of contemporary poetry. His work bears little relation to the most celebrated achievements of the modernist movement but refers back to older, more specifically English roots. Taking his inspiration from popular folk songs and ballads, Causley stands with writers, such as A. E. Houseman, Thomas Hardy, Rudyard Kipling, Walter de la Mare, Robert Graves, John Betjeman, and perhaps Philip Larkin, who are part of a conservative countertradition in English letters which stresses the fundamentally national nature of its poetry and the critical role of popular forms in its inspiration.

Much of Causley's poetry has been written in the ballad form. Indeed he is the most celebrated and accomplished living writer of ballads in the English language, but his achievements are not so narrowly focused as many critics believe. He has mastered an impressive variety of forms, and the true unity of his work is not found so much in any specific allegiance to a particular form like the ballad but rather in his fundamental commitment to certain traditional virtues of English poetry—simplicity, clarity, grace, and compassion. He holds the steadfast conviction that the traditional forms of popular English poetry are living modes of expression, despite the modernist revolution, choosing to write in simple, traditional forms in a period which prizes originality and complexity. He has endorsed the importance of narrative poetry in an age which has called the very notion of narrative poetry into question. This conservatism has placed Causley in a radically independent position among contemporary poets writing in English, but ultimately he is less important for his independent stance than for the excellence and integrity of his verse. He is a potent reminder that talent often travels on a path divergent from the age.

Charles Stanley Causley was born to Charles Samuel and Laura Jane Bartlett Causley in the small Cornish market town of Launceston, where except for his six years of military service he has lived ever since. Although he was too young to have any direct memories of World War I, the Great War exercised an unusual influence on his childhood. His father, who had served as a private soldier in France throughout the war, returned a hopeless invalid, and the young Causley, an only child, spent his first seven years watching his father slowly die from the effects of German gas. As a child he also watched the strange and frightening behavior of the shell-shocked soldiers who wandered through his native town. "From childhood, then," he wrote years later in his autobiographical afterword to *Hands to Dance and Skylark* (1979), "it had been made perfectly clear to me that war was something more than the exciting fiction one read about in books or saw on films."

From boyhood Causley intended to be an author. He began a novel at the age of nine and continued writing in a desultory fashion throughout his education at Launceston College. On leaving school in 1933 he spent seven gloomy years working first as a clerk in a builder's office and later for a local electrical supply company. In the meantime, however, he continued experimenting with poetry, the short story, the novel, and most successfully with drama. He had three one-act plays published in the late 1930s. During the same period Causley also played piano in a four-piece dance band, an experience which may have influenced his later predilection for writing poems in popular lyric forms such as the ballad.

In 1940 Causley joined the Royal Navy, in which he served for the next six years. Having spent all of his earlier life in tranquil Cornwall, he now saw wartime southern Europe, Africa, and Australia. Likewise, having already deeply felt the tragedy of war through the early death of his father, Causley experienced it again more directly in the deaths of friends and comrades. These experiences proved decisive to his literary career, pulling him from prose and drama into poetry. "I think I became a working poet the day I joined the destroyer Eclipse at Scapa Flow in August, 1940," he later wrote in a note on his work for the *Poetry Book Society Bulletin*. "Though I wrote only fragmentary notes for the next three years, the wartime experience was a catalytic one. I knew that at last I had found my first subject, as well as a form." Although Causley wrote one book of short stories based on his wartime experiences, *Hands to Dance* (1951; revised and enlarged in 1979 as *Hands to Dance and Skylark*), his major medium for dealing with his wartime experiences has been poetry.

In August 1945 the Pacific war ended (Causley witnessed this event, as the Japanese command in the Southwest Pacific surrendered on the flight deck of the aircraft carrier on which he was stationed). Returning to Launceston he entered the Peterborough Teacher's Training College to study English and history. Upon graduation he began teaching at the same school in Launceston that he had studied in as a boy.

In 1951 Causley brought out his first collection, *Farewell, Aggie Weston*, a small pamphlet of thirty-one poems. The distillation of Causley's years in the navy, the poems in this volume vividly recreate the alternatingly intoxicating and sobering experiences of a generation of young Englishmen who in fighting World War II discovered the wider world. Most of the poems depict the sailor's life in wartime, both on ship and in the strange port cities he visits on leave. In its colorful portrayal of navy life *Farewell, Aggie Weston* remains one of the most representative books of English poetry to emerge from World War II, and the poem "Chief Petty Officer" has become a definitive poem of the period in its capturing a kind of naval character who typified for better or worse the British military traditions that won the war. The book also has documentary importance since the poems incorporate a wealth of traditional and contemporary naval slang (much of which Causley explains in footnotes). Like Kipling fifty years before him, Causley believed that the only way he could truly capture the unique character of a group of men was to use their special language, and in so doing he provided an interesting record of a particular time and place.

Although *Farewell, Aggie Weston* is not Causley's best book, it already shows him as an accomplished poet with a distinctive voice and perspective. It also foreshadows both the themes and techniques of his later work. The book contains poems written in both free and formal verse, and Causley uses both techniques in particular ways to which he returns repeatedly in his subsequent career. His free verse is loose, cadenced speech used mainly for carefully detailed descriptive poems, whereas his metered poems, which are cast mainly in rhymed quatrains, especially various ballad stanzas, are used mostly for narrative and dramatic poems. Not surprisingly, given Causley's later eminence as a master of traditional forms, the best poems in *Farewell, Aggie Weston* are in rhyme and meter, usually in ballad form, such as his memorable "Nursery Rhyme of Innocence and Experience," which ends:

> "O are you the boy
>   Who would wait on the quay
> With the silver penny
>   And the apricot tree?
>
> 'I've a plum-colored fez
>   And a drum for thee
> And a sword and a parakeet
>   From over the sea.'
>
> "O where is the sailor
>   With bold red hair?
> And what is that volley
>   On the bright air?
>
> "O where are the other
>   Girls and boys?
> And why have you brought me
>   Children's toys?"

Thematically, *Farewell, Aggie Weston* reveals the issues which will concern him throughout his career—the harsh reality of war ("Song of the Dying Gunner"), the tragic deaths of the young and

promising ("A Ballad for Katharine of Aragon"), the fascination with foreign landscapes ("HMS *Glory* at Sydney"), and most important, the fall from innocence to experience, a sense of which pervades the entire volume. Only Causley's problematic Christianity is specifically absent from this first volume, although with the gift of hindsight one can see the elements which produced it in several of the poems about death and war.

Although Causley's second volume, *Survivor's Leave* (1953), does not mark a broadening of his poetic concerns, it demonstrates a liberating concentration. Abandoning cadenced free verse and the aesthetic of raw experience it embodies, Causley perfected the tightly formal poems for which he would become best known. All of the poems in *Survivor's Leave* are written in rhyme and meter, a common coin which he now uses in a distinctively personal way. His rhythms move with deliberate regularity, and the diction has a timeless traditional quality. His full rhymes ring loudly at the end of each line. Sometimes unsophisticated to the point of crudity, these poems often have the texture of folk poetry or popular song, which gives them an unusual openness and immediacy. In an age when most poets writing in rhyme and meter try to disguise or underplay the formal patterns of their verse, Causley is a radical traditionalist, a primitive, who is unabashedly open with his forms in a way unmatched by any contemporary poet except John Betjeman.

Survivor's Leave also demonstrates Causley's growing mastery of the ballad and contains two of his finest poems in that form, "Recruiting Drive" and "Ballad of the Faithless Wife." In these and other poems one notices the influence of Auden's work, which provided Causley with a model of how to rejuvenate this traditional form with bold metaphors and the use of archetypal figures. But while Causley learned much from Auden, his work is never derivative. Causley's well-known poem "On Seeing a Poet of the First World War at the Station of Abbeville" (a composite portrait based on Edmund Blunden, Siegfried Sassoon, and the poet's father), for example, incorporates techniques from Auden's lyric poetry, but Causley uses them to achieve effects that are particularly his own.

As his title suggests, Causley's major theme in *Survivor's Leave* is once again war, though here the conflict has been universalized beyond World War II into a tragic view of life as a doomed struggle between the evil and the innocent. The book is permeated with images of violence and deception. In "Recruiting Drive," a butcher bird lures young men to their deaths in battle. In "Cowboy Song," another young man, bereft of family, knows he will be murdered before his next birthday. Even a seemingly straightforward narrative poem such as the "Ballad of the Faithless Wife" acquires an unexpectedly dark visionary quality when in the last stanza personal tragedy is suddenly modulated into a terrifying allegory:

> False O false was my lover
> Dead on the diamond shore
> White as a fleece, for her name was Peace
> And the soldier's name was War.

Causley's vision in *Survivor's Leave* is so bleak that he even rejects God's role as guardian and savior of humanity. In "I Saw a Shot-Down Angel," for example, a wounded Christ figure crudely rebuffs the compassionate narrator's attempts to help him, thereby denying the redemptive nature of his suffering.

Union Street (1957) secured Causley's reputation as an important contemporary poet. Published with a preface by Edith Sitwell, then at the height of her influence, *Union Street* collected the best poems from Causley's first two volumes and added nineteen new ones, including three of his finest poems to date, "I Am the Great Sun," "Innocent's Song," and "At the British War Cemetery, Bayeux," the last of which Sitwell singled out for particular praise. In her preface, Sitwell placed Causley's work in its proper tradition, English folk song and ballad, but, while she praised Causley's traditional roots, she also noted his "strange individuality." Like most of Causley's admirers, however, Sitwell had difficulty in explaining the appeal of his work. To express her approval Sitwell repeatedly fell back on vague exclamations of delight, such as "beautiful," "deeply moving," and, that adjective which has followed Causley throughout his career, "enchanting." While these terms describe in some general way the effect Causley's poetry has on a sympathetic reader, they are so subjective that they shed little light on the nature of his literary achievement. Unfortunately, Sitwell's response typifies Causley's critical reception. His admirers have felt more comfortable in writing appreciations of his work than in discussing it in critical terms. This situation has given many critics unfamiliar with his work the understandable impression that while it may be enjoyed, because of its simplicity, it does not bear serious analysis.

The new poems in *Union Street* begin with "I Am the Great Sun," a formal devotional sonnet which reveals a change in Causley's Christianity.

Here Christ speaking from the cross (the poem was inspired by a seventeenth-century Norman crucifix) tells of his compassion for man:

> I am the great sun, but you do not see me,
>   I am your husband, but you turn away.
> I am the captive, but you do not free me.
>   I am the captain you will not obey.
>
> I am the truth, but you will not believe me,
>   I am the city where you will not stay,
> I am your wife, your child, but you will leave me,
>   I am that God to whom you will not pray.

This poem reverses the world view of "I Saw a Shot-Down Angel," where man shows compassion for the suffering Christ figure. Here Christ tries to guide and protect mankind, but man refuses to acknowledge him; yet, although man lives in an evil world, salvation is at least possible.

The other new poems in *Union Street* reflect this glimmer of hope without obscuring the bitter realism of Causley's earlier work. In "At the British War Cemetery, Bayeux," for example, the grief-stricken narrator walks among the graves of the five thousand slain soldiers and asks them what gift he can offer them beyond his tears. They reply that, since he cannot restore them to life, he should use their deaths as an inspiration to live "like a spendthrift lover." Love in its broadest Christian sense has become for Causley the means to redemption, but this redemption is not easy. Only one character in *Union Street* is able to achieve salvation through love—Sir Henry Trecarell, a sixteenth-century Cornish lord, who survives the sorrow of his son's death by devoting his wealth to rebuilding the local church at the request of St. Mary Magdalene. But most of Causley's characters lack the strength and wealth of Trecarell, and no saints intervene to guide them. They are tantalized by the notion of redemption but unable to achieve it.

Causley's next four volumes continue to exploit the style he mastered in *Survivor's Leave* and *Union Street*. His poems remain exclusively in rhyme and meter, though he uses form with more overt sophistication to deal with his increasingly complex material. The ballad also continues to attract a major part of Causley's attention, though one now notices a more pronounced division in the kinds of ballads he writes. Each book contains the usual diverse mixture of poems on contemporary themes written in ballad meters, but there is always an additional group of strictly narrative ballads on remote historical or legendary subjects. While Causley had experimented with recreating folk ballads from his first book on, it now becomes a major preoccupation. In his introduction to his anthology *Modern Ballads and Story Poems* Causley confesses the basis of his fascination with "the ancient virtues of this particular kind of writing." The story poem or ballad, he writes, allows the poet to speak "without bias or sentimentality." It keeps the author from moralizing, but it "allows the incidents of his story to speak for themselves; and, as we listen, we remain watchful for all kinds of ironic understatements."

Causley seems to have seen these ballads—most of which were based on historical anecdotes or legends—as providing a balance of objectivity to the increasing subjective and autobiographical poems he was also writing. While the war had provided Causley with a public subject matter in his early work, he now looked to these narrative ballads as creating another sort of accessible common ground. In so doing Causley confirms his position as an outsider from the mainstream of twentieth-century poetry. His ballads temporarily drove out the subjective, autobiographical side of his work, rejecting the notion that a poet creates a private reality in the context of his own poems. Instead they deliberately make an appeal to a common reality outside the poem, a reality presented through the most popular and accessible literary form in English, the ballad.

In this context even Causley's seemingly private Christian poems take on a public aspect since they are based on the central religious and moral beliefs of his culture. Causley can indulge his private imaginative notions freely because the meaning of the poems is firmly rooted in a common mythos. Not surprisingly then, his religious poems often have an almost surreal quality. Although most often written in simple forms, they usually present images and situations which seem extravagant and oddly proportioned. But they are not so much surreal as primitive and symbolic in their method, in much the same way that an early Renaissance painting might present a brightly colored Madonna holding a diminutive moon or castle in her hand and standing in a strange, unearthly landscape. While such art may not be realistic in a strict sense, it deals intelligibly with a widely understood set of symbols.

While Causley's next three volumes after *Union Street* present no stylistic break with the past, each of them marks a deepening of his thematic concerns. In *Johnny Alleluia* (1961) he explores his complex vision of Christ as the redeemer of mankind. Fully half the poems in this volume use Christ figures

either explicitly, as in "Cristo de Bristol" and "Emblems of Passion," or by implication, in strange transformations such as those in "For an Ex-Far East Prisoner of War" and "Guy Fawkes' Day," where the effigy burning in the holiday fire becomes a redemptive sacrificial victim. Likewise Causley alternates scurrilous parodies of the Christ story, such as "Sonnet to the Holy Vine" and the more disturbing "Master and Pupil," with his most devout meditations. Reading his many treatments of the Christian drama, one sees that Causley believes in the authentically redemptive nature of Christ's sacrifice but that he doubts man's ability to accept Christ's love without betrayal.

Johnny Alleluia is also Causley's first volume which does not deal specifically with the war. While his concerns remain basically the same, they are now reflected in civilian themes, especially in such vignettes of urban delinquents as "My Friend Maloney" and "Johnny Alleluia." Only once does World War II literally come to haunt the present—in "Mother, Get Up, Unbar the Door," where a woman's lover, killed nearly twenty years before at Alamein, returns from the grave to claim her daughter in a ghostly union. In this poem Causley shows remarkable skill at transposing a traditional ghost ballad into convincing contemporary terms. Causley also pursues his concern with the fall from innocence in "Healing a Lunatic Boy," possibly his most vivid presentation of this central theme. In this poem a lunatic boy, who originally experiences the world in a direct way reminiscent of Adam's in the Garden of Eden, is brought back to a mundane sense of reality by his cure. Causley contrasts the brilliant and metaphorical world of madness with the prosaic and literal world of sanity:

> Trees turned and talked to me,
>   Tigers sang,
> Houses put on leaves,
>   Water rang.
> Flew in, flew out
>   On my tongue's thread
> A speech of birds
>   From my hurt head.
> . . . .
> Now river is river
>   And tree is tree,
> My house stands still
>   As the northern sea.
> On my hundreds of parables
>   I heard him pray,
> Seize my smashed world,
>   Wrap it away.

In *Underneath the Water* (1968), Causley's most personal book of poems, he speaks frankly of both his childhood and adulthood. The poems about his boyhood are especially important in understanding his work, for, although he wrote a great deal of work about childhood earlier in his career, he rarely discussed his own. The childhood poems in *Underneath the Water* are therefore important for an understanding of the personal background of his most central themes. The volume opens with "By St. Thomas Water," one of Causley's most complex views of the fall from innocence to experience. Two children (one of them presumably Causley himself), looking for a jar to fish with, steal one holding withered flowers on a tombstone. Before they go, they playfully decide to listen for the dead man's voice in the grave, and much to their horror, they think they hear him murmuring indistinctly underground. Noticing the tombstone's legend, "He is not dead but sleeping," they flee in terror. The narrator then spends the rest of his life wondering what the dead man tried to tell him.

In this volume Causley also gives several views of himself as an adult, especially as a teacher of the young—a vocation he finds problematic and frightening—in poems such as "School at Four O'Clock" and "Conducting a Children's Choir." But the most disturbing view of his adult life comes in "Trusham," in which he revisits the village where his father and grandfather were born. He reads his dead father's name on the local war memorial, and even meets an old family acquaintance, who rebukes him for not marrying in order to carry on the family name. These experiences set off a crisis in the poet's mind which ends in a vision of his own cold and barren future.

Figure of 8: Narrative Poems (1969) stands both as Causley's most daring and most reactionary volume. This collection of eight extended narrative poems frankly rejects the mainstream aesthetic of contemporary poetry. At the end of the 1960s when free verse and the intensely lyric short poem were preferred and bitterly confessional verse was coming into vogue, narrative poetry seemed out of step with the times; yet, Causley blithely published a group of extended and impersonal story poems written in galumphing rhyme and meter. *Figure of 8* is Causley's most reactionary volume not only in form but content. All but one of its poems eschew contemporary subjects for those of traditional balladry (Bible stories, legends of the saints, tales of men at war). The poems' tone and diction remain archaically stylized, and although they are written with consummate skill, they imitate traditional folk balladry so closely that they border on pastiche—and, though the poems are pastiche of the highest order, they betray the predictability and tameness of derivative writing. These poems are enjoyable to read, but they lack resonance and depth.

This side of Causley's poetry has left him open to attack from critics such as Christopher Ricks, who see his attempts to revive the ballad as a quixotic pursuit of an impossible ideal. Writing in the *New York Times Book Review*, Ricks declared that Causley's poetry "embarks upon a task which is beyond its talents; true though those are, since it is beyond talent: to tap again the age-old sources which have become clogged, cracked, buried. . . . It would take genius to re-create the world, as something other than a recreation. Causley has much talent and no genius." There is much truth in Ricks's assessment. Skill alone cannot revive a dead literary form. But Ricks's criticism does not apply to all of Causley's work with equal validity. While it describes the dilute nature of Causley's most narrowly derivative work—the archaically stylized ballads on traditional themes—it does not adequately account for the persuasive authenticity of his finest poems. Causley's oeuvre is too diverse to be so narrowly characterized.

Figgie Hobbin (1970), a book of children's verse, bears an illuminating relationship to Causley's "adult" work. Although the poems in *Figgie Hobbin* are simple in structure and usually written from a child's perspective, they are almost indistinguishable from his other verse. In these children's poems he explores his major themes in a fully characteristic way. Indeed they fit seamlessly into the *Collected Poems* (1975), where they are presented without comment among his adult poems. Moreover, as a group, these tight and polished poems rank high among Causley's published work. "What Has Happened to Lou," "Tell Me, Tell Me, Sarah Jane," and "If You Should Go to Castor Town" are among Causley's most accomplished ballads; "I Saw a Jolly Hunter" is among his best humorous poems; and "Who" is perhaps the finest lyric he has ever written.

The simplicity of the poems in *Figgie Hobbin* reveals his method more clearly. Their clarity and grace epitomize the transparent style that he has striven for throughout his career. The voice that speaks in them is traditional in the purest sense of the word. Causley has so thoroughly assimilated certain traditions of English verse that he uses them naturally to translate personal experience into a common utterance, and there is no gap between private sensibility and the demands of traditional

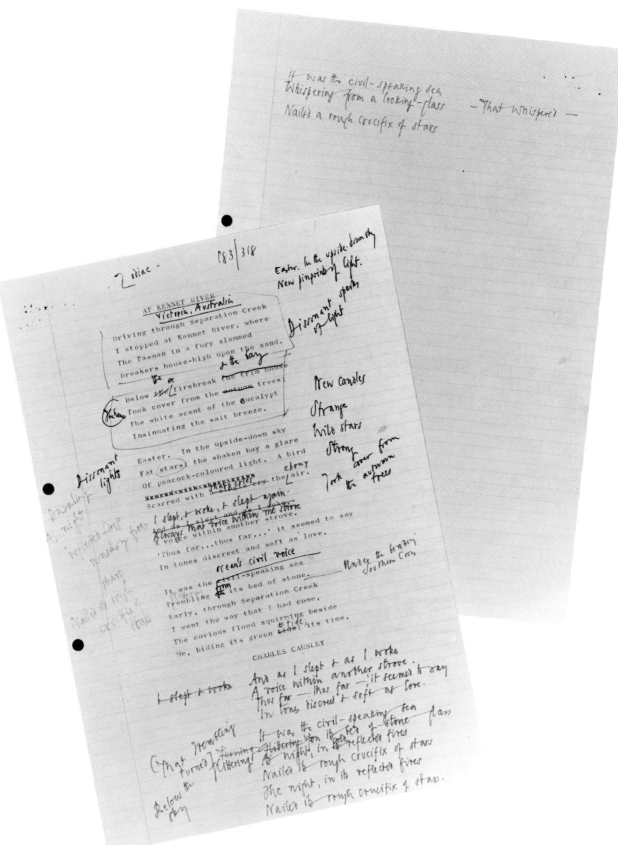

Three drafts of a poem in Secret Destinations, *a forthcoming collection (the author)*

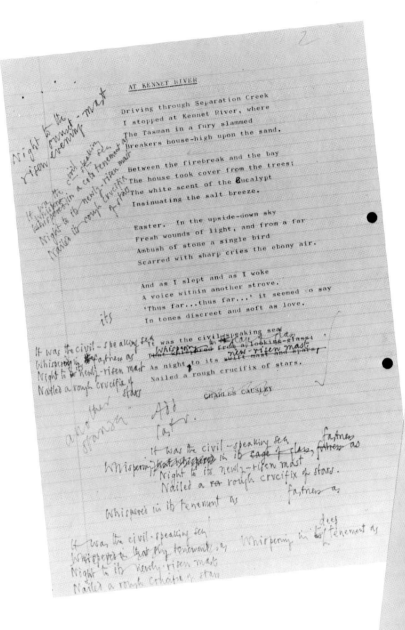

form. His work achieves the lucid impersonality of folk song or ballad, and, unlike most modern poetry, his most personal poems are often his most accessible. In "Who," for example, Causley's vision of his lost childhood remains equally authentic on either a personal or universal level:

> Who is that child I see wandering, wandering
> Down by the side of the quivering stream?
> Why does he seem not to hear, though I call
>   to him?
> Where does he come from, and what is his name?
> . . . .
> Why does he move like a wraith by the water,
> Soft as the thistledown on the breeze blown?
> When I draw near him so that I may hear him,
> Why does he say that his name is my own?

Collected Poems solidified Causley's reputation in England and broadened his audience in America. The volume was widely reviewed on both sides of the Atlantic almost entirely in a positive light, but most reviewers presented Causley's achievement in a highly reductive manner. While they admired the ease and openness of his work and praised his unwavering commitment to narrative poetry, they did not find in their readings the resonance of language which distinguishes the finest poetry. By implication therefore they classified Causley as an accomplished minor poet, an engagingly eccentric antimodernist, who had mastered the traditional ballad at the expense of other work. Only Edward Levy's essay on the *Collected Poems* in *PN Review 6* made a serious attempt to demonstrate the diversity of Causley's achievement and his importance as a lyric poet. Fortunately critics such as Michael Schmidt have followed this lead and made broader claims for Causley's work.

Most critics also missed the unexpected direction signaled by the twenty-three new poems in the collection. While continuing to work in rhyme and meter, Causley returned to free verse for the first time since *Farewell, Aggie Weston*, achieving uncharacteristic effects while liberating his talent for description. In "Ten Types of Hospital Visitor," which opens the "New Poems" section of his *Collected Poems*, Causley creates a detailed panorama of hospital life which unexpectedly modulates from realism to visionary fancy. In "Ward 14" Causley uses free verse to achieve a painful directness in his description of a man visiting his brain-damaged old mother in the hospital. These poems demonstrate a richness of description and high degree of psychological naturalism not often found in Caus-

ley's earlier work. But while mastering new techniques, Causley did not cease to regard traditional form as central to his work, and he ends the *Collected Poems* with several formal poems, most notably "A Wedding Portrait," one of his most important poems of self-definition. Here the poet's past and present, innocence and experience, are literally embodied in the scene of his middle-aged self looking at his parents' wedding photograph. His doomed father and mother appear hopeful and innocent in the portrait while the poet knows the subsequent pain they will undergo. His present knowledge cannot help them escape their plight, and he remains cut off from them now by time and death as absolutely as he was nonexistent to them on their wedding day. In a visionary moment Causley looks to his art to bridge the gap of time and restore his dead parents to him and his lost childhood self to them. The *Collected Poems* ends with this affirmation of poetry's power to triumph over death:

> I am a child again, and move
> Sunwards these images of clay,
> Listening for their first birth cry.
> And with the breath my parents gave
> I warm the cold words with my day:
> Will the dead weight to fly. To fly.

Causley's new work since the *Collected Poems* has continued to show diversity and growth. Changes in his life may have helped broaden his perspective. Retiring from full-time teaching in 1976, Causley could for the first time in his life devote himself entirely to writing. The reception of his *Collected Poems* also earned him several opportunities to teach and read his work abroad. Just as his wartime travel provided him with poetic inspiration, these recent journeys have spurred him on to new and unexpected work. While still writing about his native Cornwall in such characteristic poems as "Seven Houses" and "On Launceston Castle," he has turned his attention to foreign landscapes, especially that of Australia, which he has described in a number of new poems. He has also sharpened his gift for psychological portraiture in poems such as "Grandmother," which describes a wise and resilient old German woman who has survived World War II. When these new poems are collected in a volume, they will show Causley in his mid-sixties as a poet still broadening his reach. He has not abandoned the fundamental strengths of his earlier work while continuing to develop in new and genuine ways.

References:

Edward Levy, "The Poetry of Charles Causley," *PN Review 6*, 5, no. 2 (1977): 46-48;

Richard Pevear, "Poetry Chronicle," *Hudson Review*, 29 (Summer 1976): 314-315;

Christopher Ricks, Review of *Collected Poems, 1951-1975*, *New York Times Book Review*, 11 January 1976, p. 6;

Michael Schmidt, *An Introduction to 50 Modern British Poets* (London: Pan, 1979), pp. 291-296.

Papers:

The State University of New York at Buffalo and the University of Exeter, Devon, have collections of Causley's papers.

Jack Clemo
(11 March 1916-　)

Stephen John Lane
Newcastle University

SELECTED BOOKS: *Wilding Graft* (London: Chatto & Windus, 1948; New York: Macmillan, 1949);

Confession of a Rebel (London: Chatto & Windus, 1949);

The Clay Verge (London: Chatto & Windus, 1951);

The Invading Gospel (London: Bles, 1958; Old Tappan, N.J.: F. H. Revell, 1972);

The Map of Clay (London: Methuen, 1961; Richmond, Va.: John Knox, 1968);

Penguin Poets 6, by Clemo, Edward Lucie-Smith, and George MacBeth (Harmondsworth: Penguin, 1964);

Cactus on Carmel (London: Methuen, 1967);

The Echoing Tip (London: Methuen, 1971);

Broad Autumn (London: Eyre Methuen, 1975);

The Marriage of a Rebel (London: Gollancz, 1980);

The Bouncing Hills (Redruth: Cornish Publications, 1983).

OTHER: *The Wintry Priesthood*, in *Poems 1951*, edited by John Hayward (Harmondsworth: Penguin, 1951), pp. 169-185;

"The China Clay Country," in *My Cornwall*, edited by Michael Williams (Tintagel: Bossiney Books, 1973);

"The Clay Dump," in *Cornish Short Stories*, edited by Denys Val Baker (Harmondsworth: Penguin, 1976).

Jack Clemo's poetry is more often seen as a triumph against affliction than a literary success. His handicaps—physical, educational, social—

have served, in place of criticism, as the measure of his art. Clemo has vigorously opposed this tendency and insisted, as in "Affirmative Way":

> The insight, the forced dream,
> The theory, which a cripple shapes
> To train, sustain, explain himself,
> Falls sterile and untested.

Despite this insistence, courageous is the epithet most commonly applied to his work, which still awaits sustained critical evaluation.

Reginald John Clemo was born in the tiny Cornish clay-quarrier's cottage he inhabits to this day. His father, Reginald, after an unsuccessful attempt to make his fortune in America, had settled back into the quarriers' village of St. Austell in 1912 and married Eveline Polmounter, the daughter of a local Nonconformist preacher. The marriage was disastrous and short-lived. Reginald Clemo was conscripted into the war effort in 1917 and died shortly before Christmas that year aboard H.M.S. *Tornado*. Jack was less than two years old at the time. Despite this early death, his father, or rather, Jack's mother's recollections of her husband, were to have a strong influence upon him. Eveline Clemo sought to bring her son up strictly according to her faith and to inhibit any wayward tendencies her child might have inherited from his father. With some reason, then, Clemo has remarked upon the similarity of his background to D. H. Lawrence's.

The major themes of all Clemo's books, both verse and prose, stem from his family background:

the religious indoctrination from his mother, the uncertainty in a fatherless child. It is as though, seeking to come to terms with a father he never knew and was taught to despise, he internalized the missing figure. In poems as well as in his only novel, *Wilding Graft* (1948), he has sought to explore the conflict between grace and nature—the latter in both its human and more general form. Both at a personal level and as an artist the problem of assimilating sexuality into Christianity has been his dominant preoccupation.

A sickly child, he suffered repeated bouts of deafness and blindness from the age of five. Confined at home for long periods, he used those occasions to read widely. He soon began contributing controversial letters to the local newspaper, interspersing these with juvenile poems. In 1930 he began writing a long series of novels, none of which was published. Those that have survived in manuscript form confirm that the theme he explored in *Wilding Graft* had been with him for almost sixteen years.

His novels stem from two literary experiences. In 1930 he read an account of the relationship of Dante and Beatrice in Arthur Mee's *Children's Encyclopaedia*; five years later he read Rudolf Besier's play *The Barretts of Wimpole Street* when it was serialized in *John o' London's Weekly*. From that date he became convinced that God had "elected" him to a special kind of Christian marriage and that his role in life would be that of an evangelical propagandist. *Wilding Graft* dramatized his patient wait for the predestined bride, through the fictional character Garth Joslin.

The novel was well received, and it was quickly followed by his first volume of autobiography, *Confession of a Rebel* (1949). As the only source of information for many years on a writer who is as uniquely disadvantaged as Clemo and whose creative work rises so directly from his personal experience, this book became something of a collector's item, and popular demand caused it to be republished in 1975. The second volume of his autobiography, *The Marriage of a Rebel*, did not appear until 1980.

Wilding Graft had occupied all his energies, until his arduous struggle ended in 1945. (It was to take a further four years to have the book published.) So it was with some surprise that he found himself, in the early months of 1945, spontaneously writing poetry again after nearly six years of having written only prose. He knew at once that this new poetry was far removed from his adolescent work. Although some of its imagery and symbolism had appeared in *Wilding Graft*, it had an intensity and

Portrait of Jack Clemo by Lionel Miskin

authenticity absent from his juvenile verse. By 1951 he had accumulated enough material for two slim collections, *The Clay Verge* (poems written before 1949) and *The Wintry Priesthood* (poems after 1949). This second group of poems earned him joint second place in the Festival of Britain poetry competition and appeared in *Poems 1951*, a collection of the winning poems. Both sets of poems were republished in the 1961 collection *The Map of Clay*.

The poems in *The Clay Verge* and *The Wintry Priesthood* dramatized Clemo's theological thought, and, read in the above order, they demonstrate the development of his thought from agonizing Christian existentialism (à la Kierkegaard) to a belief in Christian fellowship and orthodox dogma. These poems contain a violence of imagery ahead of their day: the 1950s were the years of The Movement poets. Each poem is set in the devastated landscape of the china-clay quarries and articulates a series of encounters between either the poet and his God, imaged in "The Excavator" as "that broken mouthed gargoyle," or the poet and preadolescent girls, relationships with whom Clemo saw as spiritual rehearsals for contact with womanhood. Some of the poems fantasized about this maturer relationship.

The poems are remarkable for qualities associated on the one hand with metaphysicals such as Donne and Herbert and on the other with symbolist and postsymbolist poets. These characteristics are remarkable in Clemo's poetry, as he had no acquaintance until 1950 with the metaphysical poets and no knowledge of symbolist poetry until the mid-1960s. "Who needs forgiveness now?," he taunts God in "Prisoner of God," setting out his case in a way strongly reminiscent of Herbert. "These are my facts," the poem concludes, "what shall my verdict be?" In "A Calvinist in Love" the persona attempts to woo a woman in a "bare clay-pit" and argues his beloved into accepting the rude surroundings as more fitting a love that transcends material considerations. All seventeen poems of *The Clay Verge* and a smaller number in *The Wintry Priesthood* employ imagery that is ugly, twisted, and tormented; rust, mud, rain, and grass and flowers trampled and destroyed by the ever-present industrial activity. Poems such as "The Plundered Fuchsias" and "Sufficiency" are paeans offered in celebration and homage to the destruction and ugliness; for within these poems such destruction serves a clear theological purpose. The clay-tip worker, in the poem of that title, is the agent of redemptive vision, rather like Andrew Marvell's mower. His destruction of nature replaces "Creation's mood" (wayward and fallen) with "redemptive vision."

The Clay Verge presents an extreme, idiosyncratic interpretation of landscape. That Clemo is still primarily known as the author of these poems is testimony to their powerful evocation of a wholly original vision. Events within his life, however, were to set him firmly on a course that would take his poetry far from the weird, violent world he had created. In 1949 Clemo began a correspondence that was to change his outlook on nature, God, and sex. For several months he exchanged letters with a young woman, a Christian and a nature poet. Marriage, at last, seemed a real possibility, but her parents, fearful of their daughter's involvement with a poverty-stricken, deaf poet, brought the relationship to an end. It was not to be the Barrett-Browning romance he had hoped for, but her influence upon him in those few short months was enormous. In *The Marriage of a Rebel* he was to write of this affair, "I could never be the same man again. From 1949 onwards it was impossible for me to

express a savage glee at the destruction of earthly beauty."

The prizewinning sequence *The Wintry Priesthood* shows that influence. The opening poem, "Cornish Anchorite," presents the poet as autistic as ever:

> Deep in the clay-land winter lies my brain,
> All faculties that human growth could stain
> Dissolved to weedless nescience.

The sequence concludes with the poet's triumphant march out of his native land as he slips "The Cornish Bond." In the middle poems the poet examines his religious and literary mentors, a kind of intellectual spring-cleaning. The list of mentors is instructive, for they reveal the extent to which religious figures outnumber literary ones: Charles Spurgeon, Sören Kierkegaard, Karl Barth, T. F. Powys (here as a religious heretic rather than novelist), and D. H. Lawrence.

In 1950, following the publication of his first two volumes of prose, Clemo felt released from the claustrophobia of Cornwall, as the final poem in *The Wintry Priesthood* indicates. The wider-ranging, less introverted poems of *The Wintry Priesthood* were written for the most part during that eighteen-month period that saw the development and death of his affair and an increase in social contacts as a direct result of the publication of his prose books. One such contact enabled him to travel north of Cornwall for the first time in his life. Monica Hutchings, a writer of books on rural life, had received *Confession of a Rebel* as a Christmas present. Impressed by the earnestness she found in it, she saw an opportunity of providing Clemo with an interview with T. F. Powys, whom she knew and to whom Clemo had referred several times in that work.

The journey, which took Clemo into Hardy country as well, seemed symbolic to him: a confirmation that his future lay beyond the "crabbed patch of soil" in which he had first flowered as a writer. "Daybreak in Dorset," written during that brief visit, shows the poet rejecting Hardy's dour fatalism and, with that, his own:

> Fate-ridden land, in Hardy's view,
> Yet every mood that I have seen today
> On Dorset's face, each passionate hue,
> Puts my bleak fate away.

Reviewing his poetic output of the past, he condemns it as "crumbling jargon of mauled rock." The very language he used has come to seem redundant to him. Thus he uses the image of crossing a frontier, which had appeared earlier in two of *The Wintry Priesthood* poems.

Whatever recuperative strength Clemo gained during 1950-1951 he had need of. A second romance collapsed in 1952, and his health deteriorated badly. He began to suffer again from symptoms of blindness, which specialists confirmed would prove permanent this time. He also experienced heart trouble and sudden and frightening attacks of cerebral paralysis which left him confused and semiconscious for hours. By 1953 he had become so weakened and demoralized he managed to write only one poem in that year. Surprisingly, it expressed a determined optimism, as its title, "Clay Phoenix," suggests.

With blindness imminent, Clemo pressed on. His next venture was a spiritual autobiography. Autobiographical writing seemed the only form of sustained writing open to him. The novel was now impossible: he had not heard a normal conversation since his teens, it was becoming increasingly difficult and painful to read, and the reception of visitors was now a fruitless exercise. When, toward the end of 1955, his eyesight finally failed him, the manuscript of his testimony of faith lay on his bureau unfinished and seemingly unfinishable. Furthermore, his blindness had complicated his understanding of faith. As he wrote twenty-five years later: "I was writing a theological book and had to relate natural ills to ultimate questions of sin, guilt, punishment and expiation."

Clemo has called *The Invading Gospel* (1958) a "buoyant" book. This description may be true, strictly speaking, since it expounds the basis for Christian optimism on the "literal resurrection of Christ." Be that as it may, many readers may feel profoundly disturbed by his yoking together "the sexuality of apes" and "the marriage of atheists." But it is precisely here, in the realm of what might be termed *sexual dogmatics*, that the book is important for an understanding of Clemo's work. Within this book Clemo clarifies his attitude toward sex and its role in a Christian marriage. He applies there, for the first time, the term "trans-sexual" to consummations enjoyed under the sacrament of marriage. (Not, of course, that he naively believed all Christian marriages to be, in the truest sense, sacramental.) In "trans-sexual" consummations, he wrote, "the biology involved is eternal and incorruptible because it is covered by Atonement." Several of his poems written since this time are explorations of this idea.

The mid-1950s saw a number of American evangelical preachers arrive in Britain, among them Billy Graham and Renée Martz, and with the help of his mother, Clemo followed their missions eagerly through the media, gaining from them the inspiration and determination to go on with his own testimony. With his mother acting as amanuensis he completed *The Invading Gospel* in 1957. It was published the following year.

Three years later *The Clay Verge* and *The Wintry Priesthood* were republished in the larger volume *The Map of Clay* (1961). Some of the new poems in this volume show the influence of those religious missions. As with his predecessors Vachel Lindsay and Robert Browning, Clemo the evangelist surfaced at the cost of Clemo the poet. The year 1961 was notable for Clemo's receipt of a Civil List pension for his contribution to English literature. Apart from the honor, it supplemented his mother's war widow's pension, the only reliable source of income the Clemos had had since 1917.

More or less resigned to his deafness and blindness, Clemo concentrated upon his poetry. Even writing autobiography had become too taxing. At this point he received a letter from a woman artist and schoolteacher in Cumberland who passionately begged him not to consider her letter mere fan mail. Mary (Clemo still does not wish her surname to be published) stormed into his life and whipped him into a state of emotional and creative tension which lasted for three years. She visited him in his tiny cottage and persuaded him and his mother to visit her and tour the Lake District. Forthright and unconventional, she set about educating him in modern poetry. (Clemo's knowledge of British poets, apart from Hardy, had not extended beyond the Victorians, and he knew nothing of European poets.) Mary persuaded him to learn Braille, which he had stubbornly refused to study before, and then encouraged him to read T. S. Eliot, Gerard Manley Hopkins, Dylan Thomas, and Rainer Maria Rilke in translation. She also thought his poetry too subjective and proved to be a forceful and challenging critic. Her impact is visible in *Cactus on Carmel* (1967).

The central themes of his volumes are not changed: the alchemy of faith transmuting animal lust into a ballet of the resurrection and the ambiguity of natural beauty, at once image of the creator and a fallen universe. But Clemo's techniques were evolving. In this book one finds a compression of image, a new feel for the effects of sound, an experimentation with rhyme, and a

Dust jacket for Clemo's 1961 collection of poems that chart his developing religious faith

search for new, alternative symbols, as in "Eros in Exile":

> Locked grove, lost grove,
> Heavy air from mouldering clay-hills
> Fills the arbour and threatens the embrace.
> Nuptial bud at the lip
> Slips back into the natural stream
> Which gyrates blindly in the tense wood.

The search for a new and adequate symbolism which would replace that of the clay quarries was aided by Mary. She too hated the ugliness of the clay belt and, as he walked beside her in the Lake District, Mary wrote descriptions of the scenery in block letters on the palm of his hand and pressed leaves and flowers against his fingertips.

At times he seemed near to a resolution of his old fear of beauty, writing lyrically and with affection of what he "saw":

> Rowans—tender, shy, elusive rowans,
> Swaying, summer-warm, as a symbol
> Of a woman's gift at her nocturnal base.

But that resolution was to be incomplete. Clemo could not give himself up to Mary's romanticism. "Dungeon Ghyll," quoted above, wryly concludes:

> Why should there be beauty
> At the lip of the ledge where you're tempted?
> There could be nettles and a thorn hedge
> To keep you safe,
> Down at the base, at your innocent
>   meeting-point.

Part of the difficulty lay within the relationship itself, which was constantly wracked with self-doubts on both sides. After three years Mary was to write that "she could bear the fruitless inner conflict no longer." What had seemed a "miracle romance" was over.

While *Cactus on Carmel*, deriving in large part from this relationship, established Clemo as a poet, it seemed to mock him as a man. His "elected bride" remained as elusive as ever. Within a matter of months, however, he would find her in Ruth Peaty and reach that "true surrendered island," as he expressed it in a poem in *Broad Autumn* (1975).

From the outset the relationship seemed well omened: Ruth's first letter had been dated 12 September (for Clemo, who has a curious superstition regarding dates, this day was especially significant, as it was the date of Browning's wedding to Elizabeth Barrett). The following June they met for the first time when Ruth took her summer holiday in Cornwall. They had been together only three days when Clemo proposed marriage, and Ruth accepted. They were married on 26 October 1968. Clemo wrote of the occasion in "Wedding Eve," a celebration and vindication of the faith that had sustained him for thirty years:

> Elect for marriage — I sang
> That stubborn theme through three decades
> Of hunger, mirage, avalanche:
> When nature made hopes blanch,
> A text like a clay-bed tang,
> Like the bride's own breath, stirred in
> the shades.

Clemo's achievement is difficult to measure. Criticism of his work does not extend beyond the poems of *The Map of Clay*. His craftsmanship is evident, and the pains he takes with his work, despite his not being able to see what he writes (he never learned to type in Braille), is apparent from the manuscripts for his poems. The reason for critical neglect seems to lie more with the content of his poetry than its construction. Donald Davie has remarked that Clemo "breaks across, and muddles, all the comfortable categories of sociologists, psephologists, journalistic commentators, and party managers." Clemo set off arm in arm with Kierkegaard and Johann Overbeck, like John Bunyan's Christian with his companions. En route his sympathies have broadened to include Mariology, a study of Catholic saints, the application of holy water, and an admiration for the British royal family. Still a Calvinist, he agreed in 1972 to the republication of *The Invading Gospel*; his thinking has increasingly distinguished between "what Christianity is" and "how it works." The result has been an openness and interest in all forms of Christian belief and worship. Similarly, his love poetry has moved from worship at "the dark shrine of erotic mysticism" (as in "A Calvinist in Love") to sensitive evocations of the warmth and intimacy of married life ("Charlotte Nicholls" and "Katharine Luther"). Throughout, he has traveled along what seem to be side roads, unmarked byways far from the main highways of contemporary culture. It may well be because of this different pathway that his poetry contains much of lasting value and much that challenges the inbuilt and often unconscious assumptions of our time.

References:

Eveline Clemo, *I Proved Thee at the Waters* (Ilkeston: Moorley's Bible & Bookshop, 1976);

Donald Davie, "A Calvinist in Politics," *PN Review*, no. 9 (1979): 29-32;

Stephen John Lane, "A Reading of the Manuscripts of Jack Clemo," *PN Review*, no. 22 (1981): 6-7;

Geoffrey Thurley, *The Ironic Harvest: English Poetry in the Twentieth Century* (London: Arnold, 1974), pp. 167-172.

Robert Conquest

(15 July 1917-   )

John Press

SELECTED BOOKS: *Poems* (London: Macmillan, 1955; New York: St. Martin's, 1955);

A World of Difference (London: Ward, Lock, 1955; New York: Ballantine, 1964);

Where Do Marxists Go from Here?, as Arden (London: Phoenix House, 1958);

Common Sense About Russia (London: Gollancz, 1960; New York:. Macmillan, 1960);

The Soviet Deportation of Nationalities (London: Macmillan, 1960 / New York: St. Martin's, 1960); revised and enlarged as *The Nation Killers: the Soviet Deportation of Nationalities* (London: Macmillan, 1970; New York: Macmillan, 1970);

Courage of Genius: The Pasternak Affair (London: Collins & Harvill Press, 1961); republished as *The Pasternak Affair: Courage of Genius* (Philadelphia: Lippincott, 1962);

Power and Policy in the USSR (London: Macmillan, 1961; New York: St. Martin's, 1961);

The Last Empire (London: Ampersand, 1962);

Between Mars and Venus (London: Hutchinson, 1962; New York: St. Martin's Press, 1962);

Marxism Today (London: Ampersand, 1964);

The Egyptologists, by Conquest and Kingsley Amis (London: Cape, 1965; New York: Random House, 1965);

Russia after Khrushchev (London: Pall Mall Press, 1965; New York: Praeger, 1965);

The Great Terror: Stalin's Purges of the Thirties (London: Macmillan, 1968; New York: Macmillan, 1968; revised edition, Harmondsworth: Penguin, 1971);

Arias from a Love Opera and Other Poems (London: Macmillan, 1969; New York: Macmillan, 1969);

Where Marx Went Wrong (London: Tom Stacey, 1970);

Lenin (London: Fontana, 1972); republished as *V. I. Lenin* (New York: Viking, 1972);

Kolyma: The Arctic Death Camps (London: Macmillan, 1978; New York: Viking, 1978);

Coming Across (Menlo Park: Buckabest Books, 1978);

The Abomination of Moab (London: Temple Smith, 1979);

Forays (London: Chatto & Windus / Hogarth Press, 1979);

Present Danger: Towards a Foreign Policy (Oxford: Blackwell, 1979; Stanford, Calif.: Hoover Institution Press, 1979);

We and They: Civic and Despotic Cultures (London: Temple Smith, 1980).

OTHER: *New Lines*, edited by Conquest (London: Macmillan / New York: St. Martin's, 1956);

Back to Life: Poems from Behind the Iron Curtain, edited by Conquest (London: Hutchinson, 1958; New York: St. Martin's, 1958);

Spectrum: a Science Fiction Anthology, edited by Conquest, with Kingsley Amis (London: Gollancz, 1961; New York: Harcourt, Brace & World, 1962);

Spectrum 2 (London: Gollancz, 1962; New York: Harcourt, Brace & World, 1963);

New Lines 2, edited by Conquest (London: Macmillan, 1963; New York: Macmillan, 1963);

Spectrum 3 (London: Gollancz, 1963; New York: Harcourt, Brace & World, 1964);

Spectrum 4 (London: Gollancz, 1964; New York: Harcourt, Brace & World, 1965);

Spectrum 5 (London: Gollancz, 1966; New York: Harcourt, Brace & World, 1967);

Soviet Studies Series, edited by Conquest, 8 volumes (London: Bodley Head, 1967-1969); republished as *The Contemporary Soviet Union Series* (New York: Praeger, 1968-1969);

Petr. I. Yakir, *A Childhood in Prison*, edited, with an introduction, by Conquest (London: Macmillan, 1972; New York: Coward, McCann & Geoghegan, 1973);

The Robert Sheckley Omnibus, edited, with an introduction, by Conquest (London: Gollancz, 1973);

Tibor Szamuely, *The Russian Tradition*, edited, with an introduction, by Conquest (London: Secker & Warburg, 1974; New York: McGraw-Hill, 1974);

Aleksandr Solzhenitsyn, *Prussian Nights*, translated by Conquest (London: Harvill, 1977; New York: Farrar, Straus & Giroux, 1977).

There have been in the past fifty years numerous poets and novelists who have sounded off about current affairs with a confidence that has often been in inverse proportion to their knowledge, just as there have been academics and publicists who have tried their hands at fiction or literary criticism or even a book of verse. It is rare for a man to be accepted by his fellows as an imaginative writer and, at the same time, as an authority on political matters. During the past thirty years Robert Conquest has established a reputation in a wide variety of fields: as a commentator on Soviet affairs, a poet, a novelist, a literary critic, an anthologist, and an editor. At first sight there may seem few connections between his writings in these various genres. His poems seldom deal overtly with political themes, just as his prose writings are as far removed as they can be from any trace of poeticism. But his verse and prose alike display the virtues of scholarship, intelligence, and lucidity, proclaiming a belief in the value of rational discourse, formal strength, and the power of reason to check and guide the emotions by which we live.

George Robert Acworth Conquest, who was born in Great Malvern, England, to Robert Folger W. Conquest, a Virginian who settled in England, and Rosamund Acworth Conquest, an Englishwoman, was educated at Winchester, attended the University of Grenoble in 1935-1936, and received B.A. (1939), M.A. (1972), and D.Litt (1974) degrees from Magdalen College, Oxford. Serving in the Oxfordshire and Buckinghamshire Light Infantry from 1939 to 1946, he was attached to the Soviet Army Group in the Balkans in 1944-1945, witnessing the takeover of Bulgaria. He joined the foreign service in 1946 and returned to Bulgaria as press attaché and as second secretary. He later became first secretary of the United Kingdom's delegation to the United Nations. During his ten-years' diplomatic service, he acquired a detailed knowledge of Eastern Europe; his writings on the USSR and its satellites began to appear after he had resigned his post in 1956. He was awarded the Order of the British Empire in 1955. In 1942 Conquest married Joan Watkins, by whom he had two sons. The marriage was dissolved in 1948, in which year he married Tatiana Mihailova (marriage dissolved, 1962). His third marriage to Caroleen Macfarlane in 1964 was dissolved in 1978, and in 1979 he married Elizabeth, daughter of the late Col. Richard D. Neece, U.S. Air Force.

During his tenure in the foreign service, Conquest had made his debut as a writer. In 1955 he published two books, *A World of Difference*, a work of

science fiction, and *Poems*. Although Conquest has written no more science-fiction novels, he has maintained his interest in the genre, and in 1961 he and his friend Kingsley Amis edited a collection of science-fiction stories entitled *Spectrum*, the first of a series of five such collections. He has continued to practice the art of poetry, bringing out four more volumes after *Poems*, the latest of which appeared in 1979.

The range of Conquest's interests may be gauged from the titles of the sections that make up *Poems*: "Persons and Places," "Arts and Contexts," "War and After," "The Balkans." He is unashamedly a poet who draws his sustenance from the arts and from other writers, one to whom Catullus and Turgenev are as contemporary and as familiar as Paul Klee and Hart Crane. This collocation of the old and the new is exemplified in "Guided Missiles Experimental Range," a sonnet that describes the flight of three black automata, whose "loveless haste" reminds the poet of the Furies as Aeschylus portrayed them: "*O barren daughters of the fruitful night.*" This line is a striking rhetorical trope, but some critics have wondered whether it is anything more and whether this application of Aeschylus's line about the Furies to guided missiles sheds any poetic illumination on nuclear weapons. Is Conquest, in fact, a deeply imaginative poet, or a very clever, highly cultivated man writing fluent, civilized verse? A tentative answer to that question is that he is a genuine poet whose elaborate smoothness and ingenuity sometimes muffle and smother the inner vitality of his poems.

In 1956 Conquest brought out an anthology entitled *New Lines*, which contained poems by nine poets: Elizabeth Jennings, John Holloway, Philip Larkin, Thom Gunn, Kingsley Amis, D. J. Enright, Donald Davie, Robert Conquest, and John Wain. Conquest's introduction was an attack on what he regarded as the emotional looseness and verbal deliquescence that had characterized English poetry since 1940. His anthology was a call to order, an attempt to revive certain principles that he judged to be in suspended animation: verbal control, intellectual strength, and emotional sanity.

New Lines remains the most influential anthology published in England since World War II. Although the poets represented there never constituted a formal, organized group and have long since gone their own ways, the anthology helped to prepare the way for much of the best poetry and literary criticism of the next fifteen years. On the strength of *New Lines* alone Conquest merits a place in the development of postwar English poetry.

After his resignation from the Foreign Office, Conquest was Webb Research Fellow at the London School of Economics (1956-1958), visiting poet and lecturer in English at the University of Buffalo (1959-1960), and senior fellow at the Columbia University Russian Institute (1964-1965). In 1962-1963, he was literary editor of the *Spectator*. During those years he began to publish books on various aspects of the USSR and Eastern Europe.

In 1958 he edited and wrote an introduction to an anthology of translations from works of East European poets. The title of the anthology, *Back to Life*, expressed Conquest's hope that, after the years of Stalinist oppression, the frozen life of the imagination might reawaken. He followed up the anthology with a book whose title, *Common Sense About Russia* (1960), scarcely does justice to its power of analysis and breadth of vision. Conquest has always displayed a firm hostility toward the USSR, but his views are neither irrational nor fanatical: "To assume that the Soviet Union approximates either Utopia or Devil's Island is plainly wrong." In *Common Sense About Russia* he touches on several topics that he returns to in later books: the difficulty of

collecting reliable evidence about the USSR because Soviet textbooks, encyclopedias, and even photographs are modified in accordance with new twists in the political situation; the need to remember that Soviet leaders share none of our basic assumptions and are the prisoners of a rigidly closed philosophical system; and Soviet censorship of the written word and the way in which the arts and the sciences are subordinated to the state's political requirements as defined by an intolerant, obscurantist bureaucracy. He believes that the West may, by standing firm in its negotiations with the USSR, bring about conditions in which the creative power of Russia and its latent tradition of liberalism may flower again and free the country from its present sterility.

Courage of Genius: The Pasternak Affair (1961) is concerned with two of Conquest's abiding interests, literature and the USSR. Although Pasternak was known in the West, before the publication of *Dr. Zhivago*, as a major poet and translator, Conquest points out that he had written prose fiction as early as 1915 and that his earlier fiction was a preparation for *Dr. Zhivago*.

Besides setting out the relevant documents in eight appendices, Conquest unravels lucidly and fairly the tangled story of the Nobel Prize award to Pasternak and the storm that followed. He shows clearly why Pasternak felt that he was being hounded to death, his agony intensified by the fear that his beloved Olga Ivinskaya would be left defenseless when he was gone. (Soon after his death she and her daughter Irina were charged with currency offenses and sentenced respectively to eight and three years in Siberia.) Conquest pays tribute to the fifteen hundred Russians, including some well-known artists and writers, who came to Pasternak's funeral: "It is fitting that Pasternak's burial called up the courage of the Russian intelligentsia."

Conquest's second volume of poetry, *Between Mars and Venus* (1962), resumes with even more fluency many of the themes foreshadowed in *Poems*. In "Karnobat" we are back again in the Balkans: the poet wryly balances against the historical richness of the town the sour smells and the prevalence of bedbugs. "Spotsylvania County" and "Address to an Undergraduate Society" may remind the reader of Auden's serious light verse, while the sonnets on Keats and on Kafka can only be called Audenesque. There is a charming short poem, "Art and Love," about a man whose wife is a painter. What keeps them together is not painting or poetry but "some fantasy of sweetness / And the honey smell of her skin."

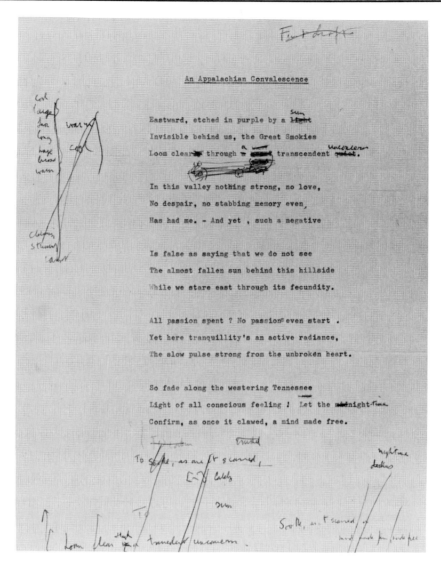

Working typescript (the author)

After his fellowship at Columbia had expired, Conquest earned his living for ten years as a free-lance writer, writing mainly on topics connected with the Soviet Union, although he continued to write fiction and poetry. In 1965 he and Kingsley Amis produced a novel, *The Egyptologists*, a comedy, or a comic farce, about the Metropolitan Egyptological Society, a learned body composed entirely of males who are far less concerned with Ancient Egypt than with certain pursuits afforded by contemporary England. The plotting of the novel is ingenious, the dialogue amusing, the characterization deft though superficial. There are lively passages that read as if they had been salvaged from the first draft of Amis's *Lucky Jim* (1954). Yet it is a disappointing book that amounts to little more than a drawn-out anecdote recounted on a wet afternoon in a club in Pall Mall.

During the late 1960s Conquest edited a number of volumes in the *Soviet Studies* series, contributing prefaces designed to put the topics surveyed in the wider context of Soviet life. Unlike these volumes, which are intended primarily for students and specialists, *The Great Terror* (1968) is aimed at the general reader, but it is widely regarded among specialists as the definitive work on the purges.

The Great Terror, which deals with Stalin's purge of the 1930s, is Conquest's longest and most substantial book, a fully documented account of the torture, execution, or condemnation to death camps of millions of people whom Stalin plotted to destroy, although nearly all were totally innocent. Conquest displays remarkable narrative skill, picking his way amid conflicting evidence, making what sense can be made of incidents that have the quality of a sickening nightmare. His analysis of character and motive is equally persuasive, and he gives vivid portraits in miniature of the persecutors and victims. His sketch of Stalin is particularly convincing, especially in its demonstration of how an apparently mediocre and colorless figure could ruthlessly transform the Communist party and the whole society. This massive, scholarly work may well be Conquest's most lasting achievement.

Conquest's third volume of verse, *Arias from a Love Opera* (1969), contains several of his best poems. "Seal Rocks: San Francisco" explores certain analogies between the gyrations of the seals and the process by which poems are shaped. The comparisons are not frigid or overintellectual, the bay exists as a sensuous reality; the seals are really there, "Big eyed, unanxious sea-things." The book's range of themes, technical skill, and poetic intelligence are apparent; and once again Conquest alludes to literature and the other arts with a natural ease. Indeed, two fine poems, "Chateaubriand's Grave," an unashamedly romantic sonnet, and "Reading Coleridge," have their origin in Conquest's veneration for great writers. In its taut elegance and richness the volume represents an advance on its two predecessors.

The Nation Killers (1970), a revised and enlarged version of *The Soviet Deportation of Nationalities* (1960), tells how eight minority nations within the Soviet Union were deported during the war—five were rehabilitated in 1957, and so were the Crimean Tartars in 1967, although they remained debarred from their ancestral homeland. Conquest uses this grim episode, in which about a half-million people died, to show how the Soviet police operate, how news can be suppressed in the USSR, and how history is rewritten by the Soviet leaders so that it may conform with current political requirements.

Although *Lenin* (1972) is only 140 pages long, it is one of Conquest's most incisive and enthralling books. In his view Lenin's dominating characteristics were a total devotion to revolutionary politics, a ruthless determination to seize power, and the ability to convince others of his infallibility as a leader. Conquest records the unpleasant aspects of Lenin's character, quoting Bertrand Russell's impression of his bigotry and Mongolian cruelty, his embracing of terror as an instrument of policy, and his total lack of scruples. But he also points to signs that, frozen within him, there were seeds of generosity and even

of love. If he was a monster, says Conquest, he was not a monster like Stalin. Yet Stalin and Stalinism were the natural heirs of Lenin, if only because his doctrine of democratic centralism had bequeathed to his successors an apparatus that Stalin was best fitted to manipulate.

Conquest returned to academic life in 1976, holding a fellowship at the Woodrow Wilson International Center for Scholars of the Smithsonian Institution in Washington, D.C. (1976-1977) and moving in 1977 to the Hoover Institution on War, Revolution and Peace at Stanford University in California, where he has remained. In 1981 he was Distinguished Visiting Scholar at The Heritage Foundation in Washington, D.C., and since 1980 he has been a research associate at Harvard University Ukrainian Research Institute.

Kolyma (1978) describes the Arctic camps, where from 1932-1954 about 3,000,000 people died. Originally founded to produce gold, these settlements became, after 1937, extermination camps where prisoners were frozen, starved, and done to death by exhaustion, disease, or bullets. Apart from the professional criminals, who were at the top of the hierarchy and encouraged to inflict violence on the political prisoners, virtually all the prisoners were innocent of the charges against them. Kolyma corrupted as well as killed: Conquest can find scarcely one act of generosity or mercy to mitigate the record of atrocious cruelty and suffering. *Kolyma* is one of Conquest's most somber and salutary books.

The Abomination of Moab (1979) brings together a number of Conquest's literary essays, with a few poems thrown in for good measure. In a combative, well-argued essay, "The Poetics of Procrustes," he launches an attack against pedantry, humbug, and drivel, in criticism as well as in poetry. He also includes his splendid review of William S. Baring-Gould's *The Lure of the Limerick* and an equally cogent survey of Charles Williams as a poet. There is sensibility as well as sense in "The Right Lines," which appeared originally as an introduction to *New Lines 2* (1963), a more eclectic, less polemical anthology than the first *New Lines*. Admirers of Ezra Pound will remain unconvinced by Conquest's assault on the master, but readers of every persuasion can rejoice in "Christian Symbolism in *Lucky Jim*," a spoof that caught some earnest readers, despite Conquest's references to wildly improbable, nonexistent works. As he points out in his postscript, "there can hardly be a real book called *The Phallus Theme in Early Amis*, (or my God! perhaps there is . . .)."

Conquest's latest book of verse, *Forays* (1979), has stylistic affinities with *Arias from a Love Opera*. It contains some admirable light verse, notably "To be a Pilgrim," in which the narrator spends two nights with his girl friend at Farringford, Isle of Wight, eager to feast on memories of Garibaldi, Swinburne, and Tennyson; "Then and There," a witty, tender evocation of a prostitute who, in the poet's youth, walked the pavement opposite St. Anne's Church, Soho; and "A Visit to the Evans Country," a dazzling parody of Kingsley Amis. Among the more ostensibly serious poems two of the best are "1944 and After," in which a wartime experience becomes a metaphor for life itself, and "On that Island," a lyric of musical intensity celebrating "the girl / Who climbs the slate-pink stair."

The New Oxford Book of Light Verse (1978), edited by Kingsley Amis, contains nine limericks, mostly bawdy, by Victor Gray and three virtuoso parodies of Winthrop Mackworth Praed (1802-1839), Chesterton, and "The Vicar of Bray" by Ted Pauker. Gray and Pauker are both pseudonyms of Conquest's. Some idea of the verses' quality may be gathered from a quotation in "A Grouchy Good Night to the Academic Year": "Then alas for the next generation, / For the pots fairly crackle with thorn / Where psychology meets education / A terrible bullshit is born."

Present Danger (1979) recapitulates themes from earlier books: the myopia of Soviet leaders, the persistence of Stalinism, the dangers of détente, the need to contain the Soviet Union. Conquest reveals that he "helped draft Barbara Castle's spirited counter-attacks on Soviet Imperialism," and that he has often found the Foreign Office ineffectual in its negotiations with the Soviet Union.

We and They (1980), dedicated to Margaret Thatcher, traces the nature and historical origins of those cultures and psychologies whose conflict threatens the world. Conquest argues that the fundamental division is between civic and despotic cultures—those grounded in custom and consent as opposed to those based on unbridled autocratic power. He profoundly mistrusts false certitude, cure-all formulae, and inappropriate "scientific" and "mathematical" policies. For light relief he meditates on the element of sheer lunacy in progressive thought, exemplified by Fourier's sincere belief that under socialism the sea could be turned into lemonade.

In the eighteenth and nineteenth centuries politicians, landowners, and manufacturers often wrote verse, translations from the classics, and essays on all manner of topics. Such versatility is uncommon nowadays, and it is therefore particularly refreshing to read the work of a writer who belongs to an older, more humane tradition. As an acknowledged expert on the nature, structure, and policy of the Soviet Union, Robert Conquest may be called a specialist, but he can justly claim the more precious title of man of affairs who is also a man of letters.

Donald Davie

(17 July 1922-)

Donald E. Stanford
Louisiana State University

SELECTED BOOKS: *Purity of Diction in English Verse* (London: Chatto & Windus, 1952; New York: Oxford University Press, 1953); second edition, with "A Postscript, 1966" (London: Routledge & Kegan Paul, 1967; New York: Schocken, 1967);

[Poems] Fantasy Poets, no. 19 (Oxford: Fantasy Press, 1954);

Brides of Reason (Oxford: Fantasy Press, 1955);

Articulate Energy: An Enquiry into the Syntax of English Poetry (London: Routledge & Kegan Paul,

1955; New York: Harcourt, Brace, 1958);

A Winter Talent and Other Poems (London: Routledge & Kegan Paul, 1957);

The Forests of Lithuania (Hessle, Yorkshire: Marvell Press, 1959);

The Heyday of Sir Walter Scott (London: Routledge & Kegan Paul, 1961; New York: Barnes & Noble, 1961);

The Poetry of Sir Walter Scott (London: Oxford University Press, 1961);

A Sequence for Francis Parkman (Hessle, Yorkshire:

Donald Davie at Trinity College, Dublin, 1954
(The Irish Times)

Marvell Press, 1961);

New and Selected Poems (Middletown, Conn.: Wesleyan University Press, 1961);

The Language of Science and the Language of Literature, 1700-1740 (London & New York: Sheed & Ward, 1963);

Ezra Pound: Poet as Sculptor (New York: Oxford University Press, 1964; London: Routledge & Kegan Paul, 1965);

Events and Wisdoms: Poems 1957-1963 (London: Routledge & Kegan Paul, 1964; Middletown, Conn.: Wesleyan University Press, 1965);

Essex Poems: 1963-1967 (London: Routledge & Kegan Paul, 1969);

Poems (London: Turret Books, 1969);

Six Epistles to Eva Hesse (London: London Magazine Editions, 1970);

Collected Poems 1950-1970 (London: Routledge & Kegan Paul, 1972; New York: Oxford University Press, 1972);

Thomas Hardy and British Poetry (New York: Oxford University Press, 1972; London: Routledge & Kegan Paul, 1973);

The Shires (London: Routledge & Kegan Paul, 1974;

New York: Oxford University Press, 1975);

In the Stopping Train and Other Poems (Manchester: Carcanet New Press, 1977; New York: Oxford University Press, 1980);

The Poet in the Imaginary Museum: Essays of Two Decades, edited by Barry Alpert (Manchester: Carcanet New Press, 1977; New York: Persea Books, 1977);

A Gathered Church: The Literature of the English Dissenting Interest, 1700-1930, The Clark Lectures 1976 (London: Routledge & Kegan Paul, 1978; New York: Oxford University Press, 1978);

Trying to Explain (Ann Arbor: University of Michigan Press, 1979);

Kenneth Allott and the Thirties (Liverpool: University of Liverpool Press, 1980);

English Hymnology in the Eighteenth Century: Papers Read at a Clark Library Seminar, 5 March 1977, by Davie and Robert Stevenson (Los Angeles: William Andrews Clark Memorial Library, University of California, 1980);

Three for Water-Music and the Shires (Manchester: Carcanet New Press, 1981);

Dissentient Voice (Notre Dame: University of Notre Dame Press, 1982);

These the Companions (Cambridge: Cambridge University Press, 1982);

Collected Poems, 1970-1983 (Manchester: Carcanet Press, 1983; Notre Dame: University of Notre Dame Press, 1983).

RECORDING: *Donald Davie Reading at Stanford*, The Stanford Program for Recording in Sound (CFS 3647), 1974.

OTHER: *"Pan Tadeusz in English Verse,"* in *Adam Mickiewicz in World Literature*, edited by Waclaw Lednicki (Berkeley & Los Angeles: University of California Press, 1956), pp. 319-330;

The Late Augustans: Longer Poems of the Eighteenth Century, edited by Davie (London: Heinemann, 1958; New York: Macmillan, 1958);

Poems: Poetry Supplement, edited by Davie (London: Poetry Book Society, 1960);

"Ezra Pound's *Hugh Selwyn Mauberley*," in *The Modern Age*, edited by Boris Ford (Harmondsworth: Penguin, 1961), pp. 315-329;

"The Relationship between Syntax and Music in Some Modern Poems in English," in *Poetics*, part 1, edited by Davie (The Hague: Mouton, 1961), pp. 203-214;

Selected Poems of William Wordsworth, edited by Davie (London: Harrap, 1962);

The Poems of Dr. Zhivago, translated with commentary by Davie (Manchester: Manchester University Press, 1965; New York: Barnes & Noble, 1965);

Russian Literature and Modern English Fiction: A Collection of Critical Essays, edited by Davie (Chicago: University of Chicago Press, 1965);

Pasternak: Modern Judgements, edited by Davie and Angela Livingstone, with verse translations by Davie (London: Macmillan, 1969; Nashville: Aurora, 1970);

"The Black Mountain Poets: Charles Olson and Edward Dorn," in *The Survival of Poetry*, edited by Martin Dodsworth (London: Faber & Faber, 1970), pp. 216-234;

"Pound and Eliot: A Distinction," in *Eliot in Perspective*, edited by Graham Martin (London: Macmillan, 1970), pp. 62-82;

Augustan Lyric, edited by Davie (London: Heinemann, 1974);

Elizabeth Daryush, *Collected Poems*, introduction by Davie (Manchester: Carcanet Press, 1976);

Collected Poems of Yvor Winters, introduction by Davie (Manchester: Carcanet Press, 1978; Athens, Ohio: Swallow Press, 1980);

The New Oxford Book of Christian Verse, edited by Davie (New York: Oxford University Press, 1981; Oxford: Oxford University Press, 1981).

PERIODICAL PUBLICATIONS: "Hopkins, the Decadent Critic," *Cambridge Journal*, 4 (September 1951): 725-739;

" 'Essential Gaudiness': The Poems of Wallace Stevens," *Twentieth Century*, 153 (June 1953): 455-462;

"Landor as Poet," *Shenandoah*, 4 (Summer-Autumn 1953): 93-105;

" 'The Deserted Village': Poem as Virtual History," *Twentieth Century*, 156 (August 1954): 161-174;

" 'The Auroras of Autumn,' " *Perspective*, 7 (Autumn 1954): 125-136;

"T. S. Eliot: The End of an Era," *Twentieth Century*, 159 (April 1956): 350-362;

"An Alternative to Pound?" [on Edgar Bowers], *Spectrum*, 1 (Fall 1957): 60-63;

"See, and Believe" [on Charles Tomlinson], *Essays in Criticism*, 9 (April 1959): 188-195;

"Remembering the Movement," *Prospect* (Summer 1959): 13-16;

"A. Alvarez and Donald Davie: A Discussion," *Review*, 1 (April-May 1962): 10-25;

"England as Poetic Subject," *Poetry*, 100 (May 1962): 121-123;

"Alan Stephens—A Tone of Voice," *Prospect*, 6 (Spring 1964): 38-40;

"Sincerity and Poetry," *Michigan Quarterly Review*, 5 (Winter 1966): 3-8;

"Beyond All This Fiddle: A Rejoinder to A. Alvarez," *Times Literary Supplement*, 25 May 1967, p. 472;

"Landscape as Poetic Focus," *Southern Review*, new series 4 (Summer 1968): 685-691;

"Eminent Talent" [on Walter Savage Landor], *Essays in Criticism*, 20 (October 1970): 466-472;

"Robert Lowell," *Parnassus*, 2 (Fall-Winter 1973): 49-57;

"English and American in *Briggflatts*" [on Basil Bunting], *PN Review*, 5 (1977): 17-20;

"Winters and Leavis: Memories and Reflections," *Sewanee Review*, 87 (Fall 1979): 608-618;

"Lessons in Honesty" [on Edward Thomas], *Times Literary Supplement*, 23 November 1979, pp. 21-22;

"A Mug's Game?," *PN Review*, 12 (1979): 17-19;

"Kenneth Allott and the Thirties," *Times Literary Supplement*, 7 March 1980, pp. 269-271;

"A Day with the DNB," *PN Review*, 18 (1980): 26-30.

Donald Davie was born in Barnsley, Yorkshire, to George Clarke and Alice Sugden Davie, received his early education at Barnsley Holgate Grammar School, and spent his boyhood in "the industrially ravaged landscape," as he called it, of the West Riding. As a Northerner, he has said that in literature he grew to like "the spare and lean." From his mother, who had a liking for poetry and knew, according to Davie, "the greater part, perhaps the whole" of Francis Turner Palgrave's *The Golden Treasury of the Best Songs and Lyrical Poems in the English Language* (1861, 1897) by heart, he developed an early interest in verse. From the art master of Barnsley Grammar School, he learned to appreciate church architecture, an appreciation expressed in a number of his poems. Of Baptist parentage, he was, to quote from an essay written in his fifties, "an Englishman bred . . . near to the heart of English Dissenting Protestantism." A considerable part of his critical writing is devoted to a defense of the conservative, orthodox, dissenting tradition—Baptist, Congregationalist, and Presbyterian—which he considers to be—at least in the seventeenth and eighteenth centuries—rational, intellectual, and enlightened. Although by the late 1970s he no longer considered himself a Baptist or a dissenter, his Baptist upbringing had a profound influence on his career as a scholar, a critic, and a poet.

In 1940 he entered St. Catharine's College, Cambridge, where he says in his memoirs *These the Companions* (1982) he had the opportunity to indulge in voracious reading of seventeenth-century pulpit oratory at the English faculty library and to pursue his second major interest, architecture. At about this time he began to have doubts about adhering to the dissenting church. Although he was in sympathy with the strong monarchical sentiment in the church, he regretted its involvement with liberalism, and he felt that when the Liberal party collapsed in England so did the dissenting church. He joined the navy in 1941, and in the summer of 1942 he was sent to northern Russia, where, successively stationed at Polyarno, Murmansk, and Archangel, he remained until December 1943. His Russian experience is vividly described in *These the Companions*, and his enthusiasm for the poetry of Boris Pasternak was an important literary development of his stay in Russia.

Nineteen forty-four found him in Plymouth, the birthplace of Doreen John, whom he married on 13 January 1945. They have three children. In 1946 Davie returned to Cambridge, where he and his wife lived in "four draughty and mouse-infested rooms over the village store in Trumpington." He became a disciple of F. R. Leavis ("*Scrutiny* was my bible and F. R. Leavis my prophet") and, with the majority of the intellectuals at Cambridge, an admirer of T. S. Eliot: "It is hard to convey the virtually unchallenged eminence that Eliot continued to enjoy in Cambridge." At this time he attempted to improve "his shore-leave sailor's Russian" and "to grapple with Pasternak." His initial interest in Pasternak developed into a serious study of Russian literature of the last two centuries, and he eventually wrote his dissertation on an Anglo-Russian subject. He also began at this time his long "Pushkin: a Didactic Poem" (included in his *Collected Poems 1950-1970* [1972] in a greatly abbreviated form), an attempt "to see how near to prose poetry can come while still remaining poetry." He received his B.A. from Cambridge in 1947, his M.A. in 1949, and his Ph.D. in 1951. In 1950 Davie went to Trinity College, Dublin, as a lecturer in English, and in 1954 he became a fellow. Among the many Irish writers and scholars he met there, he expressed especial admiration for Joseph Hone, biographer of William Butler Yeats, and the poets Austin Clarke and Padraic Fallon. After giving up his lectureship

and fellowship in 1957, he lectured at the Yeats summer school directed by his former tutor T. R. Henn. He returned as a visitor to Ireland a number of times, but by the late 1960s he "had shaken the dust of Ireland from off my feet because of I.R.A. atrocities against the innocent." His departure was commemorated with a poem, "Ireland of the Bombers," published in the *Irish Times* in 1969.

While in Dublin he produced *Purity of Diction in English Verse* (1952), which reveals his serious interest in the technical excellence of poetry and in the moral and social implications of its subject matter, an interest he was to exhibit for the next thirty years in both his creative and his critical work. He states his preference for pure diction "which comes from making a selection from the language on reasonable principles," and, arguing in favor of the restoration of genres and for the restoration of the eighteenth-century practice of selecting diction according to genre or to some scheme or tone, he objects to modern abandonment or confusion of genres and to the modern poet's belief that there are "no poetical and unpoetical words." In analyzing Oliver Goldsmith's notion of "chaste" diction as being selective and economical in the use of metaphor, Davie points out that after Wordsworth the diction of most poets (especially Keats) became increasingly impure: "Since Wordsworth, none has purified the language of the tribe." Of Gerard Manley Hopkins, for example, he says that he "has no respect for language, but gives it Sandow-exercises until it is a muscle bound monstrosity." He notes a concurrent abandonment of conventional syntax, especially in the twentieth century, as in T. S. Eliot's *Ash Wednesday* and *Four Quartets*, where (in the romantic-symbolist tradition) the structure is musical rather than logical. To abandon logical syntax, he states, "is to throw away a tradition central to human thought." In *Purity of Diction in English Verse* Davie is chiefly concerned with literature prior to the twentieth century, but its principles regarding diction and syntax have a bearing on Davie's own poetry and on the poetry of a number of his contemporaries, a group of like-minded poets in the 1950s which became known as The Movement. The Movement was, among other things, a sharp break with imagism and symbolism as they appear in the poetry of Pound and Eliot. In a postscript added to the 1966 edition of *Purity of Diction in English Verse* Davie states that he wrote the book principally so as to understand "what I had been doing, or trying to do, in the poems I had been writing. Under a thin disguise the book was, and still is, a manifesto." He goes on to say that he, Kingsley Amis, and a few others "had been moving each by his own route, upon a common point of view as regards the writing of poems." This point of view "came to be called The Movement. . . . I like to think that if the group of us had ever cohered enough to subscribe to a common manifesto, it might have been *Purity of Diction in English Verse*."

Davie shared with The Movement what he called "an angry reaction from the tawdry amoralism which had destroyed Dylan Thomas," and he mentions his indifference at that time to any poem which cannot be shown to be moral. In his 1966 postscript he rejects this latter moralistic viewpoint as extreme and an overreaction to the doctrine of art for art's sake. Nevertheless, in his poetry and criticism Davie continues to show frequent concern for the ethical implications of poetry, a concern which was influenced by the American poet and critic Yvor Winters. The Movement's break with imagism, with its emphasis on the concrete as practiced by H. D., the early Ezra Pound, and the other imagist poets, was congenial to Davie's own temperament and talent. Commenting on his early poems, he wrote, "I have not the poet's need for concreteness. . . . the idea comes into my mind more readily than the sensuous experience."

Davie's participation in The Movement became evident in 1956, when Robert Conquest edited his *New Lines: An Anthology*, which included eight poems by Davie and selections from the poetry of eight other poets—Elizabeth Jennings, John Holloway, Philip Larkin, Thom Gunn, Kingsley Amis, D. J. Enright, Robert Conquest, and John Wain. In his introduction, the editor (who later disclaimed any attempt to launch a "movement") pointed out that the nine poets represented in his volume all came to prominence in the 1950s and that they all were writing a kind of verse quite different from that which had flourished in the three previous decades, a verse which was not doctrinaire but which shared certain qualities: paraphrasable rational content, clarity of language, and a rational structure. In his introduction to the second *New Lines* anthology (1963) Conquest said that the "Poetry of the Fifties . . . had returned to the cardinal traditions of English verse."

Two poems from Davie's first book of verse, an untitled pamphlet published as number nineteen in the Fantasy Press series, drew praise from the *Times Literary Supplement* reviewer: "Homage to William Cowper" and "On Bertrand Russell's 'Portraits from Memory.'" The first of these was inspired by Cowper's "On the Death of Mrs.

Throckmorton's Bullfinch," which, Davie says, "in its controlled hysteria, is surely one of the most frightening poems in English." Davie read Cowper early in his career, praising him for rejecting the bohemia of his day and expressing admiration for his hymns. The influence of the eighteenth century is also evident in the poem on Russell's portraits in which, the *TLS* reviewer observed, the poet turns "a stilted but noble eighteenth century rhetoric legitimately to ironic uses." Both poems were included by Davie in his *Collected Poems 1950-1970* and both exhibit the characteristics of The Movement, characteristics which did not go unchallenged in the early 1950s. The Fantasy Press was attacked by Alexander Scott in the pages of the *Times Literary Supplement* for publishing the "Conundrum-Cum-Limerick School," and later, in the 1960s, Charles Tomlinson said, "I felt the Movement to be a symptom . . . of suffocation."

Davie's second book, *Brides of Reason* (1955) contains two notable poems, "Remembering the 'Thirties" and "Woodpigeons at Raheny," which appeared later in *New Lines* and in *Collected Poems 1950-1970*. In "Remembering the 'Thirties" Davie accomplishes in his own verse the aim he expressed years later in *Dissentient Voice* (1982)—to keep the language "crisp, supple, and responsible." He treats courage and the weaknesses of the generation antecedent to his with sympathy, compassion, and irony that is reminiscent of the poems of Edwin Arlington Robinson:

> It dawns upon the veterans after all
> That what for them were agonies, for us
> Are high-brow thrillers, though historical;
> And all their feats quite strictly fabulous.
> . . . .
> England expected every man that day
> To show his motives were ambivalent.
>
> They played the fool, not to appear as fools
> In time's long glass. A deprecating air
> Disarmed, they thought, the jeers of
>   later schools
> Yet irony itself is doctrinaire. . . .

"Woodpigeons at Raheny" is a charming example of Davie's many poems that emanate from a sense of place and a sense of history associated with place. In a friend's house near Dublin one spring afternoon Davie is prevented from writing a poem by the distracting thought awakened by a dove singing the old, easy phrase "tereu-tereu" and the sight of a "sandalled Capuchin's silent stride," both dove and friar arousing memories of the past.

Published in the same year as *Brides of Reason, Articulate Energy: An Enquiry into the Syntax of English Poetry* (1955) was originally intended to develop a theme announced in *Purity of Diction in English Verse*, the advantages of conventional, rational prose syntax in poetry, advantages frequently abandoned by experimentalists such as Pound and Eliot earlier in the twentieth century. The *Times Literary Supplement* reviewer of *Articulate Energy* called Davie a rational conservative out of sympathy with the imagist tradition, who expressed broad humanistic generalizations with traditional sanity and made technical observations useful and novel. In his observations on poets and theoreticians ranging from Sir Philip Sidney to Ezra Pound, Davie examines the effects of various attitudes toward syntax—traditional syntax considered as a principle of meaningful arrangement or as unpoetical (T. E. Hulme) and to be abandoned altogether; syntax as music (Eliot) or as action (Ernest Fenollosa and Pound).

In a postscript added to a 1975 reprint of *Articulate Energy*, Davie says that, while he started the book as a sequel to *Purity of Diction in English Verse*, he gradually became less polemical than he was in his earlier criticism. His critique became an inquiry rather than a manifesto, and the author became less opposed than formerly to the musical syntax used by Eliot and others and to the dislocated syntax employed by Pound. Indeed, he went on to write a fairly favorable book on Pound, and his objections to irrationality in poetry in *Articulate Energy* are softened. Nevertheless, in his 1975 postscript he expresses his horror at the abandonment of standards of reason and lucidity in literature and the other arts: "The 1960s, that hideous decade, showed what was involved: the arts of literature were enlisted on the side of all that was insane and suicidal, without order and without proportion, *against civilization*." The italics are Davie's. On the whole, *Articulate Energy*, written in the mid-1950s, is on the side of civilization. Twenty years later Davie concluded his postscript with these words: "What I wrote in 1955 I stand over now. Then what I said seemed to be timely; now it has, to my eyes, an air more forlorn. But I stand over it."

In September 1957, Davie journeyed from Dublin to the United States to become for one year a visiting professor at the University of California at Santa Barbara. During this first visit to the American West he met and became friends with the distinguished Polish critic and scholar Waclaw Lednicki, a professor on the faculty of the University of California, Berkeley, who assisted him in his study of Polish poetry and in his adaptation of Adam Mickiewicz's *Pan Tadeusz*, which Davie called *The Forests of Lithuania* (1959).

In Los Altos, California, during the 1957-1958 academic year he met Yvors Winters for the first time, although he had corresponded with him for almost ten years, and also for the first time he met British poet Thom Gunn and American poet Janet Lewis. He renewed his acquaintance with two other poets of Winters's circle, Wesley and Helen Trimpi, whom he had met as early as 1950 in England, and he became acquainted with Edgar Bowers, who was teaching at Santa Barbara. The relationship between Davie, one of the leading poets and spokesman of The Movement, and Yvor Winters and his group was an important one. Davie writes of Winters in his memoir in the *Sewanee Review*, "I had discovered him for myself before 1950, borrowing from the Cambridge Union what may at that date have been the one copy of *In Defense of Reason* [Winters's major book of criticism] in the British Isles. I had written to Winters with admiring enthusiasm. . . ." Davie's admiration is understandable, for as George Dekker says of the British poets of The Movement, "they also resembled the brilliant American 'Reactionary Generation' of Yvor Winters, Louise Bogan, the Fugitives. . . ." In a review published in fall 1957 Davie wrote "The Stanford school of poets, grouped around and schooled by Yvor Winters, seems to me perhaps the most interesting feature of the poetic scene in the U.S." From the mid-1940s on, Winters, like Davie later in the 1950s, was increasingly aware of the ethical value of poetry, and he considered the writing of a successful poem an act of moral judgment. Also, beginning with his analysis of the sixteenth-century lyric published in *Poetry* magazine in the late 1930s, he called attention to the virtues of the plain style as opposed to the ornate style, an opinion which has affinities with Davie's later advocacy of "chaste" diction. In 1968, about ten years after his first meeting with Winters, Davie joined the faculty of Stanford University where Winters, who had died on 25 January 1968, had been teaching.

In 1957 Davie's *A Winter Talent and Other Poems* was published. Of its thirty-seven poems all except one were retained by Davie in his *Collected Poems 1950-1970*. "Limited Achievement," written in smooth rhythm and restrained ironic tone, has the style of a Movement poem. Yet Davie, in depicting an artist who is successful only in "his single narrow track," may be showing impatience with the restrictions of Movement poetry. "Rejoinder to a Critic," while defending his position as a Movement poet, may also be slightly mocking it, as Florence Elon has

Janet Lewis Winters and Donald Davie on the steps to the Winters's house in Los Altos, California (Doreen Davie)

observed, and in "Cherry Ripe," says Elon, "Like Marvell [in 'The Garden'] Davie expresses an attraction to sensuous nature even as he rejects it morally and artistically." In poems in his later book *Events and Wisdoms* (1964) Davie makes a deliberate attempt to depict the richness of the sensuous world as he does to some extent in his best-known poem from *A Winter Talent*, "The Fountain." The fountain

> Feathers up fast, and steeples; then in clods
> Thuds into its first basin; thence as surf
> Smokes up and hangs; irregularly slops
> Into its second, tattered like a shawl;
> There, chill as rain, stipples a danker green,
> Where urgent tritons lob their heavy jets.

Interest in the sensuous world of nature is also evident in "The Mushroom Gatherers," praised by Thom Gunn for its precise concreteness.

The sense of place in *A Winter Talent* becomes more and more pronounced and continues in his later volumes of verse *Essex Poems* (1969) and *The*

Shires (1974), as well as in his criticism, especially in his appreciation of the use of geography in the poems of Charles Olson. Davie remarks in his *Dissentient Voice* (1982) on "the abiding relevance and imaginative richness of Geography." One group of poems in *A Winter Talent* is entitled "England," another group "Ireland," and a third "Italy." George Dekker, analyzing "North Dublin" in his article on Davie in *Agenda* (Summer 1976), finds, combined with sense of place, another recurrent theme in Davie's work, the dissenting religion of his Baptist childhood and his later interest in the Episcopalian church. To show that Davie's "sense of place poems" are seldom merely descriptive, Dekker quotes the second stanza:

> A continuous gallery, clear glass in the windows
> An elegant conventicle
> In the Ionian order—
> What dissenter with taste
> But would turn, on these terms
> Episcopalian?

Dekker also points out that in several poems in *A Winter Talent* Davie departs from the smooth rhythms and conventional syntax of his earlier work. Under the subtitle "Dissentient Voice" Davie presents four poems dealing with his Baptist childhood and his early protestant upbringing. The first of these poems begins with a side glance at the carefree innocence of Dylan Thomas's childhood, contrasted with Davie's early exposure to the ethical severities of the Baptist faith: "When some were happy as the grass was green / I was as happy as the glass was dark." The fourth and last poem in this group, "A Gathered Church," Davie calls an attempt to "win through to an apprehension of Dissent as embodied and made concrete in the personality of my grandfather." In *These the Companions* Davie, commenting on these poems, speaks of "The Dissenters' conception of 'a gathered church,' gathered *from* the world, and in tension with it. . . . And although what guided me were the writings of a Cambridge historian of the dissenting churches, Bernard Manning of Jesus, the reading was done in Dublin, where the disestablished Church of Ireland satisfied the need, bred in me as a child, to envisage my church as in tension with the state, by no means coterminous with it as the Church of England must pretend to be."

Davie and his family had visited Italy for the first time in 1952, returning in 1956 and frequently thereafter. The hills of Tuscany were a refreshing contrast to the fens of Cambridge. The "Italy" group of poems in *A Winter Talent* is the literary result of his love for Italy, as is the later "Hornet" (first published in 1962), which points up a contrast between the sun-drenched white stones of Italy, and England, "where the green mould stains before the mortar is dry."

Beginning with *The Forests of Lithuania* Davie's work showed more and more the influence of Ezra Pound, although he had objected to and continued to object to the extreme dislocation of conventional syntax in some of Pound's *Cantos*. Thom Gunn in his review of *The Forests of Lithuania* reports, "I once heard Davie say at a poetry reading that his ambition was to reconcile in his own work the style of Ezra Pound and Yvor Winters." Perhaps Davie's meeting in Dublin with an American authority on Pound, Hugh Kenner, and his temporary replacement of Kenner at the University of California at Santa Barbara in 1957-1958 were partly responsible for Davie's increased interest in Pound. Dekker refers to *The Forests of Lithuania* as a Poundian "homage." The poem is an adaptation of Adam Mic-

kiewicz's romantic epic *Pan Tadeusz* (1834), which, according to the poem itself, is the work of a fictitious Lithuanian-in-exile twenty years after the action took place (1811-1812 when Lithuania was suffering from Russian occupation).

Mickiewicz's "great masterpiece of all Slavic poetry," as G. R. Noyes called it in his introduction to his English translation (Davie's principal source), was at first intended to be merely a village idyll—*A Story of Life Among Polish Gentlefolk* as the subtitle states. But by placing the action in a period of political turmoil, during the invasion of Russia by Napoleon, Mickiewicz made the real theme of the poem the struggle between Pole and Muscovite (the Poles at that time siding with the invading French), and, while not abandoning the romantic love story and the vivid depiction of native manners and customs, Mickiewicz transformed his idyll into a national epic.

This epic quality is not preserved in Davie's relatively brief rendition of selected scenes from Mickiewicz's substantial poem. Thom Gunn (after referring to Davie as one of the most important poets in postwar England) stated that *The Forests of Lithuania* was "a series of episodes with no particular connection, which led nowhere in particular" and deplored the corrupting influence of Pound on the style and structure. Yet there are charming passages, such as "The Gathering of Mushrooms" and "The Forest," which includes a dramatic depiction of a bear hunt that has considerable power, especially as read by Davie himself. And there are interesting stylistic experiments besides those already mentioned. The description of the forest at the beginning of part four is a brilliant pastiche in the style of Andrew Marvell's "The Garden." Davie's use of the nonrhyming short line is sometimes similar to the syllabic verse of Santa Barbara poet Alan Stephens in his first book, *The Sum* (1958), which Davie praised in his review of one of Stephens's later books, *Between Matter and Principle* (1963). In the beginning of part six of *The Forests of Lithuania*, "The Year 1812," Davie makes an interesting return to the formal style of his earlier work—a series of skillfully written tercets with an interlocking rhyme scheme.

In the fall of 1958 Davie took up his duties as lecturer in English at Gonville and Caius College, Cambridge University (a year later he became a fellow). Once again Davie took up residence in Trumpington, this time on the ground floor of a late-Victorian mansion. In *These the Companions* he remembers "wistfully its vast and cold and cavernous rooms, the Ruskinian carving on certain banisters, and in particular a mossy lawn under great beech trees. Several of my poems deal directly with that house and that garden: many other poems bring the place back to me, because I remember that I wrote them there, in that ambience of solid amenity." Davie goes on to say that the house was demolished as soon as they left it and that this destruction was for him symbolic of the profound change coming over England, a change that eventually led to his expatriation: "What worried and annoyed me, when I returned to Cambridge in 1958, was the way in which the sentimental Left occupied all the same positions, and rehearsed all the same arguments, that I was just old enough to remember from twenty years before. . . . so they wasted the time staring into their beer-mugs and accusing themselves of being class-traitors because there they were, in the Little Rose or the Baron of Beef, whereas they ought to have been carousing with the South Shields football team. . . . What has been called the politics of envy, which I sometimes think of as the politics of self-pity, had sapped independence, self-help and self-respect. . . . I began to think that my habits of thought and feeling were so alien to those of my countrymen that my future, if I had one, would have to be spent out of England altogether."

The summer of 1960 found Davie in Warsaw, where he delivered an important paper at the International Conference of Work-in-Progress devoted to problems of poetics. His paper, "The Relation of Syntax and Music in some Modern Poems in English," is a refinement of the subject presented in *Articulate Energy*. In discussing Paul Valéry's statement that the symbolist poets attempted to "reclaim their own from music," Davie argues that such music is much more than obvious onomatopoeia, alliteration, and Swinburnian vowel music. What poets "envy music for is its continuity, its sustained fluency," which can be achieved by manipulation of syntax, as in Spenser's two marriage hymns and Milton's "linked sweetness long drawn out." Furthermore, Davie continues, Valéry was aware that the music of poetry has a duration in time, that the proper employment of syntax with line length will increase the effectiveness of verbal music and that the employment of the present tense to make the duration of poem's time coeval with the duration of the action depicted will give the illusion of immediacy, of the action happening *now* as in music. He quotes passages from Eliot's *The Waste Land* and Yeats's "Coole Park and Ballylee" as examples of the

successful combination of music, grammar, and syntax.

New and Selected Poems (1961) includes what Davie considered the best of his verse from *Brides of Reason* and *A Winter Talent* together with ten new poems. The volume was attacked in the pages of the *Partisan Review* as "artsy-crafty" and "minor troubadour," yet the reviewer expressed satisfaction with the irony of "The Evangelist" and with "The Life of Service" (one of the new poems), in which "a long-suffering tenacious English shrub" stands for "all the ghastliness his generation has set itself against." He also praised "Dissentient Voice." Carol Johnson, reviewing the volume in the *Sewanee Review*, liked "Gardens No Emblems," "Creon's Mouse," "Samuel Beckett's Dublin," "Hearing Russian Spoken," and "Remembering the Thirties," all reprinted from earlier books, but she appears to have liked none of the new poems and condemns especially "Killala" for what she considers its metrical ineptitude. Of the ten new poems, "Against Confidences" appears to this writer to be a successful exercise in the plain nonimagistic style of Sir Thomas Wyatt and Ben Jonson, and "Heigh-ho on a Winter Afternoon" (with echoes of Wallace Stevens's ironies) is moving in its pathos. Yet it is evident that the new poems did little to advance Davie's reputation.

Davie calls *A Sequence for Francis Parkman* (1961) "my response to North America on my first visit from September 1957 to August 1958." Brief poetic "profiles" of La Salle, Frontenac, Montcalm, and Pontiac are drawn directly from the works of the distinguished American historiographer Francis Parkman (1823-1893), author of a series of volumes, *France and England in North America* (1851-1892), of which the *History of the Conspiracy of Pontiac* (1851) is the best known. In America he is famous for this work and for his *The Oregon Trail* (1849), but apparently he is not well-known in England. A distinguished British reviewer of Davie's book thought Parkman was a personal friend of the poet's.

In 1961 Davie was British Council lecturer in Budapest. Several years later his interest in Hungarian literature became apparent when his poem on the Hungarian mathematicians Bolyai, father and son, was published in *Events and Wisdoms*. His visit to Jugoslavia in 1962 resulted in "The Vindication of Jovan Babǐc," "Across the Bay," and "Poreč," which were also published in *Events and Wisdoms*.

In June 1962, the lead writer for the *Times Literary Supplement* commented in "Language and the Self " on the debate between Davie and A. Alvarez, which had just been published as "A. Alvarez and Donald Davie: A Discussion" in the first number of the *Review* (April-May 1962), Alvarez taking the position that poetry should be primarily "serious" (that is concerned with important and timely subjects), Davie arguing that it should first of all be "aesthetic" (that is successful as a work of art). Davie renewed the argument with Alvarez several years later in "Beyond All This Fiddle," a letter to the editors of the *Times Literary Supplement* (25 May 1967), in which he attacked Alvarez for his defense of such extremism in the arts as psychic exploration enhanced by the taking of drugs. Davie found drugs a poor substitute for truth and beauty and pointed to the Russian poet Pasternak as a model for contemporary poets, superior to the three recommended by Alvarez—Robert Lowell, John Berryman, and Sylvia Plath.

In 1963 Davie visited the University of Cincinnati as the Elliston lecturer, and in this same year he produced *The Language of Science and the Language of Literature, 1700-1740* to challenge the widely held view that the whole movement of philosophy which started with Descartes was inimical to poetry. According to the *Times Literary Supplement* reviewer, Davie proves his case. This volume is one of several—beginning with the first two chapters of *Purity of Diction in English Verse*, continuing in his edition of the longer poems of the later eighteenth century, *The Late Augustans* (1958), and in his edition (with a substantial introduction) of *Augustan Lyric* (1974), in which Davie expresses his admiration for certain eighteenth-century poets, especially Christopher Smart, Isaac Watts, and William Cowper. The influence of eighteenth-century formalism and classicism is evident (though intermittent) throughout Davie's writings.

In 1964 Davie became a cofounder of the University of Essex, a professor of English there, and later pro-Vice-Chancellor. In that year he also produced two important books: *Events and Wisdoms: Poems 1957-1963* and *Ezra Pound: Poet as Sculptor*. The *Times Literary Supplement* reviewer of *Events and Wisdoms* noted that, while the poet could still write in the sophisticated, witty, and epigrammatic style of his early verse, in some poems he displayed new "metaphorical richness," "visual relish," and "sensual awareness," especially in "Low Lands," in which a river delta is described:

> Like a snake it is, its serpentine iridescence
> Of slow light spilt and wheeling over calm
> Inundations, and a snake's still menace

Hooding with bruised sky belfry and lonely farm.

The grasses wave on meadows fat with foison.

The fresh visual perception in "The Hill Field," which presents the way a landscape may be transformed into art, also received favorable comment. According to the same reviewer, this poem, "House Martin," and several others are written in quatrains similar to those of Boris Pasternak. "House Martin," the equally successful "Green River," and several other poems—in their combination of precise observation of nature, a slightly melancholy tone, and moral or philosophical comment—seem much like the poems of Robert Frost. The last poems in the volume are, according to another reviewer, dense with observation and the naming of things. William Dickey, on the other hand, in his notice in the *Hudson Review*, dismisses the volume as the work of an energetic traditional poet whose vision is that of the momentary, the trivial, the second rate.

The book on Ezra Pound is one of Davie's major critical undertakings. Although the reviewers sometimes expressed disagreement on certain issues, almost all praised the coherence of Davie's critique, which wove together some of the most important strands of Pound's career to date and demonstrated that Pound had more respect for the objectivity of phenomena than had his major contemporaries Yeats and Eliot. According to Davie, Pound is closer than they to the eighteenth-century Enlightenment, to scientific objectivity, to the scholastic medievalists, and to poets such as Cavalcanti who created a "radiant world" of hard-edged moving energies, which Pound attempted to recreate, especially during his imagist and vorticist periods and later in some of the Cantos. To substantiate his arguments Davie frequently resorts to close exegeses of individual poems, which are perhaps the most valuable parts of the book. His perceptive technical analyses of "Hugh Selwyn Mauberley," "Homage to Sextus Propertius," the Cavalcanti translations, "The Sea-Farer," several poems in *Cathay*, "Near Perigord," "Provinçia Deserta," the translation of *Women of Trachis* as well as a number of Cantos, including the series devoted to Malatesta, American history, and the Pisan and Rock-Drill Cantos, are of a quality and expertise that can come only from a practicing poet.

As early as the mid-1950s Davie, in his poem "Hearing Russian Spoken," was indicating an interest in contemporary Russia and its literature, and from 1961 on there are a growing number of refer-

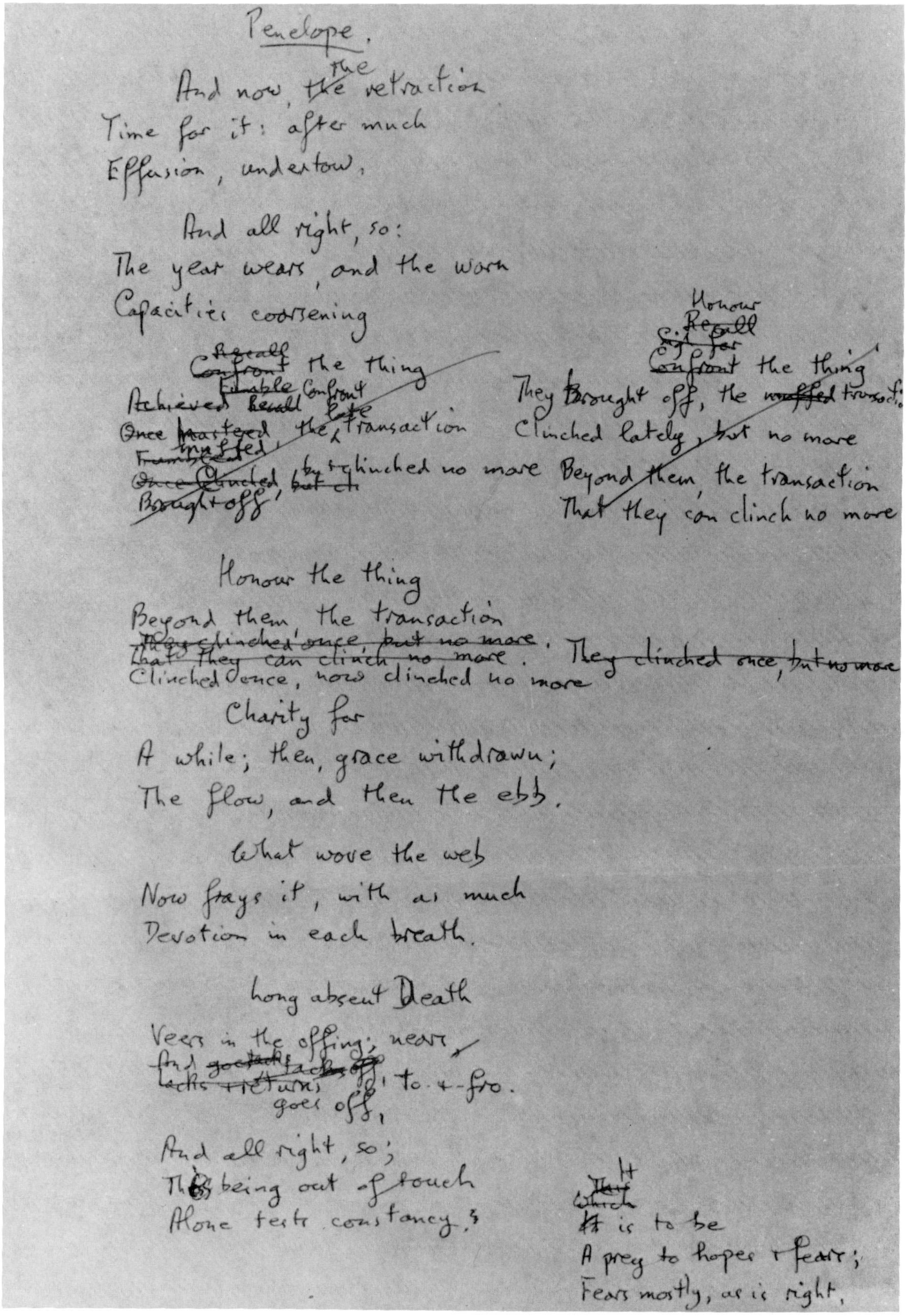

Penelope.

And now, ~~the~~ the retraction
Time for it: after much
Effusion, undertow,

And all right, so:
The year wears, and the worn
Capacities coarsening

~~Recall~~ ~~Confront~~ the thing
Achieved ~~Recall~~ Confront
Once ~~mastered~~ the, Late transaction
~~Fumbled~~ muffed
~~Once Clinched, but cl~~ but clinched no more
~~Brought off,~~

Honour
~~Recall~~
~~Sigh for~~
~~Confront~~ the thing
They Brought off, the ~~muffed~~ transac.
Clinched lately, but no more
~~Beyond them, the transaction~~
~~That they can clinch no more~~

Honour the thing
Beyond them, the transaction
~~They clinched once, but no more.~~
~~That they can clinch no more.~~ ~~They clinched once, but no more~~
Clinched once, now clinched no more

Charity for
A while; then, grace withdrawn;
The flow, and then the ebb.

What wove the web
Now frays it, with as much
Devotion in each breath.

Long absent Death
Veers in the offing; nears,
~~And goes back tacks off~~
~~tacks + returns~~ off, to-+-fro.
goes off,

And all right, so;
This being out of touch
Alone tests constancy;

~~That~~ ~~Which~~ It
~~It~~ is to be
A prey to hopes + fears;
Fears mostly, as is right,

Worksheet (the author)

ences in his writing to one of Davie's favorite poets, Boris Pasternak, whose late poems (as distinct from his early poems) Davie considers to be among "the very greatest of our time" both in practice and in theory. Furthermore, he considers Pasternak to be the only true postsymbolist poet in Russia, and he accepts Pasternak's symbolist doctrine that poetry is a kind of music and that the musical flow of language, not the poet, is actually in control of the poem. He commends Pasternak's belief that for the contemporary poet honor is more important than beauty, and he states that in *Dr. Zhivago* Pasternak gives us the "narrative of a poetic life which, simply by being lived through, challenges and criticizes and condemns the society about it."

Of Davie's three books on Russian literature—his translation, *The Poems of Dr. Zhivago* (1965); *Russian Literature and Modern English Fiction: A Collection of Critical Essays* (1965), edited with an introduction by Davie; and *Pasternak: Modern Judgements* (1969), edited by Davie and Angela Livingstone with verse translations by Davie—the first is the most relevant to Davie's own poetry. His purpose, as he explains in his introduction, is to discover the function of the poems in Pasternak's *Dr. Zhivago*, and to present verse translations as close as possible to the originals while still preserving the poetic quality. The translations were commended by the reviewers for their fidelity, firmness of texture, and lack of padding, and his detailed prose exegesis of the technique and meaning, especially the symbolic import of each poem, had an effect on his own poetry. William Dickey in his review of *Events and Wisdoms* in the *Hudson Review* noted the increased richness of metaphor and sensuous language in Davie's most recent poetry and suggested that Davie was making use of Pasternak's quatrains. George Dekker, writing in *Agenda*, called attention to the Poundian influence on Davie's poetry but stated "that, particularly during the middle and late sixties, his ways of seeing and writing probably were influenced as much by Pasternak as by Pound."

By the time *Essex Poems: 1963-1967* (1969) was published, Davie (who had accepted a professorship at Stanford University the previous year) had become a well-publicized English expatriate living in America. The English press cited him as one more example of the lamentable "brain drain" that was weakening an already culturally shaky England. Davie's decision to leave England was foreshadowed, perhaps, by his comment in a brief article, "England as Poetic Subject," which appeared in 1962 in *Poetry*. After pointing out that in England of

the early 1960s claims of civic responsibility and artistic responsibility had become irreconcilable, he said, "England is a country where even the poets are Philistines without knowing it." The theme of exile is anticipated also in the *Essex Poems: 1963-1967*. One of the most interesting, "The God of Details," is a Hopkinsian poem in praise of particulars, but it lacks the verve of Hopkins's "inscape" poems such as "Hurrahing in Harvest." The poem is subtitled "After Pasternak," and the influence of the Russian poet, here acknowledged, is evident elsewhere in the volume. Reviewers were quick to comment on a new and ominous note in Davie's verse, the sense of loss, social and personal, a kind of blankness which Davie perhaps hoped to overcome when he decided to leave England. Yet the three poems included at the end of the volume under the title "From the New World" (written in America) are scarcely more cheerful than the English poems. In the English poem "The God of Details," life is seen as a hushed "minuteness." In "Iowa," first published in 1965, he will be sorry "when the world goes piebald." He prefers the "peculiar beauty" of a kind of blankness, the "white on white" of a "framehouse amid the snow." The other American poems "Back of Affluence" and "Or, Solitude" are also bleak. In 1969 Davie had published in England a small collection entitled *Poems*, which includes another "After Pasternak" entitled "At Mid-Career," as well as "New Year Wishes for the English," in which he wishes England "the inception / Of a long recuperation."

His introduction to *Six Epistles to Eva Hesse* (1970), written from September 1969 to March 1970 and signed "D. D. California," explains that these letters in verse to Ezra Pound's German translator and the editor of *New Approaches to Ezra Pound* (1969) were written to express his reservations about Pound's experimental methods. Though they are lighthearted in tone, they advance a serious argument—that as much (or perhaps more) range and variety of experience can be encompassed in traditional verse forms as in the experimentalist forms of Pound and his followers.

Collected Poems (1972) brings together the best of Davie's verse from 1950 to 1970. The long poem "England" is a bitter expatriate Poundian sequence (reminiscent of several of Pound's historical Cantos) in which Davie does to England what Pound did to America, that "half savage country." The poet is on a polar flight from the United States to London:

> I dwell, intensely dwell
> on my flying shadow

over the Canadian barrens
and come to nothing else.

What he actually comes to in "eleven hours flying time" is London, the former imperial city, now living on the tourist trade and amusing the tourists and the natives with the theater, that facsimile of a culture:

> Beknighted actors, youth
> in tall hats, trailing feathers,
> society a congeries of roles
> ....
> Napoleon was right:
> a nation of purveyors.
> Now we purvey ourselves.
> ....
> The words of this age are spoken
> from and on a stage.

Davie in his notes cites seven of the historical works he researched while writing the poem. The focus is on England's antiheroes from her imperialist past (with frequent but not precisely annotated direct quotations from his sources) and on her degraded present:

> Brutal manners, brutal
> simplifications as
> we drag it all down.

A comprehensive review of the *Collected Poems* in the *Times Literary Supplement*, "A Candour Under Control," praised Davie for rejecting provincialisms, distrusting easy emotions, demonstrating in his own verse what as a critic he required in other poets—aesthetic control—and boldly experimenting in the styles of three centuries.

Also in 1972 Davie brought together his observations, drawn from a lifetime of reading, on the quality of Hardy's poetry and demonstrated that, for good or bad, the greatest influence on British poetry for the last fifty years has been not Yeats nor Pound nor Eliot but Hardy. In *Thomas Hardy and British Poetry* (1972), the Wessex poet is seen not as a naïf or a primitive but as a sophisticated poetic technician, a scientific humanist, and a liberal in contrast to the conservative Yeats, Eliot, Pound, and Lawrence. Hardy, in Davie's view, was a modest (though proudly expert) workman. In the early chapters of his book Davie gives a perceptive analysis of Hardy's technical skills and argues that he is usually at his very best, "self-excelling," when, as in "The Voice" and "After the Journey," he departs from his im-

periously symmetrical verse and stanza forms with perceptive irregularities. This position differs from Davie's earlier fondness for the symmetry of Augustan verse, and the change of taste is apparent in Davie's own verse. Davie's increasing use of asymmetric forms in his later years may be partially due to his careful study of Hardy.

Three awards in 1973—a Guggenheim Fellowship, an honorary fellowship at St. Catharine's College, Cambridge, and a fellowship in the American Academy of Arts and Sciences—were evidence of Davie's growing reputation in the United States and in England.

The sense of place which had been evident from the beginning in many of Davie's poems dealing with the American and the British experiences is dominant in *The Shires* (1974), in which Davie, now an expatriate, devotes a poem to each of England's forty counties. "Dorset," as George Dekker has observed, follows the Poundian method of reverie and associationism in bringing together Davie's strong interest in Thomas Hardy (Dorset's most famous writer, who showed in his Wessex poems and tales a sense of place stronger even than Davie's), John Fowles's popular novel of Dorset life, *The French Lieutenant's Woman* (1969), and the poet's own grandfather, whose voice, a "burring baritone," is most suitable to the pastoral mood of Davie's happy childhood recollections. Dekker considers the poem a triumphant example of modern pastoralism, in which Davie successfully combines the formalist techniques he learned from Winters with the experimentalist techniques he learned from Pound and the French symbolists.

Michael Schmidt, in discussing *The Shires* in *Agenda*, commented on Davie's evolution from his early imitations of eighteenth-century styles, as exemplified in "Sussex" and in poems written after the publication of *The Shires*. "Sussex" is typical of the poems in the entire volume. The material is personalized; the tone is elegiac; there is a sense of loss as well as a sense of place:

> The most poeticized
> Of English counties, and
> An alien poet's eye,
> Mine, there to endorse it.
>
> "Brain-drain" one hears no more of,
> And that's no loss, There is
> Another emigration:
> Draining away of love.

The "alien poet's eye," the eye of the expatriate, sees

into the past, present, and future of England, finds something still to love but much to regret. "Davie's peculiar relationship with his own and our common past," wrote Schmidt, "and his exploration of it, are often like Hardy's." Hardy shows the past "as un-realised," usually with reference to the development of the individual. Davie sometimes shows the past as unrealized for whole communities or societies. Yet, as Schmidt points out, what still matters for Davie are "the persistent survivals of the past." The influence of Hardy on Davie at this time was intensified by the critical reading Davie had been doing in preparation for his book on the Wessex poet.

In 1977 Barry Alpert edited and introduced a substantial collection of Davie's critical essays, *The Poet in the Imaginary Museum: Essays of Two Decades*, or more precisely, essays published from 1950 to 1977. In the same year Davie produced a small volume, *In the Stopping Train and Other Poems*. "In the Stopping Train," one of several poems that came out of the French experiences of 1972 and 1973 when Davie and his family lived much of the time in Tours, "originated," Davie says in *These the Companions*, "in a miserable journey by rail from Tours to Paris and back, through heavy rain much of the time, on a fruitless attempt to keep a rendezvous with the Irish poet John Montague." Schmidt considers the poem to be crucial in Davie's development, a spiritual autobiography of the poet, wrestling with his other self (the "He" who is in danger of going mad) on the slow train journeying from childhood innocence to the self-knowledge of maturity:

> His future is a slow
> and stopping train through places
> whose names used to have virtue.

It is a kind of parable, a modern pilgrim's progress, but the tone is bleak and, because of the lack of precise detail, charged with significance fundamentally obscure except in its general abstract intention. One would like to know, for example, at what places the train stopped and what were their lost virtues. Another poem from the French experience is "Petit-Thouars," published in its complete and final form for the first time in *These the Companions*. Named for a French naval hero, Aristide du Petit-Thouars, who lived in Touraine, the poem, according to Davie, should be classed with a number of others he wrote about British and Irish-American naval heroes whose heroic deeds for him were "inscribed less on history . . . than on charts

and maps, on geography." Much of the poem is an autobiographical reverie in the manner of Pound and Charles Olson (both mentioned), with memories of Davie and his family associated with scenes in France, California, and England.

Some of the shorter poems in *In the Stopping Train* appear to be more effective than "In the Stopping Train" and "Petit-Thouars," especially the touchingly personal "Seeing Her Leave" which has as its epigraph "gardens bare and Greek," a phrase from Winters's "On the Road to the Air Base." As in Winters's poem, there is enough perceptive detail to convey the subject effectively. Davie's poem, on the parting of the father and his daughter Diana, who is leaving California and is bound for nurse's training at St. Bartholomew's Hospital, London, is reminiscent of another Winters poem, "At the San Francisco Airport," also on the parting of father and daughter.

In 1981 appeared *Three for Water-Music*, which includes all the poems from *The Shires*. Two of the three title poems, "The Fountain of Cyane" and "The Fountain of Arethusa," are expansions of poems which appeared in the previous volume *In the Stopping Train*.

In recent years Davie has returned to his interest in religious subjects with the publication of *A Gathered Church: The Literature of the English Dissenting Interest, 1700-1930* (1978); *The New Oxford Book of Christian Verse* (1981), chosen and edited, with an introduction by Davie; and *Dissentient Voice*, a sequel to *A Gathered Church*. As the title of the first of these volumes indicates, Davie is not only investigating the tradition of dissent as it affects culture in general but more especially as it affects literature. Stating that "Distinguished individuals from the ranks of Dissent have indeed enriched our culture in every generation since 1700 but Dissent as such, as a corporate force in our society, can at a certain point be shown to have ceased to do so," he traces the cultural implications of dissent from the early decades of the eighteenth century through the period of the Wesleyans, the Evangelicals, and the Agnostics, on into the present century. His critique of English hymnology in this volume, and in his later paper published in *English Hymnology in the Eighteenth Century* (1980), is especially relevant to his career. Certainly his admiration for the hymns of Isaac Watts, Charles Wesley, and William Cowper—all substantially represented in his *New Oxford Book of Christian Verse*—has had some influence on his poetry, especially in its formative stages. In *Dissentient Voice* Davie continues his argument that the literary value of the hymns of Watts and

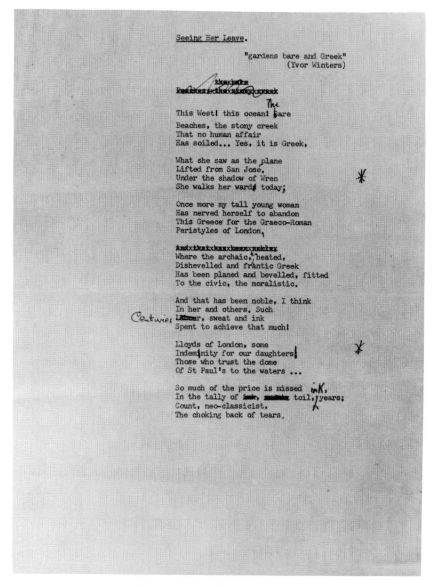

Working typescript (the author)

Wesley should be more widely recognized as being consonant with the Enlightenment and not the work of irrational religious bigots. The introduction restates Davie's abiding interest in language, which began with his first book, *Purity of Diction in English Verse*. Throughout his career he has attempted to keep the English language "crisp, supple, and responsible." As in *A Gathered Church*, Davie argues that the cultural value of dissent degenerated in the nineteenth and twentieth centuries, saying that Robert Browning as a poet of religious dissent is bad and that Rudyard Kipling is worse. In chapter nine there is a devastating analysis of Kipling's "Recessional" as the work of a diabolical poet. The poem,

according to Davie, is racist, imperialist, confused in its religious sentiments, and duplicitous.

Throughout his career, Davie has been a distinguished editor. In addition to edited books already mentioned, he has edited *The Late Augustans: Longer Poems of the Eighteenth Century* (1958), *Selected Poems of William Wordsworth* (1962), *Augustan Lyric* (1974), and *The New Oxford Book of Christian Verse* (1981). He also edited, with Angela Livingstone, and supplied the verse translations for *Pasternak: Modern Judgements* (1969) and wrote introductions to Elizabeth Daryush's *Collected Poems* (1976) and the *Collected Poems of Yvor Winters* (1978). In 1965 he had edited a collection of critical essays on *Russian*

Literature and Modern English Fiction, and in 1972 he became an editor, at its inception, of *PN Review*. In his frequent contributions—reviews, literary criticism, articles, and editorials on a variety of subjects, literary, social, religious, and political—he has become a distinctive voice in contemporary Anglo-American culture.

But it is as a poet writing in the tradition of such scholarly poets and critics as Samuel Johnson, Matthew Arnold, Robert Bridges, and Yvor Winters that Davie has made his greatest contribution to twentieth-century literature, during a period when a combination of sound learning and poetic talent in one person has been regrettably rare.

References:

George Dekker, "Donald Davie: New and Divergent Lines in English Poetry," *Agenda*, 14 (Summer 1976): 45-57;

Dekker, ed., *Donald Davie and the Responsibilities of Literature* (Manchester: Carcanet Press, 1983;

Orono, Maine: National Poetry Foundation, 1983);

Martin Dodsworth, "Donald Davie," *Agenda*, 14 (Summer 1976): 15-32;

Florence Elon, "The Movement Against Itself: British Poetry of the 1950s," *Southern Review*, new series 19 (Winter 1983): 88-110;

Thom Gunn, "*The Forests of Lithuania*," *Poetry*, 97 (January 1961): 260-270;

Frank Kermode, ed., *Ezra Pound / Donald Davie* (New York: Viking, 1976);

Michael Schmidt, "Time and Again: The Recent Poetry of Donald Davie," *Agenda*, 14 (Summer 1976): 33-44.

Papers:

The largest collection of Davie's papers is at the University of Essex, Wivenhoe, England. His correspondence with W. V. O'Connor is at the Syracuse University library, Syracuse, New York.

Patric Dickinson

(26 December 1914-   )

T. F. Healy
University of Dundee

SELECTED BOOKS: *The Seven Days of Jericho* (London: Dakers, 1944);

Theseus and the Minotaur, and Poems (London: Cape, 1946);

Stone in the Midst, and Poems (London: Methuen, 1948);

A Round of Golf Courses: A Selection of the Best Eighteen (London: Evans, 1951);

The Sailing Race, and Other Poems (London: Chatto & Windus, 1952);

The Scale of Things (London: Chatto & Windus, 1955);

The World I See (London: Chatto & Windus/ Hogarth Press, 1960);

This Cold Universe (London: Chatto & Windus/ Hogarth Press, 1964);

The Good Minute: An Autobiographical Study (London: Gollancz, 1965);

Selected Poems (London: Chatto & Windus, 1968);

More Than Time (London: Chatto & Windus/ Hogarth Press, 1970);

A Wintering Tree (London: Chatto & Windus/ Hogarth Press, 1973);

The Bearing Beast (London: Chatto & Windus/ Hogarth Press, 1976);

Our Living John (London: Chatto & Windus, 1979);

Poems From Rye (Rye: Martello Bookshop, 1979);

Winter Hostages (Hitchin: Mandeville Press, 1980);

A Rift in Time: Poems (London: Chatto & Windus, 1982).

SELECTED PLAYS: *Stone in the Midst*, London, Mercury Theatre, 1949;

The Golden Touch, Wolverhampton, 1959;

A Durable Fire, Canterbury, 1962;

Ode to St. Catharine, libretto by Dickinson, music by Bernard Rose, Cambridge, 1973;

Creation, libretto by Dickinson, music by Alan Ridout, Ely, 1973;

The Miller's Secret, libretto by Dickinson, music by Stephen Dodgson, Cookham, Berkshire, 1973.

OTHER: *Soldier's Verse*, edited by Dickinson (London: Muller, 1945);

Byron: Poems, edited by Dickinson (London: Grey Walls Press, 1949);

Aristophanes Against War: Three Plays, translated by Dickinson (London: Oxford University Press, 1957);

The Aeneid of Virgil, translated by Dickinson (New York: New American Library, 1961);

Poets' Choice: An Anthology of English Poetry from Spenser to the Present Day, edited by Dickinson and Sheila Shannon (London: Evans, 1967);

C. Day Lewis: Selections from his poetry, edited by Dickinson (London: Chatto & Windus, 1967);

The Complete Plays of Aristophanes, 2 volumes, translated by Dickinson (London: Oxford University Press, 1971);

"Seasonal," in *Chapter and Verse* (Hitchin: Mandeville Press, 1979);

Selected Poems of Henry Newbolt, edited by Dickinson (London: Hodder & Stoughton, 1981).

Patric Dickinson is more widely known for his frequent poetry broadcasts on BBC Radio Three and for his translations from Vergil and Aristophanes than for his own verse. A careful lyricist whose work remains outside the main directions taken by postwar British poets, Dickinson shares his closest affinities with those writers of the 1930s and the early 1940s who, inspired by Yeats, felt themselves continuing an English romantic tradition. A great promoter of English poetry, he has been an active editor and anthologist.

Patric Thomas Dickinson was born in Nasirabad, India, into a military family. His father, Arthur Thomas Dickinson, was killed early in World War I, and his mother, Eileen Kirwan Dickinson, returned to England, settling in Hampshire on the South Coast, initially at Petersfield and later at Brockenhurst. It is to this period of "the long bereavement in England," Dickinson states, that his early life belongs, and his feeling for his unknown father and the war became "part of his being." At school he developed an immediate love of Latin, which eventually enabled him to win a scholarship to St. Catharine's College, Cambridge, in 1933. However, having also had a deep love of English poetry since early adolescence, he decided to switch from classics to English in his third year. Even while a student Dickinson felt his own generation poetically inferior and looked nostalgically back to the immediate past. While he admired Auden and considered him a powerful voice speaking for his time and generation, Dickinson saw poets such as

Wilfred Owen as having set a standard which could not again be easily attained.

After he received his B.A. in 1936, his first job was schoolmastering at a preparatory school in Kent, but at the outbreak of World War II he enlisted in the army. Shortly after joining he sustained a back injury and caught typhoid, resulting in his demobilization in 1940. Dickinson had been writing poems since adolescence but only showing them to a small circle of friends. At the beginning of the war, however, he sent some pieces to Walter de la Mare, who encouraged him to have them published in magazines. Dickinson was briefly a schoolmaster again, this time in Yorkshire, before going to London in early 1942 to join the BBC as a radio producer. Toward the end of the war he began to read poetry on the radio, and he was made poetry editor at the BBC in 1945, a position he kept until 1948, when, winning the Atlantic Award, he became a free-lance writer. During the war he met Sheila Shannon, a minor poet, editor, and anthologist. They were married on 19 December 1947 and subsequently had two children.

The Seven Days of Jericho (1944), a versified drama, was Dickinson's first book, written while he was still working at the BBC. Although it is essentially a radio play, it was never broadcast. Adapting the biblical story of the Israelites' destruction of Jericho, this work contrasts war's destructiveness with the power of love, expressed by the harlot Rahab. Despite the gruesome annihilation of Jericho, love remains a dominant force. The play's inflated tone often unintentionally suggests a parody of the classically based drama it affects to resemble. *The Seven Days of Jericho* was not a promising start to Dickinson's career.

Dickinson's second book is more successful. *Theseus and the Minotaur, and Poems* (1946) has another radio verse play as its central work, the other poems being mostly short lyrics and epigrams. In this volume Dickinson reveals himself strongly under the influence of Yeats; the artist is an interpreter of nature: "Translating it to symbol or to thought,/Making of mud and feathers poetry." The poems introduce a number of key Dickinson themes and ideas to which he constantly returns in later books. In contrast to the permanence of nature, man is seen as a transitory, illusion-filled creature on the brink of self-annihilation, while love and poetry are the means through which the species can survive and thrive. The poet sees himself as essentially an outsider who recognizes the importance of nature's mysteries. Taking images from them in order to study the ways of love, he does not seek to

Patric Dickinson and Dylan Thomas going over the script for a BBC Radio poetry reading (BBC Hulton)

dispel their enigmas. Dickinson's world is an emblematic one, but also one deeply rooted in specific locales. In "On Exmoor" and "Kinghaven," two of the book's more successful poems, Dickinson turns to the wilder landscapes of England to discover poetry in nature's riddles. Like its predecessor, though, *Theseus and the Minotaur, and Poems* also demonstrates a basic lack of control in its inflated, immature gesturing at the grandiose and search for the profound. "Art" is continuously seen as rising phoenixlike from the destructive forces which attempt to suppress it. Dylan Thomas liked some of these early poems, but he felt Dickinson should allow himself more freedom in his use of imagery.

In *Stone in the Midst, and Poems* (1948), as the title suggests, Dickinson is still dominated by Yeatsian symbolism. The title work is a play (staged at the Mercury Theatre, London, in 1949) concerned with the "occupation" of England by a new material philistinism. Many of the poems also reveal Dickinson's unease with the postwar world and its fragile peace. In his autobiographical book *The Good Minute* (1965), he writes that "few of my poems are without war in them," and even World War II's conclusion

was an empty victory as far as the poet was concerned. "Victory Day," in which he recalls his father's going off to war, shows him unable to escape from war-induced memories:

> How much of us goes back
> The memory-trodden track
> Where obstinate echoes cling.

In 1944 Dickinson took a trip to the Yorkshire dales during a period when he sensed himself to be changing, possibly as a result of having met his future wife, Sheila Shannon. In the dales he felt he was arriving at the source of poetry, and they are celebrated in many of the poems in *Stone in the Midst, and Poems*. "Wensleydale" is seen as a magic place, where a natural synthesis fulfills body and soul, providing the right key to life. In this and other poems Dickinson deplores manmade signs and conventions, believing that mankind is too intent on mapping out nature without paying enough attention to nature's riddles, the secrets of which only love can learn. *Stone in the Midst, and Poems* establishes the English landscapes Dickinson continues to find stimulating throughout his subsequent books: the "limestone country" of the north of England and the marshes and small anchorages of the South Coast. Although many poems continue to pose too grandly, his style shows an increasing restraint and clarity of expression.

In 1948, when Dickinson became a free-lance writer, he moved to Rye, a small, ancient port in Sussex, where he still lives. The return to the South Coast, together with the death of his mother about this time, provides the background for most of the poems in his next volume, *The Sailing Race, and Other Poems* (1952). The poet feels his dead family (father, mother, and an older brother killed in the war) seeking to inhabit his poems, and he contrasts memories of childhood against the grim realities of the present. "Lament for the Great Yachts" recalls his particular fascination with the transatlantic liners he first saw off the Isle of Wight when a child on holiday: "Liners are food for the intellect." His memory provokes sadness in the present realization of the liners' demise, but it is from such sadness that poetry discovers a voice. The poems continue to reflect the preoccupations of Dickinson's earlier work. Mankind is seen as a destructive and indifferent animal, and the poet's purer natural landscapes are often shattered by the intrusion of the modern world.

Dickinson's next two volumes, *The Scale of Things* (1955) and *The World I See* (1960), show a greater lyrical conciseness, though few new themes. Where he had previously pitted the warmth of his relationship with his wife against a hostile world, his growing family (a son and daughter) here widens the positive elements in his sphere. Family continuity is seen as a hope for the future, but the family is also a vulnerable target for the "brutal world." In these volumes Dickinson increasingly sees the poet as seer. The poet's view of the world is distinct, and he cannot rest contented with day-to-day events. In observing the world of nature and the remains of the past (such as the Roman wall in Northumberland), he becomes more and more disturbed about man's direction. Identifying with nature against the modern world, he recognizes the poet's own vulnerability, his insignificance in "the scale of things." Yet natural beauty also provides solace and the strength to continue. In the sequence "Poems from Cumberland" in *The World I See*, Dickinson's lyrical resonances are most pronounced as he considers the rivers, lakes, and landscapes of the region: "We are far back in worlds/We were always of." He wishes to provoke others to share in the happiness discovered in nature while warning of the catas-

trophies man may inflict on it. Modern technology and science only serve to isolate men in the universe, demonstrating "How lonely all men are."

During the Cold War of the late 1950s and early 1960s Dickinson became depressed by his belief in an imminent holocaust and felt the poet's role was, as Wilfred Owen had suggested, to warn against war. He was earning most of his day-to-day living by presenting poetry programs on BBC Radio Three and was especially concerned with World War I poets. At the same time he was also translating Aristophanes and Vergil, using Aristophanes' comedies as part of his "warning": *Aristophanes Against War: Three Plays* appeared in 1957. During this time of growing personal crisis, he developed a drinking and sleeping-pill problem, which began to affect his marriage.

This combination of public and personal unrest resulted in the bleak vision manifested in *This Cold Universe* (1964). The poems in this volume use Dickinson's characteristic opposition of love against the impersonal universe inhabited by lonely men. His style is direct and uncompromising, and many of the poems' successes lie in the tensions created through his search for clarity in landscapes filled with paradoxes. He constantly recognizes that his uncertainties stimulate the creative forces which lead to poetry:

> Nothing must be but the sheer truth
> Of love between us two:
> O hand and planet eye and star
> So near to me so far from me.

The poems of the 1950s and 1960s have an immediate accessibility but no lasting forcefulness. Ultimately the poet's range is too limited and his language and imagery inadequate to sustain continuing interest. Dickinson marks out a topography which is his own, but each setting leads to the same generalizations. A fine control of rhythm is too often overshadowed by inflated symbolism that suggests a desire to appear a poet in the grand manner.

These problems remain in his next book, *More Than Time* (1970), but *A Wintering Tree* (1973), which won the Cholmondeley Award, reveals a new maturity and control in his vision. "Words grow fewer, meanings less," Dickinson states, and a more relaxed note begins to appear. The frantic concern for the future is modified, and he sees "humans hindered by their fears." The poems in *A Wintering Tree* return to the landscapes of Patric Dickinson's youth, the South Downs and the New Forest.

The basic theme remains unchanged: man learns from nature, but here he learns from close observation of everyday things—insects and butterflies, woods, and dandelions:

> But whether Tree or man,
> The condition of being rooted
> That gives a creature worth
> Is neither fruit nor flower.

The finer distinctions and simple but effective lyrical measures achieved in many of these poems are continued in *The Bearing Beast* (1976). Man is granted a "fragile permanence," and, although Dickinson continues to see the poet as a fighter for civilization, his view of his own insignificance now has a note of gentle ironic humor mixed with its weightier seriousness. The beauty of nature, both transitory and enduring, continues to provoke poetry, as do memory and the realization of his own passing life, but Dickinson is not so desperate to discover grand truths and imposing symbols. His imagery becomes less labored, more precise, yet subtler and, as matched with the firm cadences of his rhythms, produces some memorable lines: "The meaning of Times is the dark flying/Or at least a clue."

Dickinson's love of the classics has continued throughout his life, and there is often a classical resonance to his poetry, especially in the more relaxed manner of these later volumes. The search for the quiet life, the absolute preference for country over city, misgivings over man's destructive capacities, the celebration of love as a sustaining force, and the direct, but continuously lyrical, language Dickinson employs often recall the themes and occasionally the manner of a minor Latin poet such as Tibullus. In *The Bearing Beast* two greater classical writers, Vergil and Horace, are celebrated ("In Arcadia Ambo"), Dickinson seeing them as true poets for those growing old. Vergil is again recalled in a long, peculiar piece, "In Memory of Dylan Thomas," that attempts to imitate Vergilian hexameters, a meter regularly experimented with during the nineteenth century, though seldom with any success. The poem recalls contacts with Thomas during the 1940s. Throughout this volume Dickinson attempts to establish his own place in literary history, clearly wishing to be seen in a line originating with Vergil and Horace (a common desire among English poets), but he also tries to outline his place among more recent figures. "In Memory of Dylan Thomas" describes previous attempts to write hexameters by Arthur Clough and Cecil Day

Lewis, two poets Dickinson admires, though his own effort at hexameters cannot be said to share even their modest success. In "Obituary" the reader is introduced to Dickinson's immediate masters: William Butler Yeats, Edward Thomas, Robert Frost, and Walter de la Mare.

Poetry's importance and the place it occupies in the world are themes Dickinson touches on in most of his books, but they are especially pronounced in his next volume, *Our Living John* (1979). Poets replace the prophetess at Delphi, offering the world "Incredible realities," as poets become new enigmatic oracles for the present. In "Troy" the excitement and "reality" of Troy is to be discovered in the literature in which the city lives, not in the archaeological remains. The title poem recounts Dickinson's reaction to reading about the effect that the death of John Wordsworth had on his brother William: "I was there clenched in his raw grief." He ponders on how words can move him to feel such direct and "living" grief and also on how these words beget new words and emotions which manifest themselves in his own poem. For Dickinson a shared sense of loss and a realization of mortality become the impulses which create poems. The volume shows Dickinson employing an epigrammatic precision of form and expression to confront, with effective clarity, the dilemma of man's isolation:

> It's always like this, bits of washed up
> Bone and timber, no solution,
> Centre, comfort in the maze of silence.

Poems From Rye (1979) contains only five new pieces, collected as "Sketches from Rye," the rest of the volume being poems drawn from previous books. In the new works the town and harbor of Rye, past and present, are celebrated in a eulogy to the community Dickinson has lived in for more than thirty years.

Chapter and Verse (1979), a collection by various contemporary British poets, contains Dickinson's poem "Seasonal." A pastoral celebration of nature's continuity despite seasonal changes, it makes effective use of bird and flower nomenclature. The images Dickinson conjures are those of a traditional English Arcadia: "The greening, the golding pale shimmering short silk/Of uncut hayrills in wind."

Winter Hostages (1980) is a short collection of all new poems. The poet's life, filled with a combination of love and memories, is praised, and the tone of quiet sincerity which has been developing for nearly a decade is fully pronounced in this book. Dickinson's standpoint is now firmly that of the elder poet, and in many poems there is a sense of death, not exactly hovering, but waiting patiently somewhere nearby. The grand gesturing has dissipated, and the poet no longer sees himself as seer; having kept a secret is "divinity enough." Man has ceased being a threatening creature, his world is no longer wholly hostile to nature, and even the dead season of winter may infuse those left awake "With an instinctive hope." There is a pleasant balance to these poems, unfortunately marred by an abundance of banal lines which leave many flat and lifeless.

A Rift in Time (1982), a celebration of life by a poet clearly preparing for death, fulfills Dickinson's gentle reconciliation with the world and with himself. He no longer lives in "this cold universe." Now within the "Nameless timeless tameless/Universe of stars and planets," he knows both "how it is to be lost/And yet know where you are." There is a precision of observation matched with a lyrical delicacy in many of these poems ("A Dream," "Aubade," "Meanings," and the title poem, for instance), which rank as some of Dickinson's finest, but it is also noticeable how other poems once more demonstrate the limited and derivative nature of much of Dickinson's verse. "A Delphic Dialogue," for example, concerned with love and death and a desire for youth in age, is a poor echo of Yeats's poetic dialogues and recalls the Dickinson of the 1940s. *A Rift in Time*, though, is a touching portrait of a poet confidently at peace, radiating optimism both for himself and for his world:

> My shape may be a bark
> Yet when my flesh is gone
> It will flow on, on, on.

In many respects Patric Dickinson can be seen continuing the lyrical celebration of rural England initiated by the Georgian poets at the beginning of this century, and his poems, undoubtedly, appeal most to those with a well-established love of the countryside. He is an individual but not ultimately a distinctive poet. His best lyrics have a simple, pleasing elegance and a relaxed, meditative quality which combine to produce satisfying poetry. Throughout his career his work shows no marked diversity but a slow, yet steady, progression toward the discovery of a clear, direct, resonant voice.

Keith Douglas

(24 January 1920-9 June 1944)

Desmond Graham
University of Newcastle upon Tyne

BOOKS: *Selected Poems*, by Douglas, J. C. Hall, and Norman Nicholson (London: Bale & Staples, 1943);

Alamein to Zem Zem (London: Editions Poetry London, 1946); revised edition, edited by John Waller, G. S. Fraser, and J. C. Hall (London: Faber & Faber, 1966; New York: Chilmark, 1966); revised edition, edited by Desmond Graham (London & New York: Oxford University Press, 1979);

The Collected Poems of Keith Douglas, edited by Waller and Fraser (London: Editions Poetry London, 1951; New York: Chilmark, 1967);

Selected Poems, edited by Ted Hughes (London: Faber & Faber, 1964; New York: Chilmark, 1964);

The Complete Poems of Keith Douglas, edited by

Graham (London & New York: Oxford University Press, 1978).

OTHER: *Augury: An Oxford Miscellany of Verse and Prose*, edited by Douglas and A. M. Hardie (Oxford: Blackwell, 1940).

PERIODICAL PUBLICATIONS:
Fiction:
"Death of a Horse," *Citadel* (Cairo) (July 1942); *Lilliput* (London) (July 1944): 51-52;
"The Little Red Mouth," *Stand* (Newcastle upon Tyne), 9, no. 2 (1970): 9-11.
Nonfiction:
"Poets in This War," *Times Literary Supplement*, 23 April 1971, p. 478.

Although Keith Douglas was killed in World War II, apart from a brief selection of his poems published in 1943 with poems by J. C. Hall and Norman Nicholson, his work was not published until 1946, and the importance of his writing has been only truly recognized within the past twenty years. Geoffrey Hill summed up the situation in " 'I in Another Place': Homage to Keith Douglas," a fine review-article of 1964, when he declared that Douglas was "at once 'established' and overlooked." A hunt through standard anthologies, surveys, and histories will show how thoroughly he had been overlooked. It was in the minds of poets of his own and the subsequent generations that his achievement had been firmly established. From the 1940s on, Bernard Spencer, G. S. Fraser, Lawrence Durrell, Roy Fuller, Alan Ross, and Vernon Scannell were among those who held his work in high esteem. To the next generation of poets, Douglas's work epitomized what was absent from British poetry of the 1950s and early 1960s. Charles Tomlinson made Douglas the centerpiece of an attack upon The Movement in his 1961 essay, "Poetry Today." Tributes from poets as diverse as Geoffrey Hill, Michael Hamburger, Jon Silkin, and Ted Hughes proved Tomlinson's point of view to be no eccentric emphasis. And it was Hughes, in a broadcast of 1962, an essay of 1963, and a 1964 edition of Douglas's poems (*Selected Poems*), who brought Douglas a wider readership. The qualities Hughes so vigorously defined remain the basis of the poet's high reputation now that his *Complete Poems* (1978) and a new 1979 edition of his vivid narrative of the desert war, *Alamein to Zem Zem* (1946), make his work once more available: a fusion of intelligence and passion, a seemingly effortless lucidity of style, what Hughes termed "a burning exploratory freshness of mind" and Hill called "a fearlessness of the imagination." There has been little dissent: to Geoffrey Grigson, Douglas did not write a single line of poetry; to Ian Hamilton, he suffered from the tight-lipped insensitivity of the officers' mess. Generally Douglas is read and remembered for lying outside the impasse felt to be between the poetry of the 1930s and that of the 1940s; for an exceptionally precocious talent, writing fine poems from the age of fourteen; for the dozen or so poems written from firsthand experience of the desert war; and for the narrative of his battle experience. Perhaps the only poet of his generation to build successfully on the achievement of Wilfred Owen and Isaac Rosenberg, he is regarded as the finest British war poet of World War II and, by many, the finest poet of his generation.

Keith Castellain Douglas was born in Tun-bridge Wells, Kent, on 24 January 1920, to a solidly middle-class family finding hard times in the aftermath of war. The father, Keith Sholto Douglas, son of a doctor and trained as an engineer, had thrived on wartime military service in Mesopotamia, where he had gained the Military Cross. By choice he would have remained in the army, but he was demobilized and left restless, without employment. The mother, Marie Josephine Douglas, cherished the fact that she was a member of the Castellain family, only two generations away from French aristocrats who had fled the revolution. By the time Keith was six, his parents had separated; his mother was suffering the prolonged aftereffects of sleeping sickness; and the family was without money. For the next twelve years he went to boarding schools, spending vacations with his mother, who rarely had a place of her own. Keith grew to be rebellious, academically successful, and a powerful character who defied categories in his mix of talents and interests. He was a keen sportsman, a vigorous swimmer and rugby forward, a lover of horses and riding, a promising artist whose pictures were exhibited at school, a great admirer of things military, who rigorously and effectively supported the school's officers' cadet corps, and a poet. While a schoolboy, Douglas had poems published in Oxford magazines, anthologized in a national annual, and accepted by the influential *New Verse*.

The school poems show Douglas already fluent and expert within strict metrical forms. He uses the villanelle dexterously, the sonnet without archaism. He imitates the early Ezra Pound, Edith Sitwell, and W. H. Auden, and he efficiently translates Latin, Greek, French, and German into verse. Various styles and forms he appropriates for a justified show of skill, and yet within such poems as "On Leaving School" he already expresses a turn of mind and a voice of his own—a mix of adventurousness, boisterous observation, fine timing, and an open, extroverted awareness of feeling:

at this evening moment, when the shallow
Echoes stagger against Big School, it is awkward
Realizing happiness seems just to have started
And now we must leave it, live like trees or charlock.

One of us will be the kettle past care of tinkers,
Rejected, one the tip-top apple, the winking
Sun's friend. It will be that way, and Time on our ground
Will sweep like a maid, and where we were be clean.
Shall we find room to laugh, if turning round
We see where we have walked, how wrong we have been?

Douglas's school from 1931-1938, Christ's

Hospital, was decisively important in his development. It boasted a strong literary tradition, with Samuel Taylor Coleridge, Charles Lamb, and Leigh Hunt as former pupils. It was at once a charitable institution and highly prestigious, encouraging a sense of independence and of service. Valuing intellect in a way rare for English schools of its period and type, it was also fairly tough in its living conditions, discipline, and outlook. Set in the Sussex countryside, its roots were in Tudor London. Douglas clashed with authority there (almost being expelled on one occasion because of intransigent behavior), rebelled against the whole system, and yet loved the traditions of the institution. It was not surprising that going up to Merton College, Oxford, on a scholarship in October 1938, he had one of the school's famous and most dedicated alumni as tutor: Edmund Blunden.

Douglas's first year at Oxford was under the shadow of war: his second, during the war. Throughout that time he had a full and successful undergraduate life: an impressive and painful relationship with the daughter of a Chinese ambassador; the production (with Alec Hardie) of an Oxford miscellany, *Augury* (1940); a period as editor of the undergraduate weekly, the *Cherwell*—a task in which he so alienated would-be contributors that he virtually wrote whole issues himself. Still outside conventional categories, as editor of the *Cherwell* he felt no oddity in speaking as the voice of the undergraduates—defending students against the charge of irresponsibility, defending conscientious objectors against Blimpish smears, attacking patriotic, parental, or institutional cant. Meanwhile he mourned Oxford's decline, looked back to earlier, more glorious (and legendary) times, and deeply loved the city:

> This then is the city of young men, of beginning,
> ideas, trials, pardonable follies,
> the lightness, seriousness and sorrow of youth.
> And the city of the old, looking for truth,
> browsing for years, the mind's seven bellies
> filled, become legendary figures, seeming
>
> stones of the city, her venerable towers;
> dignified, clothed by erudition and time.
> For them it is not a city but an existence;
> outside which everything is a pretence:
> within, the leisurely immortals dream,
> venerated and spared by the ominous hours.

These stanzas from "Oxford" carry the extra tinge brought by nostalgia—for he was in the armed forces when he wrote them—but the final awareness, the sense of "ominous hours," is true to the spirit which had moved the best of his Oxford poems.

As an undergraduate Douglas had at first developed a leisurely lyrical style, frequently employing the distinctive six-line stanza of "Oxford." Alongside this, another style, more querulous and sharp, more bluntly colloquial, demanded its place. It is seen in the frankly brutal ironies of "Russians," a poem on a battalion of men frozen in death; in "The Creator," a cynical attack on God's blind inefficiency; or in "Pas de Trois," where a delicate ballet turns into a dance of death. Awareness of death, in fact, pervades these poems, but it is present in images of theater—of mimes, masks, and stage scenery—while it creates, indirectly, as a sense of precariousness, a "doom" which "hovers in the background," a part of mutability which is present in time itself, as much as in the current historical situation. But it is that situation which gives a particular poignancy to some of these poems. Already, as in "Canoe" (written at Oxford about 1940), Douglas has a seemingly effortless ability to hold the precariousness and vulnerability of the moment:

> Well, I am thinking this may be my last
> summer, but cannot lose even a part
> of pleasure in the old-fashioned art of idleness. . . .
> . . . .
> . . . What sudden fearful fate
> can deter my shade wandering next year
> from a return? Whistle and I will hear
> and come another evening, when this boat
>
> travels with you alone towards Iffley:
> as you lie looking up for thunder again,
> this cool touch does not betoken rain;
> it is my spirit that kisses your mouth lightly.

Douglas enlisted in September 1939. At Oxford he continued military training in the cavalry section of the university officer training corps, and in July 1940 he was called up. It was a strange army he joined: the anachronistic cavalry, led by the gentry and trained to do incredible things on horseback with swords. He tried to do well, but from the outset he came up against military authority. Then, in November 1940, sent to be trained for a commission at Sandhurst Military Academy, he was transferred to the mechanized cavalry. He had little love of machines and was not particularly competent with them. He missed Oxford and the friends he had made there, returning to the city on every possible occasion. The realities of army life, even at Sandhurst, little matched his games with it at school and

Keith Douglas as a cavalry cadet, autumn 1940. All of the embellishments, including the halo, are by Douglas (courtesy of The Brotherton Library, The University, Leeds).

sense of occasion which led to much of his best work, was his own elegy, should he not return from the Middle East:

> not by momentary spleen
> or love into decision hurled,
> leisurely arrive at an opinion.
>
> Remember me when I am dead
> and simplify me when I'm dead.

Sailing for the Middle East, Douglas left a typescript collection of his poems with Blunden in the hope that he would find them a publisher. Nothing came of it. In February T. S. Eliot had responded encouragingly to poems Douglas had sent him, but when the new work was sent to him, it brought no suggestion of publication. Meanwhile Douglas wasted time with the regiment he had joined on arrival in the Middle East, playing rugby in the dust, learning to make Molotov cocktails, and having disputes with his senior officers. A camouflage course led to a staff post, unwanted by Douglas because it had neither duties nor position and took him away from the regiment, which gave him a sense of identity within military life. Douglas hated to waste time, and, perhaps from boarding school experience, for all his rebelliousness he loathed the feeling of being left out. For ten months his situation was indecisive.

During that time, however, he traveled and experienced the wholly new world of the Middle East. As a schoolboy he had visited Gorizia, and its "southern" life had delighted him. A trip to Paris and a cycling holiday in France before the war had confirmed his attraction to things foreign, and now he enjoyed Palestine, despite the infuriating isolation brought by lack of contacts there. He took a brief tour through Syria to the Sea of Galilee. Helped by an air force friend, he flew to Cairo from time to time. Then, in July 1942, a posting took him to Alexandria. Poems had come from his sea voyage, from walking beside the sea in Palestine, and from the Syrian trip ("Here I am a stranger clothed/in the separative glass cloak/of strangeness"—"Syria"). A sentry seen on the Corniche, Alexandria, and a bus load of Alexandrian schoolgirls supplied the occasions for two more poems, and in each poem of place he expresses a sense of differentness or of exclusion. Then, in two poems written in Egypt in September 1942, observation is sharpened with a new political awareness. One, "Christodoulos," presents the soldiers, "weak as wounded," on leave in Cairo. They are the wastage

his childhood fantasies of it. Commissioned in February 1941, he joined the Second Derbyshire Yeomanry and spent a generally unhappy five months training with armored cars before being posted, ahead of his regiment, to the Middle East.

Douglas was dissatisfied with his writing during his army training in England. By the standards of his Oxford years, he had written little, and less had seen publication. Yet the ten poems surviving from this period show a dramatic development. In "Time Eating," "The Prisoner," and "The Marvel," he found a more impersonal, metaphysical style which carried within it a sharper sense of loss and pain. Metaphor which has earlier been descriptive is now a part of an argument, a forceful quarrel with time. Further, in "Simplify me when I'm dead," one of the best-known of his poems, this new rigor is turned upon the most dangerous and personal of subjects: his forebodings of death. Here, with a from the alchemy of the war profiteer. The other, "Egypt," personifies the country as a beggar:

> A disguise of ordure can't hide
> her beauty, succumbing in a cloud
> of disease, disease, apathy. My God,
> the king of this country must be proud.

On his travels Douglas had a succession of girl friends of various nationalities, the most significant of them being Milena, an Alexandrian of Italian stock. From the breakup of that romance, two of his finest love poems emerged: "The Knife" and "I listen to the desert wind." That reopening of the wound left by the failure of his relationship with Yingcheng, the Chinese girl at Oxford, coincided with an intensification of his sense of the futility of his part in military life. Living "more or less inside the horse's mouth" (as he expresses it in *Alamein to Zem Zem*), he knew that a huge and decisive offensive was being planned. He knew also that he was to remain out of it, behind the lines. In the most extraordinary act of his life, in October 1942, he took his truck and set off for the battlefield, in direct defiance of his orders. Accepted back by his colonel, for they had lost several officers in the previous days' fighting, Douglas was allocated a troop of tanks of a type he had never before seen and was in action the next day.

This decision and its results—Douglas's part in the fighting from El Alamein to the end of the desert campaign in Tunisia in May 1943—are best understood through his brilliantly evocative narrative *Alamein to Zem Zem*. There we see his curious place as fighting soldier—at once detached and fully participating—observant of the terrain through which he traveled, the rapid and inexplicable shifts in pace and tension which characterized such fighting, and the strange social life of a tank officer in a regiment commanded by "feudal" cavalry officers (to be depicted a few months later in his "Sportsmen": a poem at once elegiac and satiric, tender and acute). More straightforward than his poems, the narrative reveals his relish for life, his humor, his fascinated observation of character, his remorseless and impressive sense of justice, and his splendid honesty of outlook. There, too, we find exploration of war's ambiguities and paradoxes, its face at once unmistakably human and brutally destructive: an exploration he sustained in the poems written after leaving the front, wounded, in January 1943.

It appears that Douglas wrote no poems during his experience of action. An essay, "Poets in This War," probably written in May 1943, declared, in fact, that the finest poetry of the war would be written after its close. The soldier's experience, he insisted, was tautological: it had all been previously expressed by the poets of World War I. Further, the mobility of fighting in his war meant simply that there was little occasion to write. Between January and August, mainly in a hospital, a convalescent hospital, and at base depots, he telescoped his essay's time scale and wrote the war poems which are the climax of his achievement. Paralleling the concerns of his narrative but with greater intensity and more interpretative point, these poems inquire into the relationship between the living soldier and the dead; between the civilian lover mourned by the girl at home and the same man as an "enemy" soldier whose brutal death is viewed "almost with content" by his killers; between the schoolboy and the young man he had become, whose ways are known to his mother and who, as in "How to Kill," at the push of a button, can perform miracles:

> Now in my dial of glass appears
> the soldier who is going to die.
> He smiles, and moves about in ways
> his mother knows, habits of his.
> The wires touch his face: I cry
> NOW. Death, like a familiar, hears
>
> and look, has made a man of dust
> of a man of flesh. This sorcery
> I do. Being damned, I am amused
> to see the centre of love diffused
> and the waves of love travel into vacancy.
> How easy it is to make a ghost.

More frankly than any of his World War I predecessors, Douglas portrays the soldier as killer, and in doing so he writes without the personal protection of moral reserve. Being damned, he is "amused/to see the centre of love diffused." Here is the poetry of the detached killing brought to war by technology. Here also is a poetry which, without flinching, explores the transformations which war brings about, merely by one day's traveling, as in "Cairo Jag":

> But by a day's travelling you reach a new world
> the vegetation is of iron
> dead tanks, gun barrels split like celery
> the metal brambles have no flowers or berries
> and there are all sorts of manure, you can imagine
> the dead themselves, their boots, clothes and possessions
> clinging to the ground, a man with no head
> has a packet of chocolate and a souvenir of Tripoli.

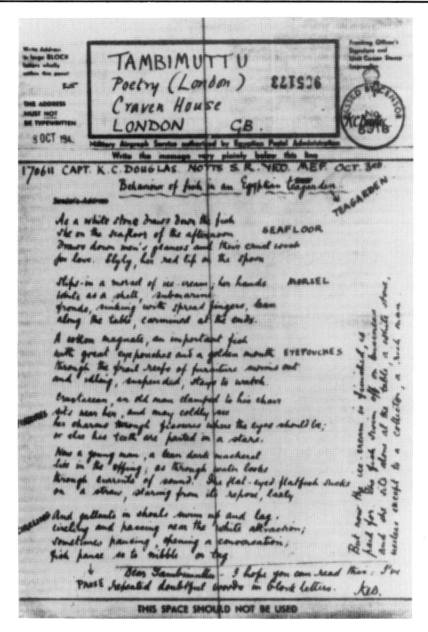

Douglas sent this poem about life in Cairo to the editor of Poetry (London) *(courtesy of the Estate of Keith Douglas)*

All along Douglas's had been a poetry of metamorphoses, of inexplicable changes of state: from love to loss, security to insecurity, cherished moment to the sinister future, life to death. Now these processes which he understood so well in his feelings and apprehended with fascination as well as pain brought him insights into the world of warfare. Still his terms are metaphysical, but new elements have entered: the literal reductions of death and the active inhumanity of killing.

In "On the Nature of Poetry," a statement published in his 1940 miscellany, *Augury*, Douglas

had said, "Poetry is like a man, whom thinking you know all his movements and appearance you will presently come upon in such a posture that for a moment you can hardly believe it a position of the limbs you know." Explaining his recent work in an August 1943 letter to J. C. Hall, however, it is on poetry's documentary value that Douglas insists: "But my object (and I don't give a damn about my duty as a poet) is to write true things, significant things in words each of which works for its place in a line. My rhythms, which you find enervated, are carefully chosen to enable the poems to be *read* as significant speech: I see no reason to be either musical or sonorous about things at present." The whole of this letter (quoted in *Complete Poems*) gives the finest insight into the emphases and purposes of Douglas's war writing, as well as into the confident sense of purpose he had now acquired. He concludes: "To be sentimental or emotional now is dangerous to oneself and others. To trust anyone or to admit any hope of a better world is criminally foolish, as foolish as it is to stop working for it. It sounds silly to say work without hope, but it can be done; it's only a form of insurance; it doesn't mean work hopelessly."

While Douglas was writing war poems, he heard that a selection of his work had appeared in England. The poet J. C. Hall, an Oxford acquaintance and admirer of his work, had included several of his Oxford poems and one from the Middle East in *Selected Poems* (1943), along with poems by Hall himself and Norman Nicholson. While it did not contain his latest work and received little notice, the appearance of his poems in this book was invaluably encouraging. Similarly encouraging, perhaps crucially so, was the interest of the editor of the magazine *Poetry* (London), M. J. Tambimuttu. Coming across some of Douglas's poems in a journal, Tambimuttu wrote to him asking to see more. Douglas responded warmly: work appeared in Tambimuttu's magazine, and Douglas sent back to him his war poems. The editor in turn invited him to make a selection for a book to be published by Editions Poetry London.

In November 1943 Douglas sailed for England. With him he had his nearly completed narrative and the mainly unpublished poems written in the Middle East. Blunden had placed a couple with the *Times Literary Supplement*, and others had appeared in *Citadel*, a magazine from the Anglo-Egyptian Institute in Cairo. There too, Douglas had published his fine short story "Death of a Horse," written while he was training in England. The more prestigious Cairo-based magazine *Personal Landscape* had also taken poems by Douglas and held his latest work for future publication. Around that magazine was a group of expatriate and exiled writers. Douglas had never been part of their circle, but one of them, Bernard Spencer, had become a friend during Douglas's visits to Cairo in 1942, and the others, including Lawrence Durrell, had, on their occasional meetings, been impressed by both him and his work. (See Durrell's preface to the 1966 edition of *Alamein to Zem Zem*.)

During his five months in England, beginning in January 1944, Douglas was mainly engaged in training for the Normandy landings. By all accounts, the conviction he had first expressed at Oxford, that he would not survive the war, had deepened into an unqualified belief. He worked with great urgency to get the poems ready for Tambimuttu and made a series of ink illustrations to go with them in a collection to be called "Bete Noir." (It was never published.) He also made ink illustrations, and one or two in color, for his prose narrative. Taking every available chance of visiting London, often without official leave, he worked with Tambimuttu or took out his editorial assistant, Betty Jesse; with the now-well-known literary and pub world around Tambimuttu at that time, Douglas, it seems, had nothing to do. His social life, like his writing, had always had little relationship with current groups of writers. Working against time, by March Douglas had publishing contracts for both the poems and the narrative, and the work was in a state complete enough for safe leaving. He wrote a graceful farewell poem to four of his earlier girl friends, a series of fragments, which were to be incorporated into the preface he wrote for "Bete Noir" ("the name of the poem I cannot write"), and a last valedictory poem of foreboding, "On a Return from Egypt":

And all my endeavours are unlucky explorers
come back, abandoning the expedition;
the specimens, the lilies of ambition
still spring in their climate, still unpicked:
but time, time is all I lacked
to find them, as the great collectors before me.

The next month, then, is a window
and with a crash I'll split the glass.
Behind it stands one I must kiss,
person of love or death
a person or a wraith,
I fear what I shall find.

On 6 June 1944 Douglas was in the main assault on the Normandy beaches. Three days later, near Tilly-sur-Seulles, he was killed.

References:
Reginald Gibbons, "A Sharp Enquiring Blade," *Parnassus*, 9 (Spring/Summer 1981): 315-331;
Desmond Graham, *Keith Douglas 1920-1944: A Biography* (London: Oxford University Press, 1974);
Graham, "Keith Douglas's Surviving Books," *Book Collector*, 30 (Summer 1981): 163-176;

Geoffrey Hill, " 'I in Another Place': Homage to Keith Douglas," *Stand* (Newcastle upon Tyne), 6, no. 4 (1964): 6-13;

Ted Hughes, "The Poetry of Keith Douglas," *Critical Quarterly*, 5, no. 1 (Spring 1963): 43-48;

Jenny Stratford, *The Arts Council Collection of Modern Literary Manuscripts* (London: Turret Books, 1974), pp. 44-61, 118-130;

Charles Tomlinson, "Poetry Today," in *Pelican Guide to English Literature*, volume 7, edited by Boris Ford (Harmondsworth: Penguin, 1961), pp. 469-471.

Papers:

The British Library has an extensive archive of worksheets, drafts, and typescripts of the poems; manuscript and typescript versions of *Alamein to Zem Zem*; letters to and from Douglas; and other papers. The Brotherton Collection at the University of Leeds has manuscripts of poems, memorabilia and other papers, surviving photographs of Douglas, and his surviving books. The Humanities Research Center at the University of Texas, Austin, has letters from Douglas to Edmund Blunden, including the texts of poems.

Lawrence Durrell

(27 February 1912-   )

Jennifer Birkett
Dundee University

See also the Durrell entry in *DLB 15, British Novelists, 1930-1959*.

SELECTED BOOKS: *Pied Piper of Lovers* (London: Cassell, 1935);

Panic Spring, as Charles Norden (London: Faber & Faber, 1937; New York: Covici Friede, 1937);

The Black Book: An Agon (Paris: Obelisk, 1938; New York: Dutton, 1960; London: Faber & Faber, 1973);

A Private Country (London: Faber & Faber, 1943);

Prospero's Cell: A Guide to the Landscape and Manners of the Island of Corcyra (London: Faber & Faber, 1945); republished with *Reflections on a Marine Venus* (New York: Dutton, 1960);

Cities, Plains and People (London: Faber & Faber, 1946);

Cefalû (London: Editions Poetry London, 1947); republished as *The Dark Labyrinth* (London: Ace, 1958; New York: Dutton, 1962);

On Seeing to Presume (London: Faber & Faber, 1948);

Sappho: A Play in Verse (London: Faber & Faber, 1950; New York: Dutton, 1958);

Key to Modern Poetry (London: Nevill, 1952); republished as *A Key to Modern British Poetry* (Norman: University of Oklahoma Press, 1952);

Reflections on a Marine Venus (London: Faber & Faber, 1953); republished with *Prospero's Cell*

(New York: Dutton, 1960);

The Tree of Idleness and Other Poems (London: Faber & Faber, 1955);

Selected Poems (London: Faber & Faber, 1956; New York: Grove, 1956);

Justine (London: Faber & Faber, 1957; New York: Dutton, 1957);

White Eagles Over Serbia (London: Faber & Faber, 1957; New York: Criterion, 1957);

Bitter Lemons (London: Faber & Faber, 1957; New York: Dutton, 1958);

Esprit de Corps: Sketches from Diplomatic Life (London: Faber & Faber, 1957; New York: Dutton, 1958);

Balthazar (London: Faber & Faber, 1958; New York: Dutton, 1958);

Mountolive (London: Faber & Faber, 1958; New York: Dutton, 1959);

Stiff Upper Lip: Life among the Diplomats (London: Faber & Faber, 1958; New York: Dutton, 1959);

Clea (London: Faber & Faber, 1960; New York: Dutton, 1960);

Collected Poems (London: Faber & Faber, 1960; New York: Dutton, 1960);

Penguin Modern Poets 1, by Durrell, Elizabeth Jennings, and R. S. Thomas (Harmondsworth: Penguin, 1962);

The Alexandria Quartet (London: Faber & Faber,

Lawrence Durrell

1962; New York: Dutton, 1962)—*Justine, Balthazar, Mountolive,* and *Clea;*

An Irish Faustus: A Morality in Nine Scenes (London: Faber & Faber, 1963; New York: Dutton, 1964);

Selected Poems 1935-1963 (London: Faber & Faber, 1964);

Acte (London: Faber & Faber, 1965; New York: Dutton, 1965);

Sauve Qui Peut (London: Faber & Faber, 1966; New York: Dutton, 1967);

The Ikons and Other Poems (London: Faber & Faber, 1966; New York: Dutton, 1967);

Tunc (London: Faber & Faber, 1968; New York: Dutton, 1968);

Spirit of Place: Letters and Essays on Travel, edited by Alan G. Thomas (London: Faber & Faber, 1969; New York: Dutton, 1969);

Nunquam (London: Faber & Faber, 1970; New York: Dutton, 1970);

The Red Limbo Lingo: A Poetry Notebook for 1968-1970

(London: Faber & Faber, 1971; New York: Dutton, 1971);

Vega and Other Poems (London: Faber & Faber, 1973);

Monsieur: or The Prince of Darkness (London: Faber & Faber, 1974; New York: Viking, 1975);

Selected Poems, edited by Alan Ross (London: Faber & Faber, 1977);

The Greek Islands (London: Faber & Faber, 1978; New York: Viking, 1978);

Livia, or Buried Alive (London: Faber & Faber, 1978; New York: Viking, 1979);

Collected Poems, 1931-1974, edited by James A. Brigham (London: Faber & Faber, 1980; New York: Viking, 1980);

Constance, or Solitary Practices (London: Faber & Faber, 1982).

PLAYS: *Sappho: A Play in Verse,* Hamburg, 1959;
Acte, Hamburg, 1961;
An Irish Faustus: A Morality in Nine Scenes, Sommerhausen, Germany, 1966.

OTHER: George Seferis, *The King of Asine and Other Poems,* translated by Durrell, Bernard Spencer, and Nanos Valaoritis (London: Lehmann, 1948);

Emmanuel Royidis, *The Curious History of Pope Joan,* translated by Durrell (London: Verschoyle, 1954; New York: Dutton, 1961);

"Studies in Genius No. VI," *Horizon* (London), 17 (June 1948); republished as the introduction to *The Book of the It,* by George Groddeck (London: Vision, 1961).

Lawrence George Durrell was born in India at Julundur in the United Provinces, of an Irish mother, Louisa Florence Dixie Durrell, and a British civil-engineer father, Lawrence Samuel Durrell. The autobiographical title poem, dated 1943, of *Cities, Plains and People* (1946) looks back on that early landscape, its horizon bounded by the Himalayas and the distant snows of Tibet; here was a sense of living in timeless harmony, which all his poetry and prose fiction would seek to evoke. "Once in idleness was my beginning," he remembers; it was a "honeycomb of silence," where time and history took on fresh dimensions and "Death marched beside the living as a friend / With no sad punctuation by the clock." The poem traces his passing from that paradise to "Pudding Island o'er the Victorian foam"—that is, St. Edmund's School in Canterbury, Kent, then bohemian London, where, in his early twenties, he made his first attempts to earn a living. He chafed at England's repressive dullness; as he wrote to Henry Miller in January 1937, "that mean, shabby little island up there wrung my guts out of me and tried to destroy anything singular and unique in me." But in England he also discovered the work of D. H. Lawrence and poet Roy Campbell, and, through the critical writings of imagist Richard Aldington, he was introduced to the literature of "the great sick-room, Europe" (as he calls it in "Cities, Plains and People"). Durrell still claims to retain a lingering affection for England, the colonial's romantic dream of home, but feels himself more a citizen of Europe, less inhibiting and less hostile to the artist. The mellower "Bere Regis" (1948) still speaks of "this lovely expurgated prose-land."

In 1935, the year of his marriage to the painter Nancy Myers, he persuaded his mother to move the whole family to Corfu, where the Greek landscape provided the antidote for what he later described in a February 1937 letter to Henry Miller as "the English death." From Corfu he regularly visited both London and Paris, where in September 1937 he met Henry Miller, with whom he had been in correspondence since August 1935, after *Tropic of Cancer* (1934) had restored his faith in the integrity of art. Miller introduced him to T. S. Eliot, on the editorial board of Faber and Faber, which in 1937 published his second novel, the thriller *Panic Spring*, under the pseudonym Charles Norden, the name of a character in *Tropic of Cancer*. (His first novel, *Pied Piper of Lovers*, a light romance, had appeared in 1935.) Durrell's career at this stage seemed about to slide into the writing of potboilers, but Miller helped him resist Faber and Faber's urgings to allow them to publish an unexpurgated version of his first important work, *The Black Book* (1938), a vituperative satire on the decay of English society. In Paris in 1937 and 1938, Miller, Durrell, Alfred Perlès, and others edited the avant-garde little magazine the *Booster* (retitled *Delta* in April 1938), and together Miller and Durrell entered into an abortive venture in publishing, heavily funded by Nancy Durrell. The three books published in their Villa Seurat Library series by Jack Kahane of Obelisk Press were Miller's *Max and the White Phagocytes* (1938), Anaïs Nin's *Winter of Artifice* (1938), and the full version of Durrell's *The Black Book*, published after the Durrells had returned to Greece. This novel proved to be a succès de scandale.

Durrell had been writing poetry and having it published since the age of twenty, but to little effect;

and in 1936 Faber and Faber turned down a selection of his poems. In February 1937 he told Miller that he felt his poetry was improving and that he was concentrating on "those tiny bitter mosaics which you can't do in prose; tight as diamonds and very brightly coloured"—what he called "ikons" in later collections. The war years—pressing him into a career of travel and making of him a professional communicator—teacher, observer, reporter, press officer—gave the final impetus.

In 1939 he was back in Greece under the auspices of the British Council, teaching at the British Institute in Athens. In 1940 his daughter Penelope Berengaria was born, and in 1941, he became Foreign Press Service Officer at the British Information Office in Cairo. He was still at this post when in 1943 *A Private Country*, written out of his first, delighted confrontation with Greece, established his poetic reputation.

In this collection, Greece welcomes the divided, alienated, self-conscious personalities of European culture—the missionary Fangbrand, Hamlet, and "the observer in the tall black hat" lurking in the mirrors of "Je est un Autre," dedicated to Rimbaud. Though part of Europe, Greece exists for Durrell in a different dimension—as the cradle of those fertile and renewing myths that the rest of Europe has allowed to die. These myths are richly recreated by the language of the poet, as in "Letter to Seferis the Greek":

> Her blue boundaries are
> Upon a curving sky of time,
> In a dark menstruum of water:
> The names of islands like doors
> Open upon it: the rotting walls
> Of the European myth are here
> For us, the industrious singers,
> In the service of this blue, this enormous blue.

The landscape invites the human self to physical and spiritual dissolution into its own greater totality, a mystical identification with the universe that abolishes all distinctions, including that of life and death. The poems urge that time is not linear development but duration, simultaneously particular and eternal, rendering what Durrell describes in his *Key to Modern Poetry* (1952) as "a sort of immediacy of impact—the impact of all time crowded into one moment of time."

In 1943, Lawrence and Nancy Durrell parted company, and in 1944 he became press attaché with the British Information Office in Alexandria, where he remained until summer 1945. He hated the city, despite its intense atmosphere of sexuality and death (he was fascinated by the linking of love and death), and loathed its obsession with money and status at the expense of music, art, and gaiety. In the spring of 1944, he complained to Miller that it made him write poetry that was "dark grey and streaky, like bad bacon." In April 1946, after he had gone to Rhodes to be director of public relations for the Dodecanese Islands, a letter to T. S. Eliot gave a slightly different reaction. In the near Levant, wrote Durrell, people were so saturated with passionate sexuality that paradoxically they were free of sex, and "able to devote [themselves] to art or God or whatnot, and make the whole world an Eros—but an eros of contemplation and real biblical love."

Out of Durrell's experiences in Cairo and Alexandria came *Cities, Plains and People* (1946), a collection of poetry which places even greater emphasis on the poet's sense of fragmented personality. The fragmentation is reflected in his personae: for example, the exiled "Conon in Alexandria," perched on the "Ash-heap of four cultures" and tormented by "nightly visitations/Of islands," Byron, La Rochefoucauld, and Horace. It appears too in the structure of the poetic narrative, such as the truncated tale of the "Pearls" ("this broken torso of a poem"). But the notion of an informing totality is still present from start to finish in "A Prospect of Children," the last of the "Eight Aspects of Melissa" on which the collection opens, and in the familiar icon at the center of the book, "Delos," in which islands, blue sea, still sky, and eternal star hold up towns and rivers to the air "like repairing mirrors." The closing poem, which gives its name to the collection, brings together the diversity of Durrell's private history, his journey from the unconscious wholeness of his Indian childhood to the hard-won, anguished unity of adult and poet. Even the anguish, though negative, is part of the whole. Even the venality of the "Levant" ("Something money or promises can buy") is matter for poetic redemption. In the furnished rooms of dark, windy "Alexandria," among the driftwood thrown up on his shore, the poet finds "objects for my study and my love" and maintains, "As for me I now move/Through many negatives to what I am." The persona at the close of "Cities, Plains and People" is Prospero, the magician:

> For Prospero remains the evergreen
> Cell by the margin of the sea and land,
> Who many cities, plains, and people saw

> Yet by his open door
> In sunlight fell asleep
> One summer with the Apple in his hand.

Personal reality for Durrell continued, however, to be less serene than his metaphysics. Having divorced Nancy Durrell, he married his second wife, Eve Cohen, in 1947. He continued his round of administrative postings to uncongenial places, leaving the Dodecanese Islands in 1947 to become director of the British Council Institute in Córdoba, Argentina, until the end of 1948. The title poem of *On Seeming to Presume* (1948), elevating his particular condition to the general, bitterly satirizes the plight of modern man, perpetual prey of ugly constraints, "This caliban of gloom," a Hamlet, divided, frustrated, estranged from his true desires. Even more depressing was Belgrade, where he spent three years as press attaché to the British Legation (1949-1952), irked by a political system totally alien to his temperament and experience. In Rhodes, in 1946, his humanitarian conscience had been stirred by seeing the effects of the war on Greece. "Only the rich still glitter," he told Miller in May of that year, and he went on to describe his new understanding of economics and how society is constructed, and to explain how he felt art could help the destitute: "For it's false that the work of art doesn't have an effect on every corner of the body politic. It even brings down the price of bread, or at least offers the staff of life as a substitute." This naive, if well-intended, version of the relationship of art and hunger was a complete volte-face from autumn 1936, when he told Miller that art and politics were utterly unconnected.("Art is not politics, i.e. averages. It is men. It is not the outer struggle but the inner.") The new perception had no chance of surviving Belgrade. Communism seemed an insult to the elitist conscience of the liberal humanist; it paid its intellectuals to keep quiet, he wrote to Miller in July 1949, and was a phenomenon so evil that "the U.S.A., witch-hunting and all, is taking a far more sensible line than anyone else" (27 October 1949). In January 1950, with the Labour government coming up for reelection, he told Miller that "Europe is a sheepfold full of bleating woolly socialists" and that he hoped sincerely that Churchill would be restored to power. In July, Durrell applauded America's intervention in Korea.

In 1953, Durrell moved to Cyprus with his daughter Sappho-Jane (born 1951), working first as a teacher and then as director of public relations for the British government. As a result, and despite Eve Durrell's breakdown and departure, *The Tree of*

Painting by Durrell of fishing boats at Kalymnos, one of the Dodecanese Islands (Lawrence Durrell)

Idleness, published in 1955, is able to diminish the unhappy experience of Yugoslavia by framing it in a familiar and much more satisfactory perspective. At the heart of the title poem is misgiving, lack, absence, but the poet contrives to calm these feelings into harmonious silence, inventing bearable landscapes in past, present, and future, until, once again, all change is abolished, life and death are indistinguishable, and the only surviving reality is the articulation of the poem:

> Tap out on sleeping lips with these same
> Worn typewriter keys a poem imploring
>
> Silence of lips and minds which have
>   not spoken.

To the reiteration that time is not discrete, fragmentary, chronological, but a continuum, the cyclic repetitions of everyday life ("Mneiae," "Chanel," "Deus Loci"), Durrell adds an emphasis on the function of the poet as punctuator of the continuum, "descrying" the form within the moment. "At Strati's" celebrates the mutuality of the process, in which nature participates, in the romantic tradition:

> You say I do not write, but the taverns
> Have no clocks, and I conscripted
> By loneliness observe how other drinkers
> Sit at Strati's embalmed in reverie:
> Forms raise green cones of wine,
> And loaded heads recline on loaded arms,
> Under a sky pronounced by cypresses,
> Packed up, all of us, like loaves
> Human and plant, memory and wish.

Reality is invented by art, created by form. The poet is "Orpheus," bringing the dead, past and present, to life, albeit only in "A paper recreation of lost loves"; the "bite" of his words draws a "thread/Of blood" ("Style").

Durrell remained in Cyprus until 1956, witnessing the dawning and tragic development of the struggle for Enosis, graphically described in *Bitter Lemons* (1957). For him, it was a time of dilemma, with his pro-British and proestablishment sympathies put into direct contradiction with his sense of justice, propriety, fair play, and affection for the Greeks, among whom he had found a spiritual and emotional home. Britain, he complained, saw merely a colonial problem, not a fundamental issue of European politics. His own attempts at practical responses to the situation were hamstrung by rigid colonial bureaucracy. Westminster neglected the economic and cultural welfare of the island and refused to acknowledge the rising tide of disorder and dissent. Durrell argued to the last moment for concessions, rather than militaristic solutions, but in the end he allowed what he saw as the logic of his situation to align him with the British rulers of the island, his employers. He expressed admiration for the man sent to run Cyprus under the military regime. Sir John Harding, like himself, was a competent executor of orders. But the end of his contract brought a sense of relief from the burden of defending the indefensible, of having been driven by history into a false position.

None of these political events finds direct expression in Durrell's poetry. Rather they are displaced into the inner struggle, the realm of the metaphysical, and the basic structures of the poems. His political frustration emerges in a sense of fatalism, the desire for apathy, the claim that man is controlled by forces beyond his control (his so-called autonomous acts the product of unknowable forces), and the exhortation in the poetry to dissolve self into landscape. These feelings are imaged in George Groddeck's concept of the It, which in his introduction to Groddeck's *The Book of the It* (1961; written in 1948) Durrell describes as "an unknown, a forever unknowable entity, whose shadows and functions we are." The It subverts Freudian notions of a conscious ego and negates rationalist concepts of responsibility and free will. In his *Key to Modern Poetry* (1952), Durrell places Groddeck's vitalist psychology, source of his own psychosexual ideas, higher than Freud's, explaining that Groddeck is "of interest to me because his equating of mind and body does, in the medical field, roughly what Einstein has done in the realm of physics with the concepts of space and time."

In this same text, which is based on poetry lectures Durrell gave to his students in Argentina, are attacks on contemporary socialist poets. Though prepared to align himself with radical criticisms of what was wrong in the system, Durrell completely refused to advocate radical cures.

Likewise political is the desire to invent through art an alternative landscape, a new and purportedly liberating disposition of space and time that substitutes for the notion of history as linear progress one of synthesis and cyclical repetition. Here Durrell's ideas on time and space link up not only with Einstein but also with a well-known right-wing European tradition. In a December 1959 letter to Richard Aldington, he acknowledged the influence of Aldington's literary generation; particularly, he noted that his " 'space' business" is from Wyndham Lewis's *Time and Western Man* (1927). He was delighted to find these concepts echoed in Eastern mysticism, especially Zen and Taoism. Origins of ideas, though, matter little for Durrell in themselves; ideas, he wrote to Aldington in February 1959, are "fun and not *facts*. Everything we believe today will be disproved sooner or later." Probably more important is the idea's function as a pretext for fine poetry and as a justification for opting out of the flow of history through the imagination—a kind of conservatism by default. Similar evasions are implied in the notion of identity which appears in Durrell's poetry and which is less complex than that which he develops in his prose narratives. In the romantic tradition, after Byron and Browning, the poetic personality seeks liberation by generating a variety of often-contradictory personae: in imagination, and through his art, the poet transcends and heals the divisions of his own and his generation's history. As often as not, however, the product is less a sense of freedom than of impotence and fragility, and Durrell's poetry itself acknowledges the emptiness at the heart of the romantic sense of self, and its tragic failure to touch history. *Cities, Plains and People*, addressing the Horatian persona, denounces the poet's defection from the life of Rome—the duties of the citizen. Through the figure of Byron, Durrell acknowledges the challenge Greece made to his assumptions and prejudices, poking fun at Byron's weakness and posturing but also picking out his torment ("places where I walk alone/With Conscience, the defective") and ending with a plangent appeal for understanding the poet with good intentions but unclear aims:

You, the speaking and the feeling who come after:
I sent you something once—it must be
Somewhere in *Juan*—it has not reached you yet.

O watch for this remote
But very self of Byron and of me,

Blown empty on the white cliffs of the mind,
A dispossessed His Lordship writing you
A message in a bottle dropped at sea.

Some values, though, are clear for Durrell, especially after his experiences in Cyprus. In September 1958, writing to Aldington, Durrell distanced himself completely from the older 1930s generation for which Aldington still spoke. Aldington had expressed some sympathy for British fascist Oswald Mosley; Durrell's response was prompt and unambiguous: "I can't go along with Mosley, who is a dangerous little pathologue. You know, Richard, I believe if you could see what happens in a Fascist state—could see the behaviour of the Cyprus police, Malaya, Palestine police, you would be scared at the strong vein of brutish fascism the British have in their unconscious. . . . I can't go along with people who could wear Per Ardua Ad Buchenwald on their shoulder flashes. . . . And if I am a Royalist it is in the biological sense—the only political creed possible to a poet, I think, who is ultimately interested in values and not politics at all. . . ."

Having left British government service without a pension to become a full-time writer, Durrell settled in Provence in 1957 with Claude-Marie Vincendon, whom he married in 1961. In 1957 he published the first of his diplomatic sketches, *Esprit de Corps*, and, more important by far, *Justine*, the first volume of the *Alexandria Quartet*, the translation into prose of his efforts to produce what he called in a 1959 interview "a kind of *demonstration* of a possible continuum" (*Paris Review*). As his correspondence with Aldington indicates, the next few years were happy and fruitful ones. *The Ikons and Other Poems* (1966) contemplates in poems such as "Stone Honey" the enduring sweetness and fullness of life, as seen through the poet's eye. Yet there are intimations of unease. The exquisite "harmony of reciprocal functions" which was Ancient Greece ("Persuasions"), abolishing the separateness of the human, concludes in a maternal, protective embrace which is strangely terrifying: "the same horizon softly insisted:/'The perfect circle is incapable of further development.' " "Moonlight" pinpoints the problem. Human desire will not be satisfied with perfect wholeness because it means ending, stasis, and man has no real wish to conclude: "how to stop the perpetual bleeding?/I cannot tell."

Claude Durrell died in 1971, and the same year, Durrell published *The Red Limbo Lingo: A Poetry Notebook for 1968-1970*, a harsh, bitter mixture of poetry and prose, harkening back to his surrealist beginnings, challenging contemporary culture, European history and its values, railing against the dying of the light: night "cancels in me the primal vision" ("Avignon"). As G. S. Fraser says, *The Red Limbo Lingo* has all the violence and frankness of *The Black Book*; yet it is unique in Durrell's poetry: it exposes the raw anguish which elsewhere is glossed over by studied form. The penultimate poem, "Mistral," opens on a positive note ("One head full of poems, cruiser of light/Cracks open the pomegranate to reveal/The lining of all today's perhapses"). But it concludes with the negative. The poet cannot enjoy life; poetry is "the purest selfishness"; atheists have no one to thank for Being; the end is aridity: "Freedom is choice: choice bondage./Where will I next be when the mistral/Rises in sullen trumpets on the hills of bone?"

The vision of the book is severe. Modern life is bloodless, drained by science, rationalism, and Christian idealism—Christ is the vampire. The subjects that preoccupy the community are despicable, and so is its language; modern man "As journalist must always brag/Of blood, vagina and the flag." But poetry provides the only alternative. Poetry, unlike the computer, answers questions never asked. In the unique synthesis of the poetic vision, idiosyncratic, human associations enter the formula; apparently disparate, fragmented lines of inquiry converge on unthought-of targets. The language of the poet, who suffers his own humanity and recognizes "the full horror of the human predicament," invigorates and redeems: "It is not generally known that words, if cut open, will also bleed; a poem of pith may at once accuse, persuade and assuage. The *Red Limbo Lingo* holds a bloody flag up to nature." The poet sacrifices himself in the struggle to punctuate the continuum of existence, to provide the reader with a mystical, musical, total experience in which no meaning should be puzzled out, no explanations asked for. What emerges, sadly, is not mystic wisdom but mystification. A firework display of images, thundering, outraged cadences, or cold assertion demand that the reader capitulate to a poetry alternately manic or depressed, locked in its own death wish, as in "?":

all you can say is: Look, it's manifest
And nobody's to blame: it has no name.
. . . .
A bird or a woman calling in the mist
Asking if anything remains, and if so

Which witch? Which witch? Witch!
I am the only one who knows

In 1973, the poet married Ghislaine de Boysson (whom he divorced in 1979). *Vega and Other Poems*, published in the same year, includes new poems and the poems of *The Red Limbo Lingo*, except for the wild introductory poem. The new collection has a calmer, less bitter tone, but it is still dark and arid. "Vega" itself brings a new richness of colors, dialogue, and movement, with a female figure joined to the search for silence. The end is still pessimistic: "Ah! The beautiful sail so unerringly on towards death/Once they experience the pith of this peerless calm." But the poem for the dead poet Seferis redresses the balance. Beyond death, poetry lingers on, a gift to future generations, so that "even to die is somehow to invent."

Durrell's poetry is not major, either in the context of his own work or in the larger poetic tradition. His range is wide—bawdy ballads, satires, dramatic monologues, surrealist prose poems, love lyrics (for woman or landscape), translations, verse dramas—but his themes are limited—the nature of time, the relativity of personality, the omnipresence of death. His techniques are skillfully applied, but all of them borrowed: from the symbolists and surrealists, from Browning, from Auden (whose use of colloquial language Durrell much admired, though loathing his politics). Often, despite his own and Eliot's attempts to prune, his poetry is too lushly romantic, has too much superficial color. Its emotions are strong, but its metaphysics are simplistic and dubious. In this characteristic, though, perhaps lies its strength, translating the violent and often confused desires of his generation, one that is still with us and whose influence is still renewed in us. In its essential lyricism, Durrell's poetry expresses aspirations both personal and collective. Durrell himself puts it best, in language drawn from the mysticism of Groddeck but expressing perfectly the traditional function of the poet in history: "some-one who has, by the surrender of his ego to the flux of the It, become the agent and translator of the extra-causal forces which rule us."

Letters:

Art and Outrage: A Correspondence about Henry Miller between Alfred Perlès and Lawrence Durrell, with an Intermission by Henry Miller (London: Putnam's, 1959; New York: Dutton, 1960);

Lawrence Durrell/Henry Miller: A Private Correspondence, edited by George Wickes (New York: Dutton, 1963; London: Faber & Faber, 1963);

Literary Lifelines: the Richard Aldington-Lawrence Durrell Correspondence, edited by Ian S. MacNiven and Harry T. Moore (London: Faber & Faber, 1981).

Bibliography:

Robert A. Potter and Brooke Whiting, *Lawrence Durrell: A Checklist* (Los Angeles: University of California Library, 1961).

References:

G. S. Fraser, *Lawrence Durrell: A Critical Study* (London: Faber & Faber, 1968; revised, 1973);

Julian Mitchell and Gene Andrewski, Interview with Durrell, in *Writers at Work: The Paris Review Interviews, Second Series* (New York: Viking, 1963), pp. 257-282;

Alfred Perlès, *My Friend Lawrence Durrell* (Northwood: Scorpion Press, 1961);

John Unterrecker, *Lawrence Durrell* (New York: Columbia University Press, 1964).

Papers:

There are collections of Durrell's papers at the University of California, Los Angeles; the University of Illinois, Urbana; the University of Iowa; and the University of Texas, Austin.

D. J. Enright

(11 March 1920-   )

Anthony John Harding
University of Saskatchewan

SELECTED BOOKS: *Season Ticket; poems* (Alexandria, Egypt: Aux Editions du Scarabée, 1948);

Commentary on Goethe's "Faust" (Norfolk, Conn.: New Directions, 1949);

The Laughing Hyena and Other Poems (London: Routledge & Kegan Paul, 1953);

Academic Year (London: Secker & Warburg, 1955);

The World of Dew: Aspects of Living Japan (London: Secker & Warburg, 1955; Rutland, Vt.: Tuttle, 1956);

Literature for Man's Sake (Tokyo: Kenkyusha, 1955; Folcroft, Pa.: Folcroft Library Editions, 1972);

Bread Rather than Blossoms (London: Secker & Warburg, 1956);

Heaven Knows Where (London: Secker & Warburg, 1957);

The Apothecary's Shop (London: Secker & Warburg, 1957; Philadelphia: Dufour, 1957);

Some Men Are Brothers (London: Chatto & Windus, 1960);

Insufficient Poppy (London: Chatto & Windus, 1960);

Robert Graves and the Decline of Modernism (Singapore: Craftsman Press, 1960; Folcroft, Pa.: Folcroft Library Editions, 1974);

Addictions (London: Chatto & Windus / Hogarth Press, 1962);

The Old Adam (London: Chatto & Windus / Hogarth Press, 1965);

Figures of Speech (London: Heinemann, 1965);

Conspirators and Poets (London: Chatto & Windus, 1966; Chester Springs, Pa.: Dufour, 1966);

Unlawful Assembly (London: Chatto & Windus / Hogarth Press, 1968; Middletown, Conn.: Wesleyan University Press, 1968);

Selected Poems (London: Chatto & Windus, 1968);

Memoirs of a Mendicant Professor (London: Chatto & Windus, 1969);

Shakespeare and the Students (London: Chatto & Windus, 1970; New York: Schocken, 1970);

The Typewriter Revolution and Other Poems (New York: Library Press, 1971);

Daughters of Earth (London: Chatto & Windus / Hogarth Press, 1972);

A Kidnapped Child of Heaven: The Poetry of Arthur

Hugh Clough, Nottingham Byron Lecture, 1972 (Nottingham: University of Nottingham, 1972);

Man Is an Onion (London: Chatto & Windus, 1972; New York: Library Press, 1973);

Foreign Devils, Covent Garden Poetry, no. 3 (London: Covent Garden Press, 1972);

The Terrible Shears (London: Chatto & Windus, 1973; Middletown, Conn.: Wesleyan University Press, 1974);

Rhyme Times Rhyme (London: Chatto & Windus, 1974);

Penguin Modern Poets 26, by Enright, Dannie Abse, and Michael Longley (Harmondsworth & Baltimore: Penguin, 1975);

Sad Ires and Others (London: Chatto & Windus, 1975);

The Joke Shop (London: Chatto & Windus, 1976; New York: McKay, 1976);

Paradise Illustrated (London: Chatto & Windus, 1978);

Wild Ghost Chase (London: Chatto & Windus, 1978);

A Faust Book (Oxford & New York: Oxford University Press, 1979);

Beyond Land's End (London: Chatto & Windus, 1979);

Collected Poems (Oxford & New York: Oxford University Press, 1981);

A Mania for Sentences (London: Chatto & Windus, 1983; Boston: Godine, 1984);

The Oxford Book of Death, edited by Enright (Oxford & New York: Oxford University Press, 1983).

OTHER: *Poets of the 1950's: An Anthology of New English Verse*, edited by Enright (Tokyo: Kenkyusha, 1955);

The Poetry of Living Japan, edited by Enright and Takamichi Ninomiya (London: Murray, 1957; New York: Grove, 1957);

A Choice of Milton's Verse, edited by Enright (London: Faber & Faber, 1975);

The Oxford Book of Contemporary Verse, 1945-1980, edited by Enright (Oxford & Melbourne: Oxford University Press, 1980);

The Oxford Book of Death, edited by Enright (Oxford & New York: Oxford University Press, 1983).

Among the 1950s poets who rejected the modernist tradition, D. J. Enright deserves a secure place. Though sometimes associated with The Movement and sharing The Movement's dislike of the esoteric and their cultivation of vernacular diction and accessible imagery, Enright is distinguished by his exceptionally candid, unpatronizing portrayal of working-class conditions, his mild but devastating irony, and his ability to render scenes as various as Berlin and Bangkok with convincing precision. He avoids both private symbolism and political phrasemaking. Though fully aware that to appoint oneself observer of others' lives, whether in Asia, Africa, or Europe, is a morally precarious position to take, he demonstrates the power that such observation can have, where there is humaneness, frankness, and a concern for ordinary decency.

Dennis Joseph Enright has claimed that his parentage and Midlands working-class upbringing left him with the gift of being unable to grasp religious, racial, or political ideologies. His father,

George Enright, a postman, was Irish (and a lapsed Catholic), his mother, Grace Cleaver Enright, English with possibly "a touch of Welsh" and "vaguely a chapel-goer." His education, at Leamington College, Warwickshire, and then at Downing College, Cambridge, was also anomalous, for the scholarships he won offered him a route out of the narrow and suffocating gentility of Leamington, yet he found he was expected to demonstrate considerable gratitude for these awards, as if English society were showing remarkable generosity and lack of prejudice by making an exception, in his case, to the usual rules. Enright's claim that his skeptical attitude toward dogma derived from his parentage and working-class background is a typically modest one, however, which at best only partially accounts for his mature liberal-humanist stance.

Tutored at Downing by F. R. Leavis and James Smith, Enright began his literary career within the general ambit of *Scrutiny*. Though he was by no means a carbon-copy Leavisite, between 1940 and 1952 Enright wrote regularly for *Scrutiny*: his first contribution was an essay on Jonson, but most of his subsequent contributions were on German literature—Goethe, Hölderlin, Rilke, Thomas Mann, and Stefan George in particular.

Enright was granted a B.A. with honors in 1944 and an M.A. in 1946. Finding that British universities in the 1940s were reluctant to hire "Scrutineers" because of their reputation for Leavisite zeal and their open contempt for the urbane, belletristic style of many senior academics, he began a long career as a university teacher overseas. His first post (1947-1950) was at the then King Farouk I University in Alexandria, where on 3 November 1949 he married Madeleine Harders, a teacher of French literature. Also in 1949 he earned a D.Litt. degree from King Farouk I University. Between 1950 and 1970 Enright held a succession of lectureships and professorships in Asia and (for one year) Germany, with only one brief spell in England, as a teacher of extramural classes for Birmingham University, from 1950 to 1953. From 1953 to 1956 he was a visiting professor at Konan University, Kobe, Japan; during 1956-1957 visiting professor at the Free University of Berlin; in 1957-1959 British Council Professor at Chulalongkorn University, Bangkok; and from 1960 to 1970 professor of English at the University of Singapore. Many of Enright's most vivid poems, as well as the four novels *Academic Year* (1955), *Heaven Knows Where* (1957), *Insufficient Poppy* (1960), and *Figures of Speech* (1965), express the expatriate Englishman's admiration and bafflement at the ways of both non-Europeans and other European exiles; but the observation is never tinged with Eurocentric snobbishness or the sentimentalism of the travel writer greedy for "local color." Enright is able to render the careful manners of a geisha in Kyoto, and the poised alertness of a fisherman in the Nile Delta, for what they are, expressions of the human spirit and of a quality Enright finds notably lacking in the English: grace.

It is ironic, then, that Enright's career as "mendicant professor" should have been marked by a number of tangles with governmental and university authorities, most of them originating in unlikely or even farcical misunderstandings. Fortunately the irony was of a kind Enright is fully able to enjoy. At one point, as Enright puts it, he "wantonly attacked some fifteen Thai policemen, finally obliging them to beat me up in self-defence." Driving home from a party late one night in Bangkok, Enright and his wife found the road near their house blocked by a car with one of its doors standing open. Madeleine Enright closed the car door so they could drive past. The two of them were immediately set upon by a group of policemen who streamed out from a brothel nearby. The car had been borrowed by one of the policemen, and he and his friends somehow had the impression that Enright and his wife were dangerous vandals, about to damage the borrowed vehicle. This incident—which is described in *Memoirs of a Mendicant Professor* (1969)—merely confirmed the view already held by the British Council representative in Thailand, that Enright was an undesirable element and a troublemaker. (Enright's admission that he smoked opium occasionally had also contributed to official distrust of him.) It led to the termination of his period of service in Bangkok, though he was paid his British Council salary for a further year, during which he lived in London, officially as an adviser on overseas appointments.

The most notorious of Enright's tangles with authority took place in Singapore, in 1960, just as Enright began his duties as Johore Professor of English in what was then the University of Malaya. In his inaugural lecture (17 November 1960) on "Robert Graves and the Decline of Modernism," he made some general remarks to the effect that culture could not be created *ex nihilo* by government directive, but emerged from the activities of a people who read and wrote books, composed music, painted pictures, and observed life. Some officials in the socialist government of Singapore saw Enright's remarks, which had been selectively reported in the *Straits Times*, as an attack on the gov-

ernment's policy of encouraging an authentically Malay culture. Enright was publicly rebuked, found himself treated as a champion of free speech by opposition politicians and by a specially convened meeting of students, was advised by some of his compatriots to resign his professorship as a gesture of protest, and decided instead to accept the compromise terms offered by the government, which had quickly begun to feel embarrassed by the overhasty reaction of their minister of culture. According to these terms Enright was to write a brief letter to the Acting Minister of Labour and Law, explaining that he had no intention of sneering at Malay culture, nor of interfering in the politics of Singapore. This letter, together with a reply from the minister, would be published in the *Straits Times*. Both letters were duly written and published, and the "Enright Affair" laid to rest, although some of Enright's compatriots continued to criticize him for not quitting the country in protest at the way he had been treated. Such incidents as this undoubtedly strengthened Enright's already distrustful attitude toward officialdom, whether of the Right or the Left, and his native sympathy for the less privileged or wary victims of official persecution.

Enright's first substantial collection of poems, *The Laughing Hyena and Other Poems* (1953), draws on poems written during the Birmingham interlude and reprints a few poems published in Alexandria (in a pamphlet called *Season Ticket*, 1948). The title poem is "after" a work of Hokusai, "The Laughing Hannya," depicting a demon, the hannya, featured in some Noh plays. The poet finds Hokusai's demon refreshingly singleminded in its commitment to evil, by comparison with the "sententious phantoms" of twentieth-century literature: "It, at least, / Knows exactly why it laughs." Enright's point is a good one, and yet there is something wrong with such a highly self-conscious poem that tries to praise unselfconsciousness. There is genuine allusive wit, but it is brought to the subject from outside, like the cozy jokes made by a lecturer to his audience, and not discovered within the subject. The same cajoling lecturer's tone interferes with the attempt to disparage Freud and substitute a certain Goethean stoicism in "Baie des Anges, Nice": "Was Goethe wholly wrong?" Believing, as he claims to in "Life and Letters," that poems themselves should not be "phantoms," Enright is at his best when he lets his subject speak for itself free of arch commentary. "Arab Music," for instance, avoids redundantly describing the Western listener's attitude or "impressions" and instead evokes the unexpected dignity and self-assurance of the

Nubian singers. "Black Country Women" achieves truth and compassion as Blake achieved them, through honesty rather than a parade of sentiment. The same clear-eyed vision is present in "The Egyptian Cat" and "A Demonstration." "Chagall's 'Calvary' " (not in *Collected Poems*) is worth seeking out for its intelligently drawn contrast between the narrated version of an event (pallid and wizened like the narrator), and the stark horror of the event itself.

Enright's experience of postwar Japan gave his developing liberal-humanist values a still severer shock than Alexandria had. During his term as visiting professor at Konan University (1953-1956) Enright visited Hiroshima, an experience which profoundly affected his work. In addition, he found Japanese manners and morals stifling, and the pervasive Japanese politeness kept him, he felt, from developing any very close relationships within the middle classes. Some of the poems in *Bread Rather than Blossoms* (1956) accordingly suffer from a certain note of wryness, a rueful humor which is too much the expected defensive posture of the Englishman abroad. "Standards" and "Akiko San," however, exhibit that empathy with the life of the working class (here represented by the bar girl and the prostitute) and that ability to render the working class vividly without patronizing it, which constitute one of Enright's best gifts. "Standards" compels us to ask who is really culturally deprived, the overeducated English educational theorist with his "cold and silent and derivative sneer," or the generous and considerate bar girl, whose warmth of nature would appear to the overeducated Englishman as sentimentality. "Akiko San" foresees the prostitute's translation to a blessed hereafter where she can rest her blistered feet. In this volume, Enright finds his proper voice: not self-consciously "earthy" nor overly intense or strident, but level, mild, honest, lucid. The particular difficulties of this style are the avoidance of bathos and the achievement of rhythmic variety. "How right they were, the Chinese poets" avoids bathos but is quite rigidly end-stopped. "Akiko San" and "Purchas His Pilgrimes" (a humanist meditation which summarizes the history of East-West warfare from the first Portuguese explorations up to the time of Hiroshima) achieve more rhythmic variety, as well as the consistent level tone that enables Enright to say the things he wants to say in quiet astonishment at the extent of human cruelty and stupidity.

The note of rueful, defensive humor which occasionally intruded into Enright's first two collections is absent from *Some Men Are Brothers* (1960), *Addictions* (1962), and *The Old Adam* (1965); or rather it is confined to those poems which openly deal with the naive surprise of the liberal Westerner at a world which seems quite able to get along, in its casually cruel way, without liberal, Western notions. *Some Men Are Brothers* and *Addictions* both draw on Enright's year in West Berlin (1956-1957), as well as on his experience of Bangkok. Enright did not feel at home in Berlin, being somewhat repelled by German ideas of correctness ("No Offence," "Am Steinplatz"), and the German ability to sanitize ugly truths with a wash of "culture" evoked one of his most bitterly ironic poems, "Apocalypse." The poem throws into sharp relief the question that must preoccupy any humanist scholar, critic, or poet in the second half of the twentieth century: what value can he possibly place on "culture" after Belsen, Dresden, and Hiroshima? Is "civilization vindicated" by the continued production of novels, paintings, and symphonies? Enright's approach appears too indirect to achieve the bitter power of a poet such as Sylvia Plath, but the air of detachment assumed in the opening stanza is deceptive. By the end of the poem the absurdism and grotesqueness of Enright's imagery, set against the urbane mockery of the opening, have given strong voice to the outraged European conscience.

The clutter and spoil of Asia provided a more fertile homeland for Enright's alert imagination than bland, hypocritical Europe, despite the guilt he inevitably bore as the representative of an exhausted colonialist power ("Entrance Visa"). But the temptation to sit back and enjoy the parade, to let the humanist conscience fall asleep, treating the exotic as "a rest from meaning" ("Reflections on Foreign Literature"), had to be resisted. Perhaps the Westerner does not "fit in" in Asia, but, as Enright asks, "who does?" Conscious of his position as tolerated outsider, Enright realizes that any protest against the determined or even accidental cruelty of an autocratic Asian regime may seem futile or ridiculous: but it has to be made. Caricaturing the voice of the fussy professor in "An Unfortunate Poem: II: Warm Protest," about the shooting of a man against the wall of a library, he asks, "How shall I ever (never easy, as you know) / Persuade the boys and girls to use the Library now?" In the second of two "Words without Songs" in *Some Men Are Brothers*, Enright speaks more to the plain humanist point. A man has been killed:

> For his occupation--
>
> I'm no UNESCO Fellow, this no report on
>   peasant skills
> (Anyone can die, and he was helped to).

> Simply, he was human, did no harm, and
> > suffered for it.

The same lucid and unesoteric realism characterizes "News" and "Fort William" (in *Addictions*).

Enright's ability to demystify is the motive force in several poems on the use of opium. It was his openness about this subject that embarrassed the British Embassy and British Council staff in Bangkok and contributed to their view that he did not quite "fit in." "Confessions of an English Opium Smoker," with somewhat puzzled glances at Coleridge, De Quincey, and Yeats, gives an alternate picture of the opium experience, far less exotic than theirs.

> I regain these images:
> Rocked by the modern traffic of the town,
> A grubby, badly lighted, stuffy shack.

"The Burning of the Pipes" is a mournful, wry commemoration of the Thai government's public bonfire of opium pipes in 1959, it having been officially decided that opium smoking was noxious and debilitating and discouraged civic-mindedness. Enright's poem is no portentous defense of opium smoking. Rather, it juxtaposes the mild innocence of the opium user with the heavy-handed moralism of government.

Official intolerance is a pervasive evil of the century, not confined to Asia, and as Enright realizes, it is as often rooted in what he calls "goody-goodiness" as in malice. This is the theme of "To Old Cavafy, from a New Country" (in *The Old Adam*). Enright shares with the Alexandrian poet a love of those roughnesses which make men various and a distrust of the moralism that tries to smooth them away. The poem to Cavafy is also a fine instance of Enright's growing interest in the satirical possibilities of religious language, incongruously transposed into the key of the secular, a technique he uses with outstanding precision in *Paradise Illustrated* (1978) and *A Faust Book* (1979).

Unlawful Assembly (1968) contains a number of poems which reflect something approaching despair about the erosion of Old World tolerance and grace. The poet's helplessness in combating propaganda is cleverly conveyed in "It's an Art," in the shift from "the art of poetry is / Not to say everything" to "The art of poetry is not to say a thing." The context of the poem is the liberal humanist's reaction to the war in Vietnam: the theme, the marginalization of poetry in a time when to try to be humane is to be ignored, silenced, or laughed at.

Even romantic rebellion, as seen in "The Last Romantics," is now made a tool of Moscow, Washington, or Peking; heroism and freedom are passé. In a similar vein, "They Who Take the Word" depicts poets as archaic survivors from some long-past age, primeval monsters stuck in the mud of the centuries.

One of the most striking poems in the collection, however, is "Roman Reasons," which praises Shakespeare's Enobarbus for not taking refuge in the anonymity of mass immorality after he had defected to Caesar's side. The others who abandoned Antony soon anesthetized any pangs of guilt they might have felt by joining in the triumphal war cries of Caesar's army. Enobarbus's last act of candor, choosing an ignominious death instead of the easy self-righteousness of the majority, plainly speaks to the situation of the poet writing in the 1960s.

In general the tighter, conciser verse forms are more successful in *Unlawful Assembly* than the free verse. Lines such as "Sensibility alters from generation to generation, and / The general feeling is that people who get into trouble / Are troublesome" ("After the Gods, after the Heroes") lack bite by comparison with such poems as "The Small War" (which effectively uses both rhyme and half-rhyme) and "Unlawful Assembly":

> In this vale of teargas,
> Should one enter a caveat,
> Or a monastery?

This more aphoristic manner appears also in *Daughters of Earth* (1972). "The Sensitive Philanthropist," "Highmindedness of an English Poet," and the title poem in that volume have an acidulous wit that bears comparison with Auden. More peculiarly Enright's, in its cool anger at the absurdity of institutionalized racism, is "Terminal," about the child of an English father and Chinese mother who is faced with a choice of queues at the immigration desk, Caucasian and Other. There is no obscurity, cleverness, or fashionable angst in the poem: only a quiet rage at the way in which those absurd categories debase everyone's humanity.

Enright returned to England in 1970, having served for ten years as professor of English at the University of Singapore. He taught part-time at Leeds University for a year and then worked as a reader for Chatto and Windus, later (in 1973) joining their board of directors. He was also coeditor of *Encounter* from 1970 to 1972. In 1975 Enright was appointed honorary professor of English at Warwick University, where he remained until 1980. Since his return from Asia Enright's work has taken

Charles Osbourne of the British Arts Council with poets Dannie Abse, Peter Porter, D. J. Enright, and Jeremy Robson embarking on a 1971 reading tour of Israel (Jeremy Robson)

several new directions and established his mastery of a number of new modes. First, in *The Terrible Shears* (1973), Enright tenderly and bitterly recreated the world of his 1920s Midlands childhood. The poems have the clear-eyed compassion of "Black Country Women," but they also have a greater pungency and at times a deeply felt amazement that such things were done, said, and tolerated in a proud country. The poems are wholly free from sentimentality or false pathos on the one hand, and from a posturing angry-young-man brashness on the other. Read alongside the best work of Wain and other Movement poets, poems such as "They: Early Horror Film," "Sunday," "Geriatrics," and "Class" demonstrate— with a clarity achieved by few other poets—the driving force behind the 1950s' rejection of urbanity and the esoteric tradition in poetry.

Paradise Illustrated and *A Faust Book* represent a reflowering of Enright's comic and parodic strain, both of them affectionately rather than bitingly satirical, full of buoyant if at times rather donnish wit and a relish for the quirks of language. Whether the subject is Adam deflating the paternalistic condolences offered by the Archangel Michael, or Faust's lechery deflating the sententious regrets of Mephistopheles, the effect is simply one of a holiday from high seriousness. A consistent reading, reinterpretation, or misinterpretation of *Faust* and *Paradise Lost* is not attempted—rather what is offered is a sort of hermeneutic circus. The humor is entirely linguistic. If an alternative metaphysic is presented, it is an antimetaphysic created by mischievous subversion of the traditional one, not a true alternative, like those resulting from the inversion technique practiced by some romantic poets. Enright is not of the devil's party without knowing it, but of Adam's party, and he knows it very well. Yet the linguistic subversion, the technique of the poet-as-trickster, is associated in *Paradise Illustrated* not with Adam, who is merely slow, irreligious, and slightly boorish, an unlucky simpleton at the mercy of an unscrupulous prankster, but with Satan, "fond of artful sound." Even so, *Paradise Illustrated*, which is about the fall into the commonplace, is

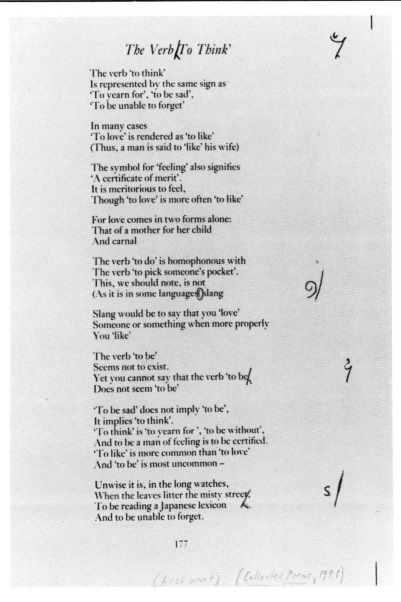

Corrected proof (the author)

perhaps more consistently successful than *A Faust Book*, where Enright tries to present Mephistopheles and Faust as unequal coconspirators in a jolly lark but constantly has to remind us of the salvation drama being played out behind the grease paint, a drama that still seems all too real. Milton's creaky metaphysical machinery may be fair game for a jest, but the abyss where Faust stands is still too close, salvation and damnation too immediate a choice, to stand being subverted, even in a secular age. More generally it may be observed that parody is too narrow and inbred a field for Enright's talents. In 1981, the same year his *Collected Poems* was published, he received the Queen's Gold Metal for poetry.

Enright's work since 1979 has shown that he still wields dexterously the humanist's sharpest tools—those of irony and iconoclasm: and surely human stupidity and intolerance, ever-productive of new varieties of folly, provide the richest field in which he can continue to exercise his rare gifts.

Reference:

William Walsh, *D. J. Enright: Poet of Humanism* (Cambridge: Cambridge University Press, 1976).

G. S. Fraser

(8 November 1915-3 January 1980)

Paul Schlueter

SELECTED BOOKS: *The Fatal Landscape and Other Poems* (London: Editions Poetry, 1941?);

Home Town Elegy (London: Nicholson & Watson / Editions Poetry, 1944);

Vision of Scotland (London: Elek, 1948);

The Traveller Has Regrets and Other Poems (London: Editions Poetry/Harvill Press, 1948); abridged and republished as *Leaves Without a Tree* (Tokyo: Hokuseido Press, 1953);

News from South America (London: Harvill Press, 1949; New York: Library Publishers, 1952);

Postwar Trends in English Literature (Tokyo: Hokuseido Press, 1950); revised and expanded as *The Modern Writer and His World* (London: Verschoyle, 1953; New York: Criterion, 1955; revised edition, London: Deutsch, 1964; New York: Praeger, 1965);

Three Philosophic Essays (Tokyo: Eibunsha, 1951?);

Impressions of Japan and Other Essays (Tokyo: Asahi-Shimbun-Sha, 1952);

W. B. Yeats (London: Longmans, Green, 1954; revised, 1962; revised again, 1965);

Scotland (London: Thames & Hudson, 1955; New York: Studio Publications, 1955);

Dylan Thomas (London: Longmans, Green, 1957; revised, 1964);

Vision and Rhetoric: Studies in Modern Poetry (London: Faber & Faber, 1959; New York: Barnes & Noble, 1960);

Ezra Pound (Edinburgh & London: Oliver & Boyd, 1960; New York: Grove, 1961);

Lawrence Durrell: A Study (New York: Dutton, 1968; London: Faber & Faber, 1968; revised, London: Faber & Faber, 1973);

Conditions: Selected Recent Poetry (Nottingham: Byron Press, 1969);

Lawrence Durrell (London: Longman, 1970);

Metre, Rhythm, and Free Verse (London: Methuen, 1970);

P. H. Newby (London: Longman, 1974);

Essays on Twentieth-Century Poets (Leicester: Leicester University Press, 1977; Totowa, N.J.: Rowman & Littlefield, 1977);

Alexander Pope (London: Routledge & Kegan Paul, 1978);

A Short History of English Poetry (Somerset, U.K.:

G. S. Fraser (photo by John Waller)

Open Books, 1979; Totowa, N.J.: Barnes & Noble, 1981);

Poems of G. S. Fraser, edited by Ian Fletcher and John Lucas (Leicester: Leicester University Press, 1981; Atlantic Highlands, N.J.: Humanities Press, 1981);

A Stranger and Afraid: Autobiography of an Intellectual (Manchester: Carcanet New Press, 1983; Atlantic Highlands, N.J.: Humanities Press, 1983).

OTHER: Henry Treece, ed., *The New Apocalypse*, includes poems by Fraser (London: Fortune Press, 1940);

102

Treece and J. F. Hendry, eds., *The White Horseman*, introduction by Fraser (London: Routledge & Kegan Paul, 1941);

Victor Selwyn and others, eds., *Oasis: The Middle East Anthology of Poetry from the Forces*, includes poems by Fraser (Cairo: Salamander Productions, 1943);

Treece and Hendry, eds., *The Crown and the Sickle*, includes poems by Fraser (London: King & Staples, 1944);

Patrice Arthur Elie Humbert de la Tour Du Pin, *The Dedicated Life in Poetry, and the Correspondence of Laurent de Cayeux*, translated by Fraser (London: Harvill Press, 1948);

Gabriel Marcel, *The Mystery of Being*, translated by Fraser (London: Harvill Press, 1950);

The Collected Poems of Keith Douglas, edited by Fraser and John Waller (London: Editions Poetry, 1951); revised edition, edited by Fraser, Waller, and J. C. Hall (London: Faber & Faber, 1966; New York: Chilmark, 1967);

Gabriel Marcel, *Men Against Humanity*, translated by Fraser (London: Harvill Press, 1952);

Jean Mesnard, *Pascal: His Life and Works*, translated by Fraser (London: Harvill Press, 1952);

Serge Moreuz, *Béla Bartók*, translated by Fraser and E. deMauny (London: Harvill Press, 1953);

Springtime: An Anthology of Young Poets and Writers, edited by Fraser and Ian Fletcher (London: Owen, 1953);

Poetry Now: An Anthology, edited by Fraser (London: Faber & Faber, 1956);

Selected Poems of Robert Burns, edited by Fraser (London: Heinemann, 1960; New York: Macmillan, 1960);

Adi-Granth, *Selections from the Sacred Writings of the Sikhs*, revised by Fraser (London: Allen & Unwin, 1960; New York: Macmillan, 1960);

Vaughan College Poems, edited by Fraser (London: University of Leicester Press, 1963);

Dante's Inferno, translated by Fraser and others (London: BBC Publications, 1966);

Keith Douglas, *Alamein to Zem Zem*, edited by Fraser, Waller, and Hall (London: Faber & Faber, 1966; New York: Chilmark, 1967);

Workshop 8, edited by Fraser and others (London: Workshop, 1969);

John Keats: Odes, a Casebook, edited by Fraser (London: Macmillan, 1971);

Donald B. Moore, *The Poetry of Louis MacNeice*, introduction by Fraser (Leicester: Leicester University Press, 1972; New York: Humanities Press, 1972);

Return to Oasis: War Poems and Recollections from the Middle East, 1940-1946, edited by Fraser and others (London: Shepheard-Walwyn / Editions Poetry London, for the Salamander Oasis Trust, 1980; New York: Flatiron Books, 1983).

Though G. S. Fraser is far better known as a critic and literary historian, it is as a poet that he wished to be remembered. A writer of published verse by age sixteen, Fraser turned to literary journalism and teaching in order to make a living. The promise of his early poetic work, which was usually occasional in nature, was rarely realized in his later poetry, and, as a consequence, his poems often appear to rely on sentimental, hackneyed, or otherwise undistinguished topics and techniques. Fraser once stated that he "never had the time to think out a theory of poetics," and much of his poetry is marked more by lyrical effusiveness and romantic sensitivity than by a carefully reasoned set of aesthetic convictions. As an "occasional" poet, he is of interest for his well-intentioned sincerity and a few memorable lines, not for technical innovation; as he observed, "Like many Scottish poets I am old-fashioned in my taste for strict metrics and explicit poetic statement." Late in his life he attempted, though only tentatively, to break away from such metrical conventionality, but his best work remains carefully controlled, measured verse of the sort that has dominated much of English literary history. In this sense, he is in a line that includes such other recent poets as Robert Graves, Edmund Blunden, W. H. Auden, and John Betjeman. And though the number of Fraser's poems that will endure as anthology pieces is small, with his primary reputation likely to be based on his criticism, his verse is a solid, workmanlike, "civilized" accomplishment.

Born in Glasgow to George Sutherland Fraser, who was employed in the town clerk's office, and Ada Jones Fraser, the younger George Sutherland Fraser was educated at Glasgow Academy and Aberdeen Grammar School. In 1933 he was awarded a bursary (scholarship) at St. Andrews University on the basis of having received the Medal for Modern Languages in school; his first published work—an article in a literary review—appeared the same year. In his first year at St. Andrews he won an annual competition with a one-act play about Marlowe, and in 1936-1937 he edited the *St. Andrews University Magazine*, which was suppressed by the university authorities because Fraser published controversial material, including a socialist manifesto. He graduated from St. Andrews in 1937, receiving a second-class honors M.A. in combined English and history; since his work in history had all been given firsts, his views on literature were evidently the cause for his having received less than a first in English. Though he recalled no distinguished teachers at St. Andrews, he claimed later that Edwin Muir's talks to the literary society impressed and inspired him. After graduation Fraser worked until 1939 as a journalist for the *Aberdeen Press and Journal*, learning as much as possible about reporting, editing, reviewing, and—most important, perhaps—about writing quickly and versatily on a variety of topics, a characteristic evident in the quantity and range of his later criticism.

He volunteered for military service in 1939 and was inducted just before Christmas, but his physical awkwardness thwarted any possibility that he be made an officer. Serving in England until May 1941, he became a part of a neoromantic group of poets reacting against the "Puritan verse" of Auden, Spender, MacNeice, and Day Lewis; this group, composed primarily of Scots, Welsh, or Northern Irish poets, included Fraser, Henry Treece, Norman MacCaig, Vernon Watkins, and Alex Comfort, among others, and took its name, the New Apocalypse, from the title of its 1940 anthology, the first of three published by the group during the war. Fraser's description of the New Apocalypse notes that it was a "dialectical development" of surrealism, with an emphasis on the movement's psychological importance, a "certain permanent clinical value for the human race."

After Fraser was shipped to Egypt in May 1941, he worked primarily on various army publications. Though he was eventually promoted to warrant officer, another effort to rise to officer status was blocked by his continued lack of physical dexterity. While in Cairo he befriended the writers connected with *Personal Landscape*, a literary magazine offering British reaction to Eastern Mediterranean life: Lawrence Durrell, Bernard Spencer, Olivia Manning, Robin Fedden, Terence Tiller, and Keith Douglas. He also met many other writers, including John Gawsworth, who had made Cairo their temporary exile, and he became a part of the Salamander Society of Poets (headed by Keith B. Bullen, nephew of A. H. Bullen, noted Elizabethan scholar and translator), which included some of the writers from the *Personal Landscape* group. The Salamander Society met each Sunday evening for poetry reading and discussion, out of which came the five issues of the magazine *Salamander* and the collection *Oasis: The Middle East Anthology of Poetry from the Forces*, all published in Cairo in

1943. In 1943-1944 Fraser served in Asmara, Ethiopia, where he edited a half-English, half-Italian newspaper, the *Eritrean Daily News (Il Quotidiano Eritreo)*. Reassigned to Cairo to write for the Ministry of Information, he produced numerous anonymous articles that were reprinted in local Arabic, French, and Italian papers.

Much of Fraser's early poetry was published while he served in the Middle East. The poems in his first two volumes, published in 1943 and 1944, are distinguished by their lyrical clarity and the obvious influence of Yeats. Much of this early verse, an attempt to capture—emotionally as well as geographically—his youth in Scotland, mixes elation and sorrow in recalling a world he knew was irrevocably lost, a world changed not only by his maturing but also by the effects of the war. To some extent Fraser's early poetry is an exercise in escapist nostalgia; yet there is a sensitivity, a sensuosity, an awareness of the ephemeral nature of love and beauty that transcends the usual self-indulgence and narcissism of youth. The war had forced Fraser to become an emotional as well as a physical expatriate. His later extended stays away from Britain—three months in South America in 1947, eighteen months in Japan in 1950-1951—seem to have added to this initial sense of isolation from the world of his youth, for he wrote reminiscences of life in Scotland throughout his career, even though he rarely returned there after his adolescence.

Fraser's first two books of poetry are very much the work of a young man, even though they appeared when he was in his late twenties. Many of the poems are conventional romantic effusions, with repeated emphasis on abstractions (often capitalized) such as Time, Death, Pity, and Eternity. All but three of the poems in *The Fatal Landscape and Other Poems*, an eighteen-page pamphlet published about 1941, were republished in *Home Town Elegy* in 1944. Some of the poems are conventional exercises in patriotism; others are clearly offered as tributes to his Scottish heritage (for example, "Meditation," "Home Town Elegy," and "To Hugh MacDiarmid"). Others reflect his lifelong fondness for imitating, paraphrasing, or translating the works of poets of other languages; in these initial collections, for example, there are poems based on works by Guy Rosey, Catullus, and Horace. Fraser's obvious poetic gifts were immediately evident to reviewers of *Home Town Elegy*. In the *New Statesman and Nation* Stephen Spender noted Fraser's "great promise," and concluded that despite Fraser's being "loquacious and argumentative" in some of his poems, the book was "well worth buying." The reviewer for the

Times Literary Supplement noted both the poetry's obvious Yeatsian elements—"its intensely personal note and . . . its ceremonial style"—as well as its formal precision. Both these critics regretted Fraser's excessive emphasis on himself and his own situation—"romantic self-preoccupation," as the *TLS* reviewer called it—but both essentially praised him as a writer of talent.

Aside from topical and patriotic verse, the one overriding emphasis in these first two collections is death: six of the forty-four poems have the word *elegy* in their titles, and death is treated in many of the others as well. Yet aside from "Rostov," none of the poems reflect wartime occurrences, even though Fraser had witnessed and survived the 1941 Blitz in London and had certainly had some firsthand knowledge of wartime horrors during his Middle East years. To a great extent, however, death, along with other grand emotions, is a mere abstraction, grist for a young man's poetic mill rather than a suggestion of deeply felt emotion arising from the depths of Fraser's life and experience.

"Problems of a Poet" reminds the reader of T. S. Eliot's "The Love Song of J. Alfred Prufrock" in its use of a self-conscious, questioning persona who is incapable of reconciling the ideal and mundane:

> "What will you write about? Trees,
> > politics, women . . ."
> I shall write about nothing at all.
> They shall say, his basket was emptied early,
> He bowed, but did not come for the
> > curtain call.

In this poem the refrain "I shall make conversation" further enforces the Eliotic parallels, while the self-conscious dropping of Osbert Sitwell's name in a casual conversation suggests a certain effort on Fraser's part to make the poem appear more sophisticated than it otherwise is. The persona's dreading woman's "soft plump hands" and "sweet inaneness of their cooing breath" introduces a tentative sensuosity found in Fraser's later work as well.

A number of these poems are self-conscious manifestations of a young man's awakening emotional and physical natures, and several are simply adolescent effusions. "Early Spring," for example, is a Shelleyan consideration of the possibility of death in the midst of emergence of new life, and "The Fatal Landscape" (accompanied by a suitable epigraph from Hemingway) is similar in tone. Fraser sometimes combines his flair for imitations

with his sensuous awareness of the possibilities of language in such adolescent utterances: "Lean Street," for instance, is a modern version of Blake's "London." But it is Yeats who comes to mind most often: "Tramp's Song," with the refrain "The lean dogs are howling to the moon" ending each stanza, seems Yeatsian, and "For Yeats" and "Elegy for Freud and Yeats" make the connection explicitly. Even when the ostensible subject or recipient of a poem is someone other than Fraser—as in "A Letter to Anne Ridler"—it is clear that the poem's focus is still on Fraser and his awareness of his own emotional life. Fraser's continual sense of the passing of an era, not just from the effects of the catastrophic war and his own involuntary exile from home, is especially well captured in the Yeatsian refrain from the otherwise jejune "Meditation of a Patriot": "With Byron and with Lermontov / Romantic Scotland's in the grave"—a refrain that echoes Yeats's line "Romantic Ireland's dead and gone." All in all, these first two volumes are an auspicious debut for a young poet, despite their excesses and predictability. Even though some of the poems date from Fraser's university days, they are balanced by the wartime poems.

In 1945 Fraser was discharged from the army and moved to London to live with his now-widowed mother in Chelsea. He began working as a freelance journalist and received the Hodder and Stoughton Literary Bursary for former service writers for 1946-1947. In 1946 he married Eileen Lucy Andrew, with whom he had two daughters and a son. He continued to earn his living as a free-lance writer, reviewer, broadcaster, anthologist, and translator until 1959, having his criticism published in a wide variety of British and American journals (*Times Literary Supplement, Encounter, New Statesman, Observer, Listener, London Magazine, Partisan Review, Commentary, Poetry, Chicago Critical Quarterly*, and *New York Review of Books*). Always fond of travel, he made two extensive cultural-mission trips during these years. He spent three months in South America in 1947, staying with Pablo Neruda in Chile and also visiting Argentina, Brazil, and Uruguay. And he spent eighteen months in Japan during 1950-1951, having succeeded Edmund Blunden as cultural adviser to the United Kingdom Liaison Mission. His work for the BBC was especially important in the 1950s; his New Poetry series of anthologies with commentaries was highly praised and led to the publication of monographs on various modern poets, notably Ezra Pound, Dylan Thomas, and Lawrence Durrell. In 1958 he gave the British Academy Chatterton Lecture on Keith Douglas, whose poems he had edited.

Fraser considered his longer poems published during these years (reflective verse epistles for the most part) to be his best work, though critics have tended to praise the early work more highly. Most of these poems published during his middle years were in fact written during the war, and they exhibit the same fondness for occasional or topical subjects as the poems published at that time. There are again a number of elegies, translations, two versions of a poem for T. S. Eliot, and poems addressed to a number of other poets, including Lawrence Durrell, John Waller, Edwin Muir, R. P. Blackmur, Anne Ridler, and Keith Bullen. The death of President Franklin D. Roosevelt and the Korean War are among the events commemorated, and one lyric poem is in French. A number of poems from this period are especially effective, but some are weak and mawkish.

The most striking verses from this middle period celebrate specific incidents from Fraser's life, in particular his years in the Middle East. "Three Profiles from Cairo," for instance, is a sensuous, evocative consideration of "X," "Y," and "Z." "X" is compared to a cat; while "Y," whose "ruined beauty" hides behind a glass of beer, but whose narcissism requires a photographer's skill for full expression, reminds Fraser of a lost child in Glasgow wandering through the brightly lit but inaccessible parts of that city; "Z" is a writer of "dreary poems" whose judgment of other poets is "cold, academical, / perception winged by spite," and "whom everybody hates / because of your reptilian coldness / and the cold-cream unction / of your inedible voice." Similarly, "Exile's Letter" is a rich, moving free-association ramble over Fraser's entire life, in which the persona writes to a loved one "as exiles will, / Half to revive and half to kill: / Revive the hope, and kill the ache." "For the Marriage of Helen Scott and John Irwin" is a worthy addition to any collection of epithalamia, and "Monologue for a Cairo Evening" transcends the significance of the list of friends contained in the poem by its bitter nostalgia and sense of the world's loss because of the war: "And Europe stinks / Of the perverted human will, is tortured / Just as our guts are tortured by our drinks." Even "Poetic Generations" is more than an easy comparison of several generations of poets because of its sense of desolation and anger at the circumstances of war so radically altering Fraser's generation of poets.

"Elegy for Adolescent Sex" and "A Bought Embrace" offer bitter reflection about the nature of youthful sexual desire, combined with guilt and fear of discovery, the first poem dealing with a furtive encounter in the dark, the second with a mere commercial sexual transaction. Fraser's fondness for traditional forms, apparent in a good deal of his early work as well, is especially well realized in two other poems also concerned with love, particularly sexual love: "A Native Girl in Decamere" is an excellent Shakespearean sonnet, and "A Lady Asks Me" is an attempt at Skeltonic meter, based on Guido Cavalcanti's poem of the same title. Poems from this period also include paraphrases or translations of other Cavalcanti poems, as well as poems by Gabriele D'Annunzio, Stéphane Mallarmé, Luisde Góngora, and Pierre Jean Jouve.

Fraser's writing during the years of 1945-1959 includes some of his richest, most sensuously romantic verse, which often rises to a height of emotional precision and effectiveness rarely achieved in Fraser's other work. Sometimes, though, the writing during his middle years is merely prosaic: in "The Time," he observes that the modern world has "So many things to die for—and death / Is not enough, unless you die / For exactly the right slogan"; "To a Lady"—one of three poems in *The Traveller Has Regrets and Other Poems* (1948) that was not included when the volume was republished in Japan as *Leaves Without a Tree* (1953)—is simply mawkish: "beauty" catches another person by the throat as a hook with a worm on it catches a fish.

In 1959 Fraser became lecturer in English at University College, Leicester (now the University of Leicester); in 1964 he was made a reader in modern English literature and, later, reader in poetry. Except for the academic year 1963-1964, when he was visiting professor at the University of Rochester in the United States, he taught at Leicester until his death in 1980. As a result of the demands that teaching made on his time, his production of verse was radically reduced; he observed that he was increasingly occupied with the writing of criticism and by "teaching students to appreciate great poetry," both activities the result of economic necessity. During these years, he noted, he had only one new poem published a year. He continued translating verse throughout these last years, though, and contributed to the BBC's Third Programme 1966 series that presented versions of Dante's *Inferno* (published in 1966) and *Paradiso*. He suffered a heart attack in 1974 and partially retired in 1979, continuing working with his graduate students till his death on 3 January 1980.

There was a brief resurgence of poetry writing in the late 1960s. *Conditions: Selected Recent Poetry*

(1969), a group of twenty poems, was the only volume published between 1960 and 1981; only a few more than that number were published but not collected until after his death. These later poems capture the tempered, meditative, philosophic quality of his maturity, which contrasts with the characteristically youthful concerns of the earlier verse.

As with the earlier poetry, a number of the later poems are occasional: some are for W. H. Auden, William Empson, George Barker, and family members; another is a "Lenten Meditation"; two others deal with Ireland and racial struggles in Leicester; "Instead of an Elegy," for John F. Kennedy, was written during 1963-1964, when Fraser taught in the United States. "Memories of Swansea" is a nostalgic reminiscence of a stay in Vernon Watkins's seaside home in Wales with Dylan Thomas and others. The more memorable later poems, however, are less concerned with specific times and places and more with Fraser's gentle philosophical perspective. "Speech of a Sufferer" dramatizes a visit from Death. "On the Persistence of Humanity" is especially good in its assertion that he wants the "bloody human race" to continue despite wars and failures. "Yin and Yang: A Dialogue," a dialectical tug-of-war between a man and woman, and "The Insane Philosophers," a satiric defense of the romantic superiority of love and children playing over tendentious intellectualizing about life, are similarly effective.

These later poems contain memorable moments; even if the verse rarely reaches the grandness of major poets' work, individual lines stand up with the best of them. "Autumnal Elegy," for example, includes these lines: "The poet pulls his scarf of commonplaces / around his chilly fate." "A Lesson in Humanity for the Children, out of Aristotle's 'Poetics,'" Fraser's poetic effort to improve race relations, observes that "We live in little tribes / Protecting our territory / And our pecking orders." A number of these more quotable late poems deal with the nature of poetry itself; "The Poem," for example, compares writing poetry with making love, in both cases as old age affects them. "Make Me an Offer," one of Fraser's last poems, compares writing poetry to a clearance sale in a store, with "only a few days" left to pick up certain bargains. In all of these late poems Fraser's controlled, gentle voice advocates moderation and civilized efforts to remain human in the best sense, and, above all, expresses an awareness of poetry's place in such efforts. "The nature of a thing may not be altered / By how we fiddle with linguistic structures," he says in "Epistle to a Young Poet"; for "when the pressures heap up all together / And we've this sense of knowing that we never / could say," there remains a sense of "There's something, and I feel it."

Ian Fletcher and John Lucas, in the introduction to the posthumous collection of Fraser's poems, astutely observed that Fraser's best poems, regardless of category or topic, "have a sweetness of regard for subject and auditor that is the hallmark of a most civilized man. This is not the same as sentimentality." At his best Fraser's wit, precision of image, and warmth of feeling enabled him to write highly readable verse of a most affecting kind, a kind of "reasonable speech," as Michael Alexander called it in his review of the posthumous collection. Though Fraser the poet did not think deeply, he most assuredly felt deeply, and his poetry stands as a monument to the civilized practice of traditional English poetics.

References:

Michael Alexander, "The Poems of G. S. Fraser," *Agenda*, 19, no. 4 / 20, no. 1 (Winter-Spring 1982): 115-117;

Bernard Bergonzi, "The Poetry of G. S. Fraser," *Critical Quarterly*, 24 (Spring 1982): 19-24;

"A Critic's Harvest," *Times Literary Supplement*, 10 April 1959, p. 210;

Babette Deutsch, *Poetry in Our Time* (New York: Holt, 1952; revised and enlarged edition, Garden City: Doubleday, 1963), pp. 68, 369, 381, 414;

Denis Donaghue, "The Common Pursuit," *New Statesman*, 5 January 1979, pp. 17-18;

Robert Hewison, *Under Siege: Literary Life in London 1939-45* (London: Weidenfeld & Nicolson, 1977; New York: Oxford University Press, 1977), pp. 111-122, 133, 162-163, 185;

Norman MacCaig, "No Niggling," *Listener*, 19 January 1978, pp. 93-94;

"The Note of Romance," *Times Literary Supplement*, 30 December 1944, p. 634;

Giles Romilly, "The Desert," *New Statesman and Nation*, 2 April 1948, p. 330;

Alan Ross, *Poetry 1945-1950* (London: Longmans, Green for the British Council, 1951);

Robin Skelton, *The Poetic Pattern* (London: Routledge & Kegan Paul, 1956), pp. 17-24;

Stephen Spender, "Four Poets," *New Statesman and Nation*, 13 January 1945, pp. 29-30.

Geoffrey Grigson
(2 March 1905-   )

Douglas Loney
University of Victoria

SELECTED BOOKS: *Several Observations: Thirty-Five Poems* (London: Cresset, 1939);

Under the Cliff and Other Poems (London: Routledge, 1943);

Henry Moore (Harmondsworth: Penguin, 1943);

Wild Flowers in Britain (London: Collins, 1944);

The Isles of Scilly and Other Poems (London: Routledge, 1946);

Samuel Palmer: The Visionary Years (London: Kegan Paul, 1947);

The Harp of Aeolus and Other Essays on Art, Literature, and Nature (London: Routledge, 1948);

An English Farmhouse and Its Neighbourhood (London: Parrish, 1948);

The Scilly Isles (London: Elek, 1948; revised edition, London: Duckworth, 1977);

Places of the Mind (London: Routledge & Kegan Paul, 1949);

The Crest on the Silver: An Autobiography (London: Cresset, 1950);

Flowers of the Meadow (Harmondsworth: Penguin, 1950);

Wessex (London: Collins, 1951);

A Master of Our Time: A Study of Wyndham Lewis (London: Methuen, 1951);

Essays from the Air (London: Routledge & Kegan Paul, 1951);

West Country (London: Collins, 1951);

Gardenage; or, The Plants of Ninhursaga (London: Routledge & Kegan Paul, 1952);

Legenda Suecana: Twenty-Odd Poems (N.p.: Privately printed, 1953);

The Female Form in Painting, by Grigson and Jean Cassou (London: Thames & Hudson, 1953; New York: Harcourt, Brace, 1953);

Freedom of the Parish (London: Phoenix House, 1954);

Gerard Manley Hopkins (London: Longmans, Green, 1955; revised, 1962);

The Englishman's Flora (London: Phoenix House, 1955);

English Drawing from Samuel Cooper to Gwen John (London: Thames & Hudson, 1955);

The Shell Guide to Flowers of the Countryside (London:

Geoffrey Grigson

Phoenix House, 1955); republished in *The Shell Nature Book* (1964);

Jean Baptiste Camille Corot (New York: Metropolitan Museum of Art, 1956);

Painted Caves (London: Phoenix House, 1957);

England (London: Thames & Hudson, 1957; New York: Studio, 1958);

Fossils, Insects, and Reptiles (London: Phoenix House, 1957); republished in *The Shell Nature Book* (1964);

The Wiltshire Book (London: Thames & Hudson, 1957);

The Shell Guide to Trees and Shrubs (London: Phoenix House, 1958); republished in *The Shell Nature Book* (1964);

English Villages in Colour (London: Batsford, 1958);

Looking and Finding and Collecting and Reading and Investigating and Much Else (London: Phoenix House, 1958; revised edition, London: Baker, 1970);

The Shell Guide to Wild Life (London: Phoenix House, 1959); republished in *The Shell Nature Book* (1964);

A Herbal of All Sorts (London: Phoenix House, 1959; New York: Macmillan, 1959);

English Excursions (London: Country Life, 1960);

Christopher Smart (London: Longmans, Green, 1961);

The Shell Country Book, by Grigson and others (London: Phoenix House, 1962);

The Collected Poems of Geoffrey Grigson: 1924-1962 (London: Phoenix House, 1963);

The Shell Book of Roads (London: Ebury Press, 1964);

Shapes and Stories: A Book about Pictures, by Grigson and Jane Grigson (London: Baker, 1964; New York: Vanguard, 1965);

The Shell Nature Book, by Grigson and others (London: Phoenix House, 1964);

The Shell Country Alphabet (London: Joseph, 1966);

Shapes and Adventures, by Grigson and Jane Grigson (London: Marshbank, 1967); republished as *More Shapes and Stories: A Book about Pictures* (New York: Vanguard, 1967);

A Skull in Salop and Other Poems (London: Macmillan, 1967; Chester Springs, Pa.: Dufour, 1969);

Ingestion of Ice-Cream and Other Poems (London: Macmillan, 1969);

Shapes and People: A Book about Pictures (London: Baker, 1969; New York: Vanguard, 1969);

Poems and Poets (London: Macmillan, 1969; Chester Springs, Pa.: Dufour, 1969);

Notes from an Odd Country (London: Macmillan, 1970);

Discoveries of Bones and Stones and Other Poems (London: Macmillan, 1971);

Sad Grave of an Imperial Mongoose (London: Macmillan, 1973);

Shapes and Creatures: A Book about Pictures (London: Black, 1973);

The First Folio (London: Poem-of-the-Month Club, 1973);

Angles and Circles and Other Poems (London: Gollancz, 1974);

The Contrary View: Glimpses of Fudge and Gold (London: Macmillan, 1974; Totowa, N.J.: Rowman & Littlefield, 1974);

A Dictionary of English Plant Names and Some Products of Plants (London: Allen Lane, 1974);

Britain Observed: The Landscape Through Artists' Eyes (London: Phaidon, 1975);

The Goddess of Love: The Birth, Triumph, Death, and Return of Aphrodite (London: Constable, 1976;

New York: Stein & Day, 1977);

The Fiesta and Other Poems (London: Secker & Warburg, 1978);

History of Him (London: Secker & Warburg, 1980);

Collected Poems: 1963-1980 (London: Allison & Busby, 1982);

Blessings, Kicks and Curses (London: Allison & Busby, 1982);

The Private Art (London: Allison & Busby, 1982).

OTHER: *The Year's Poetry*, edited by Grigson and others (London: John Lane, 1934);

The Arts Today, edited by Grigson (London: John Lane, 1935);

The Year's Poetry 1937-38, edited by Grigson and Denys Kilham Roberts (London: John Lane, 1938);

New Verse: An Anthology, edited by Grigson (London: Faber & Faber, 1939);

The Journals of George Sturt, edited by Grigson (London: Cresset, 1941);

The Romantics: An Anthology, edited by Grigson (London: Routledge, 1942; Cleveland: World, 1962);

Visionary Poems and Passages; or, The Poet's Eye, edited by Grigson (London: Muller, 1944);

The Mint: A Miscellany of Literature, Art, and Criticism, 2 volumes, edited by Grigson (London: Routledge & Kegan Paul, 1946-1948);

Before the Romantics: An Anthology of the Enlightenment, edited by Grigson (London: Routledge, 1946);

Poems of John Clare's Madness, edited by Grigson (London: Routledge & Kegan Paul, 1949);

Poetry of the Present: An Anthology of the Thirties and After, edited by Grigson (London: Phoenix House, 1949);

Selected Poems of William Barnes 1800-1866, edited by Grigson (London: Routledge & Kegan Paul, 1950; Cambridge: Harvard University Press, 1950);

John Clare, *Selected Poems*, edited by Grigson (London: Routledge & Kegan Paul, 1950);

John Dryden, *Selected Poems*, edited by Grigson (London: Grey Walls, 1950);

George Crabbe, *Poems*, edited by Grigson (London: Grey Walls, 1950);

The Victorians: An Anthology, edited by Grigson (London: Routledge & Kegan Paul, 1950);

Robert John Thornton, *Temple of Flora*, edited by Grigson (London: Collins, 1951);

Samuel Taylor Coleridge, *Poems*, edited by Grigson (London: Grey Walls, 1951);

About Britain, 13 volumes, edited by Grigson (London: Collins, 1951);

People, Places and Things, 4 volumes, edited by Grigson and Charles Harvard Gibbs-Smith (London: Grosvenor Press, 1954; New York: Hawthorn Press, 1954-1957);

Art Treasures of the British Museum, edited by Grigson (London: Thames & Hudson, 1957; New York: Abrams, 1957);

The Three Kings, edited by Grigson (Bedford: Gordon Fraser, 1958);

Country Poems, edited by Grigson (London: Hulton, 1959);

The Cherry Tree: A Collection of Poems, edited by Grigson (London: Phoenix House, 1959; New York: Vanguard Press, 1959);

Samuel Palmer's Valley of Vision, edited, with introduction and notes, by Grigson (London: Phoenix House, 1960);

Poets in their Pride, edited by Grigson (London: Phoenix House, 1962; New York: Basic Books, 1964);

The Concise Encyclopaedia of Modern World Literature, edited by Grigson (London: Hutchinson, 1963; New York: Hawthorn, 1963; revised edition, London: Hutchinson, 1970; New York: Hawthorn, 1971);

O Rare Mankind!: A Short Collection of Great Prose, edited by Grigson (London: Phoenix House, 1963);

Walter Savage Landor, *Poems*, edited by Grigson (London: Centaur Press, 1964; Carbondale: Southern Illinois University Press, 1965);

The English Year: From Diaries and Letters, edited by Grigson (London & New York: Oxford University Press, 1967);

A Choice of William Morris's Verse, edited by Grigson (London: Faber & Faber, 1969);

A Choice of Thomas Hardy's Poems, edited by Grigson (London: Macmillan, 1969);

A Choice of Robert Southey's Verse, edited by Grigson (London: Faber & Faber, 1970);

Pennethorne Hughes, *Thirty-Eight Poems*, edited by Grigson (London: Baker, 1970);

Rainbows, Fleas, and Flowers, edited by Grigson (London: Baker, 1971);

Unrespectable Verse, edited by Grigson (London: Allen Lane, 1971);

The Faber Book of Popular Verse, edited by Grigson (London: Faber & Faber, 1971); republished as *The Gambit Book of Popular Verse* (Boston: Gambit, 1971);

The Faber Book of Love Poems, edited by Grigson (London: Faber & Faber, 1973);

Poet to Poet: Charles Cotton, edited by Grigson (Harmondsworth: Penguin, 1975);

The Penguin Book of Ballads, edited by Grigson (Harmondsworth: Penguin, 1975);

The Faber Book of Epigrams and Epitaphs, edited by Grigson (London: Faber & Faber, 1977);

The Faber Book of Nonsense Verse, edited by Grigson (London: Faber & Faber, 1979);

The Oxford Book of Satirical Verse, edited by Grigson (London: Oxford University Press, 1980);

The Faber Book of Poems and Places (London: Faber & Faber, 1980).

Although he is the author of more than a dozen volumes of poetry, Geoffrey Grigson is better known for his work as a collector, editor, and critic of the works of other men of letters and the arts. This reputation as a literary entrepreneur dates from 1933, the year in which he founded *New Verse*, a highly influential poetry magazine which published early poems by W. H. Auden, Louis MacNeice, Stephen Spender, and Dylan Thomas, among a great many others. Grigson has written, edited, or contributed to scores of books on art, literature, and nature (some of these for children), has edited the works of poets from John Dryden to John Clare, and has compiled many anthologies of poetry. His often acerbic and polemical writings on art and literature have appeared in many important journals and periodicals, and several collections of his criticism have been published.

Grigson was born the youngest of seven sons to Mary Beatrice Boldero Grigson, third wife of Canon William Shuckforth Grigson, in the vicarage of Pelynt, Cornwall, when his father was fifty-nine years old. The fact of his father's rather advanced age seems to have troubled Grigson; in his autobiography, *The Crest on the Silver* (1950), he remarks wryly that he was born at the time when he "should have been thirty or thirty-five years old," and that he and his father had known but little of each other "across the unnatural gap of years." His mother he describes as having been "shrewd and a little grim," and with "no great love, as she admitted herself, for children."

Perhaps in compensation for the coolness of his childhood relationship with his natural mother, Grigson adopted a surrogate named Bessie, an unlettered but wise and clever woman of the village, of whom Grigson has written: "She could stare, like Gerard Manley Hopkins, at a piece of glass in the gravel, or be delighted with the shine which a plow puts upon a turned furrow." With Bessie, Grigson shared a love of Cornish landscapes, and the garden of Pelynt vicarage in particular, which could not be shared with his natural mother and which was to become the deepest foundation stone of his eclectic, observing, curious poetry. Already in the vicarage garden the young Grigson had discovered that the nature which he so loved could be ordered by a careful and patient art and so could achieve a significance reaching beyond its own borders: "This garden with its varying levels, its free-stone walls and its waterfall, provided the symbolic miniatures, the first editions of every possible adventure and ambition."

The years between 1910 and 1923, the years of preparatory and public schools, were for Grigson a "long purgatory," a progress "across a salt and dry desert . . . altogether unwatered by love." In the intervals between school terms, three times in each year, he would return to his sanctuary in Cornwall, to fishing and bird nesting, searching out rare plants, digging for flints in barrows and searching public records as an accomplished amateur historian and archaeologist. Near the end of his schooling at St. John's, Leatherhead, Grigson wrote antiquarian articles for the *Western Morning News* and also began to write poetry.

After a year spent "drifting," in 1924 Grigson entered St. Edmund Hall, Oxford. During his years there he had no real appetite for theater or art, little for music or even for literature, and none for scholarship; he writes: "The blue eggs of the wild duck, the adder alongside the orpine, the snoring owl, the sea-trout and the salmon slipping up out of the tide into the spate . . . all interested me more deeply (and I was right for no doubt the wrong causes) than the dry business of writing an essay on Wordsworth's ideas of nature."

Grigson brought with him to Oxford an intense appreciation of the poetry of Herbert, Coleridge, and Hopkins, for the vigor of their poetic language and their stylistic discipline, for their romantic questing, for their insistence (especially Hopkins's) on the immediate and the particular, on nature, and on nature's reflection of something rather more elusive, something of the spirit. Although W. H. Auden and Louis MacNeice were at Oxford during Grigson's years there, he did not know them; he disliked MacNeice's poetry for its too exotic flavor and had not yet begun to appreciate Auden's. Ultimately, he settled upon T. S. Eliot's work as a poetic touchstone, though he later remarked that he would have been wiser to have "balanced Hardy against . . . the urbanism and the alien quality" of Eliot's verse, that Hardy's rural accents, a counterpoise to Eliot's brittle sophistica-

tion, would have prevented him from being "traitor to the garden and the valley." It was, in fact, when he recognized such a balance in W. H. Auden's poetry that Grigson came to admire it and its author: "His mineshafts and mineral railways, his deserted waterwheels, his buzzards, his windy headlands were properties not alien at all."

After Oxford, Grigson decided (rather by default) on journalism as a means of making a living. Turned down by the *London Mercury*, he began instead at the Fleet Street offices of the *Yorkshire Post* in 1928, writing short articles and book reviews. The next year he left that paper for work on the *Morning Post* (where he went on to become literary editor), and married an American, Frances Galt.

In 1933, Grigson founded the avant-garde *New Verse*, in which he both published the works of the young poets whose various strands of modernism he by then admired and savaged his literary enemies, Edith Sitwell chief among them. Some time after the magazine's demise, Grigson repented of some of the critical violence of *New Verse*, calling it "a malignant egg . . . which was hatched with some innocence," and then defining that "innocence": "I had not grown up enough . . . to realize that the neck of a beheaded fool grows three more foolish heads. The fun and slaughter now make me, if I recall them, rather sick." Although *New Verse* boasted a circulation of only one thousand and was published only between 1933 and 1939, it made in its brief life an important contribution to letters, more perhaps in providing a forum for the works of some of England's finest young poets between the wars than for Grigson's attacks upon critics and authors who dared to disagree with him.

In 1937, Grigson's wife died soon after the birth of a daughter, the *Morning Post* closed, and Grigson was left to drift once more. He became disenchanted with *New Verse* in its last days and had the additional burden of providing care for his infant daughter. Out of this difficult time came Grigson's first book of poetry, *Several Observations* (1939).

Several Observations was dedicated to Grigson's second wife, Berta ("Bertschy") Kunert, the daughter of an Austrian major, whom he married in 1938. The title is indicative both of Grigson's eclecticism and of his insistence upon looking at the things around him, looking long and intently at even the simplest of poetic subjects, in order to be able to share with his reader a true perspective upon some several aspects of life. He commented later, "I took to writing poems from which I tried to cut away the open statement, or rather to shut the statement within the experience and the enjoyment of the senses." This principle operates in "The Calm Sunshine of the Heart," which is typical of *Several Observations* in that the speaker's perceptions are expressed simply in fragments of description, mortared with commas and colons. He suggests neither focus nor relationship among the things observed: the emphasis falls squarely on the process of observation. What the reader might expect to be central to the poem—the poet's joining of these several things which together make up "the calm sunshine of the heart"—occurs only in a final adverbial phrase:

> and the burdock leaves
> Curl over an ochre stone
>
> In the calm sunshine of the heart.

In the stripping away of false or irrelevant associations from his subjects, Grigson very often in *Several Observations* strips away the connectives and signals of relationship and order upon which the reader depends to determine the poem's focus.

Grigson and his wife left Nazi-occupied Austria under the threat of imminent war in September 1938. When war did in fact break out a year later, the Grigsons were established in England once more. Grigson suspended work on a biography of Samuel Palmer to serve in the BBC monitoring department at Evesham, auditing domestic, enemy, and allied broadcasting. Grigson so hated the experience that in his description of it he deliberately lapses into the terminology of the schools which he had so loathed: the monitors become the "Third Form," and their superior the "Form Master." The ordeal ended in March of 1942: Grigson left Evesham to work on "talks" for the BBC West Region at Bristol. The reassignment allowed him to wander through his beloved Cornwall again, albeit in a sound-recording car and on war duty. At war's end, he took his family to the Wiltshire farm which has been his permanent home ever since.

Two volumes of poetry came out of the war for Grigson: *Under the Cliff and Other Poems* (1943) and *The Isles of Scilly and Other Poems* (1946). The wartime composition of these two books of poems is not much reflected in the subject matter; in fact, both demonstrate Grigson's growing consciousness of himself as a member of the international community of poets: there are several translations from Rilke (made in defiance of the prevailing British revulsion against all things German), and allusions to Eliot, Auden, Blake, and Pound. "Oh, in the

Hollow Station" (*The Isles of Scilly*) very clearly invokes Ezra Pound's imagist poem "In a Station of the Metro": "The apparition of these faces in the crowd;/Petals on a wet, black bough." But where Pound had imposed the image's interpretation upon the reader, Grigson is true to his precept of shutting the statement within the experience:

> Oh, in the hollow station, just at dark,
> The voice of moving men, and all
> The melancholy uneasiness of going,
> Arrivals in an alien dark.

In the third line, Grigson disrupts the regular iambic meter, first with the languid "melancholy," then with the choppy rhythm of "uneasiness." The effect of the metrical disruption is to reinforce the sentence's explicit meaning. The conclusion of Grigson's brief observation describes a "young mother holding by the wall/Her heavy and clear-headed child." By virtue of the speaker's "stare" and the nimbus conferred upon the scene by a signalman's "round-eyed yellow lamp," and by application of the adjective "clear-headed," mother and child become Madonna and Child: but the analogy remains implicit only; Grigson manages not to convey an insistence (like Pound's) upon the one way of seeing the image, and his poem is the stronger for it.

One poem at least from *Under the Cliff* demonstrates something of the war's effect upon Grigson's consciousness. It is "Praise," a translation from Rilke which defines the poet's task as that of identifying and celebrating the gracious aspects of life in the face of the ungracious, the perverse, and the ugly. To the question "But the murderous and monstrous—/How endure it and submit?," the poet's persona responds simply, "I praise." Concerning those elements of life which are worthy of such praise, Grigson has said that "graces enter and exist in living; they start up, vanish, and are seen again in glimpses. It is sentimental treason to suppose that we can be anaesthetized or satisfied by these graces, but the grand treason, realizing the constancy of the bad and the worst, is not as well to admit and celebrate and be thankful for these consolatory graces, or viaticum." The fact of an ugly war cannot be wished away, not even in poetry, but praise of life's graces is at least some consolation.

In the early 1950s, Grigson was at work on many literary projects, and the flow of books on the English countryside and flora, art and literature which had begun in the previous decade increased greatly in volume. In 1953, *Legenda Suecana*, a cycle of love lyrics, was printed privately for Grigson.

(The poems were included in the 1963 *Collected Poems* under the title "Legenda.") Grigson is reticent concerning how these poems of love came to be written (and indeed refuses to add any information to that of his autobiography published in 1950): in an interview in December 1982, he would say of *Legenda* only that he did not at all agree with the many critics who have judged these poems to be his best work, that he is conscious of their distinctly seventeenth-century ambience, and that the models of Sydney and George Herbert must certainly have influenced him in their composition. The cycle describes the course of love between a man and a much younger woman, the fears and delights of such a fragile relationship, the inevitable parting, and at last his recognition that it is the finished shape of the affair, including its close, which renders it a legend and thus a part of the permanent mythology of their lives. "The Room," the fourth of *Legenda*'s twenty-five poems, begins with the lover's attempt to describe his beloved. He discovers that the difficulty is to know how or where to begin, and reasons that he should begin with a room which may contain her:

> With some room
> That lacks you where I wait
> And then—you enter.

He discovers that the setting—which he had hoped might define her—"contracts" in her, in much the same way that Donne found the world contracted in himself and his mistress under the "unruly sun." The man in Grigson's poem recognizes that the woman's body is itself the only "room" which can adequately contain her—and, even so, this discovery is at best only a partial truth:

> You live through all your sweet
> Full-breasted slender body,
> That is true,
> And yet this strong sweet body's
> Not the half or whole of you.

A *Times Literary Supplement* reviewer admired *Legenda Suecana*'s eloquent expression of "vulnerability, shyness . . . a self-surrender touching in this otherwise so often aggressive and resentful poet, and a respect for the identity and needs of the other person rare and refreshing—improbably civilized—in the love poem at any time." "The Room" is an expression of this "rare and refreshing" respect between lover and beloved, and it strikes a pleasing balance between lightness and tenderness of tone, and between verbal economy and discipline.

A later poem in the *Legenda Suecana* cycle, "The Paper in the Rain," takes for its subject the beginning of the end of the relationship: the title refers to the speaker's suggestion that he should allow the rain to smudge this, perhaps the last, poem to his beloved. He describes his self-pity with some bitterness, but recognizes wryly that when the pain goes, the woman will be gone as well; recognizes that the present pain of their love's end is to be preferred to the absence of pain with the absence of love; remarks laconically,

> I'm not compelled
> To live, that's true.
> But living—is a human habit
> All the same.

"A human habit" fairly indicates the manner of *Legenda Suecana*: the most familiar of all patterns of relationship between man and woman is set out for this thousandth time in a fresh, compassionate, ironically self-conscious and very tender and loving cycle of poems.

After *Legenda Suecana*, the flow of books written or collected or edited or touched in some way by Grigson continued unabated, but no more poetry was published until *The Collected Poems of Geoffrey Grigson: 1924-1962* in 1963, which includes only a handful of verses composed after the *Legenda Suecana* cycle. During this period, Grigson's second marriage ended in divorce, and he married Jane McIntyre, who has been variously an editorial assistant, a translator, and a writer of articles and books on cooking, and has collaborated with her husband on several books for children. *A Skull in Salop and Other Poems* (1967) and *Ingestion of Ice-Cream and Other Poems* (1969) were Grigson's first new publications of poetry in more than twenty years.

Grigson's poetry of the late 1960s is of mixed tones: the compelling voice and self-effacing wit of *Legenda Suecana* infuses some of the poems with life and beauty, but old bitterness or unexamined prejudice surfaces in others. The title poem of *A Skull in Salop* is a witty celebration of being alive: the speaker, who has squatted in a churchyard to discharge the "needs of nature," discovers a skull under his hand:

> I rise relieved, though that's
> not quite the word; and stand; and see
> azured extents below again,
> feeling the cool of air.

Dust jacket for Grigson's 1963 book, which includes only a few poems written after 1953

In his ironic apology for punning on "relieved," Grigson discards some of his accustomed reserve and speaks warmly and personally. But in a poem like "Yahoos: A Variation, and Reply," in which he lightly considers some of the "pros and cons" of humanity, the humor darkens, and the voice is impersonal: it considers, and weighs, and finds wanting, and labels offenders. In spite of his tentative expression of affection for his subject—"I think I love the human race"—Grigson's judgments seem harsh and arbitrary by the very lightness with which, ironically, he dismisses them: "True it is by me's and you's/Are burnt both Vietnamese and Jews."

Discoveries of Bones and Stones and Other Poems, published in 1971, was awarded the Duff Cooper Memorial Prize. In a prefatory note to the volume, Grigson comments on that old quality of observation in his poetry: "It isn't that I trust or celebrate objects. . . . Objects are mean, or nothing; yet can all the same, if they are discovered by the right objectifier, elicit and exert benediction." His poetic voice is by now more assured both in its tender and its comic tones. The theme of "Dead Poets: Recalling Them in November" is, again, mutability; but here

it is expressed with great compassion for those (himself included) who have been or will be taken away, while it retains a rigorous discipline over sentiment and the language of sentiment. The formal and conventional overstatement—"It is beyond bearing that you are dead"—is quickly emended to the more honest and humble "No, I bear it most days too easily." The reader of *Discoveries of Bones and Stones* cannot help but acknowledge that, even with the welcome warmth of this more personal voice, Grigson has decidedly not yielded to what he calls "the worst temptation," "to abandon everything for looseness, or easiness, untautened, unexquisite in means."

The subjects of *Sad Grave of an Imperial Mongoose* (1973) are as various as ever, and observation is still the significant poetic operation. In this volume of poetry and those which follow, Grigson is perhaps a little more preoccupied than formerly with the fact of advancing age and the transitory goodness of good things: the wit and humor remain, but there is rather more attention paid to the speaker's self-consciously gloomy consideration of his own failing years. "Observation in November" records the discovery of a lately used condom

("French letter") impaled on barbed wire next to a red-berried bush. The speaker's musings on the juxtaposition of "seeds" is twice interrupted, once when he anticipates an objection from his audience—

> Don't cosmically
> Sentimentalize
> You urge, about pale human seed
> Upon a rusted spike at this
> Cold end of November.

—and then again by his own further observation:

> But then, I must report,
> From higher trees suspended, en-
> filading berries, wire and letter,
> My cold eye took in a vegetable
> Flow of grey, all curled and grey,
> The shade exactly of my head
> And of this last cold overcast
> November day.

Grigson the naturalist knows the name of this "vegetable flow of grey" to be "Old Man's Beard": that name, with its reminder of his own advancing age, his own grayness and the grayness of the dying year, puts the speaker into an ill temper (comically described in the very epithets used to dispel it) against this fresh reminder of the inevitability of decay.

A preoccupation with the theme of mutability marks Grigson's next volume of poetry, *Angles and Circles and Other Poems* (1974), as well. The death of W. H. Auden, who had been Grigson's close friend for more than thirty years, is one occasion in which the poet takes up the theme again. Although his eulogy "To Wystan Auden" rings unmistakably with sincere love and admiration for "living's healer, loving's / Magician, for all of these years / The imposer of blessings," the words remain merely the language of eulogy, are not illuminated by example of accomplishment, or even by allusion to Auden's own words. Without such fixing of the laudatory adjectives to vivid images of the greatness celebrated, Grigson's grief and love seem at last merely conventional: they have not suffered the discipline which might have translated them into art. As a result, the poem's conclusion—that the great poet who is celebrated will live on in his poetry—seems a stale, unexamined, conventional posture.

Much more convincing is the same volume's "Grace Acts of Ourselves," where human and natural graces are made to confront the transience of life:

> Of grace acts of ourselves, of e.g. temples if in
> Ruins on red rock, and gods (the better ones)
> If with good sense now deposed, carvings
> In cliffs of Buddha, books of hours . . .
> . . . fictions—all fictions,
> Yes—in which is
> What we name our spirit . . .
> . . . .
> . . . having of all these
> Consolatory things so little sensed, is it—
> Come clean on this, my few, few friends
> Consoling that on dying soon our
> Livingness depends?

The suggestion that the fleetingness of life makes it sweet is made tentative by expressing it as a question, but the implicit assertion is supported by its strategic position: the whole thought of the poem is in fact suspended until the final line is read out. There is none of that indirectness or privacy of allusion which too often marks Grigson's reflections upon matters of the spirit of man—even his contention that religious accomplishments should more properly be considered gracious fictions, and that their goodness derives from good intentions rather than a good foundation in reality, is set out in the skillfully compressed images and comments within the poem's first few lines.

From his youth, Grigson had been not at all religious, preferring fishing to attendance at divine service in his father's church, and (as he admits) generally judging the Christian faith by the lives of some rather poor adherents to it. A scattering of verses on religious or spiritual themes exists in the volumes of poetry already considered, but in the 1978 collection, *The Fiesta and Other Poems*, Grigson's musings on the possibility of faith and the meaning potential in faith assume an unwonted prominence. "West Window" considers what seems to be the death of some few consolations of faith, as a priest looks to the stained glass window in the west wall of his church:

> Consolations were: Christ, Heaven,
> . . . .
> . . . glow of these
> Through minds stained with the bright
> Salts of cobalt, copper, iron. *And now—*
> *What now*, whispers to himself upon
> His knees the priest, *now time hurts me,*
> *Home walks away, and deserts me,*
> *And everything is beast?*

There are no answers to these questions: the window faces west toward the land of the dead and of the setting sun, the minerals used to pigment the molten glass have stained the minds of those who depended upon the reality of the "fictions" depicted there, and the priest whispers only to himself. In "Conversation with a Clerical Father," Grigson laments that the man whom he had once described as "sincerely religious" had been unable in the last moments of his life (because of the weakness of flesh and mind) to console himself with thought of heaven:

> Only your deep
> Unconsciousness then filled
> The room. No thoughts,
> You could not think at all,
> About that better land,
> My God, *that land*, you had
> Heralded to others
> Dying in their bed.

The speaker's admonition to the living to enjoy the present life and land, "there being no/Better land," is bitterly drawn from the experience of observing a death not sweetened by the benedictions bestowed during a life.

> And if you like, in being
> Thankful—though to whom?—
> Sink to an old attitude upon your knees.

Prayer is at last a graceful act only in that it is an old attitude (to which, indeed, one must now "sink"): like the priest before the west window, the readers of "Conversation" are enjoined to whisper only to themselves.

The poetry of *History of Him* (1980) is as difficult to categorize as that of any of the earlier volumes: Grigson's subjects still range from brief observations of sky or flower to memories of youth and travels and moments of love, to sour epigrams about those who dare to criticize his work. The vigor of his observation of life is as fresh as ever. Two fine poems, in which Grigson ponders the attitude appropriate to the latter days of life, are named for the last two months of the year: "His November" and "December." The first of these is a serene depiction of the jumble of sights and sounds, dreams and memories which fill the consciousness in the late days of life—"a muddle of old delights"; and, although these "late days project no fine/Materials for dreams ahead," old age is redeemed by the "graces" of experience which are still available "as long/As sense remains." But "December" is a much darker poem, less sure of an ultimate benediction for life:

> This brown cloud-cliff ends
> And light escapes, and spreads
> Goldleaf on this lower morning land
> And so, once they would have
> Said, and so . . .
>
> So, all I can say, so,
> For this while, this meaningless
> Sense of ending ends.

What would for another man and another time have been a declaration of faith, or hope, or anticipation (Grigson has admired the line from Herbert which says that death is "but a chair") is elided here. The light spilling out of the clouds and gilding the grim December landscape reminds him of the conventional comforts which can bring beauty and peace to "a meaningless/Sense of ending ends."

Grigson's late poetry is like the early in that it still reflects his eclectic fascination with "poets, towns, places unfairly neglected. Honesty and discipline of style in poetry. . . . Paintings suggestive of the unattainable Eden. Archaelogy and its dream of the different life. The structures of limestone scenery." After *Legenda Suecana*, Grigson seems readier to make explicit judgments within his verse, to write of love and human relations with more candor, sympathy, and sensitivity. He displays no more tolerance than formerly for incompetent critics, and considers it an advantage of his accumulated experience that he can

> the more easily recognize
> Squirming in his primal dirt
> Another verse-reviewing squirt.

Although he may find it impossible to affirm any lasting reality beyond that which his senses reveal, he continues to celebrate the fleeting graces which he observes in the objects and events surrounding him. Grigson's philosophy of poetry remains unchanged from the very early days: "Report well, begin with objects and events; a stone begets vision, and there's nothing to tell except truth, which 'can never be told so as to be understood and not be believed,' and there is no other way of telling it."

References:

Review of *Ingestion of Ice-Cream and Other Poems* and

A Choice of William Morris's Verse, *Times Literary Supplement*, 31 July 1969, pp. 845-846;

Review of *The Collected Poems of Geoffrey Grigson, 1924-1962*, *Times Literary Supplement*, 12 December 1963, p. 1030;

Francis Scarfe, *Auden and After* (London: Routledge, 1942).

Papers:

The British Museum and Birmingham University Library have collections of Grigson's papers.

Thom Gunn
(29 August 1929-   )

Blake Morrison

SELECTED BOOKS: *Fighting Terms* (Oxford: Fantasy Press, 1954; revised edition, New York: Hawk's Well Press, 1958; London: Faber & Faber, 1962);

The Sense of Movement (London: Faber & Faber, 1957; Chicago: Chicago University Press, 1959);

My Sad Captains (London: Faber & Faber, 1961; Chicago: University of Chicago Press, 1961);

Selected Poems, by Gunn and Ted Hughes (London: Faber & Faber, 1962);

Positives (London: Faber & Faber, 1966; Chicago: University of Chicago Press, 1967);

Touch (London: Faber & Faber, 1967; Chicago: University of Chicago Press, 1968);

Poems 1950-1966: A Selection (London: Faber & Faber, 1969);

Moly (London: Faber & Faber, 1971); republished with *My Sad Captains* (New York: Farrar, Straus, 1973);

Jack Straw's Castle (London: Faber & Faber, 1976; New York: Farrar, Straus, 1976);

Selected Poems 1950-75 (London: Faber & Faber, 1979; New York: Farrar, Straus & Giroux, 1979);

The Passages of Joy (London: Faber & Faber, 1982; New York: Farrar, Straus & Giroux, 1982);

The Occasions of Poetry: Essays in Criticism and Autobiography (London: Faber & Faber, 1982).

OTHER: *Poetry from Cambridge 1951-52*, edited by Gunn (London: Fortune Press, 1952);

Five American Poets, edited by Gunn and Ted Hughes (London: Faber & Faber, 1963);

Selected Poems of Fulke Greville, edited by Gunn

(London: Faber & Faber, 1968; Chicago: University of Chicago Press, 1968);

Ben Jonson: Poems, edited by Gunn (Harmondsworth: Penguin, 1974).

The paradox of Thom Gunn's achievement is best characterized by the ambiguities inherent in the word *fashion*. He is a "fashioning" poet, in the old-fashioned sense—a writer preoccupied by the problems of "shaping," "determining," and "controlling" both in life and in art. But somewhat to his surprise and quite without opportunism he has also turned out to be a chronicler of fashion—a poet in whose work one can discern various different trends of postwar culture: Sartrean existentialism; youth subculture; the communal aspirations of the 1960s; the consumption of hard and soft drugs. He is not a polemical poet, nor one who has been active in political movements; yet future social historians and cultural anthropologists wanting to learn about the texture of our times will probably find it more useful to turn to his work than to that of the other British poets who also emerged in the 1950s—Philip Larkin, Ted Hughes, Geoffrey Hill, Peter Redgrove, Charles Tomlinson. What one finds in Gunn's work is not just an unusual receptivity to the aspirations and transformations of our age but also a traditional set of humanist concerns. He is at bottom a philosophical poet, addressing himself to perennial questions of love, identity, freedom, and choice, but finding his answers in the immediate (and often deviant) present.

Gunn was born in 1929 in Gravesend, Kent, and christened Thomson William (Thom for short). His father, Herbert Smith Gunn, was a journalist with the Beaverbrook press, a gregarious and successful man who moved up from provincial papers such as the *Kent Messenger* to become editor of the *Evening Standard* in 1944 and later, in the 1950s, editor of the *Daily Sketch*. Gunn's mother, Ann Charlotte Thomson Gunn, had also worked as a journalist until the birth of Thom and his younger brother Alexander (Ander, as he is known). An independent woman, something of a socialist and feminist, she was a voracious reader and passed on to Thom the idea "of books as not just a commentary on life but a part of its continuing activity." Gunn has said that his was a happy childhood and that he had a special fondness for Hampstead, a well-to-do part of London to which the family moved when he was eight: a couple of his poems celebrate the spacious heath for which Hampstead is renowned and which he frequented as a child and teenager. There were, however, two darker events in his childhood about which he has been more reticent: the divorce of his parents shortly after they had moved to Hampstead and the death of his mother when he was fourteen. It is hard not to see a link between these events and the lonely (compensatorily macho) personae of his early poems. An uncollected undergraduate poem, "Mother Love," describes a boy who finds nothing but loneliness "as soon / As the old line of his mother's was permanently closed down."

Throughout his childhood and adolescence, Gunn read widely: according to his father he was better read at eleven than most people are at thirty-five. As a boy he read Louisa May Alcott, Charles Kingsley, and John Masefield; in his early teens Marlowe, Keats, Milton, Tennyson, and Meredith. Most crucial of all perhaps was his discovery of a broad range of poetry in W. H. Auden's anthology *The Poet's Tongue* (1941), given to him by an enlightened English teacher at Bedales school in Hampshire, to which he was evacuated for four terms during the World War II Blitz bombings of London (the larger part of his education was spent at University College School in London). He had also written from an early age (he recalls character sketches done at eight and a short, "curiously sophisticated novel" he wrote at twelve), and from sixteen onward he took his writing seriously, though "the results were immature and dispiriting."

After he left school, Gunn spent two years' National Service in the British army in 1948-1950 (National Service was at this time compulsory for young British men). It is tempting to date his fascination with soldiers from this period, but he himself dates it earlier, to just after the Blitz, when he en-

Thom Gunn

joyed "eyeing the well-fed and good-looking G.I.s who were on every street, with an appreciation I didn't completely understand." (In the poem "The Corporal" he goes even further: "Half of my youth I watched the soldiers.") After completing National Service he went to Paris for six months, working in a low-paid office job in the Metro, reading Proust, and attempting a Proustian novel of his own. Despite this apparent precocity, Gunn judges that when he went up to read English at Trinity College, Cambridge, in 1950, at the age of twenty-one, he was "strangely immature, a good deal more so than any of my friends."

Once there, however, he grew up quickly, becoming part of a lively and challenging circle of undergraduates who edited and wrote for the university magazine *Granta* and who were later to make their names as writers and literary journalists: Karl Miller, Nicholas Tomalin, Mark Boxer, John Coleman, John Mander, and Tony White. The abrasive Miller was especially influential—"When I wrote a new poem I would give it to him for criticism, and he would pin it to the wall above his desk for several days before he told me what he thought of it. . . . He matured my mind amazingly"—and Tony White, later a translator, odd-job-man, and dropout, was to become a lifelong friend. "Looking back on that time, I can see it all as a bit incestuous," Gunn has said: "we promoted each other consistently." But he has also said that he received "more education from my contemporaries than from my teachers." The one teacher he remembers with respect is F. R. Leavis, whose lectures he attended and whose "discriminations and enthusiasms helped teach me to write, better than any creative-writing class could have. His insistence on the realized, being the life of poetry, was exactly what I needed."

Gunn's first book, *Fighting Terms* (1954), is the product of these Cambridge years: he wrote all the poems in it between 1951 and 1953, when he received his B.A. Like most undergraduate collections it has not worn particularly well: Gunn himself has rightly said that it was received more kindly than it deserved because he had somehow been cast in the role of the new "Cambridge poet," of whom great things were expected. In retrospect the collection looks affected, cerebral, and overclever, a combination epitomized in the refrain from "Carnal Knowledge": "You know I know you know I know you know." Several poems are no more than elaborations of single metaphors or setting up of riddles: the reader is invited to decode or unscramble, to discern that the strange landscape described in "Without a Counterpart," for example, is that of the human body. The most common conceit in the book is love treated as war. As in "To His Cynical Mistress," sex becomes the battle of two human wills, lovers' ruses are military stratagems, seduction is a matter of conspiracy and maneuver:

And love is then no more than a compromise?
An impermanent treaty waiting to be signed
   By the two enemies?
While the calculating Cupid feigning impartial-blind
Drafts it, promising peace, both leaders wise
To his antics sign but secretly double their spies.

If that poem points to the influence of Donne (and its title to Marvell), others betray the presence of Shakespeare, Jonson, Fulke Greville, Auden, Empson, Yeats, and Graves. Such indebtedness gives the poems an air of bookish sophistication, even world-weariness—"For a Birthday" begins as if the poet were seventy not twenty-four, "I have reached a time when words no longer help"—but such seeming sophistication cannot disguise an op-

posite strain of callowness and crudity, evident, for example, in the slickly rhyming "La Prisonnière," which is based on the same pop song image that Cliff Richard was later to make famous in "Livin' Doll": "Now I will shut you in a box / With massive sides and a lid that locks. / Only by that I can be sure / That you are still mine and mine secure."

Yet the book is far from being a complete embarrassment. The obsession with soldiers, the themes of will and choice, and the strange accounts of metamorphosis anticipate the concerns of the mature Gunn. There are, moreover, a number of poems that stand up well by any standards. "Wind in the Street" nicely animates the cliché of the browsing shopper—"I only came . . . to look round"—and enlarges it with a suggestion of "uncommitted" existential questing. "The Secret Sharer" recounts an actual experience of disembodiment, or double selfhood, which Gunn had in Cambridge. "Lerici" strikingly contrasts the lives of Shelley and Byron, celebrating the romantic energy of Byron over the "submissive" qualities of Shelley (a characteristically Leavisian preference). "Incident of a Journey" is an unlikely but suggestive amalgam of Wilfred Owen's "Strange Meeting" and Edith Piaf's *Je ne regrette rien.* Above all there is the book's opening poem, one of the author's best, which features the sort of existential hero Gunn at this period was drawn to—the professional soldier willing to fight on any side and "subject to no man's breath"—and who is powerfully mysterious about the nature of the wound (emotional? physical? intellectual?) which is now incapacitating him. Few first books can boast opening lines as authoritative as these from "The Wound":

The huge wound in my head began to heal
About the beginning of the seventh week.
Its valleys darkened, its villages became still:
For joy I did not move and dared not speak;
Not doctors would cure it, but time, its patient skill.

Fighting Terms created a stir in 1954 not just because it marked the emergence of a bold new individual talent, but because it was identified with a new spirit of realism and irreverence in English poetry. Gunn shared with other recent arrivals—Philip Larkin, Kingsley Amis, Donald Davie, John Wain—a preference for tight verse forms, a respect for the tough and reasonable, and a distrust of the neoromanticism which Dylan Thomas and others had made fashionable in the 1940s (though Thomas himself Gunn did admire). Various articles of the time, most crucially a 1954 piece by Anthony Hartley in the

Spectator, gave these writers a corporate identity and public image, which Robert Conquest's anthology *New Lines* (1956) consolidated: they became known as The Movement. Gunn himself was well aware of the publicity surrounding The Movement but regarded the group as largely a journalistic invention (or convention) and was somewhat surprised to find himself being called one of its main members: whereas Amis, Larkin, and Wain did know each other fairly well, Gunn had met hardly anyone who was supposed to be part of the group. Nonetheless it is easy to see why Gunn should have been incorporated. A poem such as "Lines for a Book," which mocks at sensitives like Stephen Spender and adopts brutally hardheaded attitudes, is typical of brusque Movement ideology. It is also the early poem of his which Gunn now most regrets:

> It's better
> To go and see your friend than write a letter;
> To be a soldier than to be a cripple;
> To take an early weaning from the nipple
> Than think your mother is the only girl.

Whatever the extent of Gunn's affiliations with The Movement, links of one sort were effectively broken when, in the same year as his first book was published, 1954, he departed for the United States. His chief reason for going seems to have been his involvement with Mike Kitay, an American he had met at Cambridge and who was to become a steady companion. (Gunn was already a homosexual in Cambridge, though he found it hard to admit this fact to his friends and adopted a heavily heterosexual persona in the early poems.) A creative writing fellowship at Stanford made the transatlantic move possible, and for a year Gunn lived in Palo Alto, thirty miles south of the city in which he was eventually to settle, San Francisco. It was a productive year, one in which he wrote most of his second book and fell under the spell not only of California but of Yvor Winters: "It was wonderful luck for me that I should have worked with him at this particular stage of my life, rather than earlier when I would have been more impressionable or later when I would have been less ready to learn." Gunn was soon to become conscious of his mentor's rigidity about poetry—"The rigidity seemed to be the result of what I can only call an increasing distaste for the particulars of existence"—but for the moment the partnership flourished, as his well-known poetic tribute to Winters, "To Yvor Winters, 1955," testifies:

> You keep both Rule and Energy in view,
> Much power in each, most in the balanced two:
> Ferocity existing in the fence
> Built by an exercised intelligence.

This poem appeared in Gunn's second collection, *The Sense of Movement* (1957), a book which he has described as "a second work of apprenticeship," "more sophisticated" but "less independent" than the first. This comment is, up to a point, fair: the existentialism of Sartre and Camus, with its vocabulary of *will, choice, freedom, action, self-determination,* and *individualism,* is more intrusive in this volume than in *Fighting Terms.* On the other hand, Gunn's first book is largely lacking in a temporal context, whereas his second is vividly contemporary, adopting as subject matter motorcycle gangs, Elvis Presley, juke boxes, cafes, cityscapes, street markets, and leather fashions. In what was a fairly conservative period of British poetry, such "lowlife" contemporaneity involved Gunn in a considerable risk: he had been hailed as a strenuous traditionalist but was now seemingly to be placed with American Redskins rather than English Palefaces, with Ginsberg and Kerouac rather than Larkin and Davie. Formally, however, Gunn remained buttoned up, and this tension was indeed the key to the volume: myths of wild men explored in rigidly restrained meter, American motorcyclists celebrated in structures that took Marvell's mower poems as a model. So, too, Gunn's frantic commitment to the new was held in check by a series of historical allegories about Merlin, St. Martin, Jesus, and Julian the Apostate, and by a superb Chekhovian period piece, "Autumn Chapter in a Novel":

> Through woods, Mme Une Telle, a trifle ill
> With idleness, but no less beautiful,
> Walks with the young tutor, round their feet
> Mob syllables slurred to a fine complaint,
> Which in their time held off the natural heat.

This is one of the few poems in the book to show a sneaking regard for inaction. Elsewhere Gunn is in constant danger of elevating action and movement excessively high above thought, especially at the end of the book's celebrated opening poem, "On the Move," the philosophical implications of which do not bear close examination. Gunn is aware of the poem's moral problem—may not the restless activity of the motorcycle gang be to no purpose? may it not indeed be positively harmful to others?—but this awareness does not prevent him from identifying strongly with the gang's motto of movement for movement's sake:

> At worst, one is in motion; and at best,
> Reaching no absolute, in which to rest,
> One is always nearer by not keeping still.

This last line is fine rhetoric, but Gunn cannot have failed to realize that it is also untrue: movement can take one further away as well as toward. He may not have defined it quite in this way, but his problem for the next few years lay in shaking off the hoodlum philosophy to which his early allegiance to existentialism, in combination with a natural leaning to the severe and militaristic, had driven him. By 1957 some readers were already beginning to find his attraction to strong leaders and romantic over-reachers to be fascistic, and he was himself aware of unpalatable elements in his work. The problem was in part a formal one: meter and rhyme tended to enforce his emphasis on control and will. As he himself later put it, "in metrical verse it is the nature of the control being exercised that becomes part of the life being spoken about. It is poetry making great use of the conscious intelligence, but its danger is bombast—the controlling music drowning out everything else."

In the late 1950s, his first two books behind him, Gunn began to experiment with syllabic and free verse so as to develop what he called a "more humane" impulse in his work. It was not, in terms of poetry, a very productive period: he found it a struggle to master free forms. He was also, one suspects, finding it hard to adjust to life in the United States, much though he was excited by it, so that in personal terms, too, this was a restless and at times unhappy period of his life: a fairly tedious year's teaching in San Antonio, Texas (1955-1956); graduate work in Stanford, by the end of which (in 1958) Gunn had still failed to complete his Ph.D. and had become disenchanted with Yvor Winters; two years living in Oakland while teaching at Berkeley (1958-1960); a trip to Italy on a Somerset Maugham award (1959); then finally some months away in Berlin (1960), after which Gunn returned to make his home in San Francisco. He was reviewing regularly for *Poetry* and *Yale Review* during these years, but by about 1964 he had become "dissatisfied with the business of making comparatively fast judgments on contemporary poets," and since then he has reviewed very little; he especially regrets a hastily dismissive verdict on William Carlos Williams, a poet who was soon to become important to

him. He could not have been very happy, either, about what was being said about his own poetry back in England, where his name was being linked with that of Ted Hughes, who had been at Cambridge just after him and whose first book, *Hawk in the Rain,* was published to great acclaim in 1957. The two were spoken of by A. Alvarez, Edward Lucie-Smith, and others as the originators of a new school of violence in poetry—not toughly reasonable like The Movement, but unreasonably tough: aggressive, amoral, drawn to fascism and Nazi regalia. There was some justice in the Hughes-Gunn pairing, for there are verbal and thematic parallels in their early work. (The 1962 joint selection of their poetry brought out by Faber and Faber was a huge success and has gone on to sell over 100,000 copies.) But for Gunn, who was in the late 1950s and early 1960s trying to remake and humanize himself, it must have indeed been tough to be the subject of this sort of attention: the last thing he wanted was a "New Brutalist" label.

My Sad Captains (1961) was at least some sort of answer. The book is deliberately divided into two parts: the "old phase" of metrical verse and Sartrean will in part one; the new phase of syllabics and "tenderness" in part two, suitably introduced by a poem called "Waking in a Newly Built House." The implied clean break was, of course, a simplification: Gunn's previous book had already contained two poems in syllabics ("Market at Turk" and "Vox Humana"), just as later books were to revert to meter. But the book does undoubtedly mark a turning point, and not only its second half: the fine opening poem, for example, "In Maria Del Popolo," reverts to a familiar Gunn theme—man in his struggle against nothingness—but now concedes that contemplation, not action, may be the best means of resistance. The braggarts and tough guys who stalk the book's pages seem seedier and less confident than their predecessors, to be pitied rather than admired: fallen rakes in middle age, young black jackets whose tattoo-motto reads "Born to Lose." Human relationships generally are re-valued, the selfishness and subterfuge Gunn formerly saw dominating them giving way to the possibility of gentleness, as in "The Feel of Hands":

> The hands explore tentatively,
> two small live entities whose shapes
> I have to guess at. They touch me
> all, with the light of fingertips
>
> testing each surface of each thing

found, timid as kittens with it.
I connect them with amusing
hands I have shaken by daylight.

Above all Gunn is for the first time attentive to the natural world; its minutiae—snails, forest ferns, grass blades—are painstakingly described. The concluding title poem is thus a fitting farewell to Gunn's existential heroes (such as Alexander, Brutus, Coriolanus, Byron) and to the idolatry of action: as they "withdraw to an orbit / and turn with disinterested / hard energy," so too Gunn seems to attain a new detachment and disinterest. He will no longer propagandize on behalf of the brave and strong. Clarity becomes his new touchstone, a clarity which he finds present in the California light itself:

> on fogless days by the Pacific,
> there is a cold hard light without break
>
> that reveals merely what it is—no more
> and no less. That limiting candour,
>
> that accuracy of the beaches,
> is part of the ultimate richness.

"Limiting candour" does not sound like an exciting poetic program, and *My Sad Captains* is far from being Gunn's best book. But it is the most important transitional collection, the one that made his subsequent development possible.

With three collections under his belt and steady employment teaching at Berkeley, Gunn had now reached some sort of plateau and had begun to think of San Francisco as his home: he was no longer the English traveler abroad, but an émigré, or settler. Ironically, however, his next two books were both made possible by the one year in the 1960s which he spent away from San Francisco—a year from mid-1964 to mid-1965, when he lived in London. Though then in his mid-thirties, Gunn was living in London for the first time as an adult—"A London returned to after twelve years"—and its importance to him is admitted in his autobiographical essay, "My Life up to Now" (in *The Occasions of Poetry*, 1982), and in his "Talbot Road" sequence of poems (from *The Passages of Joy*) about the West London street and large Victorian house where he stayed. For those, like him, interested in youth culture generally and rock music in particular, this was an exhilarating time to be in Britain, the years of "Swinging London," "Carnaby Street," and the Beatles: "barriers seemed to be coming down all over, it was as if World War II had finally drawn to its close, there was an openness and high-spiritedness and relaxation of mood I did not remember from the London of earlier years."

As well as seeing a good deal of his Cambridge friend Tony White, who lived nearby, Gunn also visited his brother Ander and family in Teddington. He was much taken with Ander's photographs, and the two decided to collaborate on a book of poems and photographs commemorating contemporary English urban life. *Positives* (1966) cannot be considered one of Gunn's serious collections, and indeed nothing from it was included in his *Selected Poems* of 1979. As he has said, "I was never very sure whether what I was writing opposite the photographs were poems or captions," and some of the text does not seem to work as either. But the poems on subjects in which Gunn had already a proven interest—teddy boys, motorcyclists, pop singers, the subculture of male youth generally—have moments of genuine power: an arrogant young man gesturing at the camera, "inviting experience to try him"; a group of teenage boys shown huddled by a warehouse, their bodies "increasing in secret society"; and two concluding poems about an old tramp-woman, the first a memory of hop picking in Kent that echoes her present destitution ("she worked all day along the green / alleys, among the bins"), the second a haunting premonition of death:

> Something approaches, about
> which she has heard a good deal.
> Her deaf ears have caught it, like
> a silence in the wainscot
> by her head. Her flesh has felt
> a chill in her feet, a draught
> in her groin. She has watched it
> like moonlight on the frayed wood
> stealing toward her
> floorboard by floorboard. Will it hurt?
>
> Let it come, it is
> the terror of full repose,
> and so no terror.

At the back of *Positives* lies Gunn's growing admiration in the early 1960s for William Carlos Williams: he has said that he wanted to "anglicize" Williams, to write free verse poems of "fragmentary inclusiveness" about Britain in the mid-1960s. *Positives* does this with modest success and much visual support.

The year in London also enabled Gunn to complete "Misanthropos," the centerpiece of his next full-fledged collection, *Touch* (1967). This sequence of seventeen linked poems presents a life stripped to primitive essentials. A skeletal narrative recounts how the seemingly solitary survivor of a global war exists by himself until, to his surprise and even dismay, he encounters a group of about forty other survivors. The circumstances of the global war, and the man's escape from it, are not fleshed out: the poem is instead a meditation on first and last things, on what it would be like to be the last representative of the human race—and thus in effect the first one, Adam. It is an ambitious poem for which William Golding's novel *The Inheritors* (1955) is the acknowledged model (one notices the influence especially in sections twelve through fifteen) and which Ted Hughes's poem "Wodwo" also resembles. But both these texts point up the weaknesses of Gunn's: his poem has not their richly sensuous response to the natural world; its philosophizing takes place in a void or dust bowl. Most of the other poems in *Touch* are also disappointing, lacking in personality and bite, as if Gunn's turning away from the brutal and willed had left him without a subject and without a tone of voice. The collection is dominated by an ethic of the random and all-inclusive propounded in "Confessions of the Life Artist"—"Whatever is here, it is / material for my art," "You control what you can, and / use what you cannot." Fine in principle, this theory in practice results in a collection where few poems stand up as *poems,* as *artefacts.* The one distinguished work in the collection, arguably the best in Gunn's whole oeuvre and good enough to make one happy to pass over the rest of *Touch,* is the title poem, a superb example of free verse and in its last lines a pointer to the communal idealism which also dominates his next book:

> What I, now loosened,
> sink into is an old
> big place, it is
> there already, for
> you are already
> there, and the cat
> got there before you, yet
> it is hard to locate.
> What is more, the place is
> not found but seeps
> from our touch in
> continuous creation, dark
> enclosing cocoon round
> ourselves alone, dark
> wide realm where we
> walk with everyone.

Gunn returned to San Francisco in mid-1965, to find that he had been given tenure at Berkeley. A year later, however, he decided to give up his job,

evidently feeling that a full-time teaching job was no longer compatible either with his poetry writing or with the kind of life he wanted to lead. Possibly the atmosphere in San Francisco, as heady as and even more optimistic than the London he had left, had something to do with it. There was also his involvement with the drug LSD, which he seems to have taken then for the first time and which helped to make those years, as his excited description suggests, "the fullest years" of his life: "Raying out from the private there was a public excitement at the new territories that were being opened up in the mind. . . . We tripped . . . at home, on rooftops, at beaches and ranches, some went to the opera loaded on acid, others tried it as passengers on gliders, every experience was illuminated by the drug. . . . These were the fullest years of my life, crowded with discovery both inner and outer, as we moved between ecstasy and understanding. It is no longer fashionable to praise LSD, but I have no doubt at all that it has been of the utmost importance to me, both as a man and as a poet." For a brief golden moment in San Francisco drug taking, utopian politics, and flower power happily coexisted and created optimism in Gunn and others about communal living and the perfectibility of man.

As a poet, his dilemma was to find a way of speaking of these newfound experiences, images, and ideas. Drug experiences, being "essentially nonverbal," were difficult to transcribe: "Metre seemed to be the proper form for the LSD-related poems, though at first I didn't understand why. Later I rationalized about it thus. The acid trip is unstructured, it opens you up to countless possibilities. . . . The only way I could give myself any control . . . was by trying to render the infinite through the finite, the unstructured through the structured." Yet there was the problem of clarifying and articulating the nexus of ideas in which, partly because of drugs, he had become interested: "trust, openness, acceptance, innocence." The difficulty resulted in a temporary writing block, release from which—as he recounts in the essay "Writing a Poem" (in *The Occasions of Poetry*)—came about through the experience of seeing a naked family (father, mother, and small son) on a deserted Pacific beach. The encounter is memorialized in his poem "Three," and the parents in it, who have "had to learn their nakedness," become a sort of symbol for and inspiration to his work of the period. They not only confirm the possibility of innocence repossessed but are an emblem of what Gunn now thinks poetry should be—clean, naked, open, trusting, fused with the natural world.

The position Gunn had reached by the end of the 1960s was thus very different from that he had held in his first two books. *Fighting Terms* and *The Sense of Movement* had depicted the natural world as a threatening void; his heroes were those, whether motorcyclists or emperors, whose machines or mechanistic wills could overpower it; human achievements in life and art were a matter of conquering and ordering and subduing—"much that is natural to the will must yield." *Moly*, published in 1971, embodies Gunn's more hopeful vision of a fruitful union between man and nature, and between writing and living. The poem "From the Wave," for example, celebrates surfing (and by implication poetry) as a process not of defeating the natural but of riding it, harnessing it, working in consort with it. Watching surfers, he writes:

> Their pale feet curl, they poise their weight
>   With a learn'd skill.
> It is the wave they imitate
>   Keeps them so still.
>
> The marbling bodies have become
>   Half wave, half men,
> Grafted, it seems, by feet of foam.

Moly is dominated by such images of merging and metamorphosis, of centaurs, pantheists, men and women (and men and animals) in sexual union. Once aloof, moated, "condemned to be an individual," Gunn now embarks on a thrilling mission to dissolve, melt, commune, share, belong. This is, in part, the meaning of the title: when Hermes gave Odysseus the drug moly, it broke the Circe spell of confinement and subordination. The collection is about being set free into a new, more expansive universe.

The title has a second, connected meaning: it implies an analogy between the releasing powers of moly and those of LSD. There are at least a half-dozen poems in *Moly* which specifically describe LSD experiences and several more indirectly indebted to the drug. In none of these could Gunn be accused of self-indulgence, of the transcription of merely private dream worlds. He always edges the poems into the public domain to which he believes LSD belongs. ("By 1968 taking the drug was no longer an unusual experience, probably hundreds of thousands had had at least one experience with it, and many more knew about it without having taken it, so to write about its effects was not any more to be obscure or to make pretentious claims to experience closed to most readers.") The opening of "The Fair in the Woods" is a good example of his public mode,

its perfect iambics echoing the opening of Thomas Gray's "Elegy written in a Country Churchyard": "The curfew tolls the knell of parting day" (Gray); "The woodsmen blow their horns, and close the day" (Gunn). But the poems are public also because they are set in public places (a fair, a rock festival) and because they affirm a brave new social order of openness and trust:

> Open on all sides, it is held in common,
> The first field of a glistening continent
> Each found by trusting Eden in the human:
> The guiding hand, the bright grey eyes intent.

Gunn in his earlier work had praised "uncommitted" men with the courage of their lack of convictions. It was an easier stance than the one he takes here, which means holding convictions that are Edenic, vulnerable and, in retrospect, even gullible. But the courage makes this his most affirmative book, and his tight poetic structures help contain his utopianism to make it also, arguably, his best one. There are several strong poems at its center ("The Sand Man," "Three," "Words," "From the Wave"), and it ends superbly with "The Discovery of the Pacific," about a young couple resting at the end of their pioneering journey to the West Coast, and with "Sunlight," an ode which in its final lines provides Gunn with his most eloquent and beneficent moment:

> Great seedbed, yellow centre of the flower
> Flower on its own, without a root or stem,
> Giving all colour and all shape their power,
> Still recreating in defining them,
>
> Enable us, altering like you, to enter
> Your passionless love, impartial but intense,
> And kindle in acceptance round your centre,
> Petals of light lost in your innocence.

Moly is a buoyant book, "high" on the Edenic impulse of the late 1960s. By the time it appeared in 1971, however, that buoyancy had subsided. Already in 1970, while he was living for a spell in New York (he taught at Princeton and lived in a loft-apartment on Prince Street), Gunn had felt the beginnings of a change: "It was the time of numerous bombings—I saw a rather famous townhouse go up in smoke—and of the invasion of Cambodia. The feeling of the country was changing, and one didn't know into what. I went back to England for a few months of the summer, and when I returned to San Francisco I felt something strange there too: there was a certain strain in attempting to preserve the

Thom Gunn, 24 June 1970 (BBC Hulton, photograph by Alden)

euphoria of the sixties, one's anxieties seemed obstructive. I had a couple of rather bad trips on LSD that taught me no end of unpalatable facts about myself, to my great edification." This was the tenser, more contradictory atmosphere which Gunn and many others experienced, both privately and publicly, in the early 1970s. On the one side was a feeling of unease and violence, a desire (during the Nixon era) to draw back into the self. On the other was "edification," clear-sightedness and a chastened but persistent belief that "everything that we glimpsed—the trust, the brotherhood, the repossession of innocence, the nakedness of spirit—is still a possibility and will continue to be so." In personal terms Gunn moved between the pain of

losing his friend Tony White (who died at forty-five from injuries sustained in an accident while playing soccer) and the joy of discovering new friends, between the upheavals and nightmares that accompanied a move from one side of San Francisco to the other and his occasional association with a new sort of hedonistic community at a run-down resort in Sonoma County.

Tragedy versus joy, 1960s ameliorism against 1970s disenchantment—these are the fluctuating feelings that lie behind Gunn's next book, *Jack Straw's Castle*, published in 1976 and dedicated to the memory of Tony White. The book opens strongly with two poems which show the persistence of that fascination with cityscapes underlying the earlier "In Praise of Cities" and *Positives*. "Diagrams" describes Indian construction workers "with wrenches in their pockets and hard hats"; "Iron Landscapes" explores oppositions of iron and water, stability and fluidity, the virtues of constancy and the dangers of stubborn resistance. Even in these poems Gunn's persona seems darker and more resolute in mood than in *Moly*, and the shift is confirmed in the first of the book's two long sequences, "The Geysers." Initially the change is scarcely visible: the poem's opening two sections have rapturous, *Moly*-like celebrations of men merged in pantheistic union and are infected with the same pleasure which Gunn brings to his description of the background to the poem: "In the early seventies I went a few times with friends to the area in Sonoma County, north of San Francisco, known as the geysers. . . . We camped anywhere, on the flanks of the hills, which were warm even at night, or in the woodland, or beside the cool and warm streams. Everyone walked around naked, swimming in the cool stream by day and at night staying in the hot baths until early in the morning. Heterosexual and homosexual orgies sometimes overlapped: there was an attitude of benevolence and understanding on all sides that could be extended, I thought, into the rest of the world." But in section three the poem becomes more disquieting: the speaker's encounter with the rock and heat that underlie the geyser's watery pleasures brings him to a recognition of forces beyond his control: "Up here a man might shrivel in his source." Section four ushers in the disorder augured here, the verse changing abruptly from meter and rhyme into free-verse fragments, and the speaker losing his individuality and his sense of the past in an "uneasy" (part ecstatic, part terrifying) orgy of communal bathing:

> I am part of all
>   hands take
>   hands tear and twine
>
> I yielded
>   oh, the yield
>   what have I slept?
> my blood is yours   the hands that   take accept.

The lesson to be drawn is not that the chilly self should not be surrendered, but that the surrender may be painful and traumatic—more so than the similarly communal vision of *Moly* had implied.

The element of nightmare in "The Geysers" recurs more strongly in the second section of the collection and its second long sequence, "Jack Straw's Castle," which has obsessive images of the poet being assaulted, imprisoned, burned up, annihilated. Here the speaker has not expanded his mind but found it imprisoning him; he has not moved into an airy region of self-transcendence but has been returned to the dark "core" or "source" or "dungeon" of selfhood; he has not fellow hedonists and bathers for companions but Charles Manson, Medusa, and the Furies; and he finds not a joyous release through the senses but an oppressive regime of sweat, fungus, sour breath. In this prison he faces a horrific series of receding mirror images:

> I am the man on the rack.
> I am the man who puts the man on the rack.
> I am the man who watches the man who puts
>   the man on the rack.

In the third section of the book there is a return to daylight and poise and to a hope that seems stronger for its having been put through the ordeal of the previous section. "The Idea of Trust," for example, is an archetypal 1970s riposte-poem: that someone might steal "the money and dope / of the people he'd lived with" could not have been acknowledged in the headier days of the 1960s; facing up to the fact now, Gunn is not, however, merely disillusioned—he takes seriously, as a sort of plausible philosophical position, the culprit Jim's definition of trust as "an intimate conspiracy," and he implies that those who choose to share possessions must be prepared to lose them. Gunn seems to believe that the abolition of privacy is an ideal worth pursuing, but one must be clear that it involves risk and pain. In this final section he also finds room for at least one poetic persona who moves unambiguously from gloom and boredom to "joy," "love," and sensual fulfillment: the persona is that of a dog, Yoko, seen welcoming home his human master. The poem brilliantly overcomes the problems of anthropomorphism that usually attend such exercises to become, as its author intended, a "completely doggy" poem: in it Gunn escapes most convincingly the self that imprisons him elsewhere in the collection. Overall, however, *Jack Straw's Castle* is Gunn's most disturbing book, veering alarmingly between extremes of self-absorption and self-erasure. It is a book of middle age, both literally (written while he was in his mid-forties) and because of a new note of brooding and revaluation.

Throughout his career Gunn has shown an impressive ability to move off in unexpected directions. Sometimes they seem to surprise even him; it from notebook

WIND NOTES

The pilot said Cmon and
the two of us passengers climbed onto the wing
and into the snug plane
                            With a short run we took off
~~We became the plane when we~~
flexed, jumped, soared,
changed direction, hopped over a wind/current/tree
and found an altitude.
Silo and wood below us
like perfect toys, the field so close
you could where the tractor had turned in plowing.
And we like a perfect toy, at play:
play like the wind's work.

Like my best dreams
entering onto a wind
(that cleans out my skull cavity)
letting go until   / letting go, rising
I am a gust   / I am so much of it / I so much belong to it
part of the air   / I become a gust
mastering by being mastered

the gust
goes everywhere and nowhere
There are famous riddles
it has work to do, it plays always   / it is nowhere / nothing
it is here and not here
it is a flat clearing among ripples
a furrow in a field of grass

    .   .   .   .

                                    draw from attempted metrical
                                             version
A small wind
blows across the hedge
into the garden
The cat cocks her ears
her yellow eyes get big / the {pupil} in her yellow eyes dwindles to a speck as she stares
at the sudden change   / small pebbles rattles to hog round,
-- multitudinous cracking   twig crackles against twig, the stones &
and rustling all around --   leaves rootle all around, multitudinous
unable to locate
the one thing to pounce on /the one movement

Her name is Alert
She is still listening
when the wind has left
and is three gardens away

Working typescript (the author)

was probably no exaggeration when he wrote, a year after the publication of *Jack Straw's Castle*, that he had "no idea" what his next book would be like, nor that as late as 1980 he was claiming, "I don't see a pattern for my next book yet." So, too, even those intimate with his work, and those who had been reading his new poems as they appeared in periodicals in the late 1970s, must have been taken aback by the shape and content of *The Passages of Joy* when it appeared in 1982. Gunn's life-style had changed little during the period of its composition: he continued to live in San Francisco and to make occasional trips to London and other places; he added to a stream of earlier prizes and awards (a Rockefeller grant in 1966, for example, and a Guggenheim Fellowship in 1971, the prestigious W. H. Smith Award given to his *Selected Poems* of 1979), yet on average he continued to earn an income, as he puts it, "about half of that of a local bus driver or street sweeper." He came to believe more strongly than ever that writing was for him not a pose (as it had perhaps begun) but an integral part of his life, a way of understanding himself and others. But for all this steadiness and continuity, the new book was a distinct departure, being plainer and more direct than any of its predecessors and, in particular, franker about its author's homosexuality.

Yet *The Passages of Joy* is not a confessional book in the sense that confessionalism in poetry has come to be understood. Gunn has expressed his admiration for T. S. Eliot's theory of poetic impersonality and has expressed his skepticism about the demand that a poet have a "distinctive voice" ("Distinctiveness can look after itself, what I want is a voice that can speak about anything at all"). One of the poems in *The Passages of Joy*, "Expression," attacks young poets who have modeled themselves on confessional precursors:

> They write with black irony
> of breakdown, mental institution,
> and suicide attempt, of which the experience
> does not always seem first-hand.

But *The Passages of Joy* is the book in which Gunn "comes out" as a homosexual and is confessional in the sense that he speaks candidly for the first time about his sexual experiences with, and attraction to, other men, as in "Sweet Things":

> How handsome he is in
> his lust and energy, in his
> fine display of impulse.
> "How about now?" I say
> knowing the answer. My boy

> I could eat you whole. In the long pause
> I gaze at him up and down and
> from his blue sneakers back to the redawning
> one-sided smile. We know our charm.
> We know delay makes pleasure great.

One must not exaggerate the homosexual element in the book, as some reviewers did. Only a few of the poems are explicitly about homosexual encounters or venues; heterosexual relationships are also described in poems such as "Adultery" and "His Rooms in College" (though interestingly such relationships are unhappy); and the lines of Samuel Johnson from which Gunn takes his title—"Time hovers o'er, impatient to destroy, / And shuts up all the Passages of Joy"—are on one level to be taken simply as a memento mori, as a reference to mortality and the decay of the flesh. But of course the secondary meaning of these lines is indeed sexual: the passages, as Gunn has said, refer to "the nine channels with their nine holes through which we get most of our physical joys," and it is the joys of the eighth and ninth passages (the penis and the anus) which are highlighted. Moreover it is very difficult to imagine the book's occasionally demotic frankness before the decensorship of the 1960s and the widespread "gay liberation" campaign in the United States and Europe in the late 1970s. As Gunn says in his essay "Homosexuality in Robert Duncan's Poetry": "Most homosexual writers until at least the 1960s dealt with autobiographical and personal material only indirectly. One method was for a poet to address his work to an unspecified you, giving an occasional ambiguous hint about what was really going on to those in the know only. (This is what Auden did, and what I was to do later.)" In the new book Gunn adapts no such subterfuges: throughout he hymns the pleasures of male companionship, with himself undisguisedly at the center. The "coming out" is reflected in a style of "coming clean"—a poetic mode that eschews metaphor, symbol, and allegory and relies instead on anecdote, casual observation, and plain speech, "the real language of men." In "Song of a Camera" Gunn implies that his art may be that of a camera—the chance shot, the cut from life, the art that shows simply what it sees, leaving the audience to supply the adjectives and adverbs of moral judgment. But like the camera's, this is an art more artful than it seems—there is the subtlety of the line breaks in the opening "Elegy" to dead friends, for example, which carry the poem's grief:

> They keep leaving me

and they don't
tell me they don't
warn me that this is
the last time I'll be seeing them.

The Passages of Joy did not have a particularly good reception in England, where some reviewers felt that too many of the resources of Gunn's art had been stripped away and others that there was coming to be a rather tired antiestablishment air about his preference for dramatis personae located on the fringes of society—a drug dealer, a taxi driver, a pinball player, a body builder, a volunteer in a mental institution. But it is a collection which seems less plain the more one lives with it: it appears to hide nothing, but it does have hidden depths.

Gunn's overall reputation as a writer, from the perspective of the 1980s, is probably not as great as the initial acclaim for him in the 1950s would have led one to suspect. His work is taught widely in British schools; he has persuasive champions such as Clive Wilmer; he is ranked by many critics among the leading half-dozen British poets: but he does not arouse the same excitement or wide interest as, for example, Geoffrey Hill, Ted Hughes, or Seamus Heaney. There are in part extraliterary explanations. Like Auden, Gunn chose to make his home in the United States, and though he did not time his departure as badly as Auden, a prejudice against his "defection" persists. One can see it, for instance, in the English critic Colin Falck's part-chiding, part-pleading assessment of *Jack Straw's Castle*: "If Gunn could put away the vacant counter-cultural slovenliness of his Californian ethic . . . he might be able to recover the faith which once tied him in with English poetry's finest traditions. . . ." But for Gunn the choice "English or American?" is not a meaningful one: he belongs to both cultures (and countercultures); his Californian ethic is not a superficial grafting but part of the texture of his life. He continues to be better known in England than in the United States, of course, and it is more common (and commonsensical) to measure his achievement against that of British contemporaries than against the Ginsbergs and Snyders. In the end, however, he deserves to be seen as one in a long and distinguished line of modern poets for whom the term "Anglo-American" is a perfectly proper description—Eliot, Pound, Auden, Lowell, Plath, Charles Tomlinson, and Donald Davie are others. Whatever turn Gunn next takes (one would expect to see more

poems about his early family life), he is certain to have a secure place in that tradition.

Interviews:
Ian Hamilton, "Four Conversations," *London Magazine,* 4 (November 1964): 64-70;

Hilary Morrish, "Violence and Energy," *Poetry Review,* 57 (Spring 1966): 32-35;

W. I. Scobie, "Gunn in America," *London Magazine,* 17 (December 1977): 5-15;

John Haffenden, *Viewpoints: Poets in Conversation* (London: Faber & Faber, 1981).

Bibliography:
Jack W. C. Hagstrom and George Bixby, *Thom Gunn: A Bibliography 1940-78* (London: Rota, 1979).

References:
Alan Bold, *Thom Gunn and Ted Hughes* (Edinburgh: Oliver & Boyd, 1976);

Alan Brownjohn, "The Poetry of Thom Gunn," *London Magazine,* 3 (March 1963): 45-52;

Martin Dodsworth, ed., *The Survival of Poetry* (London: Faber & Faber, 1970): 193-215;

Colin Falck, "Uncertain Violence," *New Review,* 3 (November 1976): 37-41;

G. S. Fraser, "The Poetry of Thom Gunn," *Critical Quarterly,* 3 (Winter 1961): 359-367;

P. R. King, *Nine Contemporary Poets* (London: Methuen, 1979), pp. 77-106;

John Mander, *The Writer and Commitment* (London: Secker & Warburg, 1961), pp. 153-178;

John Miller, "The Stipulative Imagination of Thom Gunn," *Iowa Review,* 4 (Winter 1973): 54-72;

Blake Morrison, *The Movement: English Poetry and Fiction of the 1950s* (Oxford: Oxford University Press, 1980);

Neil Powell, "The Abstract Joy: Thom Gunn's Early Poetry," *Critical Quarterly,* 13 (Autumn 1971): 219-227;

John Press, *Rule and Energy* (Oxford: Oxford University Press, 1963), pp. 191-201;

M. L. Rosenthal, *The New Poets* (Oxford: Oxford University Press, 1967), pp. 251-257;

Clive Wilmer, "Definition and Flow," *PN Review,* 5 (Spring 1978): 51-57.

Papers:
There is a collection of Gunn's manuscripts at the University of Maryland.

Michael Hamburger
(22 March 1924-   )

Peter Schmidt
Swarthmore College

SELECTED BOOKS: *Later Hogarth* (London: Cope & Fenwick, 1945);

Flowering Cactus: Poems 1942-49 (Aldington, Kent: Hand & Flower Press, 1950);

Poems 1950-51 (Aldington, Kent: Hand & Flower Press, 1952);

The Dual Site (New York: Editions Poetry, London-New York, 1957; London: Routledge & Kegan Paul, 1958);

Reason and Energy: Studies in German Literature (London: Routledge & Kegan Paul, 1957; New York: Grove, 1957; revised edition, London: Weidenfeld & Nicolson, 1970); republished as *Contraries: Studies in German Literature* (New York: Dutton, 1970);

Weather and Season: New Poems (London: Longmans, Green, 1963; New York: Atheneum, 1963);

From Prophecy to Exorcism: The Premises of Modern German Literature (London: Longmans, Green, 1965);

In Flashlight (Leeds: Northern House Press, 1965);

Zwischen den Sprachen: Essays und Gedichte (Frankfurt am Main: S. Fisher, 1966);

Feeding the Chickadees (London: Turret, 1968);

Travelling: Poems 1963-68 (London: Fulcrum, 1969);

Penguin Modern Poets 14, by Hamburger, Charles Tomlinson, and Alan Brownjohn (Harmondsworth & Baltimore: Penguin, 1969);

The Truth of Poetry: Tensions in Modern Poetry from Baudelaire to the 1960's (London: Weidenfeld & Nicolson, 1969; New York: Harcourt, Brace & World, 1970);

Hofmannsthal: Three Essays (Princeton: Princeton University Press, 1972; Cheadle, Cheshire: Carcanet Press, 1974);

Travelling I-V (London: Agenda Editions, 1972);

A Mug's Game—intermittent memoirs—1924-1954 (Cheadle, Cheshire: Carcanet Press, 1973);

Ownerless Earth: New and Selected Poems 1950-1972 (Cheadle, Cheshire: Carcanet Press, 1973; New York: Dutton, 1973);

Art as Second Nature: Occasional Pieces 1950-1974 (Cheadle: Carcanet Press, 1975);

*Information Services
University of South Carolina*

Real Estate (Manchester: Carcanet New Press, 1977);

Variations (Manchester: Carcanet New Press, 1981; Redding Ridge, Conn.: Black Swan, 1983);

Literarische Erfahrungen (Neuwied, Germany: Luchterhand, 1981);

A Proliferation of Prophets: Essays in Modern German Literature (Manchester: Carcanet Press, 1983;

New York: St. Martin's, 1984);
Collected Poems (Manchester & New York: Carcanet New Press, 1984).

OTHER: Friedrich Hölderlin, *Poems*, translated by Hamburger (London: Nicholson & Watson, 1943); revised and enlarged, as *Hölderlin: His Poems* (London: Harvill Press, 1952; New York: Pantheon, 1953); revised and enlarged again, as *Selected Verse* (Harmondsworth: Penguin, 1961); revised and enlarged again, as *Poems and Fragments* (London: Routledge & Kegan Paul, 1967; Ann Arbor: University of Michigan Press, 1967; revised and enlarged again, Cambridge: Cambridge University Press, 1980);
Beethoven: Letters, Journals, and Conversations, edited and translated by Hamburger (London: Thames & Hudson, 1951; New York: Pantheon, 1951; revised edition, London: Cape, 1966);
George Trakl, *Decline: 12 Poems*, translated by Hamburger (St. Ives, Cornwall: Latin Press, 1952);
Johann Wolfgang von Goethe, *Egmont*, translated by Hamburger, in *Classic Theatre 2*, edited by Eric Bentley (Garden City: Doubleday, 1959);
Bertolt Brecht, *Tales from the Calendar*, translated by Hamburger and Yvonne Kapp (London: Methuen, 1961);
Hofmannsthal: Poems and Plays, edited, with an introduction, by Hamburger, Bollingen Series 33, no. 2 (New York: Pantheon, 1961; London: Routledge & Kegan Paul, 1961);
Modern German Poetry 1910-1960: An Anthology with Verse Translations, edited and translated by Hamburger and Christopher Middleton (London: MacGibbon & Kee, 1962; New York: Grove, 1962);
Hofmannsthal: Selected Plays and Libretti, edited, with an introduction, by Hamburger, Bollingen Series 33, no. 3 (New York: Pantheon, 1963; London: Routledge & Kegan Paul, 1964);
Günter Grass, *Selected Poems*, translated by Hamburger and Middleton (London: Secker & Warburg, 1966; New York: Harcourt, Brace & World, 1966);
Georg Büchner, *Leonce and Lena, Lenz, Woyzeck*, translated by Hamburger (Chicago: Chicago University Press, 1972);
East German Poetry: An Anthology of German and English, edited and translated by Hamburger (Cheadle: Carcanet Press, 1972);

German Poetry 1910-1975, edited and translated by Hamburger (New York: Urizen Books, 1976; Manchester: Carcanet New Press, 1977);
Paul Celan: Poems, translated by Hamburger (New York: Persea, 1980);
An Unofficial Rilke, edited and translated, with an introduction, by Hamburger (London: Anvil, 1981); republished as *Poems 1912-1926* (Redding Ridge, Conn.: Black Swan, 1982);
Goethe: Poems and Epigrams, edited, with an introduction, by Hamburger (London: Anvil, 1983); republished as *Goethe: Roman Elegies and Other Poems* (Redding, Conn.: Black Swan, 1983).

Michael Hamburger is one of the most active and multifaceted English poets and scholars working today. In addition to having more than two dozen books and pamphlets of his poetry published since 1945, he has been an influential critic of romantic and modern literature and a translator specializing in classic and modern German poetry, including works by Hölderlin, Goethe, Hofmannsthal, Trakl, Brecht, Celan, Grass, and contemporary East German writers. He frequently contributes poems, translations, and prose to the *Times Literary Supplement* and to *Agenda*, one of the most important contemporary literary magazines in England, as well as to American journals such as *Poetry*. He has been awarded Bollingen Fellowships twice, in 1959 and 1965, and has won prizes in Europe and America for his translations and verse, including the Deutsche Akademie translation prize in 1964 and the Levinson Prize from *Poetry* in 1972.

Michael Peter Leopold Hamburger was born in Berlin, Germany, in 1924 to Richard Hamburger, a pediatrician with an interest in the arts, and Lili M. Hamburg Hamburger; his paternal grandfather was a writer for German literary reviews who was interested in introducing ideas from the French avant-garde into Germany. Both Hamburger's parents and his parents' families were of predominantly German-Jewish stock, but Judaism was not a part of their family life, and it was not until Hamburger's schoolteachers in Berlin began forming the student handball players into "Aryan" and "Jewish" teams that he learned he was Jewish as well as German. In 1933, shortly after Hitler consolidated his power, Hamburger's family immigrated to Edinburgh, where his father had to repeat his medical studies to qualify as a practicing doctor. Hamburger was nine. Not only did he have to adjust to a new school and new educational system—his father placed him in George Watson's College, then the largest boy's preparatory school in Britain—but he also had to learn a new language. As Hamburger explains in his memoir, *A Mug's Game* (1973), his determined efforts to learn quickly and to fit in were successful, but the family's life in their new country was not entirely happy. After a year, Hamburger went with his family to London. But his father had to cut back his London medical practice soon after it was established because he was becoming increasingly debilitated with Hodgkin's disease. He died in 1940, the same year his son Michael received a Higher Certificate at the Westminster School, London. A year later Hamburger won a scholarship and entered Christ Church, Oxford, in modern languages but soon interrupted his education in 1943 to serve in the army as a signalman and (after the war) as a lieutenant in the Royal Army Education Corps in Austria. He then returned to Oxford in 1947 and received both B.A. and M.A. degrees in modern languages in 1948. He married the writer Anne Beresford in 1951, and is the father of three children. He traveled on the Continent and tried to make a living in London as a book reviewer, but in order to support his family between 1952 and 1955 he taught German at University College, London, and from 1955 to 1964 at the University of Reading. He resigned his position in Reading in 1964. Since then he has held temporary appointments at Mount Holyoke College (1966-1967), the State University of New York at Buffalo (1969) and at Stony Brook (1970), Wesleyan University (1971), University of Connecticut (1972), University of California at San Diego (1973), University of South Carolina (1973), and Boston University (1975, 1977). Since 1978 he has lived in England. Hamburger and his wife were divorced in 1970, but he later reconciled with Anne Beresford and remarried her in 1974.

Hamburger has crossed and recrossed the boundaries between German, English, and American culture and combined careers in scholarship and art. His divergence from the conservative and normative verse of The Movement aligned him naturally with the poets included in *Mavericks* (1957), an anthology edited by Dannie Abse and Howard Sergeant and including as well poems by Jon Silkin. Hamburger's poetry shows at all points an interest in experimental techniques and psychological intensities. His poetic style has changed sharply over the course of four decades, evolving from a formal, symbolist, Yeatsian style to more colloquial work in free verse which celebrates evolving rather than fixed patterns of meaning.

Despite such stylistic changes, however, his work consistently contrasts art's desire for order and unity with life's sometimes gentle and sometimes violent disruption of those values. Urban and rural values are also frequently compared, as are those of traveling and home building, possession and dispossession. Uniting all these terms is Hamburger's insistence that an honest understanding of land, property, language, and people involves admitting that one must share them, never possess or dominate them. The title of his volume of selected poems *Ownerless Earth* (1973) states this understanding well: true owners know that they borrow rather than own what they work with. The most rewarding property is temporary, the best marriages, friendships, and poems are what Robert Frost called momentary stays against confusion. Hamburger's ability to admit the impermanence of all we believe in has not always been so strong. His early poems express the desire for absolute perfection and order, the cold intensities of art.

Hamburger's first two volumes of poems, *Flowering Cactus: Poems 1942-49* (1950) and *Poems 1950-51* (1952), include portraits of mad, embittered, and failed old men—Prospero bested by Caliban and deserted by Ariel; the German romantic poet Hölderlin mad at the end of his life, lamenting that "I have no tears to mourn forsaken gods / Or my lost voice"; and Judas Iscariot sunk in "a hell of cold self-hatred." In Hamburger's version Judas has acted ambitiously *for* the "Master" (God) rather than against him. Yet he remains in exile: "Myopic men would hate him—so the play demanded— / But would the Master who gazed with different eyes?" Hamburger's Judas hopes to be forgiven for playing the role that was demanded of him, but he realizes too late that forgiveness will not be forthcoming: "never would he shed / His dark imprisoning skin, the dust of that long day, / Nor ever in the sweet still water bathe."

The Dual Site (1957) collects most of the poems from Hamburger's second decade of work, and although in it Hamburger feels his work still shadowed by that of the great modernist masters, several poems show that he is also beginning to struggle against their tradition. There are also intimations not only of Hamburger's turn to free verse in the 1960s but of his mature themes—the different ways we experience time, travel, and ownership.

Both "Palinode" and "Narcissus" dramatize Hamburger's attempt to reject what he thinks is Yeatsian rhetoric. A palinode is a formal statement of retraction, but it is clear from the poem that Hamburger still finds the symbolist ideals of perfection attractive and intimidating: "A daily vision broke my rage: / The beauty of a cold white page." Yet Hamburger's use of the past tense in this line suggests that he has distanced himself from such an impossible ideal of perfection. Thus he prepares us for the ironic perspectives of "Narcissus," in which he mordantly shows how narcissistic is the grandiose symbolist quest for transcendent images of perfection. Only a narcissistic artist can achieve it, and at the price of excluding the world:

> poised above his image on the water,
> Too much himself, he'd left no space for love,
> Remote from her as heron, crane, or swan,
> Rooted in his own stillness like a flower.

The images in "The Dual Site," the volume's title poem, are partly drawn from the Gower Peninsula in South Wales, where Hamburger used to visit his friend and fellow poet Vernon Watkins. In the poem the speaker contrasts his urbane, "polyglot" ways with those of his country "twin," who has "learnt the ways of otter and raven" and "knows what I do not." This country twin, who may teach the poem's speaker how to invent a plainer, more direct style less weighed down with the "marble and metal" of symbolist dreams of perfection, writes to the city poet:

> Have no fear for your dwelling
> Though dry-rot gnaws at the floors;
> Only lighten their load of marble and metal,
>   Keep clear the corridors,
>
> Move out the clocks that clutter your study,
>   And the years will leave you alone:
> Every frame I know of lasts long enough,
>   Though but cardboard, wood or bone.

The "frame," not only the poet's house but also the stanzas or rooms of a poet's art, will endure beyond the poet's lifetime. The letter (and the poem) concludes with the hope, not for reconciliation but for the discovery of a common ground, "the dual site / Where even you and I / Still may meet again and together build / One house before we die."

Several poems in *The Dual Site* attempt to speak with such a colloquial and worldly wise voice, most notably "Travellers," dedicated to the poet Edwin Muir. Although many of them opt for plainer speech they still employ rather heavy-handed symbolism and the formal devices of parallelism, antithesis, syntactic inversion, and emphatic alliteration. Moreover, the poet's concern with im-

permanence remains, though it is less melodramatically expressed, as in "Season and Circumstance":

> Love led me always. Love detains me now.
> A one-way course, one river I follow,
> Rushed with it shallow, deeper go slow.
>
> The water feeds which brushed the rooted willow
> To lay bare wood for the slow rain to kill
> And with its rot replace eroded soil.

In other poems, such as "After Christmas," Hamburger betrays his uneasiness at such a style by parodying it and trying to dismiss it. He writes mock pastoral:

> Gone is that errant style. The shepherds rise
> And, packed in buses, go their separate ways
> To bench and counter. . . .

Hamburger's next volume, *Weather and Season* (1963), however, contains several poems which sound like none of his previous ones, including "Man of the World," "Tides," "The Moment," and "Homage to the Weather," the best poem in the book. In "Tides" he rejects "the metronome [that] was in my own head" for more various rhythms and subject matter which he associates with the natural voice of the sea. This newer and more various music is both stately and filled with the content and rhythms of contemporary speech:

> Milk bottles, rattle; familiars, gabble "good morn-
>   ing";
> Breed, hatch, digest your weeds and fishes, sea,
> Omit no beat, nor rise to tidal waves.
> Various enough the silences cut in
> Between the rock cave's boom and the small wader's
>   cry.

In "Man of the World," "Conformist," "Bird Watcher," and other portrait poems, Hamburger seeks to include more of the "gabble" of everyday speech than he has ever done, choosing characters inspired by life rather than literature, while in "Homage to the Weather" he calculatedly employs the "various" silences and rhythms of free verse. New sights, sounds, and cadences emerge amid the ruins of his older style:

> Where, till this moment, were the bees?
> And when no hum made for the honeysuckle,
> Fumbled,
> Became a body,

Clung and drank,
Spindrift, disowned, the petals hung,
And wait, let go was what the summer meant.

"Homage" also introduces a distinction between "weather" and "season" which is central to Hamburger's poetry in the 1960s and 1970s. "Season" for Hamburger represents a more abstract and programmatic approach to time and the world; he associates it with his early style. "Weather," however, is subtler, freer, more "natural." It does not impose an abstraction on a long and various temporal period (three months) and call it a season with set characteristics. Rather, like the weather itself, it emphasizes surprise, irregularity, change—the nature that evades our supposedly "natural" names and categories. Thus "Homage to the Weather" celebrates not spring or winter but spring-in-winter, nature's irregular and inspiring combination of both in early spring. Free verse, similarly, will for Hamburger combine complete and incomplete sentences, regular and irregular rhythms:

A tide, high tide of golden air.
. . . .
Between two gusts, cold waves, the golden tide.

Weather and Season is thus the pivotal volume in Hamburger's career in his gradual move from formal to free verse.

The subject matter of *Weather and Season* and Hamburger's next volume, *Travelling* (1969), are similarly varied. Hamburger emphasized this variety by dividing up the part of *Ownerless Earth: New and Selected Poems* (1973), which contains selections from these two volumes separated into several sections, "Weather and Season," "Observations and Ironies," "Dream Poems," and "Of Time and Place." (These sections also include new or previously unpublished poems.) During the 1960s, he extended his range of subjects as he had expanded his prosody. This growth had been foretold by "Travellers" in *The Dual Site* and poems such as "Man of the World" in *Weather and Season* which held a mirror up to contemporary mores, but it is most fully represented by the poems included under "Observations" and "Of Time and Place" in *Ownerless Earth*.

Many of Hamburger's poems of the 1960s satirize materialism, employing the traditional satiric devices of hyperbole, slang, parallelism, and punning. "Sick Transit" is about the international fashion model Gloria Mundy, thus playing on the Latin epigram *sic transit gloria mundi* ("thus passes

the glory of the world"); "In Philistia, Thoughts After a Public Reading of New Verse" begins, " 'To affirm the affirmative.' Yes."; "Little Cosmology" parodies The Gospel of St. John ("In the beginning was business."); "Lines Discovered in a London Dustbin" describes a poet's self-destruction, beginning "Hung up on true love and all that jazz / I looked for a woman among / the miniskirts miniminds maxipresumptions"; and "Life and Art I and II" explore the contradictions between life and art using mundane details and understated irony. Other poems deal with contemporary material less satirically, especially "In a Cold Season" (on Adolph Eichmann and the banality of evil) and "Between the Lines" and "Treblinka," which are dramatic monologues about prisons and concentration camps during World War II. The speakers move in and out of blank verse, speak plainly and powerfully, and build their moral authority by criticizing their own actions while they were imprisoned as well as the actions of the authorities like Eichmann:

to live is not good enough: everything, anything
Proved good enough for life—there, and not
only there.
Yet we lived, a few of us, perhaps with no
need but this:
To tell of the fire in the night and briefly flare
like the dead.

The voices of these ghosts from World War II (including that of Hamburger's grandmother, who died in the camps) contrast sharply with the well-fed and self-righteous figures who are attacked in Hamburger's satiric poems. When such poems are placed together in *Ownerless Earth* we see that the contrast is not just between different life-styles but between the self-sacrifice of the 1940s and the self-indulgence of the 1950s and 1960s.

Other poems from *Weather and Season* and *Travelling* veer away from public topics. In *Ownerless Earth* they are collected under the heading "Dream Poems." Many deal with disorientation, sexual fears, and despair more directly than any poetry Hamburger had previously written. In "Memory" the speaker is pursued by a corpse—his own self-doubts and despair. This twin is a grotesque parody of the strength-giving double in "The Dual Site":

But by the knee a stranger
Clawed me, held on;
I fought: my grappling hand
Slid deep into rotten flesh,
A hole behind his ear.

Fair copy (the author)

"By the Sea" is a paranoiac nightmare about a mermaid who eats the corpses of men washed up on the beach.

One group of new poems in *Ownerless Earth* shows, in its reflective and ironical manner, little of the hallucinatory intensity of the dream poems. In "Gone," a poem about a friend who drowned himself in the Thames, Hamburger ironically catalogues examples of the banality of death— "Paid his rent to the day, / Put on his raincoat and beret, walked out, / Leaving all he possessed, and one library book, overdue." "For a Family Album" fuses Hamburger's dreamlike and documentary modes, creating an imaginary snapshot of a woman and her children working together under the light of a lamp. But that peaceful union is soon dis-

rupted. The very light that allows the scene to be captured on film, that shapes the shared, peaceful space under the lamp, turns sharp and violent, reversing and negating the image:

> I cannot even describe them, caught no more
> Than a flash of light that ripped open
> The walls of our half-lit room;
> Or the negative—a black wedge
> Rammed into light so white that it hurt to look.

The speaker's family becomes both present in his memory and irrevocably absent—blown apart as if by a bomb: "Tied to my rooted bones / In your chairs you were flying, flying."

Many of Hamburger's poems of the late 1960s

seek to merge the private and public concerns of his speakers rather than to separate them as he does in the poems in "Dream Poems" and "Observations and Ironies." In *Weather and Season*, particularly in the poems "Omens," "Errors," "Old Poacher," and "After Attica," and in several of the best poems in *Travelling*, including "S-Bahn, Berlin 1965," "The Witness," "At Fifty-Five," "For a Family Album," "The House Martins," and "Home," Hamburger includes more details to locate the poems in place and time, and several seek to define precisely that line where private and public history intersect. Hamburger's emphasis on place and time extends to his prosody as well, for the plain speech, eclectic materials, and seemingly offhand, spontaneous form of these poems emphasize how Hamburger now trusts improvised forms of order. In poems such as "Omens" details of the present are noted in lists, as in a journal entry:

> The year opens with frozen pipes,
> Roads impassable, cars immovable,
> Letter delivery slow;
> But smallpox from Pakistan
> Carried fast from Yorkshire to Surrey.

And Hamburger continually emphasizes the fragility of our ability to order art or life. "Omens" later asks,

> How do we dare to live?
> Brashly building, begetting
> For a town besieged,
> Crumbling, patched again, crumbling
> And undermined?

Hamburger's language, much like that of Ted Hughes and Geoffrey Hill, echoes the violence of European history.

Similarly, "After Attica" is both about a vacation in Greece and a voyage to discover whether Greece may still provide a model for Western civilization. The speaker who catalogues the detritus of consumer society also confronts our need for myths—eternal forms of order—which allow us to transcend our history. Most of us remain blinking, uncomprehending barbarians when we contemplate what Greece has to teach us. This ironic view of the contemporary sensibility dissolves, however, into a final prayer for an original pastoral wholeness:

> Pray for eyes that blink
> At unblinking eyes,

> Outgazed, like us all.
> That ceiling too will go
> Despite our propping, patching:
> May there be eyes here to blink
> At the sun
> And be outgazed,
> Hands to water lettuce,
> To tend the bees.

Greece may still teach order, but its order is represented by the natural rhythms of agriculture rather than the unnatural and static emblems of perfection that haunt Hamburger's early work.

After the publication of *Travelling* and *Ownerless Earth*, the critical response to Hamburger's poetry became more thorough and balanced. Hamburger has recalled the largely hostile but contradictory responses to his early poetry in his memoir, but he noted that it "confirmed my resolve to write what I must, how I must, and let the work take care of itself." Critics are still in disagreement about his later poems, but they have noted the change in style and the greater variety of subject matter beginning with *Weather and Season*. For example, the *Times Literary Supplement* reviewer praised *Travelling* for its "subdued yet inventive" metaphorical patterns and "tersely observant tone," while other commentators, for *Poetry* and *Encounter*, remarked on its diversity and intimacy while also noting how strongly other poets had influenced it. *Ownerless Earth* was reviewed more widely still, and some attempts were made to characterize the shape of Hamburger's career as it had so far evolved. The *Encounter* reviewer generalized that in Hamburger's work "the properties of urban gardens and loved landscapes are generally involved with a sense of personal unrest, spiritual exile, uprootedness, and disappointed love." And in a 1975 essay in *Agenda* assessing Hamburger's work, Val Warner stressed how his poetry has pointedly responded to both his own and this century's disruptive history. Using Remy de Gourmont's distinction between an uprooted and a transplanted psyche, she suggests that, throughout his life, Hamburger has striven to find what de Gourmont called the new vigor that can come after the initial shock of being uprooted and transplanted. Hamburger, however, states emphatically that his poetry should not be read as autobiography, that his concerns are metaphysical rather than confessional.

Hamburger's two most recent books of poems, *Real Estate* (1977) and *Variations* (1981), have dealt with his perennial concerns—time, travel, and ownership—more subtly than any of his earlier volumes. *Real Estate* is a collection of separate poems written in the 1970s, many after 1978. In one of the best, "Birthday," the speaker, on a hot August afternoon, slips into a recollection of his childhood— "Fifty years melt in the hot air"—but he then envisions his mother as an aged woman and muses on his dead father:

> Elsewhere, my mother at eighty-eight
> Lies on a deck chair, drowning
> In that same space. Were my father alive
> Today he'd be ninety, the tissue
> Undone in him larger by thirty-five years;
> But the sounds and the silence round him
> The same; here, to receive him, the space.

Another fine poem is "The Old Man of Berkshire," in which a Wordsworthian epiphany briefly fuses past and present, England and America:

> Already
> The memory of that remembering fades out
> In evening light, the shapes of leaves
> On the trail, the waterfall high up
> In the rocks, and the horses, passing.
> Such distances lie between. We do not walk
> Down the lane from village to village,
> Suburbs by now, nor shall again.
> So, for less than a minute, let
> Him walk there still. . . .

Variations is a long sequence in two parts. The poems in the first part, "Travelling," were written in the late 1960s and early 1970s, and, in fact, not until two years after the first "Travelling" poem was published in *Travelling*, did Hamburger conceive of it as the first part of a sequence. The setting of "Travelling" is various. It begins in the North of England, jumps to Austria, Greece, and the Great Lakes region of the United States, switching continually both in space and time. The second section of *Variations*, "In Suffolk," returns the speaker to England and provides a sense of renewal. Constructed as a series of meditations on the weather and the seasons of a single year, it is as concentrated as "Travelling" is heterogeneous. This element of recurso in *Variations* may make it the most complete and satisfying volume of Hamburger's verse to date.

In "Travelling," he recreates a traveler's restlessness and disorientation:

> Thirty years back. Three hundred.
> It's the same earth.
> With beer can-openers lying
> Inches away from arrowheads,

> Flint, and fossils barely covered.
> The sameness confuses. If now
> A rabbit screamed I'd be elsewhere,
> By Thames or Windrush or Taw
> Moving as I now move
> Through one death to the next.

The credo for the entire sequence is that of "needing less, knowing / That at last a rightness must come / Of so much unlearnt." The end of the sequence describes the speaker's return to England. Loss has led to a kind of "rightness," a new strength and humility:

> Together we've walked, and apart,
> . . . .
> Out of ourselves, beyond
> "I", "you," and there
> Brought to a meeting again
> After difference, barer;
> Hardly daring to speak
> The other's name or the word
> Of sameness in otherness, love.

"In Suffolk" is about transplantation and renewal, not rootlessness, but instead of advancing claims for stability and the right to name, define, and own, it argues that true ownership and true naming must be tentative and transitory, never settled. A poet's poems must recognize "manyness" and celebrate beginnings rather than conclusions. The following stanzas, from the sequence's opening, turn upon the meanings that Hamburger gives the final word "tenure": here, it connotes "tenuous" and "tenancy" (both connected to it etymologically) rather than "fixed ownership":

> So many moods of light, sky,
> Such a flux of cloud shapes,
> Cloud colours blending, blurring,
> And the winds, to be learnt by heart:
> So much movement to make a staying.
> . . . .
> So much delving down
> With fork, spade, bare hands
> To endangered roots before,
> Weighed, breathed in, this earth
> Made known its manyness
> Of sand, humus, loam,
> Of saturation, and so
> Began to permit a tenure.

The "manyness" of forms, music, and subjects which Hamburger has sought is captured more fully in *Variations* than ever before. The rhythms in this passage are both earthy and airy, and its diction is harmoniously abstract and particular ("tenure" and "saturation" versus "wrenched," "fork," and "loam"). The music of the poem well fits its matter. Also characteristic of the volume as a whole is this passage's confident pairing of particular details and assigned symbolic meaning ("Such a flux of cloud shapes" becomes "So much movement to make a staying").

Since the start of Hamburger's career, he has probably been better known as a translator and critic than as a poet. He established his name with the 1943 and 1952 editions of his versions of Hölderlin's poems and with his critical volume *Reason and Energy: Studies in German Literature* published in 1957, and he is presently recognized as one of the best translators of German literature now publishing. Recently, his translation of poems by Paul

Celan, an exiled German-speaking Rumanian Jew with whom he feels much affinity, was published to great acclaim. But Hamburger's most recent volumes of poems, especially *Variations*, represent a new consolidation of the craft and moral intelligence of his own verse, and it is proof that although his poetry may be less known than his other work, it is still flowering.

References:

Jon Glover, "Across Frontiers: Michael Hamburger as Poet and Critic," *Stand*, 11, no. 4 (1970): 52-57;

John Matthias, "Travellers," *Poetry*, 124 (April 1974): 45-55;

Val Warner, " 'Loyal to Water': A Reading of the Poetry of Michael Hamburger," *Agenda*, 13 (Autumn 1975): 47-68.

John Heath-Stubbs
(9 July 1918-   )

A. T. Tolley
Carleton University

BOOKS: *Wounded Thammuz* (London: Routledge, 1942);

Beauty and the Beast (London: Routledge, 1943);

The Divided Ways (London: Routledge, 1946);

The Charity of the Stars (New York: Sloane, 1949);

The Swarming of the Bees (London: Eyre & Spottiswoode, 1950);

The Darkling Plain (London: Eyre & Spottiswoode, 1950; Folcroft, Pa.: Folcroft Press, 1970);

A Charm Against the Toothache (London: Methuen, 1954);

Charles Williams (London: Longmans, Green, 1955);

The Triumph of the Muse and Other Poems (London & New York: Oxford University Press, 1958);

Helen in Egypt and Other Plays (London: Oxford University Press, 1958);

The Blue-Fly in His Head (London & New York: Oxford University Press, 1962);

Selected Poems (London & New York: Oxford University Press, 1965);

Satires and Epigrams (London: Turret, 1968);

The Verse Satire (London: Oxford University Press, 1969);

The Ode (London: Oxford University Press, 1969);

The Pastoral (London: Oxford University Press, 1969);

Artorius Book I (Providence, R.I.: Burning Deck, 1970);

Thomas Blackburn and John Heath-Stubbs (Harlow: Longmans, 1970);

Penguin Modern Poets 20, by Heath-Stubbs, F. T. Prince, and Stephen Spender (Harmondsworth & Baltimore: Penguin, 1971);

Artorius (London: Enitharmon, 1973);

Four Poems in Measure (New York: Helikon, 1973);

A Parliament of Birds (London: Chatto & Windus, 1975);

The Watchman's Flute (Manchester: Carcanet New Press, 1975);

The Mouse, The Bird, and the Sausage (Sunderland: Ceolfrith Press, 1978);

Birds Reconvened (London: Enitharmon, 1980);

Naming the Beasts (Manchester: Carcanet New Press, 1982).

OTHER: *Poems from Giacomo Leopardi*, translated by

Heath-Stubbs (London: Lehmann, 1946);

The Forsaken Garden: An Anthology of Poetry 1824-1909, edited by Heath-Stubbs and David Wright (London: Lehmann, 1950);

William Bell, *Mountains Beneath the Horizon*, edited by Heath-Stubbs (London: Faber & Faber, 1950);

Aphrodite's Garland, translated by Heath-Stubbs (St. Ives: Latin Press, 1951);

Thirty Poems of Hafiz of Shiraz, translated by Heath-Stubbs and Peter Avery (London: Murray, 1952);

Images of Tomorrow: An Anthology of Recent Poetry, edited by Heath-Stubbs (London: SCM Press, 1953);

The Faber Book of Twentieth Century Verse, edited by Heath-Stubbs and David Wright (London: Faber & Faber, 1953; revised, 1965; revised again, 1975);

Giacomo Leopardi, *Selected Poetry and Prose*, translated by Heath-Stubbs and Iris Origo (London: Oxford University Press, 1966; New York: New American Library, 1967);

"Dryden and the Heroic Ideal," in *Dryden's Mind and Art*, edited by Bruce King (Edinburgh: Oliver & Boyd, 1969), pp. 3-23;

Alfred de Vigny, *The Horn/Le Cor*, translated by Heath-Stubbs (Richmond, Surrey: Keepsake Press, 1969);

Homage to George Barker on His 60th Birthday, edited by Heath-Stubbs and Martin Green (London: Brian & O'Keeffe, 1973);

Dust and Carnations: Traditional Funeral Chants and Wedding Songs from Egypt, translated by Heath-Stubbs and Shafik Megally (London: TR Press, 1977);

The Ruba'iyat of Omar Khayyam, translated by Heath-Stubbs and P. Avery (London: Allen Lane, 1979);

Anyte, translated by Heath-Stubbs and Carol Whiteside (Warwick: Greville Press, 1979).

SELECTED PERIODICAL PUBLICATIONS:
"The Poetic Achievement of Charles Williams," *Poetry London*, 4 (September-October 1947): 42-45;

"Baroque Ceremony: a study of Dryden's 'Ode to the Memory of Mistress Anne Killigrew' (1682)," *Cairo Studies in English*, 3 (1959): 76-84;

"Strata," review of *The Sleeping Lord*, by David Jones, *Agenda*, 11, no. 4/12, no. 1 (Autumn-Winter 1973/74): 64-67.

John Heath-Stubbs is a poet whose accomplishment spans four decades and has been marked by a steady dedication to the art of poetry. His work ranges from brief lyrics, such as make up *Birds Reconvened* (1980), to one of the few impressive poems in the heroic manner by a modern poet, his epic *Artorius* (1973). He has translated poetry from classical and modern languages and has written learnedly of Greek and Latin poetry as well as of major English poets. In the 1940s and 1950s, he did a great deal to reestablish the reputations of lesser romantic writers such as John Clare, Thomas Lovell Beddoes, George Darley, and James Thomson (1834-1882).

Born in London to Francis and Edith Marr Heath-Stubbs, John Francis Alexander Heath-Stubbs grew up near Bournemouth, on the south coast of England, and was educated first at local schools. Later, because of poor eyesight, he was sent to a progressive school, Bembridge, on the Isle of Wight. He disliked it and proceeded to educate himself by reading the *Encyclopaedia Britannica*. He went up to Queen's College, Oxford, in 1939. His poetry first appeared in undergraduate periodicals and in *Eight Oxford Poets* (1941), along with the work of Keith Douglas, Gordon Swaine, Michael Meyer, Roy Porter, Drummond Allison, J. A. Shaw, and Sidney Keyes—young writers who should have made their mark as the poets of the 1940s. They were called "the O.C.T.U. generation" by Sidney Keyes, after the Officer Cadet Training Units to which many of them belonged: by the end of the war, the three most brilliant—Keyes, Douglas, and Allison—were dead. Heath-Stubbs was not called up for military service because of his extremely poor eyesight. After Keyes and Allison had left, Heath-Stubbs became friendly with the slightly younger Oxford poet William Bell, who was not called up until 1944. Although he survived the war, Bell too was killed, climbing the Matterhorn, at the age of twenty-four, and Heath-Stubbs edited his posthumous collection, *Mountains Beneath the Horizon* (1950).

Keyes had been the initiator of *Eight Oxford Poets*, which he coedited with Michael Meyer, the editor of the undergraduate periodical *Cherwell*. In introducing the collection, Keyes wrote: "We seem to share a horror of the world's predicament, together with the feeling that we cannot save ourselves without some kind of spiritual readjustment, though the nature of the readjustment may take widely different forms . . . we are all . . . *Romantic* writers, though by that I mean little more than that

John Heath-Stubbs, circa 1950 (BBC Hulton, Picture Post)

our greatest fault is a tendency to floridity; and that we have, on the whole, little sympathy with the Audenian school of poets." While the description hardly applies to Douglas, who had in fact already left Oxford in 1940, it is valid as applied to a group of friends—Heath-Stubbs, Keyes, and David Wright (not included in *Eight Oxford Poets*)—of whom the older Heath-Stubbs was the literary leader. In a letter to David Wright, Keyes called Heath-Stubbs "the fountain head of my skill wherever I show any." Keyes, Allison, and Heath-Stubbs, at the Queen's College, were, as Philip Larkin later recalled, "the accepted poets of the University."

Larkin, Kingsley Amis, and Alan Ross were at St. John's College; and, while Meyer had been in favor of including Larkin's work in *Eight Oxford Poets*, Keyes evidently demurred.

John Wain, in his autobiography, *Sprightly Running* (1962), recalls, "The first poet I ever knew personally was John Heath-Stubbs, whose last few months at Oxford coincided with my first. A strange, gaunt figure, he wandered about Oxford with a stick to eke out his poor sight, a too-small blue trilby lodged insecurely on his gigantic thatch of hair; one saw him sauntering up the High, meditating golden lines."

Wain also comments that at Oxford during the 1940s everybody seemed to be Christian. A figure who commanded the admiration of Heath-Stubbs and his contemporaries at Oxford was the Anglican poet and publisher Charles Williams, who had been enlisted to lecture, as so many younger fellows were away at the war. According to Heath-Stubbs, Williams "exerted a lasting and deep influence" on the work of the younger generation of poets in the 1940s. In his work Williams showed an admiration for the then little-favored romantic poets and an interest in Arthurian legend and in magic. "Younger poets," Heath-Stubbs later wrote, "became interested in mythological and religious symbolism, as a means of expressing areas of experience inaccessible to the intellect alone."

At the end of the decade, Heath-Stubbs produced a critical study, *The Darkling Plain* (1950), in which he praised such neglected minor romantic poets as Darley, Clare, Beddoes, and Charles M. Doughty, together with the then frowned-upon Pre-Raphaelites. These admirations provided the literary ambience of his friendship with Keyes, and the influence of these writers is felt not only in their work but in that of David Wright, who at the time was much in awe of Keyes. Heath-Stubbs and Wright later produced an anthology, *The Forsaken Garden: An Anthology of Poetry 1824-1909* (1950), which like *The Darkling Plain* shows an orientation that was highly original in the early 1940s, when *romantic* was an unfavorable critical term. In *The Darkling Plain* Heath-Stubbs remarked: "The modern poet who deliberately rejects the Romantic tradition, rejects an experience through which the European consciousness has passed, and which has affected it profoundly."

As the 1940s progressed, the term "the New Romanticism" was widely used in the discussion of the arts and was employed by many to lump together a variety of work, from that of Vernon Watkins or David Gascoyne to that of minor contributors to the most notable journals of the persuasion, Tambimuttu's *Poetry London* and Wrey Gardiner's *Poetry Quarterly*. The "romanticism" of Keyes, Heath-Stubbs, and their friends owes little to other movements of the period, as Heath-Stubbs made clear in an article in a 1941 issue of *Cherwell*, "Tradition or Anarchy?," where he calls Tambimuttu's stance "the *reductio ad absurdum* of the Romantic method, with its emphasis on the importance of the writer's personality and his private emotions." He goes on to call for "the return to the classical tradition of English poetry." (Important for Heath-Stubbs were minor Augustan poets, such

as Lady Winchilsea and John Gay.) Indeed, a February 1941 article in *Cherwell*, "The Poetry of John Gay," seems to mark a turning point for him. His earliest undergraduate poetry is ironical and slightly Audenesque: the first poem in the Stubbsian manner seems to be "Pavanne Pour Une Infante Defunte," which appeared in *Cherwell* in March 1941. From then on we see the emergence of his characteristic early style, with its background of the lesser romantics, the minor Augustans, and the pastoral tradition.

Herbert Read, who published *Eight Oxford Poets* from Routledge, had been convinced by Sidney Keyes's poem "William Wordsworth" that Keyes "was a poet in the absolute sense." He was also impressed by some poems by Heath-Stubbs that Keyes showed him; and in 1942 he published Keyes's *The Iron Laurel* and Heath-Stubbs's *Wounded Thammuz*. The theme of *Wounded Thammuz* is the death and rebirth of the Babylonian god Thammuz, to which Heath-Stubbs gives Frazerian and allegorical undertones. In this long poem divided into sections the new and the archaic are combined to achieve a stylish pastoral quality. As these lines suggest, the movement of the verse and the interplay of sounds are handled with unusual deftness for a first collection:

> Southward, O wind, seeking the trellised vine,
> Long has the fickle-pinioned swallow flown,
> To amethystine clusters; but your breath,
> Though nursing next year's seeds, rudely shall pine
> Those birds who salt with song your bitter teeth.

Strongly literary in inspiration, recalling self-consciously Heath-Stubbs's admirations of those days, the book's originality lies in combining these influences to bring a new tone to poetry.

The next collection, *Beauty and the Beast* (1943), consists of shorter poems, several of which preceded *Wounded Thammuz*. The dramatic monologue "Leporello," included in *Eight Oxford Poets* and earlier published in *Cherwell* (leaving the undergraduate Philip Larkin "profoundly bewildered"), has as its central figure Don Juan's old servant, and it offers a striking example of Heath-Stubbs's gift for turning material that is literary in origin into an expression of individual feeling:

> Do you see that old man over there? —He was
>   once a gentleman's gentleman
> His skull is bald and wrinkled like a leathery
>   snake's egg;
> His forehead is not high, but his eyes, though
>   horny, are cunning.

Like an old jackdaw's beginning to moult a
       few grey feathers;
His nose is sharp like a weasel's, and his lips
       always a little smiling,
His narrow shoulders crouched forward,
       hinting a half-finished bow.
. . . .
He can remember his master well—those
       were the days!—
Feast days, Carnival days—fans and flowers
       and bright silk shawls
Tossing like a poppy-patched cornfield the
       wind dishevels,
And the milky moonlight flowing over close-
       kept courtyards;
And while his master climbed the balcony, he
       would keep watch,
Whistle and rub his hands and gaze at the
       stars—
His co-panders. . . .

The theme of Don Juan and his relationship to fear and death had evidently haunted Heath-Stubbs for a long time. In the preface to *Selected Poems* (1965), he recalls that "Leporello" was "conceived when I was eighteen years old, though it was not written till about four years later," and in that later volume, he placed it beside "Don Juan Muses" and "Donna Elvira," "poems, written separately and many years afterwards, which were nevertheless always closely connected with it in my mind, so that they are now presented as a single tripartite poem on a common theme" ("The Don Juan Tryptich"). That theme is associated with the figure of the Commendador in Mozart's *Don Giovanni*—the "stone death walking the castle corridors," of whom Donna Elvira says: "John, it is you he is looking for. He is your fear" ("Donna Elvira").

The stance of Leporello is characteristic in Heath-Stubbs's poetry: the outsider remembering lost experience or experience only vicariously attained. *Beauty and the Beast* includes a number of poems about exiled and departed heroes, such as "Stone-Age Woman," or "Edward the Confessor" with its thematic phrase, "Some say this world is dying, being done with." In an early article, "The Poetic Achievement of Charles Williams" (1947), Heath-Stubbs wrote: "the Europe of the Dark Ages . . . presented a picture perhaps closer to our time than that of any intervening period—the civilisation of Europe threatened by the forces of barbarism, the rise of new phases of faith and patterns of society." Such a view was natural enough in the aftermath of Hitler's Europe; but it seems to have remained an abiding vision for Heath-Stubbs. The

past is frequently associated in the earlier poems with nostalgia for a world of tenderness now shattered; and, as Alan Ross wrote when *The Divided Ways*, Heath-Stubbs's third collection, appeared in 1946, " 'The Old King' . . . may indeed symbolize a personal sense of frustration and exist validly as a direct expression of that sense of never being quite at the centre of life. . . ."

In 1943 Heath-Stubbs left Oxford, having been awarded his B.A. with first-class honors, but found it hard to get work. First dividing his time between working on his translations of the nineteenth-century Italian poet Giacomo Leopardi and writing *The Darkling Plain*, he eventually got a job in 1945 as an English master at the Hall School in Hampstead, followed by work in 1945-1946 on *Hutchinson's Twentieth-Century Encyclopedia*, for which he wrote almost all the articles on zoology, music, cookery, and theology—an activity that must certainly have added to the disparate learnedness with which his work sometimes bristles. It was during this period that Heath-Stubbs became a frequenter of Fitzrovia, the area north of Oxford Street and Soho in London, whose pubs became a meeting place during the war for younger writers and artists, frequently of a "New Romantic" disposition. There he met slightly older poets such as Dylan Thomas, George Barker, and W. S. Graham. The opening sequence of poems in *The Divided Ways*, "Nine Gothic Ballads," has something of the pseudonaive archaism favored by such neoromantics as Henry Treece. However, Heath-Stubbs's poetry does not seem, at this time or any other, to owe much to the idioms of Fitzrovia.

Heath-Stubbs remarked of Leopardi: "Since the traditional forms of religious belief seemed largely to have lost their significance, the poets constructed their own systems, taking their symbols from revived mythologies, or from their experience of erotic passion or natural beauty." These words, which resemble Yeats's much earlier statement of his artistic predicament as a young man, have a strong bearing on Heath-Stubbs's poetry. As one of the earliest studies of Heath-Stubbs's poetry pointed out, "an imagined historical event . . . is made to symbolize an actual event in the poet's personal history."

Heath-Stubbs himself has emphasized the symbolic nature of his poetry and that of Sidney Keyes in those earlier days. In *The Divided Ways* and its successor, *The Swarming of the Bees* (1950), there are translations from the French symbolist poets Gerard de Nerval and Mallarmé, as well as a sonnet on Hart Crane, who tended to use language in the suggestive manner of the French symbolists. Their influence is apparent earlier in the use of language in the symbolic sonnet sequence that concludes *Beauty and the Beast*, "The Heart's Forest"—poems that record the development of an amatory experience. One senses the presence of Mallarmé in the elusive but evocative handling of language in these lines from a sonnet in *The Divided Ways*:

> In the time of the unbearable tenderness
> of roses,
> And the small speaking bird among the
> quick-set thorn,
> The slow significance of swans, procession
> borne
> On dark but lucid streams, where softest air
> reposes.

Heath-Stubbs's early poetry is, paradoxically, freshest and most successful when it draws on literature or history for its inspiration, as in "An Heroic Epistle (from William Congreve to Anne Bracegirdle circa 1729)":

> Now it has all gone black, you are more
> than ever
> The cadence of a voice to me, the turn of a
> prose phrase;
> For my words in your mouth were a move-
> ment in time,
> Like your hand's movement spreading the
> white
> Fan, your turned wrist twisting the air;
> Or the curve of your white neck, caught in
> a slant-light,
> The tilt of your chin, and your smile mock-
> ing, mocking—
> And then your laughter—and so your voice
> again.

The movement of the voice is captured well in the fluent variation within the long lines that Heath-Stubbs favored. The poem is again an evocation of past experience or experience from which the speaker is excluded. Heath-Stubbs, at that time, recognized the literary nature of his inspiration—at once the theme and the limitation of his early poetry in "Elegy: To one long dead":

> I need your courage for my different prob-
> lems—
> To make words take their places, nor neglect
> The impingement on the world, which justi-
> fies
> The reverie in the garden, and the dream
> Of fairy countries in the enchanted hill.

In contrast to much modern poetry in English up to that time, Heath-Stubbs's early poetry is unironic—or marked by a nostalgic, romantic irony. It required originality to turn his back, as he did after a few early (but uncollected) poems, on a tone that was still so highly favored. Even though some of his early poetry may seem rather precious in style and subject matter, it had the distinction of offering a new tone—ethereal, wistful, accomplished, as in "Sestina":

> The winter moon that clambers through
> the pine-trees,
> Nor stirs the beaded rime upon their boughs,
> That haunts the forest with a pelt of ermine,
> Printing no trace upon the fallen leaves,
> And breeds a silver blossom in my heart,
> Finds the dew dry, the stream that cannot
> weep.

In 1946 Heath-Stubbs brought out his volume of translations *Poems from Giacomo Leopardi* (later revised and republished as part of Leopardi's *Selected Poetry and Prose*, edited by Heath-Stubbs and Iris Origo in 1966). It is easy to see the attraction that the work of Leopardi might have for Heath-Stubbs, who calls him "at once a Romantic and a Classicist." In his poem "To the Spring, or, Concerning the Ancient Myths" (as translated by Heath-Stubbs) Leopardi writes:

> The brooks were once a home for the white
> nymphs,
> Their shelter and their glass
> The liquid springs; and the high mountain
> ridges
> To secret dancing of immortal feet
> Trembled . . .

Heath-Stubbs writes that "Leopardi's language is highly literary and allusive. His poems contain many echoes of the Greek and Latin classics, and turns of phrase inherited from the Arcadians of the late seventeenth or eighteenth centuries in Italy." The remarks might be applied to his own poetry, particularly if "Augustans" were substituted for "Arcadians." Leopardi wrote in *endecasillabi*, the equivalent of English blank verse, and in *canzone libera*, a form akin to the freely rhyming verses of Milton's "Lycidas." In his earlier poetry Heath-Stubbs used the corresponding English forms widely, and he also wrote poems in dialogue, another form favored by Leopardi. Heath-Stubbs has also related that "The total atheism of Leopardi corresponded to mine at the time"; and it is in their poetic stances that Leopardi and Heath-Stubbs have the most in common. Like Heath-Stubbs, Leopardi had weak eyes: as with Milton, who frequently wrote as if viewing events from a place of shade, Leopardi and Heath-Stubbs look at events from the outside. In Leopardi this characteristic is associated with the sense of being excluded from experience—a feeling present in less extreme form in the poetry of Heath-Stubbs.

As the decade came to a close, historical and literary subjects seemed to evoke a less vital response in Heath-Stubbs, and *The Swarming of the Bees* is not so attractive a collection, with its translations from French and Provençal and "Alexandria's" long historical narrative whose main subject is the martyrdom of Saint Katherine and the murder of Hypatia. In the 1950s, there came a change of style, marked by the ironic "Epitaph" in the next collection, *A Charm Against the Toothache* (1954):

> Mr. Heath-Stubbs as you must understand
> Came of a gentleman's family out of Staf-
> fordshire
> Of as good blood as any in England
> But he was wall-eyed and his legs too spare
> . . . .
> Amongst the more learned persons of his
> time
> Having had his schooling in the University
> of Oxford
> In Anglo-Saxon Latin ornithology and crime
> Yet after four years he was finally not pre-
> ferred.
> . . . .
> In his youth he would compose poems in
> prose and verse
> In a classical romantic manner which was
> pastoral
> To which the best judges of the Age were not
> averse
> And the public also but his profit was not
> financial.
>
> Now having outlived his friends and most of
> his reputation
> He is content to take his rest under these
> stones and grass
> Not expecting but hoping the Resurrection
> Will not catch him unawares whenever it
> takes place.

There are hints at this time of a sense of failing inspiration, as in "Shepherd's Bush Eclogue"—"O Muse, I said then, dear sister, how long will your voice be mute?"—and of a need to explore personal roots, as evinced in "Obstinate in Non-attendance" and "Churchyard of St. Mary Magdalene, Old Milton," in which he returns to the scenes of his upbringing. The most touching writing in *A Charm Against the Toothache*—in such poems as "Address Not Known"—has a plainness and directness at odds with the earlier work:

> So you are gone, and are proved bad change,
> as we had always known,
> And I am left in London the
> metropolitan city,
> Perhaps to twist this incident into a durable
> poem—
> The lesson of those who give their love to
> phenomenal beauty.

During the late 1940s and early 1950s, Heath-Stubbs had attempted to make a living through free-lance writing, eked out by a small legacy. However, by 1952 he was running into difficulties, and Herbert Read and T. S. Eliot recommended him for the Gregory Fellowship in Poetry at Leeds University, where Bonamy Dobree was professor—a fact commemorated in one of his several occasional poems of those years, "Preface to an Anthology of Recorded Poetry: Presented to Professor Bonamy Dobree on his Retirement." Immediately after his three years at Leeds, he had two years as visiting professor of English at the University of Alexandria, an experience that had a considerable effect on his always historical imagination. During the academic year 1960-1961 he was at the University of Michigan at Ann Arbor, and for the remainder of the decade—until 1972—he lectured at the College of St. Mark and St. John in Chelsea in London. Since 1972 he has done part-time tutorial work at Oxford. In 1958 *The Triumph of the Muse and Other Poems* appeared; and in 1962, *The Blue-Fly in His Head*. These two volumes of poetry were followed by his retrospective collection *Selected Poems* (1965), which included poetry from all his earlier volumes (except the first, *Wounded Thammuz*) along with nineteen new poems. A further, shorter selection, which includes an additional eleven uncollected poems, appeared as part of *Penguin Modern Poets 20* in 1971.

In 1958 there appeared *Helen in Egypt and Other Plays*, a collection of three plays: *The Talking Ass* from 1950, "fundamentally an Aristophanic play," partly in verse; *The Harrowing of Hell* from the early 1950s, in designedly "liturgical" verse, "intended to be performed in church at Evensong on Easter Saturday"; and *Helen in Egypt*, also wholly in

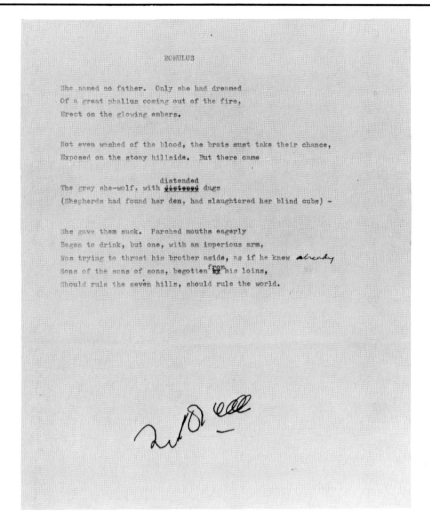

Signed typescript for a poem written to accompany a painting by John Cherrington. Because Heath-Stubbs is blind, the emendation was made by an amanuensis (the author).

verse, "written in Alexandria during the winter of 1956-7." The title play takes as its starting point Euripides' *Helena*. As Heath-Stubbs recalled, "I could see from my windows what was once the island of Pharos where, according to Euripides' version of the story, the real Helen was concealed. The circumstances in which I found myself during those months led me often to ponder the meaning of history and the destinies of nations. . . . The meaning of history and the nature of truth are . . . two of the themes of my play."

In the late 1950s, Heath-Stubbs wrote an essay, "Baroque Ceremony: a study of Dryden's 'Ode to the Memory of Mistress Anne Killigrew' (1682)," in which he called the ode a "fine poem" and a public one. This type of poetry he evidently found congenial. In a slightly later essay, "Dryden and the Heroic Ideal," he tried to show that "the

baroque heroic ideal represented for Dryden the realisation in poetic terms of a transcendental order." Heath-Stubbs is deeply versed in the traditional "forms" of poetry, as can be seen from the three introductory texts he produced in 1969—*The Verse Satire, The Ode,* and *The Pastoral*—and he clearly had a strong feeling for the type of "order" represented by the proper use of these "forms" in classical poetry. In this attitude he diverges from most modern conceptions of poetry, where the emphasis is on the authenticity of response to personal experience.

The Triumph of the Muse closes with the title poem, composed of six cantos of terza rima and having the form of a traditional dream vision, in which Heath-Stubbs sees many of his contemporary poets brought before the throne of the muse. The poem is fairly slight, and the intent critical and often satirical. More important and far more impressive (whatever one may feel about what is attempted) is his heroic poem *Artorius* (1973), which must have taken his best poetic energies of the late 1960s and early 1970s.

Artorius, described as "A Heroic Poem in Four Books and Eight Episodes," is a modern attempt at what was traditionally regarded as the highest literary form—and as an essentially public one—the epic. The subject is King Arthur; or, as it was termed in the Middle Ages, the "matter of Britain." The immediate impulse to attempt it may have come with the appearance of Gavin Bantock's *Christ* in 1966, and examples that must have been ever-present to Heath-Stubbs would be the Arthurian poems of Charles Williams, such as *Taliessin through Logres* (1938). Another early admiration was C. M. Doughty's *The Dawn in Britain* (1906), a twenty-four-book poem of early British history and the birth of Christianity that Heath-Stubbs described in *The Darkling Plain* as "the only full-length epic poem in English which might not be lessened in comparison with Milton's masterpiece." The matter of Britain has a long tradition in English literature, stretching back through Tennyson to Malory and to earlier medieval writers such as Geoffrey of Monmouth and Wace. Heath-Stubbs is personally familiar with this whole body of writing and was consciously aware of it in composing his epic. Indeed, his intimate familiarity extends to the whole body of European poetry, classical and modern, in the epic form. As he remarked in *The Darkling Plain*, "The history of epic poetry from Virgil to Milton is an epitome of the history of European Civilisation."

Artorius embodies many features of the epic identified in neoclassical criticism: the exemplary hero of historical importance to the culture in which the poem is written (Artorius or King Arthur); the invocation to the muse; battles (that begin and end Arthur's career); the descent into the underworld with a vision of future history; debates in which are discussed the nature of true religion (the synod at Oxford), the nature of poetry (the discussions of Gwion, Daegrafn, and Phyllidulus), and the nature of government (the conference at London). In the third book, the structure and its significance are explained by Myrddyn (Merlin):

> In the sign of the Bull, the bishops in synod
> Determined by dogma the *limes* of doctrine;
> In the sign of the Twins, song and sentence,
> The lines of communication, by your
>   laureates were cleared;

> The conduits of rhetoric were cleansed of
>   rubble:
> The frogs of the fens found their vocabulary;
> In the sign of the Crab, I sent you to
>   Ceridwen,
> From the maddening moonlight to the
>   Mother's cauldron,
> To face your futurity, and encounter your
>   fears
> And your utmost anxieties—an inner order
> Was created in that descent to the darkness
>   of her cavern.
> . . . .
> Now is the time for this knowledge to be
>   translated
> Into forms of government, to guide those
>   who follow.

Here another structural device is mentioned, the relationship of the various episodes to the signs of the zodiac.

It is through the episodes mentioned by Myrddyn that the epic's traditional exemplary function is made explicit in the poem: these discussions of religion, art, and politics relate as much to the present as to the past in which they take place. This contemporary relevance is emphasized by incidents that have an anachronistic quality, such as the rejection of religion by Cerdic the Saxon, who ends his speech before the opening battle with the Marxist echo: "In the freedom of the knowledge of necessity we fight them"; or "the psychedelic and spotted scarlet toadstool" that Fergus gulped down to attain a "lucid brightness/Of terrestrial paradise." One humorous episode is overtly anachronistic—the lecture on "The Possible Historical Basis for King Arthur's Conquest of the Roman Empire"; while the most amusing portions of the poem are Phyllidulus's lectures, brilliant parodies of the style of the Cambridge critic F. R. Leavis, whose writings had attained such a dominant position in the decade before *Artorius* was written. These humorous episodes have the function too of protecting the poem from the grandeur of its own ambitions in an age in which the "grand manner" would imply unqualified certainties, vulnerable to the ironic perspectives of our time. "Take down, Calliope, your trumpet from its tack," the poem opens, invoking the muse with a colloquial irreverence that implies that a similar feeling is part of the author's attitude to his own poem.

While the traditional structure of the epic provides the overall form for Heath-Stubbs's poem, a continuous narrative in the grand style is not a possibility for the modern poet. The four "books" are narrative, for which Heath-Stubbs uses a variant of the long line that he manipulated so successfully in his earlier poetry: in *Artorius* he modified it to make it a version of the alliterative meter of English medieval poetry, traditionally associated with the "matter of Britain" in poems such as Layamon's *Brut* (circa 1205) or the fourteenth-century *Morte Arthure* (circa 1360). The "eight episodes" are in a variety of forms, ranging from the lyric to prose, one episode being in the form of the Japanese Noh play, and another, the death of Arthur, being in the form of a classical Greek tragedy.

The vision of *Artorius* is traditional and conservative: "Law is love in action" is a premise of the debate on government. The author sees himself as living "somewhere near the beginning of the Third Dark Age of European civilization" (the previous two being after "the collapse of the Minoan-Mycenean culture" and after the fall of the Western Roman Empire). This pessimistic historical vision has been an enduring one with Heath-Stubbs and goes hand in hand with his traditionalist conceptions, which allow little place for any idea of progress. Heath-Stubbs clearly does not feel at home with the attitudes of the age in which he lives; and *Artorius* is not in the main line of the literature of the period. Indeed, it is a tour de force in its adaptation of a form that most would have regarded as outmoded. Marked by an awareness of and reference to literature at all levels of the poem, it will appeal to those who like this and repel those who do not.

The years following the publication of *Selected Poems* in 1965 were not very fruitful for Heath-Stubbs in terms of shorter poems. In 1968 he produced *Satires and Epigrams*—in large measure a demonstration that his talent is not well suited to this form of "public" poetry. The one memorable poem is "Lyke-Wake Dirge," written for the death of Louis MacNeice. His short poems, composed since 1965 (including the new ones in *Penguin Modern Poets 20*) were brought together in *The Watchman's Flute* (1975), a collection of some fifty poems, representing the work of nearly a decade and a half. Six are light, occasional poems; three are translations from the Greek; several, such as "Homage to J. S. Bach," take art as their subject; while others such as "Volund" or "The Twelve Labours of Hercules" or "Quetzacoatl" draw their material from mythology or history. Many are brief. Few arise directly from an event in the poet's own experience, but there are strongly felt poems for the deaths of Vernon Watkins and Brian Higgins, as well as the

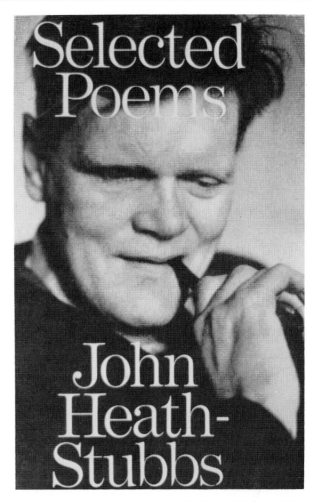

Dust jacket for Heath-Stubbs's 1965 book, in which he included poems from all his earlier collections except the first, plus nineteen new poems

one for Louis MacNeice. "A Formality" (written in memory of T. S. Eliot) states Heath-Stubbs's latter-day credo: "I would rather emulate those/ Who countered despair with elegance, emptiness with a grace." "To the Queen," written for the Silver Jubilee in 1977 (the kind of public poem with which most poets do not succeed), is one of the best—engaging in movement and touching in sentiment:

> Because the heart is finite, and can give
> Its love and loyalty only to particulars—
> Seeing in the known village, city, country,
> A partial revelation of that one good place
> Where all the just are citizens. . . .

The Watchman's Flute impresses more than it moves one. Wholly delightful, in contrast, are *A*

Parliament of Birds (1975) and its companion, *Birds Reconvened* (1980), poems about English birds remembered with perception in their natural settings, as in "The Yellow Wagtail":

> Red and white, the gentle Herefords wander
> Through the lush water-meadow, plashy
> and green—
> And gold with butter-cup gold, white with
> moon-daisies,
> Lady-smocks, meadowsweet.
> They go in a placid cowpat dream—with a
> flash
> Of yellow breast and throat, the wagtail
> Darts in and out among them, and snaps
> At the black and buzzing flies that are the
> beasts' annoy.

Equally heartening is *Naming the Beasts* (1982), a collection of some forty poems produced in the preceding four years, that attests to a happy return to the short poem. There is a plainness about even the poems on literary subjects and an emotional directness throughout that is particularly touching, as in "A Butterfly in October":

> What can I do?
> What can we ever do—the weft and warp
> Of all existence being so utterly shot through
> With innocent and irremediable suffering?
> So I deliver you to the stark airs of death—
> But you will die free.

This quality is manifest in the poems in which Heath-Stubbs remembers or addresses literary friends—"Funeral Music for Charles Wrey Gardiner," "In Memoriam Herbert Read," and "Letter to David Wright." In the poem for Wright he says,

> The journey is towards
> Silence and darkness. Who, if not you and I,
> Should know the only silence to be feared
> Is that residing in
> The unresponsive heart, the darkness
> which possesses
> The self-obfuscating mind?

Heath-Stubbs sees himself "as an exile and ambassador" ("His Excellency's Poetry") in the world of the 1980s; yet *Naming the Beasts* has a freshness and naturalness of engagement with experience that does not suggest a writer out of tune with the age into which he has lived.

The reservations one may have about *The Watchman's Flute* might be voiced concerning the body of Heath-Stubbs's shorter poems since the mid-1950s. Despite the poetic self-confrontations concerning his earlier poetry in "Epitaph," the inspiration for his later poems remains decidedly literary. *The Triumph of the Muse*, *The Blue-Fly in His Head*, and the new work in *Selected Poems* include poems on classical subjects—"Plato and the Waters of the Flood," "Titus and Berenice," "Tiberius on Capri"; poems about artists or works of art—"A Sonata by Scarlatti," "Mozart and Salieri"; exercises in older poetic modes such as "A Little Bestiary"; a large number of poems about poets, poetry, and language—"To Constantine P. Cavafy," "Ars Poetica," "Poetry Today," "Footnote on Epic Diction," "Use of Personal Pronouns." In this respect, the latter part of Heath-Stubbs's career is much like that of W. H. Auden, whose later books are full of occasional poems, light poems, poems based on incidents in legend, and poems about poetry and the arts, not to mention long poems in which traditional forms are revived or modernized, such as Auden's eclogue in alliterative verse, *The Age of Anxiety* (1948). Like Auden's later poetry, the poems in *The Blue-Fly in His Head* are urbane, natural in diction (though leaning to the recondite), and accomplished. Yet, as with the later Auden, the emotional temperature is low. Opinion may prove to be as divided about Heath-Stubbs's poetry as it is about Auden's, where admirers of the early work often decry the later.

It is of course true that Heath-Stubbs's poetry has always taken its subject matter from history, legend, and literature; so that, in this respect, it might be argued that it has changed less than poems such as "Epitaph" suggest. Yet it might equally well be maintained that early poems, such as "Leporello," that took their inspiration from the arts, give a sense of a more complex resonance with personal concerns than do later ones of similar inspiration. Many of the later poems before *Naming the Beasts* seem to have a simpler relationship to concerns that are themselves more conscious, and do not give the impression of exploration that the earlier poems did. They often seem no more than occasions for writing poems on attractive themes; while the classical "properties" of the early poetry are a feature of its symbolist mode. In the later poetry, references to the muse, for instance, seem often no more than an oblique, though decorative, manner of speech.

Heath-Stubbs's career is one of the best sustained and most impressive among British poets of his generation. It was not merely death and the war that were the enemies of the poets born between 1917 and 1925. The 1940s provided a difficult and deceptive ambience for new writers. Larkin, Amis, and Wain, who emerged as poets of individuality in the 1950s, made little mark with their work of the 1940s. Most of those who found the idiom of the period congenial discovered later that they could not stay with that idiom, but they were unable to reestablish themselves as poets in a new mode. Of that ultimately prolific group at Oxford in the early 1940s, only Heath-Stubbs and Alan Ross have made sustained poetic careers by writing in a manner that derives from the one that brought them attention in their early years. Through a long and impressive career, Heath-Stubbs has brought to English poetry a voice distinctive and accomplished. He stands apart from the age in which he has written, bringing to it a criticism that derives from an erudite aware-

ness of the legacy of past greatness, from which so much of his best work derives.

References:

Aquarius, special Heath-Stubbs issue, 10 (1978);

Thomas Blackburn, *The Price of an Eye* (London: Longmans, 1961; New York: Morrow, 1961);

Anthony Curtis, "John Heath-Stubbs: A Symbolist Poet," *Poetry Quarterly*, 10 (Spring 1948): 26-30;

George Every, *Poetry and Personal Responsibility* (London: SCM Press, 1948);

John Press, *Rule and Energy* (London: Oxford University Press, 1963);

Alan Ross, Review of *The Divided Ways, Poetry Quarterly*, 9 (Summer 1947): 115-117.

John Hewitt
(28 October 1907-   )

Terence Brown
Trinity College, Dublin

BOOKS: *Conacre* (Belfast: Privately printed, 1943);

Compass (Belfast: Privately printed, 1944);

No Rebel Word (London: Muller, 1948);

Those Swans Remember: A Poem (Belfast: Privately printed, 1956);

Tesserae (Belfast: Festival Publications, Queen's University of Belfast, 1967);

Collected Poems 1932-1967 (London: MacGibbon & Kee, 1968);

The Day of the Corncrake: Poems of the Nine Glens (N.p.: The Glens of Antrim Historical Society, 1969);

The Planter And The Gael, by Hewitt and John Montague (Belfast: Arts Council of Northern Ireland, 1971);

An Ulster Reckoning (Belfast: Privately printed, 1971);

Out Of My Time (Belfast: Blackstaff Press, 1974);

Scissors for a One-Armed Tailor (Belfast: Privately printed, 1974);

The Chinese Fluteplayer (Lisburn: Privately printed, 1974);

Time Enough (Belfast: Blackstaff Press, 1976);

Colin Middleton (Belfast: Arts Council of Northern Ireland, 1976);

Art in Ulster: 1 (Belfast: Blackstaff Press, 1977);

The Rain Dance (Belfast: Blackstaff Press, 1978);

John Luke, (1906-1975) (Belfast: Arts Council of Ireland, 1978);

Kites In Spring, A Belfast Boyhood (Belfast: Blackstaff Press, 1980);

The Selected John Hewitt, edited by Alan Warner (Belfast: Blackstaff Press, 1981);

Mosaic (Belfast: Blackstaff Press, 1981);

Loose Ends (Belfast: Blackstaff Press, 1983).

PLAY: *The Bloody Brae*, BBC Northern Ireland, 1954; Belfast, Lyric Theatre, March 1957.

SCREENPLAY: *I Found Myself Alone*, Arts Council of Northern Ireland, 1978.

OTHER: *Coventry, The Tradition of Change and Continuity*, introduction by Hewitt (Coventry: Coventry Corporation, 1966);

The Poems of William Allingham, edited, with an introduction, by Hewitt (Dublin: Dolmen Press, 1967);

The Rhyming Weavers, and other country poets of Antrim and Down, edited by Hewitt (Belfast: Blackstaff Press, 1974).

PERIODICAL PUBLICATIONS:
Nonfiction:
"The Bitter Gourd: Problems of the Ulster Writer,"
    Lagan, 3 (1945): 93-105;
"Poetry of Ulster: A Survey," *Poetry Ireland,* 8
    (January 1950): 3-10;
"Some Notes On Writing in Ulster," *Bell,* 18 (July
    1952): 197-202;
"Planter's Gothic, An Essay in Discursive Autobiog-
    raphy," as John Howard, *Bell,* 18 (January
    1953): 497-510;
"Planter's Gothic—II," as Howard, *Bell,* 18 (March
    1953): 605-612;
"The Course of Writing in Ulster," *Rann,* 20 (June
    1953): 43-52;
"Planter's Gothic—III," as Howard, *Bell,* 18 (Au-
    tumn 1953): 94-103;
"From Chairmen and Committee Men, Good Lord
    Deliver Us," *Honest Ulsterman,* 6 (October
    1968): 16-22;
"The Family Next Door," *Threshold,* 23 (Summer
    1970): 14-19;
"No Rootless Colonist," *Aquarius,* 5 (1972): 90-95;
Editorial, *Threshold,* 31 (Autumn/Winter 1980):
    1-2—Hewitt was guest editor of this issue.
Drama:
The Bloody Brae, Threshold, 1 (Autumn 1957): 14-32.

Since the 1930s John Hewitt has produced a
body of verse which, because of its assured
craftsmanship, its steady, persistent moral seriousness, and its exploration of the complex issue of
Irish identity, has come to be recognized as one of
the most significant achievements by an Irish poet
in the twentieth century, to be set beside those
of Louis MacNeice (1907-1963), Austin Clarke
(1896-1974), and Patrick Kavanagh (1905-1967), all
poets who like Hewitt himself began their careers in
the decades in which Ireland's greatest poet, W. B.
Yeats (1865-1939), achieved his greatest fame.

John Harold Hewitt was born in Belfast in
1907 in that part of Ireland which was to become,
following the partition of the island, Northern Ireland. Both his parents, Robert Telford and Elinor
Robinson Hewitt, were teachers and, like his ancestors on both sides of the family, loyal Methodists,
observing the strict moral code of that creed while
maintaining its traditional respect for education
and self-improvement. Hewitt was educated at the
Methodist College in Belfast and at the Queen's
University in that city, where he graduated with a
degree in English. From 1930 until 1957 he worked
in the Belfast Museum and Art Gallery. In 1957 he
became director of the Herbert Art Gallery and

John Hewitt

Museum in Coventry, where he remained until his
retirement in 1972.

Hewitt's origins in the nonconformist section
of Ireland's population were to be of considerable
significance to him as a poet, contributing in no
small measure to the central concerns of his work.
His earliest influences enforced on him a respect for
dissent in all its forms, even though the political
developments of twentieth-century Northern Ireland were to make such respect a rare phenomenon
in his native province. Likewise, the poet's voice,
resolutely defending the rights of individuals to
political unorthodoxy, was often a lonely one indeed.

Until the 1970s, when Hewitt underwent a
remarkable late rebirth of original poetic energy,
the poet's most obvious concerns had been, first, the
relationship of his people (the Protestant planters of
the North of Ireland) with the earlier inhabitants of
the country (the Irish Catholic majority—though
they constituted a minority within the six counties of
Northern Ireland), and second, his own relationship with the Ulster and Irish countryside to which,
as he ruefully confesses in one poem, he may have
turned "because men disappoint me" ("The Ram's

Horn"). These themes, expressed throughout much of his career, were conveyed in a controlled, carefully crafted, formally unadventurous but skilled verse that critics have tended to identify as the poetic equivalent of the Northern Protestant psyche, blending reserve with moments of firm, direct speech, quiet irony with occasional romantic longing.

Hewitt began writing poetry in the late 1920s (AE, the editor of the *Irish Statesman,* that nurturer of so many budding Irish talents, published his work in 1929), and throughout the 1930s he continued to have poems published steadily and fairly widely in British and Irish periodicals. During this period of his life, together with his wife, Roberta Black, whom he married on 7 May 1934, he was involved both in political groups concerned to protect civil liberties in Northern Ireland and with a group of artists known as the Ulster Unit, which hoped to bring developments in modern art to the attention of Northern Ireland's considerably provincial public. No full-scale collection of Hewitt's work appeared until 1948, when *No Rebel Word* saw the light of day. Nevertheless in 1943 the poet had privately printed *Conacre*, a poem of almost four hundred lines, and in 1944 *Compass*, a short collection comprising a short poetic epigraph and two longer pieces, was also privately printed. In both of these works the poet's sense of his personal isolation as a man who does not readily identify with the political assumptions of his fellows and his sense of release in the Irish landscape are present.

Crucial to Hewitt's sense of alienation from many of his fellow countrymen in the 1930s and 1940s was his political and cultural sensitivity. He early came to believe that the Protestant majority in the new state of Northern Ireland, predominantly the descendants of colonial settlers of the seventeenth century, could not but come to terms with their ambiguous inheritance and mongrel identity if they were to live with any hope of a decent future in the country of their birth. They could not depend indefinitely on the Parliament at Westminster to protect their position in an Ireland that sought full independence from Britain, nor could they in justice or in terms of simple self-interest persist in treating the Catholic national minority in Northern Ireland and the Catholic nationalist majority on the island as a whole as social inferiors. As early as 1936 or 1937 (the poet himself is unsure of the date and no clear record exists) Hewitt had written *The Bloody Brae*, a dramatic poem for six voices (it was eventually published in a 1957 issue of *Threshold*), which acknowledged the guilt that the inheritors of the

seventeenth century's acts of dispossession must inevitably bear on their shoulders and contained "a plea for forgiveness for the wrongs of our past and tolerance between the communities." As a stimulus to this political and cultural enterprise Hewitt in the 1940s became a proponent of the concept of regionalism. Writing of the period he observed in 1972: "my thought stimulated by the ideas of Le Play and Patrick Geddes, mediated through the successive books of Lewis Mumford, found itself directed towards and settled upon the concept of Regionalism." The world, becoming so centralized and controlled by vast bureaucracies, had to be broken down into smaller, more human units:

> In a word, the Region, an area of a size and significance that we could hold in our hearts.
> It seemed obvious to me that the Province of Ulster was indeed such a Region; so I set about deepening my knowledge of its physical components, its history, its arts, its literature, its folklore, its mythology scrupulously examined and assessed, its weaknesses confronted, its values recognised. It seemed also to hold the hope and promise that in this concept might be found a meeting-place for the two separated communities which dwelt within its limits, where the older and less old peoples might discover a basis for amity and cooperative progress.

Associated with the Belfast-produced literary and cultural magazine *Lagan* (of which Hewitt was associate editor in 1945-1946), the concept had some currency for a few brief years among writers and critics in Northern Ireland, for which fact Hewitt was chiefly responsible. From his absorption in the concept came too some of his best poems on the Northern Irish Protestant's sense of ambiguous identity, a number of which found a place in his first major collection, *No Rebel Word*. Of these, probably the best-known is "Once Alien Here" (written in 1942), in which the poet accepts that his people are comparative newcomers in Ireland but that he (and the people) is

> because of all the buried men
> in the Ulster clay, because of rock and glen
> and mist and cloud and quality of air,
> as native in my thought as any here.

That collection, as well as poems on the poet's relationship with the majority of the island's inhabitants, contains a number of his very skillful landscape poems. These poems, which owe something to the English eighteenth-century tradition of to-pographical verse with their exact eye for detail, their informed botanical and ornithological content, for example, are not unrelated to the poet's concern to define his people's relationship to the island on which they find themselves. They are the poems of a city man for whom the country is an area of psychic release from urban concerns, irritations, and constraints. As such they are almost unique in the Irish poetic tradition, which in the main has found its center of gravity in rural Ireland, taking the life of the country entirely for granted as a primary reality. Hewitt experienced the city as primary reality, the country as a novel, fascinating territory to be explored, learned of, and perhaps comprehended. In approaching the Irish countryside in this manner he, almost unconsciously, highlighted his distinctiveness as a Northern Protestant writer in the Irish twentieth century, one whose early experience, like that of so few of his compatriots, had been entirely urban.

Two features of the Irish countryside attracted Hewitt's attention in particular. He was respectful of a landscape that displayed the ordering and controlling hand of man. A planted countryside suggested social progress and human resource, but the planted landscape of Ireland could not be celebrated unambiguously by the poet, with his knowledge of the association of planting and colonial plantation. In the ordered fields of the Ulster rural scene he could read a history of dispossession and racial grievance, and at moments the poet became aware of the Irish rural world as containing darker, more primitive energies than could be easily absorbed by the principles of human order. The tension between these two apprehensions of the Irish countryside accounts for some of Hewitt's most interesting poetic achievements in *No Rebel Word*. A compelling example is "The Glens," where the poet expresses his deep love for the Glens of Antrim but recognizes the distance that lies between him and the inhabitants of the district:

> Not these my people, of a vainer faith
> and a more violent lineage. My dead
> lie in the steepled hillock of Kilmore
> in a fat country rich with bloom and fruit.

In the late 1940s and in the 1950s (*No Rebel Word* contains no poem written later than the first half of 1944), as the poet's commitment to the concept of regionalism became less immediate, and paradoxically as he came to know more and more about his native region, Hewitt's vision of Ireland became

more complex. Partly aided by the work of the human geographer Estyn Evans, the author of *Irish Heritage* (1942) and *Irish Folk Ways* (1957), and partly by his own knowledge of the material aspects of Ulster's social and cultural history, Hewitt began to hope that beneath the apparent divisions of his native province, which had their most virulent expression in what appeared to be religious bigotry and sectarianism, lay a shared environment which had perhaps determined a common consciousness more resilient and permanent than current factionalism might suggest. The imagery of the old Celtic and pre-Celtic lore of the countryside, deriving from intimate relationship with place, was therefore employed in *Those Swans Remember* (a long poem of over two hundred lines, which the poet had privately printed in Belfast in 1956) to imply the common sources of the Irish mind.

In 1968 Hewitt's *Collected Poems 1932-1967* allowed his readers to appreciate the consistent quality of his craftsmanship. It also permitted them to realize how the poet's two main concerns—the Protestant Irishman's identity crisis (adumbrated most directly with a controlled power in a long poem of 1949, "The Colony") and the common Irish heritage, which a shared environment had inevitably bequeathed to all the inhabitants of the island—were part of a larger poetic vision that gave an overall integrity to his achievement to that date. That vision was of man as a creature of his environment, who participated in the endless movements of nature through his own acts of making: artifacts, buildings, philosophies, nations, and smaller groupings of people. Hewitt's art could be read as a series of acts of attempted definition in which the limits of man's activities are identified and set against the natural order, which also has its limits of time and space. A sense of continuity and change as the essential dialectic which absorbed his imagination seemed the center of his art. This vision, mediated in what was predominantly a tone of calm, sane, generalizing reflection, was one that could command respect, could humble the reader in its awareness of vistas, perspectives, the round of the seasons, and the inevitable dominance of nature even over man's most magnificent creations. But what one also noticed was that this imagination, driven to define, explain, reflect, was also one touched by a sense of isolation, even alienation. Despite moments of an almost Wordsworthian, sober joy in nature, one sensed also a sensibility haunted, in its awareness of man's endless peregrinations about the globe, by a fear of final homelessness. And, as in "A Country Walk in March," a basic wish to belong pulses beneath the calm surfaces of many of the poems in the volume:

> the sad wonder if in any place
> my passing leaves a more enduring trace,
> and if the verses that I rush to print
> are worth as much as these stray wisps of lint.

This impression that alienation was a crucial aspect of Hewitt's sense of life was consolidated in 1969 when he produced *The Day of the Corncrake: Poems of the Nine Glens.* The fruit of a truly detailed, respectful knowledge of the Glens of Antrim, these poems nevertheless reflect, at a local and personal level, the poet's self-conscious awareness of the divisions between people and individuals, of boundaries invisibly staked out but real enough for all that.

In 1972 Hewitt returned from Coventry to his native Belfast. His return coincided with one of the worst years of political violence that the city had known for many generations. Hewitt had already, in a privately printed pamphlet of 1971, registered his protest and dismay at the outbreak of violence which had begun in his native province in 1969. Entitled *An Ulster Reckoning,* the poems in this pamphlet express a humanist distress, but do not transcend their rather journalistic occasions in effect. In 1970 the poet had tried to do his own small part in responding to the political crisis that was unfolding when he toured a number of Northern Irish towns with his fellow Ulster poet John Montague under the auspices of the Arts Council of Northern Ireland, their joint enterprise resulting in the pamphlet *The Planter And The Gael* (1971), which includes poems by both poets to "complement each other and provide illuminating insights into the cultural complexity of the Province."

Hewitt's return to Belfast in 1972 coincided with more than a recrudescence of political crises and civil unrest in Northern Ireland. Since the middle 1960s a resurgence of interest in poetry had occurred among the educated young in the province, and a number of young poets had begun to make their mark—Derek Mahon, Seamus Heaney, James Simmons, and Michael Longley being the best known of these—and since that date many other names have entered the poetic lists, as their elders have consolidated substantial reputations. For a few years the repatriated Hewitt served as something of a father figure to this youthful body of writers. Generous of time and advice, he found that his retirement from art-gallery work allowed him opportunity for a wide range of activities, which included readings, broadcasts, serving as writer in

residence at the Queen's University of Belfast (1976-1979), writing and publishing a number of works of art criticism, as well as an edition, based on his 1951 M.A. thesis at Queen's, of a selection of the work of the weaver poets of late-eighteenth-century, early-nineteenth-century Ulster. His contribution to Irish letters was recognized by the New University of Ulster, which awarded him an honorary doctorate in 1974. The years since his retirement and return from Coventry to Belfast have also seen a steady harvest of new volumes of poems. There have been six to date, excluding two pamphlets (*Scissors for a One-Armed Tailor,* subtitled marginal verses 1929-1954, and *The Chinese Fluteplayer,* both privately printed in 1974) and *The Selected John Hewitt* (edited with an introduction by Alan Warner, 1981). The years which have elapsed since the publication of his *Collected Poems 1932-1967* allow us to see how the poet's work has developed and deepened since then; for such a process has undoubtedly taken place, and it has been one of the events in Irish poetry of the last decade for which one should be most grateful.

For all the strengths of Hewitt's work exemplified in *Collected Poems 1932-1967,* the critic would, in 1968, have felt justified in offering Hewitt's oeuvre great respect but in regretting certain absences. The qualities of detachment which had allowed so observant an eye its proper exercise, the continual practice of discrimination, qualification, and definition, the sobriety of overall mood, had tended to exclude human warmth, personal feeling unprotected by rhetoric, and the direct expression of intense emotion. So often had the poet taken upon himself the responsibility to speak for the group, for his people, or for himself as type—planter, dissenter, socialist, curator of local lore, city man, traveler—that the self seemed oddly absent, unrevealed. In the last ten years that self has, as Hewitt's poetry has subtly altered, been allowed freer, more heartfelt expression. In "On The Canal" (in *Out Of My Time,* 1974) the poet accepts that "I am equipped / for report, comment, comparison," but in "Clogh-Oir: September 1971," a poem in the same volume, he allows himself a poignant reverie on his wife's childhood, diffidently acknowledging that he is a poet of the kind "who seldom name such stirrings, or yield words / for the dialectic of the heart." Amid poems that seem continuous in matter and mode with those in the *Collected Poems 1932-1967,* that use the same equipment, greater room is allowed in the volumes Hewitt has had published since 1974 for that difficult dialectic in verse that depends less frequently on the iambic line than hitherto, achieving a new assured flexibility. Poems salute named individuals with more open love and affection than they had done. Where his subject had been man, now it is also men and women. And one of those women is his wife, Roberta, who died as the result of a brain tumor in 1975. In *The Rain Dance* (1978) a sequence of poems, "Sonnets for Roberta," bears eloquent testimony to the poet's love (it is most revelatory of this poet's tact and restraint in a confessional age that these poems had been originally composed in 1954), and their last days together are remembered with heartbreaking immediacy in "The Last Summer, for Roberta (1975)."

The poet's father too becomes a dominant figure in his later collections, his life and particularly his death haunting the aging poet. Thoughts of wife and father, the poet's primary dead, seem also to have opened a vein of familial curiosity, memory, and piety as in each of his new volumes the poet gives poems to his kin so that his subject, man, now receives a very local habitation and very particular names. This process reaches its climax in what is a blend of autobiography, reminiscence, genealogy, and family portrait album, the volume of sonnets and photographs *Kites In Spring, A Belfast Boyhood* (1980).

The subtitle of this volume suggests another way in which Hewitt's poetry has developed since 1968. For not only has it deepened in its capacity to express immediate, intimate feeling for individuals and for the poet's personal past, but it has begun to accept the urban world which earlier he had rejected for poetic excursions to the Irish countryside, where metaphors for poetry could be found. In *Conacre* he had asserted of Belfast:

> And yet should these high chimneys tumble down,
> the gantries sag and fall, and nettles crown
> the festered mounds of rust above the marsh,
> and herons nest, and kittiwakes cry harsh
> over the banks where bridge and rigging met,
> there is but little that I should regret.

Kites In Spring proves otherwise of the poet in old age, for it is largely an urban world which is remembered with genuine affection. It is also an urban or suburban world in which a recent volume concludes, with its poem "Vigil" (in *Mosaic*, 1981; an earlier version had opened *The Chinese Fluteplayer* in 1974), encapsulating Hewitt's central concern with man on his earth, touched here with a deeply personal sense of how one man, a poet, has spent a life

Front cover for Hewitt's 1980 collection of sonnets about his family. The children in the photograph are Hewitt and his sister Eileen.

which now approaches its final phase:

> I wait for a meaning in the coming words
> sure as the earth of seasons, sure as a street
> of the familiar tread of postman's feet,
> or as a winter tree is sure of birds;
> for earth is what the seasons happen to,
> and in the branches crotch a tattered nest
> still wisps in wind, and in the houses, you
> to whom th' expected letters are addressed.

Hewitt's reputation ripened slowly. The publication of his *Collected Poems 1932-1967* in 1968 won him widespread respect in Ireland and in the United Kingdom. When the work of the last fourteen years and what he may still have in store come to be assessed together with the earlier work, and when the range and depth which recent years have added to his achievement are fully appreciated, that respect can only increase and be joined by something more celebratory.

Interviews:

Eavan Boland, "The Clash of Identities," *Irish Times,* 4 July 1974, p. 10;

Timothy Kearney, "The Planter and the Gael: An Interview with John Hewitt and John Montague," *Crane Bag,* 4, no. 2 (1980): 85-92.

References:

Terence Brown, *Northern Voices* (Dublin: Gill & Macmillan, 1975), pp. 86-97;

Brown, "The Poetry of W. R. Rodgers and John Hewitt," in *Two Decades of Irish Writing,* edited

by Douglas Dunn (Cheadle Hulme: Carcanet Press, 1975), pp. 81-97;

John Wilson Foster, "The Landscape of Planter and Gael in the Poetry of John Hewitt and John Montague," *Canadian Journal of Irish Studies,* 1 (November 1975): 17-33;

Seamus Heaney, "The Poetry of John Hewitt," *Threshold,* 22 (Summer 1969): 73-77;

John Montague, "Regionalism into Reconciliation," *Poetry Ireland,* 3 (Spring 1964): 113-118;

Douglas Sealy, "An Individual Flavour: *The Collected Poems of John Hewitt,*" *Dublin Magazine,* 8 (Spring/Summer 1969): 19-24.

John Holloway
(1 August 1920-   )

John Ferns
McMaster University

SELECTED BOOKS: *Language and Intelligence* (London: Macmillan, 1951; Hamden, Conn.: Archon, 1971);

The Victorian Sage: Studies in Argument (London: Macmillan, 1953; New York: Norton, 1965);

[Poems], Fantasy Poets, no. 26 (Oxford: Fantasy Poets, 1954);

The Minute and Longer Poems (Hessle: Marvell Press, 1956);

The Fugue and Shorter Pieces (London: Routledge & Kegan Paul, 1960);

The Charted Mirror: Literary and Critical Essays (London: Routledge & Kegan Paul, 1960; New York: Horizon, 1962);

The Story of the Night: Studies in Shakespeare's Major Tragedies (London: Routledge & Kegan Paul, 1961; Lincoln: University of Nebraska Press, 1961);

The Landfallers: A Poem in Twelve Parts (London: Routledge & Kegan Paul, 1962);

The Colours of Clarity: Essays on Contemporary Literature and Education (London: Routledge & Kegan Paul, 1964; Hamden, Conn.: Archon, 1964);

The Lion Hunt: A Pursuit of Poetry and Reality (London: Routledge & Kegan Paul, 1964; Hamden, Conn.: Shoe String Press, 1964);

Wood and Windfall (London: Routledge & Kegan Paul, 1965);

A London Childhood (London: Routledge & Kegan Paul, 1966; New York: Scribners, 1968);

Widening Horizons in English Verse (Evanston: Northwestern University Press, 1967);

Blake: The Lyric Poetry (London: Arnold, 1968);

New Poems (New York: Scribners, 1970);

The Establishment of English: An Inaugural Lecture (Cambridge: Cambridge University Press, 1972);

The Proud Knowledge: Poetry, Insight and the Self, 1620-1920 (London: Henley & Boston: Routledge & Kegan Paul, 1977);

Planet of Winds (London: Henley & Boston: Routledge & Kegan Paul, 1977);

Narrative and Structure: Exploratory Essays (Cambridge & New York: Cambridge University Press, 1979).

OTHER: *Poems of The Mid-Century*, edited by Holloway (London: Harrap, 1957);

Selected Poems of Percy Bysshe Shelley, edited by Holloway (London: Heinemann, 1960);

"Style and World in 'The Tower,'" *An Honoured Guest: New Essays on W. B. Yeats*, edited by Denis Donoghue and J. R. Mulryne (London: Arnold, 1964), pp. 88-105;

Charles Dickens, *Little Dorrit*, edited by Holloway (Harmondsworth: Penguin, 1967);

Later English Broadside Ballads, edited by Holloway and Joan Black, 2 volumes (London: Routledge & Kegan Paul, 1975, 1979; Lincoln: University of Nebraska Press, 1975-   );

"How Goes the Weather?," in *Yeats, Sligo and Ireland*, edited by A. Norman Jeffares (Gerrards Cross: Colin Smythe, 1980), pp. 89-97.

PERIODICAL PUBLICATIONS: "The Critical Theory of Yvor Winters," *Critical Quarterly*, 7 (Spring 1965): 54-68;

"Yeats and the Penal Age," *Critical Quarterly*, 8 (Spring 1966): 58-66;

"Robert Lowell and the Public Dimension," *Encounter*, 30 (April 1968): 73-79;

"The Waste Land," *Encounter*, 31 (August 1968): 73-79;

"Science & Literature: A Reply to Sir Peter Medawar," *Encounter*, 33 (July 1969): 81-85;

"The Death & Resurrection of the Folk Tale," *Encounter*, 35 (October 1970): 53-61;

"'Sincerely, Lionel Trilling,'" *Encounter*, 41 (September 1973): 64-68;

"What Do Poets Do?," *Lugano Review*, 5 (1975): 28-39;

"Three Poems, Three Obscurities: Eliot, Mandel'stam, Montale," *New Lugano Review*, 1 (1979): 17-28;

"Yeats and The Poetry Of Public Life," *New Lugano Review*, 3 (Summer 1980): 16-25;

"Varieties of Dialogue: Wilson, Trilling, Leavis," *Encounter*, 56 (February-March 1981): 67-77.

Christopher John Holloway, professor of modern English at Cambridge University since 1972, is widely known as a scholar and critic as well as a poet. He was one of a number of university-educated poets who emerged in England after World War II and whose work, appearing in Robert Conquest's *New Lines* (1956), was hailed as constituting a new "Movement" in English verse. As Elizabeth Jennings notes, "In 1956 and 1957 the words most commonly used about the current poetry were 'consolidation,' 'clarity,' 'intellectual

John Holloway in the West of Ireland

honesty,' and 'formal perfection.'" Following in some cases the work of Robert Graves, in others that of Edwin Muir, The Movement poets rejected the neoromanticism of Dylan Thomas and the experimental obscurities of earlier modernism. Though invited to contribute to *New Lines*, John Holloway has never considered himself a Movement poet. It is significant that his work did not appear in *New Lines 2* (1963). Holloway has pursued a path of independence even if it has sometimes been a stony track. Associated initially with The Movement, Holloway's work is now thought, in its fresh openness, to reach beyond the violence and pessimism of his more highly regarded contemporaries Ted Hughes and Geoffrey Hill.

Born in London to George and Evelyn Astbury Holloway, he was educated at the County School in Beckenham, Kent, and went from there to New College, Oxford, where as an Open History Scholar (1938-1941), he received a first-class degree in "Modern Greats" (philosophy, politics, and economics). He served in the war from 1941 to 1945, first in the Royal Artillery and later in intelligence. Returning to Oxford in 1945 as a temporary lecturer in philosophy, he married Audrey Good-ings in 1946 (a daughter was born to them in 1961, a son in 1965), completed his D.Phil. in 1947, and became a fellow of All Souls College. His revised doctoral thesis became his first book, *Language and Intelligence*, which appeared in 1951. Holloway's interest, however, turned from philosophy to liter-ature, and he accepted a lectureship in English at the University of Aberdeen, where he remained from 1949 to 1954, producing his well-known criti-cal book *The Victorian Sage* (1953). His change of professional interest was preceded by his beginning to write poems in the late 1940s (J. R. Ackerley was the first editor to publish one of Holloway's poems, in the *Listener* around 1950).

Holloway's major concern is to preserve the integrity of individual vision and the pursuit of truth in a hostile, modern world. These concerns he explores in short lyric and longer narrative poems. His mastery of a variety of verse forms (sonnet, ballad, longer stanzas, terza rima, and free verse) is impressive. He dwells in his work on individual, political, and social life and, if anything, has become more open and optimistic in his view of human possibilities as he has proceeded. His most recent volume, *Planet of Winds* (1977), takes a fresher and livelier view of life than his first book of poetry, *The Minute and Longer Poems* (1956). In Holloway's po-etic career we can see romantic vision struggling at times toward a religious sense of truth. His most recent long poem, *Civitatula* (about Cambridge), four of whose six parts appeared in *New Lugano Review* in 1979-1980, presents in places the author-ity of religious truth:

> Here in the filtering light I am thinking how
>   The Philosopher falters to Christ: more
> than at first a man can believe.

However, the pursuit of religious truth is an elusive and incidental rather than a central and governing concern in Holloway's work.

A quarter of a century earlier *The Minute and Longer Poems* presented moments of romantic vi-sion, a search for rootedness, and a religious rever-ence for life. Initially, Holloway interested himself in what in "Poem For Deep Winter" he calls "Inner things and outer, muddled together." The volume's title poem announces this investigation of the rela-tion between inner and outer experience:

> Up from the mind's deep middle jet,
> Clear as a bird, the sudden gleam
> Shot like a double day; and yet

> He scarcely saw the moment when
> The gentle current's crystal stream
> Turned ice turned diamond and took light
> And stole the secret of the sun
> To fuse and flare and make one bright
> Minute: and then the thing was done.

"Apollonian Poem," which immediately follows it, shows Holloway's ability to imitate the metaphysi-cals' style, while "Journey To The Capital" reveals how barren modernity empties the self, "Lost at some corner: or lamp-post. / A gallows. And I seem the ghost." "The Confluence" again reveals the literary imitativeness of some of Holloway's early work with echoes of the metaphysicals, Tennyson, Eliot, Arnold, and Keats packed into a three-stanza poem. "The Actor" subtly presents the poet as role player but stresses too the urgency and universality of his human concern: "I have been the poor Yorick of every mortal trade, / But I think it was chiefly Everyman that I played." "For tell me, which is dream / And which is mere reality?," the actor asks. It is "mere reality" that needs to be grasped, and Holloway begins here to see the need for unity and for roots. Of his college philosophers in "Elegy For An Estrangement" we learn:

> But none of these could half reveal
>   To either one of them
> How by some gentle yet insistent art
> To graft together what trended [*sic*] apart.

Can Holloway, then, discover a "gentle yet insistent art" capable of healing division and returning him to a rooted wholeness of being? He comes closer to attaining this end later in *A London Childhood* (1966) than in many of his obscure earlier poems. In "A Voice For Winter" in *The Minute and Longer Poems* he notes that "gross distance is a mode of pain / Like age: never to be mitigated." He harks back to "real roots" which in the winter of modern life are hard to find. "Once they might all have made a single circle / In a walled city with a simple centre." In his Vil-lonesque "The Petty Testament of Peter The Clerk" he sees that:

>   the blind groping of the root
> To find its soil, strikes everyone
> At first for lack of, then through friends.

The human world alone is, in Holloway's view at this point, unable to provide rootedness and stability, yet religious certainty remains elusive. The only possible renewal remains paradoxically personal in "A Voice For Winter":

> Remotest hour.
> Trumpet and tree
> Miraculously
> Blaze or flower. But no
> Epiphany
> Straddles the year. They grow
> Calmly within. Mere
> Renewal of eye and ear.

The disparaging "Mere" returns us to the "mere reality" of "The Actor." An acceptance of "mere reality" is necessary.

The years between the publication of his first book of poems and his second, *The Fugue and Shorter Pieces* (1960), saw John Holloway establish himself as a university lecturer at Cambridge, edit anthologies of modern poetry and of Shelley, and visit the Indian subcontinent in 1958. His book of critical essays, *The Charted Mirror*, appeared in the same year as *The Fugue*. At this period he also read deeply in the works of and became friendly with the poet Edwin Muir.

In *The Fugue* Holloway's poems oscillate between the delicately perceived and the stark and bitter. They are not always free from an obscurity of style which is Holloway's besetting limitation. "A Roundsman's Horse," however, combines subtle description and observation with a mythic sense of primordial male power (perhaps influenced by Muir) which anticipates Holloway's presentation of his father in *A London Childhood*:

> Among the billowed parsley's hills of white,
>   And swell of green that seems to flow
> Up from a deep sustained pelagic flow
> Into the shadows of first morning light,
>   He stands, a placid isle; or lifts
>   One ponderous hoof; and as he shifts,
> The grasses crunch and swathe, under his tread;
> Then surge up, sun-slow, from the meadow bed.

Holloway's poems are, in fact, at their best when shafts of insight break through a too frequent opacity, as in his direct challenge to Archibald MacLeish in "A letter to a Writer": "Poems dare not merely be. They mean." Such forceful statements help to make the thorny journey through other poems worth the carriage. Indeed, "Instructions to a Painter" emerges as Holloway's strongest statement about the nature of art to this point:

> Painter, never restore
> A younger colour to the hand or face.
> Give every line or shadow its established place
>   Firmly; put more,
>   Rather than fewer: if they lose the scars,
> Veterans will come to doubt they saw
>   the wars.
> . . . .
> Up in the mind's long harbours—you must
>   squint and toil
>   All day, must try
> To make paint irresistibly show
> What eyes just barely glimpse; teach what
>   we know.

Holloway shows respect for known paths, so in the poem "In The Park" he presents the rootedness of the teacher, farmers, and gardeners:

> The teacher spoke or read,
> Her voice perhaps hard, it had endured
> Decades of making easy: yet to teach,
>   One might have said, she almost sang;
> At home using a warm, a local twang
> Richly unstandard, rooted. A right speech
>
> For farmers, gardeners, men who work
>   with plants.

Holloway's love of the "Richly unstandard" "local twang" is presented nostalgically as a childhood memory of a class of boys in July listening to their teacher beneath the limes. He wishes that all those who had to do with "the sustenance / Of growing things, live individuals" had the same warmth and rootedness. That they do not leads to an awareness of social division. Division is the main problem in *The Fugue*. Here, as in Eliot's *Four Quartets*, an interest in Dante emerges, an interest in encountering the other self as with Eliot's "compound ghost." Sonnet three of "The Gates of Janus" presents this problem head on:

> Just on the sky-line where the landscape changed,
> Two travellers confronted face to face.
> Each met (as if to meet were pre-arranged)
> The other's eyes in full, slow, total gaze.
> That was all. They had no common ground,
> No contact, nothing to say. Each, being quite
> Alien, passed to the other's country, and
> They plodded back to back down out of sight.
> As the distances diminished them,
> Closer and closer still they seemed to come.

The tragic rift between seeming and being emerges in the last line.

Dante emerges again as an influence upon the form of Holloway's next volume of poetry, *The Landfallers: A Poem in Twelve Parts* (1962), a modern epic or long narrative poem written in terza rima, which was immediately preceded by his study of Shakespearean tragedy, *The Story of the Night* (1961). The poem presents two refugees who are being held for trial in a Pyrenean landscape, and, as the anonymous reviewer for the *Times Literary Supplement* explains, one of the refugees is "unprepossessing, one outwardly attractive." The poem also includes an interrogator-judge who argues with his wife and bullies his subordinate, Johnson. In the end the interrogator-judge seems to doubt his own condemnation of the unprepossessing refugee and even begins to feel a certain amount of sympathy with him. The attractive refugee, who is judged guiltless, is dependent upon and clearly involved with his less prepossessing companion. Johnson is also holding in detention another refugee, a woman called Anna. Johnson and Anna fall in love, and their love is celebrated in the poem's concluding aubade. As the *Times Literary Supplement*'s reviewer comments, "The message presumably is that we are all part of the human family, depending on and sharing the nature of one another."

Indeed, this perception is Holloway's, confirmed in the aubade in which we learn of the lovers that:

> These two, in the recurring
> Endearments that reciprocate their love,
> Through the blind dark, without a word
> being spoken,
> Had sought each other like a hand its glove.

Developing from this concern with love between two individuals is Holloway's sense of the further essential relation between the individual and society:

> Below the bustle of the morning hour
> In deeper rhythms, total and benign,
> The city opens like a tranquil flower.

Holloway's narrative poem, then, contains a double affirmation. He affirms the importance of love between man and woman but also between man and society as he presents finally "a world / Released; landfallen; fruitful; strong; fulfilled."

The question which the poem poses is: how can human and social harmony be attained? Thus, earlier in part ten, "The Verdicts," the process by which life reaches beyond tragedy and suffering is dramatized in a way with which Holloway would have been familiar from his studies of Shakespearean tragedy:

> how the present seems to hold
> The past within it, wefted—no, engrained,
> Till the new blossoms always from the old.

These lines, in part, provide an answer to the persistent problems of division and rootlessness which resurface in part five, "Line and Colour": "What can uprooted creatures do, but fail?"

Related to division and rootlessness is moral blindness, which is the stumbling block in *The Landfallers*. If human love and social harmony are to be attained moral blindness must be overcome. This central problem is presented most forcefully in part nine, "Vine's Defence . . . Declined":

> if I have done
> Harm, to have entered in the social act
> The way I have—I am the unlucky one:
> I (it may be) did suffer: and in fact
> I do sense something filmed and cloudy in
> My gaze: a kind of moral cataract,
> As if my senses grew a kind of skin,
> Sensitive but transforming: or have felt
> Some burden like a vast unwitting sin
> That swaddles, yet debars: that seems to melt
> And yet, rigidify; till I am left
> Drained, somehow, like an ageing salmon kelt.

The poem's final affirmations of love and social unity have to overcome the moral wilderness presented here and move us toward a renewed sense of liveliness and wholeness.

Two critical works, *The Lion Hunt* and *The Colours of Clarity*, both published in 1964, were followed by *Wood and Windfall* (1965), Holloway's fourth volume of poetry, which reflects his time spent as Byron Professor of English at the University of Athens between 1961 and 1963. A new openness to experience and a new freedom of form date from this volume. Miranda's response in the volume's first poem is a response to the human world. Holloway's "Miranda" seems to be a reflection upon Shakespeare's Miranda in *The Tempest*:

> Her ear now first alive, and sharply hearkening
> (This wonderment half fear) she thinks she hears,
> Faltering, almost harsh, a scrambled tune
> Among the seemly concert of the others.
> Beautiful ordinariness: the human sound.

Holloway's new sensitivity to life involves a new awareness of the feminine, as in the sonnet "A Trick to Catch the Old One," in which "The Sea Queen stood there, changeless as a star." In "Reflections As A Journey" returning to England from Greece reveals that returning home entails discovery of renewal:

> And then I reached the ferry over the river
> I'd used so often once . . . The moored
>   ships ranged
> Across the estuary. The old pastel light,
> Friendly Dickensian dirt. Nothing
>   had changed.

Finding the feminine, the original and familiar gives the poet a real sense of essential being that is finely dramatized in the title poem, the last in the volume:

> A sudden light
> And windfall and stillness. Simple as
> The act of a good woman
> At the pool of her glass, the day dons
> Diamonds and drabness flashes.
> Flashes. Light-falls. Observe
> The lamps of, moons of, their festivals.
>
> Wind falls. Observe
> That timber of the usual
> Which dreams in the rich yard and
> Sweetens with seasoning and
> Firms its grain into
> Hardwood, heartwood.

The subtle concluding movement from object to feeling provides one of the most resonant moments in Holloway's poetry.

The years between *Wood and Windfall* and the publication of *New Poems* (1970) in the United States saw Holloway complete his *Widening Horizons in English Verse* (1967), his autobiographic *A London Childhood* (1966), an edition of *Little Dorrit* (1967), and a study of Blake's lyric poetry (1968). His work on Blake and Dickens and the exploration of his own roots help to give Holloway's *New Poems* fullness of feeling. He discovers here what he describes later as "the task the poet sets himself . . . not just to chronicle and record, in a vivid lively way, but to meditate and explore, then the boundless depth of fecundity that the exploration reveals to him and so to ourselves naturally leads to a poetry of celebration and praise."

The source of "celebration and praise" is identified in "Turning the Tables" as our own hu-manity, certainly the place to begin:

> Other rooms, another table,
> All is steel, formica, glass,
> Yet those people too are able
> There to live as live as grass,
> Sweet as timber, staunch as stone
> Through humanity alone.

In "Primary Sources" Holloway finds meaning in simple activities such as restoring his house: "The house, / As I tend it, burnishes." Anne Stevenson has noted his preoccupation with fire. It is also worth noting his recurrent presentation of the natural world, as in "Beef-Apple":

> The ghost of a fruit-tree!
> So old, yet now such a
> Snow—such an icy glitter.
> An ocean plant:
> The boughs are flocked with flowers as
> Large as sea-gulls, they
> Alight, on the grey wood,
> And quiver in the western wind. A tree
> Unhurriedly demanding: it
> Waits, to cup its darkness, to round it
> All in the red of the beef-apple.

Crabbed obscurities dissolve in the face of the familiar. The essential development in Holloway's work is from an initial complex opacity toward an increasing articulateness and simplicity of statement. "Grain To The Daily" reveals again how we can find significance in ordinary experience:

> rarer by far is to find
> in stubble a harvest again so
> commend more than those,
> the one who is grain to the daily:
> yourself in the usual.

This search continues into Holloway's latest volume, *Planet of Winds* (1977), which reveals an even greater freedom of expression and form. Having lived in West Suffolk during the decade 1963-1973, Holloway spent the years immediately preceding the publication of his most recent volume in Ely, Cambridgeshire, and has lived in Cambridge since 1977. During these years appeared the first volume of *Later English Broadside Ballads* (1975), edited by Holloway and his second wife, Joan Black, whom he married in 1978, and a further critical study, *The Proud Knowledge: Poetry, Insight and the Self, 1620-1920* (1977).

The free verse of *Planet of Winds*, as in the

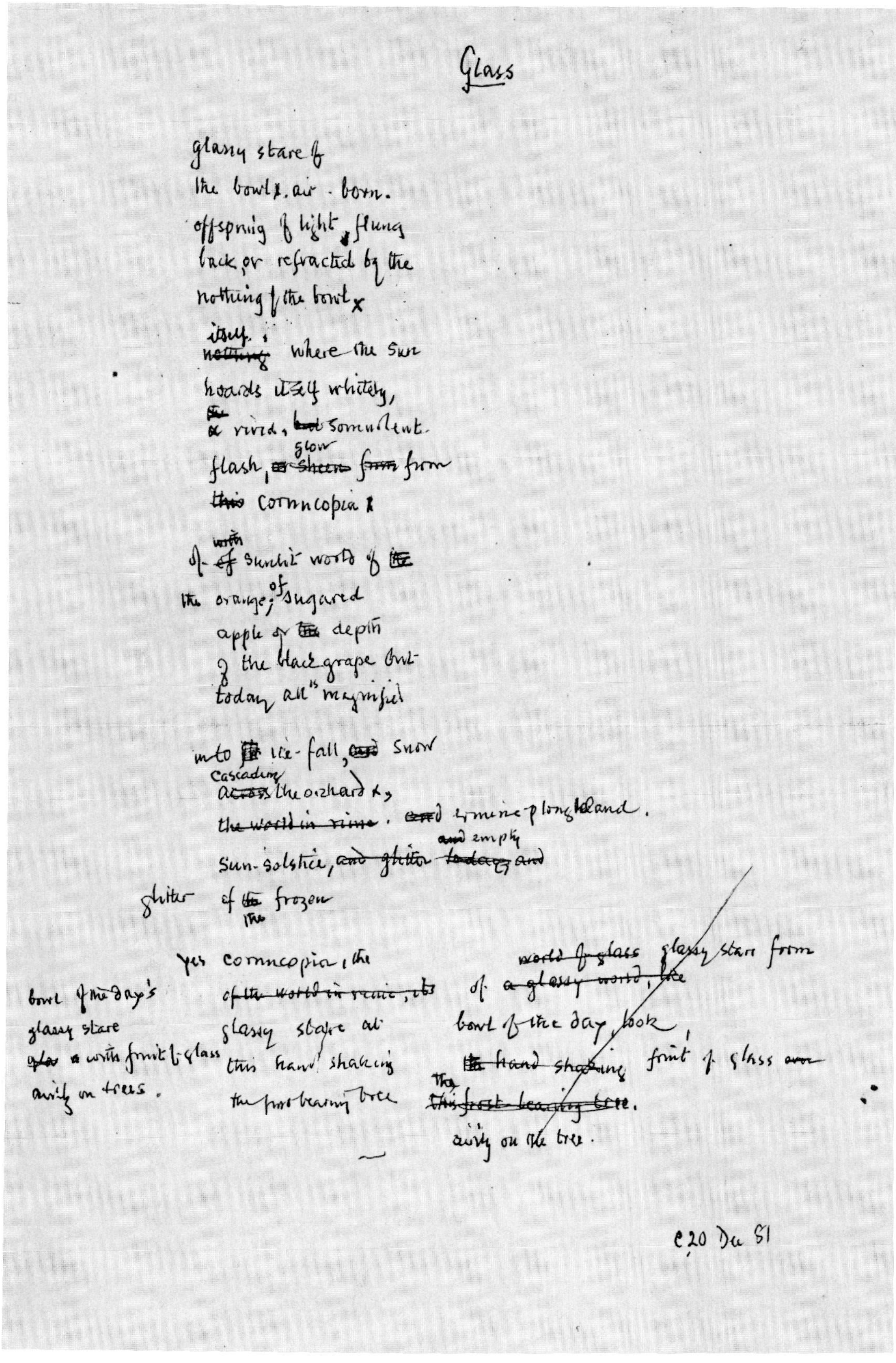

Working draft (the author)

opening "A Poem for Breakfast," is reminiscent of Lawrence:

> Look!
> We have a great frost. An
> Arrival of north.

"Stars in the House" sustains this sense of a fresh and vital response to life:

> Stars in the house! They waterfall the stairs
> From the big window. Rain has sweetened
> The air into clearness.

"Structure to 'Found'" provides an arresting insight, "What is the good / of what cannot be true?," and, as the volume draws to a close, Holloway invites the reader, in "Slack Water," to participate in simple contemplation of the world around him:

> Close your book, look up reader, and outside
>   see if the sea is quickening, sharp
> of the flood tide in outcome and inroad
>   moving with the moon toward the land.

The final poem, "Westerly," reveals, in conclusion, how the poet's essential purpose is to restore us to ourselves, to express what we have always known but, without the poet's help, have never been able to articulate even to ourselves. Such a perception appeals to our deepest bond as human beings, the way in which together and only in collaboration we can create reality:

> Those fountains
> more light than water, leave them to do
> for us, what they cannot but do: which you
>   must know
> before I tell you, on this planet of winds.

Holloway's development as a poet has been a labor of simplification, a labor from a difficult to a direct and simple style of expression. In this respect he can be compared with Yeats, a poet whose work has been of great interest to him. Holloway's present importance in comtemporary British poetry is that this new directness and simplicity offer a vital and necessary alternative to the violence and pessimism of his more highly regarded contemporaries.

Though John Holloway is respected by academic critics and reviewers, he can hardly be thought to be a popular poet or one whose audience reaches much beyond the unhappily decreasing readership that regards poetry as a crucially important art in a world that runs against it.

Bernard Bergonzi has called attention to Holloway's limitations as a poet, censuring "a pervasive sense that the will was too much involved in the production of Holloway's poetry." He thinks that many of Holloway's poems are "well-written and carefully structured, but somehow lacking in content or point." He concludes, "this tendency has become more pronounced in his subsequent poetry, much of which is frankly dull. The dedication to the ideal of writing poetry remains strong and commands respect but the spirit seems lacking." Apart from objecting to the unspecific nature of these charges, one can point out in Holloway's defense that in some of his poems he answers these objections in his own terms and fulfills his own ideal of what a poet should be, "an explorer of reality at a profound level precisely because he has, as a means for that, language, the self-renewing and inexhaustible bank, constructed from, and embodying, the experience and meditation on experience that mankind have accumulated over generations."

John Holloway continues to write and have his poetry published in such periodicals as *Art International, Encounter*, the *Hudson Review*, the *London Review of Books*, the *Times Literary Supplement*, and *Stand*. His long poem "Civitatula: The Little City" will possibly appear in an illustrated edition, after which he will be ready to publish another collection of shorter pieces. His work is moving from a complex and difficult to a simpler presentation of human and natural experience.

References:

Kenneth Allott, Note on Holloway, in *The Penguin Book of Contemporary Verse 1918-1960*, edited by Allott (Harmondsworth, U.K.: Penguin, 1962), p. 312;

Elizabeth Jennings, *Poetry To-day* (London: Longmans, Green, 1961);

William Van O'Connor, *The New University Wits and The End of Modernism* (Carbondale: Southern Illinois University Press, 1963), pp. 117-120;

Anne Stevenson, "Poetry And The Profession of English: The Poetry And Criticism of John Holloway," *New Lugano Review*, 1 (1979): 45-53, 62.

Elizabeth Jennings

(18 July 1926-   )

William Blissett
University of Toronto

BOOKS: [Poems] Fantasy Poets, no. 1 (Swinford: O. Mellor & R. Smith, n.d.);

Poems (London: Fantasy Press, 1953);

A Way of Looking (London: Deutsch, 1955; New York: Rinehart, 1956);

A Sense of the World (London: Deutsch, 1958; New York: Rinehart, 1959);

Let's Have Some Poetry! (London: Museum Press, 1960);

Poetry Today 1957-60 (London: Longmans, Green, 1961; Folcroft, Pa.: Folcroft Press, 1970);

Every Changing Shape (London: Deutsch, 1961; Philadelphia: Dufour, 1962);

Song for a Birth or a Death and Other Poems (London: Deutsch, 1961; Philadelphia: Dufour, 1962);

Penguin Modern Poets 1, by Jennings, Lawrence Durrell, and R. S. Thomas (Harmondsworth: Penguin, 1962);

Recoveries (London: Deutsch, 1964; Philadelphia: Dufour, 1964);

Frost (Edinburgh: Oliver & Boyd, 1964; New York: Barnes & Noble, 1966);

Christianity and Poetry (London: Burns & Oates, 1965); republished as *Christian Poetry* (New York: Hawthorn, 1965);

The Mind Has Mountains (London: Macmillan/New York: St. Martin's, 1966);

The Secret Brother and Other Poems for Children (London: Macmillan/New York: St. Martin's, 1966; Chester Springs, Pa.: Dufour, 1969);

Collected Poems (London & Melbourne: Macmillan, 1967; Chester Springs, Pa.: Dufour, 1967);

The Animals' Arrival (London & Melbourne: Macmillan, 1969; Chester Springs, Pa.: Dufour, 1970);

Lucidities (London: Macmillan, 1970);

Relationships (London: Macmillan, 1972);

Growing-Points (Cheadle: Carcanet New Press, 1975);

Seven Men of Vision (London: Vision Press, 1976);

Consequently I Rejoice (Manchester: Carcanet New Press, 1977);

After the Ark (London & New York: Oxford University Press, 1978);

Elizabeth Jennings

Selected Poems (Manchester: Carcanet New Press, 1979);

Moments of Grace (Manchester: Carcanet New Press, 1979);

A Dream of Spring, text by Jennings, illustrations by Anthony Rossiter (Stratford-upon-Avon: Celandine Press, 1980);

Italian Light & Other Poems, text by Jennings, illustrations by Gerald Woods (N.p.: Snake River Press, 1981);

Celebrations and Elegies (Manchester: Carcanet New Press, 1982).

163

OTHER: *The Batsford Book of Children's Verse*, edited by Jennings (London: Batsford, 1958);

An Anthology of Modern Verse 1940-1960, edited by Jennings (London: Methuen, 1961);

Michelangelo's Sonnets, translated by Jennings (London: Folio Society, 1961, Allison & Busby, 1969; Garden City: Doubleday, 1970);

A Choice of Christina Rossetti's Verse, edited by Jennings (London: Faber & Faber, 1970);

The Batsford Book of Religious Verse, edited by Jennings (London: Batsford, 1981);

In Praise of Our Lady, edited by Jennings (London: Batsford, 1982).

PERIODICAL PUBLICATIONS: "The Difficult Balance," in "A Poetry Symposium," *London Magazine*, 6 (November 1959): 27-30;

"The Making of a Movement," *Spectator* (2 October 1964), pp. 446-448.

Having published since the early 1950s some twenty books of verse (including two substantial collections), together with several anthologies and critical works, Elizabeth Jennings is a well-known writer on both sides of the Atlantic. Her poetic voice—which sounds also in her prose work—is unmistakable: quiet, controlled but not tight, always thoughtful but never ideological. Her admirers must assent to Wordsworth's dictum that "the human mind is capable of being excited without the aid of gross and violent stimulants." From there they go on to discover in her a poet of more variety than sameness, more experiment than consolidation: in her many short poems there are many small surprises. She has a wider curiosity than Henry Vaughan, a greater range of feeling than Christina Rossetti, is more delicate than Robert Frost, and less prosy than Edwin Muir. They of course surpass her in their own ways, but it is in such good company that she must take her place.

She is, as she says of Frost, a personal but not an autobiographical writer (she attempted an autobiography but did not repine when her publisher rejected it). In a book written for young readers, *Let's Have Some Poetry!* (1960), she discloses a good deal about her early development. Born in 1926 in Boston, Lincolnshire, the daughter of Henry Cecil Jennings, a physician, she attended Oxford High School and then read English at St. Anne's College, Oxford, graduating in 1949. Her discovery of poetry had occurred at age thirteen: G. K. Chesterton's "Battle of Lepanto" was followed quickly by Coleridge's "The Rime of the Ancient Mariner" and the odes of Keats. From the beginning her interest

gravitated to lyric rather than to narrative or dramatic poetry. She began writing poetry about the same time, encouraged by one of her teachers and by her uncle-godfather, himself a poet, who took her seriously and never praised what he could not admire. Her earliest poems showed regular rhyme and meter and were "pure and uncontaminated—though bad." When she showed them to her mentor, he surprised her by passing over some ambitious pieces and singling out what she now regards as her first real poem—these four lines on a bird:

> I held it in my hand
> With its little hanging head;
> It was soft and light and whole,
> But it was dead.

This rhymed stanza grasps a moment, an observation, a feeling; the mature Elizabeth Jennings is already heard in this little girl's voice.

Some of her later poems, especially those written for children, demonstrate her ability to retain the child's simple vision, but she was not confined within this mode, even in her midteens. "A small part of me still, I think, wanted to be a child. But a much larger part was intensely eager to feel more and to understand more. Religion, for example, quite suddenly became a real and important part of my life, and *because* it was important it tended to give me a lot of worries. . . ." The religion to which she refers is the Roman Catholic faith in which she was brought up and to which she adheres. Growing up during World War II (she was thirteen when it began in 1939) meant "to be denied the tranquillity, the slow growth, the sense of plenty of time in which to learn and understand." The anxiety she experienced during this period seems related to her concept of poetic inspiration: "a poem often announces itself by that nervous feeling one sometimes gets before an examination. . . " (or an air raid, one is tempted to add). Some of that religious worry and some of that anxiety remain in the finished poems, but she insists that "poetry has nothing to do with madness," that, instead, "the poem should make us *want* to understand it fully—it should . . . cast a spell on us."

One other thing she stresses, talking of her younger self to young readers, is the need for "a lot of what you fancy" in youth—plenty of reading of other poets, plenty of writing so as to achieve habits of facility, or readiness to write through thick and thin, in sickness and in health. As a young woman with a literary bent, who was to read English at

Oxford from 1945 to 1949, to work in the Oxford City Library from 1950 to 1958 and as a publisher's reader for Chatto and Windus from 1958 to 1960, she read all the poets she needed for her own development. As early as sixteen she found the poetry of T. S. Eliot liberating, little realizing then how disciplined it was. Later she discovered William Empson and Robert Graves, as did other poets of her generation; but the two twentieth-century poets who have influenced her most deeply are Edwin Muir and Robert Frost. *Every Changing Shape* (1961) has a chapter on Muir, and in 1964 her study of Frost appeared.

At Oxford she "found the most congenial kind of atmosphere in which a poet can write—friends who were themselves poets and who also seemed to be as interested in my work as they were in their own. I received ruthless criticism, certainly, but I always felt that the people who criticized my work really wanted me to write better, really believed in and cared about me." These friendships were the beginning of what J. D. Scott, in an article in the *Spectator* (1 October 1954), named The Movement. Writing retrospectively ten years later on "The Making of a Movement" for the *Spectator* (2 October 1964), Elizabeth Jennings observed that the name "might suggest the uniform, the drilled, the similar; I know that I myself have strong resistance to being linked with other poets who would seem to me to share little but nearness in age, and sometimes not even that." She goes on to suggest that there was nevertheless a deeper compatibility than literary politics or publicity involved, making two observations: "one is that none of these poets and novelists ever consciously *formed* a movement; the similarities were natural, the qualities they shared were almost a matter of chance. Secondly, they shared this fact with the poets of the Thirties." Certainly, the nine poets usually referred to as The Movement—Kingsley Amis, Robert Conquest, Donald Davie, D. J. Enright, Thom Gunn, John Holloway, Elizabeth Jennings, Philip Larkin, and John Wain—have gone their separate ways, but those ways were close and intertwined well before the naming of The Movement.

Having already had poems published in *Oxford Poetry 1948*, she found that her work suited the taste of the new editors for 1949, Kingsley Amis and James Michie, who, having called for toughness and modernity, included six of her poems, three of which ("Weathercock," "Winter Love," and "Time") were to be included in *Poems* (1953) and *Collected Poems* (1967). She knew Philip Larkin and John Wain too; Robert Conquest, editor of the two *New*

Lines anthologies (1956 and 1963), which were to include all nine Movement poets, did not meet any of the Oxford poets before 1952, nor did John Holloway before 1954. Blake Morrison, now the main source of information on The Movement, notes that "Jennings's part in the Movement has sometimes been disputed," and Conquest recalls that "someone once described her association with us as comparable to that of a schoolmistress in a non-corridor train with a bunch of drunk marines—a slight slander on both sides." Yet Morrison concludes that "it is doubtful whether her work would have developed as it did had it not been for her exposure to the Oxford climate of the later 1940s and early 1950s."

The poem "Delay," which stands first in the 1953 *Poems*, in *Collected Poems*, and in *Selected Poems* (1979), and is included by Philip Larkin in *The Oxford Book of Twentieth-Century Verse* (1973), has the marks and virtues associated with The Movement:

> The radiance of that star that leans on me
> Was shining years ago. The light that now
> Glitters up there my eyes may never see,
> And so the time lag teases me with how
>
> Love that loves now may not reach me until
> Its first desire is spent. The star's impulse
> Must wait for eyes to claim it beautiful
> And love arrived may find us somewhere else.

The poem argues consecutively and syntactically, stating the analogy between the speed of light and the speed of love and implying the astronomical distances between lovers. Its diction is plain but exact, its stanza form regular but handled with finesse, especially the leap from the first to the second stanza at the word "love"; such a line ending as "until" would ordinarily be merely flaccid, but here it suggests a long reach of mind. The last line, which sounds Empsonian, is an effective end to a love poem of some delicacy as well as an argument of some toughness. No other Movement poet would say a star "leans on me," with its suggestion of mild, slightly tedious importunity.

She shares with other members of The Movement a common generation and an Oxford propinquity, a love of simplicity, a dislike of any factitious mystification or decoration, and a willing acceptance of rhyme and metrical regularity. She differs from most of them (as Christina Rossetti differed from her associates) in her lifelong Christianity in a largely nonreligious milieu, in her love of Italy when the others were aggressively insular, and in her not being a university teacher. A resident of Oxford and a graduate of the university, she is not at all donnish in her poems about literature or even in her criticism: rather, she is like a good librarian recommending appropriate books to readers.

The poems of Elizabeth Jennings to date show a marked continuity of theme and style. This is not to say that they are repetitious, only that small surprises might occur anywhere. An attempt to find, or force, a pattern of "development" from book to book would be futile. "I write swiftly and revise very little," she observed in her interview with John Press. In the ninety-one poems from *Collected Poems* that reappear in *Selected Poems* there are only three verbal changes, all slight. She never "works up" a poem to a high polish and vibrancy; if a poem survives, it survives with its imperfections. If the hand of the reviser is light, that of the exciser is heavy. Of 243 poems in the six volumes that precede the collection of 1967, 207 are printed there, but only 91 survive in the selection of 1979, at which later date, with three more volumes to draw from, self-criticism and the exigencies of space have allowed only 103 of 363 poems to be printed. As one would expect, the poems dropped are usually either weak exercises in her own style or unsuccessful experiments in styles not her own. Nothing Audenesque survives: "Deception" and the second and third parts of "Sequence from Childhood" disappear after *Poems*; "Lost Symbols" is in the collection but not the selection, as is "Happy Families," with its moralizing objectivity and its inventions of allegorical figures:

> Someone upstairs is weeping on his bed
> (Families can hurt much more than strangers do).
> No one consoles; we take our cards instead,
> Watching Miss Grit and Mr. Satin go.

Recoveries (1964) and *The Mind Has Mountains* (1966), clearly written during a time of great mental distress, contain many exercises, possibly therapeutic in motive, to "loosen up" the writing; the results are mainly negative, and this fact is reflected in the disappearance of three-quarters of these poems between the collection and the selection. One somewhat regrettable loss is that of "Sea," which calls Salvador Dali "a smooth operator" and recalls his "only true picture"—"a child lifting the edge of the sea."

Before considering the themes and concerns that pervade her poetry, it will be useful to observe the distinctive range of sound and movement of her verse. She proves to be an iambic poet, a stanzaic

poet, a poet at home in rhyme. She adheres to the main tradition of English verse and to the normal unit of "impassioned speech," as is shown by the great preponderance of iambic pentameter and other iambic lines in her verse. However, only a few of her poems scan regularly throughout, and some, recognizably deriving from or moving toward a regular iambic pattern, allow themselves so many small hesitations, inversions, extra or missing syllables—in the interests of tentativeness in the present moment—that purists might be disturbed by her licenses. It is not the iambic line but the regular stanza that gives firmness and structure to her poetic work. Only a handful of her poems reach a second page; in every volume a majority are stanzaic and most of these rhymed. When John Press asked her if she had "any ambition to write a long poem," she replied, "Yes, I have, often, but it will never come off yet." "The splendid stanza echoing itself" is her own phrase, but it is not her way of making stanzas. The great narrative stanzas that can be sustained through cantos and books—the Spenserian, rime royal, ottava rima—are (like blank verse) all eschewed; and when she comes to deal with such a theme as the seven deadly sins, her treatment, compared to the amplitude afforded to Spenser by his stanza, must seem skimpy. There is, however, a good deal of terza rima. This religious poet, for all her quatrains and quinzaines, never (as Emily Dickinson does) echoes a hymn tune, nor does she write religious poetry that could ordinarily be sung by a church congregation or choir (in this, like the equally devout Christina Rossetti). And yet, so strong is the stanzaic impulse that she even, in "Choices" (*A Sense of the World*, 1958), separates couplets into stanzas, following very clearly, in theme as well as form, the example of Robert Frost in "The Tuft of Flowers":

> They have disguised a way to live and I,
> Clothed in confusion, set their choices by:
>
> Though sometimes one looks up and sees me there,
> Alerts his shadow, pushes back his chair
>
> And, opening windows wide, looks out at me
> And close past words we stare. It seems that he
>
> Urges my darkness, dares it to be freed
> Into that room. We need each other's need.

Among her best poems is "Visit to an Artist," dedicated to David Jones (one of her *Seven Men of Vision*, 1976), whose world of art and thought is evoked in this fine example of unobtrusive stanza building and rhyming. The three stanzas are quite naturally three. The first evokes one of David Jones's watercolor drawings:

> Window upon the wall, a balcony
> With a light chair, the air and water so
> Mingled you could not say which was the sun
> And which the adamant yet tranquil spray.
> But nothing was confused and nothing slow:
> Each way you looked always the sea, the sea.

The second describes the quietness that came over them in the presence of such pictures:

> And every shyness that we brought with us
> Was drawn into the pictures on the walls.
> It was so good to sit quite still and lose
> Necessity of discourse, words to choose
> And wonder which were honest and which false.

The third recalls the relevance of words written by the Catholic Jones in his essay "Art and Sacrament" in *Epoch and Artist* (1959):

> Then I remembered words that you had said
> Of art as gesture and as sacrament,
> A mountain under the calm form of paint
> Much like the Presence under wine and bread—
> Art with its largesse and its own restraint.

The stanzas give the impression of being equal, but the first is one line longer than the others; the rhyming is as delicate as a David Jones watercolor: in the first stanza the reader begins to think the poem is unrhymed and dependent only on regular lines and slight repetitions of sounds as in "balcony" and "spray," "so" and "sun," yet as he reads further he finds that "slow" rhymes definitely with "so," "sea" indefinitely with "balcony." In the second stanza "us" attunes with both "walls" and "lose," which proves later to rhyme with "false" and "choose"; in the third the important word "sacrament" agrees with "said" in vowel, in consonants with "paint," while the rhyming pairs are "said" and "bread," "paint" and "restraint." A frequent device of the poet, the simple repetition of a word or phrase—one which can give the desired impression of helplessness or floundering—here, in "the sea, the sea," is used (like Dante's "*Intorno, intorno*" and T. S. Eliot's "quietly, quietly") to convey rapt attention.

It is often useful to turn from metrics to imagery, but the poetry of Elizabeth Jennings is not characterized by notable recurring images, and like other poets of The Movement she is alien to the heavy emphasis on imagery that one finds in the poems of Edith Sitwell, Dylan Thomas, or W. R. Rodgers. Her poems are all lyrics, most of them short, sometimes the pure and simple record of a moment of experience, more often meditative or ruminative. They may incidentally reveal the poet's personality and circumstances, but they never relate sequences of events and most certainly do not project dramatically a character (fictional or autobiographical) in conflict with others or with herself. Places, works of art, close or strained personal relationships, and, above all, religion are the subjects of these ruminative meditations. It is always the spirit of place and not its topography that she tries to catch. Her many Italian poems, culminating in the handsome *Italian Light & Other Poems* (1981) and the Bibbiena poems in *Celebrations and Elegies* (1982), are highly evocative of the historic pagan and Catholic land and its people, but they do not prompt the reader to make an expedition or detour to some specific place. Again, there are many poems dealing with life in a mental hospital, in which she was confined in the early 1960s, that are highly alert to changing states of mind, to the personal and professional behavior of the staff, to the plight and the hopes of the patients, but give little impression of the size and shape of the institution, whether it is urban or rural, cold or warm, quiet or noisy.

As a faithful though troubled "cradle Catholic," Elizabeth Jennings has access to the graces of sacrament and prayer, but her poems record the effort of meditation, of working out her salvation in fear and trembling, more than the impulse to praise and give glory. Her titles are significant. One of her collections is named, from Gerard Manley Hopkins, *The Mind Has Mountains*—"cliffs of fall/Frightful, sheer, no-man-fathomed"; another, from T. S. Eliot, *Consequently I Rejoice* (1977)—"Having to construct something/Upon which to rejoice." The allusions are apposite, so too the dismay and the grinding effort they bring with them, along with the sense of an intensely private experience of a great common religion, an experience much plagued by distraction but working through to resting places or "growing-points" of "lucidity" and "recovery." A fine exercise on this theme is "To a Friend with a Religious Vocation" (*Song for a Birth or a Death and Other Poems*, 1961), which includes this stanza:

> Your vows enfold you. I must make my own;
> Now this, now that, each one empirical.

My poems move from feelings not yet known,
And when the poem is written I can feel
    A flash, a moment's peace.
The curtains will be drawn across your grille.
My silences are always enemies.

Of the many returns to the theme of poetry as a religious vocation or quasivocation, one of the most moving, from *Moments of Grace* (1979), is "An Answer to Odd Advice," which concludes thus:

        Hope is needed
  If in a dark world some, like me, will try
To last through mankind's new Gethsemane

And be near any Christ again who's pleaded
For friends, for comfort, and not yet to die.

After the quietness of most of the poem, the throwaway phrasing, the easy fit of meter and syntax, the final line stands out strongly indeed. The three things she cries out for, her poetry celebrates all along: friendship, whether with other persons in the ordinary course of life or vicariously in response to the arts; the comforts of grace and nature and of an enduring and thriving talent; and in the face of a threatening world the prospect of holding off the last enemy for a time.

In each of the volumes at least one poem is devoted to friendship: the variety of treatment is as notable as the continuity of theme. "Identity" (*Poems*) is a meditation on the psychology of association involved in "making friends." "A Conversation in the Gardens of the Villa Celimontana, Rome" (*A Sense of the World*) shows how two friends, by exchange of words and by simply sharing the spirit of place, share the same thought. "My Grandmother" (*Song for a Birth or a Death*) records how the poet as a child refused to go out with her grandmother, who kept an antique shop, from "perhaps a wish not to be used like antique objects." The concluding stanza of this fine poem sums up the reciprocal failure of friendship:

And when she died I felt no grief at all,
Only the guilt of what I once refused.
I walked into her room among the tall
Sideboards and cupboards—things she
                never used
But needed: and no finger-marks were there,
Only the new dust falling through the air.

An adult relationship, wary, of attraction and opposition, is caught in "A Game of Cards" (*Recoveries*), where

Determined to be peaceful, we played cards,
Dealt out the hands and hid from one
                    another
Our power.

Edmund Spenser put his tribute to his poetic master, Chaucer, in book four of *The Faerie Queene*, the Legend of Friendship, and any deep and sustained response to an artist, especially a fellow-artist, is more than merely analogous to friendship. In the poem "For Edward Thomas" (*Consequently I Rejoice*) Elizabeth Jennings records "a strange hunt" for that quiet, honest, elusive, congenial poet among scenes his poems had evoked:

    Suddenly I learnt
  Your art of being reticent,
  Of leaving birds, trees, hills alone.

In style and theme it invites comparison with Robert Frost, who had been a friend of Thomas's. "Elegy for W. H. Auden" (*Growing-Points*, 1975) does just the opposite: it assembles affectionately the "spoor" such as Thomas had been careful not to leave—carpet slippers and leather skin, late epigrams and limestone, Christ Church and Wren's Tower, grand operas, shouting orators, and mirrors shining. It is a personal poem of farewell and godspeed. "Van Gogh" (*The Mind Has Mountains*) is written out of fellow feeling at the time of her own mental distress:

There is a theory that the very heart
Of making means a flaw, neurosis, some
Sickness; yet others say it is release.
I only know that your wild, surging art
Took you to agony, but makes us come
Strangely to gentleness, a sense of peace.

Other poems of friendship include the warm and heartfelt compliment to a fellow poet in "A Letter to Peter Levi" (*The Animals' Arrival*, 1969) and the wonderfully aloof "In Memory of Anyone Unknown to me" (*Relationships*, 1972), seemingly empty yet replete with solidarity with the dead:

Sentiment will creep in. I cast it out
Wishing to give these classical repose,
No epitaph, no poppy and no rose
From me, and certainly no wish to learn about
The way they lived or died. In earth or fire
They are gone. Simply because they were
                  human,
  I admire.

Friendship is a widely inclusive category, but there are still the other needs—"comfort" and "not yet to die." Under comfort may be placed the large number of poems of religious themes, together with those that celebrate such creature comforts as are not subsumed under friendship. In "At Noon" (*A Sense of the World*) the poet is simply comforted, strengthened, edified by the happy coexistence of the sunlit world and the book she is reading. A similar place of safety within opposite experiences is evoked in "San Paolo Fuori le Mura, Rome" (*A Sense of the World*), where the roar of sunlit streets outside is somehow necessary to the stillness within; it ends:

> For me the senses still have their full sway
> Even where prayer comes quicker than an act.
> I cannot quite forget the blazing day,
> The alabaster windows or the way
> The light refuses to be called abstract.

"Harvest and Consecration" (*Song for a Birth or a Death*), a record of a friendly talk with a priest after Mass, belongs to the context just established, of unity in opposition, this time of nature and grace, of passionate awareness of what is being said and done and the calm necessity of doing and saying them. "I see," it concludes, "The wine and bread protect our ecstasy." A more recent poem, "I Count the Moments" (*Moments of Grace*), gathers together in muted terza rima this whole aspect of her work: "I see for one crammed second, order so/Explicit that I need no more persuasion." And yet "Poetry is pain as well as passion," or, to use the image of "The One Drawback" (*Celebrations and Elegies*), dark as well as light:

> To move in dark is a fate
> But I know also the gold
>
> Dawns of the world outside me, and within
> Dawns in which words break into fresh song,
> My mind is raided by a dazzling light,
>
> Sun is where I belong
> But I'm an expert on night.

The echo in the last line of Frost's "I have been one acquainted with the night" is unmistakable, but the source of light—the moon in his poem, the dawn in hers—brings them out of similarity into contrast.

The third plea is made many times in many ways—"not yet to die." Quite early in the work of this meditative, reasonable, ruminative, lucid, sometimes humdrum poet, there occur sudden shocks or unexpected indications of deep disquietude; "The Shot" is an example of the first; of the second, "A Fear" (*A Sense of the World*). Both point the way to mental breakdown and the preoccupations of *Recoveries* and *The Mind Has Mountains*. The poems of mental distress there find the reader pulling for the poet, as a doctor might, or a concerned friend. John Wain's fine and compassionate "Green Fingers," dedicated "to Elizabeth Jennings in Oxford," evokes the sort of delusions she must have had to keep at bay:

> You must stay there, queen of that fungus town
> Throned amid nightmares, till the Thing relents,
> Opens the door, and with wondering frown
>
> You climb, and find us here. Between descents,
> You live like us: books, walks, the telephone:
> All that long patience Oxford represents.
>
> Green-fingered artist, I see you never doubt
> Even in those lost days, denying, stark,
> What is the work that you must be about.
> . . . .
> Your art will save your life, Elizabeth.

Her asylum poems are sane, painfully so, except a few rather willed efforts at a sort of automatic writing (all excluded from *Selected Poems*): no surrealistic nonsense here about achieving states "in no way inferior to madness." Instead, a clear recognition that she cannot talk "About These Things" (*Songs for a Birth or a Death*) as she can talk about the realities of the world and of the mind. "It does not seem a time for lucid rhyming," she writes in "A Mental Hospital Sitting Room" (*The Mind Has Mountains*), and yet there and in the "Sequence in Hospital" (*Recoveries*) she writes sanely about being insane.

Emerging from this context is a poem of high achievement, "An Abandoned Palace" (*Growing-Points*). Presenting a sort of allegorical "House," it gives the impression of being immensely long, and its lines of about twenty syllables labyrinthine. In the palace only two figures linger, a rheumatic old woman finishing her embroidery and "the undeposed but rejected and uncomplaining Queen," with mildewed crown, who sends by moulting carrier pigeon the message "find me"—

> hoping for
> Rescue, reprieve, an escape from a palace
> now a prison where hope itself
> Taunted her continually with its expert
> disappointments,

Its refusal to gaze back at her long, caught in
its own desperate incapacity.

That last phrase brings to mind "Euthanasia" (*Moments of Grace*), a recent poem that is her first to address itself to a public issue yet springs from the deep silent plea "not yet to die" as well as from religious conviction:

> The law's been passed and I am lying low
> Hoping to hide from those who think they are
> Kindly, compassionate. My step is slow.
> I hurry. Will the executioner
> Be watching how I go?
> . . . .
>   Old age seems good.
> The ache, the anguish—we could bear then we
> Declare. The ones who pray plead with their God
> To turn the murdering ministers away,
> But they come softly shod.

The rare reader will want to read all the poems of Elizabeth Jennings because they are all hers, as one might decide to read the whole of Henry Vaughan or Christina Rossetti or Edwin Muir or Robert Frost, to name again four poets particularly congenial to her talents. The common reader would probably want all the poems cited here and twice as many more, to include her own favorite, "Fountains," and the two others, "Fisherman" and "For a Child Born Dead," chosen by her for her *An Anthology of Modern Verse 1940-1960* (1961), the title poems of *A Way of Looking* (1955) and *Song for a Birth or a Death*, many of the religious poems in *Consequently I Rejoice*, the Christmas Suite from *Moments of Grace* and several of the very recent *Celebrations and Elegies*.

The student of literary history will discern in Elizabeth Jennings the marks of her generation and The Movement—the continuity of rhyme and reason, of syntax and stanza (as if Ezra Pound had never lived), the easy rhythms, the eschewing of decoration, the control of metaphor; but he will also notice how the one woman and the one Catholic stands apart from the others, in the special insights given her by the enjoyment of Italy and the suffering of illness, by her librarian's nonacademic love of literature, and by her lifelong religious concern.

Interview:

John Press, Interview with Elizabeth Jennings, in *The Poet Speaks*, edited by Peter Orr (London: Routledge, 1967), pp. 91-96.

Thomas Kinsella
(4 May 1928-   )

Thomas H. Jackson
Bryn Mawr College

BOOKS: *The Starlit Eye* (Dublin: Dolmen Press, 1952);

Three Legendary Sonnets (Dublin: Dolmen Press, 1952);

Per Imaginem (Dublin: Dolmen Press, 1953);

Death of a Queen (Glenageary, Ireland: Dolmen Press, 1956);

Poems (Dublin: Dolmen Press, 1956);

Another September (Dublin: Dolmen Press, 1958; Philadelphia: Dufour, 1958);

Moralities (Dublin: Dolmen Press, 1960);

Poems and Translations (New York: Atheneum, 1961);

Downstream (Dublin: Dolmen Press, 1962);

Wormwood (Dublin: Dolmen Press, 1966);

Nightwalker (Dublin: Dolmen Press, 1967);

Poems, by Kinsella, Douglas Livingstone, and Anne Sexton (London & New York: Oxford University Press, 1968);

Nightwalker and Other Poems (Dublin: Dolmen Press/London: Oxford University Press, 1968; New York: Knopf, 1969);

Tear (Cambridge, Mass.: Pym Randall Press, 1969);

Notes from the Land of the Dead (Dublin: Cuala, 1972);

Butcher's Dozen: A Lesson for the Octave of Widgery (Dublin: Peppercanister Press, 1972);

A Selected Life (Dublin: Peppercanister Press, 1972);

Finistère (Dublin: Dolmen Press, 1972);

Notes from the Land of the Dead and Other Poems (New York: Knopf, 1973);

New Poems (Dublin: Dolmen Press, 1973);

Vertical Man (Dublin: Peppercanister Press, 1973);

The Good Fight (Dublin: Peppercanister Press, 1973);

Selected Poems 1956-1968 (Dublin: Dolmen Press, 1973; London: Oxford University Press, 1973);

One (Dublin: Peppercanister Press, 1974);

A Technical Supplement (Dublin: Peppercanister Press, 1976);

Song of the Night and Other Poems (Dublin: Peppercanister Press, 1978);

Peppercanister Poems 1972-1978 (Dublin: Dolmen Press, 1979; Winston-Salem: Wake Forest University Press, 1979);

One and Other Poems (Dublin: Dolmen Press/ London: Oxford University Press, 1979);

Poems 1956-1973 (Winston-Salem: Wake Forest University Press, 1979);

Fifteen Dead (Dublin: Dolmen Press/Peppercanister Press, 1979).

OTHER: *The Breastplate of Saint Patrick*, translated by Kinsella (Dublin: Dolmen Press, 1954; republished as *Faeth Fiadha: The Breastplate of Saint Patrick*, Dublin: Dolmen Press, 1957);

The Exile and Death of the Sons of Usnech ("Longes Mac n-Usnig") (Dublin: Dolmen Press, 1954);

Thirty Three Triads, translated from the XII Century Irish (Dublin: Dolmen Press, 1955);

The Dolmen Miscellany of Irish Writing, poetry section edited by Kinsella (Dublin: Dolmen Press, 1962);

The Táin (Dublin: Dolmen Press, 1969; London & New York: Oxford University Press, 1970);

Davis, Mangan, Ferguson? Tradition and the Irish Writer, essays by Kinsella and W. B. Yeats (Dublin: Dolmen Press, 1970);

Seán Ó Tuama, ed., *An Duanaire, An Irish Anthology*, translation into English verse by Kinsella (Dublin: Dolmen Press, 1981; Philadelphia: University of Pennsylvania Press, 1981).

S. *Cashman*

Thomas Kinsella is unquestionably one of the leading Irish poets of our day. One of a number of young Irishmen who began to write in the years following World War II, he has played a major role in invigorating the moribund world of Irish verse. There were good modern poets before him, but Ireland had not seen the like of his verse for decades. His technical virtuosity and the profound originality of his subject matter set him apart from his contemporaries.

Born in Dublin to John Paul and Agnes Casserley Kinsella, he is the son of what he terms a typical Dublin family. His father, a Dublin man, was a lifelong socialist, a member of the Labour party and the Left Book Club (his membership in this club of course precluded any possibility that books could be a mere ornament to the household). It was exceptional for the children of such families to attend university — Kinsella's parents did not — but a series of grants and scholarships enabled Thomas to attend University College, Dublin. Pursuing at first an interest in physics and chemistry, he ultimately took a degree in public administration, and in 1946 he joined the civil service of Ireland. Two important relationships were formed during his post-university years — his friendship with Sean Oriada, who became Ireland's leading musician and composer and was a much-loved participant in the poet's growing intellectual life, and his relationship with Eleanor Walsh, whom the poet married on 28 December 1955. He has often pointed to this relationship as a crucial factor in the development of poetry as a serious pursuit for him. He had been writing in private for some time when in 1952 he met Liam Miller, founder of the Dolmen Press; between 1952 and 1956 Miller published several pieces of Kinsella's work, and Kinsella became a director of the press.

In 1958 Dolmen brought out *Another September*, Kinsella's first major collection, which in addition to being awarded the Guinness Poetry Prize for the year was made a Poetry Book Society selection. The reviews sounded two notes that would recur throughout most subsequent criticism of the poet's work: the *Times Literary Supplement* warned of "a fascination with verbal patterning for its own sake" and complained of a willful obscurity. John Montague, on the other hand, described it in *Poetry* as "clearly one of the best books of poetry produced by an Irishman since the war" and "one of the most poetic books I have read by a contemporary." Montague was thinking of the personal or private focus of the poems. They are indeed nonpolitical and militantly nonlocal. Like many first collections, the volume as a whole is something of a miscellany; there are love poems, meditative descriptive poems about various human figures, one Audenesque ballad ("In the Ringwood"), and meditations on various modes of human life and death (such as "Priest and Emperor," "Death of a Queen," and "Death and the Professor"). The volume is already marked by a characteristic tension between a somber aesthetics of loss and a bravura technique boldly proclaiming the poet's form- and order-making powers. Thematically the book bears out Kinsella's own description of its contents as tending to "make real . . . the passing of time, the frightening exposure of all relationships and feeling to erosion," but here is no decadent aesthete falling on the thorns of life.

Two aspects of the book are helpful to an understanding of Kinsella's development: its record of an early stage in the forming of his style and his pursuit of order.

Some of the poems echo Auden and Yeats, the earliest influences on Kinsella's poetry, but what strikes the reader most is Kinsella's own virtuosity. Though many of the poems pursue rhymed stanza forms, the rhyming effects are greatly subtilized. In the first stanza of "An Ancient Ballet," for example,

the enjambment of the third and fourth lines purposely de-emphasizes the rhyme:

> In the deep reaches of the night
> The ticking stars keep order
> That when the sleepless border
> On marvel they shall sleep light.

Often rhyme fades into near-rhyme and assonance:

> It looked so when her face filled
> My window one endless hour.
> Brightly her darkness downpoured
> Delusion, radiantly skilled.
>
> Presently this room,
> Much used for music, lined with books,
> Where a faith died and a little lacks
> —And once a panther came—

But this skill is as nothing compared to the intricacies of some of the poems, and when to techniques such as these is added the use of long phrases, as in "Baggot Street Deserta," the result is an original and exciting kind of language:

> The window is wide
> On a crawling arch of stars, and the night
> Reacts faintly to the mathematic
> Passion of a cello suite
> Plotting the quiet of my attic.

Kinsella may somehow have learned from Auden's work how to do such things, but the things done are his own entirely.

The real theme of *Another September* is order, the fruit of art, which in Kinsella's view is one major form of the mind's stance against mutability and corruption. Poem after poem, but "Baggot Street Deserta" most extensively, confronts with stoic acceptance the grim fact of loss as a chief keynote of life. The pursuit of order which the poet mounts against loss and decay takes three general forms in *Another September*, the first of which is difficult to name; it is evinced by poems touching on real or hypothetical historical events, such as in "Death of a Queen," "Lady of Quality," and "King John's Castle"—the *imposed* order of monarchy, the hospital, the military citadel. Other poems speak of the order-making power of love, which, in poems such as "Soft, To Your Places," is felt to be a way of escaping the entropy of time:

> O when beauty's brought to pass
> Will Time set down his hour-glass

And rest content,
His hand upon that monument?
Unless it is so, alas
That the heart's calling is but to go stripped and
                                                    diffident.

Soft, to your places, love; I kiss
Because it is, because it is.

But the irony of other poems, such as "Tete à Tete," ("Their happiness when they forgave each other/ Made neither ready to have faith in either") suggests that love too is subject to decay.

A third ordering force stands above these other two: the force of poetry itself. Kinsella's technical virtuosity in these poems is itself a manifestation of ordering power, and he has spoken of the poetic act as a manifestation of order. In an interview in 1962 he remarked that "one of the main impulses to poetry . . . is an attempt more or less to stem the passing of time; it's the process of arresting the erosion of feelings and relationships and objects which is being fought by the artist." The stoic poise of "Baggot Street Deserta" represents the attainment of a measure of order, and the formal structure of the poem is a validation of the poise.

In some of the poems the ordering powers of love and art are brought together as stabilizing forces. In "First Light" the poet muses on how his beloved's lips "were seen to break the crests of speech in fair order":

Whereupon all manner of birds
Exploded across the estuary. Winds
Opened out white leaves:
A stylus, guided by the horizon, printed and
                                                    mirrored.

The beloved here is a muse or anima figure, and as the love brings shape and stability to feelings, poetic utterance gives stability and lastingness to the experience. In "Who Is My Proper Art" love and poetry are even more intertwined. At first one cannot tell whether the poem is a love poem or a poem about the muse; but it is a love poem, the verse being a shapely and shaping tribute to the beloved, the beloved serving as topic and matter for the verse:

                                        That latest
Look she drew from the world's sweetest
        Well, that scene lying
Imagery for her, I will make
Fix its true stare for her sake
        Into my clearer, blinder
Eyes, Who is my proper art,

Who rested here her soaring heart,
        The fashioner, the finder.

Life is a tide of loss, disorder, and corruption, and the poetic impulse is an impulse to stem that tide, to place form where time leaves disorder and pain.

In *Another September* we see Kinsella setting out, so to speak, settling into his style and his themes. Both are strikingly mature and self-possessed, but the air of fatalism—as in "A Lady of Quality," whose conviction of the inevitability of disasters is reminiscent of Auden's "Lay Your Sleeping Head, My Love"—creates in the book as a whole a narrowness of emotional and intellectual tone not characteristic of work to follow. Kinsella's subsequent work turns to more interesting inner problems. The London *Times* reviewer noted that "Mr. Kinsella's language at its best has a chilly control," which he found "the poise of a Romantic dandy," and the first part of the remark, perhaps, was not unjust.

Another September and *Moralities*, a sequence of short lyrics which was published by Dolmen in 1960, attracted attention in America, where Atheneum published *Poems and Translations* in 1961 as a volume in a series of works by younger Irish and British poets, including R. S. Thomas, Peter Redgrove, and Norman MacCaig. In *Poetry* that summer, Marya Zaturenska wrote that "the best volume in the . . . series is by Thomas Kinsella," whom she described as "already a poet of considerable originality." In the same year Kinsella was awarded the Irish Arts Council Triennial Book Award.

For the next few years he pursued his duties in the Finance Department of the Irish civil service and had his verse published in periodicals in Ireland and abroad. By 1962 there was already enough significant new work for another collection, *Downstream*, which also included five poems published in 1960 as *Moralities*. The insistent pursuit of formal experimentation is relaxed in this volume, and thematically the poetry turns more to the things people actually do in and with their lives. That many of the poems' titles refer to jobs, types of people, and life choices signals the linkage of the temporal and the abstract, the deeply buried and the visibly lived, a new stance for the poet's work—here, in short, experimentation is thematic.

The collection is exceedingly well articulated. The first section deals overtly with the phenomenal world in the choices and orientations of the characters—as in "The Laundress," "Portrait of the Engineer," and "Dick King," for example— phenomena on whose underlying principles part three constitutes a series of meditations. The poems of *Moralities* are inserted between these two groups as part two—a group of poems on love, faith, death, song, the geological ribs of the book as a whole. The return to short lyrics in part four is a return to the order of phenomena, better understood.

The very title of the book thrusts forward that preoccupation with the passing of time—change as dying, change as birth—that has marked Kinsella's poetic mind from very early on. The thematically central poem, "Cover Her Face," is essentially a picture of the failure of conventional forms of order—religion, family, art—to give shape and meaning to the death of a young woman. "Who understands," the speaker asks, "The sheet pulled white and Maura's locked blue hands?," and there is no answer. A similar (and very Yeatsian) inconclusiveness marks "Scylla and Charybdis." None of the three characters in this brief poem—greengrocer, butcher, poet—has any hope of total fulfillment. Life forms entail hunger for what lies outside them, and the banality of the "form" this truth takes in Kinsella's stoic comedy here underscores the pathos of day-to-day life. Kinsella has said many times that art has to do with the eliciting of order from significant experience, adding always that eliciting order does not allow imposing it; yet the forms in these two poems impose rather than elicit order. Of course, the day-to-day concerns of a greengrocer may not constitute quite what Kinsella means by "significant experience," but in any case the order involved would be limited. With another poem, "Old Harry," the issue is more dramatic, and imposed order flames in horror. "Harry" is Harry Truman, and the poem is about his ordering the atomic bombing of Hiroshima and Nagasaki. This is the one early poem in which Kinsella allowed himself the luxury of partisan engagement. The savagery of the simplistic moralism involved in unleashing holocaust is spectacular commentary on the fruit of order imposed:

> He raved softly and struggled for righteous-
> ness,
> Then chose in loneliness near the blurred
> curtains
> The greater terror for the lesser number.
> ....
> Lascivious streets before they shriveled up
> Heightened their rouge and welcomed baths
> of pure flame;
> In broad daylight delicate creatures of love
>
> Swayed in a rose illumination of thighs,

> Their breasts melted shyly and bared the
> white bone;
> At that sight men blushed fiercely and be-
> came shades.

Such verse is meditation only in a special sense.

The volume returns to the thoughtful realism of "Cover Her Face" in the two long poems, "A Country Walk" and "Downstream"—the earliest of Kinsella's journey poems. The stroll, the walk, the boat ride—these are his favorite early devices for long meditative operations. "A Country Walk" is an elegiac meditation on the moral running down of history, but it observes in its complicated Kinsellan way that history never did have much to offer in the way of order or fruitful occasions. "Downstream" is even more somber, though the power of its form is suggested by P. N. Furbank's description of it as "a dazzling poem of its kind." It recounts a kind of quest, the goal of which is "ancient Durrow," an old center of learning and devotion—and downstream, of course, is both a deliberate and an inevitable direction; one way or another all of us are moving toward Durrow and its devout dead. But mortality is not the poem's main concern. The poem is built around visions of violence and loss and certain attempts to deal with them—the strivings of Durrow being one. Another is poetry: the speaker has a copy of Pound's *Cantos* under his jacket, and speaking as he does of his orientation toward "the silken kings . . . epochal men/Waging among the primal clarities/Productive war," he allies himself stylistically with Yeats and Wordsworth, though as the attainment of an order, however limited, the poem must be accepted for itself alone: it is no vehicle for some redeeming vision or idea. Its shape alone, as the finely crafted villanelle it is, is its sole testimony to the possibilities of coherence in the universe.

The speaker's consciousness teeters between order and chaos. The landscape and the river have their tentative modes of harmony surrounded by radical disorder. The sunset is a "fiery complex" and the river itself is a shifting quality, a complex of shape and fluidity, hospitality and threat:

> Drifting to meet us on the darkening stage
> A pattern shivers; whorling in its place
> Another holds us in a living cage
>
> And drifts to its reordered phase of grace.
>
> ....
> The black cage closed about us. Furred
> night-brutes
> Stopped in the rat-trails. . . .

It is, in fact, this sensed threat in the ambience that during the journey silenced the speaker's more naive impulses toward poeticizing—such impulses at any rate that could be realized in the outworn language of a latter-day Wordsworth, with its "brimming flood" and its "starry host."

The river no longer runs with the blood of its historical victims, and the dimness of ancient history and the rendition of acts of mayhem into harmless words ("epochal men/Waging among the primal clarities/Productive war," for example) perhaps disguises these attempts of primitive politics to order the world. As against the abstract violence of the anciently dead, a story of a man who "one night fell sick and left his shell/Collapsed, half-eaten, like a rotted thrush's," in the woods through which the river passes forces the speaker to a more concrete understanding of more recent mayhem:

> the soil of other lands
> Drank lives that summer with a body thirst
> While nerveless by the European pit
> —Ourselves through seven hundred
> years accurst—
>
> We gazed on barren earth obscurely lit
> By tall chimneys flickering in their pall,
> The haunt of swinish man. . . .

Nature viewed in a certain mood or light may have its "rat-trails," but it takes mankind really to activate the rodent principle.

The speaker has a glimpse of order of a sort in his contemplation of the stars, but that mood does not last. From time to time, in such moments, the natural world seems to offer some promise of order—a sleeping swan, for example, near the end of the poem leads the poet to a momentary vision of celestial order when he raises his glance to the stars again—but the vision is blotted out by the "wall of ancient stone" the friends confront at their destination. The poem ends on its one gesture of persistence as the speaker and his companion search "the darkness for a landing place." Cold comfort, solemn stoicism, but informed, aware, and honest, not fantasizing order, but creating it on the one hand and living it, apparently, on the other.

It is in the strength of the stoic persistence of "Downstream" that the poems of part four are to be read. The tough-minded "Mirror in February," for instance, is not so committed to unmitigated gloom as might first appear. True, the instances of renewal around the speaker—day, the plowed earth, the "awakening trees"—evince a renovation not open to him:

> Now plainly in the mirror of my soul
> I read that I have looked my last on youth
> And little more; for they are not made whole
> That reach the age of Christ.

But his shaven jaw is not really "hacked clean" as the trees are, and he is not "defaced":

> Below my window the awakening trees,
> Hacked clean for better bearing, stand de-
> faced
> Suffering their brute necessities.

Shaving, fortunately, is not really mutilation, and the insistent rhyme *defaced*/*distaste* is ultimately cancelled by the near-rhyme, *grace*—this last an attribute of the speaker's, not of the trees:

> And how should the flesh not quail that span
> for span
> Is mutilated more? In slow distaste
> I fold my towel with what grace I can,
> Not young and not renewable, but man.

The analogies that link man to, and by their defectiveness separate him from, nature are perceived and formed by the poetic imagination; the trees may be renewable, and they may "awake," but the last word is the defining consciousness of a human artist, and this is an important index to Kinsella's main theme. Reviewers were concerned about the poet's stylistic facility. Three separate reviews took issue with what one of them, P. N. Furbank, called "a slippery, phrasemaking ease about his style which is both attractive and suspect." It remained for Margaret Bottrall to see what the issue was: "Kinsella," she said, "undoubtedly the leading Irish poet of the post-Patrick Kavanagh generation, has gone farther than almost all his fellow-bards in solving the problems of making new structures which shall be simultaneously of our day, and of our history." *New structures*—the phrase must have delighted the poet if he saw it, for it went to the heart of his enterprise.

The year after *Downstream* appeared Kinsella was able to take a leave of absence from the Finance Department, where he was by then assistant principal officer. Though he had no thought of staying away permanently, the experience of a whole year free for the writing of poetry was clearly food for thought, and in 1965 the poet—by then a member of the Irish Academy of Letters—made a major change in his life when he accepted an invitation from Southern Illinois University to join their faculty as poet in residence. Being Ireland's leading younger poet was no longer a part-time job. He was given the Denis Devlin Memorial Award for *Wormwood* (1966). He became professor of English at Southern Illinois, and the productivity of the years since *Downstream* was attested to by a remarkable new volume, *Nightwalker and Other Poems* (1968). The book includes a number of poems that had appeared in Irish and American periodicals and the long ruminative poems, as well as "Nightwalker" and the ambitious "Phoenix Park." This book made a strong impact. Writing for the *Listener*, Martin Dodsworth called it "the best book of new poems I have read this year," and several reviews proclaimed that in this book Kinsella truly came into his own.

Two things that stand out in this new collection are its formal advances and some important changes in thematic focus. Rhyme is almost entirely gone and both line and stanza forms become interestingly ad hoc—each poem exploring its own material form. As for theme, there is a new stance, a sense which will grow from *Nightwalker and Other Poems* on of potential meaningfulness in the pain that the poet seems driven to record.

Reminded by an interviewer of what he had written of this collection of poems, that "their subject in general is a developing view of life as an ordeal," Kinsella replied, "I see it now as . . . given . . . one is presented with a lifespan which manifests itself largely as ordeal, stages through which one is tested more and more deeply." The somberness of much of his work (and certainly of *Downstream*) makes it important to emphasize the concept of ordeal—not pain or violence as such; the idea of stages "through which one is tested more and more deeply" implies coherence. That spirit unquestionably informs *Nightwalker and Other Poems*.

The first group of poems in the book gives voice to different ways of forming response to death and decay. "Office for the Dead," "Landscape and Figure," "Museum," and "The Serving Maid" all turn one way or another on the question of death or the loss of vitality. As might be expected by now, Kinsella's speaker has little patience with conventional rituals; "Office for the Dead" concludes,

> *Sanctus*. We listen with bowed heads to the
> thrash of chains
> Measuring the silence. The pot gasps in its
> smoke.
> An animal of metal, dragging itself and
> breathing . . .

The "grief chewers" are wrapped in the only mea-

sure they know to deal with the death of the old woman, but these measures of imposed order do not meet the unique needs of just this case. A more ambivalent expression of the issue appears in "Museum," which contrasts the creative chaos of untrammelled art to the squat stasis of the museum ("Its blocks of granite, speechless with fatigue . . ."), but there is at least something to be said for having flux disperse "in order everywhere." "The Serving Maid," getting herself ready for her periodical visit to her late employer's grave, reveals how she has shaped a life around her mistress's needs, as a poet might shape his around service to the muse. The entire group turns on the problem of ordered response to life's endless losses and continues the move begun in *Downstream* toward the inclusion of more and more concrete outward things in the poetry's scope.

The tendency is immensely complicated in "Nightwalker" itself, a long nocturnal meditation on Ireland past and present, on the poet's consciousness as a source of order amid decay and betrayal—a move which one of the more acute reviewers perceived when the book came out: Hugh Maxton, an Irishman, saw that "the range" of *Nightwalker and Other Poems* was wider than the personal: "the decay and suffering include the decay of public life," and this was a new note in Irish poetry. In "Nightwalker" the poet ponders the desecration of art, religion, and language and the decay of communal longings into the mess of modern politics, where even education is misused in the service of ideology. The form of the poem is misleadingly loose—in fact, it anticipates the phantasmagoria of his later work. It bears some resemblance to T. S. Eliot's "Rhapsody on a Windy Night" (a fact which dismayed one reviewer): a poet-wanderer is somehow in the grip of the moon, his consciousness and thus the shape of the poem more or less at the mercy of whatever comes to him. The lurid light of the moon in this case is a symbol or pattern of the bluish glare of television and its substitutes for consciousness, of the sickly pallor of the city in general, its citizens, its failed and corrupted heroes, its commercial visitors. This is not the inspiring moon of the conventional romantic, but the ghastly moon of Coleridge and Poe, the true source of lunacy, hanging in the sky,

> A mask of grey dismay sagging open
> In the depths of torture, moron voiceless moon.
> That dark area, the mark of Cain.

The speaker ironically mouths the slogans of the

new economic development, then recalls the visit to his office by two Germans, brother and sister, the sister fronting for her "otterfaced" brother in some money-making scheme, their presence enshrouded in the speaker's memory of the horrors their co-nationals visited upon their racial victims in the Holocaust. These thoughts modulate into a rumination on modern Irish politics in the form of a sardonic popular myth involving a Bridegroom (Kevin O'Higgins), his Best Man (Rory O'Connor), and "The Fox" (Eamon de Valera, who alone of the three survived the string of political murders they were involved in). The poem goes on to recall scenes at school, where the promotion of Gaelic becomes the vehicle for tired clichés of Irish history (tinged by self-praise of the Christian Brothers), and these recollections flow into a pondering on the communion, a sad fusion of down-at-heels religion and opportunist politics:

> The Blessed Virgin smiles
> From her waxed pedestal, like young Victoria;
> A green snake wriggles under her heel
> Beside a vase of tulips.
>
> > Adolescents,
> Celibates, we offer up our vows
> To God and Ireland in Her name, grateful
> That by our studies here they may not lack
> Civil servants in a state of grace.

The ambiguities of the words *civil servants* (servants of conquering England beaten into civility, or Ireland's bureaucrats?) and even of *Her* (the Virgin, Victoria, or Ireland?) testify to the confusion even of language in this great game of sacrificing moral order for a less worthy sort.

As the poem approaches its close, the speaker's vision of his wife's "dear shadow" on the blind at home is thrust aside by a meditation of the multiple figure fusing Kathleen ni Houlihan, the legendary heroine of Ireland's communal longings for identity, with Mary and the dominant female presence, Queen Victoria, whose "concern" over Ireland fizzles out into banality:

> a meaningful drama
> . . . reaching through the years to unknown
> > goals
> In the consciousness of man, which is very
> > soothing.

The poem ends on the phantasmal arrival of the poet on the surface of the moon — or is it Ireland seen truly as the desolation it is?

> > no wind stirs
> On the dust floor. Far as the eye can see
> Rock needles stand up from the plain; the
> > horizon
> A ring of sharp mountains like broken spikes.
> Hard bluish light beats down, to kill
> Any bodily thing
> . . . .
> > . . . A true desert, naked
> To every peril. . . .
> I think this is the Sea of Disappointment.

In the poem, of course, the public institutions touched upon are all forms of imposed order, imposed moreover for impure purposes. It is the poet's sad duty to elicit the real order hidden by threadbare machinations. He makes no grand claims for himself, invoking the spirits of Joyce and Yeats as an aid to survival, not power.

In mentioning names and referring to concrete cases in this poem, Kinsella has added the parameter of human will to his view of the active evil in history. Heretofore the one conscious figure in his desolate landscapes has been the poet; in "Nightwalker" specific persons from many walks of actual life are called to account. It is as if he comes to generalize the strategy of "Old Harry." He is not interested in merely fixing blame; but in a universe where things are done by people with first and last names the possibility that the pain of human life may be an explicable ordeal rather than random and unending loss is considerably stronger. "Nightwalker" may stand, then, as a watershed in Kinsella's work: the point where poetry as *solace* becomes poetry as *assertion*.

The culminating poem in the collection, "Phoenix Park," is an ambitious composition that shows how far the poet has come since his earliest work. The title is the name of Dublin's largest park, but it bears connotation of the phoenix itself, the bird that rises from the ashes of its own cremation to live another millenium. The poem takes up the implications of the *Wormwood* group, where the lovers' marriage is seen as a powerful form which overcomes loss and the chaos of life. Their love is "the one positive dream" to which the speaker of "Phoenix Park" refers as the exception to the fact that "There's a fever now that eats everything." The poet and his wife are about to leave Dublin; as they pass by various places meaningful to them, the poet recalls their significance or associations for the lovers, and in describing the process by which he was prepared for and moved toward his part in the one positive dream, he reviews various symbolic moments of his life, where he partook of possibilities which his children came to pursue or re-enact. He expatiates on the implications of their love as evincing the "laws of order," on their love as ordeal, a continual wounding and healing, and a continual growing, and arrives at a sense of existence as a necessary ordeal—when we think we have attained some abstract "ultimate," living must end. The realistic trappings that are customary in earlier Kinsella poems of this sort are casually dismissed at one point ("The road divides and we can take either way, Etcetera. . . ."), and in the final long section the sorts of places and times that in earlier poems have been seen as regrettably drained of meaning by the failures of history actually take on significance through their associations with the love of the poet and his wife. Thoughts of the actual Dublin are dismissed in favor of review of their relationship—a meaningful past, not pain free, certainly fragile, but unbetrayed. The poet recalls their lovemaking in his Baggot Street room, seeing it as fully creative ("My past alive in you," he recalls, "a gift of tissue/Torn free from my life in an odour of books"). The sense of order recorded in earlier poems ("Baggot Street Deserta" especially) was abstract, intellectual; here the order is concrete, at once fleshly and mental—the couple's three children live, and the poet's review of his life renders their marriage a coherent result of his preparation. The solitary male poet of "Baggot Street Deserta" has been replaced by the unity-structure of male and female, idea and flesh—and overall, poet and muse.

The poem clearly constitutes a more conclusive handling of the theme of suffering and order than has heretofore appeared in Kinsella's work. His characters have not simply faced pain; they have accepted it as a test and as an impulse toward new growth. Life and growth themselves are a function of the eternal discrepancy between reach and grasp—and imagination's (or the heart's) very power to conceive or yearn for the unattainable is a source of life.

The book was most enthusiastically received. Ralph Mills in *Poetry* put his finger on an important issue by saying that "By tremendous strength of word and image [Kinsella] has succeeded magnificently in transmuting personal bitterness and despair into durable poems." Martin Dodsworth in the *Listener* was equally approving: "All through *Nightwalker* the qualifications one might make melt away before the superior force with which the poems are shaped as a whole. The faults arise from excess of talent, not from the opposite." If this comment

faintly echoes earlier critics' concern about Kinsella's facility of expression, Marius Bewley's praise in *Hudson Review* for one of the poems in the *Wormwood* group clearly does not: "I cannot think of a short passage of poetry," he wrote, "in which so many complex and tangled emotions find such concentrated expression . . . all resolved at last through an acceptance in love." Only John Montague, it seems, was unimpressed. He felt that Kinsella had not developed any new strategy for dealing with the "cliché" of "urban discontent" (it was precisely the development of new structures that Margaret Bottrall found so exciting in *Downstream*), and, coming close to an important point but missing it, he complained that the *persona* of "Nightwalker" was "depressingly close to early Eliot." Apparently the reviewer could not credit the idea that Kinsella's poem has a scope and conclusiveness far beyond the ironic close of "Rhapsody on a Windy night."

Nightwalker and Other Poems was published while the poet was on a Guggenheim Fellowship, granted for the pursuit of his translation of *Táin Bo Cualinghe*, the Old Irish saga, which he had been working on more or less casually for some time. But he continued his writing as well, and the years following *Nightwalker and Other Poems* saw a steady stream of significant poems. *The Táin* was published in 1969; several major poems appeared in periodicals that year and the next, and in 1971 the Kinsellas left Carbondale, Illinois, to take up residence near Philadelphia, where the poet was named professor of English at Temple University. He had by now won the Devlin Award for the second time (1971). Nineteen seventy-two saw the completion of several major poems: *Butcher's Dozen*, written in the white heat of rage after the release of the Widgery Report on the investigation into the shooting down of thirteen Irish civil rights marchers by British paratroopers in 1972, *A Selected Life* on the death of Sean Oriada, *Finistère*, and *Notes from the Land of the Dead*. In the same year, Kinsella set up the Peppercanister Press—*Butcher's Dozen* was its first production—a small publishing program operating out of his home in Dublin, where he lived when not teaching at Temple University. Its main function was to provide opportunity for limited printings of his work in progress. The poet's early books had been conventional gatherings of poems in hand, but Kinsella came more and more to compose in terms of whole books, and the Peppercanister releases were useful preliminary steps. The first fruit along these lines was the remarkable new collection, *Notes from the Land of the Dead and Other Poems*, published in 1973

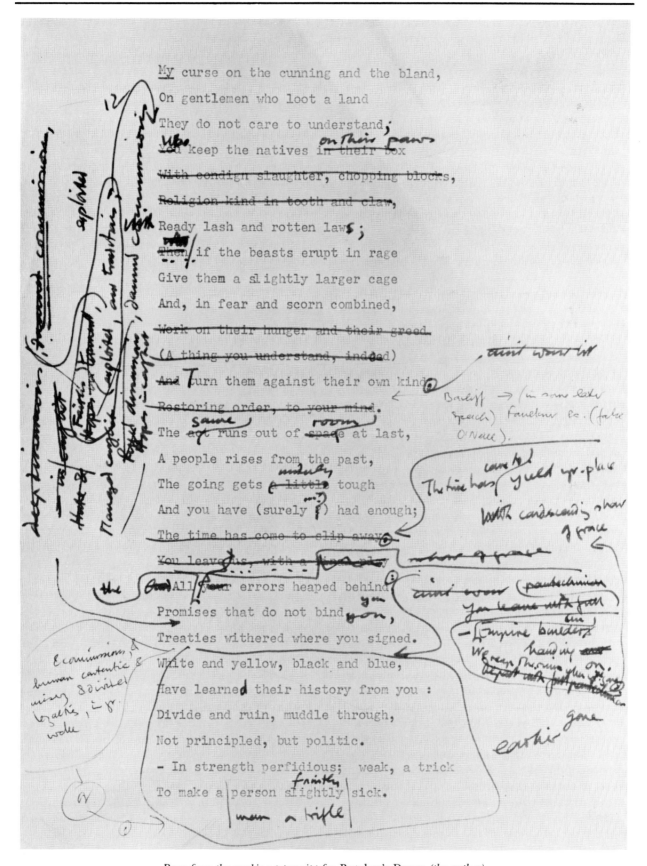

Page from the working typescript for Butcher's Dozen *(the author)*

after *Notes from the Land of the Dead* was published alone in 1972. Unlike the earlier gatherings, it does not include any poems previously included in earlier books—that function was left to *Selected Poems 1956-1968*, published by Dolmen in 1973.

But in more important ways as well *Notes from the Land of the Dead and Other Poems* is remarkably different from Kinsella's earlier books, full of new attainments. An untitled prologue that can only be described as a mystical version of a Kinsellan wandering poem recounts the speaker's descent into a psychic underworld, a reversion to the embryo stage. He is on a mystic quest to seize a seething cauldron tended by "naked ancient women," and the book is the witches' pot that now boils before us. The poems that follow are a species of myth-making wherein the poet reaches back into his psychic and familial past to find his fuller self.

The radical change in the nature of imagery in these poems signals what the new development is. The images in earlier poems are perfectly adequate to the needs of the verse, but they are not radically out of the ordinary in the context of English-language poetry. In *Notes from the Land of the Dead and Other Poems* Kinsella undertakes a whole new methodology: his images interrelate in a way not characteristic of his earlier work; a hollow shape may be the female locus of male sexual ecstasy, a devouring mouth, a fearful dark cave, a womb, a grave—or, more exactly, any one of these is apt to be a murky version of any or all of the others. Here, then, Kinsella's images are less designative than resonant, and what they resonate with are the deepest desires, terrors, and confusions of the psyche.

The poet-speaker's grandmother, an object for him of awe and fascination, is sometimes seen as an amiable, disquieting witch; her rooms—the shop, the back room, the scullery—are work places, but tonally they are witches' caves, the lairs of mysterious beings. "Survivor," a mythlike poem narrated by the lone survivor of a primordial migration into ancient Ireland, focuses on another female, an all-devouring hag (and behind that may be the bitter characterization of Ireland as the sow that eats her farrow). In "Nuchal" another mystical female creature creates the four rivers of Paradise by trailing her hand in the flowing water of the First River, and even the White Rock girl appears in one poem, called "Touching the River."

There are two reasons for dwelling on these examples. First, they embody an important theme in this book—the idea of the female principle as a creative component of the self, the female ancestor out of whom the male poet has sprung, and, second,

they show the new orientation of Kinsella's thought. Not only are the images resonant, they are synthetic, unlike the more usual analytic imagery of Kinsella's earlier work, but very like images as conceived by C. G. Jung, whose work Kinsella had begun to read in 1963. Where the earlier work was so concerned with the idea of suffering and pain as the motives of growth, the ordeal as a linear meeting of successive tests, these new poems take up the Jungian idea of a creative union of opposites. The ordeal of suffering and growth becomes the more comprehensive rhythm of destruction and creation, decay and regeneration, death and birth. The idea in "Phoenix Park" that "Giving without tearing is not possible" becomes something more profound. Kinsella has spoken of the "Jungian aim" as "the spending of one's life in such a way as to perfect one's capabilities, to fulfill one's life." Jung's aim, of course, is the integration of the various energies of the psychic life, an orientation that quite precludes operating on a principle of exclusion. A spirit of negation is seen as a strong force answering to the spirit of assertion; the drive to destroy is the shadow of the urge to create, the frenzied dark, the necessary concomitant of the rational light. Kinsella spoke of the "land of the dead" in terms openly similar to these: "I called the book *Notes from the Land of the Dead* [because] the land of the dead is not merely a place where things terminate. Some things do, but other things originate. The interesting thing there, is that part of Munster . . . where some of the poems are set, appears in some of the myths as a land of the dead, but also as the land of beginnings—and offshore are the Isles of the Blessed."

One interesting result of this Jungian orientation is that while there are many threatening, fearful figures in the poems, there is no evil. In a poem significantly titled "At the Crossroads" the speaker is confronted by a white face—a female face, "her mouth ready"—an owl, whose "choice" it is to swoop on its prey, carry it off, tear it to bits and devour it, "Her brain, afterward/staring among the rafters in the dark/until hunger returns." The picture is grim, but not "evil," and the poem is not so much a lament for the ugliness of life as the rendition of a piece of grim wisdom. Why is this phantasmagoric vision of the rational principle nestling amidst its dark need for torn flesh *not* a vision of evil? In large part it is Kinsella's new technique, which leaves the level where good and evil are at issue. For this reason, too, the poems are less transparent than his earlier work—some of them uncompromisingly elliptical. Much less committed to the complete sentence, they are studded with shards and fragments of suggestive thoughts, of musings broken off, of enigmatic things named but not pursued—as in the last two lines of "Survivor"—

> Hair. Claws. Grey.
> Naked. Wretch. Wither.

This new technique was too much for one hapless critic, Calvin Bedient, who complained that the poems were chiefly fragments and saw little or no point in either ellipses or shards, taking them as evidence that "The dream poems are conceptually tired." But the poems abandon syntax, of course, because they have left the world to which syntax is relevant and moved to the world of dream, phantasm, and myth, the world in short of psychic exploration. "In these poems," Kinsella has said, "I am trying to plunge into the land of the dead to find my own roots. That past has a psychic geography which is vitally important for the present." This kind of search cannot be carried on in purely rational terms, unless you want to pursue your search for roots on the level of where little Joe got his red hair. Kinsella has been bold enough to assert with some pride that no one digs into the psyche as he does, and in *Notes from the Land of the Dead and Other Poems* he is dramatizing that primordial and necessarily amoral struggle of the psyche toward consciousness.

The low point of coherent consciousness in this exploration is "All is Emptiness and I Must Spin." The title suggests either the forming of a protective cocoon and its implications of transformed life to come, or a sensibility bereft of all comforts, or a hanged corpse slowly twisting in air. It is not easy to tell whether the poem describes a phantasmagoric birth ("It was not Death, but Night . . . tears of self forming") or a scene in a German death camp ("Our hands touched lightly/in farewell . . . A distant door clangs"). The poem declares its formlessness in its trailing close:

> The sterile: it is a whole matter in itself.
> Fantastic millions of
> fragile
> in every single

Darkness is rehabilitated in "Good Night," where we witness a less ambiguous coming-into-being as consciousness dissolves into sleep. The speaking consciousness of the poem drifts off to sleep hearing snatches of conversation from another room and wanders in and out of dream-visions. Interwo-

ven with strands of semi-conscious visions, the overheard conversation marches on—"Would you agree, then, we wont/find truths, or any certainties"—contrapuntally to the discoveries of the irrational:

> where monsters lift soft
> self-conscious voices, and feed us
> and feed on us, and coil
> and uncoil in our substance,
> so that in that they are there
> we cannot know them, and that,
> daylit, we are the monsters of our night.

The last words of the poem are pleasantly ironic: "and ungulfs a Good Night, smiling"—a drowsy reference to the departing guest-talker, whose conventional phrase of nocturnal farewell speaks more profoundly than he—but not we or Kinsella— knows. To create a dramatic poetry out of psychic experience at this level is a remarkable achievement—here there are no abstractions, no allegorical monsters, and very little of the superficial trappings of day-to-day consciousness, and yet we are clearly in the midst of a gripping process of development.

The subrational darkness is the nutriment of consciousness, and it forms the substratum upon which the other poems in the volume stand. These are more and less complicated meditations or dramatizations on the theme of human limitations and possibilities. One, "St. Paul's Rocks: 16 February 1832" (the reference is to Darwin's *Voyage of the Beagle*), seems a straightforward, conscious-world rumination on the processes of life in terms of who eats whom; but its observations, concerns, and imagery actually reflect the concerns of the whole book—for examples, the last stanza:

> In squalor and killing and parasitic things
> life takes its first hold.
> Later the noble accident: the seed, dropped
> in some exhausted excrement, or bobbing
> like a matted skull into an inlet.

The language of this stanza glances at evolution, at Irish political history, at the process of procreation, at death—and aspects of its imagery can be found everywhere in *Notes from the Land of the Dead and Other Poems*, an astonishingly unified and adventuresome volume.

Critical reception was almost as complicated as the poetry; the book called forth some of the best and some of the most inept criticism Kinsella had so far attracted. The difficulty of the verse left some critics nonplussed or unhappy. The *Times Literary Supplement* reviewer complained of the poems' obscurity and their use of ellipsis, charging that Kinsella's "images fail to construct a consistent and coherent para-reality"—a complaint that of course highlights the book's very principles, especially that there can be no "coherent para-reality." One academic critic, writing in *Poetry* (January 1975) dismissed the whole book out of hand, irritated by what he felt to be its unfinished obscurity. Yet even Bedient concluded his review with the remark that "The more you read the poems the more they impose themselves as passionately delicate constructs. You listen and seem to hear, from something falling, tiny silvery strings, plucked as if by the air itself," and another anonymous reviewer for the *Times Literary Supplement* said that "Beset by this central blankness, several of the poems stagger to a halt, lapse into broken phrases or totter finally into silence; but there is no doubting the control with which these effects are brought off"—a perceptive assessment of the meaning of the breaking-off. The book called forth one of the best pieces of Kinsella criticism to date, a long and complete review by Vernon Young in *Parnassus* that is still the fullest and most knowing treatment of Kinsella's work. All in all critical praise outweighed censure, but with the partial exception of Young, none of the reviewers seemed conscious of the highly interesting direction of Kinsella's overall development, an evolution which would issue in the staggering achievements of his next book, *Peppercanister Poems, 1972-1978*.

After the 1973 Knopf publication of *Notes from the Land of the Dead and Other Poems*, Wake Forest University Press approached the poet about a volume of selected works. *Selected Poems 1956-1968* was being brought out by Dolmen and Oxford University Press, and Wake Forest undertook to publish *Poems 1956-1973* in connection with Dolmen. (It appeared in 1979.) Kinsella's preoccupation with Ireland and its past had been growing for some time, though his earliest work had sedulously avoided both, and even though he devoted several years to working on the translation of *The Táin*. In 1976 he founded Temple University's School of Irish Tradition in Dublin; taking the directorship of the program enabled him to continue dividing the academic year between Philadelphia and his native city, and the succeeding years have seen no diminution of his interest in the affairs of Ireland. Like many sons, he apparently had to leave in order to go back at all. At any rate, *Peppercanister Poems 1972-*

1978 (1979) includes many major poems which are not only about Ireland but about Ireland in connection with the poet; they follow a line of thinking much more complicated and committed than any of his earlier poems that touch on Ireland.

The collection is unquestionably a major work. In both technical bravura and thematic scope it is most imposing; thematically it runs the whole gamut from intimate to political and public, and it makes even more remarkable use than *Notes from the Land of the Dead* of the ability of Kinsella's poems to evoke their own powerful contexts. It is a complicated volume, a gathering of various publications of Kinsella's Peppercanister Press. To the two poems *Butcher's Dozen* and *A Selected Life*, carried over from *Notes from the Land of the Dead*, are added a later poem on Sean Oriada, "Vertical Man," and "The Good Fight," on the tenth anniversary of the assassination of John Kennedy. These are followed by *One* and *A Technical Supplement*, which continue the themes of *Notes from the Land of the Dead*. *One* includes *Finistère* and "The Oldest Place," imaginative renditions of legendary migrations into Ireland, and several poems dealing with the poet's family history and himself as artist. *A Technical Supplement* is a remarkable sequence of twenty-four poems on subjects ranging from mystical dreams to the slaughterhouse of Swift & Co. The contents of *Peppercanister 7* (*Song of the Night and Other Poems*, 1978) follow, comprising what might be called poems of reminiscence (Kinsellan reminiscence, to be sure—which is not always like other people's); and the volume closes with "The Messenger," a long and moving poem in memory of the poet's father.

The best commentary on the volume is Kinsella's own. About the zero or egg in *Notes from the Land of the Dead* and the numeral *one* which entitles a large section of *Peppercanister Poems*, he said, "The zero . . . is nothing, it's a hole, it's the opening 'from which' . . . The '0' is wide open, and everything is for later consideration. *One* is the first stroke of order. . . . It isn't the forcing of order: it is a way of finding, suddenly in *One*, that the poems can organize their own behavior. That's why the device for the volume is a snake: a unitary living thing. . . . It is an organizing thing, in Amargin's spine, when he steps onto land for the first time. . . . The 'maggot of the possible' wriggling 'out of the spine into the brain'—carries the same idea: 'the zero uncoiling and striking up.'" In *One* especially that Jungian sense of impulses merging into one another, of psychic forces manifesting themselves on a multitude of levels and in a multitude of forms, is at work. The communal migration of "Finistère" is a version of the family moves mentioned to young Thomas in "His Father's Hands"—the legendary underpinning that gives spiritual depth to the history of the family; in its aspect as an exploratory move, an undertaking, it associates with the poet's launching into verse, his exploration of his and his people's past. It is thus an association—a precedent, even—that unites the poet to his predecessors and validates the poetic act in historical terms. Similarly, the grandfather's cutting tool in "His Father's Hands" is a creative version of the slashing knives in the grisly poem about a tour of the slaughterhouse, and of the apparently murderous knives in the two "cutting" poems, four and five, of *A Technical Supplement*. The knives in those two short poems that imagize in cruel detail how knives penetrate flesh are, after all, like the little cobbler's nails driven into the grandfather's workbench—and all these associate with the "penetrating sense" of poem sixteen. "Going in" can be *any* going in, surgical, sexual, murderous, navigational, agricultural—creative, destructive, or casual.

The moral implications of these associational clusters can be seen in the book's handling of the theme of death. Visually, the ugliest presentation of death in the book occurs in the tour through the slaughterhouse. But brutal as they are, those killings feed human beings. The implications are a commentary on the questionable underpinnings of human culture (Englishmen slaughtered Indians to establish colonies; colonists slaughtered Englishmen to found an independent nation; Irish patriots slaughtered each other . . .)—but also offer a feasible justification of the slaughter of animals in the poem. On the other hand stands the slaughter of Irish Catholics in *Butcher's Dozen* and in the ignoble distortions and evasions in the Widgery Report: the humane bearing of *that* slaughter is like and unlike that in the meat plant. Then there is the enigmatic death of Kennedy. "What did it signify?" the poem seems to ask. Chance? Destiny? And there is the death of Sean Oriada in *A Selected Life*, death as loss, leaving the poet with one of those ordeals he used to write of. But though Oriada's death is waste and the other deaths senseless butchery, the death of the poet's father becomes, in "The Messenger," an immensely important inspiration to meditation and review, a passing on of the impulse toward order, moral and political in the father, psychic, moral, and aesthetic in the son. The father as messenger becomes the son as poet. These dyings describe a continuum of meaning—in fact, a continuum of nurture, from heedless murder, through ghastly but unfortunately meaningful slaughter, to

a dying which is more than a dying.

The book is a full scrutiny of the content of human life, a scrutiny which unfolds the factual and the everyday to reveal their archetypal content. Again and again events and phenomena "crack open" in the book, as the poet's perception of himself in a distorting mirror in poem twenty-two of *A Technical Supplement* ("It began to separate, the head opening/like a rubbery fan . . ./The thin hair blurred and crept apart . . . as the forehead opened down the centre . . ."). As always in Kinsella's later work, life in its fullness has a large element of the savage—hence the marvelous vision of the aquarium in poem nine, with the shark and the morays "peering up at a far off music of slaughter." The eerie beasts of the sea are a reminder of where we came from (in several senses), and the volume as a whole reminds us that we have not left them all that far behind.

The point is not that life is ugly. Jung and Kinsella's idea that creation and destruction, love and hate, life and death are interinvolved is an attempt to reclaim the wholeness of existence, not to deny its beauty. The poems here actually enact that stance: out of the death of a friend, of a father, or political martyrs comes poetry before our very eyes. Nor is being rooted in the prerational the same as being confined to it. In *Song of the Night and Other Poems*, the group of poems just before "The Messenger," the vision of the primordial seen by the poet and his children at the seaside is "Silvery sand-eels" that "Shivered and panicked through the shallows/. . .vanished—became sand . . . little whips fainted away in wet small palms, in an iodine smell"—a satisfying experience enriched by, not disqualified by, its echo of the aquarium poem. But all must be included, or the result is lies, like the Widgery Report: "it is we, letting things *be*," the speaker says in the poem on Kennedy's assassination, "Who might come at understanding." The poet's job is to elicit, not impose, order.

This latest volume was reviewed in the *New York Times*, the *Sewanee Review, Eire-Ireland,* and the *New England Review*. Writing in the *New York Times Book Review*, M. L. Rosenthal, himself a poet and a long-time authority on contemporary literature, described Kinsella as "At 52 . . . among the true poets, not only of Ireland but among all who write in English in our day," and welcomed *Peppercanister Poems* and *Poems 1956-1973* as giving Americans a view of the whole sweep of Kinsella's work. He was perceptive enough to see that "His Father's Hands" is "as it were, the personal history of Ireland's common people" and praised Kinsella as "a true elegist

```
IMF


I

For days I have wakened and felt immediately

half sick at something, a remote worry

in the meat.  Hour follows hour
     and
but my shoulders

are chilled with expectation.


It is more than mere "Loss"

burgeoning daily (though your image

certainly blackens, in the mind        drip and

surrendering its tissues and traps.

My leaden root curled on your lap.)

Or "the things you missed".  Or the things "we" miss

              which are Nothing

but things of the spirit — a yearning of the flesh

toward an impossible Possible       Nothing more.

(The conceiving hand exhausts in mid-reach.)
                          and
Sloppiness supersedes desire.)


Deeper.  A suspicion in the bones

as though they too could melt in filth.

Something to discourage goodness.

A moist movement within .

A worm winds on its hoard.
```

Page from the working typescript for "The Messenger" (the author) with a bitter, grieving, melodious tongue." Calvin Bedient, writing for the *Sewanee Review*, was again of two minds, complaining at the outset that "his sensibility is so grim that the real if rational delights of his ear and sense of form seem a necessary mercy," and that Kinsella's "reality-smiting . . . turn for quaint sick fantasy—poetic expressionism— has become more pronounced"—an impatient remark that does not argue any sweeping understanding of what the poems are all about. But after a nostalgic allusion to Kinsella's former pursuit of the everyday he concludes that "the subtle uncongenial art of the new volume develops like a negative with repeated immersions, and Kinsella is still the Irish poet most worth following."

Never committed to nor especially patient with the pursuit of "Irishness" in his poetry, Kinsella has explored Irish themes more and more in his later verse, but only in terms of exploring his own consciousness and consciousness in general. Currently, after a frightening bout of dangerous illness, he seems busy and relaxed, alternating between his academic duties in Philadelphia and in Dublin and writing poetry of ever-increasing depth. In 1981 appeared an anthology of Irish poetry from 1600 to 1900, a collaboration between Seán Ó Tuama as editor and Thomas Kinsella as translator. The poet has an *Oxford Book of Irish Verse* in preparation. Ireland may have lost a gifted assistant principal officer when Kinsella left Ireland in 1965—but it has surely gained a major poet.

Interviews:

Daniel O'Hara, "An Interview with Thomas Kinsella," *Contemporary Poetry: a Journal of Criticism*, vol. 4, no. 1 (n.d.): 1-18;
Peter Orr, "Interview with Kinsella," in *The Poet Speaks: Interviews with Contemporary Poets*, edited by Orr (London: Routledge & Kegan Paul, 1966), pp. 105-109;
Viewpoints: Poets in Conversation with John Haffenden (London & Boston: Faber & Faber, 1981), pp. 100-113.

Bibliographies:

Hensley Woodbridge, "Thomas Kinsella, a Bibliography," *Eire-Ireland*, 2, no. 2 (1967): 122-133;
Frank L. Kersnowski, C. W. Spinks, and Laird Loomis, *A Bibliography of Modern Irish and Anglo-Irish Literature* (San Antonio: Trinity University Press, 1976).

References:

Calvin Bedient, *Eight Contemporary Poets* (London: Oxford University Press, 1974), pp. 119-138;
Maurice Harmon, *The Poetry of Thomas Kinsella: "With Darkness for a Nest"* (Dublin: Wolfhound Press, 1974);
Hugh Kenner, "Thomas Kinsella: An Anecdote and Some Reflections," *Genre*, 12 (Winter 1979): 591-599;
Frank L. Kersnowski, *The Outsiders: Poets of Contemporary Ireland* (Fort Worth: Texas Christian University Press, 1975), pp. 73-84;
Edna Longley, "Thomas Kinsella," in *Two Decades of Irish Writing*, edited by Douglas Dunn (Philadelphia: Dufour, 1975);
M. L. Rosenthal, *The New Poets: American and British Poetry Since World War II* (New York & London: Oxford University Press, 1967);
Robin Skelton, "The Poetry of Thomas Kinsella," *Eire-Ireland*, 2 (1967): 86-108;
Vernon Young, "Raptures of Distress," *Parnassus*, 3 (Spring-Summer 1975): 75-80.

James Kirkup
(23 April 1918-   )

Laurence Steven
Laurentian University

BOOKS: *Indications*, by Kirkup, John Ormond Thomas, and John Bayliss (London: Grey Walls, 1942);

The Cosmic Shape: An Interpretation of Myth and Legend with Three Poems and Lyrics, by Kirkup and Ross Nichols (London: Forge Press, 1946);

The Drowned Sailor and other poems (London: Grey Walls, 1947);

The Submerged Village and other poems (London: Oxford University Press, 1951);

The Creation (Hull: Lotus Press, 1951);

A Correct Compassion and other poems (London & New York: Oxford University Press, 1952);

A Spring Journey and other poems of 1952-1953 (London & New York: Oxford University Press, 1954);

Upon This Rock: A Dramatic Chronicle of Peterborough Cathedral (London: Oxford University Press, 1955);

The True Mistery of the Nativity (London & New York: Oxford University Press, 1956);

The Descent Into the Cave and other poems (London: Oxford University Press, 1957);

The Only Child: An Autobiography of Infancy (London: Collins, 1957);

The Prodigal Son: Poems 1956-1959 (London & New York: Oxford University Press, 1959);

Sorrows, Passions and Alarms: An Autobiography of Childhood (London: Collins, 1959);

The True Mistery of the Passion: Adapted and Translated from the French Medieval Mystery Cycle of Arnoul and Simon Grelan (London & New York: Oxford University Press, 1962);

The Love of Others (London: Collins, 1962);

These Horned Islands: A Journal of Japan (London: Collins, 1962; New York: Macmillan, 1962);

Refusal to Conform: Last and First Poems (London & New York: Oxford University Press, 1963);

Tropic Temper: A Memoir of Malaya (London: Collins, 1963);

England, Now (Tokyo: Seibido, 1964);

Japan Industrial: Some Impressions of Japanese Industries, 2 volumes (Osaka: PEP, 1964-1965);

Japan Marine (Tokyo: Japan P.E.N. Club, 1965);

Japan, Now (Tokyo: Seibido, 1966);

Frankly Speaking (Tokyo: Eichosha, 1966);

Tokyo (London: Phoenix House, 1966; South Brunswick, N.J.: A. S. Barnes, 1966);

Paper Windows: Poems from Japan (London: Dent, 1968);

Filipinescas: Travels Through the Philippine Islands (London: Phoenix House, 1968);

Bangkok (London: Phoenix House, 1968; South Brunswick, N.J.: A. S. Barnes, 1968);

One Man's Russia (London: Phoenix House, 1968);

Japan Physical: A Selection, edited, with Japanese translations, by Fumiko Miura (Tokyo: Kenkyusha, 1969);

Streets of Asia (London: Dent, 1969);

White Shadows, Black Shadows: Poems of Peace and War (London: Dent, 1970);

Hong Kong and Macao (London: Dent, 1970; South Brunswick, N.J.: A. S. Barnes, 1970);

Japan Behind the Fan (London: Dent, 1970);

The Body Servant: Poems of Exile (London: Dent, 1971);

Broad Daylight (Frensham, Surrey: Sceptre Press, 1971);

A Bewick Bestiary (Ashington, Northumberland: Mid Northumberland Arts Group, 1971);

Transmental Vibrations (London: Covent Garden Press, 1971);

Insect Summer (New York: Knopf, 1971);

Zen Gardens, text by Kirkup, illustrations by Birgit Skiöld (Guildford, Surrey: Circle Press, 1973);

Many-Lined Poem (Sheffield: Headland Poetry, 1973);

The Magic Drum (New York: Knopf, 1973);

Heaven, Hell and Hara-Kiri: The Rise and Fall of the Japanese Superstate (London: Angus & Robertson, 1974);

Zen Contemplations (Osaka: Kyoto Editions, 1978);

Enlightenment (Osaka: Kyoto Editions, 1978);

Scenes From Sesshu, text by Kirkup, illustrations by Skiöld (London: Pimlico Press, 1978);

Prick Prints (Tokyo: Privately printed, 1978);

The Bad Boy's Bedside Book of Do-It-Yourself Sex (Tokyo: Privately printed, 1978);

Steps to the Temple (Osaka: Kyoto Editions, 1979);

An Actor's Revenge: An Opera in Two Acts, libretto by

James Kirkup (Yamaguchi Takeyoshi)

Kirkup, music by Minoru Miki, based on Otokichi's "Yukinojo Henge" (London: Faber/Faber Music, 1979);

The Tao of Water, text by Kirkup, illustrations by Skiöld (Guildford, Surrey: Circle Press, 1980);

Dengonban Messages (Osaka: Kyoto Editions, 1981);

Scenes From Sutcliffe (Osaka: Kyoto Editions, 1981);

I Am Count Dracula!!! (Tokyo: Asahi Press, 1981);

I Am Frankenstein's Monster!!! (Tokyo: Asahi Press, 1982);

Ecce Homo: My Pasolini (Osaka: Kyoto Editions, 1982);

No More Hiroshimas (Osaka: Kyoto Editions, 1982);

Fellow Feelings: My Blue Period—Poems Grim and Gay (Osaka: Kyoto Editions, 1982);

The Damask Drum, libretto by Kirkup, music by Atli Heimir Sveinsson (Copenhagen: Edition Hansen, 1982); with music by Paavo Heininen (Helsinki: Edition Pan, 1982);

Contrasts and Comparisons (Tokyo: Seibido, 1983);

To The Ancestral North: Poems for an Autobiography (Tokyo: Asahi Press, 1983);

When I was a Child: An Autobiographical Interpretation and Appreciation of Mother Goose Nursery Rhymes (Tokyo: Taibundo, 1983);

The Glory that was Greece (Tokyo: Seibido, 1983);

King Lear (Tokyo: Asahi Press, 1983);

The Sense of the Visit (Taunton, England: Sceptre Press, 1984).

PLAYS: *Upon This Rock: A Dramatic Chronicle of Peterborough Cathedral*, Peterborough, Peterborough Cathedral, 1955;

Masque: The Triumph of Harmony, London, Albert Hall, 1955;

The True Mistery of the Passion: Adapted and Translated from the French Medieval Mystery Cycle of Arnoul and Simon Grelan, BBC-TV, 1960; Bristol Cathedral, 1960;

The Physicists, Kirkup's translation of Friedrich Dürrenmatt's play, London, Aldwych Theatre, 1963; New York, Martin Beck Theatre, 1964;

The Meteor, Kirkup's translation of Dürrenmatt's play, London, Aldwych Theatre, 1966;

Play Strindberg, Kirkup's translation of Dürrenmatt's play, New York, Forum Theatre, Lincoln Center, 1971; Newcastle upon Tyne, University Theatre, 1972;

The Portrait of a Planet, Kirkup's translation of Dürrenmatt's play, Brighton, Gardner Centre, University of Sussex, 1973;

The Magic Drum, Newcastle upon Tyne, University Theatre, 1974; musical version, London, National Theatre, 1977;

The Conformer, Kirkup's translation of Dürrenmatt's play, Sheffield, Sheffield Crucible Studio, 1975;

Frank the Fifth, Kirkup's translation of Dürrenmatt's play, Cardiff, Sherman Theatre, 1976;

The Prince of Homburg, Kirkup's translation of Heinrich von Kleist's play, New York, Chelsea Theater Center, 1976;

An Actor's Revenge, libretto by Kirkup, music by Minoru Miki, London, Old Vic Theatre, 1979;

Friends in Arms, libretto by Kirkup, music by Charles David Barber; Cardiff, Sherman Theatre, 1980;

The Damask Drum, libretto by Kirkup, music by Atli Heimir Sveinsson, Reykjavik, Iceland, Reykjavik Festival of Music and Opera, 1982.

TELEVISION PLAYS: *The Peach Garden*, BBC, 1954;

Two Pigeons Flying High, BBC, 1955;

The True Mistery of the Nativity, BBC, 1960.

OTHER: *Aspects of the Short Story: Six Modern Short Stories with Commentary*, edited, with commentary, by Kirkup (Tokyo: Kaibunsha, 1969);

Shepherding Winds: An Anthology of Poetry from East

and West, edited by Kirkup (London: Blackie, 1969);

Songs and Dreams: An Anthology of Poetry from East and West, edited by Kirkup (London: Blackie, 1970).

TRANSLATIONS: Todja Tartschoff, *The Vision and Other Poems*, translated by Kirkup and Leopold Sirombo (London: Newman & Harris, 1953);

Camara Laye, *The Dark Child* (New York: Noonday, 1954; London: Collins, 1955); republished as *The African Child* (London: Collins, 1959);

Laye, *The Radiance of the King* (London: Collins, 1956; New York: Collier, 1971);

Doan-vinh-Thaï, *Ancestral Voices* (London: Collins, 1956);

Hertha T. von Gebhardt, *The Girl From Nowhere* (London: University of London Press, 1958; New York: Criterion Books, 1959);

Simone de Beauvoir, *Memoirs of a Dutiful Daughter* (Cleveland: World, 1959; London: Weidenfeld & Nicolson/Deutsch, 1959);

Pierre Boileau and Thomas Narcejac, *The Sleeping Beauty and The Evil Eye*, *The Sleeping Beauty* translated by Kirkup (London: Hutchinson, 1959);

Heinrich von Kleist, *The Prince of Homburg*, in *Classic Theatre 2*, edited by Eric Bentley (Garden City: Doubleday, 1959);

Heinrich Emil Klier, *Summer Gone* (London: Geoffrey Bles, 1959);

Johann von Schiller, *Don Carlos*, in *Classic Theatre 2*, edited by Eric Bentley (Garden City: Doubleday, 1959);

Jeanne Loisy, *Don Tiburcio's Secret* (London: University of London Press, 1960; New York: Pantheon Books, 1960);

Margot Benary-Isbert, *Dangerous Spring* (London: Macmillan, 1961);

Simone Martin-Chauffier, *"The Other One"* (London: University of London Press, 1961);

Ernst Salamon, *The Captive* (London: Weidenfeld & Nicolson, 1961);

Herbert Wendt, *It Began in Babel* (London: Weidenfeld & Nicolson, 1961; Boston: Houghton Mifflin, 1962);

Fritz Brunner, *Trouble in Brusada* (London: University of London Press, 1962);

Christian Geissler, *Sins of the Fathers* (New York: Random House, 1962; London: Weidenfeld & Nicolson, 1962);

L. N. Lavolle (Hélène Chaulet), *Nuno* (London: University of London Press, 1962);

Gine V. Leclercq, *Fast as the Wind* (London: University of London Press, 1962);

Modern Malay Verse, translated by Kirkup, Oliver Rice, and Abdullah Majid (London: Oxford University Press, 1963);

Jerzy Andrzejewski, *The Gates of Paradise* (London: Weidenfeld & Nicholson, 1963);

Paul Christian (Christian Pitois), *The History and Practice of Magic*, translated by Kirkup and Julian Shaw, edited by Ross Nichols (New York: Citadel, 1963);

Leclercq, *My Friend Carlo* (London: University of London Press [printed in Holland], 1963);

Friedrich Dürrenmatt, *The Physicists* (London: French, 1963; New York: Grove, 1964);

Jacques Heurgon, *Daily Life of the Etruscans* (London: Weidenfeld & Nicolson, 1964; New York: Macmillan, 1964);

James Kruss, *My Great Grandfather and I* (London: University of London Press, 1964);

Jean Robiquet, *Daily Life in the French Revolution* (London: Weidenfeld & Nicolson, 1964; New York: Macmillan, 1965);

Erwin Wickert, *The Heavenly Mandate* (London: Collins, 1964);

Theodor Storm, *Immensee* (London: Blackie, 1965);

May d'Alençon, *Red Renard* (London: University of London Press, 1966);

Erich Kästner, *The Little Man* (London: Cape, 1966; New York: Knopf, 1966);

Tales of Hoffman (London: Blackie, 1966);

Jules Supervielle, *Selected Writings*, translated by Kirkup and others (New York: New Directions, 1967);

Heinrich Kleist, *Michael Kohlhaas: from an Old Chronicle* (London: Blackie, 1967);

Laye, *A Dream of Africa* (London: Collins, 1968; New York: Collier, 1971);

Kästner, *The Little Man and the Big Thief* (New York: Knopf, 1969);

Kästner, *The Little Man and the Little Miss* (London: Cape, 1969);

Paul Valéry, *The Eternal Virgin* (Tokyo: Orient Editions, 1970);

Dürrenmatt, *Play Strindberg* (London: Cape, 1972; New York: Grove, 1973);

Henrik Ibsen, *Brand*, in *The Oxford Ibsen*, volume 3, edited by James Walter MacFarlane (London: Oxford University Press, 1972);

Takagi Kyozo, *Selected Poems of Takagi Kyozo*, translated by Kirkup and Michio Nakano (Cheadle, Cheshire: Carcanet Press, 1973);

Dürrenmatt, *The Meteor* (London: Cape, 1973; New York: Grove, 1974);

A. R. Davis, ed., *Modern Japanese Poetry* (St. Lucia: University of Queensland Press, 1978; Milton Keynes, U.K.: Open University Press, 1979);

Han Shan, *Cold Mountain Poems* (Osaka: Kyoto Editions, 1980);

Laye, *The Guardian of the Word* (London: Fontana, 1981);

Petru Dumitriu, *To the Unknown God* (London: Collins, 1982; New York: Seabury Press, 1982);

Tete-Michel Kpomassie, *An African in Greenland* (London: Secker & Warburg, 1982; San Diego: Harcourt Brace Jovanovich, 1983);

Tierno Monenembo, *The Bush Toads* (London: Longman, 1983);

Miniature Masterpieces of Kawabata Yasunari, translated by Kirkup and Tsutomu Fukuda (Tokyo: Eichosha, 1983).

PERIODICAL PUBLICATION:
"Dear Old Joe" [memoir of J. R. Ackerley], *London Magazine*, 15 (April/May 1975): 19-37.

James Kirkup is remarkable for his prodigious output in a number of genres: poetry, travel writing, drama, autobiography, and children's literature, as well as for his translations and editing. Since the early 1950s hardly a year has gone by without the appearance of a book acknowledging his involvement in some capacity. With more than twenty-five volumes of poetry to his credit, he is, as James Dickey aptly comments, "one of those poets to whom writing is a continuous process, natural, simply a part of living."

Born to James Harold and Mary Johnson Kirkup, James Falconer Kirkup describes himself as "the only son of very poor working-class parents living at South Shields, County Durham, on the River Tyne, an area of coal mines and ship-building industries." An "inborn sense of deep solitude and apartness" contributed to his being "decidedly the Odd Boy Out" at South Shields Secondary School, where he began writing his first serious poetry. This sense of apartness took tangible shape when, on taking his B.A. with double honors from Durham University in 1941, Kirkup sought, and was eventually granted, conscientious-objector status. Assigned to work on the land for five years, he spent time both as a farm worker and in Forestry Commission labor camps. During this time Wrey Gardiner of Grey Walls Press printed Kirkup's first selection of poems in *Indications* (1942). Poems by

John Ormond Thomas and John Bayliss were also included, though Kirkup knew neither of these poets. On his release in 1946 he took a position teaching German and French at the Downs School in Colwall, Gloucestershire, and while there he collaborated with Ross Nichols on *The Cosmic Shape: An Interpretation of Myth and Legend with Three Poems and Lyrics* (1946). The belief that archetypal and mythic patterns formed realities beyond the conscious surface of life appealed to the streak of romantic solipsism in Kirkup's makeup: "These shapes and the worlds they inhabit, though based on our present existence and all our conscious and unconscious life, are more real to me than the human beings and the events in the world around me."

This lack of connection with a significant human reality characterizes Kirkup's first solo collection, *The Drowned Sailor and other poems* (1947). The volume is dominated by a determinedly mythic and abstract quality which, in straining for the original image or concept, strays perilously close to obscurity and, at times, as in "Love and Apocalypse," unintentional hilarity:

> In the bolt-upright sepulchres
> the organ's crimson motors now emerge
> like wedding-monsters
> electrocuting no one.

The longer poems in the volume—"Elegy," "The Drowned Sailor," and "The Sleeper in the Earth"—are too long. In "Elegy," for example, the flowers, fruits, pathways, and other features of the garden lament the death of their archetypal gardener in such similar voices, over five pages, that what begins interestingly soon becomes sentimental and finally monotonous. Judicious pruning would certainly have improved these poems, and the lack of such editing can probably be attributed to the element of the subconscious "automatic prompting" that Kirkup says contributes to his work. The subconscious may prompt one to write, but it is a fallacy to believe that whatever results is necessarily good poetry. Conscious craftsmanship is still required to shape the promptings into a coherent whole.

This conscious craftsmanship does characterize two poems which point to Kirkup's real strengths as a poet: "The Vigil" and "View From the North-East." "The Vigil" is an early example of Kirkup's ability to enter into human situations (in this case the death of someone close to him), in a humble and sympathetic fashion which transforms the commonplace into the poetic without strain. This unpretentious stance allows the reader genuinely to participate in the poem and so to see his familiar world in a new way:

> Now that you are silent once again,
> and still, and full of a familiar peace,
> I cannot feel alarm,
> and for a little while
> I watch beside you, waiting
> for your eyes to open, and your lips to smile.

"View From the North-East" (dated South Shields, 1945), impressively captures Kirkup's skills as an observer. The "sense of deep solitude and apartness" which suffused his childhood is embodied in a careful choice of detail and minimum of abstract comment:

> Across the end of every street the piled-up
>   sea,
> the sky and the indelible horizon stretch
> like some faintly-stirring backcloth, in front
>   of which
> the pillar-box, the street-lamp and the tree
>   detach
> their elemental shape with spectral poi-
>   gnancy.

In subsequent volumes these strengths are more apparent. The esoteric and archetypal-mythic elements abate to a large degree, becoming the exception, rather than the rule they are in *The Drowned Sailor*.

In 1948, after four terms at the Downs School, Kirkup moved to London and worked at various occupations, from two terms of teaching at Minchenden Grammar School in Southgate (where he was "sacked" because he "was utterly unable to keep order"), to reviewing for magazines such as the *Listener*, whose editor, J. R. Ackerley, became a close friend. It was Ackerley who revealed to him "the cruelty and bitchiness of literary life in England," and Kirkup's estrangement from the English literary milieu dates from this time. In "Dear Old Joe," a memoir of Ackerley in the *London Magazine*, Kirkup claims that because of its BBC subsidy, there was "some kind of journalistic vendetta going on against *The Listener*, against Joe [Ackerley] and his regular contributors." These contributors "found it difficult or impossible to get their works printed outside *The Listener*, and, after Joe's retirement, not even there."

Despite these difficulties Kirkup received a certain recognition. In 1950 he held an Atlantic Award in Literature from the Rockefeller Foundation, and, with the help of Herbert Read, he was appointed the first Gregory Poetry Fellow at Leeds University for the term 1950-1952. The appointment was a fruitful one; 1951 saw the appearance of *The Submerged Village and other poems*, which was followed in 1952 by another collection, *A Correct Compassion and other poems*. *The Submerged Village* contains a number of poems inspired by paintings, a number that explore the theme of narcissism, and sundry other pieces ranging from the eyes-open realism of "In a London Schoolroom" (written while he was teaching at Minchenden Grammar School), to the platitudinous sentimentality of "The Brotherhood of Human Need." The unfortunate aspects of the longer poems in *The Drowned Sailor* reappear in "The Last Man," a poem which takes sixteen pages of phantasmagoric repetition-with-variation to say that man's pride caused his fall from paradise. The title poem, "The Submerged Village," says in essence much the same thing, yet the musings of the poet, however whimsical, are linked to a common life and common emotion, which gives the poem a poignant authenticity reminiscent, in tone if not in quality, of Hardy.

A Correct Compassion and other poems is one of Kirkup's finest collections. Though not unmarred, its proportion of satisfying poems is far greater than in earlier books, indicating that Kirkup was coming into his own. A welcome comic element appears in "The Bowl of Goldfish: A Fable" and "To Puffin, A White Cat"; there are, again, pieces inspired by the other arts as well as traditional seasonal poems such as "Winter Dusk" and "Song for All Souls." Some of the most impressive poems gathered here are those inspired by the north of England, where Kirkup spent his youth. With their concern for clarity of detail in the evocation of setting, poems such as "A City of the North," "Tyne Ferry: Night," or "The Harbour: Tynemouth" are models of poetic respect for his subjects. Here, for example, is the opening stanza from "Wreath Makers: Leeds Market":

> A cocksure boy in the gloom of the gilded
>   market bends
> With blunt fingers a bow of death, and the
>   flowers work with him.
> They fashion a grave of grass with dead
>   bracken and fine ferns.

The major flaw in this volume is Kirkup's consciousness of himself as a spiritual exile. Though not problematic in itself, this stance leads him—in "To a Painter" for example—into a facile dualism in which the imaginative creations of the poet and painter are considered "reality" while the everyday world is "ghostly." From this perspective it is only a short step to the melodrama of "The End of the World" or to the saccharine sentimentality of "The Caged Bird in Springtime." In "The Fountain" it is difficult to distinguish the stance of romantic solipsism from mere self-indulgence.

The needed corrective to this tendency is seen in what, after thirty years, is still one of Kirkup's finest poems: "A Correct Compassion." Written after he witnessed a heart operation in the General Infirmary at Leeds, the poem is remarkable for its exactness of detail. The surgeon makes his first incision, and

> A garland of flowers unfurls across the
>   painted flesh.
> With quick precision the arterial forceps
>   click.
> Yellow threads are knotted with a simple
>   flourish.
> Transfused, the blood preserves its rose,
>   though it is sick.

At the same time, as John Cotton has remarked in *Contemporary Poets*, Kirkup uses "the whole as a prolonged and deftly handled metaphor":

> —For this is imagination's other place,
> Where only necessary things are done, with
>   the supreme and grave
> Dexterity that ignores technique; with proper
>   grace
> Informing a correct compassion, that per-
>   forms its love, and makes it live.

Kirkup's precision here parallels the surgeon's in its unselfconsciousness. By maintaining "a correct compassion" toward his poetic subject Kirkup, like the surgeon, "makes it live."

From 1953 to 1956 while Kirkup was visiting poet and head of the department of English at the Bath Academy of Art in Corsham, Wiltshire, he produced two more collections of poetry, *A Spring Journey and other poems of 1952-1953* (1954) and *The Descent Into the Cave and other poems* (1957). "A Spring Journey" and "The Observatory," both in the first volume, are the kind of poem at which Kirkup excels: close detail offering a fresh perspective on a familiar scene, as in these lines from "A Spring Journey":

> A ploughman on a crimson tractor cut black
>   and brilliant furrows,

> And in the decent villages of stone the
>   housewives wiped
> Great sweeps of blue before their steps, white
>   doorways blazed with brass.

Kirkup does not intrude; he presents what he sees, vividly, and his eye becomes the reader's, making one feel the wonder he does.

The title poem of *The Descent Into the Cave and other poems* is a thirty-four-page narrative describing a caving expedition that Kirkup undertook into the Mendip Hills with members of the Bristol University Spelaeological Society. While Anne Ridler has said that "to go caving in order to write a poem about the experience is, alas, to put the egg before the hen," James Dickey is far closer to the truth when he says the poem is simply "magnificent." This description of stalactites and stalagmites exemplifies the poem's appeal:

> They yearn towards each other silently,
> Weeping carbonic-acid tears of far-
> Fetched rains, and savour for a lifetime
> Their protracted meeting, in a kiss
> That, once begun, will never end; that binds
>   them
> Ever closer, till like immortal lovers
> They become one body, their pure embrace
> A single pillar, smooth and hard, of dusky
>   alabaster.

In spite of the poem's having been read on BBC Radio three times prior to its 1957 publication, J. R. Ackerley had to inform Kirkup that he was having difficulty finding anyone to review the volume for the *Listener*. "It was the beginning," writes Kirkup, "of the systematic suppression of my work in the journals of the 'fifties and 'sixties." By this time, however, Kirkup's estrangement from Britain had become physical. After "shaking the dust of Corsham" from his feet, he spent a year (1956-1957) in Stockholm as traveling lecturer for the Swedish Ministry of Education, and in 1957-1958 he served as professor of English language and literature at the University of Salamanca, Spain. In 1959 Kirkup made a move that was "the start of a new existence" for him. On the recommendation of Stephen Spender (who, according to Kirkup, "when he couldn't find any other poet willing to go, was persuaded by Joe [Ackerley] to recommend me"), he took a position as professor of English at Tohoku University in Sendai, Japan. In a 1978 interview he records his first reactions: "I felt I had lived there in a previous existence, and for the first time in my life I did not feel a stranger on the earth."

These moves are reflected in *The Prodigal Son: Poems 1956-1959* (1959), in sections on Sweden, Spain, and Japan. Although "Suite Salamanca," in the Spanish section, is an arresting sequence of love poems, it is the Japanese section that attracts the greatest interest. One sees immediately that Kirkup's eye for the precise detail that will inform a scene with a sense of wonder is well served by Japanese poetic tradition. This influence is apparent in the second of "Two Pictures From Japan," "All and Nothing":

> In the mist of the paper
> Two boats leave a single ripple.
> They are very small.
>
> High in the far
> Corner of the air, a peak
> Hangs on nothing. That is all.

In longer poems as well there is a sense of calm, of place, which is not felt with such assurance in earlier work. Such awareness is apparent in the concluding stanza of "Sakunami":

> In the new morning at Sakunami
> I sip a bowl of fragrant tea, feeling a quiet joy
> As I watch from the floor of our tranquil
>   room
> The mountains soundlessly rising in the fall-
>   ing snow.

Though the volume is not free of the familiar Kirkup indulgences (mainly in the sentimentally pretentious fourth section, which includes poems with such titles as "The Truth," "The Nature of Love," or "Camera Obscura"), the Oriental material adds a true richness to his work.

Kirkup stayed at Tohoku University until 1961. In October of that year, following a brief sojourn in England with his ailing mother, he took up a position as lecturer in English literature at the University of Malaya in Kuala Lumpur. After almost a year of "extreme misery" he "just up and left, leaving behind nearly all [his] worldly goods." He flew to Tokyo on 30 June 1962 and was back in England in September. Being made a fellow of The Royal Society of Literature (1962) did not strengthen Kirkup's ties to England, and in 1963 he was back in Japan as literary editor of the American-Japanese magazine *Orient/West*. He held this post until the magazine folded in late 1964, by which time he had been appointed professor of English literature at Japan's Women's University in Tokyo, a position he held until 1970.

Refusal to Conform: Last and First Poems (1963), like *The Prodigal Son*, is various in subject and uneven in quality. There are translations from the French, sections on Japan and Malaya, and two more general sections. The weaknesses in the book involve two kinds of poem: those in which the poet seems to be addressing himself in a private language of image and detail (most of these appear in the section "First Aesthetics" and were originally written in the early 1940s, a fact which may offer an explanation for their opacity) and those in which clichéd rhetoric and self-indulgent spleen replace craftsmanship. In the first group are "Ten Pure Sonnets," a sequence so pure that its luxuriant surface detail acts as a hermetic seal preventing the reader from entering or meaning from escaping. The second weakness is found in poems such as "A General Protest" or "Statement," where righteous indignation alternates with misanthropy at the expense of a balanced poetic perspective.

Again the Japanese poems are the strongest in the collection, their strength being the result of Kirkup's genuine interest in the Japanese people and culture, an interest he clearly wants to convey. In "East meets West," for example, Kirkup (who could not speak Japanese at the time) helps a blind Japanese across a busy intersection. His depiction of this simple human gesture has a power that his stridency rarely manifests:

> And so, mute allegory, it is the dumb leading
>   the blind
> As we slowly pick our steps across the street
> Whose grosser agitations we successfully
>   disturb.

In 1964 Kirkup's poem sequence *Japan Marine* (1965) won first prize in an international literary contest sponsored by the Japan P.E.N. Club in commemoration of the Tokyo Olympics. The club published the poem the following year, and in 1968 Kirkup made the sequence the centerpiece of his collection *Paper Windows: Poems from Japan*. The poems in this volume span Kirkup's time in Japan, and the subject matter ranges from the homely simplicity of a wooden Japanese bathtub to the bombing of Hiroshima and Nagasaki. The volume is a clear success, and one of Kirkup's best. As Miura Fumiko wrote in reviewing the book for *Japan Quarterly*: "It is extraordinary that a British poet, with his freshly penetrating insight, could offer such delicate and poignant glimpses of a Japan which is both physically vigorous and spiritually refined, ancient and modern, familiar and unfamiliar."

Dust jacket for Kirkup's 1969 selected poems, with Japanese translations by Fumiko Miura

Kirkup attempts the traditional Japanese forms of haiku, tanka, and senryù with a large measure of success, as in "Spring Haiku":

> Snow, soft and soundless,
> All winter. But now the spring,
> Hard rain on loud roofs.

And in the prizewinning sequence "Japan Marine" he combines these Japanese forms with Western free verse to produce a poem of strange power. Just as it oscillates between East and West in form, "Japan Marine" oscillates between the physical and social landscapes, between high and low subject matter, and it ends with a hymn to the muses, to the creative imagination which alone can hold these disparate elements together.

In 1968 Kirkup accepted a one-year appointment as poet-in-residence and visiting professor at Amherst College in Massachusetts. That same year he received the Mabel L. Batchelder Award for his translation of Erich Kästner's *The Little Man and the Big Thief*. In 1970 he left Japan's Women's University to become professor of English at Nagoya Uni-

versity, Japan, where he stayed until 1972. It was during this time that his last substantial book of poetry appeared.

If *Paper Windows* is a strong volume, *White Shadows, Black Shadows: Poems of Peace and War* (1970) is not. Its best poems are three about Emily Dickinson, written while Kirkup was at Amherst College. Much of the rest of the collection is reminiscent of the righteously indignant poems in *Refusal to Conform*. Often a good image is spoiled with rhetorical excess. In "White Shadows," for example, the central image is a white shadow left on a wall by a man destroyed in the Hiroshima atomic blast. There is potential for employing the talents of Kirkup the vivid reporter but instead Kirkup the preacher draws the image out tediously over four pages, through repetition disguising as rhythm. In many of the poems one gets the impression that one is reading a first draft, and that honing is necessary.

That Kirkup is able to hone his work down is made clear in the numerous volumes of haiku poems he has produced throughout the 1970s and into the 1980s. Since the publication in 1971 of *A Bewick Bestiary* and *The Body Servant: Poems of Exile* (which, with its poems that spotlight every part of the human physique, is a kind of body bestiary), Kirkup has turned more consistently toward the East in both form and content, as a sampling of titles indicates: *Zen Gardens* (1973), *Zen Contemplations* (1978), *Steps to the Temple* (1979), *The Tao of Water* (1980).

The hiatus in his poetry writing between 1973 and 1978 seems to have been caused, in part at least, by his absence from Japan. After leaving Nagoya University in 1972 Kirkup spent time in England, the United States, Morocco, and Ireland. While located in Dublin he held an Arts Council Fellowship in Creative Writing at the University of Sheffield (1974-1975). He spent 1975-1976 as Morton Visiting Professor of International Literature at Ohio University, and during 1976-1977 he was playwright in residence for the Sherman Theatre at University College, Cardiff. In 1977, in a move that seems somehow characteristic of Kirkup's personality, he both took up residence in the principality of Andorra (which remains his permanent home) and accepted a position as professor of English at Kyoto University of Foreign Studies (which he still holds). He now spends "half of the year in Japan, and half in Europe and the USA, seldom going to Britain, and then only for a couple of days or so." The return to Japan gave a renewed impetus to Kirkup's writing of poetry. In 1978 he established his own publishing company—Kyoto Editions—which to date has produced eight volumes of his verse, the majority of a decidedly Oriental cast. In 1979, in

recognition of his "outstanding contribution to Modern Poetry," Kirkup was elected a Knight of Mark Twain.

Though the Orient has proved to be fertile ground for Kirkup's work, one still reads "A Correct Compassion" and "The Descent Into the Cave" with an undeniably fuller satisfaction. As early as 1960 James Dickey hoped that Kirkup would descend into some Japanese caves. That hope still stands.

Bibliography:
Takeyoshi Yamaguchi, *Preliminary Checklist of the Writings of James Kirkup* (Tokyo: Published by Yamaguchi at Japan's Women's University, 1972).

References:
William Bedford, "Necromantism and Masochism: An Interview with James Kirkup," *London Magazine*, 18 (July 1978): 58-63;
Neville Braybrooke, ed., *The Letters of J. R. Ackerley* (London: Duckworth, 1975);
James Dickey, *From Babel to Byzantium* (New York: Farrar, Straus & Giroux, 1968), pp. 131-132;
James Kirkup Newsletter, edited by Michio Nakano (November 1979-   );
Robin Skelton, *The Poetic Pattern* (London: Routledge & Kegan Paul, 1955), pp. 10, 23, 53-54, 139-142, 193.

Philip Larkin
(9 August 1922-   )

Bruce K. Martin
Drake University

SELECTED BOOKS: *The North Ship* (London: Fortune Press, 1945; enlarged edition, London: Faber & Faber, 1966);
Jill (London: Fortune Press, 1946; revised edition, London: Faber & Faber, 1964; New York: St. Martin's, 1964);
A Girl in Winter (London: Faber & Faber, 1947; New York: St. Martin's, 1963);
XX Poems (Belfast: Privately printed, 1951);
[Poems] Fantasy Poets, no. 21 (Oxford: Fantasy Press, 1954);

The Less Deceived (Hessle, Yorkshire: Marvell Press, 1955; New York: St. Martin's, 1960);
The Whitsun Weddings (London: Faber & Faber, 1964; New York: Random House, 1964);
All What Jazz. A Record Diary 1961-68 (London: Faber & Faber, 1970; New York: St. Martin's, 1970);
High Windows (London: Faber & Faber, 1974; New York: Farrar, Straus & Giroux, 1974);
Required Writing: Miscellaneous Pieces 1955-1982 (London: Faber & Faber, 1983).

Alan Marshall

RECORDINGS: *Listen presents Philip Larkin reading The Less Deceived*, Listen LPV 1 (Hessle, Yorkshire: Marvell Press, 1959);

Philip Larkin reads and comments on The Whitsun Weddings, LPV 6, Listen records; the Poets Voice series, edited by George Hartley (Hessle, Yorkshire: Marvell Press, circa 1966);

British poets of our time, Philip Larkin; High windows; poems read by the author, Argo PLP 1202 (London: Arts Council of Great Britain and the British Council, circa 1975).

OTHER: *The Oxford Book of Twentieth-Century English Verse,* edited by Larkin (London: Oxford University Press, 1973).

PERIODICAL PUBLICATIONS: "Wanted: Good Hardy Critic," *Critical Quarterly,* 8 (Summer 1966): 174-179;

"It could only happen in England," *Cornhill,* 1969 (Autumn 1971): 21-36.

In a time when popular reception of poetry is perhaps more tenuous than in any period since the Wordsworthian revolution, Philip Larkin has managed to capture a loyal, wide, and growing audience of readers. He has been acclaimed England's "unofficial poet laureate" and "laureate of the common man," as a representative spokesman for the British sensibility since World War II. He has emerged as the center, if not the starting point, of most critical debate over postwar British verse. He is the best known and most acclaimed—critically and popularly—of the figures who made up the so-called Movement in the early 1950s and as an avowed enemy of the literary modernism scorned by The Movement. His scant four collections of poems, written over thirty years, as well as the two novels he brought out shortly after the war, continue to go into new printings, hardcover and paperback, on both sides of the Atlantic. While he denies being a "Great Poet," only Ted Hughes among his English contemporaries rivals him in terms of international recognition. For all of his self-proclaimed insularity, Larkin is known and responded to as no other British poet since Dylan Thomas.

Two incidents from Philip Larkin's career illustrate the tone of his life, at least as he has chosen to project it in his writing. The first occurred shortly after he had had his small collection *XX Poems* (1951) published at his own expense. At first wondering why the writers and critics to whom he had sent copies failed to acknowledge them, he soon discovered that, because of a postal rate hike of which he had been unaware, the copies had been received with postage due. Self-deprecating irony, as well as a strong sense of ill-timing and chances missed, connect this incident with the personality seen in so many of his poems.

Also revealing are the circumstances attending his 1982 *Paris Review* interview. With his well-known reluctance to grant interviews, he insisted that, rather than meet his interviewers face-to-face, he be sent a series of questions, the first set of which he took five months in answering. The paradox of his consenting to the interview but on such a condition—his sense of a place on the literary map yet his refusal to be a public figure—accords with the combination of wariness and fascination toward all relationships, even the most private, seen throughout his poetry.

Philip Arthur Larkin was born in Coventry, England, on 9 August 1922, to Sydney and Eva Emily Day Larkin. Whether his childhood was "unspent," as he claims in one of his wittier poems ("I

Remember, I Remember"), there is no way of telling. His father's job as the city treasurer afforded the family a measure of solidity and financial security. His activities included the typical routines of young friends, games of football and cricket, seaside holidays. Family trips to Germany when he was a teenager established a distaste for foreign travel which has persisted. To the extent that Larkin remembers his childhood at all, he remembers it as more boring than unhappy. However, he has recalled vividly the misery brought on by near-sightedness, which went undetected for a long time, and by stuttering, which continued well into adulthood.

Perhaps these difficulties help account for his rather patchy academic performance at King Henry VIII School in Coventry, which he attended throughout the 1930s. Most certainly they relate to the shyness he attributes to himself as a child and as an adult, as well as to the preoccupation with the solitude-society issue evident in so many of his poems. Despite—or perhaps because of—such defects, Larkin soon began cultivating habits of wide reading and a lively imagination, both of which fed a youthful interest in writing. His father's well-stocked library put him in touch with authors considerably advanced for a schoolboy of the time—including George Bernard Shaw, D. H. Lawrence, Somerset Maugham, and George Moore—and these young Larkin supplemented with frequent trips to the public library.

For Larkin serious writing began sometime not too late in his period at King Henry VIII School, with a class assignment to write a poem, and quickly developed into a nightly routine. Though he has dismissed his school writings as typically adolescent, from 1933 until leaving school in 1940 he contributed regularly to the *Coventrian,* the school magazine. In late 1940 he made his first appearance in print outside school publications with a poem in the *Listener.*

The autumn of 1940 also saw Larkin's arrival at Oxford and the beginning of a vital stage in his personal and literary development. The power of his experience there is suggested by one of his most moving poems, "Dockery and Son," written twenty years after he left Oxford, which turns on his frightening realization of how much time has elapsed and how much has changed since his university years and on how he can never return. In his introduction to the 1964 edition of his novel *Jill* (first published in 1946), Larkin has spoken eloquently of how wartime Oxford served to mature the young undergraduate. For the first time in his life he was introduced to circles of friends who were especially interested in things which especially interested him. While he has recalled feeling surrounded by thousands of people cleverer than he, apparently he was able to hold his own—judging from the reports of close friends he made there, such as Kingsley Amis and John Wain—and eventually to distinguish himself academically, with a first-class honors degree in English (1943). The opportunity to specialize in English proved a chance to exercise an interest which had been held partly in check by the broader school curriculum he had encountered prior to Oxford.

Oxford stimulated Larkin's bent toward writing, too. He contributed to student literary magazines and to anthologies of student poetry. Despite his wariness of the Oxford "Aesthetes"—and his preference for the "hearties" among his fellow students—he attended poetry readings and lectures. Yet the most dramatic result of his time at Oxford came after he took his degree. The poems composing *The North Ship* (1945), as well as his two novels, *Jill* (1946) and *A Girl in Winter* (1947), were all completed within two years of his leaving Oxford. So intense an outburst of activity, which he has attributed to "creative relief" at being freed from academic pressure, surely must be credited in part to that same Oxford atmosphere and experience.

Larkin recalls how a few months after he left Oxford, the Ministry of Labour politely inquired what he was doing with himself. Having failed the physical exam for the military, he nevertheless felt obligated to answer in some definitive fashion and happened to notice a newspaper advertisement for a small-town librarian's job in Shropshire. As a result, he became the town librarian for Wellington, a job that partly inspired the rather grim setting in *A Girl in Winter,* in which the main character likewise joins the library staff in a city, where she feels alone and unappreciated.

Thus began his career as librarian. Three years later, in 1946, Larkin went to Leicester, as assistant librarian at University College, and, according to Kingsley Amis, he served as the model for Jim Dixon in *Lucky Jim* (1954). Larkin has expressed some skepticism about Amis's claim, though the years at Leicester were his most frustrating as a writer. He was able to take an Oxford M.A. in 1947. The best years—or at least the best conditions for writing—came, he feels, when he went to Belfast in 1950, as sublibrarian at Queen's University.

The youthful style and outlook informing the poems in *The North Ship* resulted directly from an

Oxford encounter, and subsequent consultations, with Vernon Watkins, friend of Dylan Thomas's and disciple of Yeats's, who impressed upon the younger poet the importance of Yeats as a poetic model. Larkin's first collection was invited by the owner of the small Fortune Press. He has since remarked that, despite his excitement at the time, the circumstances of his book's publication were "next door to a vanity press." And, reflecting on the poetry itself, he has said, "It seems amazing that anyone should have offered to publish it without a cheque in advance and a certain amount of bullying."

Most readers have found the poems of *The North Ship* greatly inferior to what Larkin was to write later. Generally they reflect an infatuation with Yeatsian models, a desire to emulate the Irishman's music without having undergone the experience upon which it had been based. Indeed, Larkin has confessed to "limbering up" with his edition of Yeats—significantly the 1933 edition, which lacks the final poems—each evening before he began working on poems for *The North Ship*. Most of those poems are vaguely plaintive. They speak of love affairs terminated or threatened by unspecified causes, of an unfriendly natural environment, and of a pervasive atmosphere of doom— perhaps a natural result of their being written in wartime. Such complaints, ungrounded by particulars of setting or motivation, however, ultimately appear self-indulgent whimpering, the products of a sensibility bent upon being unhappy and unable to face up to the possibility of relief or self-help. Such a poetry, its arguments and situations appearing so senseless, is forced to depend on image and prosody. Yet, even in these it generally fails, as there is a monotony of predictable rhymes and stanzas, of uninterestingly bleak images, and of wearisome tone throughout the collection. The emphasis in a few poems upon dream and vision introduces only another dimension of dullness to the collection's landscape, a landscape without social reality or humor. Potentially concrete settings—such as the train carrying the Polish air girl (number twelve), the snowy field through which the girl is dragged (number twenty), or the railway platform on which the man stands (number twenty-two)—invariably give way to vague expressions of misgiving or despair. Because the speaker in these poems exists only as a voice mouthing complaints—and not as a character with either compelling dilemmas or qualities of personality beyond self-pity—he inspires at best uninterest, and at worst extreme annoyance.

Larkin has since seen in *The North Ship* several abandoned selves, including the would-be Yeatsian. The process by which such abandonment occurred, and by which the central Larkin mode emerged, was long and tortuous. "I didn't choose poetry: poetry chose me," he told an interviewer. This remark has special relevance to the period 1946-1950, when he experienced extreme frustration in trying to determine what he ought to be writing. Part of his problem stemmed from having written and published two novels in a relatively short time, *Jill* having come out in 1946 and *A Girl in Winter* the next year. Where *Jill* was little noticed at the time, except by Oxford insiders, the second novel, Larkin's first book under the Faber and Faber imprint, was reviewed widely and quickly commanded a coterie of admirers.

Such success would understandably inspire an author barely into his mid-twenties to attempt a third novel, which is precisely what Larkin did for the next five years. His failure to get very far with that project led to his gradual abandonment of another one of his selves. Because even today he retains his admiration for the novelist's craft—he continues to insist that novel writing is much more demanding than the writing of poetry and that a novel is a much more impressive achievement than any number of poems—this dismissal of the novelist-self must have been especially difficult.

Nevertheless, he did dismiss it, and in the process perhaps unwittingly came upon something he preferred over novel writing. His notebooks for this period record the slow beginning, developing, and revising of poems that would not appear in print for several years. For Larkin the chief difficulty was to find a kind of poetry which could satisfy the various, and deeper, selves which remained. Yeats had clearly proven a dead end. Indeed, by this time he seems to have relegated *The North Ship* to that category already containing his juvenilia. He needed a newer concept of poetry, as well as a definitive model, to fill the vacuum created by the dismissal of Yeats.

The solution appears to have come through his discovering, or rediscovering, the poetry of Thomas Hardy. Though Larkin had admired Hardy's fiction, he had brushed aside the poetry as gloomy and inelegant. His rethinking of this position, according to Larkin himself, began with his reading Hardy's "Thoughts of Phena At News of Her Death," which quickly led to a rereading and reappraisal of other Hardy poems he had forgotten. While he had had his ear for prosody sharpened by other models—notably Yeats and

Auden—he had his feel for content sharpened by encountering Hardy. Hardy taught him not to be afraid of the obvious and commonplace in his writing—indeed, to nurture them—and, above all, to engage only actually felt emotion in his poems. Armed with this basis for what ultimately would become his mature poetic, and stimulated by moving to Belfast in 1950, he rather quickly completed and gathered together those pieces that would become *XX Poems*. "I felt for the first time I was speaking for myself," he has explained.

Despite the mailing mishap, and despite the fact that *XX Poems* received almost no critical attention when it appeared, this small pamphlet proved extremely important to Larkin's development as a poet. For one thing, he retained half of its contents for *The Less Deceived* (1955); thus the basis for that collection's phenomenal success was already set several years before its publication. Poems such as "At Grass," "If, My Darling," and "Deceptions," all of which first appeared in *XX Poems*, have remained popular and critical favorites among Larkin's writings and have continued to find their way into anthologies. They mark his advance away from vague plaintiveness toward specified setting, character, and moral issues, as well as toward a kind of diction, primarily telling metaphor, which reinforces such specificity.

Larkin has referred to his novels as "oversized poems" in their preciseness of detail and language. Equally valid is the notion of his mature poems as miniature novels, in terms of the concrete fictional quality they exude. Although based on a retired racehorse—or, to be more precise, on a newsreel of a famous racehorse in retirement—"At Grass" moves through a long series of realistic particulars defining the British obsession with "Cups and Stakes and Handicaps" to an implicit comparison of horses with people and the question of how our adjustment to life's later passages measures up to theirs. "If, My Darling" more amusingly shows its speaker caught in mock worry over what might happen were his girlfriend to "jump, like Alice" into the cesspool he knows the stream of his consciousness to be. The metaphors with which he renders his mind and its workings operate as credible expressions of guilt plaguing a witty young man caught between old-fashioned love and emancipated sexuality. The poem's effect depends on an ironic perspective central to *Jill*—Larkin's novel about a naive undergraduate newly arrived at Oxford—but wholly absent from *The North Ship* poems. Relatedly, the exclusion from *The Less Deceived* of those pieces in *XX Poems* that hearken back most to the poems of *The North Ship* reflects Larkin's growing confidence in realism, irony, and humor as components of the poetry he wished to write.

Of the earlier poems retained in *The Less Deceived,* none is more powerful than "Deceptions," originally titled "The Less Deceived." Here again is the lesson of Hardy through concrete fictionality, the poem's essence of person and place. Here, too, is Larkin's fusion of his fiction into his verse in the issues of moral responsibility and disillusionment which the poem shares with *A Girl in Winter.* The germ of the poem—a passage from Henry Mayhew's *London Labour and the London Poor* (1851-1864), where a young prostitute movingly recalls being kidnapped, drugged, and raped to initiate her into her trade—spurred Larkin to consider, through almost-emblematic metaphors, the profound grief she must have felt, but then to observe how, compared with the exactness of her suffering, her attacker's desire must have involved "erratic" readings of whatever satisfaction the attack would bring him. He concludes therefore that, whatever her pain, she was less deceived than her attacker, "stumbling up the breathless stair / To burst into fulfillment's desolate attic." Larkin's rendering of the distinction between suffering and desire, and its various ramifications, takes on significance far beyond the girl, the rapist, or even the nineteenth century in which he found them.

The 1955 publication of this and about two dozen other poems as *The Less Deceived* proved a mild sensation in poetry circles. The owner of the small Marvell Press, George Hartley, had written Larkin for a collection, and once published it gained instant notice and favorable comment in many reviews, very quickly sold out the first printing, and went into several additional printings. Its author became recognized as a significant poet. Additionally, after the appearance of *The Less Deceived* Larkin began to have poems, reviews, and occasional essays published in periodicals much more frequently. Clearly his long-sought poetic was succeeding.

The newer poems in *The Less Deceived* further solidified the issues and techniques toward which he had been moving and which have come to be identified with him ever since. Perhaps foremost among such techniques, especially in comparison with *The North Ship*, is the engaging "I" of Larkin's mature poetry. Whether humorous or serious, the speaker in most of these poems presents a compelling contrast to the bland personality in Larkin's earlier verse. The result is that subjects only vaguely developed before take on a vividness, a viewpoint, and a feeling to which the reader can respond readily.

Various poems dealing with relationships illustrate these newer tendencies and techniques. In the wittily titled "Lines on a Young Lady's Photograph Album" a young man's excitement over his girlfriend's finally allowing him to examine old snapshots of herself turns to the realization that he is on his way out of her life. Only in a sadly ironic sense will a photo permit him to hold her, "Unvariably lovely there, / Smaller and clearer as the years go by." In "Maiden Name" one sees perhaps the same character at a later stage in his life and in his relationship with his former lover, as he meditates, with philosophical bitterness and cynicism, on the strange implications of the name change wrought by marriage and on how only her old name "shelters" his fidelity to her as she was, in her youthful beauty. In each of these instances the speaker examines a personal dilemma in terms of conceptual complexities surrounding it. In "Reasons for Attendance" and "Places, Loved Ones" Larkin again develops the viewpoint of the outsider looking in, or back, on possible relationships he has lost, but with the character more aware of his power to rationalize and thus less satisfied with the answers such power yields.

Much of the mature art of Philip Larkin turns on telling metaphors, particularly as the credible "I" uses them to define a feeling or problem. In one poem he calls his work a toad and wonders why he does not "drive the brute off" with his wits, as others seem to do. Elsewhere he labels his skin an "Obedient daily dress" and thinks of the old age as a sort of "white swaddling." Then, in "Whatever Happened?" he combines two metaphorical patterns—the passage of a ship through a dangerous latitude and the developing of a photograph—to suggest a traumatic experience and the later attempt to make sense of it.

All such poems deal at least in part with the riddle of time, which by the mid-1950s had become one of Larkin's preoccupations. Because those lyrics concerned with relationships tend to question the irrevocability of previous choices, they necessarily ask in what sort of medium choices develop and harden. While in "I Remember, I Remember" Larkin deprecates his youth by wittily inverting the clichés of romantic poetry and fiction, he also suggests there that time and the human proneness to illusion and self-deception conspire to make memory highly unreliable. The same process by which the perspective afforded by time turns out to misrepresent events as experienced is, of course, at the center of "Whatever Happened?" Yet another poem, "Triple Time," gives Larkin the opportunity

to develop the puzzle of time even further, as he observes how the present ("a time unrecommended by event") is, ironically, both the future once wildly anticipated and the past soon to be recalled with nostalgia or regret.

Several attributes of the entire collection coalesce in "Church Going"—the single piece of writing most responsible for establishing, and sustaining, Larkin's reputation. Naturally it exhibits the realistic detail of setting and motivation of most of the other poems in *The Less Deceived*. As Larkin's longest poem to that time, it incorporates into its very structure the honesty and self-scrutiny increasingly evident in his writing. Its agnostic speaker admits himself to be "bored and uninformed" and discovers in his puzzling over the attraction old churches have for him—which amounts almost to an irresistible magnetism—an empiricist basis for his own set of religious values. Here, too, is Larkin's careful orchestrating of stanzas, the play between stanza and syntax which by this time had become for him a central technical resource, and the careful placing of metaphors—which, in fact, do not occur until very late in the poem, when the speaker is well toward solving his puzzle.

Republished in the *Spectator* soon after its initial appearance, "Church Going" quickly became celebrated as the definitive Movement poem, in the traditional aspects of its form (notably stanza, rhyme, and subdued imagery) and the modest dimensions of its subject and resolution. The Larkin character in "Church Going" became a prototype of the thoughtful postwar Englishman: skeptical of the merely material comfort afforded by the welfare state yet equally dubious of the promise held out by political, religious, or artistic extremists. To a generation of sensitive readers in England and America "Church Going" defined the spirit of secular humanism.

The years between the initial appearance of *The Less Deceived* in 1955 and the publication of *The Whitsun Weddings* in 1964 were probably the most eventful of Larkin's career. Just as the earlier book was coming out, he left Belfast to accept the position of librarian at the Brynmor Jones Library at the University of Hull, a situation which has apparently suited him for over a quarter-century. His affection for that area of England he expressed in "Here," the opening poem of *The Whitsun Weddings*. The poem's panoramic tribute to Hull's common people ("A cut-price crowd, urban yet simple") and their way of life extends to the surrounding countryside, where one is said to have a sense of "unfenced existence: /

Facing the sun, untalkative, out of reach." Recently Larkin explained that literary celebrity has made him even more appreciative of Hull, as strangers eager to see or meet him (especially Americans) tend to be discouraged by the difficulty of getting there by rail. As for his library position—which he has referred to as "that nice little Shetland pony of a job you so confidently bestride in the beginning [which] suddenly grows to a frightful Grand National Winner"—he likes its combining of academia and administration and definitely prefers it to the alternatives of teaching or giving readings by which other poets are forced to earn their livings. In his years at Hull, Larkin has seen buildings erected and collections and staff expanded, for which he feels some pride of accomplishment.

In addition to his professional work and the writing of poetry—which continued at a steady if modest pace—Larkin's first decade at Hull included his debut as a jazz writer. Though beginning with occasional reviews of books on jazz, in 1961 he became a regular reviewer of jazz recordings for the *Daily Telegraph*, an assignment which lasted well into the 1970s. The first eight years of the *Daily Telegraph* reviews were later assembled into a collection titled *All What Jazz* (1970). His enthusiasm for jazz had begun back in the mid-1930s, when, according to Larkin, the emotional impact of the great jazz artists on sensitive youth was comparable to that of the great romantic poems a century earlier. So obsessed with jazz has he been as an adult that, adapting Baudelaire, he has claimed he can live a week without poetry but not a day without jazz.

Besides providing apparently boundless listening pleasure, jazz represents for Larkin what he terms a "telescoped art," since, though not even a century old, it has passed through stages which took centuries to unfold in painting or poetry. Specifically, he sees in the shift from traditional to progressive jazz an analogue to the move from realism to modernism in the other arts, a move he has come to dislike intensely. Thus Charlie Parker joins the modernists of other art forms as a special target of Larkin's invective. In his introduction to *All What Jazz* he criticizes the products of modernism ("whether perpetrated by Parker, Pound or Picasso") as "irresponsible exploitations of technique in contradiction of human life as we know it," adding that modernism "helps us neither to enjoy nor endure. It will divert us as long as we are prepared to be mystified or outraged, but maintains its hold only by being more mystifying and more outrageous: it has no lasting power."

He holds in similar scorn the industry of expli-

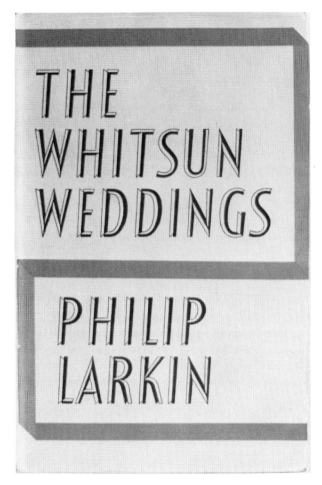

Dust jacket for Larkin's 1964 book, the central volume in his poetic canon

cation which has grown up from the mystique of modernism: "The terms and the arguments vary with circumstances, but basically the message is: Don't trust your eyes, or ears, or understanding. They'll tell you this is ridiculous, or ugly, or meaningless. Don't believe them. You've got to work at this: after all, you don't expect to understand anything as important as art straight off, do you? I mean, this is pretty complex stuff: if you want to know how complex, I'm giving a course of 96 lectures at the local college, starting next week. . . ." For Larkin, continuity and clarity—rather than violent discontinuity or obscurity—are the proper aims of human art, in keeping with the aims of human life. Modernism in most of its manifestations he rejects as elitist, pretentious, and antihumanist.

Given this poetic of continuity, *The Whitsun Weddings* represents an extension of, rather than a departure from, *The Less Deceived*. In fact, none of Larkin's three mature collections differs markedly

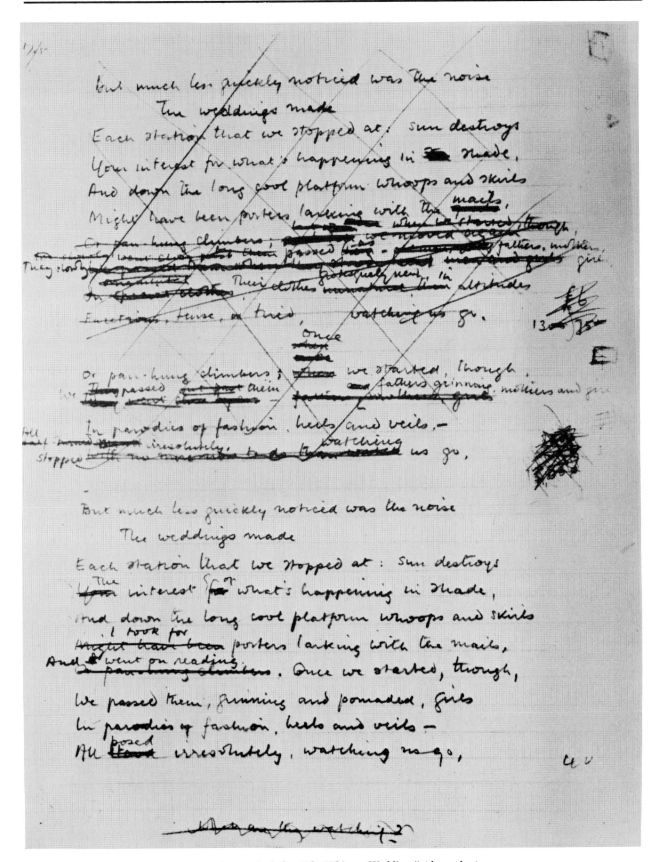

Page from a draft for "The Whitsun Weddings" (the author)

from the other two in any respect. More than the books of most other contemporary poets, they partake of the same character, which is rooted in traditional technique, gentle irony, and sympathy with the commonplace. With *The Whitsun Weddings,* the feel of continuity with the earlier poems is especially genuine, as newer pieces began appearing in periodicals almost immediately after the publication of *The Less Deceived* and continued at the steady rate of two to four each year until the later collection was pulled together. After *The North Ship,* the notion of distinctive phases in Larkin's career as poet becomes virtually impossible to sustain.

Commercially, as well as artistically, *The Whitsun Weddings* proved an even greater success than its predecessor. It quickly won favorable opinions in influential quarters, went into several printings, and gained awards for its author, including the Arts Council Triennial Award and the Queen's Gold Medal for Poetry. Such notice, of course, depended in part on the reputation gained him earlier by *The Less Deceived.* Nevertheless, most reviewers saw in the newer book a sharpening of the talent which had first delighted them ten years before. Yet, because the debate over The Movement was at its height, Larkin had begun to have detractors, in both England and the United States, who regarded him as representative of a narrowness of vision infecting postwar Britain.

Without question *The Whitsun Weddings* represents the full fruition of Philip Larkin's search for a comfortable poetic and style. In every way it is his central book. More consistently there than even in *The Less Deceived* does he define the world of his poetry as postwar Britain. By the time he was writing his best poems, England had been recovering from the war; postwar prosperity accelerated the movement into mass culture which had begun for Britain between the wars, to produce a society immersed in consumer goods and a sense of the contemporary, but not at all certain how to bear the burden of its considerable past.

Much of this emergence of mass culture is captured by Larkin in *The Whitsun Weddings,* as he devotes entire poems to such mundanely contemporary subjects as stylish billboards ("Essential Beauty") or an American evangelist's crusade through England ("Faith Healing"), graffiti on a sexy resort poster ("Sunny Prestatyn"), big-city ambulances ("Ambulances"), and even a workingman's department store featuring "Bri-Nylon Baby-Dolls and Shorties" ("The Large Cool Store"). Even poems devoted to historically more remote topics suggest a very recent viewpoint. Notably,

"MCMXIV," while picturing the details of the Edwardian England which disappeared with the beginning of World War I, invests that picture with a degree of reverence only possible to one growing up with the worship of "The Great War" and viewing prewar times from the perspective of several decades.

In *The Whitsun Weddings* Larkin manages a much wider range of tones and effects than before. This greater variety is due in part to the greater proportion of either third-person poems or first-person poems featuring characters not to be equated with Larkin himself. "A Study of Reading Habits"—the speaker of which has moved from naive romanticism through sensationalism and now finds himself bored by the all-too-familiar routine of realism—illustrates Larkin's playful irony. Besides "Toads Revisited," a sort of sequel to his earlier critique of the work ethic, he adds the more topical and biting satire of "Naturally the Foundation Will Pay Your Expenses," an attack on academic gamesmanship. Another new piece, "Mr. Bleaney," illustrates an extreme of the chillingly effective Larkin poem, as its speaker, upon renting a seedy room, reflects at length with scorn at the former tenant's simplemindedness and then realizes, with muted horror, that he has chosen the same "hired box" but without even the saving naiveté of the simpleton.

All of these poems are essentially negative in resolution. As if to counter such a tendency and to suggest a set of positives even behind such irony and gloom, three poems—"Love Songs in Age," "An Arundel Tomb," and "The Whitsun Weddings"—turn on the possibility of strength and triumph. The first describes a widow's rediscovering the romantic sheet music of her youth as she empties out the piano bench. After being momentarily tempted by the songs into their attendant ideal of love—"still promising to solve, and satisfy, / And set unchangeably in order"—she recognizes in herself a realism which can no longer tolerate such youthful illusions, so that "to cry, / Was hard, without lamely admitting how / It had not done so then, and could not now." An equally sensible valuation of love comes in "An Arundel Tomb," where Larkin finds in the sculptor's detail of clasped hands on the tomb of an earl and countess that emblem of love in all its forms, profane as well as sacred, which transcends the ephemera of life that they, and we, consistently overvalue. "What will survive of us is love," he concludes in this moving meditation.

Perhaps more than any of his other poems except "Church Going," the title piece of *The Whit-*

sun Weddings suggests the richness and emotional power of his writing. Interestingly, the central figure seems to be Larkin himself, recounting his own discovery. The occasion was a train journey from the north of England—presumably Hull—into London on a Whitsun Saturday afternoon. With loving detail worthy of a chronicler of contemporary England, where for most people trains are the principal mode of travel, Larkin traces his pilgrimage through the Lincolnshire countryside, through towns and suburbs, and gradually into the urban sprawl of London. Paralleling this movement is an adventure of mind and emotion, by which the narrator-protagonist slowly becomes aware of the newlyweds being picked up at each station and of the "frail travelling coincidence" linking his life with the profound changes beginning in all of theirs. Initially unaware and then cautiously curious, he ultimately comes to feel at least temporarily involved in these marriages. The warmth of his recollecting what clearly has been a meaningful realization for him is tempered, though, by the somewhat saddening irony that only a bachelor like himself can have the solitude and perspective to appreciate so tenuous a connection. Certainly the newlyweds have not noticed him. The unmarried observer, a staple in Larkin's poetic world, thus enjoys only a curious and highly limited kind of communion with those he observes.

The years following *The Whitsun Weddings* saw Larkin repeatedly honored as probably Britain's principal living poet. Thus the BBC feted him with a special "Larkin at 50" broadcast in 1972. Not the least of such recognitions was his being asked to edit *The Oxford Book of Twentieth-Century English Verse,* published the next year. Indeed, by the time *High Windows* (1974) appeared, the pattern of his career had become so clear to critics that the regular appearance of a Larkin collection roughly ten years after the last was fully anticipated.

The object of this waiting interested all of his readers and pleased most. The majority of the *High Windows* poems reflect a continuing observation of contemporary English life. Thus the subject of "The Building" emerges only gradually as a modern hospital, for the reader first is taken through the urban scene: "Traffic; a locked church; short terraced streets / Where kids chalk games, and girls with hair-dos fetch / Their separates from the cleaners." Such contemporaneousness extends throughout the collection. Here one finds, also, the same Larkin emphasis on continuity with the past, in particular poems—notably "To the Sea" and "Show Saturday," which celebrate the British rituals

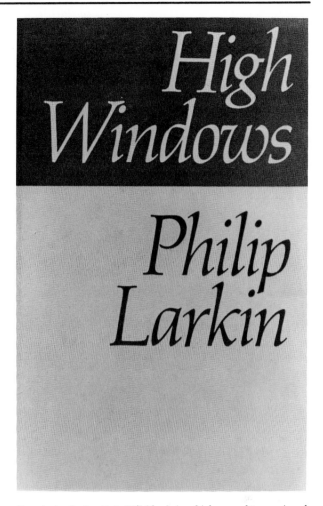

Dust jacket for Larkin's 1974 book, in which several poems signal a return to his early Yeatsian mode

of seabathing and country shows, respectively—and in the traditional forms in which virtually all the poems are cast. That poem which is arguably the most radical in terms of subject and tone, "The Card-Players," employs the same sonnet form as one of the collection's quietest pieces, "Friday Night in the Royal Station Hotel."

The characters of the poems also link with Larkin's earlier writings. "Forget What Did," where he expresses relief at having stopped keeping his diary, exhibits the same self-deprecating tone as several prior poems. "This Be the Verse" connects with all of Larkin's earlier speculations on the source of human error, as well as with the wariness of family humorously expressed by several speakers in the other collections. And *High Windows* reveals the same literary personality as before, a Larkin definitely in middle age, but still brooding on his solitude, on choices made long ago and on the strange, troubling fruits of time—all in the same wryly humorous, bitingly sympathetic tone as before.

Yet almost all critics have sensed a difference here, at least of degree. In a sense, if there is continuity and sameness, it spells out a vital difference. Many of the newer poems reveal a significant shift in age of the persona from that in the earlier poetry. Lately the Larkin emphasis is not merely on time passing or on his being caught somewhere in middle age—anywhere from thirty to fifty—but on his moving into old age. If earlier he seemed prematurely, though humanely and perhaps wisely, concerned with aging and death, such concern seems timely in *High Windows*. Thus the stocktaking of Larkin's more recent poetry, as in "Sympathy in White Major" and "Money," takes on a starker and maybe more desperate coloring. Though "High Windows," one of the most moving and beautiful of these latest lyrics, looks back to the sense of human community affirmed in "Church Going" and "The Whitsun Weddings," it rests on more final considerations as well as it ultimately focuses on "the deep blue air, that shows / Nothing, and is nowhere, and is endless." Nor is it an accident that this poem recounts a habitual discovery, implying perennial forgetting and a desperate need to remember; the "When" of the opening line ("When I see a couple of kids") clearly means "Whenever." As before, the Larkin speaker is unmarried and alone, but now the prospect of death is more of a reality for him: "Sad Steps" ends not with simply the puncturing of romantic illusion, but with the recognition that this illusion "is for others undiminished somewhere." Contrary to his rejection of love and the crowd in so many previous poems—albeit an uneasy rejection—in "Vers de Societe," he joins the party once scorned, as he explains:

> Only the young can be alone freely.
> The time is shorter now for company,
> And sitting by a lamp more often brings
> Not peace, but other things.

An awareness of "other things" is further suggested by the greater topicality of his most recent collection. Where Larkin's previous poetry contains virtually no reference to contemporary historical events, several of the *High Windows* selections depend almost entirely on such reference for their effects. Two argue didactically against developments in contemporary Britain: "Going, Going" against the encroachment of litter and tourists threatening to turn England into the "first slum of Europe," and "Homage to a Government"

against the British government's decision to close its last military bases east of the Suez. A third poem, "Annus Mirabilis," while not directed to a specific event, refers to such historical particulars as the ban on *Lady Chatterley's Lover,* the Beatles' first album, and possibly the Profumo Scandal, as its speaker complains in typical Larkin fashion of having just missed out on the sexual revolution. In "Posterity" Larkin for the first time makes use of another development from contemporary history, his own rise to literary prominence, in satirically describing an opportunistic young American scholar ("Jake Balakowsky, my biographer") bent on "doing" Larkin ("one of those old-type *natural* fouled-up guys") to gain academic tenure.

Though striking, such topicality is scarcely so startling as the emblematic-symbolic quality of several other *High Windows* poems. Many critics have seen in this development Larkin's return to his Yeatsian mode, and indeed he has said of one of these poems, "Solar," that it is "more like *The North Ship*" than anything he had written for many years. Certainly "Solar" and several others—including "Dublinesque," "How Distant," and "The Explosion"—depend on lyric suggestiveness more than concrete realism and on image more than metaphor. Though poems from *The Whitsun Weddings* and *The Less Deceived* resemble them in these regards, they seem to go beyond the others in avoiding a rooted and defined speaker and in evoking vaguely Platonic impressions. However, despite this Yeatsian flavor, each of these newer poems manages sadness without the annoyingly personal plaintiveness of *The North Ship* and without the imagistic monotony plaguing that collection. Each moves from concrete particulars to its own symbolic suggestion. In each Larkin maintains prosodic and syntactical control. Each is recognizably, if not typically, a Larkin poem.

Larkin has repeatedly expressed the wish to write the kind of poetry ordinarily not associated with him. The topical and imagistic poems in *High Windows*—not to mention the surrealistic "Card-Players"—indicate he may have succeeded. On the other hand, he has written no new poetry since *High Windows* and has expressed no intention or even desire to do so. His most recent book, *Required Writing* (1983), which won the 1984 W. H. Smith Literary Award, is a collection of prose pieces written between 1955 and 1982.

Certainly in terms of its developing persona, Larkin's poetry implies a limit which may have been reached. Certainly, too, his integrity as a poet would prevent him from writing, or at least publishing, a poem in which he could not believe; he has been most vocal in renouncing earlier work, such as *The North Ship,* despite critical acclaim.

It is this same honesty which has made him admired. Besides the charge of narrowness and insularity, the most frequent complaint against Larkin's poetry is that it is cold and unfeeling. But anyone reading carefully much of his mature work must agree with Larkin himself that, if anything, it sometimes borders on the sentimental. At his best, though, he projects a humane concern with the basic problems troubling his readers: love, loneliness, aging, personal and cultural discontinuity, and the need for metaphysical comfort in a culture bereft of metaphysics. His decision to write no more poetry, at least for some time, is perhaps regrettable. That he has given us so many moving and quietly elegant poems clearly is not.

Interviews:

Ian Hamilton, Interview with Larkin, *London Magazine,* new series 4 (November 1964): 71-77;

Dan Jacobson, "Philip Larkin—a profile," *New Review,* 1 (June 1974): 25-29;

Miriam Gross, "A Voice of Our Time," *Observer Review,* 16 December 1979, p. 35;

John Haffenden, "The True and the Beautiful: A conversation with Philip Larkin," *London Magazine,* 20 (April/May 1980): 81-96;

Robert Phillips, "The Art of Poetry XXX: Philip Larkin," *Paris Review,* no. 84 (Summer 1982): 42-72.

Bibliography:

B. C. Bloomfield, *Philip Larkin. A Bibliography* (London & Boston: Faber & Faber, 1979).

References:

John Bayley, *The Uses of Division* (New York: Viking, 1976), pp. 157-182;

Calvin Bedient, *Eight Contemporary Poets* (London, New York & Toronto: Oxford University Press, 1974), pp. 69-94;

Merle Brown, "Larkin and his Audience," *Iowa Review,* 8 (Fall 1977): 117-134;

Donald Davie, "Landscapes of Larkin," in his *Thomas Hardy and British Poetry* (London, New York & Toronto: Oxford University Press, 1972), pp. 63-82;

Seamus Heaney, "Now and in England," *Critical Inquiry,* 3 (1976-1977): 471-488;

P. R. King, "Without Illusion," in his *Nine Contemporary Poets. A Critical Introduction* (London & New York: Methuen, 1979), pp. 1-43;

Lolette Kuby, *An Uncommon Poet for the Common Man. A Study of Philip Larkin's Poetry* (The Hague: Mouton, 1974);

Edna Langley, "Larkin, Edward Thomas and the Tradition," *Phoenix,* 11/12 (Autumn & Winter 1973/1974): 63-89;

Bruce K. Martin, *Philip Larkin* (Boston: Twayne, 1978);

James Naremore, "Philip Larkin's 'Lost World,'" *Contemporary Literature,* 15 (Summer 1974): 331-343;

Simon Petch, *The Art of Philip Larkin* (Sydney: Sydney University Press, 1981);

Anthony Thwaite, "The Poetry of Philip Larkin," in *The Survival of Poetry: A Contemporary Survey,* edited by Martin Dodsworth (London: Faber & Faber, 1970), pp. 37-55;

David Timms, *Philip Larkin* (New York: Barnes & Noble, 1973);

Chad Walsh, "The Postwar Revolt in England Against Modern Poets," *Bucknell Review,* 13 (December 1965): 97-105;

A. Kingsley Weatherhead, "Philip Larkin of England," *ELH,* 38 (December 1971): 616-630;

Terry Whalen, "Philip Larkin's imagist bias: his poetry of observation," *Critical Quarterly,* 23 (Summer 1981): 29-46.

Papers:

A manuscript notebook for 5 October 1944-10 March 1950 is held in the British Library Department of Manuscripts.

Laurie Lee
(26 June 1914-   )

Linda M. Shires
Syracuse University

BOOKS: *The Sun My Monument* (London: Hogarth Press, 1944; Garden City: Doubleday, 1947);

Land at War (London: His Majesty's Stationery Office, 1945);

We Made a Film in Cyprus, by Lee and Ralph Keene (London & New York: Longmans, Green, 1947);

The Bloom of Candles: Verse from a Poet's Year (London: Lehmann, 1947);

The Voyage of Magellan: A Dramatic Chronicle for Radio (London: Lehmann, 1948);

An Obstinate Exile (Los Angeles: Privately printed, 1951);

A Rose for Winter: Travels in Andalusia (London: Hogarth Press, 1955; New York: Morrow, 1956);

My Many-Coated Man (London: Deutsch, 1955; New York: Coward McCann, 1957);

Cider with Rosie (London: Hogarth Press, 1959); republished as *The Edge of Day: A Boyhood in the West of England* (New York: Morrow, 1960);

[Selected Poems] (London: Vista, 1960);

The Firstborn (London: Hogarth Press, 1964; New York: Morrow, 1964);

As I Walked Out One Midsummer Morning (London: Deutsch, 1969; New York: Atheneum, 1969);

Pergamon Poets 10, by Lee and Charles Causley, edited by Evan Owen (Oxford: Pergamon Press, 1970);

I Can't Stay Long (London: Deutsch, 1975; New York: Atheneum, 1976).

OTHER: *Poets of Tomorrow, Third Selection*, includes poems by Lee (London: Hogarth Press, 1942).

Though Laurie Lee's poetry is highly subjective, he was not one of the neoromantic Apocalyptics, nor is his work as intellectually rigorous or esoteric as that of other contemporary poets dubbed "romantic," such as John Heath-Stubbs. And while his work reflects a gentle humility, he is not an overtly Christian poet like Anne Ridler. Yet he shares with all these writers an emphasis on personal vision. Reacting against the poetry of slightly older contemporaries from the Auden generation,

who insisted that a poet's main concerns must include social protest or social reportage, Lee is part of a general redirection of poetry in the early 1940s toward reinstating the validity of personal vision. Essentially a lyric poet, Lee was often moved by the countryside around him and by memories of his childhood in the Midlands. This emotional intensity resulted in a slender, but always sensuously arresting, poetic output.

Laurie Lee was born into a working-class family in Stroud, Gloucestershire, a village in the Cotswolds, on 26 June 1914. The eleventh of twelve children, he was educated in the village school and at the Stroud Central School. Leaving home at the age of nineteen, he walked to London, where he worked as a laborer and as a violin player. A. T. Tolley reports that Lee "was one of the poets—among them Dylan Thomas, David Gascoyne, and Ruthven Todd—who appeared in the *Sunday Referee* poetry column around 1934."

Though sympathetic to the Republican cause in the Spanish civil war, Lee did not fight in Spain, as did some of his British contemporaries. In fact, during 1935-1939, he was traveling as a tourist in Spain and in the Mediterranean region. His gradual confrontation with the coming of war in that area is documented in his second autobiographical volume, *As I Walked Out One Midsummer Morning* (1969), where he confesses that he "hung back" from fighting "as from some family affair in which I still doubted I had a part." As in his poetry, he remained an observer of public events from a distance. Safe aboard a British Navy destroyer sent from Gibraltar to evacuate British subjects marooned on the Spanish coast, Lee watched the countryside he had grown to love recede from view. His nostalgic description of this farewell illustrates one of his greatest literary strengths—the vibrant color and texture of his diction—and characteristically bemoans the loss of an exotic, alternate world: "From that seaborn distance, cut off and secure, I seemed only then to begin to know that country; could smell its runnels of dust, the dead ash of its fields, whiffs of sour wine, rotting offal and incense, the rank hide of its animals, the peppery skin of its

Laurie Lee, 12 January 1960 (BBC Hulton)

men, the sickly tang of its fevered children." This richly visualized memory is important for more than its style. Lee emphasizes that the moment of leavetaking marks the start of new awareness and understanding. As he watched the mountains east of Málaga recede into the distance, he realized, "In that instant of leaving them I felt them as never before." Paying close attention to the margins of consciousness, Lee, like Hardy, carefully charts significant shifts in emotional perception.

During World War II, Lee worked first with the General Post Office Film Unit (1939-1940) and later with the Crown Film Unit (1940-1943) as a scriptwriter. From 1944 until 1946 he served as publications editor in the editorial section of the Ministry of Information in London.

His friends from those years, who included C. Day Lewis, Kenneth Bredon, Rosamond Lehmann, and her brother, John Lehmann, remembered Lee as an "inveterate joker." Lee and his friends at the Ministry of Information delighted, for instance, in concocting mock-literary works, such as the periodical *A Hope for Poultry*. Such antics and repartee at the ministry offices were repeated on weekend visits out of London. Sean Day-Lewis remembers that of all his father's literary friends who visited the family at Brimclose, Lee was the most vivacious. Both childlike and volatile, he was "able to become a boy again, initiating games, making bows and arrows, giving out intimations of mischief." Lee's circle of acquaintances and friends during these years proved highly significant for his career.

One friend, John Lehmann, published some of Lee's poems in *Poets of Tomorrow, Third Selection* (1942) and in his magazine *Folios of New Writing*, and C. Day Lewis also helped get Lee's work published.

The poems in Lee's first book, *The Sun My Monument* (1944), deal with love, nature, and childhood. At times Lee's strained metaphors seem too much like the worst of those by the strident neoromantics, as in "Fields of Autumn," when he writes: "slow from the wild crabs' bearded breast/ the palsied apples fall." His best lines, however, remain simple and direct.

In the nostalgic "Thistle" he explores one of his major themes, the enchantment of the golden world of childhood and the wound which nature has inflicted on him as he moves from youth toward age: "Now from your stabbing bloom's/nostalgic point of pain/ghosts of those summers rise/rustling across my eyes." More than time violates his pastoral world, however. The final two poems act as pendants to each other in their separate visions of innocence and cruelty. In "Day of These Days," "time/ piles up the hills like pumpkins,/and the streams run golden." But in "Black Edge" even the sun is malevolent and the "sweet earth/is foul and full of graves." The most interesting poem in the volume is "To a Painter," where Lee defines his artistic goal and comments on his personal strength. His sensual technique is like the painter's method of evoking a landscape: "Your hands/. . . draw forth/its incandescence"; "You can catch the pitchpine hour and keep its flame/pinned at the point of heat."

The Sun My Monument received favorable notices. On the basis of this one publication, in fact, Stephen Spender selected Lee for comment in his *Poetry Since 1939* (1946). Though Spender judged that Lee had not achieved the technical versatility or the developed poetic philosophy of a Vernon Watkins, he called Lee a poet of great charm, who could make spontaneous and immediate poetry from experiences that "evidently have an explosive effect in his mind." Hardiman Scott, reviewing *The Sun My Monument* for *Poetry Quarterly* (Autumn 1944), praised Lee's original images and "singing" diction. Tracing Lee's quality of breathlessness and final discord to Lorca, he commended Lee for a "craftsmanship" rare in contemporary poetry.

In 1947, while he was working as a filmmaker for the Green Park Film Unit, Lee's second volume of poems, *The Bloom of Candles*, was published. Like its predecessor, it is a thin volume, including twelve brief lyrics that had first appeared in *The Sun My Monument* and three new pieces. With this book, subtitled *Verse from a Poet's Year*, however, Lee at-tempted to shape the individual poems into a larger whole by ordering them according to the calendar. *The Bloom of Candles* ends more positively than *The Sun My Monument*. From ruins, bitterness, and January ice-bound thoughts, the poems move through the year and, with December, to the renewal promised by the birth of Christ. In addition, the poems written expressly for this volume demonstrate a new austerity of language, a paring down of adjectives, and a tightening of metaphoric expression.

Married in 1950 to Catherine Francesca Polge, Lee worked the following year as chief caption writer for the Festival of Britain. With his third book of poetry, *My Many-Coated Man* (1955), Lee refined his technique to the extent that in each poem few extraneous words or images interrupt the flow toward a sustained, unified effect. The fifteen poems in this volume exhibit little metrical variety, and their themes are similar to those in earlier books.

Yet the volume is noteworthy for its elaborated metaphors. In "Bombay Arrival," for example, Lee transforms a group of islands into a string of hollow-sided Indian cattle:

> Slow-hooved across the carrion sea,
> Smeared by the betel-spitting sun,
> Like cows the Bombay islands come
> Dragging the mainland into view.

London, in "Sunken Evening," is a place beneath the ocean, where, "Submerged, the prawn-blue pigeons feed/In sandy grottoes round the Mall."

Although in *My Many-Coated Man* Lee continues to emphasize the rebirth of the adult, as he did in *The Bloom of Candles*, he strikes a new note by accepting the irrevocability of the passing of youth. The forms of rebirth he celebrates include the coming of the Christ child every year, the dawn of each day, and nature's cyclical renewal. The adult is perpetually reborn every morning: "from the edge of day I spring/Alive for mortal flight" ("The Edge of Day"). But the boy in Lee has now vanished forever, "time-fixed in ice." He is "fabulous" but "lost" in "Boy on Ice," the opening poem of the volume. While memories of childhood still remain, Lee senses a loss of vitality. In "The Abandoned Shade," he admits "the voice of the boy, the boy I seek,/within my mouth is dumb."

Over the next five years, 1955-1960, Lee won both the Foyles Poetry Award (1955) and the W. H. Smith Award for Literature (1959-1960). He included several new poems in his 1960 volume of selected poems, but these do not depart in any significant way from previous work. He has not had any volumes of poetry published since 1960.

Both contemporary reviewers and later critics have agreed that, while his thought did not develop substantially, Lee succeeded in honing his poetic talents. In 1951 Alan Ross classed Lee with Norman Nicholson as a writer of "richly imaged poetry." Declaring the surface of Lee's realistic poetry to be "dazzling," Ross noted Lee's effective use of adjectives, "as if to shock new beauty into familiar sights." A year later, Lawrence Durrell ranked Lee with Roy Fuller and Terence Tiller as promising poets of already "solid achievement."

Assessing Lee's work in 1975, A. T. Tolley agreed that the use of clear metaphors and images is the most outstanding characteristic of Lee's poems. He commended Lee as the only poet of any talent in the 1930s or early 1940s to have come from a working-class background with minimal educational advantages, but he criticized him for an inability to explore intense or complicated feelings without falling into rhetoric or resorting to an unnatural manner.

Norman MacCaig also praised Lee's exact physical descriptions of the natural world, and both he and Kenneth Allott, like Scott earlier, pointed out the influence of Lorca on Lee's imagery and odd correspondences. MacCaig does not so much fault Lee, as he finds the poetry too safe and secure, uninterested in a diversity of feelings or a depth of suffering. The strain of melancholy that MacCaig identifies is never deeply explored. Lee's poems remain cameos, or miniatures, as MacCaig tags them—slight and highly individual, but also a bit old-fashioned and removed from a modern world.

Since the mid-1950s, Laurie Lee has increased his already wide reputation by writing travel books and autobiographical reminiscences. His most popular book, written on the suggestion of John Lehmann, is the autobiographical *Cider With Rosie* (1959), a celebration of his country childhood.

References:
Sean Day-Lewis, *C. Day-Lewis, An English Literary Life* (London: Weidenfeld & Nicolson, 1980);
A. T. Tolley, *The Poetry of the Thirties* (London: Gollancz, 1975), pp. 367-368.

John Lehmann
(2 June 1907-   )

A. T. Tolley
Carleton University

BOOKS: *A Garden Revisited and Other Poems* (London: Hogarth Press, 1931);
The Noise of History (London: Hogarth Press, 1934);
Prometheus and the Bolsheviks (London: Cresset, 1937; New York: Knopf, 1938);
Evil Was Abroad (London: Cresset, 1938);
New Writing in England (New York: Critics Group Press, 1939);
Down River: A Danubian Study (London: Cresset, 1939);
New Writing in Europe (Harmondsworth & New York: Allen Lane/Penguin, 1940);
Forty Poems (London: Hogarth Press, 1942);
The Sphere of Glass and Other Poems (London: Hogarth Press, 1944);
The Age of the Dragon: Poems 1930-1951 (London & New York: Longmans, Green, 1951; New York: Harcourt, Brace, 1952);

The Open Night (London & New York: Longmans, Green, 1952; New York: Harcourt, Brace, 1952);
Edith Sitwell (London & New York: Longmans, Green, 1952; revised edition, 1970);
The Whispering Gallery (London & New York: Longmans, Green, 1955; New York: Harcourt, Brace, 1955);
The Secret Messages (Stamford, Conn.: Overbrook Press, 1958);
I Am My Brother (London: Longmans, Green, 1960; New York: Reynal, 1960);
Ancestors and Friends (London: Eyre & Spottiswoode, 1962);
Collected Poems 1930-1963 (London: Eyre & Spottiswoode, 1963);
Christ the Hunter (London: Eyre & Spottiswoode, 1965);

Hans Wild

The Ample Proposition (London: Eyre & Spottiswoode, 1966);

*A Nest of Tigers: Edith, Osbert, and Sacheverell Sitwell in
Their Times* (London: Macmillan, 1968); re-
published as *A Nest of Tigers: The Sitwells in
Their Times* (Boston: Little, Brown, 1968);

In My Own Time: Memoirs of a Literary Life (Boston:
Little, Brown, 1969) — revised and condensed
version of *The Whispering Gallery, I Am My
Brother,* and *The Ample Proposition*;

Holborn: An Historical Portrait of a London Borough
(London: Macmillan, 1970);

Photograph (London: Poem-of-the-Month Club,
1971);

The Reader at Night and Other Poems (Toronto:
Basilike, 1974);

Lewis Carroll and the Spirit of Nonsense (Nottingham:
University of Nottingham, 1974);

Virginia Woolf and Her World (London: Thames &

Hudson, 1975; New York: Harcourt Brace
Jovanovich, 1975);

Edward Lear and His World (New York: Scribners,
1977; London: Thames & Hudson, 1977);

*Thrown to the Woolfs: Leonard and Virginia Woolf and
the Hogarth Press* (London: Weidenfeld &
Nicolson, 1978; New York: Holt, Rinehart &
Winston, 1979);

Rupert Brooke: His Life and Legend (London: Weiden-
feld & Nicolson, 1980); republished as *The
Strange Destiny of Rupert Brooke* (New York:
Holt, Rinehart & Winston, 1981);

The English Poets of the First World War (London:
Thames & Hudson, 1981; New York: Thames
& Hudson, 1982).

OTHER: *New Writing*, edited by Lehmann (1936-
1939);

Poems for Spain, edited by Lehmann and Stephen
Spender (London: Hogarth Press, 1939);

Folios of New Writing, edited by Lehmann (1940-
1941);

Penguin New Writing, edited by Lehmann (1940-
1950);

Daylight, edited by Lehmann (1941);

New Writing and Daylight, edited by Lehmann
(1942-1946);

Poems from New Writing, 1936-1946, edited by
Lehmann (London: Lehmann, 1946);

French Stories from New Writing, edited by Lehmann
(London: Lehmann, 1947); republished as
Modern French Stories (New York: New Direc-
tions, 1948);

Demetrios Capetanakis: A Greek Poet in England, edited
by Lehmann (London: Lehmann, 1947); republished as *Shores of Darkness: Poems and Essays* (New York: Devin-Adair, 1949);

Orpheus, edited by Lehmann (1948-1949);

English Stories from New Writing, edited by Lehmann
(London: Lehmann, 1951); republished as
Best Stories from New Writing (New York: Har-
court, Brace, 1951);

Pleasures of New Writing, edited by Lehmann (London: Lehmann, 1952);

London Magazine, edited by Lehmann (1954-1961);

The Craft of Letters in England: A Symposium, edited by
Lehmann (London: Cresset Press, 1956;
Boston: Houghton Mifflin, 1957);

Coming to London, edited by Lehmann (London:
Phoenix House, 1957);

Selected Letters of Edith Sitwell 1919-1964, edited by
Lehmann and Derek Parker (London: Mac-
millan, 1970).

John Lehmann is one of the outstanding twentieth-century men of letters in English. He came from a family of unusual talent: his sister Beatrix was a famous actress, while his sister Rosamond was a well-known novelist. He is widely known as the founding editor of *New Writing, New Writing and Daylight, Penguin New Writing, Orpheus,* and the *London Magazine.* With Leonard and Virginia Woolf's Hogarth Press and under his own name he published many masterpieces of twentieth-century literature. Through a long career he has written books of poetry, novels, and works of criticism. His three volumes of memoirs, *The Whispering Gallery* (1955), *I Am My Brother* (1960), and *The Ample Proposition* (1966)—collected in shortened form as *In My Own Time* (1969)—are among the notable literary autobiographies of the period. Although he was one of the group of young poets who emerged in England in the 1930s (a group that included W. H. Auden, C. Day Lewis, Stephen Spender, Rex Warner, Louis MacNeice, and William Empson), his full flowering as a poet came in the mid-1940s and after.

John Lehmann was born on 2 June 1907, the son of Rudolph Chambers Lehmann and Alice Marie Davis Lehmann. The Lehmanns had come to England from Germany in the previous generation; but Rudolph's second name derived, via his mother, from the distinguished Scottish publishing family that founded *Chambers Encyclopedia.* Alice Marie Davis was of New England stock and numbered among her ancestors John Wentworth, an early lieutenant-governor of New Hampshire. Rudolph Lehmann, who was born in 1856, was the Liberal Member of Parliament for Market Harborough in Leicestershire from 1905 to 1910. He was also a writer and a regular contributor to the humorous periodical *Punch.* John Lehmann grew up where he was born, in the family home, Fieldhead, beside the River Thames near Little Marlow. He was at school at Eton from 1921 to 1927, where he was the top scholar of his year. There he edited the periodical *College Days.* Among his contemporaries at Eton were Cyril Connolly, Eric Blair (George Orwell), Henry Yorke (the novelist Henry Green), and the philosopher A. J. Ayer.

At Trinity College, Cambridge (which granted him a B.A. in 1930), Lehmann's great friend was Julian Bell, the son of Vanessa and Clive Bell and the nephew of Virginia Woolf. Bell wrote of the English countryside with a freshness and particularity that recalled the poetry of Edmund Blunden; and his *Winter Movement* (1930) was regarded in its

day as one of the outstanding first books of poetry. The early years of friendship with Bell were for Lehmann a time of constant discussion and correspondence; and he studied Edward Marsh's anthologies, *Georgian Poetry* (1912-1922), "not merely to find the real and nourishing food I wanted, but to purge myself, by surfeit, of all contemporary clichés of attitude and metaphor and phrase-making." The economy of style that he found in the best Georgian poetry is manifested in his first book, *A Garden Revisited and Other Poems* (1931).

The image of the garden has been important for Lehmann throughout his career as poet. It has an autobiographical origin in the garden of his family home, Fieldhead, in the Thames Valley. In poems such as "Return to the Chateau" it is often associated with an element of fantasy, through which Lehmann frequently attains a subtler and more adventurous exploration of feeling than in his more explicit realistic poems:

> From the wide roof we heard the pheasants
> call,
> We saw the chestnut leaves in yellow waste,
> The glossy nuts, and dahlias by the wall,
> The ladders in late apple branches placed;
>
> We had no need of words: our thoughts were
> phrased
> By flowers, and trees, and evening sky be-
> hind,
> Summer with Autumn blending: and we
> gazed
> As down the distance of each other's mind.

In 1932 Michael Roberts edited an anthology of poetry, *New Signatures,* bringing together the work of Lehmann and Bell with that of W. H. Auden, C. Day Lewis, Stephen Spender, William Empson, and other young poets. This volume was succeeded by Roberts's *New Country* in 1933, which included poems by many of the same poets and marked the beginning of the Left-wing literary movement of the 1930s. Most of these poets came together in an admiration of the modernist poetry of T. S. Eliot, in the use of industrial and scientific imagery (conventionally regarded as unpoetic), and in revolt against a society whose mismanagement by its dominant class (from which they came) was to be seen in the senseless destruction of World War I and in the lingering repressions of Victorian puritanism. The feeling that their culture was moribund was heightened by the rising unemployment of the

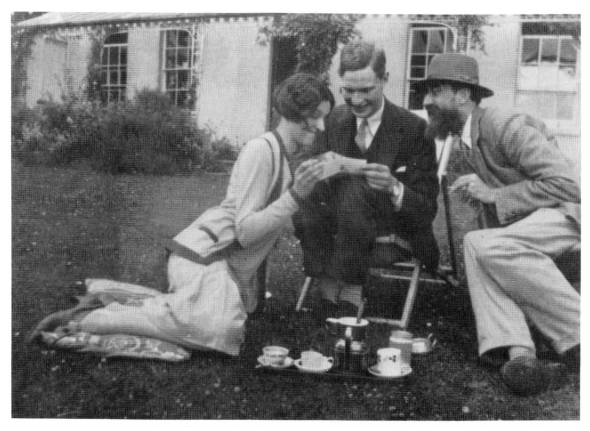

Rosamond Lehmann, John Lehmann, and Lytton Strachey, circa 1930

early 1930s and by the appearance of fascism in Germany.

These concerns were reflected in Lehmann's next book, *The Noise of History* (1934). The poems it contained were, with one exception, written in 1931 and 1932, while the prose (as he recorded in his author's note) "begins in 1933, at the time of the Nazi conquest of power in Germany, and ends soon after the suppression of the February Insurrection in Austria. Much of it was written in Berlin and Vienna." In the presence of unemployment and violence in Austria, aftereffects of World War I from which the country had never recovered, Lehmann became aware of the threat latent in Hitler's rise to power. The suffering, the listlessness, the undercurrents of violence, and the disregard for human beings characteristic of those times are reflected in poems such as "Like the Wind":

> The singers wandering before the door
> Come empty-handed from shut factories;
> Suffering is in their faces, but no greed;
> Their voices are not strong, but like the wind
> Straying in gusts about the littered road.

> Yesterday came three boys from an Alpine
> village,
> Fair, with brown skins, and one had a violin;
> They moved like twigs that fall in a sluggish
> river,
> They held out caps for coins and passed by,
> And the violin grew faint, as the voices now;
> To-morrow these too will be gone, but more
> will come.

In such poems one sees the development of those stylistic features on which Lehmann had concentrated in his Cambridge poems—firm and unassuming diction, subdued and natural rhythms. Yet there is growing subtlety and imaginative depth as he endeavors to move beyond the restricted manner of his earlier poetry toward a style involving what he later described as "a mingling of outer and inner, of the beleagured past and the dissolving present, of the conscious mind with . . . the deeper intuitive mind"—an endeavor in which he was to a large extent inspired by Rainer Maria Rilke's novel *The Notebook of Malte Laurids Brigge* (1910). This influence is felt in "Tell Me Your Name":

Now, as I lean towards your face,
A diver watching the wave smile, so soon
To leap to him, engulf, caress,
I think, still poised—this place
I fix with a falling gesture, I press,
Pressing your lips, a signet in my life,
Imprint deep, deep, this moon, this lamp,
And from the linden, after storm in June,
The smell of leaves, fresh, damp.

These developments did not show themselves in his political poems, often too explicit in their enunciation of a position. He was more successful in bringing the political crisis into the prose poems, such as "Quickened by Horror," with which he experimented at the time:

In the days before Easter, the haze vanishes early before the sun, and innumerable tips of branches are set glowing with a soft green flame. But when we look out of our windows, we see the trees as if they were dripping blood.

Down there, below the lilac-bushes, rank ivy creeps and sucks among the bulbs of the crocuses. Over the first folded heads of daffodils a shadow seems to hang, that will not turn with the turning light.

A body lies on the cobbles of an industrial city's suburb, covered with a stained green coat, and casts its shadow over these fields. The mind, quickened by horror, darkens here and now with shadows of the images of other time and place. . . .

Lehmann has been one of the few English poets to attempt the prose poem, which he thinks "has been very much neglected in this country." The poetic quality lies in the evocation of atmosphere, in the images and the transitions between them. Though Lehmann was to return to the prose poem in the 1940s and the 1960s, the group that he wrote in Vienna in 1933 remains the freshest, evoking as few English poems do the beauty and the submerged horror of Central Europe on the verge of engulfment.

In 1936, still in Vienna, Lehmann launched *New Writing*, one of the finest international reviews of the twentieth century, and one of the most important organs of the Left-wing literary movement of the 1930s. In it he published many works that are now justly celebrated, such as Christopher Isherwood's Berlin stories. The work of editing gave him less energy for his own creative work, though in 1938 he produced a novel about Vienna, *Evil Was Abroad*. He endeavored to write poetry that em-

bodied his feelings about the world situation, but he encountered "a kind of silent refusal to co-operate of some power in the inmost poetic chamber of my imagination . . . it was not until . . . the middle of the war, when I had abandoned the belief that topical passions . . . could ever be the stuff of *my* poetry, that the mysterious agency began to co-operate freely again."

These were the years of the Spanish civil war (1936-1939), which to the intellectuals of the Left seemed finally to offer an opportunity to confront the forces of fascism. No other cause of the period gave rise to such idealism. Lehmann and Stephen Spender produced an anthology, *Poems for Spain* (1939), in which they collected many of the poems inspired by the war. Several British writers of Lehmann's generation went to fight with the British Brigade on the government side, and Lehmann's friend Julian Bell was with an ambulance unit. When Bell was killed in 1937, Lehmann was deeply and lastingly moved. As he wrote many years later in his autobiography, "For me it is . . . hard to forgive the killing of Julian . . . and I have been unable to find it in my heart to visit Spain as long as Franco's regime lasts."

With the coming of World War II in 1939, the future of *New Writing* for a while seemed uncertain. Lehmann began to edit a shorter version, *Folios of New Writing* (1940-1941). In 1941, anxious to do what he could to maintain international literary contacts now that the frontiers of Europe had closed, he produced a new periodical, *Daylight*, with the exiled Czech writer Jiri Mucha. After one issue of *Daylight* was published, the two periodicals were combined as *New Writing and Daylight*, which appeared annually or biannually until 1946. However, Lehmann's greatest achievement as an editor in the war years was *Penguin New Writing*, which ran through forty numbers from 1940 to 1950 and achieved sales in its early years of 100,000 copies an issue while maintaining the highest standards. Through these periodicals, and through his partnership in the Hogarth Press, Lehmann encouraged and published the work of many of the better young writers of the 1940s, among them Roy Fuller, Laurie Lee, Henry Reed, Terence Tiller, and Alan Ross.

Despite these undertakings, Lehmann, like so many writers in those years, found himself thrown back on his own spiritual resources. The war, and the Hitler-Stalin pact which had immediately preceded it, had brought an end to the Left-wing literary movement as an aspect of the struggle against fascism. In the ferment of the doubts and dangers after the fall of France, Lehmann found poems once again forming in his mind. From "an experience of the deepest confusion and agony of spirit" he "began gradually to be aware of possibilities in experience that I would never have admitted before." The crisis is recorded in "Vigils," a group of three prose poems. One senses the pressure of Lehmann's experiences at times in a particularity of detail or argument that goes beyond the imaginative needs of the poems, which endure less well than the Vienna prose poems.

"I think it was largely owing to Demetrios's encouragement and quite extraordinarily intense perceptive interest," Lehmann wrote later, "that . . . I began to write poetry again." Demetrios Capetanakis, a Greek writer, came to England in 1939. From then until he died in 1944, he wrote steadily in English, both poetry and prose. His relationship with Lehmann as a poet was one of mutual encouragement. Capetanakis's own few, but remarkable, poems in English have a directness and starkness of symbolism that is in harmony with Lehmann's simple but rather more muted poetry.

Much of Lehmann's poetry at this time was written on visits to his sisters in the country; and one, "The Sphere of Glass," arose from a walk with Rosamond Lehmann, during which they discussed their work to the "ceaseless humming of aeroplanes; and I was aware of some strange counterpoint between . . . their constant reminder of the war . . . and the Roman dyke . . . beside which we were walking":

> Within the wood, within that hour
> It seemed a sphere of glass had grown
> That glittered round their lives with power
> To link what grief the dyke had known
> With voices of their vaster war
> The sun-shot bombers homing drone.

As Lehmann wrote in his autobiography, "Gradually, the sense of a civilisation that had lost its way, a world out of control began to dominate my thoughts . . . but also that somewhere in the speechless mounds and crumbling stones . . . a secret might be found that would tell us . . . what belief or intuition we had lost." In a longer poem written during World War II, "The Age of the Dragon," he tried to realize what he later called "the contrast between the violence of the present and the symbols of permanency, the reapers in the field and the megalithic burial chambers and temple stones":

> Just before sunset the last stragglers came
> Riddled with cannon, like great wounded rooks

> To settle on their runways, and the lame
> Flutter of engines passed across the stooks

> Of gathered harvest . . .
> . . . .
> The marble hands imploring from the past,
> The cities and the symbols are dismissed,
> And history, our home, is changed too fast
> Till all our lives grow thin as autumn mist.

The style, as in all of Lehmann's best work, is natural and self-effacing, with a serenity that comes from acceptance—a quality most touching in a poem singled out by Christopher Isherwood, "At a Time of Death."

Lehmann had two collections of poems published during the 1940s. The first, in his own New Hogarth Library, was *Forty Poems* (1942), a retrospective selection with some new additions. More important was *The Sphere of Glass and Other Poems* (1944), which included the three prose poems "Vigils" and the poems written since the war began. It is perhaps his best single volume, and one of the enduring books of poetry of the war years. It marked his return as a poet of stature: sadly, it also marked the end of a period of poetic fluency and achievement.

In 1946, Lehmann gave up his partnership in Hogarth Press and started a publishing house under his own name. During the next six years he was to bring out more than two hundred volumes, including some of the outstanding and influential works of the period: among them were a translation of Jean-Paul Sartre's *La Nausée* (which he published as *The Diary of Antoine Roquentin*), George Seferis's *The King of Asine* (a selection of poems in translation), and Saul Bellow's *Dangling Man*. This publishing activity took him away from his creative work, and the only book of his sole authorship published during those years is *The Age of the Dragon* (1951), his first "collected poems," which contains just a few pieces not included in his four earlier volumes. The longest of these poems is "The House," written for broadcasting and produced for the BBC Third Programme in 1947 by Terence Tiller, one of the younger writers Lehmann had encouraged during the war years. Entitled "An Eclogue for the Air on themes suggested by living in an age of transition," it seems to have been inspired by the family's relinquishing of Fieldhead, the family home—a house that for Lehmann had been associated with all the social changes from his Edwardian childhood through the Depression and the war.

In 1952, under the pressure of the deteriorating financial situation of postwar publishing, Lehmann was forced to give up his publishing house. Immediately following that, he went on a holiday in the Mediterranean, and, once more free to write, he turned again to poetry. It was a brief interlude: in 1954 he took on the editorship of the *London Magazine*, which he was to edit until 1961. Only then were the poems begun in 1953 completed: they appeared as "A Mediterranean Sequence" in *Collected Poems* (1963)—the only recent poems in that volume.

Recalling those poems in his autobiography, Lehmann commented, "every time I meet face to face with the sublime monuments or ruins of Greece, I am profoundly shaken." The speaker of "In the Museum (I)" responds happily to the relics of a "race/Who dreamed a myth round everything/Mysterious to reason." In "Sunrise: Amalfi" (where he first stayed in 1953) there is a sense of benediction in the place itself:

Has the time come? The morning breeze is cool,
Ruffles the curtains, and the first cliff rose.
. . . Now the place is air and sea,
Through the wide window one blue ring that glows
Over the inchoate world that learns to be.

The best poems in "A Mediterranean Sequence," such as "The Wind Offered," have an effortless transparence through which the landscape seems to speak:

Stone by stone the court-room of our lives
Dropping into deep pools among the rocks
Translucent blue transfiguring;
Here to wake in another rhythm of gladness
Beginning again with the blue mountains
                                        above
Remembering only the inviolate bay
The ripple of foam where finger with finger
                                        locks . . .

These are among the most engaging of his poems.

Two years later, Lehmann returned to a form he had fostered throughout his career in a sequence of prose poems, *Christ the Hunter* (1965). The title derives from a Roman wall painting in which Christ appears as "a young hunter, a conqueror, a musician: in his free-flowing, youthful tunic . . . he is pictured as if striding into the mountains, the wind blowing his long curls. He is Orpheus. . . ." These prose poems in the "second wind of life" involve comparisons of Christian stories with pagan myths, always attractive to Lehmann as embodiments of

the ideal. *Christ the Hunter* reminds one in places of such modern retellings of myth as André Gide's *Theseus*, while some sections have the character of essays. As Lehmann explains in the foreword, "This sequence, originally written to be spoken rather than read, includes meditations, diary entries, imaginary letters or monologues addressed to an intimate friend, dreams, invocations, resolutions, talkings to myself in the early morning, evocations of legend or history, notes towards a definition of belief, confessions. Poems can without question be all these things. . . ." However, it is only in a few pieces, such as the meditations on waking or the dream in which he is walking on a beach, that one senses the imaginative intensity of Lehmann's earlier prose poems. The sequence was written for broadcasting, and it was produced by Terence Tiller in 1964. Possibly, when read by several voices, it attained an imaginative unity not readily retrievable by the lone reader.

Lehmann's latest collection, *The Reader at Night and Other Poems* (1974), published when he was sixty-seven, is, despite its brevity, one of his most attractive. It consists of six lighter pieces, inspired by literary and historical subjects ("The Reader at Night") and six poems of a more personal nature ("Dedications"). In nearly all the touch is sure and the tone controlled. Lehmann has seldom written better than in his moving recollection of Virginia Woolf, "The Lady of Elvedon," where the sense of her enduring presence is embodied in one of his recurring images, the garden as pastoral:

The waves close over us, and the green air
Of beach leaves meets above our heads:
We are the first explorers crouching here
To learn what the walled garden hides.
Hush: the red funguses and ferns smell strong.
Primeval fir cones fall to rot
Among the grasses; sleeping daws take wing;
And someone, see, will stay to write,

Ransomed as in eternity, between
The two long windows that face the lawn . . .

The clarity and simplicity of his best poetry here come together with his gift for fantasy to produce a deeply moving scene, expectant and reverential.

With characteristic modesty and clarity of self-appraisal, Lehmann summed up his aims and achievements as poet in the foreword to *The Age of the Dragon*: "I made it my aim to find a style in which the personality of the writing ego and his opinions should be as far as possible suppressed, and the experience, the scene communicate almost

Monk's House

How strange it is that small things often bring back the past more vividly than the big and central things. When I re-visited Monk's House a few years ago, it was not the absence of Leonard and Virginia, which of course I had been prepared for, and for Virginia's absence long before Leonard ~~himself~~ died there, but the absence of two features which I had always associated with the house during my visits when one or both of them were a living presence there. The first was Virginia's books, so many of them re-bound in fancy coloured papers prepared by herself, which filled the sitting-room shelves beside her chair and seemed so powerfully redolent of Virginia's ~~own~~ writing life. They are gone, sold to some ardent collector on the other side of the Atlantic, and replaced only by a few miscellaneous Hogarth Press publications which did nothing to fill the yawning personality gap. The second thing I missed was Leonard's potted plants: elaborately blossomed double begonias, gloxinias, and heavily perfumed lilies, which he had nurtured ~~which he had~~ in his carefully tended greenhouse in the garden and brought into the house when they were at the peak of their blossoming. He took a great pride in them, and they filled the little room with their bright colours and (sometimes) scent.

The Woolfs had first spotted Monk's House when they

Page from the manuscript for an essay about Leonard and Virginia Woolf's house at Rodmell (the author) entirely by themselves and their symbolism." He saw his work as a battle with the technical problems involved in clearing his poetry of "the sentimental echoes of the period" and finding a vehicle "for a new precision of description" that implied "a harder precision of thought and feeling." He concluded that "Poetry . . . is a hard master" and observed how often he had denied the successive urges to produce poetry, "preferring the easier calls of other endeavours" before he had "exhausted all the ideas for poems that each impulse brought with it." He is too hard with himself; though, from the time when he began his own publishing house in 1946 until he gave up editing the *London Magazine* in 1961, the writing of poetry largely came when events gave some respite from the pressure of publishing, it would be wrong to think of Lehmann as an occasional poet. He had from the beginning a firm dedication to the medium. For a period, after he started *New Writing* in the mid-1930s, poems no longer seemed to come to him; but he has returned to poetry with successful results throughout his life.

Lehmann was somewhat overshadowed in the 1930s by his brilliant contemporaries W. H. Auden, Louis MacNeice, Stephen Spender, and William Empson. Subsequently, his poetry has not had the attention it deserves—partly because of his intermittent career as poet, and partly because of the unostentatious virtues that he has cultivated in his writing. Yet it is these virtues that give his best poems their immediacy and lasting power. Perceptive, graceful, unmarred by the political attitudes with which he was so deeply involved, they remain refreshingly honest and lyrical. They constitute a body of work that makes a distinctive contribution to the poetry of the twentieth century.

Reference:

A. T. Tolley, *The Poetry of the Thirties* (London: Gollancz, 1975; New York: St. Martin's, 1976).

Papers:

There is a collection of Lehmann's papers at the Humanities Research Center, University of Texas at Austin.

Christopher Logue
(23 November 1926-   )

Peter Craven and Michael Heyward
University of Melbourne

SELECTED BOOKS: *Wand and Quadrant* (Paris: Olympia Press, 1953);

Devil, Maggot and Son (The Hague: Stols, 1956; Tunbridge Wells: Peter Russell, 1956);

The Man Who Told His Love: Twenty Poems Based on Pablo Neruda's 'Los Cantos d'Amores' (London: Scorpion Press, 1958);

Lust, as Count Palmiro Vicarion (Paris: Olympia Press, 1959);

Songs (London: Hutchinson, 1959; New York: McDowell Obolensky, 1960);

Patrocleia: Book 16 of Homer's Iliad Freely Adapted into English (London: Scorpion Press, 1962); republished as *Patrocleia of Homer: A New Version* (Ann Arbor: University of Michigan Press, 1963);

The Arrival of the Poet in the City: A Treatment for a Film (Amsterdam: Yellow Press, 1963; London: Mandarin Books, 1964);

Logue's A.B.C. (London: Scorpion Press, 1966);

Pax: from Book XIX of the Iliad (London: Turret Books: 1967);

New Numbers (London: Cape, 1969; New York: Knopf, 1970);

The Crocodile (London: Cape, 1976);

Ratsmagic (London: Cape, 1976; New York: Pantheon, 1976);

Puss-in-Boots Pop-Up (London: Cape, 1976; New York: Morrow, 1977);

Abecedary (London: Cape, 1977);

The Magic Circus (London: Cape, 1979; New York: Viking, 1979);

Ode to the Dodo: Poems 1953-78 (London: Cape, 1981);

War Music (London: Cape, 1981).

PLAYS: *The Trial of Cob and Leach*, London, Royal Court Theatre, 26 April 1959;

Jazzetry, London, Royal Court Theatre, 26 April 1959;

The Lily White Boys, book by Harry Cookson, lyrics by Logue, London, Royal Court Theatre, 27 January 1960;

Trials by Logue: Antigone and *Cob and Leach*, London, Royal Court Theatre, 23 November 1960;

Friday, Logue's adaptation of Hugo Claus's play, London, Royal Court Theatre, 23 November 1971;

War Music, Logue's adaptation of the *Iliad*, music by Donald Fraser, London, Old Vic, 25 May 1977.

SCREENPLAY: *Savage Messiah*, MGM, 1972.

TELEVISION SCRIPT: *The End of Arthur's Marriage*, by Logue and Stanley Myers, BBC, 2, 1965.

RECORDINGS: *Red Bird*, with music by Tony Kinsey and Bill le Sage (Parlophone G.E.P. 8765, 1959);

Laurie Lee and Christopher Logue reading (Jupiter jep 0C16, 1960);

The Death of Patroclus, with Vanessa Redgrave and Alan Dobie (Spoken Arts SA 926, 1962).

OTHER: *Count Palmiro Vicarion's Book of Limericks*, edited by Logue (Paris: Olympia Press, 1959);

Count Palmiro Vicarion's Book of Bawdy Ballads, edited by Logue (Paris: Olympia Press, 1962);

True Stories, edited by Logue (London: New English Library, 1965);

True Stories from "Private Eye," edited by Logue (London: Deutsch, 1973);

The Children's Book of Comic Verse, edited by Logue (London: Batsford, 1979);

The Bumper Book of True Stories, edited by Logue (London: Private Eye/Deutsch, 1980).

Christopher Logue's *War Music* (1981), a long poem in three parts, freely based on Homer's *Iliad*, is one of the major achievements of postwar British poetry. Logue is also an accomplished lyric poet and a master of comic and satirical verse. Deeply indebted to Ezra Pound and, as a creative translator, one of Pound's most eminent successors, Logue is among the few British poets to have exploited the inheritance of modernism.

Born in Portsmouth to Molly and John Dominic Logue, Christopher Logue was educated at two Catholic schools and at Portsmouth Gram-

mar School. His father was an official in the wages branch of the British postal service. In 1943 Christopher Logue volunteered for the army, and while serving with the Army Commandos at St. Ives, Cornwall, he suffered an injury which resulted in the loss of sight in one eye. After the disbanding of the Army Commandos Logue returned to the Fourth Battalion of the Black Watch, which was posted to the Middle East. In Binyamina, Palestine, Lance Corporal Logue was charged with being in illegal possession of six Army Books 64 (identity documents and/or pay books issued to other ranks) and as a consequence was sentenced to two years' imprisonment. It was around this time that Logue first became interested in poetry: the books he took into prison were Auden's *Selected Poems*, an edition of Wilde, and a complete edition of Shakespeare. On his release in November 1947 he bought a copy of J. H. C. Grierson's *The Poems of John Donne*. Unable to attend a university, Logue, who returned to England in 1948, went on the dole. He made his first literary friends in London and, armed with George Samson's *Cambridge History of English Literature*, set about building a library for himself. Logue learned most from reading Ezra Pound and T. S. Eliot: Peter Russell, then editor of *Nine*, confirmed Logue's sense of how Pound's "broken lines" could come alive in recital. In 1951 Logue grew dispirited with London and headed for the Left Bank of Paris. There his work was published in the literary magazine *Merlin* (founded by his Scottish friend Alexander Trocchi in 1952), and he was encouraged by one of its contributors, Samuel Beckett.

At that time, the dominant influence was Pound. *Wand and Quadrant*, published by Olympia Press under the Merlin imprint in 1953, is a testament to Logue's immersion in Pound's medievalism. Logue delved into everything from troubadours to falconry. Though immensely talented, the poems are reminiscent of very early Pound, dandified, uncertain, and fin de siècle. This is a young man's book, striding on stilts, but unsure of its direction.

Logue returned to England in 1956. In *Devil, Maggot and Son* (1956) there is a greater trust in song and, in spite of a residue of poetic diction, Logue starts to develop a resonant plainness which is more dramatic, less merely theatrical, as in sonnet three from "Half a Dozen approximate Sonnets":

> Woman, I loved you forever, and now
> I love you not. Forever has its day
> it is not Bethlehem or Calvary,
> or in the province of Love's god

Nell Dunn, Angus Wilson, Mr. Jones of the Arts Council, Margaret Drabble, Charles Osborne,
and Christopher Logue during a reading tour in Wales

Yeats, besides influencing this new rhetorical strength, also provides the focus for two of the poems, "The Old Canary" and "Politics." "Politics," a sustained attack on Yeats's supposed political complacency, nonetheless succeeds in being Yeatsian. In reviewing *Devil, Maggot and Son* Edwin Muir said that, although Logue was struggling against everything Yeats stood for, he yet took fire from Yeats's imagination. In 1982 Logue commented, "Certainly Muir's judgement is, by hindsight, correct."

Logue attributes his political conversion to the Left to the political atmosphere of Paris during the early 1950s. Setting out to unify his poetry and his political vision, he said in 1956, "I was writing one thing and believing another. . . . Now I shall write not just about love, but about a butcher, a baker or a candlestick maker in love." In 1957 Logue wrote an unsigned article for the *Times Literary Supplement* attacking the two leading poetry factions (The Movement and The Mavericks) for their lack of political engagement. Logue had gone to Berlin in 1956 to see Brecht, whom he described as "the only writer of any significance who could use political things without strain." Brecht had advised Logue to

return to London, to learn German, and then to come back, but Brecht's death a few months later cut short the proposed apprenticeship.

Songs (1959) remains a testament to Brecht's influence, and with this book Logue fully arrives as a poet: radical socialism provides him with a subject while the astringency of Brechtian technique disciplines his tendency to romanticism without dampening his lyrical gifts. Logue's experiments with a "popular" voice in songs such as "She Sings" and "The Song of the Dead Soldier" enable him to exploit what he has learned from Yeats's late poems in order to project his own vision. He creates a typology of downtrodden everyday life which vindicates his earlier fumblings with allegory. When Philip Larkin, reviewing *Songs* in the *Guardian*, said that Logue's lyricism was "afflicted with that *faiblesse* that nowadays inevitably attends words like King, Queen, Tom o' Bedlam," his remark was far more applicable to Logue's earlier work. Animated by a refreshing vulgarity and a wild sense of comedy, *Songs* exploits popular and traditional poetic forms with a liberating effect, using them as vehicles for satire and protest. At his most ambitious (in poems such as "The story about the road"), Logue works toward the complex immediacy of overtly dramatic speech, but the verse is ultimately more epic than dramatic: it uses a terse, telegraphic narrative voice with a sweeping cinematic effect to produce action. This voice is Logue's great poetic innovation: his major poems are film scripts for the speaking voice. The first glimpse of such poetry in *Songs* is "Achilles Fights the River." Adapted from Homer's *Iliad* (though less freely than the later poems that make up *War Music*), this coarser-grained verse is nonetheless masterfully propelled by its savage and glittering rhetoric, its driving nervous energy. The revival of verse drama in the early 1950s (in which Eliot and Christopher Fry played prominent parts) had not produced dramatic verse of such authority.

Logue was increasingly active in London cultural life: "Achilles Fights the River" was broadcast on the BBC's Third Programme; in 1957 he read at the National Film Theatre, "guided by Kenneth Tynan and Lindsay Anderson," and he also produced his first two poster poems: *To My Fellow Artists*, which deploys a taut and spare oratory to attack acquiescence in the face of nuclear armament, and *The Dead Soldier*, which caused a scandal when it appeared at the time of the Cyprus occupation.

Songs also includes a sequence of twenty poems which take their bearings from the love poetry of Pablo Neruda. Originally published in 1958 by Scorpion Press under the title *The Man Who Told His Love*, these poems of sunlit and dizzy sensuality create an erotic landscape in the manner of *The Song of Songs*. In March 1959 they were broadcast on the BBC under the title *Red Bird Dancing on Ivory*, with music by Tony Kinsey and Bill le Sage; the program combined a balance of jazz and poetry, the one illustrating the other. Frank Kermode saw the experiment as an "attempt to get the lyre back into the lyric" which should be taken "very seriously" by "everybody who cares about poetry."

Jazzetry (jazz plus poetry), incorporating much of the *Red Bird Dancing on Ivory* material, was performed at the Royal Court in 1959 with Peter O'Toole among the readers. Logue's other dramatic works of this period are the "news-play" *The Trial of Cob and Leach* (1959) and *Antigone* (1960). These, as well as *Jazzetry*, were directed by Logue's friend Lindsay Anderson.

A. Alvarez criticized the plays' reliance on Brecht; similarly, Philip Larkin complained that the success of the poems after Homer and Neruda showed that Logue was "unable to organize a strong effect without another writer in the background"; but these charges of literary grave robbing are be-

side the point: Logue has consistently tinkered with other men's masterpieces, and his mature poetry is his vindication. *Patrocleia* (1962), a free adaptation of book sixteen of the *Iliad*, is original poetry of the highest order. Donald Carne-Ross, who had commissioned the first Homeric imitation for the BBC, supplied Logue, who does not know Greek, with "a literal translation which retained the Greek word order." Logue's aim was not "a translation in the accepted sense" but "a poem in English."

Patrocleia begins with Patroclus pleading with Achilles to allow him to go into battle in his place and ends with the death of Patroclus. The poem is characterized by brutal and impacted violence alternating rapidly with ravishing lyrical interludes, which, in a piece of brilliant adaptation, Logue improvises to re-create the effect of the Homeric simile. The diction, though exceptionally wide ranging, and sometimes deliberately anachronistic, is only occasionally poetic; elevated or archaic language is used sparingly and with deliberate effect. While this verse is free, it tends to have a strong iambic base, though the influence of Pound is still discernible, particularly in the lyrical interludes. The character of Achilles is masterfully established at the outset of the poem, and, although he does not reappear, he broods over its action like the nemesis he is destined to become. *Patrocleia* is arguably the greatest tour de force in Logue's work because of the sheer difficulty of what he set out to accomplish. Logue's structural dexterity and his brilliant cinematic cutting ensure that the combat scenes are never monotonous or confusing. It was this cinematic effect that led Donald Carne-Ross to assert that in his presentation of warfare Logue was at times actually superior to Homer. It is difficult to say whether Logue is more remarkable for the imaginative license with which he departs from Homer or the empathic fidelity with which he concentrates the Homeric vision. Sometimes he will translate Homer's actual lines magnificently: "O, my sweet friend/How splendid it would be if all of them—/Greeks, Trojans, Allies, Confederates—were dead./And thou and I were left to rip Troy down alone!" More frequently he traces Homer's shadow with astonishing inventiveness.

The English reception of *Patrocleia* was mixed. Hugh Lloyd-Jones thought the poem lacked "nobility." More perceptively Louis MacNeice found it to be "not a translation" but "a remarkable achievement of empathy." The reaction from America was unambiguous. "I'm crazy about it," Henry Miller said. "Haven't seen such poetry in ages." William

Arrowsmith declared that *Patrocleia* was "the most important piece of translation since Ezra Pound's 'Propertius,'" and Guy Davenport, writing in *Poetry*, thought Logue "an incomparable poet.... He has managed to incorporate more of Homer's sense of action than any other English translator."

While working on his versions of Homer (supported by the Bollingen Foundation) Logue wrote songs for The Establishment, London's satirical nightclub. The year 1963 saw the publication of *The Arrival of the Poet in the City*, an overt attempt to use the techniques of the screenplay in order to amplify an obscene apocalyptic vision. *Logue's A.B.C.* (1966), an alphabet of comic poems, represents a rapprochement between the Brechtian poet and the English humorist. The verse is "light" but hard-edged, and the best of these rhyming jokes, with their combination of crazy humor and epigrammatic wisdom, are likely to have passed into the language when a fair quantity of "heavier" verse is forgotten.

During the 1960s Logue actively promoted poetry readings as part of his sustained involvement with popular culture. (At the 1969 Isle of Wight Festival, where Bob Dylan performed, Logue read to an estimated audience of 100,000.) Frank Kermode has said of Logue's manner of reading: "Mr. Logue reads very well, not at all 'beautifully.'" Logue's concern for bringing poetry to the people was a natural outgrowth of his political and social commitment. He read everywhere, from Eton to the Walls Sausage Factory. "A poet's shop is in his throat," Logue has said. In 1963 he wrote, "If one more person likes what I have done then, for me, it has been worth it; if a few more people are put in the imaginary know then the money is well spent."

But Logue's activities were not confined to poetry. His film appearances include Swinburne in Ken Russell's *Dante's Inferno* (1966) and Richelieu in *The Devils* (1970). He had also begun writing in 1962 a column for the satirical magazine *Private Eye*. In 1966 Bernard Stone of Turret Books published Logue's satirical poem *I Shall Vote Labour* as a poster, and it sold so well (30,000 copies) that the poster-poem industry blossomed. Heavily influenced by commercial art, Logue's poster poems incorporate cartoons, photographs, and abstract designs. The finest of the poster poems (*Crime One*, 1967; *September Song*, 1966; *Gone Ladies*, 1966) have striking visual and lyric impact. *Gone Ladies* is probably the best version of François Villon's "Ballade des dames du temps jadis" in English. As Guy Davenport has remarked, it "is not less literal than Rossetti's trans-

lation, and is much richer":

> Where in the world is Helen gone,
> Whose loveliness demolished Troy,.
> Sheba, Salome, and the wan
> Licentious Queen of Avalon,
> And where is she who could enjoy
> Caesar—and Anthony enthral,
> And she who bore God's only boy?
> Where is the snow we watched last Fall?

Pax (1967), Logue's re-creation of book nineteen of the *Iliad*, is focused on Achilles' grief at Patroclus's death and Achilles' consequent decision to go back into battle. Although lacking the dynamically orchestrated action of *Patrocleia*, *Pax* shows Logue's poetic powers at their most concentrated. From the startlingly beautiful opening, which takes Homer's stock image of "rosy fingered dawn" and unfolds it shot by shot in a magnificent visual conceit, to Achilles' final defiant shout ("I know I shall not make old bones"), the verse is fresh, sinewy, and brilliant. Logue's dramatic mastery is particularly highlighted in this poem: Odysseus is brought alive in a few brilliant touches, such as his masterful interception of Achilles' recklessness, "Wait . . . marvellous boy." Dominating the poem is the headstrong, grief-deranged figure of Achilles. If the most outstanding quality of *Pax* is its speeches, which Logue heightens in order to create an effect of heroic confrontation, without recourse to poetical diction, then it is equally true that Logue's Achilles, in the moment when he forces himself to make his peace with Agamemnon, has a stature comparable to that of Shakespeare's Coriolanus. Like Shakespeare, Logue creates a voice of immense authority in a state of exaltation and breakdown, knowing that its derangement is its claim to greatness. In the lyrical interludes Logue creates a mood of tense quiet. These passages give an effect of spaciousness, setting the scene for the main action and providing a counterpoint to the speechmaking.

With the publication of *Pax* Logue's reputation as the "grand translateur" of his generation was consolidated: Peter Levi in *Agenda* and Guy Davenport in *Arion* took him as their creative yardstick for measuring the limitations of Richmond Lattimore's "faithful" translation of the *Odyssey*. In 1968 George Steiner described Logue's version of Homer as "the most magnificent act of translation going on in the English language at the moment."

In 1969 *New Numbers* appeared. The previous

year Logue had referred to poetry as "this fostered, pampered child of the arts," and these poems represent a head-on attempt to rescue verse from the realms of cultural self-congratulation. In the introduction to *New Numbers*, Logue writes, "If this book does not change you . . . then throw it away." The collection has some hilarious moments, much wit, some sadness, and considerable satire; Logue has a keen eye for the absurd; but after *Pax*, *New Numbers* inevitably reads as the product of his "talent" rather than his "genius."

In the same year Logue wrote that the "best poetry" was "out on the streets, my darlings" and that academic criticism was as incapable of dealing with the Dylan lyric (or the Adrian Mitchell poem) as it was with the border ballad. Many of Logue's poems (the pop-song-like lyric "Woke up this morning," for example) reflect his mastery of apparently light verse which clearly calls either for performance or to be seen in relation to the medium it exploits, whether poster, newspaper, or illustrated book. *Twelve Cards* (1972) is a suite of poems printed on separate cards which reproduce pastel drawings by the poet in an attractive "mixed art" format. Sometimes these poems sound as old (and as fresh) as the origins of poetry: "Pin this to your wall/Then,/though you have no love for me,/my writing can admire your breasts." Presumably it was this kind of poetry Logue was defending when he said in 1981: "Light verse is often preferable to heavy. And good heavy is no substitute, no alternative to light."

Ratsmagic (1976) and *Puss-in-Boots Pop-Up* (1976) are magnificent illustrated children's books, with stories by Logue. *The Crocodile* (1976), also a children's book (with elegantly stylized illustrations by Binette Schroeder), gave Logue the opportunity to produce a deliciously macabre comic poem in the manner of Edward Lear or Lewis Carroll. *Abecedary* (1977), with illustrations by Bert Kitchen is basically a reworking of the earlier *Logue's A.B.C*, though this version is best seen as alternative rather than definitive.

In 1981 Logue produced *Ode to the Dodo: Poems 1953-78*. As well as including selected poems from his earlier full-length books, it incorporates work from his pamphlets of the 1970s: *Singles* (1973), *Mixed Rushes* (1974), and *Urbanal* (1975). Some of these sharp and snappy later poems were published as a series in the *Times*. Much of what is preserved in *Ode to the Dodo* is substantially revised, and the collection bears the stamp of the professional poet remedying the excesses of his earlier work. George Steiner remarked that it was "simply unfair" to read

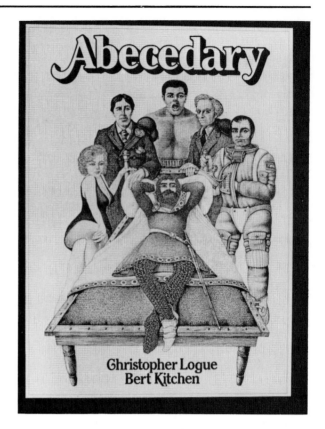

Front cover for Logue's 1977 alphabet book. He considers his comic and satiric verse an antidote to more serious poetry, "this fostered, pampered child of the arts."

these poems "in tandem" with Logue's Homerics, but the volume remains a testament to Logue's versatility, his ability to turn his hand to any occasion: political satire, poster poem, pop song, children's poetry, and translation. The collection is characterized by what is implicit in the title—a plainspoken irony about the value of the poetic, though this skepticism is made honest by Logue's experimentation with a multitude of forms.

During the 1970s Logue adapted Hugo Claus's play *Friday* (1971), wrote the screenplay for Ken Russell's *Savage Messiah* (1972), and in 1977 turned his Homer into a "music drama," *War Music*, for the Prospect Theatre Company. *War Music*, incorporating revised versions of *Patrocleia* and *Pax* together with a new interlocking section, *GBH* ("grievous bodily harm"), unites the three into a single work. Logue describes *War Music* as "a narrative poem capable of being read independently of its guessed-at parent."

The action of *GBH* centers on the Greeks' attempt to recover the dead body of Patroclus. War is presented as an invigorating obscenity—

something morally and physically degrading, though Logue is everywhere alive to its grisly excitements. *GBH* is the least lyrical of Logue's major poems, and it dispels any doubts that may have remained that there was anything pretty about his Homeric masterwork. Technically it yields nothing to *Pax* or *Patrocleia*: Logue's muscled and straining language is exactly adjusted to his subject. In a complex way it is an heroic idiom. At times the black humor is audacious and chilling: Menelaos "bows—as if to Helen on their wedding day"—seconds before he brutally slaughters his "whimpering" boyish opponent. Everywhere the emphasis is on physical extremity: Achilles' grief "pistol whips his face." His great cry of hate and pain is magnificently achieved: "He lifts his face to ninety; draws his breath;/And from the bottom of his heart emits/so long and loud and terrible a scream,/The icy scabs at either end of earth/Winced in their sleep. . . ." With Achilles' final words over the body of Patroclus, Logue has the precision that can realize the terrible emotion: "My love I swear you will not burn/Till Hector's severed head is in my lap."

Everywhere in *GBH* we can see how deeply implicated Logue is in the traditions of English narrative and dramatic verse; the use of the long line and the surging poetic paragraph even recalls Milton. If at times he seems to have pruned some rich lines from the earlier sections of *War Music*, this revision represents an attempt to purge any trace of poetical diction.

P. J. Kavanagh called *War Music* "a shining, original (whatever its source), long poem in English." George Steiner, cautioning that the term was to be used "very rarely," applied the word "genius."

In 1981 Logue defined his attitude to Homer in this way: "I sometimes imagine Homer's *Iliad* as a great radioactive lump of something at the bottom of a mineshaft. The best way for me to study it is to concentrate on the light its beam throws on the clouds above the shaft's mouth." That Logue's major poetry is, in its overall conception though not in the detail of its phrasing, a translation of Homer should only heighten our sense of his achievement. Guy Davenport has called this poetry "a miracle of the imagination" and one which deserves the title Homeric because "Homer is as much a spirit and a quality as he is an order of words."

In the 1950s Logue began as an ambitious and talented lyric poet who attempted to reconcile a

unique range of influences: Pound, Yeats . . . and *Brecht Songs* is his crossroads—although it shows a mastery of different kinds of short poem, the thrust of Logue's genius is clearly toward a highly dramatized form of abbreviated (and cinematic) epic. His dramatic prowess is huge, and its promise is fulfilled in the Homeric poems. But this dramatic talent coexists with one that is histrionic, brilliant, and a trifle meretricious. If Logue is an expert poet, at home in the role of the witty comedian or instant songster who sees the occasional poem as a slender, humorous, perhaps tender thing, of use but throwaway, he is also the opposite: a writer who breaks all the rules and whose major work defies the question of discernible influence, because the personal vision is utterly achieved. His Homer stands apart like a mountain.

Interviews:

Davina Lloyd, "Christopher Logue's Poster Poems," *London Magazine* (August 1968): 42-45;

Peter Craven and Michael Heyward, "An Interview with Christopher Logue," *Scripsi*, 1 (Spring 1981): 14-21;

"Interview with Christopher Logue," *Quarto* (November 1981): 13-15.

References:

Donald Carne-Ross, "On Looking into Fitzgerald's Homer," *New York Review of Books*, 21 (12 December 1974): 3-7;

Carne-Ross, "Structural Translation: Notes on Logue's *Patrocleia*," *Arion*, 1 (Summer 1962): 27-38; republished in *Patrocleia of Homer* (Ann Arbor: University of Michigan Press, 1963);

Guy Davenport, "Another *Odyssey*," *Arion*, 7 (Spring 1968): 135-153; republished in his *The Geography of the Imagination* (San Francisco: North Point Press, 1981), pp. 29-44;

Davenport, "From the Greek," *Poetry*, 108 (September 1966): 416-419;

Davenport, "Provender from Cathay," *Hudson Review*, 21 (Autumn 1968): 564-574;

Michael Ewans, "Homer's Christopher Logue," *Scripsi*, 1 (Spring 1981): 22-26;

Michael Heyward, "Who's Homer?," *Scripsi*, 1 (Spring 1981): 27-35;

George Steiner, *After Babel* (London & New York: Oxford University Press, 1975), pp. 252, 351, 361, 401-402.

Norman MacCaig

(14 November 1910-   )

Christopher Levenson
Carleton University

BOOKS: *Far Cry: Poems* (London: Routledge, 1943);

The Inward Eye (London: Routledge, 1946);

Riding Lights: Poems (London: Hogarth Press, 1955; New York: Macmillan, 1956);

The Sinai Sort: Poems (London: Hogarth Press, 1957; New York: Macmillan, 1957);

A Common Grace (London: Chatto & Windus, 1960);

A Round of Applause (London: Chatto & Windus, 1962);

Measures (London: Chatto & Windus, 1965);

Surroundings (London: Chatto & Windus/Hogarth Press, 1966);

Rings on a Tree (London: Chatto & Windus/Hogarth Press, 1968);

A Man in My Position (London: Chatto & Windus, 1969);

Selected Poems (London: Hogarth, 1971);

Penguin Modern Poets 21, by MacCaig, Iain Crichton Smith, and George Mackay Brown (Harmondsworth: Penguin, 1972);

The White Bird (London: Chatto & Windus, 1973);

The World's Room (London: Chatto & Windus, 1974);

Tree of Strings (London: Chatto & Windus, 1977);

Old Maps and New: Selected Poems (London: Hogarth Press, 1978);

The Equal Skies (London: Chatto & Windus/Hogarth Press, 1980);

A World of Difference (London: Chatto & Windus, 1983).

OTHER: *Honour'd shade: an anthology of new Scottish poetry to mark the bicentenary of the birth of Robert Burns*, edited by MacCaig (Edinburgh: W. & R. Chambers, 1959);

Contemporary Scottish verse, 1959-1969, edited by MacCaig and Alexander Scott (London: Calder & Boyars, 1970).

Despite the publication of fifteen individual volumes of poetry and two substantial selections over the past forty years, despite the fact that most of his mature work has been well received by critics and has won awards, and despite the inclusion of his work in such an influential anthology as A. Alvarez's *The New Poetry* (1962), Norman MacCaig's name is not nearly so well known among readers of poetry as it should be.

Perhaps one should speak of his lack of reputation among English readers of poetry, for part of the problem, undoubtedly, is geographical: MacCaig has rarely strayed far or for long from his native Scotland, and one recalls that even Hugh MacDiarmid was an old man before he became generally known south of a border that, as MacCaig has said, is a potent psychological barrier. Moreover, although he is a man of wit and erudition, MacCaig lacks the flamboyance of MacDiarmid or of such later Scottish poets as W. S. Graham or Sydney Goodsir Smith, both of whom found an audience in London. On the contrary he has lived a rather quiet and ordered life as a schoolteacher far from the main literary centers. If he is, as some believe, the most important living Scottish poet, that fact is well hidden from many outside Scotland.

MacCaig's origins, on which he lays some personal emphasis, make him seven-eighths Celtic. He has described his father, Robert MacCaig, who came from Dumfries, as a wage slave who worked in and later owned an Edinburgh chemist's shop that had been established in 1769. It was from his mother, Joan MacLeod MacCaig, who had arrived in Edinburgh from the Outer Hebrides at the age of sixteen, able to speak only Gaelic, that he claims to have inherited his poetic gift. His mother was illiterate. As he explained in a 1982 interview, "she never went to school and this gave her a wonderful free hand with the English language. If there's any poetry in me at all, it's from her. She *thought* in images." MacCaig attended Edinburgh University, where he received an honors M.A. in 1932. MacCaig studied not English but classics because from his early teens he had known both that he was to be a teacher and that he did not want to teach English. For most of the time from 1934 until 1970, with the exception of the time he spent as a fellow in creative writing at the University of Edinburgh (1967-1969), he taught in primary schools in Edinburgh. In 1940 he mar-

Norman MacCaig

ried Isabel Munn, a fellow schoolteacher. After 1970, until 1978, MacCaig was, as he puts it, "degraded to being a Lecturer in English at Stirling University." Yet MacCaig says, "I don't think of myself as a poet. . . . I don't like the word. I never call myself a poet. I say I'm a teacher." The influence of his teaching career on his writing seems to have been good, part of what he terms his "long haul to lucidity," for it has "emphasized an instinctive thing, just as the Classics emphasized," on the other hand, his "Celtic love of form." "What's the use of talking to kids," MacCaig asks, "if they don't understand you? What's the use of writing a poem if nobody can understand it?"

Yet beyond his firm control over poetic forms that are at times quite intricate, there are few overt traces of the classics in his work. Nor indeed does it show much evidence of his wide reading or his occasional travels. Although he has read and enjoyed numerous European and Russian poets—he has mentioned Miroslav Holub, Hans Enzensberger, Zbigniew Herbert, and the early Boris

Pasternak, all in translation—he claims that, aside from John Donne and Wallace Stevens, there is not a trace of literary influence in his poetry because "my bump of mimicry was amputated at birth." (With Wallace Stevens, whose work he loved and for whom he felt an affinity, he says, "I knew I had to write my way through it.") So too with his travels: although he has visited the United States, Canada, Italy, and Australia, he has written only fifteen poems on his first visit to New York, three on his Italian trip, and nothing at all on his three weeks in Australia. He is, he concludes, "an extremely local man." But here too there is a surprise, for just as his long teaching career has resulted in only three poems about children, so too he has written only a handful of poems about Edinburgh, where he was born and has lived all his life. His native city is "too close" to him; he calls it "just an old coat," though he adds, "a Joseph's coat of many colours." Where then does one of MacCaig's most striking characteristics, his sense of particular place, derive? Mostly, it seems, from the two months that he has spent every summer since the age of thirty in the Northwestern Highlands. The poet never writes while he is there but uses the experience of landscape and people to fatten his "camel's hump," on which he then lives poetically for the remaining ten months.

Although "all Scots have got generations of Calvinism in their corpuscles," MacCaig was not raised as a Calvinist: "thank God, I escaped that pollution! Neither of my parents were believers and they didn't press their belief in nonbelief upon me." He declares, "I was born an atheist and I still am. I'm a rationalist." Yet he also claims to be a kind of puritan, at least in the way that he regards material objects, and he hates it when people impose on landscapes, flowers, or creatures their human feelings. Speaking of his favorite mountain, he comments: "When I look at Suilven it's a lump of sandstone. It's very beautiful. *It* doesn't know that it's beautiful, of course. . . . It's so easy to make metaphors and symbols that *appear* to be profound." He loves physical objects, rooms as well as mountains or jugs, because they are beautiful or interesting, not for any ulterior purpose. This impatience with large abstractions and ideologies can be seen in his pacifism and rejection of extreme nationalism, and in the emphasis that especially his later books have placed on love and friendship.

Although, as some critics have pointed out, MacCaig does return time and again to certain themes, so that there is a unity of concern in most of his mature work, one can still distinguish three roughly chronological stages of development. The first is evident in the first and second books, *Far Cry* (1943) and *The Inward Eye* (1946); the second stage would include the volumes of the 1950s and early 1960s—*Riding Lights* (1955), *The Sinai Sort* (1957), *A Common Grace* (1960), *A Round of Applause* (1962), and *Measures* (1965)—while in the third would be all the works published from *Surroundings* (1966) to the present, with *Surroundings* marking his breakaway from regular meter and rhyme into more frequent, though never exclusive, use of freer forms. Such a division would not take account of the gradual darkening of tone over the last three or four volumes as MacCaig came to terms with the deaths of his close friends, but it will serve. In any case the changes throughout his mature work are more of emphasis than of any radical expansion of style or subject matter. The enduring value of MacCaig's work owes more to the clarity and consistency of a particular, idiosyncratic vision than to development through time.

Although MacCaig first attracted attention when some of his poems appeared in the New Apocalypse anthology, *The White Horseman* (1941), his first book, *Far Cry*, did not appear until 1943. The first stanza of the first poem at least illustrates the beginning poet's skill in assonance and in a kind of rhetoric, as he handles the repetition and modulation of such words as "courage," "hearts," and "crack" or "cracking":

> The crying courage that has wolves running in it
> is the only courage that outlasts a wave falling,
> and hearts heedless after mining the hearts
> of other men crack before the cracking mast.
> Where can courage sound for me its appealing
> and gentle voice, who visit the dismal courts.

The long sentences are not syntactically complex, but nevertheless they require a series of parallel subordinate clauses or phrases in apposition. The effect is curiously formal, unspontaneous.

Composed as sentences rather than metrical units, the poetry seems to lack cadence, and grammar, as the organizing influence, sometimes breaks down:

> The preying evil of a cracking thew
> spermed in the mind whose eyelids never flicker
> except from not done to the have to do
> betrays the darkness and insults the day,
> and day on day adds up the murderer,
> mingles the minds of angels in a crew
> will sink him in the sea, heeled to a star.

The cluttered effect of these lines is simply a matter

of syntax: working largely by thought association, the poem is all metaphor, and it is difficult to discern any overall architecture of meaning.

Even so, certain lines do stand out for their sharpness and directness, as in poem seven:

> At the narrow neck of the loch, half loch half
> river,
> arriving when darkness felt the first drag of
> light,
> half dark half day, we sat and watched in the
> stillness
> gulls witlessly flitting along the narrow water.

Perhaps the overtly Scottish nature of this scene contributes to its effectiveness. Certainly, MacCaig's recurrent images of sea, wind, bird, and mountain point forward to an element that has become a constant in his later work, his keen and exact sense of the natural world, glimpsed again in such moments from poem twenty-six:

> Across to you, away from the narrow ferry
> leaving behind only for a mile's moment
> the red sea-weed and the sliding blue of tide.
> Leave sand to oyster catchers for where only tread
> otter and fox, or stag slots his hoof-print.

What is lacking here that we find in later work is above all the humorous distancing, the quality we recognize in "From between two stones/in the Bay of Stinking Fish an otter protrudes/its World War One face, . . ." The immediate difference between MacCaig's second book, *The Inward Eye* (1946), and its predecessor arises from the fact that the poems in *The Inward Eye* are written predominantly in four-, five-, or six-line stanzas. The rhyme schemes are more consistent and regular, and the sentence structure likewise tends to be more straightforward, often a series of simple declarative sentences, as in "Gardener":

> Bean sticks and pea-pods are a clef for winds
> whose haulms of music shiver on my hands.
> The tongued sun quivers, the air stands up
> and down
> in regiments of colour, in globes of green

But in poems such as "The Word and the Text" we find the same kind of verbal intoxication, of local effect preempting meaning, as in *Far Cry*:

> In the straight stare of sun, outside the mask
> of silver that makes tolerable my mirror,
> the devil rubs my head, writes on my eyes,

hangs Mars and Venus on hair's heavy hooks,
and in my heart breathes breath into the saviour
whose shadow haunts me all my circling days.

Throughout the volume, whatever the ostensible
subject matter, a certain kind of vocabulary
predominates—words such as "devil," "mirror," or
"blood"—together with a tendency to feminine line
endings and frequent rather obtrusive double
rhymes. Interestingly, in the light of MacCaig's classical training, after this volume and the next
we do not encounter many references to classical
mythology until his two later books. What is more
important, perhaps, in the context of his later work
is the coexistence of rhetoric reminiscent of Dylan
Thomas's with down-to-earth and unrhetorical
terms: "curmudgeon," "harridan," and specifically
Scots words such as "brattle." There are also frequent references to the kind of natural detail that
distinguishes MacCaig's mature poetic world.

MacCaig was later very critical of his first two
books, referring to them scornfully as "balderdash
. . . too easy, too easy," and commenting that "any
idiot can be obscure." The change came about, it
seems, through a friend's commenting, "There's
your book, Norman. When are you publishing the
answers?" MacCaig has repudiated the published
work and destroyed the unpublished poems written
before he was thirty-four "because it was all rubbish." Each poem, he said, was "a vomitorium of
practically unrelated images."

After these early misdirections, MacCaig
began his "long haul to lucidity": it took him nearly
ten years "to be able to write what any other person
could understand and respond to." Nevertheless,
even though he claims never to have read a single
surrealist poem that was of any interest at all as a
poem, MacCaig will admit that some gain did accrue
from his early association with the New Apocalypse
group: "I think the whole surrealist movement
loosened up the muscles of writers' minds and imag-
inations, and they began to use figurative language
. . . in a much freer way than had been done since
the last century."

The first result is *Riding Lights*, published in
1955. The first poem, "Instrument and Agent,"
establishes the new tone, for part of the poet's
emergent wit involves playing with and renovating
existing stock phrases:

> In my eye I've no apple; every object
> Enters in there with hands in pockets.
> I welcome them all, just as they are,
> Every one equal, none a stranger.

These lines create a strong sense of the individuality
of the poet as a tolerant man, without aesthetic axes
to grind.

Such tolerance becomes affection whenever
MacCaig is dealing with aspects of the natural
world: "I love animals and plants . . . but I think I
love them in a pure way, if that doesn't sound too
boastful." He loves their extraordinary diversity of
colors and shapes, but he does not like "burdening"
lochs and mountains with his personality and is very
much aware of their separateness and distance. A
poem such as "Swimming Lizard," then, is merely
the first of a whole menagerie of poems that evoke
the particular qualities of bird or beast. Accurate
observation combines with what indeed can only be
termed affection:

> The tiny monster, the alligator
> A finger long, swam unhurried through the
>   brown;
> Each eye glittered under its heavy lid.
>
> This was his witness and his protest,
> To swim unhurried; for an unknown Cause
> He twinkled his brief texts through the brown
>   and still.

The poet remains outside the scene, "no reaching
hand, but a loving and helpless will." Nothing is too
insignificant for his attention. Thus in "Laggan-
doan, Harris,"

> A dragon-fly of mica whirs
> Off and up; then makes a thin
> Tottering grass its anchor-post,
> Changed to a small blue zeppelin.

As is the case in such poems as Andrew Marvell's
"Upon Appleton House," MacCaig compares
natural creatures to human artifacts and makes his
readers feel like Gullivers, charmed and superior.
Yet MacCaig is far from indulging mere whimsical
fancies; as "Birds all singing" proves, he is a realist,
well aware that birdsong has nothing in common
with the human concept of idyllic lovemaking.

True at times, as in "Be Easy," there is still a
fantastic, distorted edge to his imagination, but for
the most part MacCaig's evocations of nature convince because of their intense visual accuracy. In
"Wet Snow" the poet has to "turn away in terror, not
to see / A tree stand there hugged by its own ghost,"
while in "Climbing Suilven,"

> I nod and nod to my own shadow and thrust
> A mountain down and down.

Between my feet a loch shines in the brown,
Its silver paper crinkled and edged with rust.

MacCaig is at a loss to explain his strong visual bias, especially as it is music rather than painting that is his favorite art form. In high school, he says, he was the "absolute despair of the art teacher.... I proved conclusively that I was the worst artist in Europe, and yet I've got a guzzling eye. Odd."

"Country House," though something of a set piece, exhibits darker aspects of this same ability in its portrayal of the effects of dereliction, without irony but with immense resonance:

Last night the birds perched under water;
                  smoke
Hung flattened under fathoms of sodden air;
The roof, like a limpet, glistened; the lighted
                  window
Was jelly-red, an anemone in flower.

The final stanza reintroduces the forces of chaos, the "something" that "leaves on the disordered slates/ A thumbprint of green lichen" and that "Rushes down headlong from the freezing stars."

After such tactile poems it comes as something of a surprise to find also in this volume another type of poem that MacCaig has made his own in subsequent work, a kind of love poem that creates arabesques of pseudologic around the beloved in order to present less a situation or a portrait than a state of mind. Sometimes MacCaig seems consciously to be exhibiting an anti-Petrarchan bravura, as in the first stanza of "Fiat," which is close to pastiche:

I cannot stammer thunder in your sky
Or flash white phrases there. I have no terse
Exploding passion, and cannot vilify
My dulcet world through flute-holes of a verse,
But gently speak and, gently speaking, prove
The everlastingness in which you move.

More often, in quasi-metaphysical fashion, Mac-Caig uses words such as *therefore* to suggest a logical coherence, an aim underlined by stanza forms and meters of great neatness and balance. Perhaps, as MacCaig asserts in the final stanza of "Harpsichord playing Bach," "The understanding and the loving are/ Of course, the same." Certainly, both here and later, many poems that start off looking like pure philosophy end up by arguing themselves and their readers into a contemplation of love and its myriad intricacies.

It is probably *The Sinai Sort* (1957) that established MacCaig's reputation as a neo-metaphysical poet. He has admitted being under the influence of Donne, and it shows in this volume in various ways, which are not confined to his love poems, though certainly they are most striking in them.

"Particular You," for instance, in its plea to his beloved to retain disguises rather than "a horde of disclosures blackening the sun," ends with a slyly sacrilegious flourish (in the manner of Donne's "The Flea"):

Then, gazing,
I lose the loss of what I must be losing
   And find the language of disguise
Says all I want and bear to know, that we
And all the world are three, but one in three.

"In No Time at All" presents a similarly tongue-in-cheek self-apotheosis, but it is above all the ongoing sense of argument and twisted logic that gives these poems their tone. "Shadow of love," for instance, which starts colloquially enough with the question "What though I never made a mountain of it," proceeds for the rest of the poem to construct an ingenious conceit out of mountains, molehills, and stars—for "Love in the dark blinds half the stars to make/ The others brighter," the reader is told in the first stanza. But, if there is an ingenious bravura to the argument, there is certainly nothing mechanical about the verse movement, and by the time the reader reaches the fourth stanza, MacCaig's verbal dexterity is keeping the reader on the alert:

Therefore I blunder through myself, and love
The world and you and me for being the same.
Is this a molehill? A mountain of dead stars
It seems rather. And I will never frame
A hazard at a truth till I unblind
   The dark part of my mind.

Not that MacCaig becomes totally captive of this manner: in "Gifts" the point is a direct, indeed George Herbert-like, refusal to offer his beloved the usual hyperboles of Petrarchan love poetry. Characteristically for a poet with a keen sense of his own integrity, he makes her "the harder offer of all I can/ The good and ill that make of me this man." For the theme behind all these variations is the identity of lover and beloved, and beyond that, identity in general. "Growing Down" sums it up wryly. The lover is

Caught in the act of living, if to live
Is to be all one's possibilities,

A sum of generations six foot high,
Learning to live and practising to die.

This is not the "modesty" for which MacCaig has often been praised but rather a farsighted, singleminded, and, in certain aspects, blatantly egoistic concern with defining the self and emphasizing the necessarily personal and partial view of reality to which we are all doomed. As he puts it in "Lies for Comfort," "All that the eye names is disguises./That's no tree but a way of feeling." MacCaig's neutralist, value-free attitude toward natural phenomena is not only rigorously nonanthropomorphic but at times, as in "Ego," not even anthropocentric:

I see a rose, that strange thing, and what's there
But a seeming something coloured on the air
With the transparencies that make up me,
Thickened to existence by my notice. Tree
And star are ways of finding out what I
Mean in a text composed of earth and sky.

What reason to believe this, any more
Than that I am myself a metaphor
That's noticed in the researches of a rose
And self-instructs a star? Time only knows
Creation's mad cross-purposes and will
Destroy the evidence to keep them secret still.

This poem is merely one of the earlier examples in MacCaig's work of his explicit concern with the act of poetry, the act of observing and being observed. What makes MacCaig's observations, whether of animals, landscapes, or people so memorable is the combination of direct language with oblique reference, as if he had thousands of possible analogies ready and could produce them effortlessly, at will, from the widest possible range of experience and reading. Seldom is there any overt erudition involved; mostly, as in the opening stanza of "Maiden Loch," it is a matter of his having observed carefully and noted for later use:

In the round bay a drifting boat
Rides on another's shadowy back
And unreflecting lilies float,
Whose whiteness makes brown water black.

The directness of these lines, indeed of the whole poem, is an indicator of MacCaig's gradual moving away from anything that resembles rhetoric toward a greater colloquialism, and with it toward a greater self-irony.

MacCaig's next book, *A Common Grace*, pub-

lished in 1960, adds some excellent individual poems to this trend. "Goat," the "blasé lecher" who makes man feel "suddenly/Hypocrite found out" is a worthy representative in the series of vignettes, especially about birds and animals, that populates all his mature books; while "Half built boat in a hayfield" is another witty speculation based on a visual analogy elegantly carried through:

A cradle, at a distance, of a kind:
Or, making midget its neat pastoral scene,
A carcase rotted and its bones picked clean.

Then too, there are a number of fine poems, such as "Spring in a clear October" or "Ardmore," whose main point seems to be atmospheric, whether evoking unexpected springlike mildness in autumn or the end of a road in the Highlands, where "The sea, the sun/Are the next stage, with nothing in between./A quick place this to know your journey's done." Here too we find the deservedly anthologized "Spate in Winter Midnight":

Through Troys of bracken and Babel towers
                              of rocks
Shrinks now the looting fox,
Fearful to touch the thudding ground
And flattened to it by the mastering sound.
And roebuck stilt and leap sideways; their
                                        skin
Twitches like water on the fear within.

Leaving aside the rare kind of sensibility needed even to be aware of all such activity, one can only admire the accuracy of "looting," "stilt," and "their skin/Twitches like water"—all part of MacCaig's larger accuracy that refuses to distort the natural world. With "Explicit Snow," however, he does not merely present but also explains the effect on the human observer of the year's first snowfall:

As a great actor steps, not from the wings
But from the play's extension—all he does
Is move to be seen from the mysterious—

And his performance is the first of all—
The snow falls from its implications and
Stages pure newness on the uncurtained land.

And the hill we've looked out of existence comes
Vivid in its own language; and this tree
Stands self-explained, its own soliloquy.

Typically for MacCaig, the emphasis is not just on freshness and newness but rather on the total originality of the scene that transforms our vision. Indeed, in all his best poems he focuses so sharply on the visual or tactile essence of an object or scene that he makes it stand out against its context or background as if for the first time.

In *A Common Grace* there are also poems, such as "Nude in a fountain," that in their self-regarding, almost euphuistic echoing and alliterative effects seem throwbacks to an earlier manner, just as there are other poems, such as "Blue Chair in a Sunny Day," where abstract speculation has overburdened its physical starting point:

> Angle and square and pull and thrust prepare
> A balance of well-being and they make
> Chair solid in the idea of chair,
>
> Where two modes interpenetrate and are;
> An accent and a thunder clap in being;
> Existence modified; angelic nous
> Become a geometry of strut and spar.

This kind of doglike worrying of philosophical bones remains one of MacCaig's less profitable enterprises in subsequent volumes.

By contrast, MacCaig's crusade against Calvinism takes a more lighthearted and fanciful turn in "Too Cold for Words" when the unsuccessful lover, who rejects having to choose between Gabriel and the Devil, claims that he will

> little care, when we from nakedness
> Put on our fleshly appetites again,
> If you will have one black kiss to explain
> The brimstone stink that haunts your holiness.

Perhaps, as he has said, it is impossible to escape Calvinism in Scotland—MacCaig himself clearly knows his Bible—but one can at least thumb one's nose at it, and MacCaig, who has termed himself a Zen Calvinist, enjoys taking that opportunity in the most unlikely contexts. Thus in "Haycock, Achiltibuie" the mingling scents of the salt sea air and the heavy sweetness of the mown hay lead on to these lines:

> Some saints too smelled of honey when they died.
>
> A sort of holiness has been cut down
> And heaped up in one hill, with many mansions
> Where mice, its little sinners, can run in.
>
> Till comes the wintry crofter, hoisting half
> A Zion on his back, and pitiful
> Small angels fall through nights and days of frost.

One of MacCaig's recurrent impulses, important both where religion and where political issues are concerned, is to demythologize, to bring things down to size, as in "Two Ways of it," another love poem that stresses humility, the unromantic, the matter-of-factness of his love and of his beloved "not by being symbol,/Or ominous of anything but what it is." Naturally this good-humored skepticism extends also to the poet's view of himself as poet. In "Creator," for example, he is the "nosey-parker" who makes "translations he takes to be lovely/Of fish, bird, fruit: and the dead lives he mentions/Become immortal." He concludes however: "How hard to be so god-like/As one would fancy." The same virtues and deficiencies are apparent also in *A Round of Applause* (1962). The by-now-expected accuracy and vitality of natural description in poems such as "Spraying Sheep" or "Byre" (with its cows "mincing in/Swagbellied Aphrodites, swinging/A silver slaver from each chin") is expanded in "Thaw on a building site" to include inanimate objects also: "A concrete mixer cleared its throat/For a boring speech, all consonants. . . ." The book's most impressive lines come at the start of "Sound of the Sea on a Still Evening":

> It comes through quietness, softly crumbling in
> Till it becomes the quietness; and we know
> The wind to be will reach us from Loch Roe.
> From the receding South it will begin
> To stir, to whisper; and by morning all
> The sea will lounge North, sloping by Clachtoll.

One might analyze the sequence of *u* and long *e* sounds, the mild alliterations or the sibilants; yet one cannot explain away this transparently beautiful and memorably cadenced evocation, even though its devices of word music and rhythm are in themselves traditional enough. Indeed, one of MacCaig's talents as a poet is the apparent ease with which he can compose such scenes and have them seem merely an extension of ordinary speech. Asked to explain how he writes, he claims that most of his poems are "two fag poems"—composed, that is, during the time it takes to smoke two cigarettes—while quite often writing a poem takes him no longer than it would take to copy it. Often he does not make a single change and, although, not surprisingly, many poems go straight into the wastepaper basket, MacCaig claims that there is no relationship between the complexity of the poem and the speed of its composition.

Perhaps because of this poetic method some poems that are indeed ingenious but little more slip through. "Lighthouse," for instance, neat though it undoubtedly is, seems willed, an exercise in cleverness for its own sake, unlike such poems as "Culag Pier." Here, after introducing the gull that "slews in with icefloes in his eyes," MacCaig diverts the reader with thematically apt puns: "where a transcendence feeds on guts and makes/No bones of it. . . ."

MacCaig is again least successful in poems, such as "Romantic Sunset" or "Brackloch," that play solely with ideas, especially the concept of solipsism, or with ways of categorizing such things as silence or color, as he does in "Familiar." For the most part then *A Round of Applause* covers familiar territory.

Measures, which appeared in 1965, also differs more in degree than in kind from its predecessors, with metaphor not surprisingly the key indicator:

> The narrow bay
> Has a knuckle of houses and a nail of sand
> By which the sea hangs grimly to the land.
>
> A boat, deflowered
> Of its brown sail, pokes its bald pistil up,
> Fattening the seed of miles it has devoured.
> . . . .
> Around altars hung
> With holy weeds, ducks, as they skid and lurch,
> Quack soft, like laymen working in a church.

There is a similar mild ridiculing of organized religion in "Street Preacher," where "no tattered prophet" but "a rosy bourgeois" preacher howls about God every Sunday evening outside the poet's window. Another persistent motif in MacCaig poems is his skepticism about political issues, which he deflates by mocking imagery, as in "Noah by the fire":

> The fire jumps about in the grate
> Like a political agitator—
> He tries to stir us from our cold
> By burning himself up.

The poem ends: "The flames will look fine, gesticulating/Stupidly in the brand new air." What strikes one about this poem is its easy, more relaxed and playful kind of humor. But even in poems, such as "Granton," that lack these satiric aspects, the images frequently require of the reader a strong imagination that goes beyond the merely visual:

> A shunting engine butts them
> And the long line of wagons
> Abruptly pours out
> Iron drops from a bottle.

Elsewhere, in sequences such as "Movements," for instance, are poems that consist almost entirely of lists of virtuoso images:

> Lark drives invisible pitons in the air
> And hauls itself up the face of space.
> Mouse stops being comma and clockworks on
> the floor.
> Cats spill from walls. Swans undulate
> through clouds.
> Eel drills through darkness its malignant
> face.

In the same vein, some poems, such as "Betweens," turn his Neo-Apocalyptic apprenticeship to good purpose, creating a controlled surrealism for the sake of the uncanny; but other poems, such as "Environment," seem like an exuberant overflow of imagination not properly channeled, and hence fey rather than witty or charming.

Another facet of MacCaig's art, first employed in "Harris, East Side" is what seems to be an original stanza form, a tercet composed of a dimeter line followed by two pentameter lines that rhyme *abb*. He uses it three more times in this volume (in "Likenesses," "Saturday Morning," and "A Corner of the Road, Early Morning"). MacCaig seems to have been seeking alternatives to the deftly managed but rhythmically fairly limited repertoire of stanza forms and rhyme schemes that he had deployed throughout the previous ten years, and indeed such a supposition gains credence when one discovers the truncated rhyme that he experiments with in "Miracles in Working Clothes," another typical celebration of the realistic everyday:

> Not over clouds or under stones
> My homely apparitions. They gather,
> Quiet and noisy, fat and bony,
> No age at all, on any path.

As with Wilfred Owen's pararhyme, the effect here is one of dislocation and uncertainty, of jolted expectations.

Throughout all such variations, MacCaig maintains, indeed comments overtly upon, his role as poet, most explicitly perhaps in "Struck by lightning": "I in a safe place, as I always am,/Was, as I always am, observer only." In fact, one of the greatest changes that occurs gradually through the volumes published after *Measures* is MacCaig's increasingly direct involvement in his own poems. Although the dust-jacket copy for MacCaig's next book, *Surroundings* (1966), makes much of his conversion to free verse, the change is not in fact that spectacular. According to the poet himself, "at the back of every line I ever wrote [before *Surroundings*] was a ghost, a paradigm of an iambic pentameter." This statement no longer applies to poems such as "Cloud of undoing," which projects a strong sense of unobtrusively knowing just where it wants to go:

> A water splash
> On a granite stone
> Vanishes so gradually and
> So all at once
> It leaves behind it
> No smile in the air.
>
> An unravelled man
> Is spreading away
> Into disappearances.

The line breaks coincide with speech patterns so that the poem seems measured, the emphasis falling exactly on the right syllables.

Sometimes, it is true, MacCaig strikes a completely different note, as in the last two stanzas of "Pastoral," which have the monumental simplicity of ballads or folk epics:

> Let him run his fastest,
> He will not outstrip
> The slow death
> That keeps pace with him.
>
> For how many days
> Will the light darken before
> His empty cage lies, growing green
> On the green ground.

Certainly, MacCaig's abandoning of set forms has not led to any loosening of his hold on epigram. On the contrary, one feature of this book is the number of poems that deal satirically, or at least skeptically with political issues—not in any narrow partisan sense but rather with the effects of power. Thus "Progress" comments in a generalized way on the relationship between military glory and national prosperity, and "Smuggler" advises us to watch the politician

> when he opens
> His bulging words—justice,
> Fraternity, freedom, internationalism, peace,
> Peace, peace. Make it your custom
> To pay no heed
> To his frank look, his visas, his stamps
> And signatures. Make it

> Your duty to spread out their contents
> In a clear light.
>
> Nobody with such luggage
> Has nothing to declare.

"Leader of men" contrasts, though with less than his customary epigrammatic sharpness, the public and private worlds of the manipulative, ambitious politician. A similar point is made more trenchantly in fable terms by "King of Beasts":

> The only one
> There's no mistake about is
> The indifferent lion lolling
> Through the jungle in the back of
> His Rolls Royce. . . .

The same urge to epigram works to new purposes in a number of poems exploring problems of philosophy, especially aesthetics, these being again much more direct in *Surroundings* than in previous volumes. In poems such as "Not stolen but strayed" the discrete identity of observer and observed is argued at length:

> Some sorts of silence
> Embarrass me. I sing best
> Beside a waterfall or a locomotive being
> A dragon—but I don't imitate
> The waterfall or pretend
> To be a dragon. Go away, Tennyson,
> Go away every wordmonger and let
> My native vocabulary range
> Its possibility of meaning, prowling
> The familiar. . . .

The same point is made even more sharply in "Humanism," an attack mainly on the pathetic fallacy:

> What a human lie is this. What greed and what
> Arrogance, not to allow
> A glacier to be a glacier—
> To humanize into a metaphor
> That long slither of ice.

What his political and philosophical poems have in common perhaps is a greater colloquial ease, a more nonchalantly conversational tone, but it is a quality that carries over also to poems such as "Nothing so memorable," in which MacCaig compares his beloved to a trout or, rather, to the unreality of the trout's sudden leap:

A foot above the water it extravagantly
Emerged from—you remember it
A foot above the water, not coming out
Or returning to it: a still.
Can you tell me
How you manage to be an apparition
All the time?

Even if, as he states in "No word for it," "Language is a compulsive denier/Of synonyms," MacCaig cannot go far without metaphor in his efforts to make the familiar remarkable and to render the remarkable in terms of the familiar, or, as he puts it himself in "An ordinary day,"

And my mind observed to me,
Or I to it, how ordinary
Extraordinary things are or

How extraordinary ordinary
Things are, like the nature of the mind
And the process of observing.

This observation applies particularly to his three Italian poems. In "Assisi" the point is the familiar irony of tourists obediently admiring works of art that depict St. Francis's life while they ignore the contemporary hunchbacked beggars who would have received the saint's charity. In a neatly tripartite structure, "The Streets of Florence" views an interpenetration between art and life as chance faces in the street mirror those just seen in the Uffizi. "Hill streams of Abruzzi," however, shows MacCaig domesticating the foreign scene by concentrating on those aspects that have familiar counterparts in his Scottish experience:

They flow by bell-towers
Of ferocious crags,
Between murals of mountains,
Through the harsh mosaics of dead av-
                                    alanches,
They speak the world language of hill
                                    streams.

I listen and understand
That watery Esperanto—
I am
A new valley for them to flow through.

Philosophical curiosity moves beautifully through the water imagery of "Names," in MacCaig's next volume, *Rings on a Tree* (1968):

In that shallow water

swim extraordinary little fish
with extraordinary names
they don't know they've been given—
rock goby, lumpsucker, father lasher.

The same idea, but applied to flora, recurs in the second stanza; then, as so often happens with MacCaig, the particular scene opens out into the general issue of naming, before being diverted into personal relevance with the introduction of the beloved:

I know your name and who named you.
But you have selves as secret from me
as blenny or butterfish.
I sit by you and see you
with eyes ignorant as a glasswort
and I name you and name you
and wonder how it is
that the weight of your name, the most pon-
                                    derable
thing I know, should raise
my thoughts up
from one shallow pool to
another where
we move always sideways to each other, like
a velvet fiddler and a porcelain crab.

MacCaig's strongly felt conviction that there can be no complete and final knowledge of another person is one factor that constantly revivifies his love poetry. As always, it is the relationship and its effect upon the poet, rather than any single facet of the woman herself, to which MacCaig responds, both in "Names" and in the moving, and almost Roethkean, "Truth for comfort," which begins:

So much effect, and yet so much a cause—
Where things crowd close she is a space to be in:
And makes a marvel where a nowhere was.

The theme of naming recurs in "Names and their things"—"I stood with you/watching a familiar word/turn into a hickory tree"—obviously in this case, as in several other poems in *Rings on a Tree*, the result of his encounter with the New World. But there was no way that MacCaig could have assimilated and familiarized the urban jungle of New York City, so different both in scale and in intensity from his native Edinburgh, as he had done with the three Italian poems in *Surroundings*. In some cases—"Writers Conference, Long Island University" for instance—he resorts to a clever but predictable irony. Elsewhere, as in "Brooklyn Cop" or "Circle Line," his stress is on brute violence and the justifiable but by now almost-obligatory cynicism of non-Americans toward the Statue of Liberty. In "Last Night in New York" he indulges in amusing but predictable exaggeration about the city's noise, size, speed: "I plunge through constellations/and basements. My brain spins up there,/I pass it on its way down. I can't see/for the skyscraper in my eye." Only rarely, as in "The Sun comes to Earth in the Bowery" (about a dead drunk on a sidewalk), in "Hotel Room, 12th Floor" ("The frontier is never/somewhere else. And no stockades/can keep the midnight out"), and especially in "Battery Park," does he attain imaginative perspective on what he experiences:

> In the pleasant arc of the Battery, citizens
> stroll, sit, eat sandwiches
> and stare across
> the filthy water they crept out of
> millions of years ago, now chopped
> by the Staten Island ferry. . . .

Clearly MacCaig is not at ease here. He goes on to contrast the natural past and the confusing and man-made present:

> Old seamen stare across water
> at their own history. But they
> stare at a history they have
> never had and cannot
> reconstruct—where Nature
> had something to do with the colour
> green and the sound
> of clear water; where Nature
> tired muscles, not nerves; and was a wil-
> derness—
> but one where it was not so easy
> to lose your way. . . .

This more explicit treatment of history is the subject matter of another interesting poem, "Crossing the border" (that is, the border between England and Scotland), where the issues are in both senses closer to home. As the train passes ancient battlefields he thinks "of lives/bubbling into the harsh grass." The setting—"I sit with my back to the engine, watching/the landscape pouring away out of my eyes," becomes metaphorical in the last section:

> I sit with my back to the future, watching
> time pouring away into the past. I sit, being
> helplessly
> lugged backwards
> through the Debatable Lands of history.

What strikes one repeatedly wherever Mac-Caig treats large issues is his resolute concentration on concrete details, as in "Balances," which has a directness that at the time was still uncharacteristic:

> Because I see the world poisoned
> by cant and brutal self-seeking,
> must I be silent about
> the useless water-lily, the dunnock's nest
> in the hedgeback?

Two further stanzas ask analogous questions such as, "Must I love . . . not people, but only/the idea of people. . . ?" and "must a man meet only a fellow worker/and never a man?," before the final stanza's affirmation and its defiance of political ideologues and systematizers:

> There are more meanings than those
> in text books of economics
> and a part of the worst slum
> is the moon rising over it
> and eyes weeping and
> mouths laughing.

Curiously, the more overt social and political statements in this volume coexist with an increasingly playful and inventive use of language. Thus in "Rhu Mor," as if to parallel the playfulness of the imagination that sees "Gannets fall like the heads of tridents," we find a seal "struggling in the strait-waistcoat of its own skin," just as in *Surroundings* MacCaig had invented Shakespearean "micicles" to "hang by the wall" for the hunting owl.

Playfulness and self-mockery become major components in MacCaig's next book, *A Man in My Position*, which appeared in 1969. Yet, although they are attractive, its often witty and perceptive poems seem at times mildly garrulous and slighter than most of their predecessors. Still, "Uncle Roderick" is an attractive vignette:

> In the kitchen he dropped
> His oilskins where he stood.
> He was strong as the red bull.
> He moved like a dancer.
> He was a cran of songs.

MacCaig's scorn for the university's treatment of literature finds worthy expression in "Academic":

> What a job is this, to measure
> lightning with a footrule, the heart's
> turbulence with a pair of callipers.

Norman MacCaig, Sydney Goodsir Smith, Hugh MacDiarmid, Sorley MacLean, and Alastair Fowler arriving at a May 1972 Edinburgh University conference honoring MacDiarmid's eightieth birthday (The Glasgow Herald)

And what a magician, who can
dismantle Juliet, Ahab, Agamemnon
into a do-it-yourself kit
of semantic gestures.

The poet's solution is to present the academic with "a transfusion of pain." Nonetheless, and despite several remarkable observations of animals—"an owl swivelling his face like a plate" and male pigeons on the roof, "wobbling gyroscopes of lust"—there are few poems here that break new ground in subject matter or in technique. Even the long poem commissioned by BBC-TV, "A Man in Assynt," which the blurb heralds as "a new development," is not a long poem in any structural or thematic sense; indeed, MacCaig's methods of composition virtually preclude so deliberate a form. Yet it is at times an amusing, at times an angry lament for the depopulation of his beloved Western Highlands, a landscape intractable except to the elements. He asks, "Who owns this landscape?/The man who bought it or/I who am possessed by it?" and ends with a rather fragile vision of the dispossessed returning like the flood tide, "coming, at last,/into their own

again." The poem lives in its local details rather than as a whole.

One of the most interesting poems, "The Unlikely," shows MacCaig in his role as preacher—a very good preacher:

We like the unlikely. It's good
that the boundaries of the normal should be
widened.
It means—how many things there are still to
be noticed!

We like the unlikely. The terrible thing is
we like it, too, when it's terrible.
When the quiet clerk poisons his family,
when the doctor says Cancer, when the tanks
clank on the innocent frontier,
inside the fear, the rage and the horror
a tiny approval smirks, ashamed of itself.

That tiny approval has murdered more
people
than Genghis Khan. It widened the boundaries of the normal
with the explosion over Hiroshima.

> That means—how many things there are still
>   to be suffered!

This voice is among those that persist into Mac-Caig's most recent work. The structural use of a repeated phrase with slight variations—in this case "That means—how many things there are still to be noticed" and later ". . . to be suffered"—parallels MacCaig's use of incremental imagery elsewhere.

Such quasi refrains become even more prominent in his next book, *The White Bird* (1973); indeed, the threefold repetition of the phrase "No need, I say to myself" is the main structural device of the title poem. Noticeable too is a tentative return to three- or four-line stanzas, frequently rhymed. MacCaig's imagery continues to move in two totally opposed directions. One is toward the fanciful, or "dictionary of miracles," as MacCaig calls it in "Return," a poem that also includes the lines "It was a night for fat marrows/to forage grunting through the blackberry thickets,/for the moon to be singing/Ophelia songs. . . ." The other is toward more realistic sights and sounds, as in "Gulls on a Hill Loch," which attempts to render the effect of the gulls' "impossible language":

> like the cries a shell would make,
> or a corkscrew singing in the morning,
> or the leading contralto in a choir of
>   tombstones,
> or a shell-less egg, or a terrified slate.

Yet even this poem ends with typically witty and fanciful visual images of "eight swallows clothes-pegged on a telephone wire/and the village bull, as usual, pretending to be Jove."

In contrast, "Ugly Corner" or "A Sort of Eden" seems to exist solely as idea. The imagery is not specific enough, and intellectual concepts are not imaginatively worked through into sufficiently concrete detail. In other cases such details seem arbitrary, as in "Musical Moment in Assynt," where the poet makes a series of analogies between various mountains and specific composers' works or styles of music. Even "Bookworm," which builds on the fanciful, even at times almost cute conceit of "reading" Nature in the same way that one reads books, exists primarily as idea. The idea overwhelms the detail in "the second volume/of a rose" or "the Gothic script/of pine trees."

Perhaps one may generalize by saying that when MacCaig's poems fail, it is frequently for the same reason that the metaphysicals' poems sometimes failed—because the conceit has taken over, allowing ingenuity rather than aptness to dominate. At the same time, in a number of poems in *The White Bird*, image and concept combine so neatly as to become a kind of epigram. The first stanza of "Tree hung with fairy lights" reaches an epigrammatic conclusion:

> It's not additions but extensions give
> A thing its further self,
> Changed from within:
> Blossom's a sort of leaf, as nail is skin.

Then, however, the poem changes direction, as the speaker decides "But decoration contradicts the tree" and tells his lover that he loves her best "When clothed in nothing but your altered dust." The presence of another "long poem," "Inward Bound," confirms the impression given by "A Man in Assynt": despite some effective passages of nostalgic reminiscence—with occasional suggestions of the Dylan Thomas of "Fern Hill" in lines such as "I was a millionaire of sunlight and summer winds"—the poem states MacCaig's hostility to myth and advocates his realism:

> I can't make myths I can't make fables.
> When I try to invent one
> a true crow swallows real cheese
> and a real fox
> doesn't like grapes anyway.

Another poem in *The White Bird*, "Old Maps and New," most sharply foreshadows the direction of MacCaig's subsequent volumes. After dealing with early maps, on which much of the as yet unexplored globe was filled in with imaginary creatures, the concluding stanza voices a darker and more explicit distrust in mankind's fate:

> though these days it's only
> in the explored territories
> that men write, sadly,
> Here live monsters.

The realm of monsters is apparent in several poems of *The World's Room* (1974), especially in poems such as "Progress," where "the idea became/a myth" and "grew teeth/and iron wings." Like Auden in "Musée des Beaux Arts," MacCaig stresses the normalcy of what is happening—the phrase "everything was as usual" recurs three times—but in MacCaig's poem it is not a single death that is involved:

And legs arms heads were buried
in the rubble of cities. Great minds
rotted black. And everything
was as usual, everything wept beside
an endless column of refugees.
And good minds said No, good minds
kept saying No. And the word
created a silence round it
and was heard by no-one.

The personal counterpart to such poems is to be
found in "Private," where he ponders removing his
public mask and concludes that, if he did so,

How they would grieve for
that comfortable MacCaig whose
small predictions were predictable.
How they would wish back
the clean white bandages
that hid these ugly wounds.

Yet despite such presences, the volume contains
memorable love poems and further delightful bird
vignettes. A kind of crazy balance is kept between
personal and universal. As he says in "Understanding,"

Everything spoke you; for you are the word
to which all other words are a footnote.

It was an evening, one of the many
when your meaning was all the others'
and love and pity were the O in the graph
of the world's loneliness, of wars, and disasters.

What cannot be balanced out, now or subsequently,
are the changes that time brings, especially the
death of friends. Similarly, "Stag in a neglected
hayfield" observes a classical decorum that unobtrusively blends realistic detail with the most ancient
of literary symbols to evoke a sense of seasons
crossgrained with awareness of personal loss.

MacCaig has said he is glad that the poems of
the past ten years have been moving toward more
overt and specified emotion, especially regarding
the death of friends: "That's what did it. It shook
me. I've been awfully lucky. I survived two world
wars and I never saw a corpse until my parents died.
It was just an abstraction to me." Nothing is more
important than friendship to him, and MacCaig's
living room is hung with the signed photographs of,
among others, those six close friends who all died
during the 1970s, among them Hugh MacDiarmid,
Sydney Goodsir Smith, and Angus MacLeod, to

whose memory MacCaig's next volume, *Tree of
Strings* (1977) was dedicated.

From the opening line of "Stars and
planets"—to its final stanza, a sharper tone is
noticeable:

It's hard to think that the earth is one—
This poor sad bearer of wars and disasters
Rolls-Roycing round the sun with its load of
gangsters,
Attended only by the loveless moon.

In "A Sigh for Simplicity" MacCaig mockingly regrets his own passion for metaphors and similes, but
what is most striking about this volume is perhaps
less MacCaig's ability to create metaphors than his
skill in perceiving and orchestrating analogies, as in
"Notes on a winter journey, and a footnote," occasioned by the death of MacLeod:

At Inchnadamph snow is falling. The wind-
screen wipers
squeak and I stare through
a segment of a circle. What more do I ever do?
. . . .
(Seventeen miles to go. I didn't know it, but
when
I got there a death waited for me—that segment
shuts its fan; and a blinding winter closed in.)

MacLeod's death provided the impetus for two
other poems that are direct and simple. "Finality"
concludes:

The places of the world
can be visited
and the people in them.

But he's in a nowhere
without journeys, without places,
without him.

Yet these poems are made no less moving by the fact
that they do not overshadow the rest of the volume.
Part of the book's spareness and incisiveness is due
to the poems' shorter lines and perhaps also to the
increasingly taut way in which the poet presents or
juxtaposes imagery. In "Notations of ten summer
minutes,"

The schoolmaster stands looking out of the window
with one Latin eye and one Greek one.
A boat rounds the point in Gaelic.

MacCaig's self-accusation of solipsism in "Convicted" has him "admiring/the shadows of the bars/on the floor of my cell." "1800 feet up" makes a similar charge of aestheticism, ironically, in the form of a literary epigram:

> The flower—it didn't know it—
> was called dwarf cornel.
> I found this out by enquiring.
>
> Now I remember the name
> but have forgotten the flower.
>
> —The curse of literacy.

"Means Test" is one of many epigrams that starts from taking a common figurative phrase literally. Of the "stony look" he is given the poet asks, "Are you water? or diamond? I prefer things shifting/And lucid, not locked in a hard design." Then in the final stanza he asks the donor of the look to turn to him and let him know "If I'm a millionaire/of water or a pauper of diamonds."

Altogether in this volume there is a noticeable increase in the kind of metaphor that is contained in the verb, another feature that makes for intensity and conciseness. Thus water "skulks/through the cracks in rocks,/jemmying them open"; the kingfisher is "jewelling upstream"; the bar is "fire-flied with whiskey glasses"; the daddy longlegs "helicopters about the room."

In another writer it might be surprising to find, in a book so shaken by death, so many titles beginning "Praise of . . ." (a boat, a collie, a thorn bush, a road), so many vignettes evoking animals, small lochs (treated with the same kind of affection as the animals), music or love. But that kind of Protean ability to turn everything he encounters or reads about into the raw material of poetry is precisely what one has come to expect from MacCaig: he is so serious about relating everything to everything else that he has no time for solemnity.

Something of this attitude is to be found also in the opening section of MacCaig's next book, *The Equal Skies* (1980), with its twelve "Poems for Angus" (two republished from the previous volume). "Highland funeral," for instance, describes the frozen air over the dead man's house as "a scrawny psalm/I believed in, because it was pagan/as he was." The minister's voice, by contrast, "spread a pollution of bad beliefs." A year later the dead have proved able to help because "that sanctimonious voice is silent and the pagan/Landscape is sacred in a new way." Yet the accep-

tance of the physical death is final, involving a clear-eyed exploration of what he terms elsewhere "the desolate landscape of loss" and an uncompromising refusal to take comfort in any afterlife. In "A month after his death" the friends laughing and singing are all "thinking/of the one who isn't here":

> The laughter and the singing are paper flow-
>   ers
> laid on a wet grave in an empty darkness.
> For we all know we're thinking
> of the one who can't be here,
> not even as a ghost smiling through the black
>   window.

"Triple Burden" envisages the poet's own death with a similar resignation and in the most natural of images: "For a boat has sailed into/the sea of unknowing;/you are on board./And somewhere another boat/rocks/by another pier./It's waiting to take me/where I'll never know you again—/a voyage/beyond knowledge, beyond memory." This classic reticence that can speak of the strongest emotions, of grief and love, calmly and without self-indulgence, reaches a high point in "From his house door":

> I say to myself, How he enriched my life.
> And I say to myself, More than he have died,
> He's not the only one.
>
> I look at the estuary and see
> a gravel bank and a glitter going through it
> and the stealthy tide, black-masked,
> drowning stone after stone.

In the remainder of the poems in *The Equal Skies* the externals of the contemporary world enter his subject matter as never before. Thus, in the poem "Little Boy Blue" MacCaig asks, "have you been listening to the news/on the telly?—are you taking/industrial action?" MacCaig is well aware of what he is doing and of its possible pitfalls; in "One of my difficulties," he acknowledges,

> The danger is flippancy. I demand of myself
> the discipline of discipline, the bible thump
> of solemnity, the white yashmak
> of the surgeon making the first incision.
>
> But what can a camera do when it's peering
> down the horn of a cornucopia where Catullus
> skids his Honda to a halt at the door
> of the heavenly Bingo hall?

Along with MacCaig's new departures into the popular, there is a darker attitude toward some of his habitual subject matter. While some of his poems of natural description, such as "Cormorants Nesting," retain the old, untroubled affection, others, such as "Toad"—"A jewel in your head? Toad,/you've put one in mine,/a tiny radiance in a dark place"—seem now to minister to MacCaig's spiritual condition, an office that they did not overtly perform before. So too, in "Real life Christmas Card," instead of being content to evoke by human analogies the robin's characteristics, MacCaig makes other human parallels explicit: "You sing your robin song, I my man song. They're different,/but they mean the same: winter, territory, greed." The same applies to a poem such as "Me as traveller," where for almost the first time he discusses specific aspects of his autobiography, in the end settling for his own "one small part" of Scotland:

> America, Italy, Canada, I rested on you
> briefly as a butterfly and returned
> to suck the honey of Assynt
> and want no more, though that honey
> has three bitternesses in it, three deaths
> more foreign to me
> than the other side of space.

As the last poem in this book makes clear, MacCaig's journeys now are toward his own death, about which he remains ambivalent:

> There are other bad journeys, to a bitter place
> I can't get to—yet. I lean towards it,
> tugging to get there, and thank God
> I'm clogged with the world. It grips me,
> I hold it.

But the mood of this volume is perhaps best summed up by "Equilibrist," which is concerned with surviving the deaths of friends:

> Noticing you can do nothing about.
> It's the balancing that shakes my mind.
>
> What my friends don't notice
> is the weight of joy in my right hand
> and the weight of sadness in my left.
> All they see is MacCaig being upright,
> . . . .
> easy-oasy and jocose.

Self-mockery, ever-present in MacCaig's mature work, is now joined by the sardonic: in the same

poem he comments, "I switch the radio/from tortures in foreign prisons/to a sonata of Schubert (that foreigner)," while in "The Kirk" he asks, "Haven't the people learned yet that God/is an absentee landlord?" "Report to the Clan," a new use of MacCaig's epigrammatic skills, gives an unusual view of man:

> His skin is in tatters,
> he can't climb trees. He burns things
> before he eats them! His face
> is shiny, his feet have no toes.
> Run, brothers, run
> from this visitor from the past!
>
> This was said by
> the first ape that saw Darwin.

Yet, true to the image of "Equilibrist," MacCaig's ironic sense preserves proportion and recognizes wherever possible conflicting claims. Thus in "Intruder in a set scene," the little girl, "five years of self-importance" walking on the canal tow path in her own season, is oblivious both of the derelict swan's nest and to her mother's tears as she reads a letter.

In *A World of Difference* (1983) MacCaig's justifiable pessimism about the world has turned in some poems, such as "A New Age," into a withering irony directed not only toward those who commit atrocities but also against those in the Church who accept such atrocities as God's mercies:

> When the barbarians came, things were better.
> They even let us wear our clothes
> when we went into the gas chambers.
> And what gratitude we felt
> when they killed the mothers before
> they killed their babies and when they blew off
> the head of the Holy Prelate
> without gouging his eyes out first.
> . . . .
> We even revived the art of prayer. *O Lord*, we
> prayed,
> *we thank Thee for Thy present mercies,*
> *we thank Thee for leading us forth*
> *from the dark ages of civilisation.*

Although MacCaig himself seems well aware that Clio, in the poem of that name, "has long since failed to be amused/by irony, truth, lies, murder/and suicide," that knowledge does not prevent him from striking some shrewd blows of his own. Some are aimed at perennial enemies. In "Two Thieves" for instance, the first thief is the sea, which has claimed fifty yards of what was once "a smooth green sward" where the second thief, the Duke of Sutherland, "turned his coach and six." The point again is the greed-driven depopulation of the Highlands:

> There were fine strong men in the Duke's time.
> He drove them to the shore, he drove them
> to Canada. He gave no friendly thought to them
> as he turned his coach and six
> on the sweet green sward
> by the Place for Pulling up Boats
> where no boats are.

Other poems target his more recent adversary, Death (whom he refers to in "Old Man" as a cruel "playboy king capering and giggling yet again/at his one bad joke") or almost more bitterly, in "Trapped," deride man the inventor "frantic with admiration/for the grey mess inside his skull," who invented an afterlife "and can't wait/to go into it" but who has not yet invented "a way of inventing/his afterself." In the same vein, "To a dead friend" restates MacCaig's refusal to accept "a comforting fantasy," while "Recipe," a formula for survival, ends bleakly:

> And you must learn there are words
> with no meaning, words like *consolation*,
> words like *goodbye*.

There are still poems about the animal kingdom, of course, but now more frequently than before it is seen in a darker, human context: in "The first of them" the poet expresses sympathy for the snake in Eden:

> Poor snake. He crawls on his belly
> dropping amber tears in the dust and whining
> *I was only obeying orders.*

and in "Outsider" he feels envy for thrush, newt, and gannet in that they live in "a free world, a world without hypocrisy, without masks./Cramped with humanity, I envy them." As for himself, there is only the calm resignation of "Every Day":

> What's that cart that nobody sees
> grinding along the shore road?
>
> Whose is the horse that pulls it, the white horse
> that bares its yellow teeth to the wind?

> They turn, unnoticed by anyone,
> into the field of slanted stones.
>
> My friends meet me. They lift me from the cart and,
> the greetings over, we go smiling underground.

Paralleling this directness of approach is a new colloquial ease. Since his rhetorical New Apocalypse stage MacCaig has never stood on his poetic dignity, but in *A World of Difference* he has even become slangy, as in "Go away, Ariel":

> Supersonic Ariel, go zip round the world
> or curl up in a cowslip's bell.
> I'd rather be visited by Caliban.
> ....
> Phone a bat, Ariel. Leave us
> to have a good cry—to stare at each other
> with recognition and loathing.

Yet this volume contains more references to figures from classical mythology—Circe, Daedalus, and Hermes, for example—than any other volume of MacCaig's poems, though treated, as one would expect from MacCaig, from unexpected angles and without the customary afflatus. Perhaps, after all, it is these classical shades and the decades he spent on teaching them that provide the basis for that air of sturdy independence and equanimity that he maintains even in the presence of so much death and disintegration at both a personal and an international level.

MacCaig's oeuvre, then, if it appears to lack acknowledged single masterpieces, has consistently, since the mid-1950s, maintained an astonishingly high standard both in its technical finesse and in its unwavering human concerns. He has established himself not as the leader of any school of poetry—indeed, such an idea would probably be repugnant to him—but rather as a wry and independent-minded observer of, and meditator on, the human and the natural scene who frequently conflates the two. If the poet of the last few volumes is more informal, he is also whittled and bleaker, but always clear-eyed and rarely without the saving grace of wit. It is premature to forecast any final place for MacCaig in the English-language poetry of this century, especially as his skills and poetic strengths have not been among the most fashionable, but whatever his place may be, it will have been earned largely by his steadfastness in "the long haul to lucidity."

Roland Mathias

(4 September 1915-   )

Michael J. Collins
Georgetown University

BOOKS: *Break in Harvest and Other Poems* (London: Routledge, 1946);

The Roses of Tretower (Llandysul, Wales: Dock Leaves Press, 1952);

The Eleven Men of Eppynt and Other Stories (Pembroke Dock, Wales: Dock Leaves Press, 1956);

The Flooded Valley (London: Putnam's, 1960);

Whitsun Riot: An Account of a Commotion Amongst Catholics in Herefordshire and Monmouthshire in 1605 (London: Bowes & Bowes, 1963);

Absalom in the Tree (Llandysul, Wales: Gwasg Gomer, 1971);

Vernon Watkins (Cardiff: University of Wales Press, 1974);

Snipe's Castle (Llandysul, Wales: Gomer Press, 1979);

The Hollowed-Out Elder Stalk: John Cowper Powys as Poet (London: Enitharmon Press, 1979);

Burning Brambles: Selected Poems 1944-1979 (Llandysul, Wales: Gomer Press, 1983).

RECORDING: *Poets of Wales*, by Mathias and others (Argo PLP 1201, 1975).

OTHER: *The Shining Pyramid and Other Stories by Welsh Authors*, edited by Mathias and Sam Adams (Llandysul, Wales: Gwasg Gower, 1970);

David Jones: Eight Essays on His Work as Writer and Artist, edited by Mathias (Llandysul, Wales: Gomer Press, 1976);

"Literature in English," in *The Arts in Wales: 1950-75*, edited by Meic Stephens (Cardiff: Welsh Arts Council, 1979), pp. 207-238;

Anglo-Welsh Poetry 1480-1980, edited by Mathias and Raymond Garlick (Bridgend, Wales: Poetry Wales Press, 1984).

PERIODICAL PUBLICATIONS: "A Niche for Dylan Thomas," *Poetry Wales*, 9 (Autumn 1973): 51-74;

" 'The Black Spot in The Focus': A Study of the Poetry of Alun Lewis," *Anglo-Welsh Review*, no. 67 (1980): 43-78;

"David Jones—Towards the 'Holy Diversities,' "

Transactions of the Honourable Society of Cymmrodorion (1981): 137-178;

"Channels of Grace: A View of the Earlier Novels of Emyr Humphreys," *Anglo-Welsh Review*, no. 70 (1982): 64-88.

On 31 August 1969, four days before his fifty-fourth birthday, Roland Mathias resigned as headmaster of King Edward's Five Ways School in Birmingham and moved back to Wales, where he had been born. "I returned to live in Wales," he has said, "because there is nowhere else that a Welshman for whom the history and traditions of Wales mean a great deal can live. It was partly nostalgia, I suppose, but partly necessity too. My whole life had been pointing in that direction. . . . I felt I could best serve Wales by living there." Roland Mathias was not alone in his move from England to Wales (a number of important Anglo-Welsh writers moved at about the same time), and it was motivated, as he has suggested, by a commitment to Wales, by the desire to work, so far as possible, for the preservation of the distinct culture and heritage of his country. His "yearning affinity for Wales," as he calls it in a brief essay on Edward Thomas, has, to a large extent, shaped his career as a writer and made him not just a distinguished poet, but one of the two or three most important and influential interpreters of the Anglo-Welsh literary tradition.

Roland Glyn Mathias was born at Ffynnon Fawr, a farm five miles from Talybont-on-Usk, in Breconshire, a largely rural Welsh county on the border of England. He attended Caterham School in Surrey, where he was senior prefect of the school and editor of its magazine. He entered Jesus College, Oxford, as a commoner in October 1933, was awarded a Meyricke Exhibition in modern history in March 1934, and became an honorary scholar of the College as a result of his bachelor of arts examination. He received a B.A. with honors in modern history in 1936, a B.Litt. in February 1939 for a thesis on "The Economic Policy of the Board of Trade 1696-1714," and an M.A. in 1944. His interest in history has continued throughout his life. He has written a historical study called *Whitsun Riot: An Account of a Commotion Amongst Catholics in Herefordshire and Monmouthshire in 1605* (1963), and his love of history has shaped both his poetry and his criticism. In discussing his earlier poems, written for the most part outside of Wales, he has said that "it was always of tremendous importance to me to know exactly *where* I was and what mood the place engendered in me. People might help to form that mood but the moment of ignition was always (or almost always) produced by solitude, the particular place and the history of men in that place."

In 1938 Roland Mathias began his career as a schoolmaster at the Cowley School in St. Helens, Lancashire. Writing years later about his friendship with Vernon Watkins, he said, "My meetings with poets or literary personages of any kind have been, until very recently, infrequent. I have lived in a different world." Except for a period in 1941 when he was imprisoned as a conscientious objector, he

worked as a schoolmaster for thirty-one years in various schools until he resigned in 1969 to become a full-time writer in Wales. He married Mary (Molly) Hawes on 4 April 1944. During his tenure in the schools, he was a headmaster for twenty-one years first at The Grammar School in Pembroke, Wales (1948-1958), then at The Herbert Strutt School in Belper, Derbyshire (1958-1964), and finally at King Edward's Five Ways School in Birmingham (1964-1969). He was elected schoolmaster-fellow of Balliol College, Oxford, in 1961, and of University College, Swansea, in 1967. Since his resignation in 1969 he has continued to teach and has served as a part-time lecturer for the university colleges of Cardiff, Swansea, and Aberystwyth. He has also been a visiting lecturer at the universities of Rennes and Brest (1970) and at the University of Alabama in Birmingham (1971).

Roland Mathias is, among writers in English, the most distinguished man of letters in Wales today. He has written a collection of short stories, *The Eleven Men of Eppynt and Other Stories* (1956), and five books of poetry, the last two of which, *Absalom in the Tree* (1971) and *Snipe's Castle* (1979), won Welsh Arts Council Prizes for Poetry in 1972 and 1980. He has written important and influential critical pieces on nearly all the major Anglo-Welsh writers, and he served, from 1961 until 1976, as editor of the *Anglo-Welsh Review*, a magazine he established with Raymond Garlick and others as *Dock Leaves* in 1949. One of the founders of the English Language Section of *Yr Academi Gymreig* (the Academy of Welsh Writers), he was its chairman from 1975 to 1978. In 1968 he received a Welsh Arts Council award for his services to writing in Wales and in 1969 a Welsh Arts Council bursary to assist his transition to full-time writing. He was for three and a half years Chairman of the Literature Committee of the Welsh Arts Council. As his career over the last forty years suggests, Roland Mathias's work as a man of letters has been integrally connected with Wales, and he has struggled in various ways to develop and nurture an Anglo-Welsh literary tradition for the English-speaking Welsh and to preserve for all of Wales its distinct culture and heritage.

When Mathias replaced Raymond Garlick as editor of the *Anglo-Welsh Review*, he "was trying," he has said, "to create a complete spectrum of Welsh interests in English—not merely in literature but in all the humanities—because it was something *not realized* in the mind of English speakers. . . . I tried to build *The Anglo-Welsh Review* up in terms of its contacts and contributors so that it was a kind of symbol of unity of interest." The editorials he wrote, while varied and wide-ranging, reflect his concern for the preservation and understanding of the heritage of Wales. Looking back in the late 1970s over the history of the *Anglo-Welsh Review*, he explained that "it became the policy . . . to offer a conspectus of the arts in Wales and in particular to give review coverage to every significant book of Welsh interest written in English."

As a literary critic, while working to define and preserve the Anglo-Welsh literary tradition, he has also realized that "there is a sense in which there never has been an Anglo-Welsh literary tradition, any more than there has been one nation in Wales, and I have felt it necessary to identify, to draw together, in a way to create." Having written widely, intelligently, sensitively about the literature in English by Welshmen and women, he has attempted, in part because of his interest in history, "to understand the poet or prose writer *in his times*" and, as his criticism suggests, in his place. "The basic fault," he has said, "is to imagine that one can deal with a text *in vacuo*, even if one does manage to identify what the poet means to say. The validity of that meaning can only be judged satisfactorily against an understanding of the society that produced it." His own poetry, written over a period of more than forty years, makes as clear as that of any of his contemporaries, the importance of place in Anglo-Welsh literature.

Mathias brought out his first collection of poems, *Break in Harvest and Other Poems*, in 1946, and he has continued, in the midst of all his other activities, to write increasingly distinguished poetry that is generally marked by a concern with Wales, with history and particularly Welsh history, with the connection between past and present, and with the individual's relationship to all these things. As the reviewer of *Break in Harvest* wrote in the *Times Literary Supplement*, the "poetry is rooted in place, it attempts to convey the feeling of a real world, which is, however, a local world, and a world of habitual intimate experience."

The poem that opens the volume, "The Bearers," affirms the importance of place in the poems that follow. After describing, in the first stanza, the field in which he stands, the speaker suggests its impact upon him:

> Yet I am home
> With handgrip, knowing
> Something there is that turns me to the hills,
> Some bowel-moving look about me tills
> The body going
> To growth. I am turned bonewards in this
> loam.

The poems that follow often draw their strength, as the review in the *Times Literary Supplement* recognized, from the "landscape of Wales," and while the poems transcend their "local habitation," they nevertheless are shaped and nourished by it. As Mathias puts it in a poem called "Grace Before Work," "Each has his earth and mulches in it good./O backbreak past, share in the present's food."

Mathias's second collection of poems, *The Roses of Tretower* with illustrations by Eric Peyman, appeared in 1952 to fulfill what the *Times Literary Supplement* review had called the "solid promise" of *Break in Harvest*. The thirty-seven poems in *The Roses of Tretower* are marked by a wide range of theme and manner. The title poem is a long ballad set on a hill farm in Wales. A dialect poem, "A Letter," is the marriage proposal of an unnamed speaker to Ellen Skone, a widow with whom he quarreled eight years before. "Craswall" and "Argyle Street," two poems about particular places, are lyric meditations on the cultural and economic depression of contemporary Wales. "The Flooded Valley," the poem that would give its title to Mathias's next collection, mourns the displacement of a farmer from Glyn Collwng, the valley of the poet's birth, and its conversion, by flooding, to a reservoir. The Welsh critic Raymond Garlick has called the poem "one of the most vigorous . . . to come out of modern Breconshire."

The Flooded Valley, published in 1960, included both new poems and the best from *The Roses of Tretower*. The reviewer for the *Times Literary Supplement* wrote that although their "immediate attraction . . . is the exact imagist portrayal of Welsh town and country scenes. . . , the use of such clear descriptive power is not an end in itself," but rather the means by which the poet can express his bleak vision of the world. Writing ten years later about the new poems in *The Flooded Valley*, Jeremy Hooker said, "Nowhere is Roland Mathias's ability to evoke the past more vividly realized than in 'Orielton Empty' and 'Cascob.' In each poem vital physical impressions of place serve to establish a strong sense of the period associated with it." One of the best new poems in the volume, "For Warren Davies, two years dead," is a long elegy that celebrates, in an appropriately vibrant tone, the speaker's dead friend:

> How best remember? Shipwright you, quiet, wry
> As a hawk, a viking-cast dropped out of conquest,
> Averse from talk most when there were gabbers by
> And jawed like Magnus at the holocaust.

In his two most recent volumes of poetry, *Absalom in the Tree*, published in 1971, and *Snipe's Castle*, published in 1979, Roland Mathias has continued to grapple with his own relation to the past and present of Wales. "Departure in Middle Age," a poem from the earlier collection, for example, recalls the adult speaker's childhood and suggests his sense of alienation from the place of his birth.

The strength of the poem comes largely from its figures of speech. The one that ends the first stanza ("strange to myself as a stepfather encountered/For the first time in the passage from the front door") makes simultaneously clear the comforting familiarity the place once had for him and the now disturbing, even frightening alienation he feels in what was once home. The figure of speech that begins the second stanza ("plump up the pillow and shape/My sickness like courage") suggests a child in his sickbed, on a day home from school, eased in his illness by family, familiar toys on the bed, visiting friends, and it contrasts with the isolated adult, shivering alone in the dark, disturbed by the river whose sound he was once presumably accustomed to and perhaps comforted by. The final metaphor ("exile is the parcel I carry") evokes beautifully an image of the departing visitor and emphasizes the sad paradox of his life. It is not the gray, cloudy day that makes his departure bleak: as the mountains around his valley suggest, he is an exile in both his homes—the place he was born and the place he now lives.

While "Departure in Middle Age," as Mathias puts it, "was intended as a personal poem, reflecting (with some internal anger) upon the inevitable diminution of grief and its replacement by a kind of indifferent despair," it suggests as well the plight in Wales of those English-speaking men and women who have felt cut off both from their Welsh heritage and from the largely English world in which they live and work. "They Have Not Survived," in *Absalom in the Tree*, describes the historical migration of poor farmers to the mining valleys of Wales and their subsequent failure to improve their own or their children's economic condition. But the poem ends with a question suggesting that the speaker feels his own success in the English-speaking world may be a betrayal of his nation, his heritage, and his people:

> Why am I unlike
> Them, alive and jack in office,
> Shrewd among the plunderers?

The rhythm of these last lines and the use of the

Dust jacket for Mathias's 1979 book, his fifth volume of poetry. Mathias has commented that, in writing poems, "I have to wait for my creative energy to top up, so to speak—and the poem that is waiting often has to signal for some time before it gets itself written."

phrase "jack in office" suggest that the speaker has learned the language of survival (both the language of the English and a kind of knowing slang) and, as a salesman of himself, has indeed made his way, shrewdly and somewhat selfishly, in the English-speaking world.

He treats much the same theme in a more complex poem in *Snipe's Castle*, "Memling," which is written in blank verse. Here again, the source of the poem is historical, but this time it is not the history of Wales, but of fifteenth-century Europe. Hans Memling, the poem reminds us, was a German (born in Seligenstadt near Frankfurt am Main), an outsider who found wealth, recognition, and respectability as an artist in the Flemish city of Bruges. And yet, the poem suggests, this successful burgher-artist saw in the story of Ursula, a Welsh saint martyred at Cologne in the third or fourth century, something of himself and his national history. As Ursula was ravished by the Huns, Memling, himself a German, was, by his own choices, ravished—culturally, as an artist—by the Flemish world which he served with great success and of which he became a prosperous, respectable citizen. In making the reliquary, which depicts the life and martyrdom of Saint Ursula, he sought to reveal some part of himself and "to exorcise" his sense of ancestral guilt.

"The history we choose speaks largely of ourselves." The last line of "Memling" (which suggests the way Mathias often uses history and the relationship of the poem to some of his other work) refers not just to Memling, but to the speaker as well. "Alive and jack in office/Shrewd among plunderers," yet conscious of his Welsh heritage, the Anglo-Welsh speaker is alienated both from his Welsh-speaking countrymen and the Anglicized world in which he lives. He too has been ravished and has lost, with his culture and his language, the stuff out of which his art should be made. And like Memling, he feels a sense of guilt, for not only does he fail the heritage he would affirm and conserve, he also, through his work as an artist in the English-speaking world, cooperates in its ravishment and hastens its destruction. While "it is all/Safely transposed, the ravisher and the ravished" are one.

As he explained in a lecture on Anglo-Welsh literature at Fordham University in 1978, Mathias, like many of his contemporaries, has had to work back and possess by deliberate effort his Welsh heritage. And yet for him the feeling of alienation persists, as does the fear that such effort is ultimately doomed to failure and "a kind of grief that a loved society or way of life is dying." In the last stanza of "Porth Cwyfan," in *Snipe's Castle*, as he returns from visiting an island chapel said to have been built by the little-known saint for whom the place is named, the speaker encounters a family of tourists:

> A man on the beach, a woman
> And child with a red woollen cap,
> Hummock and stop within earshot,
> Eyeing my blundering walk. "Can
> We get to the island?" he asks, Lanchashire
> Accent humble, dark curls broad. And I
> Am suddenly angry. But how is my tripright
>   sounder,
> Save that I know Roger Parry and he does
>   not?

The question that ends the poem suggests the speaker's doubts about his ever being more than a tourist himself in Wales. While he has done the work, learned the history, knows the life of Roger Parry, an obscure historical figure who was buried near the chapel at the beginning of the nineteenth century, he may finally be no more Welsh than the man from Lancashire.

The alienation and grief the speaker feels are, in the cultural and linguistic depression of Wales, shared by many. In a long and beautifully written poem in *Snipe's Castle*, "Brechfa Chapel," the speaker has evidence that a community of culture and belief has passed away. After describing in the long first stanza the terrain and water birds around the place, he turns his attention, in the second stanza, to the chapel itself. The chapel no longer draws men and women into a community or provides, as it did in the past, a place where the distinct culture of Wales is preserved. The farmers now come "singly" to the chapel and "keep counsel." The "militant brabble" of the modern world, represented by the noisy water birds, has fragmented the old community of believers. A consciously shared faith and a shared heritage (traditionally interconnected through the nonconformist churches in Wales) are now impossible. Each must find for himself, individually, what a communal belief and culture once provided—a way of making sense of things and giving significance to his life.

While these more or less personal poems in his most recent collections suggest Roland Mathias's central concerns as a poet, they do not finally make clear the full range of his work. *Absalom in the Tree*, for example, includes two fine dramatic monologues—the title poem and "For Jenkin Jones," whose speaker is the poet Henry Vaughan. *Snipe's Castle* contains "Madoc," a long verse play of voices commissioned by the BBC in 1971 and based on the story of Madoc's reputed voyage to America and the subsequent reports of a tribe of Welsh Indians in what is now North Dakota; "Tide-Reach: A Sequence of Pembrokeshire Poems written for Music," the libretto for a cantata by David Harries; and another dramatic monologue, "Sir Gelli to R. S.," the imagined response of a late sixteenth-century Welshman to a poem by R. S. Thomas. As Peter Elfed Lewis wrote in a review of *Snipe's Castle* in *Poetry Wales*, Roland Mathias has "considerable range in various kinds of poetic forms, long and short, dramatic and lyrical." He is, to put it simply, a skilled and distinguished poet.

Roland Mathias's career as a writer has been integrally connected with the progress, over the last thirty or forty years, of Welsh literature in English.

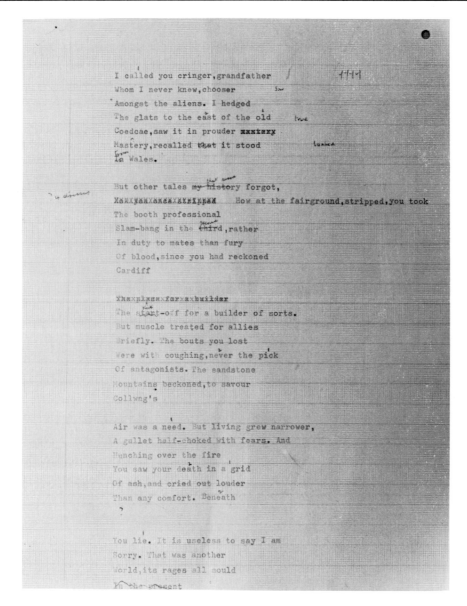

Page from the second draft for "A Kind of Expiation" (the author)

As a critic and editor, he has contributed significantly to the recognition and understanding of the Anglo-Welsh literary tradition. His generosity and encouragement to individual writers and critics are widely acknowledged in Wales. Simultaneously, with all the demands on his time and energy, he has produced five volumes of increasingly distinguished poetry, and as the recently published collected edition suggests, he has come to be recognized as one of the best poets writing in Wales today, one whose work deserves a wider audience than it has had so far. Mathias's achievements as a writer and his inordinately generous service to Wales and its literature in English have made him, among English-speaking writers, the most distinguished man of letters in Wales today.

References:

Jeremy Hooker, "The Poetry of Roland Mathias," *Poetry Wales*, 7 (Summer 1971): 6-13;

Glyn Jones, *The Dragon Has Two Tongues* (London: Dent, 1968), pp. 138-139;

Jones, "Poetry in Wales," *British Poetry Since 1960*, edited by Michael Schmidt and Grevel Lindop (Oxford: Carcanet Press, 1972), pp. 125-127.

Edwin Morgan

(27 April 1920-   )

Alan Young

SELECTED BOOKS: *The Vision of Cathkin Braes and Other Poems* (Glasgow: Maclellan, 1952);

The Cape of Good Hope (Tunbridge Wells: Peter Russell, 1955);

Starryveldt (Frauenfeld [Switzerland]: Eugen Gomringer Press, 1965);

Scotch mist (Cleveland, Ohio: Renegade Press, 1965);

emergent poems (Stuttgart: Edition Hansjörg Mayer, 1967);

gnomes (Preston: Akros Publications, 1968);

The Second Life (Edinburgh: Edinburgh University Press, 1968);

Proverbfolder (Corsham, Wiltshire: Openings Press, 1969);

Penguin Modern Poets 15, by Morgan, Alan Bold, and Edward Braithwaite (Harmondsworth: Penguin, 1969);

The Horseman's Word: a sequence of concrete poems (Preston: Akros Publications, 1970);

Twelve songs (West Linton: Castlelaw Press, 1970);

Instamatic Poems (London: Ian McKelvie, 1972);

The Whittrick: a poem in eight dialogues . . . 1955-1961 (Preston: Akros Publications, 1973);

From Glasgow to Saturn (Cheadle: Carcanet Press, 1973);

!?,. Nuspeak 8, being a visual poem (Glasgow: Scottish Arts Council, Glasgow Centre, 1973);

Essays (Cheadle: Carcanet Press, 1974);

Hugh MacDiarmid (London: Longman, 1976);

The New Divan (Manchester: Carcanet New Press, 1977);

Colour Poems (Glasgow: Third Eye Centre, 1978);

Star Gate: science fiction poems (Glasgow: Third Eye Centre, 1979);

Provenance and problematics of "Sublime and alarming images," The Warton Lecture (London: British Academy, 1979);

Poems of Thirty Years (Manchester: Carcanet New Press, 1982);

Grafts/Takes (Glasgow: Mariscat Press, 1983);

Sonnets from Scotland (Glasgow: Mariscat Press, forthcoming 1984).

TRANSLATIONS: *Beowulf* (Aldington [Kent]: Hand & Flower Press, 1952; Berkeley: University of California Press, 1962);

Jessie Ann Matthew

Poems from Eugenio Montale (Reading: Reading University School of Art, 1959);

Sovpoems: Brecht, Neruda, Pasternak, Tsvetayeva, Mayakovsky, Martynov, Yevtushenko (Worcester: Migrant Press, 1961);

Selected Poems: Sándor Weores, translated, with an introduction, by Edwin Morgan; bound with *Selected Poems: Ferenc Juhász*, translated by David Wevill (Harmondsworth: Penguin Books, 1970);

247

Wi the haill voice: 25 poems by Vladimir Mayakovsky,
translated into Scots, with a glossary, by Morgan (Oxford: Carcanet Press, 1972);

Fifty Renascence love-poems (Reading: Whiteknights
Press, 1975);

Rites of Passage: translations (Manchester: Carcanet
New Press, 1976);

August Graf von Platen-Hallermünde, *Platen:
selected poems* (West Linton: Castlelaw Press,
1978);

*The Apple-tree: A medieval Dutch play in a version by
Edwin Morgan* (Glasgow: Third Eye Centre,
1982);

Master Peter Pathelin (Glasgow: Third Eye Centre,
1983).

Edwin Morgan's principal achievement in
poetry has been to revive some of the modernist
spirit of linguistic adventure and play, otherwise
mostly defunct in Britain for several decades. His
poems and translations demonstrate an excitement
about the possibilities of poetic innovation, an excitement that has taken him into unusual experimental idioms. In the early 1950s his writing was
influenced by British surrealism, by the romantic-
symbolist modes of Dylan Thomas, and by science
fiction, for which he has shown an abiding passion.
Soon, however, he was to recognize strong affinities
with American moderns such as William Carlos
Williams, the Black Mountain poets, and the Beats.
From their examples he was to learn a new creative
freedom. In 1962 he discovered the Brazilian
Noigandres group of "concrete" poets, and he
began to create visual and phonic poems. His delight and energy in developing experimental
methods and also in making a simpler, spontaneous
poetry (and poetic) of direct experience have made
Morgan's a rare kind of attainment in contemporary British writing.

Romantic attitudes to both poetry and life are
to be found in Morgan's work throughout his
career, even in his earliest translations from
Anglo-Saxon poetry. He can write indignantly and
compassionately of human suffering: the deprivation and the violence of life in the modern city—
especially in his native Glasgow—are among Morgan's main concerns and repeated themes. He can
also write movingly about the personal anguish of
love and separation. Fundamentally, however, he
chooses to be optimistic about the outlook for modern man in his technological society. Mistrusting
tradition, Morgan shares a confident sense of his
own time with certain futurist poets—especially the
Russian Mayakovsky—and he has a strong feeling

for the living present, which leads him to try to
capture in his poetry the living moment as it passes.
As he has said, "I like poetry that comes not out of
'poetry' but out of a story in today's newspaper, or a
chance personal encounter in a city street, or the
death of a famous person: I am very moved by the
absolute force of what actually happens, because,
after all, that is it, there is really nothing else that has
its poignance, its razor edge." At his best, he succeeds in capturing a vivid immediacy. When he fails,
there is frequently a slackness of form or a reliance
on mere formulae, with a consequent loss of finesse
in his language. Morgan's games of poetic making
can become "mere games" where methods are arbitrary or mechanically rigid, not very productive,
and followed more in hope of a result than with
genuine inspiration. Happily, he succeeds much
more often than he fails.

Edwin George Morgan was born in Glasgow to
Stanley Lawrence and Margaret McKillop Arnott
Morgan. His father worked as a clerk with a company of iron and steel merchants, and Edwin Morgan was educated at Rutherglen Academy in Glasgow, Glasgow High School, and Glasgow University. During the Second World War he served with
the Royal Army Medical Corps (1940-1946); his
wartime postings included a period in the Eastern
Mediterranean. In 1947 he completed his master's
degree at Glasgow University, and then he lectured
in English there until 1980 (he was a professor of
English from 1975 until his retirement). His writing
life began in school, where he wrote fantastic prose
narratives based partly on his reading of science
fiction. Until he went to university his poetry was
limited to romantic models, but during his university years he began to take an interest in modern
verse and in poetry from several languages including Anglo-Saxon, Scots, and nearly all the major
European languages. His first published work, *The
Vision of Cathkin Braes* and a translation of *Beowulf*,
appeared in 1952. By that time *Dies Irae* had been
completed also, though it did not get into print until
thirty years later, as a part of Morgan's collection
Poems of Thirty Years (1982).

From his earliest poems it is obvious that Morgan has a fine natural ear for stylistic parody as well
as a tendency toward sentimental whimsy. The
poem "Dies Irae," for example, was written at a time
when the New Apocalypse group of poets had all
but vanished from the center of the British literary
scene, but the poem shows the influence of that
group as well as Anglo-Saxon models:

The boomerang drum-roll doubling and re-

dounding a hundredfold,
The blistering fulgor fire-runnelling the livid
vault,
The thunder and the blaze of heaven I bore.

"Stanzas of the Jeopardy," another poem from Morgan's *Dies Irae* collection, is a New Apocalyptic version of St. Paul's Apocalyptic Letter to the Corinthians. Morgan's *Dies Irae* also contains lively translations of several Anglo-Saxon poems, including "The Ruin," "The Seafarer," and "The Wanderer." *The Vision of Cathkin Braes* contains a charade poem ("Ingram Lake or, Five Acts on the House"), which parodies the narrative methods and attitudes of five popular contemporary playwrights, including Tennessee Williams, T. S. Eliot, and Jean-Paul Sartre. Morgan imitates James Joyce too in "Verses for a Christmas Card," a poem which reveals an early enthusiasm for almost pure sound. The first stanza ends:

Froral brookrims hoartrack glassling,
Allairbelue beauheaven ablove
Avalanchbloomfondshowed brrumalljove.

Morgan's next two volumes—*The Cape of Good Hope* (1955) and *The Whittrick* (written by 1961 but published only in 1973)—show a continuation down much the same poetic paths. *The Cape of Good Hope* is a four-part work which echoes several poets of the modern period, especially Eliot, Auden, and, yet once more, the New Apocalyptic imitators of Dylan Thomas. *The Whittrick* is self-conscious game playing in many styles, including more literary models such as Hugh MacDiarmid, James Joyce, Charlotte and Emily Brontë, and Jean Cocteau. The reader is again made aware of Morgan's love of stylistic imitation. The "whittrick" itself is a curious random linguistic visitant in all sections of the poem which it gives a title to, though it hardly works as a structuring device.

First signs of a radical change in Morgan's approach to poetic language come with *Starryveldt* (1965), *emergent poems* (1967), and *gnomes* (1968). By the late 1960s he had adopted some of the perspectives of "concrete poetry." In *emergent poems* he created visual poems, each of which recombines the letters which make up a single line taken from a well-known work; Brecht, Burns, Dante, Marx, and Engels composed the original texts selected by Morgan for such a treatment. The formalistic limits which Morgan sets himself provide a necessary discipline to facilitate escape from the romantic whimsy of his earlier poetic world. Some of the poems in *gnomes* were influenced by Eugen Gomringer's ideas of typographical spacing, while other poems (including "The Computer's Second Christmas Card") reflect Morgan's playfully serious interest in new possibilities for poetry latent in technological developments, including computers and computer programming.

The Second Life, published in 1968, is probably Morgan's most important volume in terms of his poetic development; it is certainly an original and richly varied book. On the contents pages the date of composition is given for each poem, as if Morgan is anxious to show how much of his poetry by this time had become an immediate response to events. The volume begins with three elegies—to Ernest Hemingway, Marilyn Monroe, and Edith Piaf—written between August 1962 and October 1963. Each elegy has a distinctive style which reflects strongly the life-style of the subject. The Hemingway elegy parodies, seriously, the novelist's style, though the end of the poem becomes flat and sententious. The power of the elegy for Marilyn Monroe drops too when it lapses into a rather naive and dull moralizing tone of address. This schoolmasterly manner is a recurring fault in *The Second Life*, especially noticeable when Morgan writes with apparent spontaneity. The concrete poems in this volume, by contrast, are nearly always successful precisely because they are objective and fully controlled. Morgan handles concrete poetry techniques with subtlety and adroitness, indulging his love of formal games with chance elements within them ("The Computer's First Christmas Card" and "The Chaffinch Map of Scotland," for example). But that he has learned more from the example of modern American poetry is apparent too. Some poems reveal a freedom of informal expression while keeping a sure sense of musical cadence, as in the title poem:

All January, all February the skaters
enjoyed Bingham's pond, the crisp cold
evenings,
they swung and flashed among car head-
lights.

This less formalistic mode enables him to face and express honestly some raw-nerved personal experience which would have been impossible in the merely playful charade verse of his early poetry. He is able to work successfully in quite distinct modes, endeavoring always to balance together several different accounts. *The Second Life* contains the most convincing and moving of Morgan's "emergent" poems ("Message Clear") as well as "Pomander," which is a fascinating and complex calligram. The style of his later *Instamatic Poems* (1972) is already worked out in bright celebratory impressions such as "Linoleum Chocolate" and "Trio," and there are several effective love poems written in his newly discovered free-verse style. This same style is used for several breathlessly rhapsodic space- or science-fiction poems including the fantasies "In Sobieski's Shield" and "From the Domain of Arnheim." These poems celebrate the wonder of strange worlds—worlds which include much suffering as well as joy. They may be seen as extended metaphors for the pains and triumphs of the positive human spirit in choosing a second life.

The gap in Morgan's creative life between the publication of *The Cape of Good Hope* in 1955 and *Starryveldt* in 1965 is bridged to a certain extent by two books of translations. *Poems from Eugenio Montale* came out in 1959, followed by *Sovpoems*, versions of Brecht, Neruda, and several Soviet poets, in 1961. These translations helped his imagination and craft not only to stay alive during a bleak period but to forge a distinctive though many-faceted identity. The influence of Mayakovsky, for example, one of the poets whose work he translated for *Sovpoems*, cannot be overestimated. Through Mayakovsky Morgan absorbed some of the confident and energetic attitudes of Russian futurism. Morgan's most persuasive collection of translations is *Wi the haill voice: 25 poems by Vladimir Mayakovsky*. This volume, published in 1972, makes spirited use of Scots dialect. According to Morgan: "Mayakovsky's exclamatoriness, the abrupt changes of tone, the unusual mixture of fantasy, lyricism, and direct civic and moral concern—all seemed recalcitrant to the English medium . . . but with the use of Scots, I found that many of the problems quickly dissolved. It is possible to tap a Scottish tradition both of grotesque exaggeration and fantasy and of linguistic extroversion and dash that goes back through MacDiarmid, Burns, and Dunbar." A few lines from "Wi the Haill Voice" may serve to illustrate this viewpoint:

> my voice
>> will tyauve
>>> and break through Grampian
>>>> time
>
> and shaw itsel—rouch,
>> wechty,
>>> sichty,
>>>> like

> some aqueduct
>> survivit
>>> sin langsyne
>
> when Roman slave-chiels
>> biggit brick and dyke.

(*tyauve*:struggle; *sichty*:striking)

If *The Second Life* was a key volume in Morgan's creative development, his next larger collection of poetry—*From Glasgow to Saturn* (1973)—marked a shift upward in his popularity with readers of poetry. The book was deservedly a choice of the British Poetry Book Society. There is an increased sureness of control and communication in *From Glasgow to Saturn*, and this more confident mastery of craft, especially noticeable in the lyric poems, allows Morgan to present a generally more relaxed, less sententious manner, without losing a hard and biting edge when his poems call for it. Some of the lyric poems celebrate simple, delighted experiences ("Oban Girl" and "The Apple's Song," for example), while others belie a songlike surface; "Tropic" begins: "ring river riding silver/forest flashing waterfalls" but ends:

> bastinado and electrode
> swelling jails with filth and pain
>
> Christ of the Andes paper tiger
> head in clouds and feet on skulls.

Heavy-handed moral indignation is lightened here by the ironic changes of the poem's music. In other poems too Morgan allows the sufferers (including himself) to sing their grievances. "Fado" begins:

> Fold those waves away
> and take the yellow, yellow bay
> roll it up like Saturday.

"From the North" presents a painful separation through use of words with a Northern ring to them: "What is left till I see you?/This anorak, these knuckles, that kyle." "Blue Toboggans," "Song of the Child," "Lord Jim's Ghost's Tiger Poem," and "Flakes" are all varieties of formal lyric; once more, a given structure permits Morgan to write with apparently spontaneous grace. "The Loch Ness Monster's Song," a sound poem, has become one of Morgan's most popular performances, especially in the version produced by him with the assistance of BBC's Radiophonic Workshop. The monster sinks into the uncharted depths of Loch Ness while uttering its deep and plaintive call:

        blm   plm
        blm   plm
        blm   plm
        blp.

The most original and characteristic experimental work in the collection is in "Interferences." In this sequence of nine poems Morgan changes normal word structure very slightly to suggest dislocations in actuality, as in these lines from a meditation about John Cage, silence, and the final silence of death:

    and there is space in the rose in the glass
    and in the two nurses whispering
    there was such whispering as a plane passed
    and the clack of feet what is this silen

"The First Men on Mercury"—an imagined dialogue between an earthman and an inhabitant of Mercury, each learning the other's language—is one of Morgan's most entertaining studies in linguistic dislocation and translation. "Stobhill," by contrast, is the most dramatically intense poem in the volume. Morgan presents to the reader the guiltiness and self-deceit of five characters who are responsible in different ways for the death of a fetus in its seventh month. These are the doctor who aborted the unwanted child, the boilerman who nearly burned it alive, the mother, the father, and the hospital porter. Only the mother feels deep remorse and has any understanding of what has happened. In "Stobhill" an ear for parody is turned to serious use with memorable effect. The porter's soliloquy concludes the sequence and ends with lines (in a Scots accent) which are intended to echo in the mind, and do so:

    Don't answer nothin incriminatin, says the
                                        sheriff.
    And that's good enough fur yours truly.
    And neither ah did, neither ah did,
    neither ah did, neither ah did.

Finally, the ten "Glasgow Sonnets" succeed in combining formal control, observation of a modern city's squalor, and a compassionate dignity. The sestet of the final sonnet has all these qualities:

    And stalled lifts generating high-rise blues
    can be set loose. But stalled lives never budge.
    They linger in the single-ends that use

    their spirit to the bone, and when they trudge
    from closemouth to laundrette their steady
                                        shoes
    carry a world that weighs us like a judge.

Morgan's next collection—*The New Divan*—appeared in 1977, three years after publication of a collection of essays and one year after his selected translations (*Rites of Passage*). In translating, he says in his introductory note, he worked "directly" from original texts and did not allow himself the sort of freedom of approach used by such translators as Ezra Pound and Robert Lowell: "I have tried to work with a sense of close and deep obligation to the other poet." This attitude may have produced a less exciting collection of versions or imitations, but, throughout, Morgan shows complete respect for his poets, even when he reworks part of *Macbeth* into Scots. Lady Macbeth's speeches, from this new angle, are as powerful and cold as they were in Shakespeare's English:

        Cwa to thir breists o mine
    you murder-fidgin spreits, and turn their
                                        milk
    to venim and to verjuice, fae your sheddows
    waukrife ower erd's evil! Cwa starnless nicht,
    rowed i the smeek and reek o daurkest hell,
    that my ain eident knife gang blinly in,
    and heaven keekna through the skuggy thack
    to cry "Haud back!"

Rites of Passage includes versions of concrete poems by such writers as Haroldo de Campos, Edgard Braga, and Eugen Gomringer, as well as selections from Morgan's translations of Montale, Mayakovsky, Pasternak, Quasimodo, Lorca, and several others.

"The New Divan," the title sequence of his 1977 collection, consists of one hundred poems which exhibit quite remarkable variety and control. A *divan*, as Morgan informs his readers, is a state council, a couch or bed, or a collection of poems. The most famous poetic divan was written by the fourteenth-century Persian poet Hafiz, who composed poems of love and confident joy during a period of great political and emotional turmoil. Morgan "imitates" the celebratory optimism of Hafiz, though he too is well aware of all the degrees of human distress. "The New Divan" is Morgan's most personal utterance, although he never allows his ego to take any direct part. His verses celebrate sensual delight in the natural world as well as the wondrous strangeness of human existence. Moods and settings change continually, from poem to

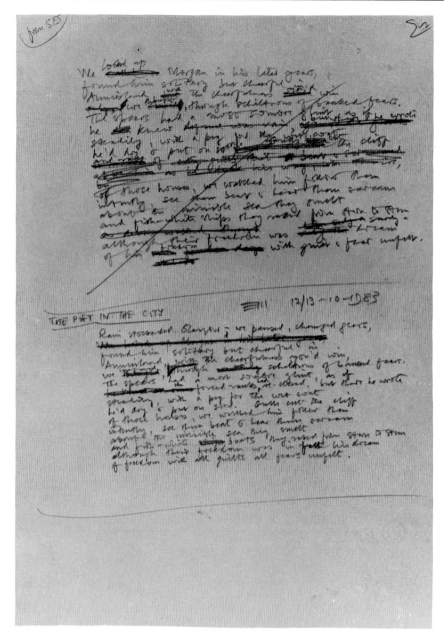

Working draft for "The Poet in the City," published in Sonnets from Scotland *(the author)*

poem, so that grief and pain are always balanced by delight and awe, the remote past against the "instamatic" present, human love against the cruelty of power. His wartime experiences in the Near East are often evoked, but these too are deliberately kept at a distance by rapid changes of feeling and scene within the sequence. A bleak vision of war with atomic bombs ("Pale children/break the grass-blades in their hands") soon gives way to a simply articulated harbor scene and a vision of young love which ends:

> The next
> bride waits for summer,
> turns in her bed to have
> everybody's dreams. Houses
> line the quayside with upper
> windows lit. Below
> a mended sail shines clean.

Other poems in *The New Divan* are developments of Morgan's many styles, including concrete poetry, "instamatic" verses of the future ("Pictures

Floating from the World"), and some effective free-verse sequences ("Five Poems on Film Directors," "School's Out," and "Adventures of the Antisage"). The final group of poems—beginning with "Smoke" and ending with "Resurrections"—though personal and unsentimental is very moving.

Morgan has continued to experiment. His *Colour Poems* (1978) literally make use of many-colored inks, while *Star Gate* (1979) moves into new realms of science-fiction poetry. *Grafts/Takes* (1983) includes poems which transform lines discarded by the poet Michael Schmidt. The recently completed *Sonnets from Scotland* (1984) is a new exploration of a traditional form. These fifty sonnets vary in mood from knockabout humor to deep pathos, but always with a positive delight in the interplay of language and form. *The Apple-tree* (1982) is a lively version of a medieval Dutch play, and *Master Peter Pathelin* (1983) captures the rumbustious character of fifteenth-century French farce. It is surprising that Morgan's sensitive ear for speech and his imaginative dramatic sense have not led him to write original plays.

In his art Edwin Morgan communicates, above all, a vulnerable but controlling poetic self. His explorations of language have taken him into new experiments with both formal and freer styles of poetic making, and his distinction has been to develop a gift for literary parody into a rich and humane poetic voice.

Interviews:

Marshall Walker, "Edwin Morgan: An Interview," *Akros*, 11 (December 1976): 3-23;

William Barr, Interview with Morgan, *English Ayr*, 7 (March 1982): 22-39.

References:

Robin Fulton, "Edwin Morgan," in his *Contemporary Scottish Poetry: individuals and contexts* (Loanhead: Macdonald, 1974), pp. 13-40;

Fulton, "Two Scottish poets: Edwin Morgan and Iain Crichton Smith," *Stand*, 10, no. 4 (1969): 60-68;

Robin Hamilton, "The poetry of Edwin Morgan: translator of reality," *Akros*, 15 (April 1980): 23-39;

Michael Schmidt, "Edwin Morgan," in his *An Introduction to Fifty Modern British Poets* (London: Pan, 1979), pp. 314-320;

Alan Young, "Three neo-moderns: Ian Hamilton Finlay, Edwin Morgan, Christopher Middleton," in *British Poetry since 1970: a critical survey*, edited by Peter Jones and Michael Schmidt (Manchester: Carcanet Press, 1980), pp. 112-124.

Norman Nicholson

(8 January 1914-   )

Margaret B. McDowell
University of Iowa

BOOKS: *Selected Poems*, by Nicholson, John Hall, and Keith Douglas (London: Bale & Staples, 1943);

Man & Literature (London: SCM Press, 1943; Folcroft, Pa.: Folcroft Editions, 1974);

Five Rivers (London: Faber & Faber, 1944; New York: Dutton, 1945);

The Fire of the Lord (London: Nicholson & Watson, 1944; New York: Dutton, 1946);

The Old Man of the Mountains: A Play in Three Acts (London: Faber & Faber, 1946; revised, 1950);

The Green Shore (London: Nicholson & Watson, 1947);

Rock Face (London: Faber & Faber, 1948);

Cumberland and Westmorland (London: Hall, 1949);

H. G. Wells (London: Barker, 1950; Denver: Swallow, 1950);

Prophesy to the Wind: A Play in Four Scenes and a Prologue (London: Faber & Faber, 1950);

William Cowper (London: Lehmann, 1951; Folcroft, Pa.: Folcroft Editions, 1977);

The Pot Geranium (London: Faber & Faber, 1954);

A Match for the Devil (London: Faber & Faber, 1955);

The Lakers: The Adventures of the First Tourists (London: Hale, 1955);

Provincial Pleasures (London: Hale, 1959);

William Cowper (London: Longmans, Green, 1960);

Birth by Drowning (London: Faber & Faber, 1960);

Portrait of the Lakes (London: Hale, 1963); revised as *The Lakes* (London: Hale, 1977);

Enjoying It All (London: Waltham Forest Books, 1964);

Selected Poems (London: Faber & Faber, 1966);

No Star on the Way Back: Ballads and Carols (Manchester: Manchester Institute of Contemporary Arts, 1967);

Greater Lakeland (London: Hale, 1969);

A Local Habitation (London: Faber & Faber, 1972);

Wednesday Early Closing (London: Faber & Faber, 1975);

Cloud on the Black Combe (Hitchin: Cellar Press, 1975);

Stitch and Stone: A Cumbrian Landscape (Sunderland: Ceolfrith, 1975);

The Shadow on Black Combe (Ashington: Mid Northumberland Arts Group, 1978);

Sea to the West (London & Boston: Faber & Faber, 1981);

Selected Poems, 1940-1982 (London & Boston: Faber & Faber, 1982).

OTHER: *An Anthology of Religious Verse Designed for the Times*, edited by Nicholson (Harmondsworth & New York: Penguin, 1942);

Wordsworth: An Introduction and Selection, edited by Nicholson (London: Phoenix House, 1949);

William Cowper, *Poems*, edited by Nicholson (London: Grey Walls Press, 1951);

"The Second Chance," in *Writers on Themselves* (London: British Broadcasting Corp., 1964);

A Choice of Cowper's Verse, edited by Nicholson (London: Faber & Faber, 1975);

The Lake District: An Anthology, edited by Nicholson (London: Hale, 1977).

Although Norman Nicholson identifies himself as a poet, he has also written regional geography, literary criticism, autobiography, literary biography, and novels. Nearly all of his work reveals deep feeling for the South Cumberland coastal area bordered on the west by the Irish Sea and on the east by the Lake District. An area settled in the ninth and tenth centuries by Vikings from Ireland and Iceland, its rugged landscape has inspired in Nicholson a nature poetry less idyllic than that of Lake District poets such as Wordsworth.

Much of Nicholson's poetry depicts life in Millom, a small South Cumberland industrial and mining town, where, except for nearly two years during 1930-1932 that he spent in a tuberculosis hospital in Hampshire, Nicholson has lived all his

life in the house where he was born. His writing reveals his conviction that an individual can find the wisdom of the universe in his hometown, and it emphasizes the value of community and nature in human development, as well as the need to center one's life in Christian faith and principle.

In 1860 the discovery of hematite iron ore just outside Millom brought to the area a rush of new settlers, including Norman Nicholson's grandparents. The town had no schools, churches, or streets when his Grandmother Nicholson arrived to join her husband. According to a family story, she so despised what she saw ("ram-shackle furnaces, the grey anthills of slag, the half-made-up roads") that she urged the carter to turn the horse around and take her away. Instead, she remained, bore fourteen sons in the next sixteen years, moved thirty years later from her first home to another just a half-mile up the street, and—though she lived to

1928—never boarded a train. Millom's population reached four thousand by 1875, continued to rise until 1890, and slowly declined during the Depression and World War II. The iron mill imported ore long after it exhausted the local iron mines but finally closed in 1968. The abandoned mines, the mountainous slag pile at the edge of the town, the spire of the sandstone church, the shabby "tin Bethel" chapel of the Nonconformists, the rocky sea coast, the cold becks, and the wall of rugged fells that isolates the coastal strip from the Lake District mark the little mining and steel-mill town. They mark nearly all of Nicholson's writing as well.

Millom provides not only the setting for Nicholson's poems, plays, and novels, but also the major symbols for his religious expression. In his artistic merging of his area's ancient natural beauty and modern industry he produces a sense of discord, which precludes easy sentimentality, as he extols nature, strong faith, and optimism even in the presence of ugliness and frustration. His unmitigating praise of the provincial world and of the mysteries of an unseen heaven are lent credibility by his humor, his common sense, and his eye for realistic detail. The shrewd provincial human beings who people his work—fishermen, miners, steelworkers, farmers, and shepherds—nonchalantly assume that the mining town and its bleak environs are at the outskirts of the City of God. Through rustic scenes and comic characters, he introduces in his fiction and drama, as well as in his poems, a lively mixture of disturbances and pleasures, virtues and vices.

The son of Joseph Nicholson, a tailor, and Edith Cornthwaite Nicholson, who died when her son was five, Norman Cornthwaite Nicholson frequently employs in his writings the circumstances of his early life and the people who enriched it—his grandparents, his many uncles and their families, neighbors, customers in his father's tailor shop (the family lived in rooms above it), and patrons of his stepmother's piano shop a few doors down the street. (His father remarried when Norman was eight.) The family looked forward to Wednesdays, when the tailor shop was closed at noon, and in *Wednesday Early Closing* (1975), where Nicholson writes of his life up to his return from the sanatorium in 1932, he comments that his father's pleasure in that short workday prepared his son to accept a quiet life in which all workdays were short because his early debilitating illness made it mandatory.

An Anglican all his life, Nicholson maintains that his poetry has been influenced more by his early attendance at Methodist worship with his stepmother. Like the religious practice he encountered in the Wesley Chapel and Sunday School, his poetry is often strongly personal, emotional, colloquial in diction, and conversational in rhythm. Less often, the poems echo the hymns, liturgy, and formal prayers of the traditional Anglican service.

For several years in the mid-1930s, after returning at eighteen from hospitalization for tuberculosis, Nicholson struggled with continuing fatigue and low-grade infection but persisted in his hope to leave Millom. In "The Second Chance" (1964), he recalls his resentment of the ugliness and grime of Millom and his longing for the Hampshire forest, where his hospital bed was kept outside day and night. In Millom, he hiked daily in all weather, but, fearful "of dust and fog and noise and traffic," he went no closer than a mile to the steel mill. Finally, his study of wild flowers drew him to the ironworks, near which the best flowers grew on the seawall and in cracks in the quarry. In this place he began to feel that from birth he had been "part of the rock" on which Millom was built, and he reconciled his new interest in the town's industrial activity with his love of the natural beauty of seacoast and cliffs.

During these years, Nicholson developed as a literary critic and poet, in part through the support of the Reverend Samuel Taylor, vicar of the local church, and Brother George Every, a literary editor and contributor to the *Criterion*. Through Every, with whom he corresponded for several years, Nicholson met T. S. Eliot in 1938, after Eliot had read and responded favorably to some of his unpublished poems. Nicholson had become interested in Eliot's work in 1934, and *The Wasteland* (1922) led him to the study of Frazer's *The Golden Bough* and to the use in his own poems of symbols connoting dichotomies such as life-death, death-resurrection, and winter-spring. Eliot's religious verse dramas, such as *Murder in the Cathedral* (1935), stimulated Nicholson to work in that genre. He also studied Wordsworth and Cowper. As early as 1938 he lectured on literature at meetings of the Worker's Educational Association in several towns and at a conference of the Student Christian Movement. These lectures appear in *Man & Literature* (1943). Two of his early poems, "Song for 7 p.m." (1938) and "Sonnet for an Introvert" (1939), appeared in *Poetry* (Chicago), thus exposing his work to American readers. Yet of the thirty poems he wrote between 1937 and 1942, Nicholson now thinks few were worth saving.

By 1940 Nicholson had formally renewed his

membership in the Anglican church, a sign that he had resolved earlier frustrations, doubts, and confusion, and by the early 1940s he had clearly found his vocation as a writer. In 1942 he edited the Penguin *Anthology of Religious Verse* and prepared a dozen poems for inclusion, with poems by J. C. Hall and Keith Douglas, in *Selected Poems* (1943). Between 1943 and 1950 he published a number of books in addition to his collection of lectures: two novels, *The Fire of the Lord* (1944) and *The Green Shore* (1947); two collections of poems, *Five Rivers* (1944) and *Rock Face* (1948); two verse plays, *The Old Man of the Mountains* (1946) and *Prophesy to the Wind* (1950); and a biography, *H. G. Wells* (1950). He also edited and wrote the introduction for a selection of Wordsworth's poems (1949).

In spite of his isolation, Nicholson's work even in this first decade of his career received considerable attention, most of it favorable. The *Saturday Review of Literature* mildly praised *The Fire of the Lord* as a novel "of quality and accomplishment." Here, as well as in his later novel, he used extensively the landmarks of Millom, though he called the fictional town 'Odborough, a corruption of Hodbarrow, the section of Millom where mines were located. While neither of Nicholson's novels is a major accomplishment, both show Nicholson's versatility, and both, through hermit figures who return to the town of 'Odborough, reveal the author's own conviction that living in a quiet rural setting may offer less spiritual challenge than living in a bustling town like Millom. As such, the novels provide some insight into Nicholson's life and thought at the beginning of his career as a poet.

Nicholson's verse dramas, like T. S. Eliot's, draw upon medieval mystery plays and folk ritual. Written to be performed before small village audiences meeting in church halls, they, like the medieval drama cycles that were performed in streets on guild holidays, are peopled by stereotypical biblical figures as well as individuals not mentioned in the Bible, and the plays are marked by colloquial diction with vivid and sometimes racy imagery drawn from folklore, comic sequences of astringent repartee, and the occasional use of startling and profound rhetorical questions directed to the audience. Nicholson is didactic in all his plays, directing his audience to choose between true and false gods, to balance the benefits of modern industrialism with the need to conserve natural resources, and to appreciate the virtues of humility, courage, and steadfastness.

While such overt sermonizing tends to mar the plays for some contemporary audiences, others re-spond favorably to Nicholson's lively satire of human folly. In his essay "Modern Verse Drama and the Folk Tradition" (1960) he explains that plays such as his provide an opportunity for members of the audience to act out their own fantasies vicariously as they identify with the figures on the stage and thus to resolve their own moral conflicts and religious doubts. The actors perform on behalf of the audience, and the members of the ideal audience—because of these moments of "shared belief"—become a community as they watch the play, much as they would through the sharing of an ecclesiastical sacrament.

The Old Man of the Mountains, based on the life of the prophet Elijah, opened in London the year before its publication, as part of a series of religious dramas performed at the Mercury Theatre, the small theater where Eliot's *Murder in the Cathedral* had had a successful run in 1937-1938. Reviews were generally favorable; amateur performances appeared with frequency for two decades; and it remains Nicholson's own favorite among his plays.

Nicholson skillfully varies the speeches in *The Old Man of the Mountains* from poetry to prose depending on subject, tone, and character. God's messages are all in poetry, while, after being raised from the dead, the widow's child speaks only in simple prose. The other characters all move easily from poetry to prose, from formal to colloquial usage, as the occasion demands. The play's chief distinctions may well be Nicholson's stress on the conservation of natural resources as a basic religious principle and his unconventional conceptions of Ahab and Elijah. God's messages—spoken by two personified figures from nature, the Raven and the Beck (brook)—declare that land and water must not be misused, for these are God's gifts to all people, and that secular work is essential and need not preclude one's listening to the "still, small voice" of God.

The most radical change in Nicholson's treatment of the biblical source appears in his characterizations of Ahab and Elijah. Unlike his biblical counterpart, who is a powerful, tyrannical king, Nicholson's Ahab is a greedy farmer. Nicholson's Elijah is a man so filled with doubts about himself and the power of his God that he is surprised whenever he sees the miracles that result from his prayers and continues to be diffident about the efficacy of his prayers even at the height of his career as a prophet. After the deluge proves that Jehovah is mightier in mercy than Baal, the Raven chides Elijah for idleness and advises him to go back to his farm and work: "Return and seek a liturgy in your labors." While Nicholson's intent was to make of these biblical characters common men and women with whom the audience could quickly identify, he overemphasizes their ordinariness and, thereby, diminishes the strong dramatic effect that should ensue when, in answer to Elijah's prayers, the heavens open after years of drought or a child is raised from the dead.

Prophesy to the Wind differs decidedly from Nicholson's other three verse plays, because it is not based on biblical sources and is set in the future. In its impressive prologue, voices frantically scream, "Fire!" while the winds sweep the protagonist, John, up a chimney and into the future. He arrives in a primitive Viking village among shepherds who know only vaguely about an atomic age that existed before the nuclear holocaust destroyed most of the world. He and a beautiful woman, Freya, fall in love, and together they build a generator around a fragment of an ancient machine. John hopes—and the others fear—that with this key to "ancient" knowledge he can develop again the scientific technology of the atomic age. To prevent this possibility, Freya's relatives murder John, but she already has conceived her lover's child, and that child may some day discover the secrets of nuclear science, the knowledge that his father almost recovered from the past.

Nicholson's poetry possesses great variety. For example, Vikar, the rough sailor, exclaims coarsely of his fellows, "They'll cram their gullets with beans and fat bacon,/And flush it down with a swill of sour beer," but a moment later, he expresses his grief over the death of Freya's mother with eloquent restraint: "But—dead?/And dead so young? I would as soon/Expect to hear the wind is dead." For the most part, the verse is lyrical, as in this description of John's arrival: "He comes like an arctic sea bird/Blown to our coast, broken-winged and hungered./Prodding the salt sand." After T. S. Eliot saw this play performed in Ealing in 1949, he commented to Nicholson that he should be "a very happy man," and others who saw the play performed in Ealing and in Newcastle the same year were also complimentary. Yet its postpublication performance in London in 1951 brought less favorable reaction. Written for small audiences of people who share his views on religion and his sacramental attitude toward nature, Nicholson's plays have fared less well with larger, secular audiences. Only *The Old Man of the Mountains*, which had its London premiere under conditions closer to those for which it was intended, was favorably reviewed in London newspapers. London reviews for the other plays have, for the most part, not reflected the reactions

of those who saw the plays under the more auspicious circumstances for which Nicholson designed them. Yet, by the time his second play opened in London, Nicholson had decided that he "didn't quite own" this play, which he had undertaken because the Little Theatre Guild had assigned him to write a "post-atomic play." He has not again attempted any extended exercise in fantasy laid in the future.

Nicholson undertook the writing of *A Match for the Devil* (1955) on a commission from the Religious Drama Society early in 1952. Depicting the marriage of the prophet Hosea and Gomer, a former temple prostitute, the play was to be produced in churches in small industrial towns by the New Pilgrims touring company. After the play had gone into rehearsal, the society withdrew its sponsorship because the members feared that the play might associate prostitution with the modern church; because they felt that the play's comic tone was inappropriate for the depiction of a tragic marriage; and because they believed the couple's child (one not mentioned in the Bible), was made to seem more important than the prophet Hosea. In 1953 the London Club Theatre Group took the play to the Edinburgh Festival, where the large audience and several Scottish newspapers praised it, but London critics were unanimously negative, citing its loose structure or its heaviness (in spite of the high proportion of scenes devoted to comic repartee between Hosea and various other characters).

Nicholson's originality in his interpretation of Hosea's forgiveness of Gomer is noteworthy. Ordinarily readers of the Bible interpret this action as symbolic of God's unlimited forgiveness for the unworthy. Here, however, Nicholson presents Hosea as the lesser of the two people because of his unacknowledged pride, which motivates him to think he can judge his wife, then forgive her, assuming a kind of superiority and detachment not consistent with his own human sinfulness. Later, after struggle, Hosea accepts her as an equal partner, believing he recognizes God's pleasure in their decision to reconcile: "I hear it in the . . . laughter of the wind among the palms/And my wife and I will share the joke with Yahweh,/The holy joke of marriage." The dialogue is often coarsely suggestive, and the play provides robust domestic comedy.

Nicholson wrote *Birth by Drowning* (1960) in 1957 for the Committee for Religious Drama in the Northern Province. A play about Elisha, it was part of a commemoration for the Community of the Resurrection in July 1959. The play was presented by theology students, and the audience in the open-air Quarry Theatre at Mirfield, Yorkshire, numbered nearly four thousand. Though critics applauded its vigorous dialogue and humor, they generally judged *Birth by Drowning* to be Nicholson's least serious effort, an evaluation that may have discouraged him from further efforts in this genre.

To help his audiences identify with the prophets in his verse plays, Nicholson stressed the ordinary natures of his protagonists, rather than their dramatic uniqueness. Similarly, he has sought in his lyric poetry to speak to ordinary people as a balladeer might, rather than as a poet with a sophisticated audience. In his essay "The Comic Prophet" (1953) he argues that it is necessary for a poet of his generation to emphasize kinship with readers in a time when many poets emphasize their isolation or alienation. Nicholson's poems refer almost constantly to everyday experience, common objects, and basic human aspirations and conflicts. Only in his second collection, *Rock Face*, does he sometimes use literary allusions, and even in this volume, where his preoccupation with verse techniques, such as internal rhyme, makes some poems seem artificial and distracting, he continues to use natural speech rhythms. In the two later collections—*The Pot Geranium* (1954) and *A Local Habitation* (1972)—he keeps primarily to his simpler mode of writing. Clear statements, unguarded revelations, anecdotal scenes, and conversational or colloquial style are the primary characteristics of Nicholson's most consistent mode of stylistic expression.

Nicholson's poems are more accessible than the poems of the contemporaries he admires (such as T. S. Eliot, W. H. Auden, Marianne Moore, Robert Lowell) and some of the poems of his great predecessor in northern regional poetry, William Wordsworth. Nicholson's poetry, in many respects, resembles that of the late-eighteenth-century poet William Cowper. Nicholson has written two critical books on Cowper (1951 and 1960) and has edited two collections of his poetry (1951 and 1975). Like Nicholson, Cowper lived in one village all his life and wrote poems about ordinary people living in close proximity to nature and poems celebrating the joy to be found in nature itself. Like Cowper, Nicholson reveals in his poems an engaging sense of humor, and he expresses abstractions only as they develop inevitably from the lives and experiences of ordinary people. Both poets often reveal complexities in thought, feeling, and versification; and irony, paradox, and symbols implying multiple dimensions of meaning pervade their poetry. Nevertheless, their poetry seldom strikes the reader as obscure. Though Nicholson may leave some is-

sues in his poems unresolved, he formulates them with clarity and persuades his readers to ponder them.

By the time *Five Rivers* and *Rock Face* were published in the 1940s, Nicholson had gained considerable recognition through the appearance of many of the poems in at least ten anthologies and a number of respected periodicals such as *Horizon*, *New Statesman and Nation*, *Poetry* (Chicago), *Poetry* (London), *Poetry Quarterly*, the *Listener*, the *Spectator*, *Time and Tide*, *Transformation*, *Voices*, *Welsh Review*, *St. Martin's Review*, and the *Fortnightly*.

Five Rivers, widely and favorably reviewed, went through three printings in thirteen months and in 1945 won the Heinemann Prize for poetry. The title poem describes the main rivers in south Cumberland and introduces a series of poems describing certain towns and topographical features of the region, which consists of a thirty-mile strip from the port of Whitehaven on the north to Millom on the south, with the Irish Sea to the west and the iron and coal cliffs to the north. In "Five Rivers" Nicholson describes a locomotive of the West Coast Railway as it "canters along the curve" and crosses five rivers on its way south to Whitehaven from Millom. Though generally light in tone, the rhythm of the poem varies subtly to suggest the poet's changing moods, the speed of the train, and the currents of the rivers. The waters of the first river, the Ehen, described in the second stanza, are "red as rhubarb" from iron ore mined at Egremont and Cleator Moor. Nicholson suggests through his use of a harsh diction the violent wresting of the ore from the rock, which had lain undisturbed for centuries: "Here drill and navy break the stone/And hack the living earth to the bone;/Blood spurts like water from the stricken rock;/Seeps into drain and gully. . . ." In contrast, the third stanza presents the Calder River, whose placid hum derives from its "memory of plainsong and choirboys' trebles" heard as it flowed past a deserted abbey "of blood-red stone." The next three stanzas describe the other three rivers—Irt, Mite, and Esk—as they move past less industrialized towns, where life seems more relaxed and sociable. As the rivers merge in a marshy area and flow past Ravenglass, "The slow rain falls like memory." The memory draws him back through centuries of history to the Roman invasion at Ravenglass. Finally, the fresh waters and the salt waters mingle, as the rain from the sky mingles with the waters of the earth.

"Egremont," "Cleator Moor," and "Whitehaven" express Nicholson's continuing conflict between his love of unspoiled nature and his appreci-

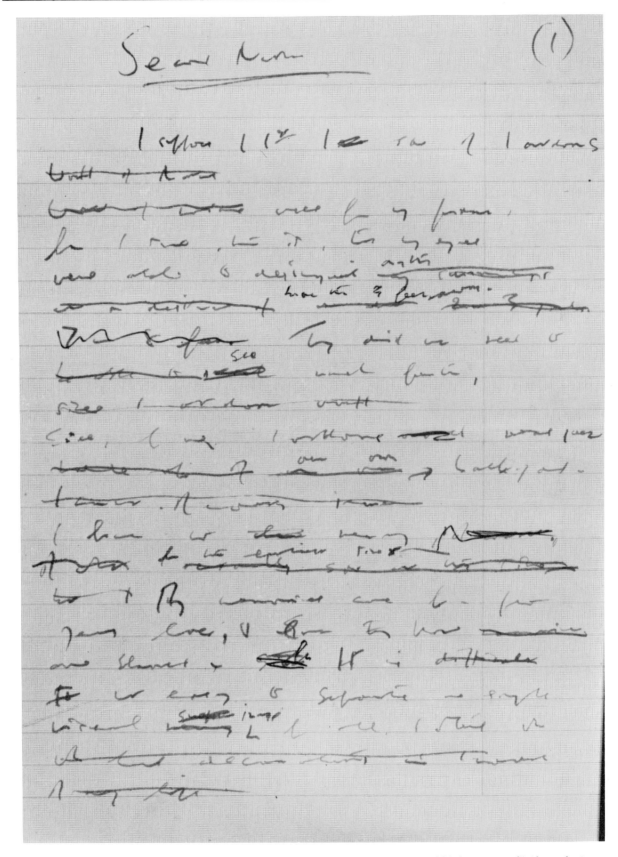

First page from the manuscript for an essay about "the relation between the poet and his home ground" (the author)

ation of the benefits of industrial development. In both "Egremont" and "Whitehaven" the final lines predict that a judgment from heaven will fall upon the greedy exploiters of nature. In "Cleator Moor" Nicholson uses ironically a jaunty, sing-song measure to narrate the prosperous history of the local mines, which have recovered from the Depression, but only because the steel mills are using the iron to turn out bullets for use in World War II. Nicholson presents in the last stanza a miner with bleeding hands, who "feels the iron in his soul," as if he himself is being struck by the bullets he is helping to produce.

The volume's long religious poems, such as "The Council of the Seven Deadly Sins," "The Holy Mountain," and "The Bow in the Cloud," fall short of mastery. Yet in the brief and coarsely worded poem "The Preachers" the poet reveals a dexterity and a virtuosity appropriate to a comic poem, as he depicts St. Francis preaching to the birds on the sickness that Adam and Eve suffered after they ate of the apple. The birds scornfully reply that berries give *them* "no bellyache," and God laughs to hear them preach to the saint.

The best poem in this first volume is "To the River Duddon," a thirty-two-line poem on Wordsworth, who wrote a sequence of sonnets on this same river. As Wordsworth did in many of his sonnets, Nicholson addresses the River Duddon, but more casually, especially in his references to the earlier poet: "I wonder, Duddon, if you still remember/An oldish man with a nose like a pony's nose. . . ." Somewhat jauntily, Nicholson talks of Wordsworth as a boy going fishing here with a piece of bread and cheese in his pocket, as a middle-aged conservative pensioner with a doting sister, and as a seventy-year-old poet still walking the Duddon shores. Nicholson quotes part of Wordsworth's lofty paean to the river—"Child of the clouds. Remote from every taint/Of sordid industry. . . ."—and then adds, "But you and I know better, Duddon lass." Now the tide is purple with ore; muddy gullies pollute the river; and dust covers even the farmyard damsons. Though he chides Wordsworth's failure to observe that modern industry was already polluting the Duddon in his lifetime, he acknowledges that the older poet knew what he has just now begun to learn—that the elemental aspects of nature are relatively firm and solid amid the more obvious flux which surrounds them. In the closing seven lines Nicholson contrasts the transient aspects of nature with the "living rock" which undergirds them: "Thirty thousand feet of solid Cumberland."

Rock Face does not represent an advance be-

yond *Five Rivers*. This second collection, however, includes several lyrics which equal those in the first. For example, "The Candle" defines poetry as that nebulous state "where the candle turns/To smoke, solid to air/. . . . The flame is not an aim,/Nor the brightest light/Any justification for its burning." In "To a Child Before Birth" he tells an infant in the womb, living where no seasons can exist, about the perfect summer of his mother's love to which the unborn cannot respond before "the sun stings his eyes" in August. As life develops within her, the mother feels a transcendent closeness to all nature, "So in her blood for you the bright bird sings."

While Nicholson's experiments in versification produced the monotonous and mechanical exercise "The Pendulum," they also led to the superb "Winter Song," where in the last stanza especially he achieves grace and harmony through intricately modulated rhythms, inexact rhymes, alliteration, and assonance.

"Thomas Gray in Patterdale" refers to the scholar-poet Thomas Gray's 1769 ten-day tour of the Lake District, during which he sent notes on his observations to a sick friend. Gray excitedly experimented on this tour with a Claude-glass, a convex lens laid over black foil in sunlight or over silver foil in cloudy weather. Facing away from the scene, the observer sees in the mirror the landscape, framed and ordered like a carefully composed small picture, motionless and silent. Nicholson portrays Gray as turning his back to the reality of the natural beauty and gazing on its mirror image, but sounds, movement, and warmth interrupt his reverie. He hears the wind, sees the mountain trees drop October leaves on his scattering papers, and feels the heat of the sun. Suddenly he realizes that he cannot control the vitality of nature through the manipulation of art and that he cannot appreciate the beauty of nature from a remote position but must be involved closely as part of nature himself. Closing with a series of disturbing questions about his relationship to nature, asked with breathless speed, the poem thus demonstrates Nicholson's skill in changing the dynamics of his work to reflect changing moods and meanings—in this case, from Gray's quiet contemplation of the ordered landscape to his fuller involvement with natural beauty.

In the best of the poems in this book, "Silecroft Shore," Nicholson considers geological phenomena as they relate to the development, dying, and spiritual rebirth of the individual: "Stone is the earth's Cool skeleton,/And bone the rock/That flesh builds on." In the second section the poet on the shore studies a pebble intently, recognizing its history and its perfection at this moment. Snapped from a mountain and carried by a glacier to the sea, it has been "planed flat" by ice, then polished "in the dice-box of the surf." In the pebble's beauty—it is "self-axelled and self-bounded. . . . / . . . acknowledging no way/other of being than this"—Nicholson sees an analogy to human life: the individual who can survive in his environment gains strength, beauty, and contentment through the struggle.

The third section suddenly shifts from one pebble to the entire rock surface of the planet, which is personified as a giant with feet on either pole of the earth and arms encircling the tropics. The creation of this giant has taken God thousands of years, and God becomes an analogue for the artist, who must reveal similar care and patience. The fourth section reverts in theme and imagery to the volume's short title poem, as it sketches a stone man sitting in a waterfall, being eroded by falling water, but inviting the water animals to shelter in his hollowed and disintegrating body. The destruction of the stone man provides a contrast to the creative processes described in the earlier section. In the final section Nicholson ends on a note of uncertainty. The poet accepts relentless change—his bones will molder to molecules of "limestone generations of the dead"—but he also recoils from the realization that with this return to inanimate nature comes the loss of all individual consciousness.

Nicholson shares Wordsworth's veneration for the unchanging stability of rock, and, throughout his own work, rock is both artifact and symbol. Repeatedly in the poems ore-bearing rock provides for a joining of nature and industry, and rock also serves in the traditional sense as a symbol of religious faith or Christ himself, as the reader recalls Christ's words to Peter following his confession of faith, "On this rock, I will build my church." The significance of rock becomes especially insistent in Nicholson's third volume of poems, *The Pot Geranium*, which may be his best. In the title poem he speaks of his circumscribed life confined "to one small radius of rock." (In 1951 the British Council had invited him to lecture in India, but he had declined because of poor health.) "Millom Old Quarry," a dialogue between the poet and an old man, reveals not only that the town of Millom was built from the quarry but also that the dead generations of the town are "swept, shovelled/Back in the quarry again/All that was mortal in five thousand lives." Most ominously, in "Gathering Sticks on Sunday" Nicholson predicts that soon only rock will be left on an unpeopled earth—"And moon and earth will stare at one another/Like the cold, yellow skulls of child and mother." In "The Outer Planet" he prays for violence—that the rocks will be utterly broken apart so the fire of God will melt the hearts of recalcitrant people. Nicholson closes this collection with "The Seven Rocks," in which the sections describe species of rock that are common to the area and are allegories of the seven virtues. The poem generally lacks intensity.

In the best poem in this volume, "The Pot Geranium," the poet looks from the window over the roofs of Millom and watches a box kite of crimson calico strain as at "a rag of dreams." Fatigued, he turns from the window and sky and goes to his bed in the small room, where the slanted ceiling and the white walls wrap him round and his body becomes "clamped to the mattress." Desolate and removed from the presence of wind and sun, he notices that in his window "A pot geranium flies its bright balloon." In his imagination it carries him to tropical forests, and he finds that he now possesses equator, sky, and sun even on his "one small radius of rock." The excellence of this poem lies in its simplicity and vivid imagery. The energy of the first and third parts of the poem contrasts with the total depletion of the sick man before he happens to look at the geranium.

Still another notable poem in this collection is "Rising Five," which begins with the comment of a boastful four-year-old that he is "rising five." The poet goes on to suggest that, by living in anticipation all our lives, we never fully enjoy the present moment: "we never see the flower/But only the fruit in the flower; never the fruit,/But only the rot in the fruit." On the other hand, he leads the reader to the realization that the process of dying is losing this power to anticipate life itself: "not living/But rising dead," playing on the ambiguity of the word *rising*—a colloquial word for "almost" but also "resurrection." Paradoxically, the time arrives when one must not dwell in the present but hopefully anticipate the future—to become the "rising dead."

The decade following the publication of *The Pot Geranium* saw the appearance of Nicholson's third and fourth verse dramas and a television script containing songs, *No Star on the Way Back*, which was produced in 1963 and published in 1967. He also wrote some prose works, including *Provincial Pleasures* (1959), *William Cowper* (1960), *Enjoying It All* (1964); and three works on regional geography, *The Lakers* (1955), *Portrait of the Lakes* (1963), and *Greater Lakeland* (1969). *Selected Poems* (1966), which includes poems from his first collections, revived Nicholson's reputation as a poet. In 1967 he shared with Seamus Heaney and Brian Jones the Cholmondeley Award for Poetry, and in 1969 he received a grant from the Northern Arts Association. Eighteen years after the publication of *The Pot Geranium* a fourth collection of new poems appeared. *A Local Habitation*, the autumn 1972 selection for the Poetry Book Society, widened his audience to include a new generation of readers. Nicholson commented that the poems in this book were more direct and colloquial than his earlier ones; and—though he has retained strong interest in nature and the Cumberland region—the poems in *A Local Habitation* "deal more with people than with places, and in particular with the people of Millom, with my family and other memories of childhood and youth."

One is not surprised then to find him returning in "The Whisperers" to his hospitalization and sharing with the reader his experience of not having spoken one word aloud for twenty months. He also commemorates people and scenes that he has known intimately, and he refers frequently to his grandparents and many uncles. In "Hodbarrow Flooded" he casually describes the old mine, now filled with shallow water, and recalls how "At seventy fathom/My Uncle Jack was killed./With half a ton of hematite spilled on his back." Several poems recreate scenes with his sharp-tongued paternal grandmother, who bore fourteen sons in sixteen years. At first glance, "The Tune the Old Cow Died Of" appears to be a comic poem, its title being the grandmother's teasing name for whatever tune Nicholson's uncle plays on his flute. But the poet goes on to say that during her childhood his grandmother had feared the death of the family cow because it might well bring starvation to the family. Later in Millom, where there were no cows, this fear began to symbolize for her a more general fear of hunger. Whenever the town fire alarm screamed, she could "find no words to ease her fear" that it might be the tune a cow would die of. As the poem develops, the sardonic replaces the comic, and the sharp-tongued grandmother is understood in a new way.

In "Boo to a Goose" the poet recalls his grandmother's chiding him when, at age eight, he was beaten up because he was too timid to defend himself. After she accuses him of being afraid to say "boo" to a goose, he describes to himself the geese he has known—and fifty years later he acknowledges that he is still afraid to say "boo" to one of them. In "Have You Been to London?" he recalls running into his grandmother's house on a cold Saturday to read to her. (Not until he had read to

her for many years did he learn that she could not read, even before her sight failed.) At the beginning of the poem she asks the question, and near the end she explains primly to him that boys in *London* are taught to close the door after themselves. These family poems have the liveliness and energy of the best scenes in Nicholson's verse dramas.

"September on the Mosses" develops the theme of transience and the necessity for human beings to accept change, affirming its value as well as the value of permanence. The speaker, overcome by autumnal beauty, seeks to make it last by crying to the sea in a repeated refrain: "Wait, tide, Wait." Eventually, he recognizes that all reality is vulnerable to change, and because beauty's actual presence is fleeting, the illusion and memory of beauty that last in one's consciousness become the more precious. When he realizes that the apparently transient can become permanent in the spirit, he welcomes change and rewords his refrain: "Come, tide, Come."

Some of the poems in this volume refer to the fact that Nicholson and his wife, Yvonne Gardner Nicholson, a teacher whom he married on 5 July 1956, have no children. He was an only child, and none of his thirteen uncles' few sons is still alive. The family name will die with him. He uses this fact as the subject of "The Seventeenth of the Name," where he imagines his grandparents and their fourteen sons all in heaven, seeing the family name only on gravestones. When people ask what he is going to do about the situation, the poet can only "hem and haw." In "The Cock's Nest" Nicholson recalls that, while his father died in February, the family did not feel "the bruise" and notice the empty rooms until March. In early March a sparrow had built its nest near the drainpipe, but at the end of March the nest was still empty. His grief for his father merges with his sense that the family name is coming to an end in the final, factual statement: "The cock's nest with never an egg in,/And my father dead."

In the 1970s Nicholson revised *Portrait of the Lakes* as *The Lakes* and completed a volume of autobiography, *Wednesday Early Closing*. He also edited two anthologies: *A Choice of Cowper's Verse* (1975) and *The Lake District* (1977). He continues to receive honors: a Society of Authors Bursary in 1973, an Arts Council Bursary in 1977, the Queen's Gold Medal for Poetry in 1977, a Manchester Polytechnic Fellowship in 1979, and a Litt.D. from Liverpool University in 1980.

In 1981 Nicholson published *Sea to the West*, which he considers to be his best book. Already it has received more attention from critics than any of his earlier books. S. Toulson declared that Nicholson "is recognized as one of the most important poets writing in English today"; William Scammell called him "a regional poet *par excellence*"; and Robert Nye concluded that this volume "reveals him at the height of his considerable powers." More than ever, Nicholson excels in the simplicity and grace of a single phrase, line, or word, such as his use of an unusual verb in these lines from "Nobbut God": "The mountain ousel/Oboes its one note." In perhaps the most notable of the new poems, "Comprehending It Not," Nicholson describes through his eyes as a child of seven a Christmas at his grandmother's house following the death of his mother. He seldom portrays people in his poems, but here he sharply delineates his grandmother and his boisterous unmarried uncles as they interact with the grieving child. At a subtler level in the poem Nicholson communicates the compassion of the adults, which as a child he did not perceive. Of much interest to readers of Nicholson's writings is "Dismantling of Millom Ironworks," in which the poet regrets the razing of a huge foundry. In many previous poems the iron mill has served as center for the town's daily activity, and in others it has been the ugly—but vital—force that contrasts with the natural beauty of the mountains and sea. The mill's closing threw hundreds out of work and completed the decline begun years before when the iron mines gave out. The poet resents the ghost of Wordsworth—"seeing further than I can"—which may gaze with satisfaction over the now-unblemished landscape and now-unpolluted river. The reversion to nature as it had once been has exacted too high a price in human suffering. Other significant poems in this volume are "Sea to the West," "Haley's Comet," and "At the Music Festival." In 1982 Nicholson published *Selected Poems, 1940-1982* and chose to include even fewer poems than he had in his 1966 *Selected Poems*.

Norman Nicholson continues the tradition of writing a simple, sensuous, and impassioned verse like that of the Georgian poets and Wordsworth. Unpretentious, originating in his love of nature and in the lives of ordinary people in his native Cumberland, Nicholson's poetry derives from the romantic poetry of Wordsworth and proto-romantic eighteenth-century poets such as Cowper, Gray, and Burns. Like Wordsworth, he is a romantic poet who writes about ordinary people as they are subject to the vagaries of nature. Yet his concern, more than Wordsworth's, extends to the spoliation of the environment by modern industry, the effect of such misuse of nature upon ordinary people, and the responsibility of all individuals, in the light of Christian morality, to respect the creation of God on earth. His scholarly interests in geography, geology, botany, and literary biography all enter his work naturally. His Christian faith informs his poetry and allows him to interpret the daily life he leads in his native town in the light of history and eternity and in terms of the celebration of courage and endurance. The attitudes expressed in his poetry lie between pessimism and optimism. Suffering, pain, privation, and evil are ever-present realities, but fortitude, the exercise of free will, and a sense of integrity can mitigate these forces and render life, on the whole, a positive experience. His poetry reveals also the sane perspective provided by a rich and earthy sense of humor. Nicholson is an artist whose poetry provides for him a way of living, not a way to make a living or to achieve celebrity. His poetry is authentic, and its merit will continue to impress readers regardless of trends in literary fashion.

References:

Philip Gardner, "No Man Is an Island: Norman Nicholson's Novels," *Review of International English Literature*, 3 (January 1972): 44-53;

Gardner, *Norman Nicholson* (Boston: Twayne, 1973);

Kathleen E. Morgan, "The Word in Creation," in her *Christian Themes in Contemporary Poets* (London: SCM Press, 1965).

Papers:

Nicholson's manuscripts are deposited in the National Collection of Poetry Manuscripts, London, and the Northern Arts Manuscript Collection, Newcastle upon Tyne.

Leslie Norris

(21 May 1921-   )

Thomas Emery
DePauw University

SELECTED BOOKS: *Tongue of Beauty* (London: Favil Press, 1942);

Poems (London: Resurgam Press, 1946);

The Loud Winter (Cardiff: Triskel Press, 1967);

Finding Gold (London: Chatto & Windus/Hogarth Press, 1967);

Ransoms (London: Chatto & Windus, 1970);

Glyn Jones (Cardiff: University of Wales Press, 1973);

Mountains, Polecats, Pheasants and Other Elegies (London: Chatto & Windus/Hogarth Press, 1973);

His Last Autumn (Rushden, Northamptonshire: Priapus Press, 1976);

Sliding And Other Stories (New York: Scribners, 1976; London: Dent, 1978);

Ravenna Bridge (Knotting, Bedfordshire: Sceptre Press, 1977);

Merlin and the Snake's Egg (New York: Viking, 1978);

Water Voices (London: Chatto & Windus/Hogarth Press, 1980);

Walking The White Fields, Poems, 1967-1980 (Boston: Little, Brown, 1980).

PERIODICAL PUBLICATIONS:
Fiction:

"Three Shots for Charlie Betson," *Atlantic*, 238 (September 1976): 51-57;

"Shaving," *Atlantic*, 239 (April 1977): 42-45;

"Lurchers," *New Yorker*, 54 (3 July 1978): 26-32;

"Sing It Again Wordsworth," *Atlantic*, 244 (August 1979): 65-68;

"A Piece of Archangel," *Shenandoah*, 33, no. 1 (1981-1982): 69-77;

"Gamblers," *Shenandoah*, 33, no. 3 (1982): 51-59;

"A Seeing Eye," *Shenandoah*, 33, no. 4 (1982): 89-101.

Poetry:

"The Stone Poems," *Tar River Poetry,* 21 (Spring 1982): 37-38;

"Tree, Stone, Water," *Atlantic,* 250 (September 1982): 61.

When Leslie Norris, poet and storywriter, read Dylan Thomas's "Fern Hill" at the unveiling of the memorial to Thomas in Poet's Corner at Westminster Abbey on 1 March 1982, his gentle,

Leslie Norris (courtesy of the Welsh Arts Council)

mellifluous Welsh voice bore a strong resemblance to Thomas's own. The sounds, the techniques, even the scenery of the poem were familiar and comfortable to Norris, seven years Thomas's junior, an early imitator of him, and briefly, an acquaintance.

At the time of Dylan Thomas's death in 1953 at the age of thirty-nine, Norris was still ten years away from beginning his own mature career, one that would bring him only in his forties and fifties some of the growing attention in England and America that Thomas had enjoyed from his early twenties. Even when Norris's late recognition came, it was initially not so much from literary "establishments" as from younger poets and editors, attracted (perhaps mistakenly) to the seeming freeness of his forms and the spontaneity of voice in his poems and stories, writings that lock with keen and precise focus on the beauty, harmony, even cruelty, of nature and on man's place in it, insisting on man's need to persevere in his day-to-day life, facing obstacles in a decent, humane way.

The son of George William and Mary Jane Jones Norris, Norris was born on 21 May 1921, near Merthyr Tydfil, one of the world's first industrial cities. Merthyr Tydfil had grown from a town of 7,000 in 1800 to a rough, teeming iron, coal, and steel center of 70,000 by 1900 and then, for all practical purposes, died in the 1930s during the Great Depression. Norris attended Cyfarthfa Castle School from 1931 to 1938 and recalls being at times the only child in his class whose father held a job (farmer and milkman). From that rough and poverty-stricken environment, where policemen would walk in pairs and threes and where boxing was a most popular sport and pastime, Norris would escape into the enormously contrasting beauty of the area surrounding the Brecon Beacons, sandstone peaks in Brecknockshire, from which his grandfather, a horseman, had emerged. This juxtaposition of the natural beauty, serenity, and mystery of the mountains to the poverty and gloom of the stagnating city, together with Norris's father's death of stomach cancer at the age of forty-three, would be the source for many if not most of the themes of his later work. Norris left Merthyr Tydfil in 1940 to receive training in the Royal Air Force at Little Rissington, Gloucestershire, but he was discharged for a physical disability in 1941. From 1942 to 1947 he worked in the treasurer's department of the city of Merthyr Tydfil. He has spent most of his adult life in England. It would educate him, employ him, but it would make him wait more than twenty years for any substantial recognition of his literary art.

Norris had two small books of poetry published in the 1940s, although he describes himself as having had "no real connection with the literary world at all, no other writer, nobody." After attending the City of Coventry College in 1947-1948 and marrying Catherine Mary Morgan on 30 July 1948, he became an assistant teacher at the Grass Royal School in Yeovil, Somerset, where he worked from 1948 to 1952, when he left to take the position of deputy head of the Southdown School in Bath. Resigning that post in 1955, he attended the University of Southampton in 1955 to 1958, receiving Dip.Ed. and M.Phil. degrees. From 1955 to 1958, he served as head teacher at the Aldingbourne School in Chichester, and from 1958 to 1973 he was principal lecturer in degree studies and then an administrator at the College of Education in Bognor Regis, Sussex. Norris resigned the Bognor Regis position

in 1973 after a visiting lectureship at the University of Washington, Seattle, and has spent his time since writing poetry and fiction and lecturing. He returned to Seattle in 1980 and has lectured in several other English and American universities. He was resident poet at Eton College in 1977.

Norris's honors include the Welsh Arts Council awards in 1967 and 1968, the Alice Hunt Bartlett Prize for *Ransoms* in 1970, the Welsh Arts Council prize and the Cholmondeley Prize in 1978, and the Katherine Mansfield Triennial Award in 1981 for the best short story ("Waxwings") of 1978, 1979, and 1980.

Norris's first book of poetry was a small chapbook, *Tongue of Beauty*, published in 1942 by Peter Baker as one of the Resurgam Younger Poets series. *Tongue of Beauty* was well reviewed, particularly the sequence of religious sonnets which formed the major part of the collection and which reflected Norris's childhood attendance at Baptist services with his grandmother. On the whole the poetry was that of a young writer uncertain of his voice, the influence of Dylan Thomas being obvious.

In 1946 Baker published from the Resurgam Press in London a larger selection of Norris's poems. *Poems* includes all the poems from the earlier pamphlet as well as those written since that time. The new poems remain lyrical and often introspective, but a few poems touch on the war experience. Norris's concern with the natural world and other themes that he explores in his later work can be seen emerging in these poems. After the appearance of *Poems*, Norris did not have another book published for twenty-one years. Of this "silence," Norris says he did not stop writing, but he was involved in building his own career as a teacher and administrator, and it was difficult to get his work published. "The times were wrong for what I wrote," he says. "Poetry was rather an intellectual affair, with very stringent and, I think, restrictive verse-forms. I am a formal poet, but people didn't think so."

In 1967 a small press in Wales, the Triskel Press, published a book collecting some of the poems written during this long interval, all of which had been previously published in periodicals or broadcast. *The Loud Winter* is the product of a mature voice. The book's distribution was confined largely to Wales, but it was soon followed by a more substantial selection, *Finding Gold*, published later in the same year by Chatto and Windus in London. The poems in *Finding Gold* range from recapitulations of the poet's childhood and youth in Merthyr Tydfil—"Picking Coal," "Dead Boys," "The Strong Man"—to celebrations of the Sussex landscape in which he was then living—"Clymping," "Sussex," "Driving Home"—and poems written from his experience as a teacher—"Man and Boy," "Snow." Also in this collection is "The Ballad of Billy Rose," a vigorous poem about a boxer blinded in the ring, which had already been broadcast and published many times and was for years Norris's best-known poem, although it is in many ways untypical and written in a ballad form he did not continue to use.

Norris began writing his finest poems after the publication of *Finding Gold*. At that point, he began to work on the book that became *Ransoms* (1970), which contains many poems that Norris calls "celebratory elegies," moments of intense experience that the poet captures to keep them alive. In "Cardigan Bay," dedicated to his wife, Kitty, a couple looks out to sea, and the poet concludes, "For those who live here/After our daylight, I/Could wish us to look/Out of the darkness/We have become, teaching—Them Happiness, a true love." "Water" has a dairy family leaving out by the road a jug of water and glasses for shy mountain children who pass by in the hot summer, "But they never looked at us./Their eyes were full of the mountain. . . ." "Early Frost" invokes an adult's memory of an incident in his childhood, when he returned near-frozen to home and father: "But I knew what he meant/With the love of his rueful laugh, and my true/World unfroze in a flood of happy crying,/as hot on my cheek as the sting of this present Frost. . . ."

"A True Death" is a memorial for his friend, teacher and mentor, Welsh poet Vernon Watkins, who also was a personal friend and private critic of Dylan Thomas's. It speaks of a dying summer when they sat together in Watkins's garden and compares the narrator's childhood on "scarred hills where industrial/Fires for a hundred years had grieved/All things growing . . ." to Watkins's knowledge and love of the sea, things living. For most of his life Watkins would not leave his job as a bank clerk because employment elsewhere would force him to leave his beautiful Gower coast. The poem ends, "he spoke of the little tormentil,/Tenacious flower; growing there still."

Two poems in this collection particularly deserve attention for their own sake but also as moments when Norris's perspective is announced in themes that continue through all of his mature work, both poetry and fiction.

"Ransoms" details a chance moonlight passing of the former home of English critic and poet Edward Thomas, who volunteered for World War I in his forties and was killed in battle. Norris, who claims he learned from Thomas the secret of being able to write poetry in a quiet voice, has his narrator, coming from a journey of "dry irritation," observe wild garlic blooming in the moonlight, something Thomas may have seen many times, but which apparently never served as a source of inspiration for him. The key moment in the poem is when the narrator observes: "I have my small despair/And would not want your sadness; your truth,/Your tragic honesty, are what I know you for."

The poem was triggered, Norris says, by his seeing *ramsons*—the common name for wild garlic—spelled incorrectly as *ransoms*. The notion of the garlic's moonlight blooms serving as ransoms works on several levels, including their releasing Norris's creative powers both as human and poet, just as Thomas's poems have served Norris's art. But the poem also implies sadness that, while Norris has found truth in the sight of the blooming garlic ("And clean the smell of ransoms from the wood,/And I am refreshed. . . ."), the same sight did not serve to relieve Thomas's restless quest for truth.

"Now the House Sleeps" is an ambitious and provocative poem that questions the nature of reality. The house "sleeps" while the lane has "quietly gone/Down the cold hill. . . ." The narrator trusts his senses, what he sees, knows, has lived, "half/ignorant, half understood. . . ." In a memorable couplet, the narrator declares, "But at the edge of what I know/The massed, appalling forests grow." Trucks have ground the highways all night, cities' oppressions have continued, "Forced by a crude growling. Yet all/Are Plato's shadows on the wall." Near the end, the narrator declares, "clear eternities of light/Shine somewhere on the perfect world/We cannot know. My shadowed field/Lies in its flawed morning. . . ." As in "Ransoms," Norris celebrates as a whole the world he knows and in which he lives, the "flawed morning" rather than the "perfect world we cannot know." The poem suggests a profound suspicion of theoretical concepts, of absolutes, of ideology in favor of the known and verifiable functions of the flawed earth and its natural constituents.

Another important poem in this volume is "Space Miner," about an aged former coal miner lying in a hospital who "had worked deep seams where encrusted ore,/Too tight for his diamond drill, had ripped/Strips from his flesh." The poem is saved from being simply a protest of exploitation by its fine specificity and verbal agility, but its tone of protest is a thread in Norris's poetry (no surprise for a Welshman) that provides continuing tension with the acceptance of inevitable conflict in man and nature, with inevitable winners and losers.

Mountains, Polecats, Pheasants and Other Elegies (1973) continues this tension. "At the Publishers' " (also published separately in 1976) details a meeting with C. Day Lewis. With W. H. Auden and Stephen Spender, Day Lewis is said to have dominated much of English literary taste in the 1930s, 1940s, 1950s, and even beyond with his preference for strong intellectual, even ideological, content dressed in traditional poetic forms, so unlike Norris's. (Day Lewis in his preface to the first edition of *Contemporary Poets of the English Language* complained that free verse "enables the poem to be truly 'organic'/ whatever that may mean.")

In the poem Day Lewis comes from behind his desk to talk to the narrator, explaining that a Welshman whose poetry he had rejected once told him: "I allow no man sitting in a bloody office . . ./ . . . to tell me how to write poetry." The narrator asks Day Lewis to lunch, but Day Lewis declines and remains. The poem ends: "Next day you were announced the new Laureate./ You knew, of course, but hadn't said a word./ No, like the swollen cancers you carried with you,/ You waited for the proper day to come." Here again Norris seems to reject artificial propriety in life as well as in art because this sort of form denies the all too real content.

"A Small War" invokes Norris's childhood bicycle riding from Merthyr Tydfil to the Senni Valley, "an Eden fourteen miles from home," and recalls that when Evan Drew sent his sons to World War II, they rode their ponies to the station and then "circled the spitting sky above Europe." The narrator says he would not fight for Wales, not for its language, but he would fight for the forty people in Senni, who, "with frailest barriers of love and anger," try to prevent the building of a dam that would flood their fields. The narrator concludes, "When I open the taps in my English bathroom/ I am surprised they do not run with Breconshire blood"—as strong a statement as can be found in Norris's poetry.

"Beachmaster," one of Norris's finest poems, is a sensitive evocation of the turning of a generation of seals, in which the reader comes to realize and accept—"The way nature does these things"—that the bull seal guarding his herd will eventually be killed by one of his pups that are now nursing on the beach. The poem, like many of Norris's, is measured by a syllabic line (seven in this case) and does not have a fixed rhyme scheme, but it is full of rich internal rhyme, off-rhyme, and alliteration. The last line forms (unconsciously, Norris says) a perfect example of a medieval Welsh form,

the cynghannedd: "his sons, small,/ Weak, wait for white fur to fall."

In *Water Voices* (1980), written after Norris left academe, the forms become freer, his voice slightly more conversational, but still clearly measured. "At The Sea's Edge, In Pembrokeshire" was commissioned for the nine-hundredth anniversary of Winchester Cathedral but actually was written about St. David's Cathedral in Wales. Its lines are short, often no more than five or six syllables; the strategy is to make the poem physically resemble the building of a cathedral, stone by stone. The language is direct, economical, largely monosyllabic, and the poem contrasts the cathedral's builder, Peter de Leia ("dead eight hundred years"), to Saint David, who had been chosen archbishop when the ground under him miraculously rose before his fellow priests. De Leia on the other hand "saw/ his masons bleed if the chisel slipped. One fell in his sight/ from the brittle scaffolding/ and the two legs snapped/ audibly, hitting the ground."

De Leia "Knew that right/ building was a moral force, that/ stone can grow. . . ." Near the end of the poem is a short, surprising burst into polysyllables (a characteristic Norris strategy):

> De Leia built well, saw stone
> vault and flower. A plain man,
> building in faith where God
> had touched the saint, he saw
> the miracle, which is not swift
> visitation, nor an incredible
> suspension of the commonplace,
> but the church grown great about us,
> as if the first stone were a seed.

Other poems in this collection reflect on aging and, alternatively, celebrate the vitality and ruthlessness of youth and nature. "Eagle and Hummingbird" has the narrator fishing in a river with spinners that combine the beauty of the hummingbird with the sharp cruelty of the eagle in "the one forgiving world/ In whose veined heart I stand in a blue morning/ Beneath the flash of hummingbirds, the smoulder/ Of fishing eagles. . . ."

Several poems reflect Norris's travels on both the east and west coasts of America. "A Reading In Seattle" causes the narrator briefly to think of Dylan Thomas reading in the same room ("I thought I heard his voice/ Everywhere, after twenty years/ of famous death . . ."). In "Travelling West" the narrator is back home in southern England late at night. Observing a violent rainstorm beating from the west, he reflects on his travels west and on westward travel as a traditional symbol of moving toward death: "a small Odysseus,/Having as best I could, followed the sun./. . .hearing/The storm, knowing no end to the journey." The poem ends, "We'll begin once more,/Travelling west, travelling west."

Walking The White Fields, Poems, 1967-1980 (1980, a collection of the poems from *Ransoms; Mountains, Polecats, Pheasants and Other Elegies*; and *Water Voices*) received strong praise from reviewers in *Choice, Library Journal,* and *World Literature Today.* Norris writes, they said, "simply and eloquently," with an eye for detail "and the meaning of that detail." His poems are "tight and potent," the rhythms are "quiet and conversational [and] are tightened at appropriate moments with remarkable effectiveness."

Norris's short stories, published largely in America and in some of the most prestigious magazines (the *New Yorker*, the *Atlantic*, *Esquire*), account for a large part of his reputation in this country. Like the poems, they rely heavily on convincing voice and selection of sharp detail, drawing the reader into them as if there were no artifice about them. Frequently Norris uses a first-person narrator, often a child but equally often an adult who looks back into childhood, allowing a dual perspective on the experience. Norris has said that "the art of telling the story still remains the thing that most pleases me. I am a person who in other times would have sat at the fire corner and told the story, and in a way, I'm delighted to have people in the palm of my hand. . . ."

Sliding And Other Stories (1976) received good reviews, some of which compared Norris to such writers as D. H. Lawrence, Joyce, and Hemingway. A reviewer for *Choice* said that Norris's work should also go alongside that of Poe, Steinbeck, and Chekhov. On the other hand, more than one critic saw the stories as nostalgic, and one observed that the stories are "not symbolic, not difficult," and "not heavy or demanding on the reader. . . ."

Norris has described his fiction as composed of "spots of time" in the Wordsworthian sense (moments of ordinary experience rendered luminous through imaginative recollection in which, as Wordsworth wrote, "our minds/Are nourished and invisibly repaired. . . ." This element is important in Norris's poetry as well, representing a thread of acceptance as opposed to an impulse that might incline the poet to reach out, to protest fact or reason.

"Shaving," a story written after the publication of *Sliding*, exemplifies this sense of acceptance. In a very short, deft, and subtle story, extremely moving without being sentimental, Norris has a seventeen-year-old football player shave his father, near death from a long, slow illness. It is a ceremonial act, the boy trimming away some of the slight mortality that remains, preparing his father for death. As the boy holds the father in his arms, the father worries, "You're too young . . . to have this happen." The boy says he is not; he is bigger than most men; and at the crucial moment, the father agrees and releases his body's force to the boy's strong hands: "He had let go all his authority, handed it over." The father says he will not worry then "about anything." The story ends sadly, but in the way many of Norris's stories end, oddly healing, curative, resolved to life as it comes, with death as a part of it, without guilt.

Norris is difficult to categorize. He is Welsh by birth but declines any association with a Welsh "school" of writing. His models are diverse and eclectic, ranging from Wordsworth to Dylan Thomas (Norris says "his influence was not entirely for the good") in poetry and from Daniel Defoe to William Saroyan and Ernest Hemingway in fiction. His work is both modern and traditional. His poems often appear very "free" in form, as if consciously scrubbed of poeticisms, yet they are highly structured internally. Norris says of his poetry, "I just love formal verse. I just adore it. The making of the poem, after I've caught it, so to speak . . . the polishing of it, the making sure that nobody ever sees the joints—that's what I adore above everything else." His fiction is completely accessible but on close inspection reveals surprising substance and enormous technical skill. While his subject matter often is from another time, his themes are modern in their insistence on the world of the here and now, not some ideal or theoretical world.

Now in his early sixties, Norris has seen his collected poems published to strong reviews and respectable sales; *Sliding and Other Stories* has been republished in England in a mass-market student edition; he has written ample poems and stories for additional volumes of each, and he continues writing (and publishing) steadily. In accepting an appointment as poet in residence at Brigham Young University in Utah for 1983-1984, Norris once again returned to the America of which he has always been fond and which he thinks has worked to loosen his own poetic style, bring him closer to what he wants to say in "bolder (oddly enough) . . . plain, unadorned statements." In fiction, he would like to extend his range, to deal more with contemporary voices, perhaps urban settings, but he is set against moving from the short story to the novel: "I can do anything in the short story that I could do in the novel."

It is difficult to assess what the future will bring to Norris in terms of popular and critical regard. He deserves a wider audience. His lucidity, wordplay, sheer entertainment, coherent system of thought, and reasonable humane appeal set him apart from a literary world heavily preoccupied with self-consciousness, irony, and a diminution of the human spirit. It is clear that he has written poems and stories that deserve a place next to some of the best in the English language.

References:

Glyn Jones, *The Dragon Has Two Tongues* (London: Dent, 1968), pp. 9-38;

Thomas Parry, *A History of Welsh Literature*, translated by H. Idris Bell (London: Oxford University Press, 1955), p. 389.

Papers:

Norris's papers are at the National Library of Wales, Aberystwyth.

John Ormond
(3 April 1923-   )

Michael J. Collins
Georgetown University

BOOKS: *Indications*, by Ormond (as John Ormond Thomas), John Bayliss, and James Kirkup (London: Grey Walls, 1943);

Requiem and Celebration (Llandybie: Christopher Davies, 1969);

Definition of a Waterfall (London & New York: Oxford University Press, 1973);

Penguin Modern Poets 27, by Ormond, Emyr Humphreys, and John Tripp (Harmondsworth: Penguin, 1979);

Graham Sutherland, O.M.: A Memorial Address (Cardiff: National Museum of Wales, 1981).

RECORDING: *Poets of Wales: John Ormond and Raymond Garlick*, Argo (PLP 1156), 1971.

OTHER: "Ceri Richards," in *Ceri Richards Memorial Exhibition* (Cardiff: National Museum of Wales, 1973), pp. 7-11;

"*John Ormond Writes:*," in *Corgi Modern Poets in Focus: 5*, edited by Dannie Abse (London: Corgi, 1973), pp. 133-135.

PERIODICAL PUBLICATIONS: "Ceri Richards: Root and Branch," *Planet*, 10 (February/March 1972);

"R. S. Thomas: Priest and Poet," *Poetry Wales*, 7 (Spring 1972): 47-57;

"Four Poems," *Poetry Wales*, 16 (Autumn 1980): 8-11.

On Saint David's Day, 1 March 1982, some two thousand people gathered in Westminster Abbey for the unveiling and dedication of a memorial to Dylan Thomas. Among those present was John Ormond, a poet, filmmaker, and friend of Dylan Thomas, who had, like Thomas, grown up near Swansea. He had been invited to read Thomas's "Poem in October," and his presence and participation that day reflect his friendship not just with Dylan Thomas, but with the other great poet from Swansea, Thomas's good friend, Vernon Watkins. Ormond had met Thomas and Watkins when he was a young man, had been influenced by their work, and shares with them a commitment to the craft of poetry and the longing, in a lovely, fragile world, for the permanent and transcendent. From one point of view, John Ormond's career as a poet has consisted largely of his finding his own distinctly articulated answers to the questions raised by Thomas and Watkins. In the process, he has become one of the finest poets writing in English today.

The son of Arthur and Elsie Ormond Thomas, John Ormond was born John Ormond Thomas in Dunvant, a village to the west of Swansea:

> Upstairs in this stone house,
> Up the twelve crooked stairs
> My mother climbed to bear me.

At eleven o'clock on a spring night
I fell from her dark into candlelight,
Came to my own flesh as the string was cut
And lay alone on the bloody sheet.

He grew up in a small, closely knit community. His father was the shoemaker of the village, and many of his relatives worked in the nearby coal mines. (The village and its people have remained an important part of Ormond's life and have provided the material for some of his best poems.) He attended Dunvant Council School and Swansea Grammar School and then, in 1941, entered University College, Swansea (one of the four constituent colleges of the University of Wales), where he earned a final degree in philosophy in 1944 and an honours B.A. in English language and literature in 1945. (Years later, when he was offered a teaching fellowship at Swansea "to talk about poetry and film," he commented, "It was lovely to be asked. My parents had such trouble to keep me when I was scholarshipless at university.") At the same time, thinking he would become a painter, he attended classes in life-study drawing at the Swansea School of Art. Although his creative work has been in other media, his interest in painting has continued throughout his life, and he has written on the work of Graham Sutherland and Welsh painter Ceri Richards, who was also born in Dunvant. Moreover, his training in the Swansea School of Art and his lifelong interest in painting have influenced both his poetry and his films.

At the university, he read the poetry of Wilfred Owen and Dylan Thomas with particular interest and began, as he has put it, "to try to write." He published a good number of poems in magazines in England and Wales, and in 1943, Grey Walls Press brought out *Indications*, a collection by John Bayliss, James Kirkup, and John Ormond Thomas. The book was generally well received, and Ormond's promise as a poet was recognized in the reviews. As the *Times Literary Supplement* put it on 21 August 1943, Ormond "tends as often to exploit . . . imagery for his clever purposes as to create it out of an inward necessity. But there is more than cleverness in his verses, a lyrical probing of the dark mine of experience and a sinuous verbal craft that promises much." Randal Jenkins later said that "the encouragement confirmed the young poet in his vocation."

When he left the university in 1945, Ormond became a staff writer for *Picture Post* in London and thus began his career as a journalist. As he recently

John Ormond

explained, "I merely wrote and asked for a job and when asked for samples of my writing I sent every poem I had managed to publish. On the strength of that . . . [Sir Thomas Hopkinson] took me on as one of the six writers on the staff of a major journal which helped change the face of Britain after the war." He married Glenys Roderick on 21 September 1946, and in 1949 he became a subeditor for the *South Wales Evening Post* in Swansea. He moved to Cardiff in 1955 as television-news editor for the BBC and two years later became a producer and director of documentary films for the BBC Wales Television Service. In 1958 he completed *A Sort of*

Welcome to Spring, the first of more than two dozen films he would make for the BBC, eventually as senior documentary film producer and director.

John Ormond has had a distinguished career as a filmmaker with the BBC, and his work is highly regarded both in Britain and abroad. His films on other Anglo-Welsh poets are among his best and include *Under a Bright Heaven*, on Vernon Watkins (1966), *A Bronze Mask*, on Dylan Thomas (1968), *The Fragile Universe*, on Alun Lewis (1969), and *R. S. Thomas: Priest and Poet* (1971). A second film on Dylan Thomas, *I Sing to You Strangers*, the last Ormond made for the BBC, was shown in November 1983, to commemorate the thirtieth anniversary of the poet's death. Writing in a book called *Factual Television* in 1966, Norman Swallow recognized Ormond's distinguished achievement as a filmmaker. "It may well be," he said, "that the television of our own time will . . . be remembered . . . for the programs of a small group of men who have used the television documentary as a means of expressing their own vision of our age." He then named John Ormond as one of these filmmakers, who have in "the personal documentary" given television "its finest creative moments."

Although he continued to write and publish poetry after he left the university, Ormond had been advised by Vernon Watkins not to collect his poems again until he was thirty. As the years passed, he grew dissatisfied with his work, and by the time he was thirty he had come to regard it as "rubbish." His poetry up to this point had been heavily influenced by that of Dylan Thomas, and it was characterized by what Dannie Abse has called Thomas's "wordy mannerisms." As the reviewer in the *Times Literary Supplement* noted, Ormond's poems in *Indications* often used "imagery for . . . clever purposes," and "sound," as John Ormond put it later in an essay on his work, "heavily overbore sense." The result of his growing dissatisfaction with his early poetry, Ormond explained in a 1982 letter, "was a great bonfire on the potato patch when I came home from London to Dunvant, one August, of perhaps 300 or more pieces. I mean not drafts, but 'complete.' Though in those days I hadn't much of the pattern of revision and rewriting that later became the norm." He continued to write but had his work published only intermittently in the 1950s and early 1960s, and his career as a poet seemed finished. But then, in 1965, with the writing of a poem called "Cathedral Builders" and its publication in *Poetry Wales*, he entered upon a new phase of his career and began producing the apparently un-

adorned, resonant, carefully crafted poems upon which his reputation now rests.

> They climbed on sketchy ladders towards
> God,
> With winch and pulley hosted hewn rock into
> heaven,
> Inhabited sky with hammers, defied gravity,
> Deified stone, took up God's house to meet
> Him,
> And came down to their suppers and small
> beer;
> Every night slept, lay with their smelly wives,
> Quarrelled and cuffed the children, lied,
> Spat, sang, were happy or unhappy,
>
> And every day took to the ladders again;
> Impeded the rights of way of another sum-
> mer's
> Swallows, grew greyer, shakier, became less
> inclined
> To fix a neighbour's roof of a fine evening,
>
> Saw naves sprout arches, clerestories soar,
> Cursed the loud fancy glaziers for their luck,
> Somehow escaped the plague, got rheuma-
> tism,
> Decided it was time to give it up,
>
> To leave the spire to others; stood in the
> crowd
> Well back from the vestments at the conse-
> cration,
> Envied the fat bishop his warm boots,
> Cocked up a squint eye and said, "I bloody
> did that."

Although it is neither his best nor his most ambitious poem, "Cathedral Builders" was, in 1965, an important achievement for Ormond. He wrote the poem after his first trip to Italy, where he had gone on a filmmaking assignment. In "Arezzo, the city of Piero della Francesca. Up in the campanile of Santa Maria della Grazie I had heard the hammering and the singing of workmen as restoration went on. Some time later I wrote the one sentence of the piece (not knowing it was one sentence) in about 20 minutes and it was like nothing else I had ever done. . . . But at that moment I learned, or had somehow contrived, to use details of memory."

The poem has none of the conspicuous verbal techniques that characterize his earlier work. In fact, it seems so simple and direct as to need no comment at all. Yet the poem is put together as carefully as the cathedral whose builders it celebrates: the choice of words ("sketchy," "sprout," "defied gravity/Deified stone," for example), the alternating rhythms of the first three stanzas, the periodic structure of the whole poem and the last stanza particularly all combine to make it a deft and effective celebration of man's creative labor in the face of his inescapable mortality. As Ormond describes the process of writing it, "Cathedral Builders" seems one of those rare poems that is given to a poet. But his description is also misleading, for the poem seems finally the result of more than ten years of work to hone and perfect his craft, to make, as he does here, technique and meaning one.

In 1968, "to exorcise the devil of that long silence," he decided at last to have a collection of poems published, and in the following year Christopher Davies brought out *Requiem and Celebration*. The book includes poems written over more than twenty-five years. The opening poem, "First Sleep," for example (whose last stanza, beginning "Upstairs in this stone house," describes his birth), is a revised version of a poem that was first published in the *Welsh Review* in 1946. The last poem, "City in Fire and Snow," a long, eight-part sequence in memory of "the Swansea destroyed by bombing," was written between 1948 and 1952. Although the book was well received and awarded the annual Welsh Arts Council Prize for Literature, critics generally felt that the later, less elaborate poems in the book were more effective. Robert B. Shaw, writing in *Poetry* (Chicago), said that "although some of the pieces . . . have a weighty sonority and womb-tomb imagery too close to Dylan Thomas, Ormond breaks through often to an attractive, quieter music and vision of his own." While *Requiem and Celebration* contains many excellent poems ("My Grandfather and His Apple Tree," "Johnny Randall," "Design for a Tomb," and "Definition of Waterfall," to name just four), the shortest of them, "At His Father's Grave," completed in 1951, suggests the characteristic virtues of Ormond's later work:

Here lies a shoe-maker whose knife and
hammer
Fell idle at the height of summer,
Who was not missed so much as when the rain
Of winter brought him back to mind again.

He was no preacher but his working text
Was *See all dry this winter and the next.*
Stand still. Remember his two hands, his
laugh,
His craftsmanship. They are his epitaph.

The poem is written, appropriately enough, in heroic couplets. Its simple, direct, inconspicuous language seems utterly ordinary and familiar, and it follows the traditional curve of the elegy as it moves from death and loss to a quiet celebration of the shoemaker's life. The rhythmic movement of the last two lines (with the enjambment and the long pause) helps give the poem its triumphant conclusion. The mention of summer and winter is a clear and familiar reminder of time and change, of the transience and fragility of life and joy in a fallen, finite world. Yet the poem ends in affirmation as it suggests, with the simplest words, the quiet virtues and human decency of a man remembered with love. The poet's skill makes the poem a moving and effective tribute to his father and balances it deftly between joy and sorrow, requiem and celebration. "At His Father's Grave" offers Ormond's characteristic affirmation of life in the face of its inevitable passing.

In the years that followed *Requiem and Celebration* John Ormond continued to publish individual poems in a variety of magazines in and out of Wales. In 1971 Argo Records released a recording by Ormond and Raymond Garlick on which Ormond reads some of his later poems (*Poets of Wales: John Ormond and Raymond Garlick*). Soon afterward Jon Stallworthy, then an editor at Oxford University Press, accepted a collection of Ormond's poems for publication, and *Definition of a Waterfall* appeared in 1973. Like its predecessor, it was awarded the Welsh Arts Council Prize for Literature. As David Shayer put it in a review in *Poetry Wales*, "John Ormond . . . consolidated the achievement of *Requiem and Celebration* . . . with this volume."

A collection of twenty-eight poems (eleven of which appeared in *Requiem and Celebration*), *Definition of a Waterfall* is an excellent book. Writing in the Autumn 1980 issue of *Poetry Wales*, Cary Archard called it "one of the best books of English language poetry to appear in the Seventies." It contains such finely written poems as "The Key," perhaps his best poem about the village in which he grew up; "In September," a beautiful love poem; and "Salmon," a long poem of ninety-six lines which "took four and a half years to complete and went through about thirty drafts and three hundred or so worksheets." Jeremy Hooker, writing in *The Anglo-Welsh Review*, said, "I believe that in *Definition of a Waterfall*, which he publishes at the age of fifty, John Ormond has emerged as a major poet."

The new poems in *Definition of a Waterfall* are marked by the same deft and resonant simplicity that characterized the best poems in his previous collection. At the same time, he returns again to what he has called his continual concern "with 'life's miraculous poise between light and dark,' " to his affirmation of life and joy in the face of time and change:

> Again the golden month, still
> Favourite, is renewed;
> Once more I'd wind it in a ring
> About your finger, pledge myself
> Again, my love, my shelter,
> My good roof over me,
> My strong wall against winter.

While the simple, domestic images and the quiet, gentle rhythms of "In September" make it a beautiful and moving declaration of love, words such as "still," "again," "once more" recall the passing of time. As he does in many of his poems, John Ormond at once celebrates the joys of ordinary life and mourns their inevitable loss.

In 1973 Ormond was awarded a Welsh Arts Council Major Bursary for Writing, and in 1979 a group of twenty-eight of his poems appeared in *Penguin Modern Poets 27*, which also includes poems by Emyr Humphreys and John Tripp. Of the poems by Ormond, eight had not been previously collected. One of the most interesting among them is "Homing Pigeons," which first appeared in the *Times Literary Supplement*'s special issue on Wales (4 March 1977):

> Out of a parsimony of space unclenched,
> Into the not known and yet familiar,
> They ascend out of their hunger, venture
> A few tentative arcs, donate new
> Circumflexions to the order of strange sky;
> Then blend to a common tangent and so ren-
> der
> Themselves to the essence of what they are.
>
> What beguilement shepherds the heart
> home?
> Not what we know but some late lode-stone
> Which, far, was always there, drawing us
> To a meaning irreducible, to a fixed star.
>
> Why then the falling, all the fumbling
> As tumbler pigeons, fools flying, with the
> most
> Inept of masteries? But flying still
> And, despite awkwardness, being, as best we
> can,

> Committed, in the chance weather we ap-
> proach,
> To what and where, without a sense of re-
> ward,
> We may reach and trust to be fed.

The poem is characteristically rich and carefully crafted. The alliteration, which becomes more insistent as the poem progresses, not only suggests, with the rhythms of the poem, the flight of the pigeons, it also recalls the traditional Welsh poetic forms that are characterized by strict patterns of alliteration. This formal allusion shapes and enlarges the poem's definition of home and suggests it is meant to be seen, in part, as the heritage and traditions of Wales through which the nation and its people can become distinctly, essentially themselves. But the poem gives no guarantees. The broken rhythms of the last stanza and the ambiguity of the word "may" in the last line make tentative and guarded its final affirmation.

As "Homing Pigeons" makes clear, Ormond has, for all his individuality, been influenced as a poet by Wales, where he was born, grew up, and has lived for most of his life. "I don't particularly like the term 'Anglo-Welsh,' " he once wrote, "although I can see its usefulness as a short-hand description of those Welshmen who write in English. As far as I am concerned the first thing I ask of 'Anglo-Welsh' poems is that they should be good poems in the English Language. The Welshness, if it is to be there at all, will look after itself." The Welshness has in fact done so, for while John Ormond has written many fine poems in English that grow out of his life in Wales, they finally transcend the particulars of place and speak to men and women everywhere.

"Homing Pigeons," for example, is not only about Wales, but about the universal human desire to make sense of things, to find meaning for our lives. Like tumbler pigeons, whose flight is broken by their tumbling, we struggle to reach the place where our hunger for meaning can be satisfied. The broken rhythms and the insistent alliteration of the last stanza, which suggest the labored flight of the pigeons, recall as well John Ormond's continuing effort in his poetry to make sense of the human condition.

The longing for permanence, for perfection, for meaning and order is a constant theme of John Ormond's poetry. And if they are sometimes found by the characters he portrays (the cathedral builders who take "up God's house to meet Him"; the shoemaker whose craft is his epitaph), they are at

Homing Pigeons

Out of a parsimony of space unclenched,
Into the not known & yet familiar,
They ascend out of their hunger, venture
A few tentative ups, donate new
Circumflexions to the order of strange sky;
Then blend to a common tangent & so render
Themselves to the essence of what they are.

What beguilement shepherds the heart home?
Not what we know but some late lode-stone
Which, far, was always there, drawing us
To a meaning irreducible, to a fixed star.

Why then the falling, all the fumbling
As tumbler pigeons, fools flying, with the most
Inept of masteries? But flying still
And, despite awkwardness, being as best we can,
Committed in the chance weather we approach,
To what and where, without a sense of reward,
We may reach and trust to be fed.

John Ormond

Inscribed for Michael J. Collins as greeting and
in gratitude for his understanding   1980

Fair copy (the author)

best momentary and elusive. In his film on R. S. Thomas, Ormond introduces Thomas's poem "The River" with these words: "Signals from an ever present reality, glimpses of the eternal; sources at which a man can strengthen and renew his vision of an order beyond time." John Ormond looks for such signals in his poetry, but he finds in the end nothing more than the world of time and change which gives reason to mourn and rejoice.

In "A Lost Word," a poem he included in *Penguin Modern Poets 27*, he describes those moments when the signals seem about to come clear, when one is on the edge of vision. Sometimes, he writes,

> One cannot escape the feeling that something
> Almost at hand eludes us, that characters im-
>   printed
> On the other side of a page, in parallel, press
>   through
> On what we are trying to say, and would dis-
>   close
> News or perhaps solace, some almost obvious
> Simple sentence which would complete
> The heart's short story of magnificence.

But in John Ormond's world "the lost word" is never heard, revelation never comes:

> Unable to sleep, shaving at half-dawn,
> Unwilling to gaze full into the eyes
> Of the latest forgery in the bathroom mirror,
> Today's bad copy of an earlier work,
> I have no lust for secrets. It is enough that the
>   blade
> Is sharp, that the sun lurks then rises over my
>   garden's
> Blown roses and its brown turmoil of leaves.

The speaker is content with the cycle of new days that reveal both blown roses and brown leaves, with the growth and decay, the joy and sorrow that characterize his existential condition. In John Ormond's poetry one lives in a fallen, finite world that brings both requiem and celebration.

The resignation of "A Lost Word," however, is not finally John Ormond's dominant tone. In a poem called "The Gift" he affirms the value of life even as it is lived without metaphysical knowledge.

> From where, from whom? Why ask, in tor-
>   ment
> All life long when, while we live, we live in it?
> As pointless to ask for truth in epiphanies
> That throb in the fire, rustle, then fall into
>   ash;
> Or why stars are not black in a white firma-
>   ment.
> Enough that it was given, green, as of right,
>   when,
> Equally possible, nothing might ever have
>   been.

If the world is all there is in John Ormond's poetry, it seems more than enough. In joy or in sorrow, with a sure and exquisite skill, he celebrates the fragile, finite world and returns us to it with a renewed sense of its inestimable goodness and worth. John Ormond is one of the finest poets writing in English today, and his generous, carefully crafted poetry deserves wider recognition than it has so far received.

Bibliography:

Chris O'Neill, "Notes Towards a Bibliography of John Ormond's Works," *Poetry Wales*, 16 (Autumn 1980): 34-38.

References:

Dannie Abse, "John Ormond," in *Corgi Modern Poets in Focus: 5*, edited by Abse (London: Corgi, 1973), pp. 127-133;

Michael J. Collins, "The Anglo-Welsh Poet John Ormond," *World Literature Today*, 51 (Autumn 1977): 534-537;

Collins, "Craftsmanship as Meaning: The Poetry of John Ormond," *Poetry Wales*, 16 (Autumn 1980): 25-33;

Jeremy Hooker, "The Accessible Song," *Anglo-Welsh Review*, no. 51 (Spring 1974): 5-12;

Randal Jenkins, "The Poetry of John Ormond," *Poetry Wales*, 8 (Summer 1972): 17-28;

Richard Poole, "The Voices of John Ormond," *Poetry Wales*, 16 (Autumn 1980): 12-24.

Henry Reed

(22 February 1914-   )

Douglas Cleverdon

BOOKS: *A Map of Verona* (London: Cape, 1946;
New York: Reynal & Hitchcock, 1948);
The Novel Since 1939 (London & New York:
Longmans, Green, 1946);
*Moby Dick: A Play for Radio from Herman Melville's
Novel* (London: Cape, 1947);
Lessons of the War (New York & London: Clover Hill
Editions/Chilmark Press, 1970);
The Streets of Pompeii, and other plays for radio (Lon-
don: British Broadcasting Corp., 1971);
Hilda Tablet and Others: four pieces for radio (London:
British Broadcasting Corp., 1971).

RADIO SCRIPTS: *Moby Dick*, BBC, 1947;
Pytheas: A Dramatic Speculation, BBC, 1947;
The Unblest, BBC, 1949;
The Monument, BBC, 1950;
Return to Naples, BBC, 1950;
A By-Election in the Nineties, BBC, 1951;
The Streets of Pompeii, BBC, 1952;
The Great Desire I Had, BBC, 1952;
A Very Great Man Indeed, BBC, 1953;
The Private Life of Hilda Tablet, BBC, 1954;
Vincenzo, BBC, 1955;
Emily Butter, BBC, 1955;
A Hedge, Backwards, BBC, 1956;
The Primal Scene, as it were . . ., BBC, 1958;
The Auction Sale, BBC, 1958;
*Not a Drum Was Heard: The War Memoirs of General
Gland*, BBC, 1959;
Musique Discrète, BBC, 1959;
The Complete Lessons of War, BBC, 1960.

TRANSLATIONS: Ugo Betti, *Three Plays* (Lon-
don: Gollancz, 1951; New York: Grove, 1958);
Betti, *Crime on Goat Island* (London: French, 1960;
San Francisco: Chandler, 1961);
Dino Buzzati, *Larger than Life* (London: Secker &
Warburg, 1962);
Honoré de Balzac, *Eugénie Grandet* (New York: New
American Library, 1964).

Henry Reed's reputation was established in
1946 by a single slim book of poems, *A Map of
Verona*, which includes his much-anthologized war
poem "Naming of Parts," one of three poems

Henry Reed, circa 1965 (University of Washington, Seattle)

grouped together as *Lessons of the War*. While he has
occasionally had poems published in periodicals
and an expanded version of *Lessons of the War* appeared in 1970, no other volume of his verse has
been published; yet he continues to be well known
in England because of his works for radio. The
twenty years after World War II saw a flowering of
creative talent among the younger poets,
dramatists, and composers who found in BBC
Radio a fulfilling and reasonably profitable outlet
for their work. The BBC Drama Department was
the first to sponsor productions of plays by Samuel
Beckett, Harold Pinter, Tom Stoppard, Giles
Cooper, and other now highly regarded dramatists.

276

BBC Features, whose staff producers included such poets as Louis MacNeice, W. R. Rodgers, and Terence Tiller, covered a wide range of programs. In this company Henry Reed was preeminent in the consistently high quality of his radio creations: in the compelling tragic beauty of his two verse plays on Giacomo Leopardi, *The Unblest* (1949) and *The Monument* (1950), no less than in the series of plays that depict hilarious satirical delights of Hilda Tablet and her circle—*A Very Great Man Indeed* (1953), *The Private Life of Hilda Tablet* (1954), *Emily Butter* (1955), *A Hedge, Backwards* (1956), and *The Primal Scene, as it were* (1958).

Born in Birmingham in 1914 to Henry and Mary Ann Bell Reed, Henry Reed was educated at King Edward VI School and later at the University of Birmingham, where Louis MacNeice, then a young assistant lecturer in classics, was a stimulating influence on a group of intelligent undergraduates, several of whom later became BBC radio writers and producers. Taking a first-class honors degree in languages and literature in 1934 and later an M.A., Reed conceived a profound admiration for Thomas Hardy, and for several years worked on a biography, while occasionally contributing poems and book reviews to literary and other journals—in particular the *Listener*, whose editor, J. R. Ackerley, had a considerable respect for Reed's abilities.

Having taught for a year at his old school, St. Edward VI in Birmingham, he was conscripted in 1941 into the Royal Army Ordnance Corps and then transferred to the Foreign Office where he worked with Naval Intelligence. As he later told Vernon Scannell, he developed a capacity for comic impersonations of drill sergeants, a knack he perfected in the sergeant's voice in "Naming of Parts." Equally terse and ironic was his note for *Who's Who* about his last days of military service: "released VJ day, 1945; recalled to army, 1945; did not go, 1945; matter silently dropped, 1945."

In 1946 Reed produced *A Map of Verona*, which revealed an unmistakably individual mode of writing. The first group of poems, "Preludes," is largely personal in origin. The title poem, "A Map of Verona," reflects his love of Italy: the enchantments of towns already known, the anticipation of "the small strange city" of Verona, the "cautious questioning/Of travellers who talk of Juliet's Tomb and fountains/And a shining smile of snowfall, late in Spring." Other poems recall travel with a loved friend. "Naming of Parts" intersperses the ambiguities of the sergeant's instructions to the squad about the manipulation of the rifle with descriptions of goings-on in the neighboring garden: "And

rapidly backwards and forwards/The early bees are assaulting the flowers:/They call it 'easing the Spring.'" "Chard Whitlow" (often solemnly regarded as a serious poem) is a brilliant parody of T. S. Eliot.

In the second group of poems, "The Desert," Henry Reed's imaginative power creates images of distant oceans and lands, where "You, I, or we/Finally, certainly, may,/Skirting the shattered fragments,/Wander and praise." In the third group, "Tintagel," four poems—"Tristram," "Iseult Blaunchesmains," "King Mark," and "Iseult La Belle"—evoke the tragedy that each suffered. Finally, in the last two poems, Chrysothemis and Philoctetes re-enact their lives in the world of Greek mythology.

On its publication in 1946, *A Map of Verona* aroused considerable admiration. Of "this remarkable first volume" the critic for the *New Statesman & Nation* wrote: "Mr Henry Reed is a rare poet in more senses than one. He writes very little; that little is

Dust jacket for Reed's first book, which contains "Naming of Parts," the poem Vernon Scannell has called "the most complete and poignant articulation we have of the consciousness of the reluctant conscript. . . ."

highly finished and exactly chosen. . . . Already Mr Reed has a mastery of the blank-verse line as extended by Eliot. Where he will go to one can't tell, but all the hints seem to be here of larger work."

In the same year Reed wrote a short but comprehensive monograph, *The Novel Since 1939*, which was published by Longmans, Green, for the British Council. Thereafter all his major works were written for broadcasting on the BBC Third Programme. The first was a two-hour adaptation of *Moby-Dick*. As he wrote in his preface to the published text, "it is upon the book's symbolism and tragedy alone that an adaptor must concentrate." To retain all the most dramatic scenes would merely result in "a series of roaring climaxes." Thus the script contains a number of reflective poems that concentrate on the experience of whaling, the whiteness of the whale, and the aura of the Pacific. Also, during the final three-days' pursuit of the whale, the second day is described in a verse intermezzo spoken by Ishmael. This radio version was imaginatively produced in 1947 by Stephen Potter, with Ralph Richardson as Ahab, and with music by Anthony Hopkins. In the same year he wrote his first full-length and original play for radio, *Pytheas: A Dramatic Speculation*, concerning the Greek traveler who sailed from Marseilles into the Atlantic in search of Ultima Thule.

Reed has a profound admiration for the poems of the nineteenth-century Italian poet Count Giacomo Leopardi. In 1949 and 1950 he wrote two verse plays on Leopardi, using a sprung pentameter throughout. The first, *The Unblest*, evokes the cloistral atmosphere of the Palazzo Leopardi in the little provincial town of Recanati, where the children's lives are made miserable by the obsessive piety of their bigoted, domineering mother. Giacomo Leopardi, the eldest, a hunchback and half-blind, is never allowed out alone and lives vicariously through the people he sees from his window:

> Innocent passers-by, you do not know
> How you companion my waking nights, how
> you are forced
> To meet my shut eyes' gaze, when I wake in
> the morning.
> Clod-hopping youth, hold your arms tight
> round that girl.
> In the waning day, draw her into the
> shadows;
> Let the shadows embrace you both as you
> embrace.
> You cannot escape me; while your mouth
> Lies upon hers, she has been also mine.

Imagining the sexual passions of all he sees, he also hopes for release from his obsessions:

> Help me, incredible God! unmake my fever,
> Give me my unhorizoned innocence,
> Or send me him who shall restore me to it,
> And it to me. Send me Giordani. . . .

The scholar-priest Pietro Giordani comes and takes Leopardi for a few hours to Macerata, and at last, in a deeply moving scene, Giacomo's father, realizing his son's despair, overrules his wife and allows Giacomo to leave Recanati for Rome. In *The Monument*, Leopardi is in Bologna eight years later, renowned as a poet, moving in the cultured circles of the city, but suffering the anguish of unrequited love:

> And now she goes
> Between the insensible stone and the heedless
> fountain,
> By the trees that do not see her, as she passes
> Where I dare not go with her, where I only
> follow,
> To let the shadows that have fallen upon her
> path
> Fall upon mine a moment after. . . .

At the end of the play, he is drawn back to Recanati by memories of his sister and his brothers.

Return to Naples (1950) is semiautobiographical, a young Englishman's recreating five visits, over a period of twenty years, to an Italian family in Naples, and reflecting their vicissitudes between 1930 and 1950. The father, a passionate stamp collector, and the mother, ample and warm but perpetually harassed by the domestic cares of bringing up four sons, have marvellously funny discussions (on stamp collecting, or on the incomprehensible mores of the English), while they also reveal their anxieties and frustrations as attitudes change over the years. The Italian ambience is brilliantly conveyed by an occasional Italian epithet or a literally translated turn of phrase.

Reed regards his next play for radio, *The Streets of Pompeii* (1952), as "a sort of dramatic poem," although much of it is written in prose. The play opens with the formal, elegiac verse of the Sibyl of Cumae recalling the destruction of the town, in stanzas based on Leopardi's poem about the yellow broom growing on the slopes of Vesuvius:

> Once more, once more, once more:

These plains once more with barren ashes
                                      covered,
Once more the lava, once more turned to
                                      stone;
The traveller's feet once more clink over it,
Once more, once more.
And the snake nests and coils in the sun's
                                      heat,
The rabbit seeks its familiar winding home
Once more.
. . . .
And to this place,
Let him come bravely now, whose wont it is
To praise man's power and chance; here let
                                      him see
How the harsh Nurse covers her children's
                                      eyes.
On these bright shores full-painted let him
                                      see
Here of the human race
The magnificent, progressive destinies.

A crescendo of music brings a flashback of the
Pompeians' panic as the mountain erupted. Silence
ensues. A young Italian architectural student encounters a girl from Naples. As the hours pass from
morning to dusk, their appreciative exploration of
the ruins is often expressed in a loose, graceful
pentameter. Their growing love is voiced in two
deeply felt sonnets as each sees the other sleeping.
The young woman says,

He sleeps, Attilio sleeps, sleeps lightly, sleeps
                                      by me.
I must not watch him, and I must, as there he
                                      lies.
I must not watch too long, lest when he wakes,
                                      his eyes
Open to mine. I must not. It must not be.
I must watch instead the lizard or the tree,
Or the stones he knows so well: which recog-
                                      nise
The warm bright glance, affectionate and
                                      wise,
He turns upon them; so that I may not see
The sunlight fall on his mouth, nor the sur-
                                      render
To sleep of his dark hair, nor clear and sweet
The curve of his silent cheek, the golden
                                      splendour
Of his throat and his arms and his thighs
                                      and his sandalled feet.
I will watch the lizard, or the stone, or the
                                      sky above him,
Lest he should see, when he wakes, dear
                                      Attilio, how dearly I love him.

A traveler contemplates the scene, while ar-
chaeologists make their way to the Villa of the Mysteries; four high-spirited young English tourists
enjoy themselves; and a lizard basks in the heat.
There follows an interchange between the Sibyl and
the traveler as they evoke the erotic drama of the
frescoes of the Mysteries. As evening falls, an elderly Englishman and his wife, recalling earlier visits to Pompeii, encounter the young Italian couple.

Technically this play is a skillful piece of
dramatic writing, with continuing interaction and
contrast between one group and another, between
Roman Pompeii and the contemporary world,
marked by subtle changes of mood and tension, and
by smooth transitions from lighthearted badinage
to passages of great force and beauty. In its evocative power it is essentially a poet's creation. First
broadcast in 1950, it received an award from the
Italia Prize jury in Palermo a few months later.

Although *The Great Desire I Had* (1952) and
Vincenzo (1955) are not in verse, most of the narra-
tions and soliloquies in these two radio plays are
written in a heightened prose that is purely poetic in
feeling and style. In *The Great Desire I Had* (the title is
from *The Taming of the Shrew*, where Lucentio expresses "the great desire I had/To see faire Padua,
nurserie of Arts"), Reed was prompted to imagine
the visit that Shakespeare, in his thirtieth year,
might have made to Italy. Meeting with a company
of Italian players—including, of course, women instead of boys to play the female roles—Shakespeare
appreciates their different approach to the art of
the theater. Accompanying them to Mantua and the
Gonzaga palace, where they are to perform before
the well-known late-Renaissance patron Duke Vincenzo I, Shakespeare finds himself alone in the vast
salon with Giulio Romano's huge Trojan frescoes
sprawling over the walls. As Reed conceives it,
Shakespeare has for ten years been planning an epic
poem on the siege of Troy, but his work as actor and
playwright has prevented its completion. Duke Vincenzo Gonzaga comes into the room, but does not
disclose his identity to the Englishman. In their
conversation Shakespeare speaks of his ten years'
frustration. Vincenzo sensibly advises him to give
up the Trojan epic and write something shorter—
fifty lines, say, describing Giulio Romano's frescoes,
just to satisfy his conscience; the lines might come in
useful later. After the initial shock, Shakespeare
sees the point, and the eventual outcome is *The Rape
of Lucrece*.

Altogether *The Great Desire I Had* is a diverting
jeu d'esprit, with lovely evocations of sixteenth-
century Padua, Verona, Venice, and Mantua, both

in the narrative passages and in Shakespeare's own soliloquies. But it is a minor work in comparison with *Vincenzo*, which covers the life of Vincenzo Gonzaga from his nineteenth year, as an irresistibly handsome wanton young prince with the beautiful Ippolita, whom he calls Andromeda, as his favorite mistress, through his marriages, first to the fourteen-year-old Margherita Farnese (annulled when she proved childless), and then to Eleanora de Medici, who bore him four children and, at Vincenzo's insistence, brought up with them Silvio, his child by the Marchesa Agnese del Carretto. By this time Vincenzo is middle-aged, self-centered, and pompous, and fancies himself as a military commander, giving instructions to Rubens for paintings that will immortalize his exploits in his forthcoming campaign against the Turks.

The linking narrative is carried forward by the four women in Vincenzo's life, Ippolita, Margherita, Eleanora, and Agnese. Finally Margherita's brother Renuccio, now Duke of Parma, who has always hated Vincenzo, seizes Agnese's young lover and some other Mantuans in a sudden frenzy of suspicion. Fearing for their lives, Agnese persuades Vincenzo to offer remarriage to Margherita, in order to establish good relations between Parma and Mantua. For thirty years Margherita has lived in a convent, resigned to the religious life. In prayer she welcomes God's mercy in allowing her to return to his world and to walk among his fields and woods. But before the papal dispensation can be secured, she learns that Vincenzo has died, leaving her totally bereft.

Vincenzo is a remarkable work. Its understanding of human character, its erotic power, and its deep compassion are conjoined with delicate satire and delicious comedy. The language ranges from enchanting descriptions of the rose gardens of Colorno to witty bantering between lovers or the biting invective of family quarrels or the anguish of love nobly controlled. There are scenes that haunt the memory: Francesco de Medici, Grand Duke of Tuscany, and his mistress Bianca Cappello lying together on their deathbed, unable to reach each other for one last kiss, but never renouncing their love though it condemned them to an eternity of damnation; or Vincenzo and his five-year-old Silvio sharing, entranced, the sufferings depicted in the seventeenth-century composer Monteverdi's "Lament of Ariadne" as she mourns the departure of Theseus. After Vincenzo explains that "in the end you will see that she is rescued and made happy by Bacchus, the god of wine," Silvio asks, "Are unhappy ladies always rescued from their sorrow by

the god of wine?," and Vincenzo responds, "Very frequently, yes."

Meanwhile Reed had decided to abandon his unfinished biography of Hardy. He had worked at it intensively at first, and later sporadically, for twenty years, ever since he was at Birmingham University; and it was now a millstone round his neck that had frustrated the development of his true creative gifts. One offshoot of his research, however, was a lighthearted feature, *A By-Election in the Nineties* (1951), regarding a by-election in Dorchester of which Hardy must have been aware. And, just as Voltaire's jeu d'esprit, *Candide*, brought him far greater renown than his vast philosophical writings, so from the ashes of the life of Hardy arose that incomparable phoenix of radio, Hilda Tablet: the "composeress" of twelve-tone music, whose personality and achievements so impressed musical circles in London and elsewhere that (through the intermediation of Henry Reed and of Donald Swann who "realised" her compositions) she ultimately received the accolade of a two-column profile in the London *Times*.

One must regret that Hilda Tablet, diverting though she was, diverted Henry Reed from continuing to exercise his poetic creativity in more substantial radio works of the caliber of *Vincenzo* or *The Streets of Pompeii*. His succession of masterpieces for the BBC Features Department had established his reputation as second only, perhaps, to Louis MacNeice, the most distinguished and most consistently successful of the poets who were enlarging the frontiers of radio during the twenty years following the war—MacNeice, David Gascoyne, Dylan Thomas, Sylvia Plath, Ted Hughes, David Jones, Stevie Smith, as well as others less well-known. But the temptation to exploit in radio form his tribulations as a biographer of Thomas Hardy proved irresistible. In September 1953, the BBC Third Programme broadcast *A Very Great Man Indeed*, in which Henry Reed's other self, Herbert Reeve, an earnest but ingenuous young biographer, strives to collect material for his life of a famous novelist, ten-years dead, named Richard Shewin. Reeve's narrative is a delicious parody of literary-pompous biographese; the people he interviews range from the literary executrix ("The legal documents, Mr Reeve, will certainly be available as from February 22nd, 2017. . . ." "What a charming coincidence. It will be my hundred and third birthday") to the two Miss Burkleys, "so courageously living out their spinsterhood in their little flat in Shepherd Market" (traditionally inhabited by high-class prostitutes). The part of Hilda Tablet was played so magnificently by Mary O'Farrell that a few months later Henry Reed produced a sequel, *The Private Life of Hilda Tablet* (1954), in which Hilda browbeats Reeve into making herself, not Shewin, the subject of his biography ("not more than twelve volumes, Bertie, I beg you. It was enough for Gibbon, it was enough for Proust. Let it be enough for you, Bertie"). She first suggests the transference in a hilarious bathroom scene, in which—as Reed later described it—"full frontal nudity was heard on radio for the first time, the writer being quite unaware of what a trail he was blazing."

All features producers for the BBC Features Department were contracted as writers also and worked in close collaboration with their free-lance radio writers, composers, actors, and technical staff. Office hours were largely disregarded, and it was in the BBC studios and two adjacent taverns (the George and the Stag) that creative radio was nurtured. Reed was never a frequenter of pubs, but he was closely and affectionately involved with the group of brilliant players who regularly took most of the leading roles in his radio pieces. They virtually constituted a permanent company. Consequently in much of his work for radio he wrote with particular players in mind, and their individual abilities often spurred his creative imagination. Certainly without Mary O'Farrell's inspired performance as Hilda Tablet there would have been no sequel to *A Very Great Man Indeed*; and each of the subsequent programs was prompted by some ingredient in its predecessor. *The Private Life of Hilda Tablet* led inevitably to a brilliantly satirical evocation of the Covent Garden premiere of Hilda's opera, *Emily Butter* (1955). In contradistinction to Benjamin Britten's recent all-male opera, *Billy Budd*, the artistes in *Emily Butter* (at first provisionally entitled "Milly Mudd") were all female, except for "a plain-clothes police lady," whose role was sung by a basso profundo. Britten's "realisations" of Purcell and other early composers were reflected in the BBC closing announcement that "Hilda Tablet's score was realised by Donald Swann; the production was suddenly realised by Douglas Cleverdon." As a large proportion of the program consisted of operatic performance, *Emily Butter* was not included in the BBC collection *Hilda Tablet and Others* (1971). It was followed by *A Hedge, Backwards* (1956), in which Reeve is perplexed by confusing and contradictory biographical details from members of Richard Shewin's family, including a brother-in-law, General Gland—superbly characterized by an outstanding radio actor, Deryck Guyler.

Meanwhile Reed had conceived the idea of a major dramatic work on Clytemnestra. The BBC accordingly sponsored a visit to Mycenae (in a ship specializing in cultural tours to the Mediterranean). Unfortunately the Clytemnestra project was never completed; instead, Hilda Tablet and her entourage embarked for a Mediterranean voyage in a vessel owned by a Greek millionaire (who had sent back a Henry Moore sculpture because there was a hole in it). The trip was recorded in *The Primal Scene, as it were* (1958). In this psychoanalytical milieu General Gland's contribution was so outstanding that Reed went off at a tangent with *Not a Drum Was Heard: The War Memoirs of General Gland* (1959), which had some overtones of General Montgomery. In 1959 the wheel came full circle with *Musique Discrète*, a request programme of compositions by Dame Hilda Tablet, including her latest explorations into her own brand of "*musique concrète renforcée.*"

In September 1958 the BBC Third Programme broadcast *The Auction Sale*, a partly rhymed poem of about 300 lines. The narrative describes a humdrum country auction of household furniture and ornaments of no particular interest or value until a large gold-framed painting of Venus and Mars is displayed. Its Renaissance beauty is never stressed, but the mood of the poem changes as the painting is described:

> Effulgent in the Paduan air,
> Ardent to yield the Venus lay
> Naked upon the sunwarmed earth.

Evocative passages describing the picture are interspersed with the narrative, as two dealers from London compete against each other. At £2000 a quiet, inoffensive young man "from over Henstridge way" joins in the bidding:

> And still within the Paduan field,
> The silent summer scene stood by,
> The sails, the hill-tops, and the sky,
> And the bright warmth of Venus' glance
> That had for centuries caught the eye
> Of whosoever looked that way,
> And now caught theirs, on this far day.

But after £4025 the young man responds no longer to the bidding; his sweating face is glowing red, with a look almost of pain. An hour later a child sees him striding beneath the sodden trees along the Henstridge Road:

> He went on, through the soaking grass,
> Crying: that was what she said.

Bitterly, she later added.

Crying bitterly, she said.

In the broadcast, the descriptive passages were spoken by Reed, with another voice carrying the narration. He did the same (with Frank Duncan as the sergeant instructor) when in February 1960 a sequence of five poems was broadcast under the title of *The Complete Lessons of War*. The sequence contains the three that had been included in *A Map of Verona* and two later poems, "Movement of Bodies" (added in 1950) and "Returning of Issue" (added in 1960), in the same vein. In "Movement of Bodies" the sergeant displays a model of a characteristic battle-terrain (ambiguously recalling a woman's body): "somewhat hilly by nature/with a fair amount of typical vegetation/disposed at certain parts/..../And here is our point of attack." The final poem, "Returning of Issue," marks the ending of the war. A prodigal son seeking his father's home, the soldier returns too late: "father, you could not hear me now,/where now you lie, crumpled in that small grave/like any withering dog." He rejoins the army, with its "military garments, and harlots, and riotous living." He has nowhere else to go.

In 1970 the five poems were published in a limited Clover Hill Edition as *Lessons of the War*. During the previous two decades a number of Reed's translations were published, including Ugo Betti's *Three Plays* (1951) and *Crime on Goat Island*

(1960), Dino Buzzati's novel *Larger than Life* (1962), and Balzac's *Eugénie Grandet* (1964); many of Reed's translations of works by French and Italian playwrights have been broadcast by the BBC.

From 1964 through 1966, Reed spent some terms as visiting professor of poetry or assistant professor of English at the University of Washington in Seattle. In 1971 BBC Publications published several of his most successful radio scripts in two volumes: *The Streets of Pompeii, and other plays for radio* and *Hilda Tablet and Others*. They bear comparison with Evelyn Waugh's novels in their satirical wit, their compassion, and their impeccable style; and they are no less stimulating to read than *Decline and Fall* or *Brideshead Revisited*. Belated recognition of Henry Reed's outstanding radio achievements came in 1979, when he received from the Society of Authors the first of the Pye Golden Awards for Radio. As for *The Auction Sale* and the other poems that have accumulated over the last thirty years, Reed's long-continuing ill health and his own high standards of perfection have delayed their final revision.

References:

Roger Savage, "The radio plays of Henry Reed," in *British radio drama*, edited by John Drakakis (Cambridge: Cambridge University Press, 1981), pp. 158-190;

Vernon Scannell, "Henry Reed and Others," in his *Not Without Glory: Poets of the Second World War* (London: Woburn, 1976), pp. 134-171.

Alastair Reid
(22 March 1926-   )

Jennifer Birkett
Dundee University

BOOKS: *Twelve Poems* (St. Andrews: Privately printed, 1949);
To Lighten My House (Scarsdale, N.Y.: Morgan & Morgan, 1953);
I Will Tell You of a Town (Boston: Houghton Mifflin, 1956; London: Hutchinson, 1959);
Fairwater (Boston: Houghton Mifflin, 1957);
A Balloon for a Blunderbuss (New York: Harper, 1957);
Allth (Boston: Houghton Mifflin, 1958);

Ounce Dice Trice (Boston: Little, Brown, 1958; London: Dent, 1960);
The Millionaires, by Reid and Bob Gill (New York: Simon & Schuster, 1959);
Oddments Inklings Omens Moments (Boston: Little, Brown, 1959; London: Dent, 1960);
Supposing (Boston: Little, Brown, 1960);
Passwords. Places, Poems, Preoccupations (Boston: Little, Brown, 1963; London: Weidenfeld & Nicholson, 1964);

Alastair Reid (© Jerry Bauer)

To Be Alive (New York: Macmillan, 1966; London: Collier-Macmillan, 1967);

Uncle Timothy's Traviata (New York: Delacorte, 1967);

La Isla Azul (Barcelona: Editorial Lumen, 1973);

Weathering: Poems and Translations (Edinburgh: Canongate, 1978; New York: Dutton, 1978).

OTHER: Jorge Luis Borges, *Ficciones*, edited by Anthony Kerrigan, translated by Reid and others (New York: Grove, 1965; London: Weidenfeld & Nicolson, 1965);

Pablo Neruda, *We Are Many*, translated by Reid (London: Cape Goliard, 1967; New York: Grossman, 1968);

Neruda, *A New Decade: Poems 1958-67*, translated by Reid and Ben Belitt (New York: Grove, 1969);

Dannie Abse, ed., *Corgi Modern Poets in Focus 3*, includes poems by Reid (London: Corgi, 1971);

Mario Vargas Llasa, *Sunday Sunday*, translated by Reid (Indianapolis: Bobbs-Merrill, 1973);

Jose Emilio Pacheco, *Don't Ask Me How the Time Goes*

By, translated by Reid (New York: Columbia University Press, 1978);

Neruda, *Isla Negra: A Notebook*, translated by Reid (New York: Farrar, Straus & Giroux, 1981; London: Souvenir Press, 1982);

"Reflections," *New Yorker*, 57 (5 October 1981): 59-125.

In a talk he gave on BBC radio in November 1980, Alastair Reid warned critics against attempts to isolate particular poems in particular moments of his history. Thematically, chronological development is far less important in his poetry than its cyclical quality; every collection returns to preoccupations that the poet has made central throughout his whole life. And yet, as Reid also acknowledged in that talk, historical placing of a poem provides it with an illuminating perspective. What in fact his poetry considers is the relation of the particular moment to the continuity: the view through a single moment to the fluid, multilayered continuum thoughtlessly called "I"; the perpetual rediscovery, or invention of selfhood, through the landscape of the present, which encloses the many landscapes of the past. A moment of epiphany in present time and space, the thrill of memory retrieving past places and past selves, triggers the sense of what he described in his radio talk as "living through time, not just in time"—achieving the equilibrium between being rooted in a particular history and yet still free. The poet escapes being trapped in history; instead, as Reid writes in "Maine Coast," he stands at its center, seeing simultaneously past, present, and future:

> Though sun burns books, blinds eyes,
> I see through to the bone and the beginning.
>
> Tomorrow waits for the net; today tells
> time in circles on the trunks, in tides.

Born in Whithorn, Wigtonshire, Scotland, to a minister, William Arnold Reid, and his wife, Marian Wilson Reid, Alastair Reid acknowledges the indelible imprint of his Scottish upbringing. Reid's radio talk refers to his debt to his minister father for his first awareness of the difference between everyday language and the language of poetry (through the King James Version of the Bible and the liturgy heard in his father's church, and his father's own "loving care" in the use of language), and he notes in *Passwords* (1963) how in observing his father's ministry he absorbed his "extraordinary reverence for things." Also in *Passwords* he describes the compelling force of the landscapes of childhood: "Childhood landscapes are an entire containment of mystery—we spend a good part of our lives trying to find them again, trying to lose ourselves in the sense in which children are lost. We come away with no more than occasional glimpses, whiffs, suggestions, and yet these are enough, often, to transform suddenly the whole current of our lives. A smell recalls a whole vanished state of being; the sound of a word reaches far back, beyond memory. The beginning of poetry for me was the dazzling realization of all that seemed to be magically compressed into the word 'weather.' " Poetry and life are a journeying to recover the starting point—the soft West Coast of Galloway, or the Isle of Arran, where he spent summers as a boy, enjoying (at least in the editing retrospect of memory) a unique sense of unity between self and an endlessly changing, welcoming and harmonious outside world.

Conscripted into the Royal Navy in 1943, Reid served until 1946. After graduating from the University of St. Andrews in 1949 with an honors M.A., he took a job in 1950 at Sarah Lawrence College in Bronxville, New York, where he remained until 1955. His first commercially published collection, *To Lighten My House* (1953), assesses his progress from Scottish childhood to America, from a parochial, enclosed past to a present, open world, still to be explored. The best of that original childhood experience, recollected as nostalgia, is rediscovered in adulthood and the New World: "New Hampshire" is the child's discovery of home in the American forest.

The first half of the collection evokes Reid's own particular childhood as well as the generic experience. The sense of time without time is evoked in the flying bird of "Poem Without Ends"; continuity and renewal are figured in the changing seasons of the "agrarian round," as Reid calls it in "Reflections" (*New Yorker*, 5 October 1981), or in the cherished institution of the family. Weather, landscape, and human mood are in harmony ("Lay for New Lovers"); images of the natural and the human blend ("Song for Four Seasons," "My One High Morning"). Perception is spontaneous, fresh, delighted, and perpetually *amazed* (a word Reid uses frequently), a view on and from a world still to be comprehended and mapped. The little girl roller skating among the stolid adults in "Saturday Park" lives in a limitless present endowed with energy and intensity. Children see vividly the immediate and the particular, and give each thing its own special importance. They possess too what Reid calls in

Passwords a magical "power to transform," experiencing all the delights and terrors that imagination installs in nature. They also have the power to wish, enshrined in "Nursery Songs," and overwhelming confidence in the possibilities of the world and their own ability to tame them. The nostalgic "Spell on Five Fingers" recalls how once the world could be unhesitatingly counted into the grasp of a hand.

The serpent in this Eden is the fear of losing vision, enthusiasm, and the poetic gift. By the age of seven, Reid had realized that the Scotland that cradled him was also a straitjacket. Behind the innocent, flowery peace of "The Village," the mountains stand in cold critical judgment, listening to "your quietest thoughts." Correspondingly, "Reflections," Reid's autobiographical article in the *New Yorker*, pinpoints the painful contrast between the soft, fluid landscape and the hard, flinty, judgmental Scottish character, wedded to rules, hostile to spontaneity and change, riddled with a sense of "rueful doom." "Poem for my Father" traces the historical origins of the Scottish blight to agricultural neglect, war, and economic waste, and the *New Yorker* article speaks of the sense of impotence that derives from Scotland's "colonization" by the English. There is, however, no hint of nationalist sympathies in "Poem for my Father." Indeed in one essay in *Passwords*, dated 1961, Reid completely disavows the nationalist cause: "While I was growing up in Scotland, the clishmaclaver of aggressive nationalism rang continuously in my ears, but when I had exhausted the roles of terrorist, martyr, agitator, and cold logician, I found that, after all, it was possible to live quite fruitfully under what we used to call 'the English yoke,' and that the persecution we suffered was either statistically hypothetical or romantically imagined." What the poem expresses instead is an acceptance of a personal moral responsibility to remake the Scottish inheritance through the articulation of poetry and private life.

The second half of the collection shows the sea change into adulthood: the woods of infancy give way to images of the sea, the poet's "green" love turns "salt," the dross of the past is purged ("Four Figures for the Sea"), but there still remains the refusal to accept habit and decay, desire for the new, eagerness to learn, and longing to be rooted in love. The child's instinctive and entirely physical oneness with nature is replaced by the adult poetic ability to articulate both difference and similarity. In "The Waterglass," language breaks open the distinction of self from landscape yet still holds the two united:

Mirrored, I saw my death
in the underworld in the water,
. . . .
till I spoke to my speaking likeness,
and the moment broke with my breath.

Dannie Abse's introduction to Reid's work in his *Corgi Modern Poets in Focus 3* (1971), while unfairly dismissing most of this collection as not particularly good, overderivative of Dylan Thomas, singles out this poem, together with "New Hampshire," as evidence of Reid's first discovery of an authentic voice. In "The Seasons of the Sea," love is no longer simple pastoral but bitter desire, perpetually aroused, thwarted, and rekindled; sea, life, and woman (mother, beloved, and whore) are fused into the eternal feminine, through which man journeys in endless cycles, "linking the chain of the baffled love/that anchors the endless man to his sailor living/alone in a loft with the fish falling back into the sea." Again there is the tension of living contradictory desires: to be rooted but also to be free. Man finds himself on pilgrimage ("Directions for a Map"); yet his symbol is also the island, tree-covered, deeply rooted, but lapped by the open sea ("Maine Coast," "Isle of Arran"). The title poem, closing the collection, affirms the determination to live with a tradition transformed:

And patiently, into my bruised dark house,
light breaks like a birthday
as, shouldering the weather of this place, I
wake in
the nowhere of the moment, single-willed
to love the world.

Oddments Inklings Omens Moments, published in 1959, the year Reid became a staff writer and correspondent on the *New Yorker*, is, as its title suggests, a kaleidoscope of epiphanies. Scents, sights, sounds, and emotions freshly experienced provoke the rewriting and transformation of familiar memories. "Ghosts" gives new meaning to childish terrors. Ghosts are the elements of collective and personal history that are the makers of our landscape and the shapers of our language:

No, they are there. Let your ear be gentle.
At dawn or owl-cry, over doorway and lintel,
theirs are the voices moving night towards
morning,
the garden's grief, the river's warning.
Their curious presence in a kiss,

the past quivering in what is,
our words odd-sounding, not our own—
how can we think we sleep alone?

This new version of mood and landscape—of internal and external temper—emerges elsewhere in "Rain in Spain," a poem which recalls his first liberating encounter with an alternative culture in the 1950s; he had found the Spanish people quite unlike the Scots, at ease with their own humanity and physicality. "Poet with Sea-Horse," dedicated to Robert Graves, recalls their meeting in Spain during the 1950s and a friendship that substantially influenced Reid's prose, if not his poetry. (In his radio talk Reid expresses admiration for Graves's work, but not for his poetic elitism. He himself prefers, as a disciple and friend of Louis MacNeice, to write poetry for the general audience, embracing the social, political, and economic preoccupations of everyday life.) "Cat-Faith" returns to what Reid has called the "Jekyll and Hyde" contradictions in the Scottish character and evokes what he would also hold to be a fundamental polarity in all human nature. Though opting firmly for the cat's desire for adventure, he confesses to also sharing the dog's attraction to security and routine.

The collection comes into focus around a sequence of love poems which elaborate the theme adumbrated in *To Lighten My House*—desire frustrated is the basis of being. Giving a new, painful dimension to the concept of journey and return, these poems place against the desire for sexual contact and total self-oblivion in the "sea" of the other, fear of commitment and the round of stale habit which is desire fulfilled. The grotesquely wistful "Small Sad Song" of the lady midget expresses the emptiness of one who never risked the experience of sexuality; yet in "Calenture," love is death, ecstatic drowning in delusions that destroy. "In such a Poise is Love," writes the poet: it is between the "bewildering" and the "familiar," torn between the "twin fears, of losing and of having." Home is only desirable once lost ("Childhood Landscape"). Time together is spent in wounding, in retaliation for failure to answer an ideal; parting is sad but an inevitable relief. Time itself kills love; the Edenic garden ("Casa d'Amunt") is only rented. The fulfillment of desire is the end of desire, in the dual sense of both "extinction" and "goal." Ulysses' return in "A Homecoming" is not triumph but defeat, the faithless lover tormented by his own betrayals: perhaps Penelope too succumbed to others? The end of journeying, the absence of desire, opens a space flooded by uncertainty and self-doubt, with the conclusion—a rare note—that freedom is loss and pain. The sequence gives way to "Spain, Morning," in which the night's "dream of tall women" fades and the poet turns for comfort to his "blank desk." Only the transformations of art make love bearable.

The uncertainties and self-doubt of the love sequence run through this whole collection, and are summed up in the concluding poem, "What's What," in which Reid tries on, with an ironic whimsy, the role of the fairy-tale Younger Son. The adventurous, personal quest for an idiosyncratic destiny is clearly still felt to be the right vocation, but it seems also a slight one, mildly "ridiculous." "He's going nowhere/and, what's more,/he doesn't care" rings hollow; solitude is hard to bear.

Passwords, a collection of prose and poetry, celebrates the restoration of a sense of meaning. Partly this is the liberation achieved through life in Spain, whose society and politics are captured in prose pieces on Madrid, Gibraltar, and Barcelona, and whose language offered Reid a change of personality. Prose and poems evoke the delight of being foreign, "properly lost, and so in a position to rediscover the world, from the outside in." The fundamental role of language in shaping human experience comes increasingly to the forefront. The range of languages an individual can speak, within and outside his native tongue, proliferates different personalities within him, liberating, but also creating unease. "Disguises" asks if these selves are mere masks, costumes, while "The Figures on the Frieze" questions whether communication is possible in so many different tongues. "Speaking a Foreign Language" affirms in answer the possibility of effecting "the translation of/syntax into love." "The Syntax of Seasons" speaks with equal confidence of the material reality of language, informing nature ("we fall to silence under the burning sun,/and feel the great verbs run").

But equally, if not more important, in this collection is the presence of Reid's son Jasper, born in Madrid in August 1959, and whom Reid takes pride in having brought up himself from the age of four. *Passwords* is dedicated to Reid's father and to his son; Reid, the Younger Son, finds a new dimension in another childhood, the rediscovery of hope and excitement ("Wishes"), and in another future, to which to hand on for renewal the tradition of adaptability, of feeling independent, yet at home, in a variety of different worlds ("To a Child at the Piano"). "The Spiral," the autobiographical poem that closes the collection, extends the mapping of

self within the individual to the generations of others:

> Across the spiral distance,
> through time and turbulence,
> the rooted self in me
> maps out its true country.
>
> And, as my father found
> his own small weathered island,
> so will I come to ground
>
> where that small man, my son,
> can put his years on.
>
> For him, too, time will turn.

In the 1960s and 1970s Reid combined his writing for the *New Yorker* with continued forays into the academic world, despite what he described in his radio talk as a deep-rooted fear of the power of academic institutions to crush poetic spontaneity. The origins of this attitude would seem to lie mainly in his undergraduate experience of the "stony" stuffiness of St. Andrews, caught in *Weathering* (1978) in the light but serious humor of "The Academy." The navy, as Reid wrote in the *New Yorker*, had already provided one brief release: "I left [St. Andrews] after a brief first year to go into the Navy, and by the time I got back, after the end of the Second World War, I had seen the Mediterranean, the Red Sea, the Indian Ocean, and enough ports of call, enough human variety, to make St. Andrews seem small and querulous." But American academic life in the 1960s was quite different. In the *New Yorker*, Reid evokes the passionate excitement of exchanging deeply felt ideas, with Woodstock and Kent State standing on the horizon as the reward and the cost of radicalism. During this period he was a fellow in writing at Columbia University (1966); a visiting professor of Latin-American studies, first at Antioch College (1969-1970), then at Oxford University and St. Andrews University (1972-1973). Subsequently he served as a visiting professor at Colorado College (1977 and 1978) and at Yale University (1979). In 1966 and 1969 he gave lectures for the Association of American Colleges.

More important, from 1965 onward he began translating the works of Spanish and Latin-American writers: Jorge Luis Borges, Pablo Neruda, Mario Vargas Llasa, and Jose Emilio Pacheco. In the act of translation he enjoys both a sense of anonymity and the experience of trying on someone else's personality. For him translation amounts to the writing of original poetry. In

Dust jacket for Reid's 1978 collection, his farewell to formal poetry, which he calls "something of an artificial gesture, like wearing a tie"

Weathering he quotes Octavio Paz's dictum that all poetry is a translation and transmutation of the world: "Everything we do is translation, and all translations are in a way creations." Working with Pablo Neruda, whom he first met in February 1964, he chose to concentrate on that part of Neruda's production with which he personally felt the most affinity—the warm, abundantly human poems, "self-questioning yet affirmative," which express Reid's own values. The result is a fusion of two voices, from two different languages, speaking in communion.

Reid's most recent collection, *Weathering* (1978), collects, with some new work, poems published in previous books, some of them slightly revised; it marks, then, both continuity and variation. It is also a farewell to formal poetry, which, as Reid says in his foreword, "seems to me now something of an artificial gesture, like wearing a tie." The first section revives roots in Scotland and the past, as a final settling of accounts. The image of the family house reappears in "The Manse," where the returning poet, finding the old home burned down, rejoices in the "luck" of being rid of old memories and the discovery of his hard-won ability to live independently of the security of origins. Even so the conclusion is ambiguous, and the syntax leaves the reader uncertain whether speaker or vanished house is the truly insubstantial. A second cluster of poems reviews a range of moods linked to women and love: sexual contact is good, but love recollected

in books, at a distance, is better—a "dilemma" encapsulated in a wickedly witty "Mandala." Revisiting landscapes, the poet reasserts the need for "Curiosity" as well as the desire to live "through" time, not just "in" it, and he offers further considerations on the nature of language. A closing section gathers some of Reid's translations.

In the poems on language, Reid seems to revert again to hesitancy. "The Syntax of Seasons," with its ringing, positive assertions, is followed by the more uncertain "Visiting Lecturer," still claiming, from a far more abstract vocabulary, that new language is new self, and that words are a home, and "Home/is where new words are still to come," but including the plaintive query: "Even though words are portable,/where can they come to rest?" The beautifully constructed "What Gets Lost/Lo Que Se Pierde" evokes the translator's, and the poet's, dilemma. Translators are "ghosts who live/in a limbo between two worlds"; language itself, though it is the only means to articulate experience, is not experience; for "lovers or users or words," experience is always "what gets lost."

After his travels, Alastair Reid is now "anchored," as he says, in New York City, which is "a good place to be when one has not quite decided just where to live—although I think I have chosen looking for such a place over finding it." He has changed his metaphors. As he says in "Reflections," "I think, in fact, that I am done with the metaphor of roots. I prefer that of a web, a web of people and places, threads of curiosity, wires of impulse, a network of the people who have cropped up in our lives, and will always crop up—the 'webbed scheme,' as Borges calls it."

But the change in metaphor brings a loss, whose analogue is found in Reid's switch from poetry to prose. Reid's *New Yorker* writing, aimed at a mid-Atlantic clientele, is entertaining and pleasant, but of necessity it lacks the intensity and substantiality of his poetic form. What sets his poetry apart is his ability to encapsulate in the "artificial gesture" of a poem a sense of life, an act of faith in the moment caught in the act of language, what he calls "the raw act of containing something unsayable in words." "Poem without Ends," in *To Lighten My House*, fixes the impossibility of fixing the moment, capturing the feeling of an eternal present with a syntax of short, rhythmical phrases held by juxtaposition in apparent contradictions that resolve unexpectedly into fluid motion: "The process is continuous as wind,/the bird observed, not rising, but in flight,/unrealized, in motion in the mind." "Once at Piertavit," in *Oddments Inklings Omens Moments*, with its muted echoes of Hopkins (with John Crowe Ransom and W. S. Graham a major influence) uses short, two-stressed lines of simple, swinging rhythm and simple language to create an incantation of ordinariness, shattered by the mo-

ment of horror when the casually thrown apple strikes a bird, which miraculously survives, and time almost stops: "The whole sky curdled/over Piertavit." "An Instance," also in *Oddments Inklings Omens Moments*, evokes the special privilege of the poem, catching an epiphany in a blaze of words. The reality gone, the language replaces it, concentrated, intense, and eternal: "their moment burns again, restored/to its spontaneity. The poem stays."

But as the same poetry has said, an aim achieved is an end, as Ulysses found, and as the poet warned: "Say the soft bird's name, but do not be surprised/to see it fall/headlong, struck skyless, into its pigeonhole" ("Growing, Flying, Happening"). Another kind of commitment means the beginning of a search for another form; there is, perhaps, a limit to the number of times a poet can repeat the miracle of Piertavit.

Reference:

Dannie Abse, "Alastair Reid," in *Corgi Modern Poets in Focus 3*, edited by Abse (London: Corgi, 1971).

Papers:

The State University of New York, Buffalo, and the National Library of Scotland in Edinburgh have collections of Reid's papers.

I. A. Richards
(26 February 1893–7 September 1979)

John Paul Russo
University of Miami, Florida

SELECTED BOOKS: *The Foundations of Aesthetics*, by Richards, C. K. Ogden, and James Wood (London: Allen & Unwin, 1922);

The Meaning of Meaning: A Study of the Influence of Language upon Thought and of the Science of Symbolism, by Richards and Ogden (London: Kegan Paul, Trench, Trubner/New York: Harcourt, Brace, 1923; revised edition, New York: Harcourt, Brace, 1927);

Principles of Literary Criticism (London: Kegan Paul, Trench, Trubner, 1924; New York: Harcourt, Brace/London: Kegan Paul, Trench, Trubner, 1925);

Science and Poetry (London: Kegan Paul, Trench, Trubner, 1926; revised, 1935); revised again as *Poetries and Sciences* (London: Routledge & Kegan Paul, 1970; New York: Norton, 1970);

Practical Criticism: A Study of Literary Judgment (London: Kegan Paul, Trench, Trubner, 1929; New York: Harcourt, Brace, 1929);

Mencius on the Mind: Experiments in Multiple Definition (London: Kegan Paul, Trench, Trubner, 1932; New York: Harcourt, Brace/London: Kegan Paul, Trench, Trubner, 1932);

Basic Rules of Reason (London: Kegan Paul, Trench, Trubner, 1933);

I. A. Richards, circa 1928

Coleridge on Imagination (London: Kegan Paul, Trench, Trubner, 1934; New York: Harcourt, Brace, 1935);

The Philosophy of Rhetoric (New York & London: Oxford University Press, 1936);

Interpretation in Teaching (New York: Harcourt, Brace, 1938; London: Kegan Paul, Trench, Trubner, 1938);

How to Read a Page (New York: Norton, 1942; London: Kegan Paul, Trench, Trubner, 1943);

Basic English and Its Uses (London: Kegan Paul, Trench, Trubner, 1943; New York: Norton 1943);

Speculative Instruments (Chicago: University of Chicago Press, 1955; London: Routledge & Kegan Paul, 1955);

Goodbye Earth and Other Poems (New York: Harcourt, Brace, 1958; London: Routledge & Kegan Paul, 1959);

The Screens and Other Poems (New York: Harcourt, Brace, 1960; London: Routledge & Kegan Paul, 1961);

Tomorrow Morning, Faustus! An Infernal Comedy (New York: Harcourt, Brace & World, 1962; London: Routledge & Kegan Paul, 1962);

So Much Nearer: Essays Toward a World English (New York: Harcourt, Brace & World, 1968);

Design for Escape: World Education Through Modern Media (New York: Harcourt, Brace & World, 1968);

Internal Colloquies. Poems and Plays (New York: Harcourt Brace Jovanovich, 1971; London: Routledge & Kegan Paul, 1972);

Beyond (New York: Harcourt Brace Jovanovich, 1974);

Poetries: Their Media and Ends, edited by Trevor Eaton (The Hague: Mouton, 1974);

Complementarities: Uncollected Essays, edited by John Paul Russo (Cambridge: Harvard University Press, 1976; Manchester: Carcanet New Press, 1977);

New and Selected Poems (Manchester: Carcanet New Press, 1978).

OTHER: *The Wrath of Achilles. The Iliad of Homer, Shortened*, translated by Richards (New York: Norton, 1950);

A Leak in the Universe, in *Playbook: Five Plays for a New Theatre* (New York: New Directions, 1956), pp. 241-293.

When Ivor Armstrong Richards began writing poems in his sixtieth year, he was likened to the aging Socrates who learned to play the lyre. Richards already had two complete careers, one in literary criticism, another in language training and theory of education. He had lived and taught in England, China, and America, and had written twenty books. His late calling to poetry was endowed with a wealth of human experience and an unrivalled analytical knowledge of the technique of poetry. Four collections of an original, highly textured poetry and three verse plays appeared over twenty-five years. He had nurtured in effect a third career.

The son of a Welsh chemical engineer, William Armstrong Richards, and a Yorkshire woman, Mary Anne Haig Richards, Ivor Armstrong Richards was born in Sandbach, Cheshire. In 1904-1905 he suffered the first of three severe attacks of tuberculosis that nearly cost him his life (the others were in 1912-1913 and 1915-1916). He said he recuperated by rock-climbing in the mountains of North Wales. He attended Clifton in Bristol and was graduated in 1915 from Magdalene College, Cambridge, where he read moral sciences. In 1917-1918 he pursued premedical subjects. After World War I he lectured on contemporary literature and the theory of criticism in the newly founded English School at Cambridge, and he collaborated with C. K. Ogden on *The Meaning of Meaning* (1923), a pioneering study of semantics. "New millions of participants in the control of general affairs," wrote the authors, "must now attempt to form personal opinions on matters which were once left to a few." They pleaded the urgency of raising "the level of communication through a direct study of its conditions, its dangers, and its difficulties." Thus was struck the practical keynote of Richards's life work: how to develop skill in reading and communication for the better governance of self and world. *The Meaning of Meaning* went through ten editions and remains in print after sixty years.

As a literary critic Richards was one of the main founders of the modern school of criticism and the acknowledged father of New Criticism. In *Principles of Literary Criticism* (1924) he applied the findings of various schools of European and American psychology to the study of poetry and the theory of value. He was criticized for building an eclectic Benthamite model—its behaviorist component was particularly objectionable and widely misinterpreted—and for jumping beyond evidence to his conclusions. But many of his conclusions were so insightful and stimulating that his readers accepted them and ignored the psychology. *Science and Poetry* (1926) is a popularization of his major ideas. Richards was married to Dorothy Eleanor Pilley, a journalist and professional mountaineer, on 31 December 1926 in Honolulu.

Practical Criticism (1929) revolutionized the method of studying poetry. Richards analyzed hundreds of reports by undergraduates on not especially cryptic poems; he classified types of error and offered numerous strategies for improved reading. His critical approaches to sense, irony, ambiguity, feeling, authorial tone, and intention provided the matrix of strategies for New Criticism. In *Coleridge on Imagination* (1934) he demonstrated how Coleridge used an Idealist metaphysics to study mental action, anticipating modern psychology; the book, however extreme in its point of view, founded modern Coleridge studies. *The Philosophy of Rhetoric* (1936)—on metaphor, *Interpretation in Teaching* (1938)—a "practical criticism" for prose, and *How to Read a Page* (1942)—responding to Mortimer Adler's *How To Read a Book* (1940), completed his system. The originality and influence of Richards's criticism can be shown by the number of terms he put into circulation, terms that became the currency of debate for almost half a century: *close reading, tone, context, pseudostatement, stock response, tension, equilibrium of opposed attitudes, tenor and vehicle of metaphor, emotive and referential language*.

Richards began a second career in language training and education in the mid-1930s in Peking, shifting his operation to Harvard in 1939. He spent thirty-five years on the teaching and development of Basic English, invented by C. K. Ogden, and subsequent models (Every Man's English). Basic English is an analytically simplified version of the language based on 850 words and key grammatical patterns. Both a first step toward learning English and an international "second" language, it is not a substitute for Standard English. With Christine M. Gibson, Richards directed a nonprofit institute, Language Research, and created the Language Through Pictures series. As technology advanced, he adapted the series to film, records, television, videotape, and cassette, capitalizing on the unique qualities of the media. His major innovations were in the areas of sequencing with maximum efficiency, audio-visual-manual interplay of channels, contiguity programming, technological aids, and economy of items to be remembered. Integration was always a key theme, for where it was absent there was wasted effort. His collected papers on language training appeared in *So Much Nearer: Essays Toward a World English* (1968) and *Design for Escape: World Education Through Modern Media* (1968). In these books Richards was addressing "the planet"; his final trip, undertaken in his eighty-seventh year, was to China to "pick up and restart work (on The Design of elementary English & First Steps in Literacy and Literature) done there 42 years ago." His last major book, *Beyond* (1974), studies man's dialectical relation to his gods, his highest self-images, in Homer, Plato, the book of Job, Dante, and Shelley.

Richards's third career was in poetry and verse drama. He collected four volumes of poems: *Good-bye Earth and Other Poems* (1958), *The Screens and Other Poems* (1960), *Internal Colloquies* (1971), which includes the poems from previous books as well as "Further Poems" from 1960-1970, and *New and Selected Poems* (1978), which contains "New Poems" (1971-1977). He published three plays: *A Leak in the Universe* (written in 1954 and published in 1956 in *Playbook*), *Tomorrow Morning, Faustus!* (1962), and *Job's Comforting*, a verse translation of the book of Job, which appeared in *Internal Colloquies*. There are also an unpublished play in three acts, "Erna: an Extravaganza," and unpublished poems.

The reviews that Richards's poetry received were mixed but respectful. George Steiner praised the "taut metaphors," the "delight in risk, the poised delicacy of technique, the impish fun in a certain esotericism" (*PN Review*). The poetry as a whole is marked by "sweeping intellectual range alive in a perpetual crackle of local wit" (John Holloway, the *Guardian*), by Socratic (John Hollander, *Poetry*) or Lucretian (Robert Lowell, *Encounter*) insight, by abrupt turns, startled halts, and giddy vistas, by "astonishingly alive curiosity" (Marvin Maddocks, *Christian Science Monitor*), by a "dialectic battle" and a "profound and tender regard for the power of the human organization" (Sidney Richman, *Wisconsin Studies in Contemporary Literature*). Many poems are "difficult, too difficult" (W. D. Snodgrass, *Hudson Review*), "homely, often scratchy" (Dudley Fitts, *New York Times Book Review*), "not so much sinewy as muscle bound" (Richmond Lattimore, *New Republic*), "wispy exercises" (Janet Fiscalini, *Commonwealth*), "chirpy eupeptic pipings" (Donald Davie, *Spectator*). The poems "remind one of the awkward

rightness" of Hardy (Samuel French Morse, *Poetry*); William Empson is often mentioned as an influence; and in a letter Marianne Moore noted the "impact of Hardy and Donne without a greater debt than innate similarity—(than analogous idiosyncrasy is better)." Finally, Robert Lowell spoke of Richards's "unrivalled *élan* from the momentary to the absolute, his wavering intricate modern mind is joined to an old joyful simplicity." Lowell defended Richards's verse as "innocent, intelligent, unconventional . . . the most cherished pages in his immense work" (*Times Literary Supplement*, 14 July 1972).

Richards wrote well of what he knew best and felt most strongly. Old age, resignation, and courage before death are the subjects of many poems. High mountaineering, his favorite pastime, offered the backdrop for many others. The interaction of opposites, dialectical strategies, choice, the growth of the self, are studied in the philosophical poems. Finally, he treats creativity and language itself, the *logos* as bearer of man's traditions: "Do we often enough . . . reflect what an august and perdurable a being a language is—lasting so far longer than any of the minds it makes?" (1978). Indeed language is man's greatest model for integration, apart from language's nearest analogue, the mind itself (though Richards thought language "concrete by comparison" to thought). Not to play down the "emotive" function of language, Richards put a high premium on "reference" in his own poetry.

As his themes are few, so are his voices. Two stand out: the Cambridge strain—inquisitive, analytic, scientific, learned, skeptical; and, less noticeable, a Welsh strain—oracular, magical, exigent, nature-oriented, gnomic. The poems gain from crossing patterns, the oracular with the scientific, the gnomic with the philosophical. An extraordinarily effective speaker of poetry and lecturer, Richards read frequently from his verse in his last years.

While themes and tones are few, however, Richards's choice of stanzaic patterns and the range of his free verse are extremely broad. From the sonnet to the sestina, from the ballad to verse drama, he experimented continuously. He learned Greek in middle age and translated *The Iliad*. The only other English philosopher to have done so was Hobbes. As a young man he had known Hardy, and his last work, "Friends Beyond," is a "pastiche poem" made partly from lines by Hardy.

A Leak in the Universe, a play in verse and prose, in which Richards published his first significant poetry, is a science-fiction fable that takes place among professors at an Institute for Advancing Studies. A Faustian Conjuror (played originally by Richards in 1954) urges "fellow Conjurors" in the audience to root the action in "your ground"; it (that is, creative growth, self-knowledge, inheritance) is "about itself and so are you." He warns that the symbol is not the reality, that the image is not the god, though image and god "sustain" each "instrument through which you strain to see," like the "self-supporting" attitudes that compel intellectual and emotional growth in *Principles of Literary Criticism*. The Conjuror throws many such Richardsian themes into the hat.

The action of the play centers around the investigation of a box in which everything disappears, the "leak" in the universe. The Conjuror has lost his pen, watch, key, and magic wand (see Richards's poem "Forfeits"), that is, his writing, ebbing life, place in the world, and inspiration. He wants desperately to conjure them back though he knows it is impossible. As the plot proceeds, the box stands for a dustbin, a coffin, Plato's cave, a spinning boxwood top, the center of all things, the thing in itself, a rebel, human consciousness on the brink of the unthinkable, the as-yet-unsayable nothingness out of which all is created, and the artist "lost" in his work.

To aid the investigation the Conjuror consults three professors and a medium. The Nobel Prize-winning physicist proves helpless; science is stymied. Then, the medium Mrs. Nemo ("no one") speaks in a trance. Her lines evoke the withdrawn Achilles in his tent in the *Iliad*:

> How could I choose
>   Or it choose me,
> To save the world
>   Or let it be?

Mrs. Nemo and the Conjuror listen to the mysterious tape-recorded report of Sir Glendoveer Pearks (a play on the name of Glendower, the Welsh nobleman in *Henry IV, Part I*); his verse becomes the text upon which the rest of the play turns:

> Then voluble and bold, now hid, now seen
> . . . .
> Voluble box will you do for my centre—
> That still point all things turn on, all things seek?
> That centre lay betwixt
> Our Satan's haunches fixt
> While all the spheres swept round the shaggy Sleek.
>
> Fallen fallen light renew?

> Fallen from Paradise too
> Our glassy essence clouded.

Professor Zocca ("good-for-nothing") then gives the first New Critical explication in drama: The text alludes to Vergil's *volubile buxum* or "spinning top" (in the *Aeneid*) and introduces the concept of a mental eddy or equilibrium, though in Vergil *volubile buxum* describes the Fury Allecto lashing Queen Amata into madness (see Richards's "Rainbow" and "Sunrise"). Dante's Satan and Eliot's "still point" or godhead are superimposed; Richards believed in their interchangeability, depending on what man did in their name. Blake's "Fallen fallen light renew" (from "Hear the voice of the Bard") invokes the idea of redemption through meditation on the peaks of literature; "glassy essence" is Shakespeare's description of the mirror of the soul in *Measure for Measure*. The form of the pastiche poem enacts its meaning: voices of the past coil within each other, contrast and resolve, at least partially. The author is not the complete creator of his work but a medium.

The physicist announces that the box confirms a fundamental convention of modern physics, but Professor Omori, a Japanese Buddhist, has the last word: "The contriver of THIS/Let's call him a Waker, someone who has started/Out from the dreaming we call living." The contriver is perhaps Lucifer as rebel but also the creative artist; the box is the artist's disappearing into his work, a dying into life, and thus a teacher "like all the greatest," alive in the light shed upon subsequent generations. The box is an "invitation"; Richards would later call Pepys's motto ("*Mens cuiusque is est quisque,*" "it is the mind that is the man") an "invitation to endless reflection" and use it as the epigraph of his poem "Here & There." Professor Omori even guesses how the box works: "Maybe no more/Than a little switch of attention, a lifted stress/A break in a circuit, a shift of love." The state of attention ranks among the highest values in *Principles of Literary Criticism*, the necessary condition for an "equilibrium of opposed impulses" or "ground-plan of the most valuable aesthetic responses." Images of circuitry, synaptic junctions, and connections that trigger mental action are common in Richards's poetry and criticism. When the Conjuror wonders whether the box is a Holy Grail, Omori cautions that the Grail offered everything, the box "nothing." It must not be compared to a doctrine but to an active force for change and progress. "The trick it teaches? 'Physician heal thyself.' " The box disappears, having served its purpose, "showing me how to remember myself./ Whatever does that is due to be . . . vilified."

"Goodbye Earth: A Farewell to the Planet" is the title poem of Richards's first collection. The elderly poet contemplates death with a comic glance at the space craze stirred up by Sputnik and suggests that we all build individual spaceships with our lives. He examines the choices through which his life was made, the "raw materials" that went into its making, and "The symbiotic tensions that impel us." With departure at hand Richards condenses in telegraphic capitals his central progress: "SUCCESS, ADVENTURE, FAILURE, COMPREHENDING." The first three headings signify his achievement in criticism, the explorations in Basic English and language training which took him around the world, and failure to win widespread adoption for his programs. He has been bold enough to fail in this "more august ambition" aimed at international understanding, and he blames others too for failing to recognize their responsibilities. "COMPREHENDING" includes the Socratic admission of *not* knowing "what its knowing is" and the study of death, for which the poet feels almost prepared by his numerous past choices, the "circuits" of the spaceship. His humanism orients him one last time: man makes his destiny; he is his own god and demon; his freedom results from an exacting control over the immense energies stored up inside him:

> Yet Man's god—tho' men be pismires yet—
> A perishable god whose clumsy hand
> Could remake anything or ruin it.

As the spaceship begins its ascent, the poet simultaneously feels a sense of "falling" like a leaf. His parting words are "Goodbye,/ And blessings welling from the word, Farewell." The benediction wells from the whole poem, in the shape of the life disclosed and its affirmative vision. "Welling" may derive from Swinburne's "The Last Oracle": "Dark the shrine, and dumb the fount of song thence welling." Richards said that as a boy "I knew Swinburne by heart—and Shelley much better."

Richards confronts the gradual impairment of memory in the sestina "To Dumb Forgetfulness." The quote, the statistic are irretrievable. The lost glance, sigh, or profile of the dead haunt him, especially when they might have revealed his "formula of fate." The first refrain urges bitterly, "Let go and let the loitering dead be dead." The second is also an imperative; the poet transforms passive loss into

active strength: "Forget, forget . . . forget what you forget." Elsie Duncan-Jones writes that the refrain "suggests ostensibly that loss is to be acquiesced in. But to forget what you forget is hard work . . . a demonstration of the art of intellectual survival" (*PN Review*, 1980). Altogether Richards has written some of the best poems in the language on being over sixty-five, an important subject and one especially difficult to find pleasure in. Lacking the alchemical imagination of Yeats, Richards has a vision of age which is bleak but courageous, unpoetical but not despairing.

"Not No," which Marianne Moore cited for its "virile diction," denies that one's life is entirely one's own; much is mysteriously lived "through *x* without or *y* within," one's family past, culture, race, and species. This short poem's propositions slide on its innumerable prepositions: *in, out, through* (six times), *without, within*. The particles tend to dissolve the self's boundaries. The mind is likened to a ruined house through which the wind passes; the poet hears "*Not mine, all this lived through in me*," and responds "Who asks? Who answers? What ventriloquy!" (a reference to Coleridge's truth as a "divine ventriloquist" in *Biographia Literaria*). But the poet declares against personal immortality. Elsewhere he avers that creative products enter "The Indivisible" and claim a secular immortality. Essentially the classical concept of fame as just reward for noble deeds is restated in modern terms.

As the self is not wholly one's own, so the poem only partly belongs to its poet. The rest is language's. This theme is attacked without antiromantic rhetoric and is consistent with the antibiographical, antihistorical approach that colors Richards's entire criticism. At times it is difficult to square this antibiographical attitude with his strong emphasis on choice and individual responsibility. Richards treats the language the way romantic poets treated nature, as a source brimming with truth and value. In a way he makes a garden landscape of language, fruitful in itself, but which must be cultivated to yield its truth. Many poems deal with the specific contribution of language: "Lighting Fires in Snow," the first poem in *Goodbye Earth*, "Retort," "The Ruins" ("And words it is, not poets, make up poems"), "Ars Poetica," the final poem in his last volume; also, "Verse v. Prose," his presidential address to the English Association in 1978. (In "Verse v. Prose" E. H. Gombrich found the idea that words not poets make poetry "so compelling that I decided to apply it to the history of the visual arts and of music" in his 1979 Darwin Lecture.) "Lighting Fires in Snow" is a practical lesson in which intricacies of formal design are as demonstrative of poems as of campfires:

> Tread out a marble hollow
>   Then lay the twigs athwart,
>   Teepee-wise or wigwam,
> So that the air can follow
>   The match-flame from the start:
>   As we begin a poem
>   And some may win a heart.
> . . . .
> The wise poem knows its father
>   And treats him not amiss;
>   But Language is its mother
> To burn where it would rather
>   Choose that and by-pass this
>   Only afraid of smother
>   Though the thickening snow-flakes hiss.

Perhaps only Ransom or Hardy would have the wit and nerve to rhyme poem with wigwam; Richards pronounced "poem" emphatically in two syllables, stressing the first. "No, no, it is not love" warns against thinking passion alone fans the flames of creation. Comparing Richards's mountaineering metaphor with Arnold's in "Rugby Chapel," in an

Richards in the Alps, 1958

essay published in *I. A. Richards: Essays in His Honor* (1973), Janet Adam Smith notes that Arnold's main idea is "more real" than the metaphor, whereas Richards "starts from the concrete experience." The fire does not illustrate a statement about poetry; it is there in its own right as "a lived experience . . . through which came the idea of how a poem starts."

Richards's second volume, *The Screens and Other Poems* (1960), impresses largely through its philosophical gambits: six poems on Niels Bohr's theory of complementarity; a character portrait of Wittgenstein; a reply to key passages in the *Tractatus Logico-Philosophicus* (1922); poems on semantics, psychology, and neoplatonism; end notes; and an essay on "The Future of Poetry," originally the Armstrong Lecture at Victoria University, Toronto. The volume is similar to *Goodbye Earth and Other Poems* in style and subject matter, but somehow the tone is heftier, the shadows less darkly colored. Richards is a better poet for his second book. At the same time he has temporarily exorcised the ghosts. Several lyrics written on vacations in southern Florida brighten the atmosphere, though Richards's real terrain is the high mountains.

The longer poems in *The Screens and Other Poems* involve epistemological questions. Typically, Richards sets forth sundry hypotheses and meditates upon them until a provisional resolution emerges. The poetic process of their explication is what matters. "The Screens," for example, is a multiple definition like the definitions of words such as *emotion, beauty,* and *meaning* in his criticism. He revolves half a dozen definitions of the word *screen* around the idea of complementarity: no pure image falls on any pure screen; no pure lens exists for viewing it; thus the perceiver must construct one unified image from a number of disparate but complementary images. Sometimes "rival screens" stage wars. How does one mediate between them? What prevents absolutism? Man's hope begins with the fact that, as the individual has not one but two eyes for depth perception, so the soul must have two eyes—and more: "Their vision cannot guide till they combine/To work with other Sensing":

> Words would not utter, may not formulate,
> Dare only hint, one to another one:
> Before all veils, the Lonely (and therethrough)
> Seeks for Itself as Earth veers to the Sun.
> And for that search we must be desolate.

Words cannot "formulate" the precise terms of this essentially personal quest for sincerity, but as in a poem they "Dare only hint," like the "wise *Guess*" in "A:B:B:C," the "hit or miss" of words in "The Proper Study," the "inkling without a source" in "Theology," an intellectual intuition in consort with emotion. The sense of the impersonal is maintained by treating the seeker as the abstract Lonely. Uppercase typography platonizes this seeking in search of itself, its best destiny, in which "we" participate. The seeking is like the planet; spinning to itself, it veers to the source of life and strength, never reaching it but always tending toward it. Desolate is another common word in Richards's poetic diction. For all the technological optimism, his lonely quester is like the Knight in Dürer's well-known etching.

Just as Richards's criticism contains many models for mental activity, so his poems have their "emblems." He may create a "double," or set "mind" within a larger entity like an island in a sea, a source of sound surrounded by silence, a figure against ground, even the head and neck of a giraffe, "aloof, free, delicate and calm" ("Silences"). Most often Richards portrays the mind as an equilibrium opening onto a "nothing" where "the unthinkable junctures flower" ("The Daughter Thought"). In one of the "Birthday Thoughts" he finds "Late dreaded hours" relieved in the way a deep breath calms the nerves:

> so an   I know not
> What, a gust or gale intaken
> Awakened has an overseeing eye,
> My oldest guide, who serves an endless ought.
>
> This eye—not I—took over thus and taught
> Thought mazed in by-way wonderings of late.

Rhymes connect ends to beginnings of lines, and the mind folds back circuitously on itself to gain its bearings. The "oldest guide" is Apollo, not forgetting Shelley's "I am the eye with which the Universe/Beholds itself and knows itself divine" ("Hymn of Apollo"). The neoplatonic principle, the "endless ought" or moral imperative, rules over the god himself or is identified with him. In " 'The Temporal the All,' " Richards names the source: "From/The Indivisible/All come," the unity of the true, the good, and the beautiful. In his apartment Richards had an intricately printed sign that read *Ex divina pulchritudine omne derivatur*, "From divine beauty all derives" (Pseudo-Dionysius).

The mountaineering poems are full of lonely seekers, not abstractions, but flesh and blood. Richards began climbing high mountains in his youth, and ever after, on weekends, vacations, and in a long retirement, he pursued this most dangerous and aesthetic of pastimes. He knew too much about mountains to romanticize them. The view from the summit is never the real goal. Mountains are testing grounds for endurance, technical expertise, and aspiration: "We have them in our bones:/Ten thousand miles of stones,/Moraine, debris and scree" ("Resign! Resign!"). Upper ridges look like fear and death, "Time's scythings" ("Alpine Sketches"); cliffs present problems, "Tissue of *buts* and *ifs*" ("Gravitation and Delinquency"). He glimpses the sublime: "Across the numinous gulf uprear/Sheer spires and sunlit snow"; but his tramway reels "along this ravining brink" ("Finhaut"), and death is in his eyes. In "Hope," named after a slab in Wales, Richards tries to cheer up his wife after an auto accident (Dorothy Pilley Richards is the author of the classic *Climbing Days*, 1935). Draw strength, he counsels, from remembering past exploits:

> "Leaping crevasses in the dark,
> That's how to live!" you said.
> No room in that to hedge:
> A razor's edge of a remark.

Like all of Richards's drama, *Tomorrow Morning, Faustus!* (1962) is a kind of philosophical feud in verse. The major fiends, who have gained respectability and become board members of the Futurity Foundation, make a pact with the aging Faustus (played originally by Richards in 1964): if they tell him what he most needs to know about himself, he must hand himself over forever. Matters are complicated by the fact that the fiends do not fully know what they are, since man, the "bare chameleon," reflects their own multifacetedness and lack of unity; he is the "blueprint" of what they must become. Furthermore, the character Sophia oversees the action and projects her words on an "Impending Screen" above and beyond the actors. What flashes on the screen becomes a possession of mankind.

The fiends conspire to eavesdrop on Faustus by means of "psy-rays," complementarity-free instruments of "direct inspection," while sending Mammon disguised as a member of the World Population Control Bureau. In act two Faustus discovers the ruse and tempts Mammon into joining him in new enterprises: unilateral disarmament and birth control. Mammon says that the price Faustus must pay is himself and asks that he lead the movement. In so doing, Mammon gives up the fiends' secret: they are failing badly and need Faustus to "start a new Epoch." The fiends recall Mammon and accuse him of betrayal. They decide to summon Faustus "tomorrow morning" for the dramatic confrontation which delivers him over to death and spiritual victory.

In act three Sophia predicts Faustus's fall and transfiguration. Satan tempts him with the psy-ray, the instrument that could provide answers to what he most wants to know, knowledge of the self and the "Circuits of the All." Resisting, Faustus yields up his own secret strength. Full knowledge of the self is a contradiction; it would set a limit on the self and deaden the creative drive. In the same way "We are baffled by the by-products of Being/The less they are the more we spend on them." Utopia always "Turns something else when you set out to build it." What begins as a poem ends up a "government Regulation." Only by a Faustian striving *beyond*, an unresting search, critical of one's possessions, creating out of a nothingness, can man remake himself. "An echo, a mirror rounding up a circuit?," suggests Faustus. The echo returns the sound, the mirror reflects the seeker. If the mind sees only what it projects, how can it escape beyond its ken, and view itself afresh? The answer is multiple frameworks. In the "rounding" of the circuitry (*veering, spiraling, twirling, coiling* are common metaphors for the process in Richards's poems) the act of consciousness reflects on (*re, flectere,* to bend back upon) and thereby gains on itself. "The answer to thinking's another way to think." Faustus likens life to climbers on a cliff, "biscuit thin and brittle"; every breakthrough opens up a "cold void gulf" in the self. Therein lies the challenge ("SUCCESS, ADVENTURE, FAILURE, COMPREHENDING"). As Satan and Faustus vanish together, Sophia sees them "still eddying, swept/Possessing and possessed . . . augmented far beyond/their either compass." They have absorbed each other's knowledge.

"Further Poems" (1960-1970) in *Internal Colloquies* (1971) records a lengthy conversation between Satan and Faustus, "Theodicy. An Internal Colloquy." Richards's penchant for putting his thought into dramatic form—the plays, the pastiche and colloquy poems, poems with critical notes (in "Whose Endless Jar" in *Beyond*, 1974)—stems from his belief that truth is reached by subjecting points of view to dialectical procedure. It is also a defense against dogmatic solutions. Truths of fact remain the same; emotive truths are bound to the systems that have created them and must be proved on the pulse. This belief is essentially William James's pragmatic definition of truth.

Of note in "Further Poems" and in "Whose Endless Jar" (January 1972) is the theme of man's relation to his gods. "The Eddying Ford," in which Jacob wrestles with the angel at the ford of Jabbok (Genesis 32) juxtaposes two central images in Richards's career as critic and poet: the eddy and the double or opposite. In *Principles of Literary Criticism* he prized the "equilibrium of opposed impulses." In *Coleridge on Imagination* he cited Coleridge on the life of things as the "eddying" of nature's "living soul," calling it one of his "greatest imaginative triumphs. An eddy is in something, and is a conspicuous example of a balance of forces." Like the spinning top in *A Leak in the Universe*, the Earth "a-sway in a seeming void/Stable because a-spin and swinging round" in *Tomorrow Morning, Faustus!*, the pole star ("Distinctive vortices worked out within") and wobble ("My wobble now salutes your wobble, you") in "Sunrise," the ball in "Ball Court," and the "whirl of being" in "Ars Poetica," the eddy signifies a countercurrent swirling within a current, a dynamic equipoise within a larger system that may be only very slightly knowable. The larger system is sometimes referred to as a stream, the All, or the Indivisible in Richards's idealistic moments. More often he simply leaves the matter open to doubt, stressing "the conduct of a doubt" ("Ditty"). The mountaineering poems that open onto voids come closest to expressing his belief.

The second image connected with the eddy in "The Eddying Ford" is the interaction of opposites, not a stasis, but an oscillation, something to give energy to the spin. Centrifugal and centripetal energy are an immediate example. The use of doubles in and through which individuals define themselves is another way of exploring this interaction; hence, the number of poems dealing with mutualities (another key word), janus-faced options, dynamic, logical and mechanical oppositions. Jacob's wrestling with the angel signifies the courage of the challenge and the intellectual penetration involved in matching wits:

JACOB: And what are thou?
THE EL: Thyself.
JACOB: Wrestle thou then with me!
THE EL: Myself to overcome Myself
        Will wrestle here with the thee.
JACOB: What art thou but this eddying ford
        By which I sent across,
    To save me from my brother's sword,
        My winnings and my loss.

Jacob and The El call each other an eddying ford, a

barrier to be crossed only at risk. Jacob is rewarded not for having won (The El is in command) but for having striven to his limit. His limp signifies the sacred wound that sets him apart from the rest of man. Richards takes up these motifs in *Job's Comforting* and *Beyond*.

"New Poems" (1971-1977) in *New and Selected Poems* (1978) and poems published in periodicals in 1978-1979 and posthumously review the sequence between the original of Know Thyself carved on the Temple of Delphi and meaning "Know the difference between gods and mortals, and your place below the gods," and know thyself as a Socratic quest for self-understanding and control. In "The Proper Study" he would reconcile the quests for a "variant" and "volatile" *Thyself* and "presences/ Divined as variously" of *Thy God*. Is the pursuit of this knowledge and its control over evil and suffering a "single search misguided by a double name"?

> The desolate aims
> Through which the soul is sought
> Are mirror-imaged
> In the selves they've wrought.

The aims are "desolate," forlorn, full of despair, because they are unattainable, and one must seek them, in part, alone; contrariwise, the aims have already shaped their protagonist and to that extent have partially realized their end. In "Emigrant: A Birthday Poem" (*Times Literary Supplement*, 30 March 1973), this is called a "well-lost game." The question of free will in choosing selves and ends is left in doubt. The good man's conduct derives from its inner nature "as from wise laws within him— seemingly" ("Nosce Teipsum").

The new poems in *New and Selected Poems* are wintry and impersonal; their subject matter, first and last things: "Birthright," "The First Lesson," "Possession," "Why." Richards in his eighties looks at life compassionately but from a height as great as the clouds themselves in "Annual Club Dinner":

> Even as clouds float on to hidden ends
>   So do these *convives* here converse together,
> Each spending smiles reconstituting friends,
>   While sighing at another's shortening tether.
> . . . .
> What was takes over, calls itself a Will:
>   The fleeting eddy would the Tide forget
> (The emptying soul, the unrelenting chill)
>   And hold things as they were, yes, even yet.
>
> Now does compassion, heart's eye, the unbidden,
> Find for itself what in these clouds is hidden.

Unexpected exemplars, the abolitionist William Wilberforce, the rebel "dauntless Eve," and the stoical Chinese Woman stand beside Socrates and Cicero in these poems. Yet the dominant mood is one of meditation "daunted," challenged by the mystery of death ("Espionage"). (*Dauntless, daunted,* and *daunting*, are all common words in Richards's diction; the root connotes internalized energy, challenge, apprehension before a work to be done, all presupposing a strong, resilient ego.) These thoughts on death are neither suppressed, nor quite stared out of their extremity. The importance that Richards gave to the impersonal virtues of the language and wisdom has already been noted. The long study of death releases the poet into an oblique articulation of "wise laws within" and lends the final poems an aura of almost biblical didacticism and classical fortitude.

Richards's "third" career, in poetry, was not crowned with the success of his first in criticism. Nor was it fraught with the difficulty and practical complication of his second in world literacy programs. Yet through his poems and verse plays he brought to fruition many of the themes and values that had informed his other careers: the psychology of mental integration, self-control, the quest for sincerity, complementarity, the place of ethical action. In the most personal of the poems, on mountaineering and old age, Richards explored sources of courage and offered insight into human destiny, revealing new sides of himself into extreme old age.

Bibliography:
John Paul Russo, "A Bibliography of the Books, Articles, and Reviews of I. A. Richards," in *I. A. Richards: Essays In His Honor*, edited by Reuben Brower, Helen Vendler, and John Hollander (New York: Oxford University Press, 1973), pp. 319-365.

References:
Reuben Brower, Helen Vendler, and John Hollander, eds., *I. A. Richards: Essays In His Honor* (New York: Oxford University Press, 1973);
Robert Lowell, "I. A. Richards as Poet," *Encounter*, 14 (February 1960): 77-78;
John Paul Russo, "The Mysterious Mountains: I. A. Richards and High Mountaineering," *Shenandoah*, 30, no. 4 (1979): 69-91.

Papers:
Magdalene College Old Library, Cambridge, and the Houghton Library at Harvard University have collections of Richards's papers.

Anne Ridler

(30 July 1912-   )

Joseph J. Feeney, S.J.
Saint Joseph's University

BOOKS: *Poems* (London: Oxford University Press, 1939);

A Dream Observed and Other Poems (London: Poetry, 1941);

The Nine Bright Shiners (London: Faber & Faber, 1943);

Cain: A Play in Two Acts (London: Nicholson & Watson, 1943);

The Shadow Factory: A Nativity Play (London: Faber & Faber, 1946);

Henry Bly, and Other Plays (London: Faber & Faber, 1950);

The Golden Bird and Other Poems (London: Faber & Faber, 1951);

The Trial of Thomas Cranmer: A Play (London: Faber & Faber, 1956);

A Matter of Life and Death (London: Faber & Faber, 1959);

Selected Poems (New York: Macmillan, 1961);

Who Is My Neighbour?; and, How Bitter the Bread (London: Faber & Faber, 1963);

Olive Willis and Downe House: An Adventure in Education (London: Murray, 1967);

Some Time After and Other Poems (London: Faber & Faber, 1972);

The Jesse Tree (London: Lyrebird Press, 1972).

OTHER: *Shakespeare Criticism, 1919-1935*, edited by Ridler, as Anne Bradby (London: Oxford University Press, 1936);

The Little Book of Modern Verse, edited by Ridler (London: Faber & Faber, 1941);

"A Question of Speech," in *T. S. Eliot: A Study of His Writings by Several Hands*, edited by Balachandra Rajan (London: Dobson, 1947), pp. 107-118;

Michael Roberts, ed., *The Faber Book of Modern Verse*, enlarged edition, with additional poems chosen by Ridler and an introduction by Ridler (London: Faber & Faber, 1951);

Charles Williams, *The Image of the City, and Other Essays*, edited by Ridler (London & New York: Oxford University Press, 1958);

Williams, *Selected Writings*, edited by Ridler (London: Oxford University Press, 1961);

Shakespeare Criticism, 1935-1960, edited by Ridler (London: Oxford University Press, 1963);

James Thomson, *Poems and Some Letters*, edited by Ridler (London: Centaur, 1963);

Thomas Traherne, *Poems, Centuries and Three Thanksgivings*, edited by Ridler (London: Oxford University Press, 1966);

George Darley, *Selected Poems of George Darley*, edited by Ridler (London: Merrion Press, 1979);

William Austin, *Poems*, edited by Ridler (Oxford: Perpetua Press, 1983).

Anne Ridler's poetry is stylistically uncommon: she is a modern metaphysical poet. Often her subject matter—the bombing of London, electricity, working in the City—is solidly modern, as are her unobtrusive rhythms and her distrust of exact rhyme. She has also written and worked in the very midst of modern poetry: W. H. Auden was a poetic influence; her favorite poets include T. S. Eliot and the later William Butler Yeats; and she edited *The Little Book of Modern Verse* (1941) and the second edition of *The Faber Book of Modern Verse* (1951). At Faber and Faber, furthermore, she worked closely with T. S. Eliot, serving as his secretary and helping him to choose poetry both for the publishing house and for the *Criterion*. Yet her belief, her mind, and her poetic sensibility are also firmly rooted in the seventeenth-century metaphysical tradition. Like Herbert and Donne she is a believing Christian of the Anglican communion; when she writes about human experience—marriage, love, childbearing, family—she closely links God and his world, analytically presenting this relationship in complex and detailed metaphors. As in the metaphysical poets, her metaphors are often strikingly original, and her poetic expression is difficult, fresh, highly structured, and sometimes craggy. As a modern metaphysical she has both revived the seventeenth-century tradition and, with her clear mind, has quickened and deepened twentieth-century religious poetry. She is, finally, well known and important, as a poet of marriage and of motherhood.

She was born Anne Bradby, in Rugby, War-

wickshire, the only daughter of a Rugby School housemaster, Henry Christopher Bradby, and his wife, Violet Alice Milford Bradby. In the summer of 1925, shortly before her thirteenth birthday, she went away to Downe House School in Berkshire. When she was fourteen, however, she fell ill and spent some time at home, but afterward she returned to Downe House School, where she remained until 1930. During these years she heard her first lecture by Charles Williams, novelist, poet, playwright, and essayist, who later became a significant influence on her. After leaving Downe House School, she spent six months in Italy with her parents and a school friend, learning Italian in Florence and Rome, exploring Dante, and reading history with her father. She completed her formal education at King's College of the University of London, receiving a diploma in journalism in 1933. While in London—a city she found exciting—she also attended evening extension lectures by Charles Williams. During this time Williams, a Christian apologist who taught the approach to God through an affirmation of the world's goodness and of Christ's Incarnation, developed into the major influence on her thought and life (though not on her poetic techniques). He also became a close friend and later served as godfather for her oldest child. After completing her studies at King's, Anne

Bradby, commissioned by Williams, did editorial work for Oxford University Press; she also aided the ailing Lascelles Abercrombie in editing what was to be *The Oxford Book of Modern Verse*. (Abercrombie later resigned this task; W. B. Yeats took on the editorship and produced a quite different book.) Her own edition of *Shakespeare Criticism, 1919-1935*, was published by Oxford University Press in 1936. In 1935, however, Anne Bradby herself had gone to Faber and Faber, where she worked until 1940 as a reader, secretary-assistant for Eliot and editor of *The Little Book of Modern Verse* (1941). While at Faber and Faber she was married, in July 1938, to Vivian Ridler, a Bristol native who was a printer, amateur painter, and at the time of his marriage the manager of the Bunhill Press in London. Anne Ridler's first book of poetry was published the next year.

Poems (1939) is a demanding and sometimes moving book. Difficult in syntax and rigorous in thought, it deals with love and marriage, with nature and time and God. The images are drawn from sea and land, from England and Italy, and from myth and dream; the poems, though, are meditations of the mind rather than revelries in sense experience. And although Ridler's material is often emotional and immediate, her poetic voice speaks from a reflective distance and enjoys a verbal originality. In "A Letter" she expresses her early aesthetic: "Technical problems have always given me trouble:/ . . . coming to verse, I hid my lack of ease/by writing only as I thought myself able,/ escaped the crash of the bold by salt originalities./ This is one reason for writing far from one's heart;/a better is, that one fears it may be hurt."

Complex metaphors structure many poems —a parallel, for example, in the poem "In Italy: I," involving a lake devouring raindrops, the mind devouring the heart, and her own pride threatening to devour her loved one. Underlying these complex conceits is her sense of interrelationships, especially of the similarities linking the world's creatures with each other and with their God. Such an understanding of the world came, she wrote (again in "In Italy: I"), when she "understood identity/and difference, and the doctrine of the Trinity"—how, that is, a God who is supreme in himself acts in the world and is reflected in all things. Thus her careful patterns of analogy display both theological convictions and a rare gift of perceiving and expressing complex parallels. "Old Goose of Time," for example, a prayer for her beloved through all time and into eternity, catches her theological perspective, her simultaneous passion and restraint, her original metaphors, and her complex syntax. In this poem

Time is a taxi bearing her beloved—"the Lord Almighty's precious,/the luck of Holiness"—away from her arms and her kisses. As he is borne northward through the night, she cries out to Time, "So then you can take him, I'll not cry after him,/even wishing to, my dandy, my fire/and phalanx of words against the crying demon;/bring him to his fine, excellent peace in heaven." In this and the other poems a new voice and a strong mind appear; she writes as a poet of life, of God, and supremely of married love. The contemporary critics praised Anne Ridler's first book, commenting on her fresh and precise language, her sharp visual images, her "impetuous moral sensibility" (the anonymous critic of the *Times Literary Supplement*), and her original style and perspective; the complaints involved her crabbed syntax and style and her occasional strained conceit.

Before the systematic bombing of London began in September 1940, Anne Ridler, with a child on the way, had left her job at Faber and Faber (though continuing as a reader for them) and moved to her retired parents' home, Ringshall End, in the Chiltern Hills near Ivinghoe Beacon. Her husband, Vivian Ridler, commuting between Ringshall and London, served in the fire brigade and saw their London flat bombed; he was later called up for military service. (Anne Ridler still vividly remembers the warm, sunny summer of 1940—"going through unhappiness yourself while all the world around is smiling"—and catches this pain in the idyll "Ringshall Summer" and in the anguished prayers "For this Time" and "Prayer in a Pestilent Time.") Vivian Ridler was sent north to the Orkney Islands, where his wife and their baby Jane joined him for a short, happy time; when he was ordered overseas to West Africa, Anne Ridler and Jane returned to her parents at Ringshall End.

This period of war and upset is reflected in the poet's second major collection, *The Nine Bright Shiners* (1943). These thirty-six poems, which include fourteen of the sixteen poems published in *A Dream Observed and Other Poems* (1941), show a matured and developing Anne Ridler. Gone are the overcomplexities and prickly syntax of her earlier *Poems*. Here one finds a new ease and assurance, while the tone remains as analytic and reflective as before. The metaphors are equally striking, if a bit less detailed, and the thought is more approachable though equally rich. The poems deal with war (in its public and private effects) and with her absent husband and their two babies, Jane (born in 1941) and Alison (born in 1943). Some poems—"For a Child Expected," "Crab Apple and the Crab's Tropic,"

and the extraordinary "For a Christening"—combine theological sensibility, human wisdom, original imagery, and abstract meditation. "Ringshall Summer," in the style of Marvell, links images of land and sea while contrasting beauty and war. On occasion Anne Ridler writes a poem, such as "The Cranes," which is pure description, but more commonly, as she puts it in "Aisholt Revisited," "the landscape was the occasion and the vessel" for contemplation and meditation. *The Nine Bright Shiners* ends with the surprising, playful "Jane Wakeful" and "Jane at Ten Months." In commenting on these poems the English critics, noting that "her sensibility is often markedly feminine" (the reviewer for the *Times Literary Supplement*), praised her freshness, her "luminousness" (Sheila Shannon in the *Spectator*), and her "intellectual distinction" (the *Times Literary Supplement*). And Stephen Spender, in the *New Statesman*, though noting that these poems contained "few terrors, agonies and bloody sweats," did find something of the primal woman in Anne Ridler—a touch of elemental terror with "the eternal matriarch casting her spells around her" and even (in "A Dream Observed") merging child and husband into one.

In 1945, the war having ended, Anne Ridler returned to London, where her husband taught typography at the Royal College of Art, and she continued as occasional reader for Faber and Faber. In 1948 the Ridler family moved to Oxford, when Vivian Ridler was named assistant to the printer to the University of Oxford. From that year to the present they have remained in the same Oxford house, having passed through Vivian Ridler's appointment in 1958 as printer to the University of Oxford and his retirement in 1978. During this period Anne Ridler produced four more collections of poetry, beginning with *The Golden Bird* (1951). In this book some new themes emerge: reflections on music (a longtime love of Anne Ridler's) and on Italian paintings (stimulated by a return to Florence in 1948). Unusual personal tributes appear in "To a Magician on Her Retirement" and in a sonnet for T. S. Eliot on his sixtieth birthday. The poet also experiments with a new form in the dazzling "Villanelle for the Middle of the Way." But Anne Ridler's traditional subjects dominate the book: her family, the sea, the countryside, and Christian themes such as Christmas. The poems are formal and precise in diction, intellectually clear and controlled, and rhythmic without being taut. In "To Mark Time" she commemorates her first son, Benedict (born in 1947). And in poems such as "Deus Absconditus" and "The Speech of the Dead" she shows once again how she can be emotionally powerful, strikingly original, and deeply moving. G. S. Fraser, in the *New Statesman*, stressed her propriety and her "poetry of piety and acceptance, of Anglicanism, domesticity, and a feeling for traditional ways and scenes"; the reviewer for the *Times Literary Supplement*, probing more deeply, tried to define her personal idiom: "At best her characteristic mannerisms created pointed and curiously touching effects. At worst there was a self-conscious gawkiness and quaintness." She showed a "blend of artlessness and artifice" and a mature technique. "The poetic world she creates may have its limitations, but within them there is formal and thematic variety."

In her next collection, *A Matter of Life and Death* (1959), Anne Ridler included three of her finest poems on childhood, "Choosing a Name," "The Gaze," and the title poem. This title poem, written for her last child, Colin (born in 1952), is the poet's personal favorite among all her works; it was also chosen to conclude her *Selected Poems*. In "A Matter of Life and Death," an astoundingly unsentimental but moving poem about a baby, the poet compares its growth to the gradual unfurling of an iris. As she foresees the child's growing through life in the hope of resurrection, the awed mother expresses a human and metaphysical wonder: "I did not feel the unfurling of my love." In another poem she is the craftsman, reflecting on the problem of form in poetry by means of a parallel with a flower garden. In "A Carol to Be Set to Music" she crafts a rhyming carol which, by violating rhyme in its last line, shocks the reader to insight. Some new topics appear in this collection —Thomas Cranmer, and a photograph—but most poems touch on her favorite images (the countryside, flowers, the sea) and her favorite themes (children, time, God, love). Some of the reviewers commented on a spiritual coziness and an excess of nice feelings, but the book was generally praised. Frank Kermode, writing in the *Spectator*, called it "richly satisfying," "quietly remarkable," and "formidably relaxed and lucid." "Her language," he concluded, "moves perpetually in a pure translucence, never rough or forced, yet answering faithfully the strong action of the mind beneath."

Until 1961 Anne Ridler's poetic reputation in the United States had been based on her English collections, on poems in English magazines and newspapers, and on individual poems published in such American magazines as *Poetry* (Chicago), the *Virginia Quarterly Review*, and the *New Yorker*. In 1954 and 1955, furthermore, she had won two

prizes for poems published in *Poetry* (Chicago). It was appropriate, then, for an American publisher, the Macmillan Company, to publish her *Selected Poems* (1961). This collection, which contains 46 of the 127 poems previously published in book form, prompted a new critical evaluation of the poet. She was still generally viewed as a religious poet and/or a woman poet, but the reviewer in *Poetry* (Chicago) treated her and Louis MacNeice as representatives of the two major types of modern British poetry: MacNeice was the poet of the public world, while "Mrs. Ridler represents marvelously the type of the personal, often private, putatively metaphysical writer. Her themes are private loves and sorrows." She was praised for her fresh insights, remarkable control, and lyric facility; her limitations were a lack of tension, a tendency to moralize, and an excessive self-certainty. James Dickey, in the *Sewanee Review*, curiously talked about her "pantheism" but called her work "very distinguished indeed." Hayden Carruth in *Poetry* magazine said that "Mrs. Ridler's poems about childbearing in wartime are among the few genuinely maternal poems in the language."

Anne Ridler's most recent collection is *Some Time After and Other Poems* (1972), published in England. It begins with "For a New Voice," which asks the "muse of middle-age" to grant Anne Ridler "a poet's voice again." To a certain extent a new voice does appear, for the poems are more readily understandable; God's presence in the world is less frequently mentioned; and there is a newfound sadness about the contemporary world. New topics are also broached: modern medicine, twisted love, current news, and even Soviet oppression. But even in these poems (except in "Modern Love" which parodies current life), Anne Ridler's approach is the familiar one of reflection and meditation, often through analogy. In "A Pirated Edition," contemplating how the image of a friend remains on retina and in memory, she intermingles the worlds of books, biology, and everyday experience in the mode of a seventeenth-century conceit. And in "Islands of Scilly" she parallels the islands, the fingers of a hand, and an individual's "luckiest" days. Following her personal tradition, too, Anne Ridler still celebrates her husband, her children, and her God. The poet at sixty has somewhat developed a new voice and new songs, but she also continues as a careful craftsman, a maker of complex metaphors, a master of lithe rhythm and occasional rhyme, and a poet of married love and of God. With the wisdom of years she finishes the poem "Some Time After" in a gently contented mood: "Love unillusioned is not love disenchanted." In commenting on this col-

Finches in the Castalian stream
  Wink a golden wing
And the deep ~~rocky~~ mountain cleft, where steam *in which mysterious*
  ~~condensed in~~
could stiffen into prophecy
Contains a trickle of water & no mystery.

  All the temples are open to the sky

  Arguing over the oracle
Tourists ~~try~~ to eat the plane tree's fruit
  Or choosing picture postcards try
To trap a moment's ecstasy.
  All the temples . . .

Whatever stirred the Delphic ~~seer~~
  Whether a god's whisper
  fumes of
Or cyanide ~~fumes~~, as some declare
No longer speaks. Mycenae is still red
  But w. the blood of poppies.
Something remains here to be understood.
  ~~To all the temples~~
  All the temples
~~Here is~~ the old antithesis:
~~Remains~~
  The lucid statues & the riddling darkness.

Working draft for "Delphi" (the author)

The air is blue, & sweet with cistus
  Our culture & our ignorance
Here
  Are brought to judgement (here)
  Between the shining rocks ~~within~~ in the mountain's
    Wink of gold in the stream —   trance.
  ~~The~~ Blue the air, & sweet with cistus
Dark as ever the mutter of doom

  Tho' all the temples

The air is blue, & sweet with cistus
Bright flash in the stream
A Wink of gold where finches fly
Dark as ever the mutter of doom
Tho' all the temples are open y sky.

lection the *Times Literary Supplement* reviewer noted a rather heavy moralizing, and Alan Brownjohn, in the *New Statesman*, saw a falling-off from the "tenderness and perception" of her earlier work. But Christopher Hudson in the *Spectator* found the book "as graceful and sprightly as could be wished" and the poems "quietly successful within their self-imposed limits." And Hudson, graciously writing that a new voice was not at all needed, commented on the poet's confidence and ease "as if speaking from the heart of a tradition."

Anne Ridler has also had published nine plays in verse, which range from the biblical *Cain* (1943) through the historical *The Trial of Thomas Cranmer* (1956) to the contemporary *The Shadow Factory* (1946) and *Who Is My Neighbour?* (1963). *The Shadow Factory* and *Who Is My Neighbour?* touch on modern problems such as industry's depersonalization of workers. In *The Jesse Tree* (1972), a masque for music, Anne Ridler meditates on Christ's continuing redemption in a world of concentration camps, political prisoners, and nuclear warfare. This highly poetic masque, conceived as a dream vision, draws upon Norse and Christian myths and deals with the paradox of the world's glory coexisting with the mystery of evil.

At the present time Anne Ridler continues as an occasional reader for Faber and Faber and for the Oxford University Press. She has also edited the poems of the seventeenth-century poet William Austin, published in a limited edition printed by her husband. She thus remains in close contact both with contemporary poetry and with the English tradition of the seventeenth century.

Throughout her seven books of poetry Anne Ridler has attempted a difficult task, for as a modern metaphysical she has been willing to stand partly aside from the prevailing modernism.

Working from diverse influences—Wyatt and Auden in particular, but also Donne and Herbert—she gradually developed a distinctive perspective and an individual voice. In her early work, according to Anne Ridler herself, too much of her background thinking got into the text. In her later work she distilled the underlying thought and concentrated on the human experience and its occasion. Sometimes she directly presented the occasion in a descriptive poem; more usually she used the experience as a base for reflection and meditation, often by means of a complex metaphor. With regard to her poetic voice, the critics continue to use words such as "stillness," "luminescence," "precision," "clarity," "intelligence," and "control." Underlying this calm voice are an intensity and a passion that are restrained by poetic form and given hope by family love and religious belief.

Both English and American critics recognize the importance of Anne Ridler. She writes within certain limits of material and perception, but is considered outstanding in England among religious poets and among poets who are women. She deserves a place, too, in the tradition of love poetry, as she celebrates married love, maternal love, and God's active love in the world. Although, with her metaphysical imagination, she would not be chosen to represent the typical or unique voice of the twentieth century, she continues to renew the broader poetic tradition with poems of strong-minded love and strong-minded belief.

Reference:

Kathleen E. Morgan, *Christian Themes in Contemporary Poets: A Study of English Poetry of the Twentieth Century* (London: SCM Press, 1965), pp. 144-153.

Vernon Scannell
(23 January 1922-   )

John H. Schwarz
Villanova University

SELECTED BOOKS: *Graves and Resurrections* (London: Fortune Press, 1948);

The Fight (London: Peter Nevill, 1953);

The Wound and the Scar (London: Peter Nevill, 1953);

A Mortal Pitch (London: Villiers, 1957);

The Masks of Love (London: Putnam's, 1960);

The Big Chance (London: John Long, 1960);

The Shadowed Place (London: John Long, 1961);

The Face of the Enemy (London: Putnam's, 1961);

A Sense of Danger (London: Putnam's, 1962);

The Dividing Night (London: Putnam's, 1962);

Edward Thomas (London: Longmans, Green, 1963);

Walking Wounded: Poems 1962-1965 (London: Eyre & Spottiswoode, 1965);

The Big Time (London: Longmans, 1965);

Epithets of War: Poems 1965-1969 (London: Eyre & Spottiswoode, 1969);

Pergamon Poets 8, by Scannell and Jon Silkin, edited by Dennis Butts (Oxford & New York: Pergamon, 1970);

The Dangerous Ones (Oxford: Pergamon, 1970; New York: Pergamon, 1970);

Mastering the Craft (Oxford & New York: Pergamon, 1970);

Selected Poems (London: Allison & Busby, 1971);

The Tiger and the Rose: An Autobiography (London: Hamilton, 1971);

The Winter Man (London: Allison & Busby, 1973);

The Apple-Raid and other Poems (London: Chatto & Windus, 1974);

The Loving Game (London: Robson, 1975);

Not Without Glory: Poets of the Second World War (London: Woburn, 1976);

A Proper Gentleman (London: Robson, 1977);

A Lonely Game (Exeter: Wheaton, 1979);

New & Collected Poems: 1950-1980 (London: Robson, 1980);

Winterlude (London: Robson, 1982).

OTHER: Howard Sergeant and Dannie Abse, eds., *Mavericks: An Anthology*, includes poems by Scannell (London: Editions Poetry and Poverty, 1957);

Yorkshire Post

New Poems 1962: A P.E.N. Anthology of Contemporary Poetry, edited by Scannell, Patricia Beer, and Ted Hughes (London: Hutchinson, 1962).

In *Not Without Glory* (1976), his study of poets of World War II, Vernon Scannell asserts that "the best poetry of the war, the most truthful and penetrating was written with a respect for that tradition of English verse which is informed by the spirit of Milton's words, 'simple, sensuous and passionate,' a poetry which is rooted in the ground of physical experience, suspicious of the abstract and conforming to the disciplines of provenly effective forms." He might be characterizing his own best poetry. For more than thirty years Scannell has written poems that meet the challenges of established forms while drawing on his vivid experiences as soldier, boxer, lover, husband and father, tutor and lecturer, broadcaster, drinker, and general survivor. His eventful, unconventional life allied him naturally, but briefly, in the 1950s with the Mavericks, poets as much at odds with the literary establishment as Scannell had been with social norms. Scannell concludes the introduction to his *New & Collected Poems* (1980) with these words: "I fervently, if audaciously, hope that there will be readers who will find something in these pages that will, in Doctor Johnson's words 'enable them the better to enjoy life or the better to endure it.' " While his poems may lean more to endurance than enjoyment—Scannell is a melancholy poet—the hope is not audacious.

Scannell was born in Spilsby, Lincolnshire. The family lived in a number of homes in the provinces until his father, a photographer, established himself in Aylesbury, Buckinghamshire. Scannell lived there for nine years, leaving school at fourteen to work in an accounting firm, for which his ambitions to be a writer as well as a boxing champion did not equip him ideally. In 1940 Scannell enlisted in the army, saw his first action in the Middle East, was seriously wounded near Caen in France in the summer of 1944, and spent the rest of the war recovering. Shortly after V-E Day, feeling brutalized by army life, he deserted.

For more than two years he was at large. He boxed professionally for a while in London, then moved to Leeds. There he found work tutoring and started to write and send out poems, including two that were published by John Middleton Murry in *Adelphi*. In 1946-1947 he studied at Leeds University under Bonamy Dobrée and G. Wilson Knight, both of whom encouraged him in his literary pursuits. He also joined the university boxing club and went on to win the welterweight, middleweight, and cruiserweight Northern Universities Championships.

Scannell was finally arrested in the summer of 1947 and taken to Aberdeen to be court-martialed. Acting on the advice of an army psychiatrist, the court directed that he be sent to Northfield Hospital, the "nutters joint" near Birmingham. He was soon discharged from the hospital and the army, and he returned to Leeds, where he brought out his

first book of poems, *Graves and Resurrections*, in 1948. He has since dismissed the book as "a woolly and wordy collection," referring to its consciously poetic diction and awkward rhetoric. The overall gloom, typical of the contemporary "apocalyptic" poets, is unrelieved by humor.

Scannell left Leeds in 1949. He worked on advertising layout for a trade magazine in London until his incapacity for such work was manifest. He then washed dishes and wandered a bit in France. Back in Aylesbury, he worked as a "boxing illusionist" (that is, in fixed fights) for Alf Taylor's Boxing Academy, part of a traveling fair. In 1950 he moved on to the tamer and steadier business of teaching English and history in a West London suburban school.

The job enabled him to work more methodically on his writing, and he started placing some poems in periodicals such as the *Listener, Spectator,* and *Time and Tide*. In 1952 he sold his first novel, *The Fight* (published in 1953), and wrote and delivered on BBC Radio a script about fairground boxing that was favorably received. Thus encouraged to hope for a career as a free-lance broadcaster, he resigned from his teaching post at the end of the summer term of 1952. He did more radio broadcasting but did not receive the same attention. He sold a second novel, *The Wound and the Scar*, in 1953, and it was published in the same year. Also in 1953 John Wain selected some of his poems for radio broadcast. He worked in 1953 at a cram school, preparing students for examinations, and in 1955 he wrote a column on sport and edited and lectured for the National Anti-Vivisection Society.

The hectic pace of the early 1950s was accompanied by heavy drinking. While he was at the West London school, for instance, he and a colleague would go on binges. Scannell writes of that time, "We were quite often arrested and had to spend a night in the cells." The pace slowed in October 1954 when Scannell was married to Josephine Higson. After the birth of Jane, the first of his six children, he started teaching, in September 1955, at the Hazlewood School in Limpsfield, Surrey, remaining until 1962.

Mavericks (1957), an anthology of poets whose work was not included in Robert Conquest's Movement anthology *New Lines*, published five of Scannell's poems, and he was about to bring out his second collection of poems, *A Mortal Pitch* (1957). The title, from Shakespeare's sonnet eighty-six, suggests Scannell's preoccupation with mortality, with here-and-now reality. The poems in *A Mortal*

Pitch have many of the features that have continued to mark the poet's work. "Schoolroom on a Wet Afternoon," for example, achieves its power through its unexpected ending; ordinary musings of a schoolmaster—"Is it their doomed innocence noon weeps for?"—give way to his awareness of what is hidden in the students' desks: "Vicious rope, glaring blade, the gun cocked to kill." The "woolly and wordy" writing of *Graves and Resurrections* is past; these poems show the typical Scannell qualities of brevity, directness of expression, and commitment to rhyme and standard English meters. The wit of "How to Fill in a Crossword Puzzle," the humor of "Unsuccessful Poet," the representation of marital pain in "The Complaint of the Adulterous Woman," the remembrance of war in "Gunpowder Plot" all reappear in later work. In the *Spectator*, Robert Conquest marked Scannell's "broad and uneffeminate sense of humour" and his achievement of "a passionate statement which is devoid of both alto sentimentality and tremolo emotionalism." Nevertheless, there are signs that *A Mortal Pitch* is the work of a poet who is still learning his craft. Some poems are commonplace. Flat expression weakens the effect of others. The reviewer for the *Listener* found little more than "some good near misses."

The Scannell family, by then four in number with the birth of Nancy in 1956, moved in 1958 to a larger house in Limpsfield. The extra space made writing easier. By the end of 1960 Scannell had broadcast on George MacBeth's BBC Third Programme arts review, *Comment*; he had had a play, *A Door with One Eye* (1960), produced on radio; he had written and had accepted for publication two thrillers, *The Big Chance* (1960) and *The Shadowed Place* (1961), and a novel, *The Face of the Enemy* (1961); he had been given the job, with Ted Hughes and Patricia Beer, of editing a P.E.N. anthology of verse; and he had been elected a Fellow of the Royal Society of Literature. He had also published another book of poems, *The Masks of Love* (1960). He was looking forward to the day when he would be freed from the necessity to teach, able to live off earnings from his imaginative writings as well as from broadcasting, reviewing, lecturing, and public readings.

The Masks of Love won the Heinemann Award for Literature in 1961, despite mixed reception by reviewers in 1960. John Holloway, writing in *London Magazine*, found "a diction that tags and hurries on, instead of exploring and revealing." In the *New Statesman* Donald Hall objected to sloppy meter and numerous clichés. The reviewer in the *Times Literary*

Supplement, however, expressed surprise that "Mr. Scannell has not been made more of." His kind of poetry "stops one short," and, the reviewer added, Scannell has the "ability to speak through images. On the whole these are superbly integrated poems."

The Masks of Love certainly includes some moving poetry. Scannell combines irony and compassion in telling of the "Romantic Suicide" who drowned himself because the poems he read said that was the appropriate response to a woman's rejection and whose grotesque corpse prompts a prayer for "one not wicked, merely wrong." "Simon Frailman: Ten Sonnets and an Elegiac Coda" is a quietly effective study of an average suburbanite whose death leads his wife and children to realize their love for him. In "Poem for Jane" Scannell expresses his own love for his first-born. Some poems, on the other hand, are less than inspired, such as "Silver Wedding": "I sit with a wreath of quarrels set/On my tired and balding brow."

In 1960 Scannell's wife, Jo, gave birth to twins, Toby and Benjamin, but Benjamin was born severely deformed and a few months later died at home. Scannell writes affectingly in *The Tiger and the Rose* (1971), his first autobiographical memoir, about his love for Benjamin. A fifth child, John, was born in 1961, and in 1962 Scannell's next collection of poems was published.

A Sense of Danger again elicited differences of opinion. The reviewer in the *Times Literary Supplement* thought Scannell "a little uncertain in his handling both of diction and rhythm." John Montague, in the *Spectator*, regretted Scannell's "tendency to slip into an O. Henry slickness," and Ian Hamilton, in *London Magazine*, spoke of "glibly compassionate anecdotes" with "cosily aphoristic" resolutions. Others praised the author's anecdotes. The *TLS* reviewer pointed to their similarity in art and effect to Hardy. Anthony Thwaite, in *Encounter*, remarked that "Scannell's *forte* is the anecdote, often commonplace and banal in itself but organised—seldom forced—into a poem with real depths." Thwaite also said that "Scannell's work has strengthened out of all recognition." D. J. Enright wrote in the *New Statesman*, "Here for once is a slim volume whose slimness one actually regrets." *A Sense of Danger* received a Poetry Book Society Recommendation.

A Sense of Danger is aptly named: its subjects include an incendiary, a man unaccountably weeping in a bar, a Jew beaten to death, a suicide, a dead boozer, a girl murdered in the dark near a fair, a "Juan in Middle Age" on whose eyes "kisses press

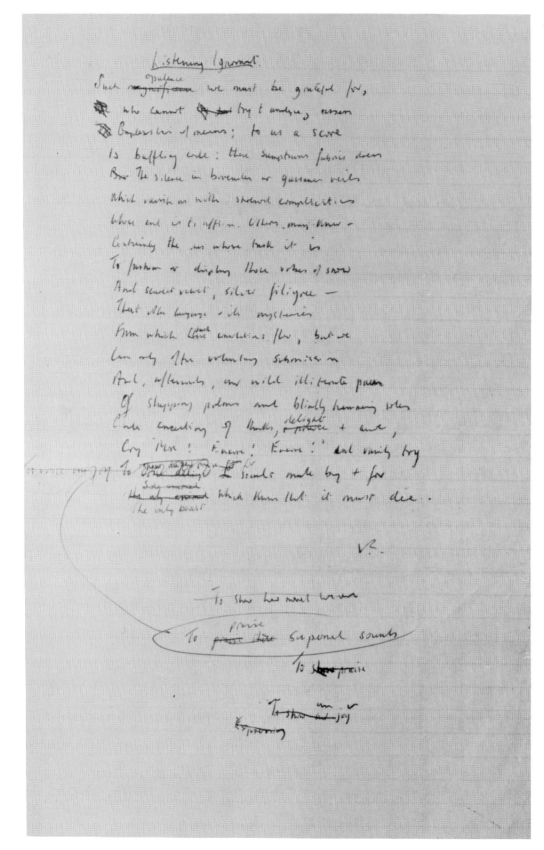

Working draft (the author)

like pennies." One of the best poems, "Cows in Red Pasture," recalls two cows seen in Normandy during the war:

> Both were still; the toffee one
> Lay on its back, its stiff legs stuck
> Up from the swollen belly like
> A huge discarded set of bagpipes.
> The piebald cow lay on its side
> Looking like any summer beast
> Until one saw it had no head.
>
> The grass on which they lay was red.

Perhaps Scannell writes so frequently of danger and death because, as he says in "An Old Lament Renewed," "I mourn the cadaver in the egg."

Scannell now felt well enough established to resign from his teaching position, though the family continued to live in Limpsfield. There he worked on the poems published in *Walking Wounded*. Of the title piece, which views wounded soldiers walking in thousands, Scannell once wrote: "I came to see that the Walking Wounded represented the common human condition: the dramatically heroic role is for the few. Most of us have to take the smaller wounds of living and we have to return again and again to the battlefield, and perhaps in the long run this is the more heroic role." The wounded are not only war veterans but people cut or bruised by modern living conditions. Writers of graffiti on toilet walls, who express "Our loneliness and lust, despair and hate," are walking wounded. So is the alcoholic old clerk of "The Old Books," talking of the way he used to keep the books: "You youngsters with your ball-points wouldn't understand." Even the boy who kills a cat and is haunted by Poesque imaginings in "A Case of Murder" is of the company.

Gavin Ewart's review in *London Magazine* was for the most part sympathetic: "These poems inhabit the real world; they concern life as it is lived today. And they are, in the very best sense, 'consolatory.' " Francis Hope wrote disapprovingly in the *New Statesman* of the poet's "way of spelling out his morals in that final verse." The reviewer for the *Times Literary Supplement* noted a "somewhat ruthless urge to moralize and a weakness for a flat ending" and called for "some restraint, some exactness and purity of language."

In 1967 Scannell spent two months in Brixton Prison for drunken driving; a sixth child, Jacob, was born; and the Scannells moved to Nether Compton, near Sherborne, Dorset. Two years later Scannell published *Epithets of War: Poems 1965-1969*. The

volume is a bit less impressive than *Walking Wounded*. He includes too many trifles: "View from a Barber's Chair" is shaped like a comb; "A Long Sentence" is just that, and not a very witty one. "Pistol" is unimaginative in its irony: "Who would deny/Any healthy boy/Such an old-fashioned and/Beautiful toy?" The title piece, on the other hand, consists of five poems that have stirring moments: the roll call of Scannell's dead World War II mates in "Eidolon Parade" or the reference in "Casualties" to raw recruits in World War I, "Children with sad moustaches and puttee'd calves/Prepared to be translated." Two additional poems of war provide Scannell's characteristic surprise endings: in "View from a Wheelchair" a mutilated soldier ends his soliloquy, "They do not know that I walk in my sleep"; "Uncle Edward's Affliction" plays off the comedy of Uncle Edward's color-blind confusion against the horror of what he must have seen in the trenches, "The rain of innocent green blood." "A Game of Shove-Ha'penny" and "A Simple Need" depict sexual suffering in sharp detail. "Growing Pain" is a gentle poem about one of Scannell's sons. "Cigarette" will have wry appeal to longtime smokers.

Alan Brownjohn, in the *New Statesman*, called *Epithets* "a rather hit-or-miss collection," though he added that "Scannell's extrovert, no-nonsense standpoint, his approachability, his alert eye for everyday detail, are attractive." The *Times Literary Supplement* critic found the war poems "for the most part, stalely conventional responses to the fighting," the overall volume sparse in subject matter, and the rhythms "slack and careless." Brian Jones, reviewing the book for *London Magazine*, thought the poems lacked adventurousness. Nevertheless, he wrote, "Scannell has, unashamedly, something to say, and has clearly worked hard to find the least pretentious, the most apposite, language by which to express his intentions."

In the next year, 1970, Scannell published a book of poems for younger readers called *Mastering the Craft*, and the eighth *Pergamon Poets* consisted of selections by Dennis Butts from the work of Scannell and Jon Silkin. *The Tiger and the Rose: An Autobiography* appeared in 1971. That same year Jeremy Robson's *Corgi Modern Poets in Focus: 4* included selections from Scannell's work and a generous estimate of the poet's achievement, and, also in 1971, Scannell produced his *Selected Poems*.

Julian Symons, reviewing the book for *London Magazine*, was not greatly impressed by *Selected Poems*: "Obviously these poems about parents, children, school and teaching, being married, the ordinary affairs of life, are written by a likeable, intelligent man. Unfortunately they are produced upon a rather low level of sensibility to words, and they have a sort of crassness or patness that alienates the well-wisher." Thwaite responded differently in the *New Statesman*: "There are 10 or a dozen poems in *A Sense of Danger* (1962) and *Walking Wounded* (1965) which stand among the best of their decade," he wrote, and he argued that the poet has never been "properly noticed" except by compilers of school anthologies.

Scannell's 1973 collection of poems, *The Winter Man*, helped win for him the Cholmondoley Poetry Prize in 1974. The reviewer in the *Times Literary Supplement* thought highly of the book. Of "Picnic on the Lawn," in which a childless woman reveals to two harassed mothers her wish to have had children, he wrote: "This sort of poem, where truth and pathos are evinced from the suggestions of a very slight situation, is notoriously difficult to bring off without sounding sugary or contrived, and it says a great deal for Mr. Scannell's delicate judgment and dramatizing skill that he avoids both pitfalls." The review praised Scannell's "fertile image-making power working comfortably within its limits" but noted "a truly monstrous piece of poetic diction," the plea in "Confessional Poem" that the reader "shed no liquid salt."

Scannell stays within his usual limits of subject matter and theme in *The Winter Man*. He examines failure in marriage in several poems. In "Confrontation" a husband and his wife's lover meet: "through the bonds of her body/We were related." The speaker of "The Widow's Complaint" has been cheated by her husband's sudden death of the chance to tell him how much she hated him: "Oh, love, my love,/How can I forgive you that?" "End of a Libertine" is less successful with its predictable ending reference to "the husband's hard black gun." "Six Reasons for Drinking" is diverting on another favorite subject, and "Battlefields" is a charming father's poem. "Incident at West Bay" tells of a man whose two children drown, after he leaves his car for a moment and it rolls off a quay. "Comeback" is the somewhat hackneyed monologue of a punchy ex-champion boxer. In the title poem a man sadly returns after a separation to a woman whose desire for him he knows is "spiked with hate."

After a second book of verses for the young, *The Apple-Raid and other Poems* (1974), Scannell's next collection was *The Loving Game* (1975). Several poems in this volume seem to grow out of the recent collapse of the poet's marriage—he had left his wife

and family in 1974 to move to Rhydyfelin in South Wales—and they make painful reading. "An Anniversary" develops the conceit of two fallen willow leaves: "They will not touch each other again,/Not now, not ever." "The Loving Game" compares loving to boxing: in loving the poet "Was hurt much worse than in the other ring." Other poems take up the subject of aging, a longstanding interest of the poet, but here, as he passes fifty, one that seems especially absorbing to him ("Spot-check at Fifty," "The Wrong of Spring," "All Things Come"). "Right Dress," a hilarious poem about a transvestite, is in a different key.

The Loving Game is not as satisfying a work as some of Scannell's earlier books, despite its having been a Poetry Book Society Choice. "*The Loving Game* has made less of an impression on me than his last three or four books. . . . some slackness seems to have got into his language," Thwaite wrote in the *Times Literary Supplement*. Peter Bland, reviewing the book for *London Magazine*, thought the language "a unique form of heightened journalism as much Kiplingesque as Chaplinesque" that works when Scannell is tongue-in-cheek but does not work so well when he is serious.

In November 1975 Scannell began living in a council flat as a poet-in-residence in the postwar "new village" of Berinsfield in Oxfordshire. He had been awarded a nine-month writing fellowship by the Southern Arts Association. The experience, recounted in *A Proper Gentleman* (1977), the second volume of his memoirs, was dispiriting. He was to give readings and deliver talks when requested, advise aspiring writers, and live among and make himself generally available to the people. In fact, he encountered suspicion and hostility from the start. When he had at last won a kind of acceptance among most of the adult villagers, local youths began harassing him, and he was literally driven out of the community in July 1975, short of his agreed nine months.

Back in Rhydyfelin, Scannell wrote *Not Without Glory: Poets of the Second World War* and *A Proper Gentleman*. In 1978 he became a writer-in-residence again, in a more hospitable environment, the Shrewsbury School, for the academic year 1978-1979. He was then appointed resident poet at the King's School, Canterbury, for the Michaelmas Term 1979, after which he moved to Leeds. In 1980 he brought out his *New & Collected Poems*.

This collection excludes *Graves and Resurrections* and other published poems that seemed on rereading to be, in Scannell's words, "false, banal or inept." The "New Poems 1975-80" section contains

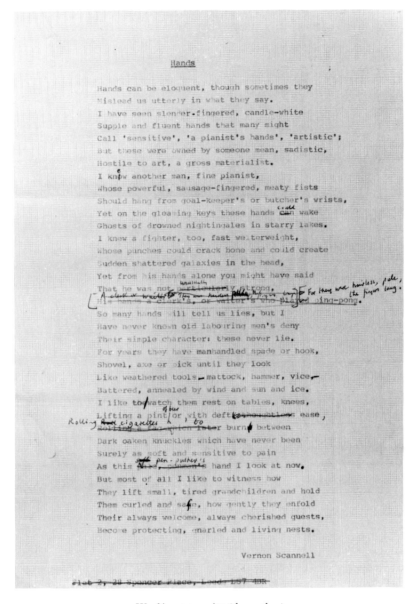

Working typescript (the author)

four works, two about aging, one about a reformed drunkard, and a long piece of political and social protest called "A Partial View."

The reviews of *New & Collected Poems* were generally positive. Alan Hollinghurst, writing for the *New Statesman*, considered "A Partial View" a failure and had other reservations; still he called the collection "a body of work of easy appeal and genuine and likeable personality." Alan Brownjohn, Gavin Ewart, and Simon Curtis spoke well of the collection. Curtis, in the *Times Literary Supplement*, singled out for praise both Scannell's clarity of expression, "There is not an obscure line

in the whole of his *New & Collected Poems*," and his skillful handling of the dramatic monologue form.

Scannell has by no means settled into retirement since *New & Collected Poems*. In April 1982 he published *Winterlude*. The new volume begins with two poems from *Mastering the Craft*; the rest are pieces written since *The Loving Game* but not included in *New & Collected Poems*. As usual the poems are traditional in form. A number of them have to do with sexual pain. "Weaker Sex," for instance, concludes, "she cannot rape him./You think he should rejoice that this is true?/Maybe, but there are worse things she can do." "Lover's Moon" expresses the bitterness of waning love. In "Sleep Talker" a husband hears his dreaming wife speak amorously to another man. Several poems explore aging and death, old Scannell ground.

Scannell relieves the melancholy in three solacing, even life-embracing, poems. "Listening Ignorant," on his love of classical music, pays homage to humankind "for sounds made by and for/The only animal which knows that it must die." "On This May Morning" celebrates the spring with almost youthful ardor: "I breakfast on birdsong." Finally, while he is "In a City Churchyard"—his only companions a homeless old lady, a drunk, and a mongrel dog—he has a glorious vision of a Day of Judgment on which angels may see "Rejuvenated lady, dancing dog,/The sleeping drinker's dream corporified."

In his sixties Scannell remains a discerning observer of the walking wounded, himself included, of modern urban and suburban life. His poetry is sometimes uninspired: the subject matter can be hackneyed, resolutions predictable, language flat. But more often his poems successfully direct the reader's eye afresh to the pathos and humor in an imperfect world. Except for the derivative *Graves and Resurrections*, his books of poetry all reveal a likable personality speaking in a distinctive voice. Reviewers more often than not have applauded Scannell's work, and he has a loyal following of readers. Judging from *Winterlude*, his powers are undiminished.

Interviews:

Hilary Morrish, "Vernon Scannell," 9 September 1963, *The Poet Speaks: Interviews with Contemporary Poets*, edited by Peter Orr (London: Routledge & Kegan Paul, 1966), pp. 219-224;

Phillip Hay and Angharad Wynn-Jones, *Three Poets, Two Children: Leonard Clark, Vernon Scannell, Dannie Abse Answer Questions by Two Children*, edited by Desmond Badham-Thornhill (Gloucester: Thornhill Press, 1975).

Reference:

Jeremy Robson, "Vernon Scannell," in *Corgi Modern Poets in Focus: 4*, edited by Robson (London: Corgi, 1971), pp. 59-64.

Tom Scott

(6 June 1918-   )

William Cookson

SELECTED BOOKS: *Seeven Poems o Maister Francis Villon* (Tunbridge Wells: Peter Russell, Pound Press, 1953);

An Ode til New Jerusalem (Edinburgh: Macdonald, 1956);

The Ship and Ither Poems (London & New York: Oxford University Press, 1963);

Dunbar: An Exposition of the Poems (Edinburgh & London: Oliver & Boyd, 1966; New York: Barnes & Noble, 1966);

At the Shrine o the Unkent Sodger (Preston: Akros, 1968);

Tales of King Robert the Bruce, Freely Adapted from The Brus of John Barbour (14th Century) (New York & Oxford: Pergamon, 1969);

Brand the Builder (Epping, Essex: Ember Press, 1975);

The Tree (Dunfermline: Borderline Press, 1977).

OTHER: *The Oxford Book of Scottish Verse*, edited by Scott and John MacQueen (Oxford: Clarendon Press, 1966);

Late Medieval Scots Poetry, edited by Scott (London: Heinemann, 1967; New York: Barnes & Noble, 1967);

The Penguin Book of Scottish Verse, edited by Scott (Harmondsworth: Penguin, 1970).

Tom Scott expressed the concerns at the core of his work in an autobiographical essay for *Contemporary Poets* in 1975. Here he depicts himself as a social idealist, whose inspiration appears both in visions of the Good Society and satires of the current social order. He is, specifically, a Scottish nationalist "more concerned with the salvation of my nation than that of my own soul." The most typical and conspicuous sign of his nationalist en-

Willie Kellock, Hugh MacDiarmid, and Tom Scott at a meeting of the 200 Burns Club, the society formed in 1959 to celebrate the bicentennial of Robert Burns's birth, Bo'ness, 1960 (The Glasgow Herald)

thusiasms appeared when he shifted the language of his poetry from the standard English of his early work to a native Scots. (His prose, however, is written in English.) All in all, his "utopian socialism" is of a "moral-aesthetic" nature, and so may be realized, he believes, as he exercises and refines the instrument of the national language, not by political activism.

Born in Glasgow, Scotland, Tom Scott was the son of a boilermaker and shop assistant, William Kerr Scott, and his wife, Catherine Newell Baille Scott. He went to Thornwood Primary School in Glasgow and then to Hyndland Secondary. In 1931 he and his family moved to St. Andrews, where his father started a new life as a builder's laborer (having previously been a foreman boilermaker on the Clyde). Tom Scott went to Madras College, St. Andrews, for a year and a half until 1933, when he left to work at various jobs, including the building trade. He gave up building work in 1938 and also an ambition to become a singer, deciding at this time

that his vocation was to be a poet. In 1939 he was about to enter Newcastle Abbey College when war broke out and he was called up. From 1939 to 1944 he served in the Royal Army Pay Corps both in Britain and Nigeria. After the war he spent some time in London, until in 1950 he won an Atlantic Award for Literature, which enabled him to go to Italy and Sicily; these travels led to his conversion to writing in Scots as his own European dialect. In 1953 he went to Newbattle, where he studied under Edwin Muir; later he went to Edinburgh University, where he took an M.A. and a Ph.D., settling in Edinburgh, where he now lives. He married Heather Fretwell in 1963.

Scott's poems were first published in 1940 in *Poetry Quarterly*, and his work appeared in various wartime anthologies, including *The White Horseman* and *Poetry in Wartime*. At this period in his life all his work was in English, and it was another ten years before he found his own voice in his native Scottish tradition. There is an affinity here with Hugh Mac-

Diarmid, whose earliest poems were also in English, and it is interesting to note that, again like MacDiarmid, Scott has returned to writing in English in his most recently published long poem, *The Tree* (1977).

Probably the most talented poet to keep alive the great renaissance of Scots as a language for poetry, which began with the poems MacDiarmid wrote in the 1920s and 1930s, Scott writes in the tradition of three great poets (often misleadingly labelled the Scottish Chaucerians): Robert Henryson, William Dunbar, and Gavin Douglas. Yet Scott is also a modernist who has succeeded in grafting the Pound/Eliot tradition onto a number of medieval Scottish and European traditions. His first important book, *Seeven Poems o Maister Francis Villon* (1953), was admired by Ezra Pound. These Scots translations belong to that small group of great translations which read like original poems and help to revitalize the poetry of a nation—the finest previous example in Scots (apart from MacDiarmid's version of Alexander Blok's "The Stranger" contained in *A Drunk Man Looks at the Thistle*) is Gavin Douglas's *Aeneid*. The close of "Ballet o the Hingit" indicates the quality of Scott's Villon:

> We hae been washed and purifee'd by rain.
> The sun has tanned our hides a leathery hue.
> Craws and pyes hae pykit out our een,
> And barbered ilka stibble-chin and brou.
> Nae peace we ken the twenty-four hours
> throu,
> For back and furth, whiles braid-on, whiles
> askew,
> Wi ilka wind that blaws we twist and slue;
> Mair stoggit nor straeberries, and juist as raw.
> See ti it *ye* never mell wi sic a crew,
> And pray the Lord shaws mercy til us aa.
>
> Prince Jesus, wha haud aa mankind in feu,
> Watch Satan duisna reive us serfs frae you;
> Wi him we'll byde nae langer nor we awe.
> Guid-fellae-men, dinnae ye mock us nou,
> But pray the Lord shaws mercy til us aa.

Only a selection of Scott's Villon translations is included in *The Ship and Ither Poems* (1963). As creative translations in the best modern tradition of Pound, they deserve to be collected and made available as a whole.

Another example of Scott's genius as a translator is his version of the Anglo-Saxon poem *The Dream of the Rood* (in *The Ship and Ither Poems*), where he succeeds in recreating this visionary poem by using the meters of St. John of the Cross:

> A dream o dreams I'll tell,
> That smooled intil my mind while I wes
> sleepan,
> Jist or midnicht fell,
> And cuist owre me a spell.
> When aa mankind ablow the claithes were
> creepen.
> There seemed to come in sicht
> A selie tree that in the lift wes leaman,
> Byordinarly bricht,
> Of a supernal licht
> That fludit the haill carry wi its beamin.

But Scott is by no means only a translator; his original work contains a number of moving lyrics. "The Annunciation" is a fine example:

> Ye'll lig your bridal nicht yourlane
> Your legs aspar til nocht but air,
> And it shall get in you a Son
> Yet nevir pairt your maiden hair.
>
> Ye'll gie your Bairn the name I say.
> And let nae lover stier ye, will ye,
> Till He has seen the licht o day
> And broached your virgin nipples til ye.
>
> Tak tent nou—I maun gang my road—
> Ilka word I've said is true:
> And aa I've envied God
> Is the bairnin o a lass like you!

Scott has also had the courage to attempt several long poems, including "The Ship," *At the Shrine o the Unkent Sodger* (1968), and *Brand the Builder* (1975). *Brand the Builder*, probably the finest of these, is in part autobiographical—in some ways comparable to Basil Bunting's *Briggflatts* (1966). A poem of place, it has a sustained lyricism lacking in Scott's other long poems:

> Say it's spring, and some wee sporty breeze
> Is makin free wi the leaves, the young rye,
> Wi lassies' frocks, wi ilkabody's hair
> And the first swallows, martins and swifts in
> the lift,
> The saut air melled wi smells o maut, mint
> And mignonette, and o new-baked bried and
> coffee
> Throu the auld West Port and alang the
> Street
> Lined wi trees and unpretentious shops,
> The scent o intangible blossom here and
> there,
> The toun kirk, no langsyne rebuilt
> By Malcolm Brand the builder, is near as auld
> They say, as the toun itsel, and it's muckle
> nock

That chimes lah fah sol doh, fah sol lah fah
At ilk hauf-'oor, is no naę common kirk
But a suitable aristokirk o kirks.

At the Shrine o the Unkent Sodger is a passionate
meditation on the horror of war from the beginning
of history until the recent crimes of the concentration camps, civilian bombing, Hiroshima, Nagasaki,
and Vietnam. There are flashes of insight, particularly into the economic causes of war—like Pound,
Scott is committed to a radical reform of our financial system as the most practical way of preventing
wars. The meter in this poem, and of "The Ship," is
a five-stress line with no end rhyme, at times making
use of a silent stress indicated by a full stop or a dash.
This line is probably closer to the natural speech
rhythms of Scots than iambic pentameter is to
present-day English, but the poem might have

gained more strength if a greater variety of meter
had been used. Scott's five-stress verse is diffuse
compared with his lyrics and relies too much on
rhetoric.

Yet Scott's long poems, including *The Tree*,
written in English, have an honesty and rough-
hewn strength which only feeling things deeply
could have produced. At a time when so much verse
writing is concerned with trivia, it is good to see a
poet with the courage to tackle major subjects. He is
not content to stay still and has that quality of
curiosity that Pound said was essential to good literature. To paraphrase Yeats, Scott always writes as if
"he had a sword upstairs"; such poets are rare, but it
is they who keep poetry alive. It is to be hoped that a
publisher will soon produce a definitive edition of
his work.

Jon Silkin

(2 December 1930-   )

Roger Garfitt

SELECTED BOOKS: *The Peaceable Kingdom* (London: Chatto & Windus, 1954; Miami: Olivant
Press, 1959);

The Two Freedoms (London: Chatto & Windus, 1958;
New York: Macmillan, 1958);

The Re-ordering of the Stones (London: Chatto &
Windus, 1961);

Flower Poems (Leeds: Northern House, 1964; revised edition, Newcastle upon Tyne: Northern House, 1978);

Nature with Man (London: Chatto & Windus, 1965);

Penguin Modern Poets 7, by Silkin, Richard Murphy,
and Nathaniel Tarn (Harmondsworth: Penguin, 1966);

Poems New and Selected (London: Chatto & Windus,
1966; Middletown, Conn.: Wesleyan University Press, 1966);

Killhope Wheel (Ashington: Mid Northumberland
Arts Group, 1971);

Amana Grass (London: Chatto & Windus, 1971;
Middletown, Conn.: Wesleyan University
Press, 1971);

Out of Battle: Poetry of the Great War (London: Oxford
University Press, 1972);

The Principle of Water (Manchester: Carcanet New
Press, 1974);

The Little Time-Keeper (Ashington: Mid Northumberland Arts Group/Manchester: Carcanet,
1976; New York: Norton, 1977);

The Psalms with their Spoils (London & Boston:
Routledge & Kegan Paul, 1980);

Selected Poems (London & Boston: Routledge &
Kegan Paul, 1980);

Autobiographical Stanzas (Langley Park, County
Durham: Taxus Press, 1984).

OTHER: Natan Zach, *Against Parting,* translated
by Silkin (Newcastle-upon-Tyne: Northern
House, 1967);

Poetry of the Committed Individual: A Stand *Anthology,*
edited by Silkin (London: Gollancz, 1973);

Dennis Silk, ed., *Fourteen Israeli Poets,* includes translations by Silkin (London: Deutsch, 1976);

Contemporary Israeli Literature, includes translations
by Silkin (Philadelphia: Jewish Publication
Society of America, 1977);

The Burning Bush: Poems from Modern Israel (London:
Allen, 1977);

The Penguin Book of First World War Poetry, edited, with translations, by Silkin (London: Allen Lane, 1979);
The Penguin Book of First World War Prose, edited by Silkin and Jon Glover (Harmondsworth: Penguin, 1985).

PERIODICAL PUBLICATIONS: "The War and Rosenberg," *Stand,* 17, no. 3 (1976);
"Edward Hicks's Peaceable Kingdom," *Stand,* 19, no. 2 (1978);
"Which England Shall We Labor For? A Reply to Donald Davie's 'Conservative England,'" *Parnassus,* 7 (Fall/Winter 1978): 280-287;
"The Rights of England," *Stand,* 20, no. 2 (1979).

Jon Silkin is a poet, a critic, an editor who has worked particularly on the poets of World War I, and the founder and coeditor of *Stand,* probably the most widely distributed small magazine in the English-speaking world, which for over thirty years has maintained a distinctive social commitment.

He was born in London, the only child of Joseph Silkin and Dora (Doris) Rubinstein Silkin. Joseph Silkin was a lawyer, but his father had been a barrowboy in London's East End, á Jewish refugee from Lithuania, who had to moonlight as a Hebrew teacher and synagogue lavatory cleaner to support his eight children. Joseph's elder brother had worked as a docker before qualifying as a solicitor and founding the family law firm. It is not surprising Joseph was aghast at Jon's intention, announced at the age of fifteen, to become a poet. "There have never been any Jewish poets," he protested. "What about the Bible, father?," was Jon's reply.

The Old Testament had a profound influence on Silkin's poetry, all the more profound because it was his own discovery. His family's Judaism was nominal, although he attended synagogue and heder. His father was an atheist, "a nineteenth century rationalist," and such Jewish observances as were kept at home were kept up by his mother. Home life ended abruptly with the outbreak of World War II. He was first evacuated to Kent with his school, Dulwich College Preparatory School, then sent to his mother's sister in Swansea, then evacuated again with his Welsh school, Parc Wern School, to Dol-au-Cothy House in Pumpsaint, a gaunt, seventeenth-century mansion lit by acetylene gas. At his next school in nearby Lampeter, he refused to attend chapel, and he was left every Sunday to his own devices—and so embarked, at the age of ten, on a solitary reading of the Old Testament.

Jon Silkin

His mother's family, the Rubinsteins, were quite different in temperament from the Silkins, more emotional, more expressive. His mother encouraged his poetry, as far as she could. Her father, a refugee from a later pogrom in Lithuania, sailed for America, but when the ship put into Swansea in South Wales to take on fresh water, he thought, "Might as well be here as anywhere," and disembarked. He struck lucky: after some lean years as a wallpaper and paint merchant, his stock suddenly acquired scarcity value in World War I. But the Swansea Jews were a small, isolated community, and this fact left its mark on Silkin's mother. From an early age she taught him that as a Jew he must tread carefully.

In the 1930s she had reason to be apprehensive. Undercurrents of anti-Semitism surfaced in England when Sir Oswald Mosley's Blackshirts terrorized the East End. When World War II broke out, she explained to him what the consequences of a Nazi victory would be. Ironically, his first direct experience of anti-Semitism came from his fellow evacuees at prep school, and his wartime fears crystallized when he read, at the age of ten, a book by a concentration camp survivor who escaped to England only to commit suicide. He began to have nightmares of imprisonment in a concentration camp; time and again he would escape, only to be recaptured. The nightmares continued until he underwent analysis in his mid-twenties. Thereafter he still dreamed of the camp, but when he escaped, he was no longer recaptured.

As the war ended, he resumed his schooling at Dulwich College. While his first creative impulse, at fourteen, was toward music, a year's struggle with the clarinet, and a growing impatience with mathematical forms, convinced him he was not cut out to be a composer. At fifteen he committed himself to poetry, of which he knew nothing beyond an imagist anthology and T. S. Eliot's first *Collected Poems.* Poetry was taught so badly at Dulwich that he was in the paradoxical position of loathing poetry at school while trying to write it at home; he was finally expelled for persistent truancy. He had matriculated for university but there was no question of sending him unless he consented to enter the family law firm. Conscription was still in force in Britain: believing that "experience was a greater tutor," he applied in 1948 for an early call-up.

Experience taught some hard lessons. Two years in the army, a rude awakening in itself, were followed by months of living from hand to mouth, first as a street photographer, then as a grave filler in Fortune Green Cemetery, West Hampstead. At one point he was reduced to sleeping rough, collapsed from malnutrition, and was taken into a hospital for three weeks. Images from this period surfaced some twenty-five years later, in the fine "Untitled Poem" in *The Little Time-Keeper* (1976). All told, he worked as a laborer for six years.

During this time he encountered Philip Inman, a young poet in rather easier circumstances: Inman worked for his father, Lord Inman, in the small publishing firm of Williams and Norgate. He became a staunch friend, and Silkin often slept on his floor. Women friends were important to Silkin, and one, Cynthia Redpath, a married woman who had left her husband, influenced him decisively. Intelligent and well read, she became Silkin's mentor, giving him "intellectual credibility" in his own eyes. They first lived together in rooms in Swiss Cottage, where their son Adam was born in 1952. The following year they moved to an unfurnished flat in Blackheath, where they remained until 1955. Unfurnished flats were rare in London, then as now, and offered security of tenure. Silkin has recalled how his poems seemed to come together "as

soon as we had a place of our own. . . . I do attribute a lot of my starting off as a poet to that. . . . I remember the image that I had of myself and of my mind: it was like a rather small but very clear film screen. As soon as I stopped, there was this film screen and my life, which was in movement, and my mind, which was still and calm, could have projected onto that screen the poems that meant something. Very curious. . . . My life could be experienced out of the stillness of my life. . . . There was a still element in my life, which was the stability with Cynthia. . . . She gave me my eyes."

If stability was the screen, it was pain that brought the poems into focus. "Death of a Son," perhaps the best known of Silkin's early poems, records Adam's death from pneumonia "in a mental hospital aged one." His second son, David Emanuel, born in 1953, survived but with a mental handicap. Silkin's work up to this point, published in small magazines such as *Poetry Manchester,* had been, in his own phrase, "emotionally convoluted": "What clarified the emotional convolution was simply the pain. And the realisation—and I think this is very important, this is why I'm a political poet as well—the realisation that the amount of desperate energy that had to go into creating the poems in *The Peaceable Kingdom* was the result of hoping for a world with better relations between the individual human beings but not being certain one could ever have that. I think that's what clarified these poems. . . . They are neither political nor not political, which I think is true of the best of my work. I'm personal, but I'm personal in relation to other people and their problems." Many of the poems in *The Peaceable Kingdom* (1954) were first published in Dannie Abse's magazine, *Poetry and Poverty,* an appropriate outlet for poems written in pencil on brown paper bags that had been slit open and smoothed into long sheets. Alan Brownjohn recalls these curious manuscripts, often shown to him on the last bus back from Soho, then in its final years as London's Montmartre. He also recalls the "visual and typographical excitement" of the early issues of *Stand,* which Silkin started in 1952. *Stand* experimented with type and with superimposing type on photographic images in ways that have since become familiar. Then "the whole feel and colour" of the magazine was new and created the impression of a vital "underground in poetry."

Silkin's third son, Richard, was born in 1954 free of any handicap, but by then the relationship with Cynthia Redpath was under severe strain from the shock of two defective children, from Silkin's "immaturity" (particularly his "inability to focus love, affection and sex together"), which resulted in continual infidelities, and from the difficulty of supporting the family on an unskilled laborer's wages. The Blackheath period, Silkin's formative period, ended in the couple's separation when Richard was one and a half.

In his introduction to the 1975 American edition Merle Brown described *The Peaceable Kingdom* as "the finest first volume of poetry written by a living English poet." It is remarkable for its singleness of purpose, each poem reflecting the central vision of that kingdom prophesied by Isaiah, where "the leopard shall lie down with the kid." In "For David Emanuel" the poet contemplates his newborn son, "I with / Two large eyes staring into his god's eyes": the language is Blakean in its proportions, in terms of Blake's paintings as much as his poems. This emblematic power was a quality Silkin found also in the American primitive painter Edward Hicks, from whose one great subject, *The Peaceable Kingdom,* he took his title. Silkin has pointed out the difference between *peaceful* and *peaceable*: "a peaceable music" is "tuned in fear." It is "the harmony composed from tension," the harmony continually broken and recomposed in his diamond stanzas of three short lines and one long line: "The spaces between the stanzas were the tensions. They increased the tension because they cut across the actual language. The space was stronger than the language." The long line "gave you time to get a complete shape out, a complete rhythmical shape." The diamond stanzas of "First it was Singing" create a sense of the poet's voice breaking out of the silence that would overwhelm it:

> From the first I was
> Given a voice
>
> To cry out with.
> It was a peaceable music tuned in fear.
> Later, it was death
> But it was singing
>
> First.

The images of "Death of a Son" circle the almost inexpressible. Each repetition represents a redefinition, a small advance—a movement characteristic of the Psalms and of traditional ballads. Ballads belonged to that "communal audience" he wanted to reach, but he has said that he "couldn't write ballads," so he wanted "to write ballad-like poems."

Blackheath was succeeded by Pimlico. Silkin lived for two years with the painter Susan Benson,

with whom he also traveled to Greece. During this period he underwent analysis with Paul Senft, a Czech Jew who had escaped the Nazis via Dunkirk. In 1956 Silkin moved to 10 Compayne Gardens, where he shared a top-floor flat with, among others, playwright David Mercer and novelist Malcolm Ross-MacDonald. Below, in the main house, lived the novelists Bernice Rubens and Rudolf Nassauer. The top floor furnished Ross-MacDonald with the uproarious bohemian menage of *The Big Waves* (1962), in which Silkin is attractively portrayed as the poet Somes Arenstein. In the novel Somes's ex-mistress, Milena (based on Ann Fraser, to whom Silkin's poem "Defence" is dedicated) reflects on his personality: "To see him seriously talking about poetry at these meetings, and to have him holding me alone, almost childlike, incoherent with his passion, was to experience two different people, reconcilable only through that transparent honesty, that sense of purpose which, although it has made him do and say the most inane things, has also enabled him to go on being just a poet. . . . There are some poets—good ones even—whom you could see equally well as actors, painters, schoolteachers, gardeners, etc., but of Somes you can only say *poet.* It shines out of him; he gives himself and his energies away at the whole business of living poetry." As if to balance her account, Milena also wryly recalls Somes's fleeting, abortive passion for a Greek waitress met in Paddington: the affair rapidly dissolved into farce but became, nonetheless, "the germ of one of those fine love poems he wrote at that time."

The late 1950s were years of transition, and the transitions are reflected in Silkin's poetry. *The Two Freedoms* (1958) has been judged by writers such as Geoffrey Hill to be too elaborate in style. Silkin was trying, partly under the influence of American poet Gene Baro, to explore his capacity for "grandiloquence." He wanted "some bass notes as well as a melodic line": but he comes all too close to the organ blasts of the New Apocalypse poets. *Stand* temporarily ceased publication in 1957, and in the two years at Compayne Gardens Silkin produced no published work, partly because he was totally drained by teaching English to foreign students, partly because he was "experimenting to see what length of line would best reflect the rhythms of one's speech." He eventually came up with the three-beat line, first used in *The Re-ordering of the Stones* (1961) and most effectively deployed in the "Flower Poems" of *Nature with Man* (1965).

In 1958 he was appointed Gregory Fellow in Poetry at the University of Leeds and entered upon one of his most productive periods. Leeds had an outstanding English department, built up by Bonamy Dobrée and sustained by Norman Jeffares, and at Jeffares's suggestion, Silkin took the chance to read for a degree himself. Thus in his second year at Leeds he was simultaneously Gregory Fellow and English undergraduate. His tutor was G. Wilson Knight, and the staff included Arnold Kettle, Harold Orton, and the poet Geoffrey Hill. Among his fellow students were the poets Ken Smith, Tony Harrison, Jeffrey Wainwright, and Jon Glover, and the actor Ronald Pickup. His successor as Gregory Fellow, in 1960, was Peter Redgrove. Silkin took a first-class honors B.A. in 1962, and his postgraduate work on the poets of World War I provided the groundwork for his critical book, *Out of Battle* (1972).

The creative ferment of Leeds led Silkin to revive *Stand* in 1960, and to publish, among other important work, Hill's "Funeral Music" and "September Song." With his coeditors Ken Smith and Catherine Lamb (his companion for some years and still a close friend), he gave *Stand* the identity it has today and established the tradition of direct selling all over Britain, tramping university campuses, working cinema and theater queues, patiently circulating pubs. The editorial judgment and the direct selling are part of the same social commitment, a commitment that Silkin discusses shrewdly in his introduction to *Poetry of the Committed Individual* (1973), a *Stand* anthology whose strength is a challenge in itself.

The short lines of *The Re-ordering of the Stones* deliberately eschew "delicious imagery or confectionery." "All the energy went into the rhythms," says Silkin, into the creation of a "romping harshness," a "harsh laughter." Terry Eagleton, assessing the book for *Poetry Review,* called it Silkin's "fall," in that all the work prior to it seems prelapsarian. Two key poems are "The Coldness," which examines the moral legacy of Jewish persecution, and "The Possibility," which reenacts a crisis in a personal relationship:

> Behind, the bay
>
>   Shifts small if
> Clear, a past become
> What it is: detached, seen, despoiling
>   Its richnesses.
>
>   If ever it
> Had them: houses
> With love in bed weaning to fullness
>   Its moment.

>   But sun
> Puts forth the light
> We move on, a track from past
>   We leave.
> ···
>   What we fear
> Is such past which
> Not destroyed yet now falls short
>   Of what we were—
>
>   As we move on
> Light, a track that leads
> From the town shrinking like a heart
>   In moral danger.

The political and the personal inform each other, both aspects of the human condition, which Silkin repeatedly characterizes as a state of "despair," "agony," "pain." Successful as the poems often are in grounding these large terms, there is still a gap between the intimacy of Silkin's concern and the generality of his language.

He solved this stylistic problem in *Nature with Man*, one of his most widely admired collections, which won the 1966 Geoffrey Faber Memorial Prize. In the "Flower Poems" he fuses detail with implication, corolla with corollary. Precisely observed through their stages of growth, the flowers enact modes of being "anticipatory" of the human world. It is drama rather than allegory: the plants become characters with human cousins, a vegetable kingdom as compelling as the animal kingdom of Silkin's first book.

There are other parallels between *Nature with Man* and *The Peaceable Kingdom*. One sequence in the later book returns to the themes of "Death of a Son," while "Something has been teased from me" is almost a companion to that poem. An impressively sustained exploration of feeling through two repeated images, it meditates on the birth of Silkin's daughter Rachel at the very time when his relationship with her mother, the writer Wendy Oliver, was breaking up. This experience, which has since become the culmination of *Autobiographical Stanzas*, took on added significance when Rachel, at the age of sixteen, came to seek her father out. Father and daughter have since developed a close relationship, which led Rachel to explore her ancestry by living for a time in Israel.

Silkin made his first visit to Israel in 1964, as one of a group of Anglo-Jewish writers. He returned there almost immediately and lived for five months in Tel Aviv, supporting himself by assisting in the translation of modern Hebrew poetry. To accommodate this "ochre or dun brown or dull green" landscape that has "rather an unwinking eye" and yet is tense with conflicts, Silkin made his first use of a long line, a line that might be composed of many short units but was "held together by the tension of being one line." All his formal innovations, the diamond stanza, the three-beat line, the long line, reflect his adherence to F. R. Leavis's principle that the basic unit of poetry is the line. To erase the unitary sense of the line, to write, for instance, simply in cadences, would be "to dismember the very being of the poem."

The Israeli poems appear in *Amana Grass* (1971), a collection that also reflects Silkin's first visits to America, in 1965 as a visiting lecturer at Denison University and in 1968-1969 as a member of the Writer's Workshop at Iowa. Merle Brown, a writer who was at Denison and then in the English department at Iowa, formed a profound friendship with Silkin, one Silkin has characterized as "never uneventful, often disturbing." In an intriguing chapter in *The Double Lyric* (1981), Brown suggests the impact on Silkin's work of "the healing emptiness of America," a phrase to which Silkin assents: "the English landscape is covered with eyes, the eyes of everyone who has ever seen it, had designs upon it, poetically or otherwise, whereas the American landscape, like the Australian, is untamed, undomesticated." Silkin took the title *Amana Grass* from the feathery grass that grows around the German Amana Colony, near Iowa City. The long lines of the long title poem dramatize "a failure in love." When he revised the poem for inclusion in *Selected Poems* (1980), Silkin cut the central section, a dialogue between the man and the woman. The opening section is a haunting evocation of the American Midwest, of the "desolating space" in which man and woman meet as two creatures on the surface of an indifferent planet.

The experience of living in America informed Silkin's response when he returned to Britain. He attempted, by redisposing his language, to break the frame of familiarity. Rather than writing of a bridge over the Spey in a way which would leave the bridge in repose as a piece of landscape furniture, he writes: "At Laggan, iron / bridges the Spey's banks, water / on these, snowed." Iron becomes an active element, a mineral and moral quality in a landscape where "the river / harshly slopes down over red shafts / of stone, milkishly tinged" and "English / soldiers meticulously abandoned their minds among rock, Scot and revolt . . . mouthing shapes of red-dressed ferocity."

Silkin reads the moral contours of a landscape, the economic and political forces that are as much

part of its shaping as the natural forces. The most extensive of such readings is the "Killhope Wheel" sequence in *The Principle of Water* (1974). In 1965, on being offered a grant for *Stand* from Northern Arts, Silkin had moved from Leeds to Newcastle upon Tyne. He found the Northeast's once-vigorous working-class culture in danger of becoming sentimentalized and commercialized, the shrewd humor of the pit ballads giving way to Geordie Passports (printed in the dialect of the people of Newcastle) and "500-whippetpower Geordiemobile" car stickers. "Killhope Wheel" is Silkin's counteraction, an attempt in the spirit of E. P. Thompson's *The Making of the English Working Class* (a seminal book whose influence can also be seen in the work of Douglas Dunn, Tony Harrison, Ken Smith, and Jeffrey Wainwright) to rally the region to its history. He imagines the wheel, a forty-foot, cast-iron waterwheel used to wash lead ore, now an industrial monument, as the setting of a strike in the last century, when

> soldiers, who do not strike,
> thrust
> their bayonets into you.

The long line is now incorporated within a tighter prosody as an occasional resource, used to impressive effect at the conclusion of "Spade," where a miner's widow contemplates her husband's summary burial:

> no psalm, leaf-like, shading the eyelid
> as the eye beneath is dazed abruptly
> in the earth's flare of black light
> burning after death.
>
> The spade digging in the sunlight illuminates
>   the face of my God.
> Blind him.

In an editorial in *Stand* (15, no. 4, 1974), Silkin argued for a fusion of narrative and image, for "the putting together what has been patiently disjoined." His own contribution was a verse play, *The People,* broadcast by the BBC in 1973, published in *The Principle of Water,* and republished in a revised and shortened form in *Selected Poems.* Once again Silkin returns to the themes of "Death of a Son," interweaving the experiences of Finn and Kye (the infant's parents in the play) with the experience of Stein, a concentration-camp survivor. The play fails, as did "Amana Grass," on the dialogue, which is so elliptical that the characters can hardly interact. But Silkin does succeed in one important respect, in his attempt "to perceive Adam's death in a whole way." Where the images of "Death of a Son" were images of silence, singularity, an imprisoning solitude, the images of *The People* are of connection, communication, continuity: the play ends with Kye's recognition that "My dead touch me, they open my care, by right."

The opening of care is Silkin's deepest concern as a poet. He sees love in the human animal as only potential, a capacity that has to be developed. He is fond of quoting Erich Fromm's remark "I kiss my child not only because I love him, but in order that I may love him." Equally, human love is not "impregnable": it is "more contingent than we would like to imagine." In *The Little Time-Keeper* love is doubly under stress: in the foreground are the intimate, societal pressures, registered in two poems that Silkin sees as "gemini," "Untitled Poem" and "Breaking Us"; in the background is the metaphysical anguish of the title sequence.

Silkin wrote "Untitled Poem" for his wife, American prose writer Lorna Tracy, whom he met in Iowa in 1968. She returned with him to England in 1969, and they were married in 1973. By a series of flashbacks to his early experiences as a homeless laborer, Silkin completely interfuses his personal and his political commitment:

> Each night the kicked man screams.
> If I help you. If I can lift you. His stain
> over stone is blue, feather light.

Love becomes a form of moral courage, a courage that has continually to be renewed, to be found over and again at the point where "My conscience, my fear, and our sex, stir." The lovemaking of "Untitled Poem" is matched by the love-breaking of "Breaking Us," where a man and woman experience the demolition of their home (during Newcastle's massive and controversial restructuring in the 1960s) as "an erasure of them as a couple":

> So much spills. The look
> you gave the house
> goes down with it.

Love is lost in the loss of what had registered it, an enactment on the human scale of the universal erasure Silkin imagines in "Entropy at Hartburn" as "The huge energies untwine, and stars / slither away on the braids." Silkin first confronted such dissolution in *The Re-ordering of the Stones,* in poems such as "The Measure." Here he confronts it in "the more elate landscape" of Northumbria, where the sad-

ness is to observe "the fruitless endeavour of all our most fecund things." It is here rather than in *The Re-ordering of the Stones* that Silkin himself would locate his "Fall," in the realization that "God was not listening to my poems." In common with other major poets of his generation, Ted Hughes and Peter Redgrove, Silkin finds himself writing "inhuman poems," poems that are forced to take a view of the universe such that "the human animal is no longer the centre of their attention." The difference in Silkin is that his lament for the loss of Judeo-Christian values is so strong as to amount almost to a reinstatement:

> Nothing's going to last
>
> the clear baptismal water, twice welcome,
> like two good hands
>
> like the olive with
> its stone of oil.

Direct colloquialisms flex a language that can properly be called majestic, a modern counterpart to the language of the Old Testament or of Silkin's other great model, Milton. Criticism has not yet taken proper account of *The Little Time-Keeper,* which deserves to be ranked alongside *The Peaceable Kingdom* and *Nature with Man* as one of the high points of Silkin's development so far.

Silkin admires Milton for being "alert, all-eyed at so many junctures in poetry: sensuously, morally, intellectually, rhythmically." Some critics have felt that his own endeavor to be "all-eyed" can lead to confusion, to a loss of focus from looking too many ways at once. In a special issue of *Poetry Review* (June 1980), to mark the publication of Silkin's most recent collection, *The Psalms with their Spoils* (1980), Anne Cluysenaar wrote that "the multiplicity of meanings and connotations which most words have as 'dictionary items' remains only too much alive. No context is provided which will settle a meaning one way or another, or even a definite selection of ways...," while Paul Mills found that "this book tries to cram, enfold, rather than to render coherent. The world has to be classified, has to be somehow digested into each sentence. The sentence soon breaks down." Silkin's own view is that "Many people ... write as if they thought poems were really versified prose.... Prose reflects the precondition of understanding which is order. The notion is that order more or less has existed since God created the universe. Well, it's clearly nonsense.... it is not a static universe.... there clearly is a great deal of conflict, stress and chaos, and . . . the good poet has . . . to create a sense out of which the clarity is emerging. But the experience of all that is extraordinarily rich. How on earth does one recreate that? Recreate it and give it value, which is another problem."

The problem of giving value is complicated by the recognition that "you cannot always come off positive." Despite the initial disclaimer of "Death of a Son"—"And there was no nobility in it / Or anything like that"—the poem does discover a nobility. But when Silkin came to write of Merle Brown's sudden death in 1978, he had to confront the fact that "there was nothing admirable about his dying,

it was awful, and the life that terminated his life was awful." Thus in "Wildness makes a form," "the only appropriate landscape . . . was this urinous marshy landscape in which nothing grows and everything decays, for which there is nothing to say but everything to say against."

If *The Little Time-Keeper* registers the loss "of a belief in God, of a sense of being protected," the poems are still enriched by the memory of belief. In *The Psalms with their Spoils* there is almost no enrichment, there is scarcely even the knowledge of what has been lost. There is only "dishevellment," "soot, darkness & lethargy," which can result in some of Silkin's densest poetry, such as the long poem "I in

```
As loam squelches through the cleft hoof
beasts pass through night-fall.  Steaming presences
and dung stained on the breaths.  Hartburn
divides light with a shutter, and xtraix closes
xexxxxhadxxxxxxxxxxxxxxxxxxxxxxxxxxxxxxxxxxxx
xexxxxxxfx
xxxxxxxxx on us.  What of that?
night
The church revives its season
xxxh a scrawny light bulb, xxxxxx xxxxxxx yellows
and
xxxxxxxxxxx
the fleeing stars.  God's light.  What
can he see by this light?

Branches tap at the stained glass




As loam squelches between the cleft hoof
beasts penetrate night-fall.  Steaming presences
and dung stains their breaths.  With a shutter
Hartburn divides night on itself.

And of that, every night.  'Mildred,
shut the night from us.'  two hundred     turns                    dark
years of decent futility.  The great stems
of sex slather to xxxxxxxx to inane fruitfulness.

At the stained glass tap the branches
upon life's mid-night.  The church is asleep.
xxxxxxxxl winter profusion of berries stares
and jingles at the glass.  Get away.
```

Working typescripts (the author)

Entropy at Hartburn

Between the hoof's cleft loam squelches;
so beasts enter night-fall. Steamy
presences; the dunged breath falters.

Hartburn divides night upon itself
with a shutter. 'Mildred clamp out the dark). The creamy
lace embroiders its holes.

The sky's larger dark grows. We're
two vicars with a single church. The squeezed stems
of sex slather to inane fruitfulness.

The sky's larger dark grows, where huge
energies untwine, stars slither ~~alongxthexbraids~~
along the braids.

The huge energies untwine, and stars
slither along the braids. The wagging stems
of sex slather to inane fruitfulness.

Not a thing to comfort us. Where the equinox
clenches upon day, seeds got by holly
tap at the church's stained glass.

The small energies out-thorn, in winter's
mid-night profusion.

Another Place," a dialogue set in hell. But it can also produce the quick, allusive movement of "Acids" or the terseness of "Joy, lined with metal":

> Where a bridge fastens two soaked banks
> there clayey waters braid; and a man plays
> a tin whistle, in an open shirt
>
> and jacket. Is the mind a loving form?
> it enters the stagnating air, and breathes
> it is the breath, it is the only thing.
> . . . .
> A man hears only his own loneliness,
>
> and if he cannot hear then he must feel.
> By this sump of fecal spillage a big
> man plays his flute for all he's worth.

There, as Paul Mills observed, the dishevellment "lies at last outside the music and yet the music is strangely encumbered with it."

Since publication of *The Psalms with their Spoils* and *Selected Poems*, two new sequences have been completed. "The Salome Poems," published in the special issue of *Poetry Review,* relate closely to *The Psalms with their Spoils* in that Salome seems to be a development from the female figure in "I in another place." The poems in *Autobiographical Stanzas* (1984) are a development from the terseness, or in Silkin's own phrase, the "curtness" of "Joy, lined with metal," an attempt to "unease" the curtness without losing the economy. They span Silkin's late childhood and early adolescence, from his evacuation at the age of eight, which he sees as the birth of his identity as a separate human being, to the birth of his daughter Rachel. The later period is telescoped, so that he is "younger in the poems" than he actually was in life.

The *Autobiographical Stanzas* are stations of self-knowledge, memories that have become allegories of inner doubt, "someone's narrative" (to quote the sequence's subtitle) of the places he has continually to reenter in his slow progress as pilgrim. They focus, as did "Untitled Poem," on the fear that inhibits moral growth:

>   If I could tear my body
> from this space . . .   I would,
> as a man lifts weights not before
> lifted, be strong.

References:

Merle E. Brown, *The Double Lyric: Divisiveness and Communal Creativity in Recent English Poetry* (New York: Columbia University Press, 1981; London: Routledge & Kegan Paul, 1981);

Anne Cluysenaar, "Alone in a Mine of Reality: a Matrix in the Poetry of Jon Silkin," in *British Poetry Since 1960,* edited by Michael Schmidt and Grevel Lindop (Manchester: Carcanet New Press, 1972);

Jon Glover, "Jon Silkin: the Voice in The Peaceable Kingdom," *Bananas,* 20 (April 1980): 39-42;

Geoffrey Hill, "The Poetry of Jon Silkin," *Poetry & Audience,* 19, no. 12 (1962);

Poetry Review, special Silkin issue, edited by Roger Garfitt, 69 (June 1980).

C. H. Sisson
(22 April 1914-   )

Sibyl Severance
Pennsylvania State University, Delaware County Campus, Media

SELECTED BOOKS: *An Asiatic Romance* (London: Gaberbocchus, 1953);

The Spirit of British Administration and Some European Comparisons (London: Faber & Faber, 1959; New York: Praeger, 1959);

The London Zoo (London & New York: Abelard-Schuman, 1961);

Art and Action (London: Methuen, 1965);

Christopher Homm (London: Methuen, 1965);

Numbers (London: Methuen, 1965);

Metamorphoses (London: Methuen, 1968);

English Poetry 1900-1950: An Assessment (London: Hart-Davis, 1971);

The Case of Walter Bagehot (London: Faber & Faber, 1972);

In the Trojan Ditch: Collected Poems and Selected Translations (Cheadle: Carcanet New Press, 1974);

Anchises (Manchester: Carcanet New Press, 1976);

David Hume (Edinburgh: Ramsay Head Press, 1976);

The Avoidance of Literature: Collected Essays (Manchester: Carcanet New Press, 1978);

Exactions (Manchester: Carcanet New Press, 1980);

Selected Poems (Manchester: Carcanet New Press, 1981);

Collected Poems (Manchester: Carcanet New Press, forthcoming, 1984).

OTHER: *Versions and Perversions of Heine*, translated by Sisson (London: Gaberbocchus, 1955);

The Poetry of Catullus, translated by Sisson (London: MacGibbon & Kee, 1966; New York: Orion, 1967);

The Poetic Art: a Translation of Horace's Ars Poetica, translated by Sisson (Cheadle: Carcanet Press, 1975);

The Poem on Nature: a translation of Lucretius's De Rerum Natura, translated by Sisson (Manchester: Carcanet New Press, 1976);

The English Sermon 1650-1750, selected, with an introduction, by Sisson (Manchester: Carcanet New Press, 1976);

Jonathan Swift, *Selected Poems*, selected, with an in-

troduction, by Sisson (Manchester: Carcanet New Press, 1977);

La Fontaine, *Some Tales*, translated by Sisson (Manchester: Carcanet New Press, 1979);

Thomas Hardy, *Jude the Obscure*, introduction and notes by Sisson (Harmondsworth: Penguin, 1979);

Dante, *The Divine Comedy*, translated by Sisson (Manchester: Carcanet New Press, 1980);

Philip Mairet, *Autobiographical and Other Papers*, edited by Sisson (Manchester: Carcanet New Press, 1981);

Wyndham Lewis, *Collected Poems and Plays*, introduction by Sisson (Manchester: Carcanet New Press, 1981).

PERIODICAL PUBLICATIONS: "Pound's Literary Programmes," *Agenda*, 17-18 (Autumn-Winter-Spring 1979-1980): 200-207;
"Sequelae," *Agenda*, 18 (Summer 1980): 9-11.

The words C. H. Sisson uses to honor David Hume identify the distinguishing qualities of his own writing: like Hume, Sisson has the ability to be "patient of the truth, as he sees it, to the point of being disconcerting," and he also shares with Hume "the sense of discovery with which he sets out, and the disillusion with which he surveys his conclusions." Because the truth he sees is sometimes opposed to current literary fashions and ideological postures, Sisson stands apart from his contemporaries. He has written: "The poetry owners cannot make me out/Nor I them." Yet such estrangement or lack of fashion, as Martin Seymour-Smith has recognized, is "only as unfashionable as seriousness." Sisson stands apart, too, because he was forty-seven before publishing his first major collection of verse, *The London Zoo* (1961). Not until 1974, with *In the Trojan Ditch*, brought out when he was sixty, was the distinction of his poetry widely recognized in England. Since that time his patience with truth, his rhythms—which measure his mind's integrity, and his lucidity have made Sisson's work essential for those who care about poetry.

Charles Hubert Sisson was born 22 April 1914 in Bristol to Richard Percy and Ellen Minnie Worlock Sisson, and he spent his childhood in a working-class district ("it is possible/To live harshly in that city"). His father had a small business as an optician and watchmaker, having come to Bristol from the North, from Kendal in Westmoreland, where his family had had a comb mill since the eighteenth century. Sisson's mother had come to Bristol from the Midwestern portion of England, Gloucestershire and Wiltshire, where her family had farmed for generations. For Sisson his mother's country village represented a life that had been essentially unchanged for 150 years before her birth.

He remembers that from this stable rural background his mother drew "a sort of solid body of lore and speech which belonged to the country of those parts. And, in a sense, I was brought up on proverbs." These sure proverbs have turned into the resolute epigrams that mark Sisson's writing. His early immersion in tradition seems to shape his

need for and use of the past, his insistence on continuity, his vision of place as symbol and of every reality as "a kind of sign." Today he has returned to the country, choosing to live in Langport, a small town in Somerset. This land is the ground of his poetry.

Although neither of Sisson's parents had a higher education, his home offered opportunities for reading because of an uncle's legacy of books, which included Mermaid editions of Shakespeare and volumes of American poets. Sisson remembers Poe and the "glitter" from an uncertain rhythm in some of Emerson's verse. He attended a "really average kind of secondary school"; it did not offer Greek, but Latin was well taught. When he was about sixteen, Sisson first heard T. S. Eliot's poetry, "through broadcasts in the days when we had a civilized radio." Although he had no money for books, he received Eliot's poems of 1909-1935 as a prize book when he left his secondary school. "It really marked the beginning of my grasp of what was going on in modern poetry. An encounter with a poet like that, at that age, is so decisive. You know, nothing is quite the same from there on."

Another significant encounter for his later writing occurred in 1931 when he first read Pound's *How to Read* (1931), followed in 1934 by *ABC of Reading* (1934). That same year, having gone on a scholarship to the University of Bristol, Sisson took an honors B.A. in philosophy and English literature. He continued to explore Pound's literary recommendations during postgraduate work in Germany and France. His tribute to "Pound's Literary Programmes," which appeared in *Agenda* (17-18, 1979-1980), affirms that he never felt "deceived" by Pound's ideas about reading, which he characterized as "blazingly illuminating."

In studying at the universities of Berlin and Freiburg (1934-1935) and the Sorbonne (1935-1936), Sisson was influenced not only by his reading but by political events in Germany and France during the mid-1930s. A "more or less complete political agnostic" when he arrived in Germany, he was repelled by the fascism he observed. On returning to England, he entered the Civil Service through the examination system. He steadily advanced in his career at the Ministry of Labour from assistant principal (1936-1942), to principal (1945-1953), to assistant secretary (1953-1962), and undersecretary (1962-1968). From 1968 to 1971 he served as assistant undersecretary of state in the Department of Employment, and finally he was director of Occupational Safety and Health until he took early retirement in 1973. During these years Sisson's government work rather than his writing was his primary concern: "it never occurred to me to do otherwise than give precedence to the work that I was paid to do."

To understand that part of his life, it is helpful to read *The Spirit of British Administration and Some European Comparisons* (1959), which wittily conveys his dedication and his belief in the theory and practicality of the British Civil Service. However, another perspective comes from his essay "Fashions in Government," which satirizes the "art of being a senior civil servant" as "a kind of discursive prostitution." Sisson's poems too, particularly the title piece of *The London Zoo*, excoriate the anonymous civil servant, seeing the officials as animals brought to London "from one of the cages on the periphery." Sisson acknowledges that he is "like the rest/Expending my best energies on the second-best."

A final perspective of the relationship between Sisson as a Whitehall official and Sisson as a writer comes from his questioning in *Art and Action* (1965): "Can it be that the discipline of practical life affects the writer more deeply, so that his work is tempered by it? . . . some of the best books in the language were written by people who were not literary men . . . but men concerned with the government of church or state." Such men would include Andrew Marvell, Charles Maurras, George Herbert, and Sir Walter Raleigh. This admiration for writers whose work grew from lives devoted to practical affairs comes from Sisson's deep conviction "that one just has to live one's life and in a sense poetry is a by-product of that."

Living one's life, in Sisson's case, included marriage to Nora Gilbertson in 1937 and the birth of two daughters, Janet and Hilary, in the 1940s. During World War II he enlisted, serving in the British Army Intelligence Corps from 1942 to 1945, briefly in Ireland, longer in India. His editor, Michael Schmidt, believes that Sisson's army service was significant in a number of ways. It was a source of his "cynicism concerning authority" and his empathy with those "who had roots and did not aspire to climb the hierarchy. . . . It was at once disorientating and defining. It threw all of his values into question but made his Englishness more pronounced." It was also "in India that he first seriously considered the Anglican Communion."

From 1937 to 1949 Sisson's writing was limited chiefly to essays and reviews of political and social concern, which he submitted to the *New English Weekly*, then under the editorship of Philip Mairet. His decision, made at age twenty, to stop writing poetry was reversed during World War II. "On a Troopship" transmits the uncertainties of that place and Sisson's "oppressive situation" in its unsteady rhythms:

> Practising my integrity
> In awkward places,
> Walking till I walk easily
> Among uncomprehended faces.

But perhaps Sisson's most important work of the war period was his translation from Heinrich Heine's *Meisterwerke in Vers und Prosa*, one of the three books Sisson carried in his pack aboard the troopship.

The 1940s were years of poetic apprenticeship. Sisson learned his craft from translating, "exercises undertaken, for pleasure and as part of my late dilatory training as a writer. . . . If I had been asked what I was after, I should have said *plainness*, not certain whether I meant in verse or in prose, and thinking more probably the latter" (*The Avoidance of Literature*, 1978). Subsequently, an urge toward plainness has shaped all of Sisson's writing and has encouraged his translations of Roman authors, especially Catullus.

Sisson's early books, a novel, *An Asiatic Romance* (1953), and his translation *Versions and Perversions of Heine* (1955), received little attention. *The Spirit of British Administration and Some European Comparisons* occasioned more discussion. Written with the assistance of a Senior Simon Research Fellowship, awarded in 1956 by the University of Manchester, it argued that the British system of training its administrative officials, through direct exposure and actual experience, was "modest and practical." The last chapter, "The Civil Service and the Crown," reflects Sisson's abiding belief in the centrality of the monarchy in British life, the conviction "that the centre of our terms of reference should be a person and not some theoretical entity or declaration."

The decade of the 1950s was also the time when another belief of profound significance for Sisson's work took formal manifestation in his baptism and entry into the Anglican church at age thirty-nine. This move marked a return to the faith of past generations in his family. In "Coleridge Revisited" he sees his Anglicanism as inevitable; it is "the religion of our fathers or the *mère patrie*, of the spirits buried in the ground, of the religion of England. I cannot help it. Of course, this in turn conceals a profound cynicism."

Thus a cynical accent falls on his religious

poems. These poems, all too aware of nothingness, struggle to identify man's nature rather than rejoice in his spiritual being. A particular debate in such poems concerns the body's power to seize identity. His language may be harsh, unadorned, anguished, or scatological, as in "The Theology of Fitness," in which the speaker imagines the resurrection that will occur when the conflict between body and spirit finds resolution: "Your spirit and your bum/Will certainly be one."

Correspondingly, the poems of *The London Zoo* bear evidence of struggle: "when I was forced into verse it was through having something not altogether easy to say." There is death in "Moritorus," or the failure of a sure personal identity in "Epictetus," or the disillusioned discoveries of "In a Dark Wood": these subjects challenge poetic craft as well as the human spirit, and Sisson, accordingly, refuses facile imagery or rhythms. In "Ellick Farm" he sees himself "turning verses, half dumb/After half a lifetime." At forty his vision is of "a sickening garbage that could not be shared." Sisson's handling of these themes shows "intelligence and maturity," according to William Cookson in *Agenda*.

One of the most remarkable poems in the volume, "Maurras, Young and Old," offers tribute to Charles Maurras in an elegant, plain style. "His eyes looked out towards the middle sea/He heard not even that murmur/But an interior music." Another fine lyric is "The Deer Park," a poem on lost or diminished wonder, on the turning of time and men until there remains "no individual sorrow/Or even identified pain." Yet mystery may come forth:

It is possible that the musk ox
Descending the glacial valley
Enters the dying vision
Of the effete hunter, or the bell
Of the emerging church-tower marks
A point in the gathering mists.

The novel *Christopher Homm*, published in 1965, was actually written much earlier, in 1952, the year before Sisson's baptism. He has called it "a slightly belated *nel mezzo del cammin*" (the first words of Dante's *Inferno*, referring to mid-life), and his prefatory poem, "In a Dark Wood," further connects the work to Dante. Through bleak and comic ironies the book details the blundering life of its protagonist. Homm's journey goes backward, beginning with his death and moving toward his birth, a physical reversal whose theology John Donne and the seventeenth-century metaphysicals would have recognized—"In my end is my beginning." The

work again testifies to Sisson's need to find the beginnings and his belief that "every sincere life, in a sense, [is] a journey to the first years" (*The Avoidance of Literature*). Correspondingly, in poems such as "Ellick Farm" in *The London Zoo*, Sisson recalls his own boyhood on the moor farm from the perspective of the mature man. The ending describes Homm, waiting to leave the womb: "Christopher crouched in his blindness. He was about to set out on the road to Torrington Street, and if he had known how bitter the journey was to be he would not have come."

Sisson's next three books were poetry: *Numbers* (1965), *The Poetry of Catullus* (1966), and *Metamorphoses* (1968). His lucid translation of Catullus is central to his own poetry at this time, for Sisson believes it granted him greater ease in achieving his plain style. "Human Relations" in *Metamorphoses* shows this mastery of clarity, as Sisson mocks his own corruption and lechery, manifested by his glib duplicity of tongue and hand: "And be impressed by the truth of my explanation./No less, lady, take my chaste hand/While the other imaginatively rifles your drawers." These poems evince Sisson's increasing skill in establishing "a link between verse and the language that is spoken" (*English Poetry: 1900-1950*, 1971).

The themes pursued are familiar, but there is a more intense focus upon the blankness and frustration of aging. While some readers objected to a poetry that was too conversational in its restrained tones and rhythms, Martin Seymour-Smith praised the wideness of its range, the profundity of its thought, the "evident stylistic distinction" and especially the "memorability and sharp-voicedness" of this collection. For example, "On my Fifty-First Birthday" considers "the immeasurable benignity of the destructive God"; the hare dances "Like a poor cat struggling at a rope's end" and "the whole hill-side is roofed with lark-song." Sisson's vision evocatively recreates the quality of mingled sound and silence:

The gulls come inland, alight on the brown
land
And bring their sea-cries to this stillness.
It was waves and the surf running they heard
before
And now the lark-song and the respiration of
leaves.

Before his next major collection of poetry was published in 1974, Sisson finished *English Poetry 1900-1950: An Assessment*, an evaluation of English poetry in the first half of the twentieth century. Remarkable for its economy and sense of connection, the work is most striking in conveying one reader's perceiving, judging mind. As one might expect, the book is both idiosyncratic and constantly revealing: "it is not a history of reputations." Sisson is accurate in locating excess or sham as well as authenticity. Single chapters are reserved for Pound and Eliot, and for Yeats, although he is disturbed by Yeats's pretentiousness and need for public posturing, which mars some of the poetry. Sisson dismisses Dylan Thomas shortly, as if his own brevity could correct the welter he finds in Thomas's lyrics. Repeatedly Sisson evaluates poets by noting how time (rhythm) conveys time (epoch). Rhythm, more than any other quality, draws him into a poem and conditions his assessments. For Sisson, the poets of the first half of the twentieth century have given genuinely when they "contributed to bringing the wayward big mouth of the public back to an exact speech which manages to correspond to the real movements of the mind and to reflect reality." John Davidson, Thomas Hardy, Edward Thomas, George Barker, as well as Eliot and Pound, are among those twentieth-century poets who, for Sisson, return us to an integrity, a wholeness of word, mind, and world.

The year after Sisson's retirement from the Civil Service, the much-praised *In the Trojan Ditch: Collected Poems and Selected Translations* (1974) was published. The book contains many of his earlier poems and a number of new ones, placed first, so that once again Sisson asks his readers to follow him back to beginnings that serve as endings. In the new work, however, the most recent poems are shadowed. We are drawn farther into his "dark wood." Dreams are more central than in the earlier work. Thus the sense of discovery as we journey backward is particularly compelling.

The *Times* celebrated the work as "the finest collected poems for a decade." A number of poems have been singled out by critics for particular acclaim. According to Michael Schmidt, "In Insula Avalonia" "is perhaps his best poem" because "Sisson taxes rhythm to its utmost, fusing religious and patriotic themes in the legend of Arthur, dreaming the centuries away on the Isle of Avalon, near Glastonbury." Arthur joins Vergil and Dante as Sisson's guides, his "dream associates" as he has called them elsewhere: "A mine of mind, descend who can that way/As down a staircase to the inner ring." Yet the interior is essential Sisson: "I do not know and cannot know indeed/And do not want a word to tell me so/A sentence is construction more than I."

Donald Davie believes "The Usk" is "one of the great poems of our time." The poem moves through many of Sisson's most urgent concerns — disorder, his art, his faith. Repeatedly in Sisson's work the concreteness of place and its creatures restores the poet, rescuing him from the abstract blank of negation. The second section of "The Usk" declares "Nothing is in my own voice because I have not/Any. Nothing in my own name." But this section continues:

> Standing beside the Usk
> You flow like truth, river, I will get in
> Over me, through me perhaps, river let me be
> crystalline
> As I shall not be, shivering upon the bank.

The anguish of telling, the fear of obscuring the lucid voice, is addressed in sections four and six: "my truth/Was not public enough, not perhaps true," and again "So speech is treasured, for the things it gives/Which I can not have, for I speak too plain/Yet not so plain as to be understood."

Another of the later poems, "Somerton Moor," speaks of the difficulty of excellence overtly and in the halt and flow of its rhythm and the ambiguities of its punctuation. The final section begins in easy cliché, "Accustomed as I am to speech" and moves to the recognition that "excellence is hard/For nothing that is facile can be heard/And nothing hard can be endured for long." The final measure confirms that hardness with straitened eloquence: "The instrument I carry is untuned."

Similar concerns join *In the Trojan Ditch* with the next poetry collection, *Anchises* (1976). (Sisson's persistent fascination with classicism and Roman legend can be seen in the two translations published in the intervening time, *The Poetic Art: a translation of Horace's* Ars Poetica, 1975, and *The Poem on Nature: a translation of Lucretius's* De Rerum Natura, 1976.) *Anchises'* poems invoke and remake the classical world, so that its restraint and reason, its clarity and losses become contemporary experience. "Troia" and "Est in Conspectu Tenedos" are particularly effective in this respect. The resonant title poem establishes Anchises' condition: "sightlessness,/The invisible pack hunting the visible air./There are those who exist, but it is not I." With terse control, the conclusion brilliantly rebuilds the speaker's wall of pride. "I came from Troy./It was not after she had ended, but before."

Other remarkable poems in this collection include "The Corridor," with its backward road, and

Page from a draft for "Eclogue" (the author)

"Over the Wall," praised by David Wright as "one of the great *public* poems of our time." Several poems on gardens anticipate the garden sequences of *Exactions*. In "The Garden" Sisson expresses rare pleasure in his life as he describes his own garden and his contentment. "Fortunate men/Love home, are not often abroad, sleep/Rather than wake and when they wake, rejoice."

In 1975, as his writing, his poetry in particular, was receiving wider recognition and acclaim, Sisson was named a fellow of the Royal Society of Literature; in 1976 he became joint editor of *PN Review*. Further confirmation of his literary stature came with the publication in 1978 of *The Avoidance of Literature: Collected Essays*. With his essays gathered

in one place, Sisson's accomplishment as a prose stylist, his wit, his passionate avowal of his values, his "bumptiousness" (as he has called it), and his ready generosity are all on splendid display to teach and delight. Although he leaves little doubt as to what he believes and seeks to preserve and forward, his work is distinguished by his practice of what he has called "the technique of ignorance." "What most needs teaching to the modern man (poor devil) is a technique of ignorance; to march without maps, compass or the sun, without more (for something one must give him) than an occasional glimpse, for a moment, between cloud and treetops, of the Bear or Orion" ("Politics and Morals"). For Sisson, then, the way he must proceed and the method he would suggest to others is to "look around and see what one sees and not pretend that you've got it all already."

A major project for Sisson has been his translation of *The Divine Comedy* (1980). Notable for its lucidity, the work bears out Sisson's belief about translation. "The only preparation is a long experience of writing poetry of one's own. . . . This is because the poet has to listen rather than dictate, to accept rather than to decide." What the translator must do is "to find both a metric and a tone in which he can give the matter of his author so that a readable English work is made out of it."

Sisson's introduction to Dante had been Eliot's essay of 1929, which Sisson read several years later when he was eighteen or nineteen. The first line of the *Inferno*, "*Nel mezzo del cammin di nostra vita*," has had a particular resonance for Sisson; it sounds again and again in his work, serving as a touchstone by which he recognizes the nature of his life and measures his progress through it. Although he first vehemently rejected the idea of translating *The Divine Comedy*, he became possessed by "the luminous clarity of Dante's line," and agreed to the project.

Absorption with Dante did not prevent Sisson from continuing to write his own poetry, gathered in *Exactions* (1980). The title denotes the theme and method of the work. Its "exactions" are the demands Sisson has faced and made upon himself. He has met these demands with precision and care, as his text testifies. This is another realization of the hardness of excellence, a reconsideration of virtue, of time passing, of absence and memory, of the grace of the particular, "the acres in which we spent our childhood" ("Place").

The terror of an unnamed, unlocated place fills the opening poem, "The Desert," with its fierce vision of disintegration into annihilating multiplicity. Not even the eyes can join or work together: "Shatter the retina so that the eyes are many." The desert too "Is frequent with images." This world of the "damned unrepairable" undergoes a metamorphosis during the book's course, passing into the tranquil surety of the eighth section of "Burrington Combe":

And that distance into which I shall have
                                            vanished
Will still be there,
It was always dear to me, is now
In the thickening air.

No distance was ever like this one

The flat land with its willows, and the great
                                            sky
With the river reflecting its uncertainty
But no more I.

The final poems are sequences of memory fastened to specific people and places, to gardens with their burden of an idyllic vision, irremediable loss, and death in "a shrivelled heap." Adam's act is the root, Sisson's aging the branch of these garden meditations. "By eating deceived, as Adam was,/I tell myself, but I do not believe it:/Belief is difficult after sixty years" ("Autumn Poems").

In addition to seeing the publication of two major works, *The Divine Comedy* and *Exactions*, in 1980 Sisson received an honorary Doctor of Literature from the University of Bristol. While he still felt possessed by his work on Dante, he continued to write new poems, looking toward the publication in the fall of 1981 of *Selected Poems*. He began work as well on a study of seventeenth-century poetry, a book promising to have as little dealing with pedantry and reputations as his earlier *English Poetry: 1900-1950*. His stature increases with each new work. The *Times Literary Supplement* and *Agenda* are his frequent publishers. *Agenda* has hailed him as "a major talent," while a review in the *Scotsman* has designated him a writer "worth a place on the short shelf reserved for the finest twentieth-century poets, with Eliot and Rilke and MacDiarmid." Although his recurrent theme of aging bears witness to his experience of that journey, his undiminished development and the wealth of his accomplishment give little evidence that he is approaching seventy.

His study in Moorfield Cottage overlooks his garden and the sweep of the Somerset distance. "To see" is what Sisson's life and poetry are most about; it is the need which his poetry discloses and fulfills. (His unpublished autobiography, written in 1964, is called "On the Lookout.") Always wary of formulaic answers and unearned resolutions ("A moral saw is not worth an I see"), Sisson moves toward the world beyond his study window, which he sees as an authenticity he may set down, as he wrote in "Sequelae" (*Agenda*, Summer 1980):

I have seen the mallard fly out of the rhine,
The snipe skip round the willow and then
                                            away;
Nothing to be touched, O the creation my
                                            friend
And the dawn will rise upon a cold field.

Interview:

John Burney, "An Interview with C. H. Sisson," *Parnassus*, 6 (Spring-Summer 1978): 167-169.

References:

Kenneth Cox, "The Poetry of C. H. Sisson," *Agenda*, 12 (Autumn 1974): 45-49;

John Pilling, "The Strict Temperature of Classicism: C. H. Sisson," *Critical Quarterly*, 21 (Autumn 1979): 73-81;

Michael Schmidt, *A Reader's Guide to Fifty Modern British Poets* (London: Heinemann, 1979), pp. 266-277;

Martin Seymour-Smith, "Some Notes on the Poetry of C. H. Sisson," *Agenda*, 8 (Autumn-Winter 1970): 207-214;

David Wright, "The Poetry of C. H. Sisson," *Agenda*, 13 (Autumn 1975): 5-17.

Robin Skelton

(12 October 1925-   )

Laurence Steven
Laurentian University

BOOKS: *Patmos and Other Poems* (London: Routledge & Kegan Paul, 1955);

The Poetic Pattern (London: Routledge & Kegan Paul, 1956; Berkeley: University of California Press, 1956);

Third Day Lucky (London & New York: Oxford University Press, 1958);

Two Ballads of the Muse (Cambridge: Rampant Lions Press, 1960);

Begging the Dialect: Poems and Ballads (London & New York: Oxford University Press, 1960);

Cavalier Poets (London: Longmans, Green, 1960);

The Dark Window (London & New York: Oxford University Press, 1962);

A Valedictory Poem (Victoria, B.C.: Privately printed, 1963);

Poetry (London: English Universities Press, 1963; New York: Dover, 1965);

An Irish Gathering (Dublin: Dolmen Press, 1964);

A Ballad of Billy Barker (Victoria, B.C.: Morriss, 1965);

Inscriptions (Victoria, B.C.: Morriss, 1967);

Because of This and Other Poems (Manchester: Manchester Institute of Contemporary Arts, 1968);

Selected Poems 1947-1967 (Toronto: McClelland & Stewart, 1968);

The Hold of Our Hands (Victoria, B.C.: Privately printed, 1968);

An Irish Album (Dublin: Dolmen Press, 1969; Chester Springs, Pa.: Dufour, 1969);

Georges Zuk: Selected Verse (San Francisco: Kayak, 1969);

Answers (London: Enitharmon Press, 1969);

The Hunting Dark (London: Deutsch, 1971);

Remembering Synge: A Poem in Homage for the Centenary of His Birth, 16 April 1971 (Dublin: Dolmen Press, 1971);

A Different Mountain (Santa Cruz: Kayak, 1971);

A Private Speech (Vancouver: Sono Nis Press, 1971);

J. M. Synge and His World (London: Thames & Hudson, 1971; New York: Viking, 1971);

The Writings of J. M. Synge (London: Thames & Hudson, 1971; Indianapolis: Bobbs-Merrill, 1971);

The Practice of Poetry (London: Heinemann, 1971; New York: Barnes & Noble, 1971);

Three for Herself (Rushden, Northamptonshire: Sceptre Press, 1972);

Musebook (Victoria, B.C.: Pharos Press, 1972);

A Christmas Poem (Victoria, B.C.: Privately printed, 1972);

J. M. Synge (Lewisburg, Pa.: Bucknell University Press, 1972);

Country Songs (Rushden, Northamptonshire: Sceptre Press, 1973);

Timelight (Toronto: McClelland & Stewart, 1974; London: Heinemann, 1974);

Fifty Syllables for a Fiftieth Birthday (Victoria, B.C.: Privately printed, 1975);

Georges Zuk: The Underwear of the Unicorn (Nanaimo, B.C.: Oolichan Press, 1975);

Robin Skelton, 1982 (P. W. Jarrett)

The Poet's Calling (London: Heinemann, 1975; New
York: Barnes & Noble, 1975);

Callsigns (Victoria, B.C.: Sono Nis Press, 1976);

Because of Love (Toronto: McClelland & Stewart,
1977);

Three Poems (Knotting, Bedfordshire: Sceptre Press,
1977);

Poetic Truth (London: Heinemann, 1978; New
York: Barnes & Noble, 1978);

Spellcraft (Toronto: McClelland & Stewart, 1978;
London: Routledge & Kegan Paul, 1978);

Landmarks (Victoria, B.C.: Sono Nis Press, 1979);

Herbert Siebner: A Monograph (Victoria, B.C.: Sono
Nis Press, 1979);

They Call It the Caribou (Victoria, B.C.: Sono Nis
Press, 1980);

Collected Shorter Poems, 1947-1977 (Victoria, B.C.:
Sono Nis Press, 1981);

Limits (Erin, Ontario: Porcupine's Quill, 1981);

De Nihilo (Toronto: Aloysius Press, 1982);

Zuk (Erin, Ontario: Porcupine's Quill, 1982);

The Paper Cage (Lantzville, B.C.: Oolichan Books,
1982);

Wordsong: Twelve Ballads (Vancouver, B.C.: Sono
Nis Press, 1983);

*George Faludy: Twelve Sonnets in English Versions by
Robin Skelton* (Victoria, B.C.: Pharos Press,
1983);

The Man Who Sang In His Sleep (Erin, Ontario: Porcupine's Quill, 1984).

OTHER: *Leeds University Poetry 1949*, edited by
Skelton (York: Lotus Press, 1950);

The Acadine Poets, Series I-III, edited by Skelton and
Derrick Metcalfe (Hull, Yorkshire: Lotus
Press, 1950-);

"John Ruskin: the Final Years," *John Rylands Library*
[Manchester] *Bulletin,* 37 (1955): 562-586;

J. M. Synge: Translations, edited by Skelton (Dublin:
Dolmen Press, 1961);

J. M. Synge, *Four Plays and The Aran Islands*, edited
by Skelton (London & New York: Oxford
University Press, 1962);

Edward Thomas' Selected Poems, edited by Skelton
(London: Hutchinson, 1962);

J. M. Synge: Collected Poems, edited by Skelton (London: Oxford University Press, 1962);

*Six Irish Poets: Austin Clarke, Richard Kell, Thomas
Kinsella, John Montague, Richard Murphy,
Richard Weber*, edited by Skelton (London: Ox-
ford University Press, 1962);

Viewpoint: An Anthology of Poetry, edited by Skelton
(London: Hutchinson, 1962);

Five Poets of the Pacific Northwest, edited by Skelton
(Seattle: University of Washington Press,
1964);

Poetry of the Thirties, edited by Skelton (Harmondsworth: Penguin, 1964);

Selected Poems of Byron, edited by Skelton (London:
Heinemann, 1965; New York: Barnes &
Noble, 1966);

David Gascoyne, *Collected Poems*, edited by Skelton
(London: Oxford University Press, 1965);

*The Irish Renaissance: A Gathering of Essays, Letters and
Memoirs from the Massachusetts Review*, symposium edited by Skelton and David Clark
(Dublin: Dolmen Press, 1965; London: Oxford University Press, 1965);

The World of W. B. Yeats: Essays in Perspective, symposium edited by Skelton and Ann Sad-
dlemyer (Seattle: University of Washington Press, 1965; revised edition, 1967);

Poetry of the Forties, edited by Skelton (Harmondsworth: Penguin, 1968);

"O, Canada!," in *Notes for a Native Land*, edited by Andy Wainwright (Ottawa: Oberon Press, 1969), pp. 80-83;

J. M. Synge, *Riders to the Sea*, edited by Skelton (Dublin: Dolmen Press, 1969; Chester Springs: Dufour, 1969);

Introductions from an Island: A Selection of Student Writing, 5 volumes (Victoria: University of Victoria, 1969, 1971, 1973, 1974, 1977);

David Gascoyne, *Collected Verse Translations*, edited by Skelton and Alan Clodd (London: Oxford University Press/Deutsch, 1970);

The Cavalier Poets, edited by Skelton (London: Faber & Faber, 1970; New York: Oxford University Press, 1970);

Herbert Read: A Memorial Symposium, edited by Skelton (London: Methuen, 1970);

The Collected Plays of Jack B. Yeats, edited by Skelton (London: Secker & Warburg, 1971; Indianapolis: Bobbs-Merrill, 1972);

Two Hundred Poems from the Greek Anthology, translated and edited by Skelton (London: Methuen, 1971; Seattle: University of Washington Press, 1972);

Synge, *Some Sonnets from "Laura in Death" after the Italian of Francesco Petrarch*, bilingual edition, edited by Skelton (Dublin: Dolmen Press, 1971);

Thirteen Irish Writers on Ireland, edited by Skelton (Boston: Godine, 1973);

Six Poets of British Columbia, edited by Skelton (Victoria, B.C.: Sono Nis Press, 1980).

Robin Skelton was born in Easington, East Yorkshire, the only son of the village schoolmaster, Cyril Skelton, and his wife, Eliza Robins Skelton. His childhood was a lonely one; his father's position contributed to his having few friends, and in response he turned inward. As he says in *The Poet's Calling* (1975)—one of five books he has written about poetry as craft and way of life—"My dependence upon my own thoughts and dreams for my entertainment and comfort was increased by the bullying of the other boys at the village school." The isolation continued at Pocklington Grammar School near York, where he boarded from 1936 to 1943 and "spent much time alone reading or, on Sundays, wandering the countryside and the fields around the school." Skelton believes it was this "habit of solitude" that first set him "to feeling a compulsion to write poetry."

His first published poems appeared in the magazine of Christ's College, Cambridge, in 1943,

while Skelton was there as a student and RAF officer cadet. He passed his academic examinations although he failed as an RAF cadet; in 1944 he entered the RAF, where he was trained as a code and cyphers clerk and posted to South Asia in 1945 with the rank of sergeant. Though he considers his two years in the East an exile, he also admitted to Linda Sandler in a 1976 interview that it was there he "began to write the first poems that made any kind of sense."

In 1947 Skelton was demobilized and entered Leeds University as a student of English language and literature. He received a first-class honors B.A. in 1950, and also in that year he made his first foray into editing and publishing when he bought The Lotus Press. He published *Leeds University Poetry 1949* (1950) and six other paperback volumes before dissolving the company in 1951. After taking an M.A. at Leeds in 1951, he accepted the post of assistant lecturer in the English department of the University of Manchester, where he stayed for twelve years. During his tenure here, as well as founding the Peterloo Group of Poets and Painters with Michael Snow and Tony Connor, he established himself as a devoted scholar and editor with a short study of Ruskin, a critical study of the Cavalier Poets, and editions of Edward Thomas, J. M. Synge, and six contemporary Irish poets. This Irish work was the beginning of an interest in Irish writing that Skelton has maintained over the years through editions, critical studies, biography, symposia, and his own poetry. In 1953 he married Margaret Lambert, but they were divorced in 1957, and he married Sylvia Mary Jarrett on 4 February of the same year (a son was born to them in December 1957, a daughter in 1959, and another daughter in 1966).

During his Manchester years Skelton produced four volumes of poetry, the first being *Patmos and Other Poems* (1955), which was the Poetry Book Society Choice for autumn of that year. The volume introduces a theme that is central to Skelton's entire poetic career, that of man's exile from a reality embodying wonder, meaning, and wholeness. Skelton's vision manifests both a Neoplatonic dualism which refers significance to a transcendent realm and a strong Jungian influence which makes the unconscious a major route to that realm. In *The Poetic Pattern* (1956) he stresses the importance of poetry in this connection: "the poetic activity, in its use of language as in its fusion of the conscious and unconscious aspects of personality, and its being opposed to the tide of differentiation, is a tendency to return to the state of unfallen man."

This statement may seem a little glib, and certainly in *Patmos and Other Poems*, though there is often definite technical skill, the theme of exile threatens to become a program, a convenient formula upon which to impose whatever form Skelton has a mind to try. The sense that many of the pieces are exercises was borne out by Skelton in 1976: "In my early experiments I was trying—quite deliberately I think—pretty near every approach a poet could make. I taught myself many of the most difficult verse forms. . . . I reckon that if you're going to take on this kind of thing, you'd better learn it properly. The result is that my early poems have a great many echoes, and are ventriloquial poems."

In spite of its being the most ambitious, and most impressive, piece in the volume, the twenty-five-page title poem "Patmos" is a definite example of Skelton's ventriloquial early manner. The poet uses John's visions while in exile on Patmos as an analogue for the power of the creative imagination to free mankind from its imprisonment in mundane human reality. This imprisonment is likened to that in a concentration camp; we are caged in by wire which only a faithful following of our visionary imagination can help us to cut:

> This is our place; the sea
> we know to be our time,
> the dead salt plain without
> the wire our doubt and wrong
> centred upon this hour.
> Yet there is power to mould
> the rock of gold if we
> have faith to see the wire,
> the tide's desire, the wrack,
> a broken lock, and find,
> where sight is blind and ear
> cannot hear, the whole
> of living soul.

Yet Skelton seems to be hobbled by chains of another sort. For all its vatic fervor the verse in this poem is bound fast to Blake, Yeats, and especially T. S. Eliot. It is not difficult to agree with David Jackel that "Skelton is a craftsman whose work shows that he has not merely studied but *absorbed* the major traditions of poetry in English, and can write with gracefully assured precision in a variety of tones and rhythmic forms" (*Canadian Forum*, August 1977). Yet "Patmos" remains curiously sterile; one feels the pupil has not only absorbed, but *been absorbed by*, the traditions of high modernism. Skelton has approached the modernist's ideal of impersonality in "Patmos," but at the cost of a distinctive poetic voice, which would of necessity be a *personal* voice, as Eliot's most definitely was.

This lack of a distinctive voice, combined with the ability to "turn" technically impressive pieces, continued through the next two volumes: *Third Day Lucky* (1958) and *Begging the Dialect: Poems and Ballads* (1960). It is interesting to note that one of the ballads in *Begging the Dialect*—"A Ballad of the Four Fishers"—is strikingly close to J. M. Synge's *Riders to the Sea*. Skelton began work on Synge's papers in 1960, and in the ensuing years has produced editions and studies of his work as well as poetry in commemoration of the man.

Begging the Dialect turns on the paradox that language both brings people together and acts as a barrier between them. In "Answering a Question," for example, the poet attempts to explain the genesis of a pattern of images and finds he cannot. Consequently he directs the reader to

>   listen
> not to the meaning but the spaces dropped
> between the words. Sun. Children. Wheels. A
>   Barn.
> Only such telling spells us to ourselves.

The problem here is that as Skelton intrudes the poetic process between the subject and the reader, his quest for meaning becomes so self-conscious it tends to obscure anything that may be discovered. The positive response to a sterile impersonality is not self-consciousness but creative relationship, which demands a responsible humility from the poet, a stance which maintains respect for the subject while bringing home to us the truth that respect is a personal gesture. This stance, in other words, would be the basis of a distinctive poetic voice.

In *The Practice of Poetry* (1971) Skelton says, "the first time I called myself a poet and meant the title to be more than an approximation used loosely in conversation to refer to someone who made poems was when I had completed my third book." Certainly with his fourth book of poetry, *The Dark Window* (1962), the appellation is justified. The distinctive voice missed earlier begins to be felt here. In this collection Skelton seems to be summing up his poetic career so far. Besides the long title poem there are two major sections—"Time Past" and "Time Present"—divided by a section of six free translations from Corbière.

"Time Past" is a strong section; the span of time separating the poet from his subject helps him to maintain his distance, allows the poem its integrity. Skelton sees the past as definitely influencing the present; primarily through Wordsworthian "spots of time" which contribute directly to the development of the poet's career, as in "The Walls," "As I Remember It," or "Westfield Lane," but also through the insistent memories of youth qualifying and putting into perspective the ordered complacencies of adult life. This insistent influence of past on present is captured simply and well in "The Birds," in which Skelton characterizes his childhood memories as birds that "pick at the laid stones/ cemented together," and as they pick:

> lime,
> (lime for the dead ones' bones),
> sand, (sand for the time
> that drags and drains away),
> and water (oh water, water)
> bonded them where they lay,
> fastened them, froze them, fixed them,
> yet out of my childhood these
> birds pick at the laid stones,
> roost in the nailed trees.

The section "Time Present" is dominated by "Poem on His Thirty-fifth Birthday." The self-restraint found in the earlier section is absent here; in endeavoring to "make truce," to "take stock, pause, reload," Skelton produces a self-indulgent compendium of cliché situations pitting the hard drinking, hard writing rebel poet against "the state," "bad laws," "prigs," and that tattered old standby the "academic sheep." His persistent and authentic sense of spiritual exile degenerates into mere role playing. Playing at being The Poet, with all the liberties (or indulgences) the role affords him, is always a temptation for Skelton, one that needs to be resisted.

In the thirty-four-page title poem, "The Dark Window," Skelton rarely indulges himself. The poem concerns the poet's need "made/in a time of wars cross-hatching Europe/to name his ghosts." Working in the tradition of the great modernists Yeats and Eliot, Skelton feels compelled to reconsider man's history and religion in the light of the breakdown, through war, of the set of values bequeathed us by the past. But whereas in "Patmos" the modernist tendency overwhelmed the personal element, here the survey of mankind's heritage is effectively counterpointed by scenes from Skelton's personal history which offer an immediacy that might otherwise be lacking. The meaningful past, for example, is embodied in the poet's father:

> And my Father leant on his spade, said
> "Everything in the right way; care,
> steadiness, labour, the true balance
> letting the spade know its own power:

> put by your strength; let the spade dig,"
> . . . .
> "The good style is the good answer,"
> his blue eyes round as a child's.

After the war, however, the poet returns to a landscape and home externally unchanged but whose intrinsic significance has been lost: "all changed; the black window/reflected the dark, said 'A good style,'/said 'The style firm, but no answer.'"

Faced with this loss of traditional meaning the poet is thrown back on himself; his responsibility both as a poet and as a man compels him to attempt a new synthesis, or at least guess a new map. Flanked by, on one side, the muse that lures him on, and, on the other, the memory of the child he was, the poet strains forward within the harness of his craft:

> And night upon night at the star's foot
> I build verses, till my hands
> stiffen like stiffening gloves torn
> with making the house of the tall queen
> who speaks my throat; yet I see plain
> the step of the child on the sea shore,
>
> and the light shines. . . .
> . . . .
> though harness gall
> my arching back, though my heart break,
> my breath's my god, my message is my own.

Though there is a confidently romantic acceptance of the poet's role expressed in these lines, there is also a distinct note of resignation, of bowing to the emotional hardship and isolation that appear to be the burden of the vocation that has chosen him.

This sense of separation, of a lack of genuine communication with those around him, was reinforced by the Manchester years. In *The Poet's Calling* Skelton recalls that in his twelve years at the university he was never asked to read his work there: "I found that this treatment did my work no good at all. I grew progressively more depressed." Consequently he jumped at the opportunity to teach abroad, and in 1962, the same year *The Dark Window* was published, he taught summer school in Canada at what was then Victoria College (now University of Victoria) in British Columbia. The fall semester of 1962 he spent as visiting professor at the University of Massachusetts. The impact of North America was profound; after a few months back in England in 1963 Skelton immigrated to Canada, taking up a position as associate professor in the English department of the University of Victoria, where he has since remained. In 1966, as well as being made fellow of the Royal Society of Literature, he was promoted to full professor with tenure; from 1967 to 1973 he was director of the creative writing program, and from 1973 to 1976 he was the founding chairman of the department of creative writing. Also in 1967 he and John Peter began the international literary magazine the *Malahat Review*. Peter resigned his editorship in 1971, and from 1972 to 1983 Skelton was general editor. In 1972 he also founded the Pharos Press and from 1976 to 1983 served as the editor in chief of the Sono Nis Press. In 1976 he was elected a Knight of Mark Twain for his services to literature, and was made a fellow of P.E.N. International.

The romantic inclination in Skelton's nature felt an immediate affinity with Canada. In an essay written for Andy Wainwright's *Notes for a Native Land* (1969) he says, "A country so seriously, and so comically, devoted to the discovery of its own identity is my kind of country." Here he found "space . . . the freedom to move, and, moving, breathe deep." This newly found freedom is reflected in a stylistic shift toward looser rhythms and shorter lines, a movement away from what he called "English gentility." "The great disease of English poetry is gentility, which masks as irony," he told Sandler. Even if the attitude expressed here misrepresents British poetry of the 1950s somewhat, there is a definite rift between the self-deprecatory gestures of the Movement writers and Skelton's self-assertion.

In one of his earliest Canadian poems, "Night Poem, Vancouver Island" (first collected in *Selected Poems 1947-1967*, 1968), the poet's relationship with the land parallels the interaction of conscious and unconscious levels of being. As Skelton told Sandler, "the sleeper is becoming part of the land, and occasionally surfaces to realize he has an individual identity." There is a duality here that undermines, to some degree, the self-assertion that was so hard won in "The Dark Window." The poem expresses an uneasiness with the fact that identification with nature, or the collective unconscious, entails a loss of personal identity and conscious human relationships. The concluding gesture, for example, in which the now-conscious speaker turns to his companion, appears as a consolation in lieu of the greater truths that conscious life is denied access to:

> Come now, if you wish.
> The wind from the west has stilled.
> Your mouth upon my mouth
> solves nothing but is good.
> Light rises from the sea

and time spreads with the light.
Put your body to mine;
we are the world we caused.

This duality appears in a self-indulgent vein in Skelton's next major book of poetry, *The Hunting Dark*, which, though completed by 1968, was not published until 1971. The poles of the dualism here, however, are the past and present; in poems such as "Forty," "The Poet at Fifty," and "At the Centre" Skelton laments the passing of youth, which he sentimentally equates with passion and meaning. He implies that in middle age only brief moments of vitality are left: "At forty, one/finds summer grown so short there's but a day/to burn away the dead" ("The Fortieth Summer"). These dramatic monologues express little more than the truism that as time passes one's blood cools. Skelton's implication that there is more to them is indicative of a tendency to idealize the youthful past. And the idealization is only a variant of a wish-fulfilling fantasy.

Besides these questionable pieces, which occur primarily in this section entitled "At the Centre," there are other and more satisfying poems. In "Sergeant Casey," a perceptively detailed study of a racially prejudiced Irish RAF man in India, the poet keeps his intrusions to a minimum. "The Friday Fish" is a two-page narrative of a fishing trip which clearly values the experience as much for itself as for the symbolic significance it affords the poet.

In 1969-1970 Skelton took a sabbatical leave and with the help of a Canada Council travel grant was able to wander around Europe and write. He visited France, Italy, Corsica, Switzerland, Ireland, England, and Mallorca, making connections both actual—Robert Graves and Ezra Pound—and spiritual—Eliot and Yeats. Intending "to make some comparisons between life in the old world and life in the new," what he found, he told Sandler, "was a cultural shock so intense that I could do no more than gape—particularly at Italy—and so I was forced into an entirely different direction." The trip became a quest for roots, an attempt to refamiliarize himself with, and so to understand, his Europeanness. The result was *Timelight* (1974), a volume of seven interrelated sections which Skelton hoped would "mingle memory/and desire,/dream and dream,/to hint a whole/beyond the vagaries/of its parts" ("Timelight").

This dualism of whole and parts is the same Neoplatonic theme that has dominated Skelton's work from the beginning. Certainly the poems in this collection are often linked by reference to this theme, but to say there is a whole hinted at beyond them is closer to willed authorial assertion than the poetic reality. And there are places that suggest Skelton is obliquely aware of this problem. In "October," for example, Skelton remembers a moment in childhood when he had fleetingly felt a presence while hiding in his "cavern" in the hedgerow. Pressing his hands into the clay, he had attempted to "rouse a pulse or a gasp/or an answering cry/from something other" than his normal world. The desire for the "answering cry" remains lodged at his center and, hence, qualifies all merely human relationships. He concludes the poem by asking his children to forgive him his sadness and help him to continue. In this plea there is an implicit recognition that his desire for the "answering cry" is self-indulgent and needs to be curbed.

The plea for forgiveness came from the poet as father; when Skelton is writing as The Poet, as in "Robert Graves in Deya, Mallorca," his twinge of conscience disappears:

> Vision lives
> that one dimension
> closer to the sun
> than all we measure by,
> and Time, absurd,
> becomes a mesh of shadows
> cast by that
> entrancing light poets enter
> to meet Death
> in every poem they make
> and be reborn
> by virtue of the poem
> which alters earth
> around them.

The evidence of self-indulgence here is in the histrionic gestures which so easily label the world of time "absurd." Skelton's susceptibility to the romantic notion of the poet impedes a due cognizance of the importance of the temporal realm he ignores. After all, were it not for that realm there would be no poetry, no human creativity, for that matter, no poet. When the histrionics and self-consciousness are set aside Skelton is able to offer a truly distinctive verse which gains from its temporality; as in his description of Robert Graves at home in Deya, from the same poem quoted above:

> So Deya is, because of him.
> He comes
> down to the terrace,
> underneath his arm
> a basket of black olives,

> on his head
> the straw hat of a peasant
> from the fields,
> a strong, warm, honoured man
> admiring earth.

The split, in *Timelight*, between Skelton as man and Skelton as The Poet continues in his next major volume of poetry, *Callsigns* (1976). This book was begun on the same sabbatical that produced *Timelight*, and in it the desire for "an answering cry" is the dominant concern. Skelton uses his wartime experience as a code and cypher clerk to develop the "central images of the callsign and the message in code" (introduction to *Callsigns*). The image of decoding clerk puzzling over his cryptic communications is made to parallel the situation of the poet wrestling with his hints of a larger message, of a whole beyond the parts. Though this overt, if not completely arbitrary, use of symbolism is effective over a short span, the mechanism is definitely creaking by the end of this ninety-four-page volume.

Within this symbolic design there is a distinctly different voice heard from time to time; in "Marchlight" it is as if a more domestic side of Skelton's psyche were straining to be heard over the esoteric side:

> House, garden, children, wife and
> custom—I
> must keep these, hold these fast:
> the other way
> is emptiness. . . .

In the poem "Divides" Skelton acknowledges the two halves in himself:

> the private man, the public man,
> the clown
> and guru, the professor
> and the poet
> and, more significantly,
> the life of flesh
> and life of spirit,
> man and unman matched.

Despite the overwhelming preponderance of spirit over flesh in both *Callsigns* and *Timelight*, the just quoted equivocations suggest that, as Anthony J. Harding says in a review of Skelton's next collection that appeared in *Canadian Literature* (Spring 1981), Skelton is "trapped in the esoteric, but wanting out."

In *Landmarks* (1979), to quote Harding again, "Skelton escapes more successfully." The choice of

1977 as the stopping point for his *Collected Shorter Poems, 1947-1977* (1981) suggests that Skelton saw the year as the end of a phase in his life and poetic development. The blurb he wrote for the back cover of *Landmarks* bears this theory out: "only now in *Landmarks* do I feel that I have made a true beginning, relating my own present self to the haunting past and the presences of this place which is, for me, the centre of the natural and spiritual world I inhabit and which inhabits me." There is a definite sense that Skelton has come to terms with the spirits of place in this most distinctively Canadian of his books. The concreteness of image and event, and the easy confidence of the predominantly trimeter and dimeter rhythms offer a sharp contrast to the almost obsessive straining after a significant message in *Callsigns*.

Yet the typical Skelton indulgences do appear. They are represented well by the self-concerned condescension of "O Lazarus" in which God wills—for Lazarus and Skelton—

> another darker claim
> upon our journey
> than his finite plan
> for other creatures
> (if such creatures be)
> that can at last
> lie down between the trees
> or in the darkness
> underneath the waves
> content to be the smallness
> of themselves.

In general, however, Skelton seems to have approached a balance between spirit and flesh, between his self-confessed extremes of "wild-eyed romantic solipsism" and "harsh social realism" (Sandler interview). The fusion of these two "voices" is dramatized in "The Visitant":

> What about Credo,
> thus and thus and thus?
> *Have you*
> *seen the*
> *leaf drop*
> *from the*
> *tree?*
>
> Well, then, Logic—
> therefore, thus, and so . . . ?
>
> *Have you*
> *seen the*

> *tree let*
> *go the*
> *leaf?*
>
> . . . .
> I feel now, at last,
> his touching hand.
> . . . .
> *You have found me.*
> *Enter now the dance.*

Entrance into the dance demands that the poet attempt to transcend the limited ego while maintaining a personal shaping. In Skelton's case he has to curb his penchant for interposing himself self-consciously between subject and reader. As Harding noted, Skelton has to avoid an "embarrassing man-observes-himself-observing gentility." Skelton's ability to approximate this ideal in longer poems such as "The Emissaries" or the title poem "Landmarks," and in shorter pieces such as "Fish Eagles" or "In the Gulf," makes *Landmarks* one of his strongest collections.

Skelton's most recent major collection, *Limits* (1981), continues this movement away from the esoteric, finding its strength in the sinew of tangible human experience captured in concrete detail, as in "Leavings":

> Dead leaves dug out
> of the old hedge bottom:
> the years we forget
>
> are there always, lodged
> in the roots, pressed
> black and solid
>
> by the enormous weight
> of fall upon fall.

The strength of the volume is not unalloyed. The relaxed, often intimate tone at times allows Skelton to mistake sentimentality for sincerity: "I guess you'll understand/that when I come myself/I'm often rather shy/and clumsy with my feet" ("In This Poem I Am"). There is still the temptation to "talk about" an experience rather than evoke it with a minimum of tampering. In "Those Afternoons," for example, the first half is a sharp description of a tavern the speaker "used to wait in": "the heavy/big glass ashtrays scratched,/their names rubbed out,/the Schlitz sharp, chilling." The second half, however, forgets the concrete evocation and gives us weak and obvious abstraction, instead:

thinking, as thought blurred,
what poems might do

or say, what I might
say or do if I

discovered, as could happen
if I waited
patiently enough, just
why I waited.

Still, the strengths of the volume clearly out-weigh the weaknesses; nowhere are these strengths seen more vividly than in four poems about Skelton's aged mother. The blend of humor, pathos, wry wit, sorrow, and love offers a depth of human involvement seldom encountered in his earlier poems. In poems such as "Blackberrying" Skelton's respect for this frail, tenacious woman is such that both sentimentality and self-consciousness—elements that focus the reader's attention on the poet rather than the subject—are absent. Here is a sample from "Blackberrying":

in the grass at her heel
is the scratched enamel
can she will spill

sometime for sure,
her shamefaced laughter
brightening the air

before she kneels
in the grass, refills
it, suddenly small

to the wide blue sky.

If *Landmarks* and *Limits* are reliable indicators of the direction Skelton's future poetry will take then we have much to look forward to.

Interview:
Linda Sandler, "An Interview with Robin Skelton," *Tamarack Review*, 68 (1976-77): 71-85.

Papers:
The MacPherson Library of the University of Victoria holds nearly all of Skelton's manuscripts.

Sydney Goodsir Smith
(26 October 1915-15 January 1975)

David S. Robb
Dundee University

BOOKS: *Skail Wind: Poems* (Edinburgh: Chalmers Press, 1941);
The Wanderer and Other Poems (Edinburgh: Oliver & Boyd, 1943);
The Deevil's Waltz (Glasgow: William Maclellan, 1946);
Carotid Cornucopius (Glasgow: Caledonian Press, 1947; enlarged edition, Edinburgh: M. Macdonald, 1964);
Selected Poems (Edinburgh: Oliver & Boyd, for Saltire Society, 1947);
Under the Eildon Tree (Edinburgh: Serif Books, 1948; revised edition, Edinburgh: Serif Books, 1954);
The Aipple and the Hazel (Glasgow: Caledonian Press, 1951);
A Short Introduction to Scottish Literature (Edinburgh: Serif Books, 1951);

So Late into the Night: Fifty Lyrics, 1944-1948 (London: Peter Russell, 1952);
Cokkils (Edinburgh: M. Macdonald, 1953);
Orpheus and Eurydice: A Dramatic Poem (Edinburgh: M. Macdonald, 1955);
Omens: Nine Poems (Edinburgh: M. Macdonald, 1955);
Figs and Thistles (Edinburgh: Oliver & Boyd, 1959);
The Vision of the Prodigal Son (Edinburgh: M. Macdonald, 1960);
The Wallace: A Triumph in Five Acts (Edinburgh: Oliver & Boyd, 1960);
Kynd Kittock's Land (Edinburgh: M. Macdonald, 1965);
Fifteen Poems and a Play (Edinburgh: Southside, 1969);
Gowdspink in Reekie (Loanhead: Macdonald Publishers, 1974);

Collected Poems: 1941-1975 (London: Calder, 1975).

PLAYS: *The Wallace*, Edinburgh, Assembly Hall, 22
August 1960;
The Stick-up, or Full Circle, BBC Radio, 8 December
1961; as libretto *Full Circle*, by Robin Orr,
Perth, Perth Theatre, 10 April 1968.

OTHER: *Robert Fergusson, 1750-1774. Essays by vari-
ous hands to commemorate the bicentenary of his
birth*, edited by Smith (Edinburgh: Nelson,
1952);
Robert Burns, comp., *The Merry Muses of Caledonia*,
edited by Smith and James Barke (Edinburgh:
M. Macdonald, for the Auk Society, 1959;
New York: Putnam's, 1964);
Gavin Douglas: A Selection from his Poetry, edited, with
an introduction, by Smith (Edinburgh: Oliver
& Boyd for the Saltire Society, 1959);
Hugh MacDiarmid: a festschrift, edited by Smith and
K. D. Duval (Edinburgh: K. D. Duval, 1962);
*Bannockburn: the story of the battle and its place in Scot-
land's history*, edited by Smith (Stirling: *Scots
Independent*, 1965);
A Choice of Burns's Poems and Songs, edited, with an
introduction, by Smith (London: Faber &
Faber, 1966).

Sydney Goodsir Smith, the author of some of
this century's finest love poetry, was also, after
Hugh MacDiarmid, perhaps the most important
poet to write in Scots since Robert Burns. The most
prominent of the second wave of poets who, under
MacDiarmid's influence, saw themselves as part of a
twentieth-century Scottish literary renaissance,
Smith performed the signal service of recapturing
for his generation some of the heady emotional,
nationalistic, and linguistic exuberance which had
helped make MacDiarmid's Scots poems of the
1920s so memorable but which had been partially
lost in MacDiarmid's more recent work. Smith's
poetic canon, despite great unevenness and some
monotony of theme and attitude, contains work of
rare quality. Almost as important, at times, was his
role, for three decades after the war, as a social focus
for some of Edinburgh's most vital literary life. His
achievement in all these respects seems the more
remarkable in that he was Scottish neither by birth
nor by education.

He was born in Wellington, New Zealand. His
mother, Catherine Goodsir Gelenick, whose family
came from Fife, had married in New Zealand. His
father was Professor Sir Sydney Smith, occupant of
the regius chair of forensic medicine at Edinburgh

from 1928 and one of the best-known forensic scientists of his day. As an infant, Smith stayed with his
parents for a short spell in Egypt, but at the age of
five he was sent to a preparatory school at Hillcrest
in Dorset, where he associated with not only certain
Scottish boys who became lifelong friends, but also
with the school's Scottish headmaster, who regularly took Smith, among others, on holidays to
Dumfries and to Heriot, Midlothian. From 1929 to
1933 he was sent to preparatory school at Malvern
(near Bristol), where he was less happy and where
he found himself at odds with the class distinctions
which the school reflected and reinforced. To
please his parents, he embarked on a medical degree at Edinburgh University in the early 1930s, but
being temperamentally unsuited for such study, he
gave up after a year and went to Oxford, where he
graduated with an M.A. in history in 1937. His years
at Oxford were followed by a brief spell in London,
but he soon returned to Edinburgh, where he made
his home for the rest of his life. He loved the city for
its beauty, its history, its paradoxes, and its cultural
life: not only was Edinburgh "this my first and onlie
hame," as he described it in a verse letter to his
friend Hector MacIver, but it also offered him an
environment of political and literary commitment.
New friendships with men such as MacIver (a
prominent Gael and a teacher at the Royal High
School) and Hugh MacDiarmid were influential in
encouraging him to make a place for himself among
Scottish writers of the day, but even more decisive
was his discovery of MacDiarmid's masterpiece, *A
Drunk Man Looks at the Thistle* (1926).

Prior to settling in Edinburgh, Smith had
written poems and fiction in English, most of which
were never published. In the late 1930s, he began to
use Scots as a poetic medium. It seems, at first
glance, astonishing that a New Zealand-born product of the English educational system should have
even attempted this step, let alone that he should
eventually attain Smith's distinction, but Smith had
been familiar with the sound of Scottish speech
from his earliest days at Hillcrest. His was no
Conrad-like assumption of an alien tongue; he had
a natural foundation of knowledge of spoken Scots
on which to base his explorations of past Scottish
literature, a knowledge he naturally reinforced in
the course of his joyous participation in Edinburgh's social life. The medium he eventually
created was a synthesized Scots spoken by none
(including Smith, whose basic accent remained an
upper-class English one), mannered and artificial
but perfectly adapted for what he wanted to write.

What that was, however, was not made entirely

*Marion and Sydney Goodsir Smith at a party during the 1947
Edinburgh Festival (BBC Hulton)*

clear with his first published volume, *Skail Wind* (1941), a substantial collection of poems in English and Scots reflecting his writing from about 1939. The weakness of these poems is not solely due to Smith's inexperience in writing Scots, though most of the poems in that medium suggest that they have been conceived in English and then translated into the less familiar tongue. In addition to this drawback, however, the *Skail Wind* poems are often blighted by a turgid intensity which was doubtless partly due to the poetic taste of the age as well as to Smith's own inexperience. Many of these poems are written in a long, self-indulgent line, allowing him scope for what is clearly an intoxication with the Scots language. Indeed David Murison, speculating on what attracted Smith to Lallans (Scots as it is spoken in the southern and eastern Lowlands of Scotland), plausibly suggests that "it seems simplest to assume that he had from the outset a liking for words as such, for their associations and history, and for the way in which they can be manipulated." Smith's adoption of Lallans was probably part of a wider and deeper commitment to Scotland, but his fascination with the language is clear in this collec-

tion, and was to become still stronger. There is a moderate thematic range, though many of the poems derive from developments in his own recent past, and many more, again, reflect the war. The volume gives little indication of his future mastery of the brief lyric of love. Taken as a whole, the collection suggests a great and sudden creative outburst, an outpouring which was in part a response to the war, which seems to have stimulated him greatly.

He had found himself essentially an observer of the war rather than a participant, for he was rejected for active service because of the asthma from which he had suffered since he was two years old. A few months after the publication of *Skail Wind*, he began his contribution to the war effort by teaching English to Polish soldiers stationed in Scotland, but this assignment scarcely impeded his literary activities or his social life in Edinburgh. His second volume, *The Wanderer and Other Poems*, appeared in 1943. The title poem takes up by far the bulk of the book, unfortunately, for it is in the songs among the other poems that clear foreshadowings of the later, and better, Smith are to be found.

His next volume, however, was something of a breakthrough, and *The Deevil's Waltz* (1946) contains several poems which can stand comparison with the best of his later work. It is partly that his command of Scots idiom has become more secure (though still occasionally fallible) and that he is now creating poems which seem to have been conceived in Scots, not just translated into it. With this new confidence in the medium comes a greater lucidity. Significant, too, is the number of love poems, so that Smith is beginning to give voice to the range of tenderness and anguish which characterizes his work in the mode. Sometimes, however, the shadow of the war falls even on the love poems, and the sense, which pervades the book as a whole, of the individual confronting great and terrible events is established by the "prolegomenon," the title poem with its evocation of a universal devil dance (this poem, significantly, is dated "Halloween, 1943"):

> O rin an rout, we birl about,
> Tae the rhythm o the Deil's jack-boot,
> Black as auld gibbet-fruit, Mahoun
> Bestrides a kenless mappamound.

> (*rin an rout:* run and bellow; *birl:* whirl; *kenless:* unknown; *mappamound:* globe; map of the world.)

The collection is divided into three parts, "Venus" (love poems), "Prometheus" (poems of social change) and "Mars" (war poems). With hindsight, it is apparent that Smith was strongest in the personal poems, but he clearly felt a necessity to write about the great public events of his day, and he expresses his detestation of war from the standpoint of a socialist and Scottish patriot. But the reader can sometimes detect an opposition, a tension, between the impulses to celebrate private experience and to confront large public issues, a tension which is more clearly expressed in his unpublished correspondence.

A crucial development in the background of Smith's poetry was his writing of the first version of *Carotid Cornucopius* (first published in 1947, then again, in a greatly expanded version, in 1964). This prose work is built round a faint suggestion of narrative, but its true concerns are the evocation of the boozing and whoring sides of Edinburgh life, and the reveling in a joke language which transforms spoken Scots by an excess of puns. James Joyce is a clear influence, but influential also was the seventeenth-century Scottish translator of Rabelais, Sir Thomas Urquhart of Cromarty. With supreme zest and wit, Smith challenges the reader's mental agility and bourgeois sensibility alike, in a style extrapolated from the outpourings of a drunkard. The result is probably unreadable to those not familiar with Scots or with Edinburgh, and only to be read slowly by those who are: "But Duncod was a retch sod apairt frae his bad-business bondintrusts, for he was Lourd and Shyster of all the money ogres of lend, numbinate Rueland or Irule, roundclosed by the Fart of Mondlethean neer by the Mirkit Crust ootby the Couthietrull or Huge Gurk of Sanct Jowls, Oddanbeery."

Carotid Cornucopius is fun to read, though opinions vary on how substantial an achievement it is. What is less doubtful is the degree to which Smith's games with the Scots language gave him a more secure and supple grasp of the medium than he had hitherto enjoyed. Furthermore, with the personifying of a side of himself in the central figure, he essentially introduced into his writing his stance (often adopted in his later poetry) of the drunken waster and lover, the impoverished, big-hearted creature of the Edinburgh night.

The work universally regarded as his finest appeared in 1948. *Under the Eildon Tree* is a sequence of twenty-four elegies exploring love as experienced by "Sydney Slugabed Godless Smith," who, it appears, has not only lost his beloved, but lost her through his own foolish unfaithfulness. In this poem, love is presented as a torture from which the victim desires no escape: Smith is blissfully enslaved by his beloved, as the legendary Thomas the Rhymer was entrapped by the Queen of Elfland in her kingdom under the Eildon Tree. Nor is this literary allusion the only one in the poem, for Smith uses a sequence of famous lovers to parallel and glorify his own situation: Antony and Cleopatra, Burns and Highland Mary, Orpheus and Eurydice, Cuchulain torn between Fann and Eimhir, Dido and Aeneas, Troilus and Cressida, Tristram and Iseult. Conversely, his own experience transforms these creatures of legend back into flesh and blood. The result is a passionate vision of the tragicomic behavior of the male in love: the poem is a sad one, but full of comedy and the ironic undercutting of its own (and its maker's) posturings. The stylistic range is immense, attaining at times a rhetorical artifice reminiscent of, and worthy of, the great medieval poems of love, while elsewhere evoking the backchat of the pub with earthy gusto. In the great Elegy XIII, Smith describes his encounter with a prostitute while on a week-long binge: this poem dazzlingly negotiates the extremes of lyrical rapture and the grossly physical. The greatness of *Under the Eildon Tree* lies in its intensity, its verbal inventiveness and the completeness of its portrayal of what sexual passion is and feels like: it is an extraordinarily honest poem in its treatment of love.

It is honest, also, in being partially autobiographical, for love was as important in his life as was drink and good fellowship. For thirty years after the war, Smith's life was that of a man of letters, but his style was closer to that of Burns rather than, say, Carlyle. He was married twice, to Marion Welsh in 1938 and to Hazel Williamson, who survives him, in 1967. In *The Author's and Writer's Who's Who* (sixth edition, 1972) he listed his occupations as "teaching, freelance journalism, broadcasting," but more vivid is his summary of his recreations: "drinking, blethering." He was, in the early and mid-1960s, art critic of the *Scotsman*, and was himself a talented painter in watercolors, an activity he kept up even after he lost an eye six years before his death. His asthma never left him, but neither did it inhibit him: he endured it not only heroically but, better still, with humor. He had a genius for friendship, and a sense of fun which pervaded the most mundane corners of daily existence; here is the address he once scribbled on the envelope to a letter to Hector MacIver, an envelope preserved in the National Library of Scotland:

Postie, gang by the *CALTON HILL*
Until ye come to the *ROYAL HIGH SCHULE*;
Look for a dominie, gray & grim,
H. MACIVER, that is him.

Deliver this billet & dinna be blate
Or he'll maybe hit ye on the heid wi a SLATE!

One other anecdote might be told. Along with various publicans and other customers in the Edinburgh pub scene, Smith once fell victim to a petty trickster who was eventually caught and brought to trial. Smith was called as a witness and, on entering the witness room, found himself in the familiar company of a host of pub managers whose hostelries he could instantly recall—all except one, and the bard, rising to the challenge, made several unsuccessful attempts to specify the particular familiar polished counter with which he thought he associated him, until he was testily informed, "Mr. Smith, I am your bank manager."

In 1951 appeared *The Aipple and the Hazel*, a pamphlet of love poems. Far more substantial, however, both in bulk and quality, was *So Late into the Night: Fifty Lyrics, 1944-1948*, which appeared in 1952 with a eulogistic preface by Edith Sitwell. This collection of very short poems, along with *Under the Eildon Tree*, is at the heart of Smith's achievement. His command of his unique brand of Scots was now secure, his verse flowing with a clarity far removed from the clogged lines of his earliest collections. Once again, love is the principal concern, but, where *Under the Eildon Tree* is characterized by a dominant passionate intensity, the depth of feeling in poems such as "Loch Leven" is partly achieved by delicacy, mystery, ambiguity, indirection. Many of them, however, are simple and direct, with a fresh innocence which is an achievement in itself.

The book as a whole has a certain monotony of theme and manner: it largely lacks the healthy self-irony which enriches *Under the Eildon Tree*. But it is full of exceptionally fine poems.

Smith's poetry of the late 1940s and early 1950s was predominantly personal in theme, and it is perhaps no accident that this is the period of his finest work and most abundant productivity. Several later poems which, from the date of their publication in book form, appear to be products of the 1960s and 1970s, were actually written earlier. He followed *So Late into the Night* with a series of pamphlets, mining still further the styles and concerns of his two great collections: *Cokkils* (1953), *Orpheus and Eurydice* (1955), and *Omens* (1955). A larger collection, *Figs and Thistles* (1959), contains a higher proportion of social and political verse than its immediate predecessors, and, while the tangled chronology of his output makes it unsafe to ascribe any individual poem to a date of origin, it is clear that he was turning outward again in his poetic

concerns, to wider public issues. This uneven but impressive collection contains some of Smith's most effective poems including, notably, his harrowing account of an encounter with a down-and-out, "The Grace of God and the Meth-Drinker"; this poem is among his most frequently anthologized.

Much of his work of around the early 1960s is more outspokenly nationalistic than before. A key work is his play about the early Scottish patriot, *The Wallace* (1960); its concern with a Scotland held down politically and culturally, and betrayed from within, is echoed in *The Vision of the Prodigal Son* (1960), an ambitious meditation on the bicentenary of Burns's birth, and in *Kynd Kittock's Land* (1965), an Edinburgh poem of a more familiar Smith cast. Another long poem, *Gowdspink in Reekie* (another tour of Edinburgh pubs, this time in the imagined company of Oliver Goldsmith), was published as a book in 1974 but had been written twenty years previously. Of these three long poems, the two Edinburgh works are the best realized, but *The Vision of the Prodigal Son* is the most interesting for its ambitious, careful structure, and for the extra subtlety with which he grapples with the familiar theme of the impoverishment of life in modern Scotland. In it and (less convincingly) in *The Wallace*, he attempts to reconcile his two instincts to celebrate womankind and to write about Scotland by personifying the nation in the image of the beloved. It does not quite work, but the poem challenges its reader to an extent reached by few of the late long poems. In addition to *Gowdspink in Reekie* Smith's final volumes include *Fifteen Poems and a Play* (1969), which also contains material written two decades earlier, and the *Collected Poems* (1975), published a few months after the sudden stroke which killed him. His death threw the arrangements for producing the collected poems into disarray, so that the volume is but a fumbled version of his life's work: it cannot be trusted textually; it fails to give a satisfactory picture of Smith's line of development; and it omits certain poems which should have been included.

Sydney Goodsir Smith's poetry is unique in content and language. In their overtly artificial idiom, his best poems convey emotional experience with a rare depth and passion. Once his language has been mastered, his poems are not obscure: he is a modern without mystification. His linguistic synthesis dates him as a disciple of the early MacDiarmid; more recent poets use versions of Scots more purely drawn from real speech. Recent assessments of his output suggest that he was more limited and repetitive than was often thought in his lifetime: his

Sydney Goodsir Smith, Hugh MacDiarmid, and Norman MacCaig, the club bards for the 200 Burns Club, at the club's first dinner, 20 January 1959, in Edinburgh (The Scotsman)

development from the mid-1950s failed to produce any innovations to equal his achievement of the late 1940s. Nevertheless, his finest work stands securely on its merits, and nearly everything he wrote after it has a gusto and a personality which should ensure that he remains what he is now, among the best-known and best-loved Scottish poets of the twentieth century.

Bibliography:

W. R. Aitken, "Sydney Goodsir Smith, 1915-75: A Checklist of his Books and Pamphlets," in *For Sidney Goodsir Smith* (Loanhead: M. Macdonald, 1975), pp. 85-91.

References:

Alan Bold, "Three Post-MacDiarmid Makars: Soutar, Garioch, Smith," *Akros*, 44 (August 1980): 44-61;

Kenneth Buthlay, "Sydney Goodsir Smith: Makar Macironical," *Akros*, 31 (August 1976): 46-56;

Thomas Crawford, "The Poetry of Sydney Goodsir Smith," *Studies in Scottish Literature*, 7 (July-October 1969): 40-59;

Robin Fulton, *Contemporary Scottish Poetry: Individuals and Contexts* (Loanhead: Macdonald Publishers, 1974), pp. 173-175;

Eric Gold, *Sydney Goodsir Smith's "Under the Eildon Tree": An Essay* (Preston: Akros Publications, 1975);

Norman MacCaig, "Introductory Note," in *For Sydney Goodsir Smith* (Loanhead: M. Macdonald, 1975), pp. 7-10;

MacCaig, "The Poetry of Sydney Goodsir Smith," *Saltire Review*, 1 (April 1954): 14-19;

Hugh MacDiarmid, "The Significance of Sydney Goodsir Smith," *Jabberwock*, 4 (February 1952): 5-10;

Sorley Maclean, "*Figs and Thistles*," in *For Sydney Goodsir Smith*, pp. 73-78;

David Murison, "The Language of Sidney Goodsir Smith," in *For Sydney Goodsir Smith*, pp. 23-29;

Alexander Scott, "Daylight and the Dark: Edinburgh in the Poetry of Robert Fergusson and Sydney Goodsir Smith," *Lines*, 3 (Summer 1953): 9-13;

Scott, "Goodsir Smith's Masterpiece: *Under the Eildon Tree*," in *For Sydney Goodsir Smith*, pp. 11-22;

Scott, "Sydney Goodsir Smith: The Art of Devilment," *Akros*, 10 (May 1969): 21-28;

Kurt Wittig, *The Scottish Tradition in Literature* (Edinburgh: Oliver & Boyd, 1958), pp. 292-296.

Papers:

The National Library of Scotland, Edinburgh, possesses a large number of Smith's letters, manuscripts, and typescripts; letters from and about him are frequently found in the library's other manuscript holdings related to twentieth-century literature.

R. S. Thomas
(1915-)

W. J. Keith
University of Toronto

BOOKS: *The Stones of the Field* (Carmarthen: Druid Press, 1946);

An Acre of Land (Newtown: Montgomeryshire Printing Company, 1952);

The Minister (Newtown: Montgomeryshire, 1953);

Song at the Year's Turning: Poems 1942-1954 (London: Hart-Davis, 1955);

Poetry for Supper (London: Hart-Davis, 1958; Chester Springs, Pa.: Dufour, 1961);

Tares (London: Hart-Davis, 1961; Chester Springs, Pa.: Dufour, 1961);

Penguin Modern Poets 1, by Thomas, Lawrence Durrell, and Elizabeth Jennings (Harmondsworth: Penguin, 1962);

The Bread of Truth (London: Hart-Davis, 1963; Chester Springs, Pa.: Dufour, 1963);

Words and the Poet, W. D. Thomas Memorial Lecture (Cardiff: University of Wales Press, 1964);

Pietà (London: Hart-Davis, 1966);

Not That He Brought Flowers (London: Hart-Davis, 1968);

The Mountains, text by Thomas, illustrations by John Piper (New York: Chilmark, 1968);

H'm (London: Macmillan, 1972; New York: St. Martin's Press, 1972);

Young and Old (London: Chatto & Windus, 1972);

Selected Poems 1946-1968 (London: Hart-Davis, MacGibbon, 1973; New York: St. Martin's Press, 1974);

What is a Welshman? (Landybie, Carmarthenshire: Christopher Davies, 1974);

Laboratories of the Spirit (London: Macmillan, 1975; Boston: Godine, 1976);

The Way of It, text by Thomas, illustrations by Barry Hirst (Sunderland: Ceolfrith Press, 1977);

Frequencies (London: Macmillan, 1978);

Between Here and Now (London: Macmillan, 1981);

Later Poems: A Selection (London: Macmillan, 1983).

OTHER: *The Batsford Book of Country Verse*, edited by Thomas (London: Batsford, 1961);

The Penguin Book of Religious Verse, edited by Thomas (Harmondsworth: Penguin, 1963);

Selected Poems of Edward Thomas, edited by Thomas (London: Faber & Faber, 1964);

"A Frame for Poetry," *Times Literary Supplement*, 3 March 1966, p. 169;

A Choice of George Herbert's Verse, edited by Thomas (London: Faber & Faber, 1967);

A Choice of Wordsworth's Verse, edited by Thomas (London: Faber & Faber, 1971).

When Rupert Hart-Davis agreed to publish *Song at the Year's Turning* (1955), R. S. Thomas's collection of all his previous poems that he wished to preserve, it was decided that a well-known poetic figure should be asked to draw attention to the volume, and the services of John Betjeman were enlisted. In his dignified and sensitive introduction Betjeman remarked that "the 'name' which has the honour to introduce this fine poet to a larger public will be forgotten long before that of R. S. Thomas." Betjeman, who has since become poet laureate (as well as Sir John), may have been excessively modest; nonetheless, R. S. Thomas, at that time barely known outside his native Wales, is now recognized as a prominent voice in British poetry of the second half of the twentieth century. Since David Jones's

death in 1974, indeed, he has strong claims to be considered the most important contemporary Anglo-Welsh poet.

Born in Cardiff in 1915 ("begotten in a drab town," as he writes in *The Bread of Truth*), Ronald Stuart Thomas was educated at Holyhead Grammar School in Anglesey and obtained a B.A. in classics at the University College of North Wales (Bangor) in 1935. After studying theology at St. Michael's College, Llandaff, he was ordained as a deacon in 1936 and as a priest of the Anglican church in the following year. Since then he has served at Chirk, Denbighshire (1936-1940), and in a number of mainly rural parishes, notably at Manafon, Montgomeryshire (1942-1954), Eglwsfach, Cardiganshire (1954-1967), and Aberdaron, originally in Caernarvonshire and now in Gwynedd (since 1967). He is married to a painter, Mildred Eldridge, and they have one son. His biography, if we ignore his poetic distinction, has been uneventful, and his succession of livings represents a continuing withdrawal to the wilder, most desolate and thinly populated parts of his country. Manafon is a parish made up of "starved pastures" in the central Welsh hill country, Eglwsfach is close to the sea, near the estuary of the River Dovey, while Aberdaron is at the extreme tip of the Lleyn peninsula in north Wales, one of the most isolated spots in the land.

Song at the Year's Turning, which caused quite a stir on its first appearance in 1955, is subtitled *Poems 1942-1954*, and it is interesting to note that the years in question correspond exactly to the span of his residence at Manafon. But although this volume introduced his work to readers outside Wales, it was in a sense a retrospective collection. His first book, *The Stones of the Field*, privately printed in 1946, had been followed by *An Acre of Land* in 1952 and *The Minister*, a radio play performed on the Welsh BBC, a year later. In *Song at the Year's Turning* Thomas included selections from the first two books, the complete but revised text of *The Minister*, and also some more recent poems.

There are four aspects of R. S. Thomas that immediately become noticeable in his poetry: the priest, the poet, the Welshman, the countryman. It is the last that perhaps strikes the reader of his early work most forcibly, though this element in his makeup becomes less conspicuous as his poetic career proceeds. Like Edward Thomas, a fellow-Welshman whom he has always admired and a selection of whose poems he edited in 1964, he is one of the urban born who has chosen to live in a rural environment, but his introduction to life in Manafon must nonetheless have been a rude shock. Throughout his life Thomas has been attracted to the poetry of Wordsworth (again, he demonstrated his admiration by editing *A Choice of Wordsworth's Verse* in 1971), but the harsh landscape in which he found himself in 1942 was very different from the gentle beauties of the Lake District, and the countrymen he met there bore little resemblance to the likes of Michael or Margaret or the leech gatherer. In this first volume we are introduced to Iago Prytherch, the laborer about whom Thomas was to write many poems in subsequent volumes. The poet has explained that "A Peasant" was written "after visiting a 1,000 feet up farm in Manafon where I saw a labourer docking swedes in the cold, grey air of a Manafon afternoon," but the poem is not about the joys of living close to the soil. Prytherch is anything but prepossessing on a first encounter. "Just an ordinary man of the bald Welsh hills," he is given "a half-witted grin," his clothes are "sour with years of sweat/And animal contact," and the poet admits:

"There is something frightening in the vacancy of his mind." Neither landscape nor countryman is idealized. Although in another poem Thomas praises "The land's patience and a tree's/Knotted endurance," and although he makes an effort to find admirable qualities in the people who inhabit this countryside, we detect from the start a tension between the poet-priest and his congregation.

Part of this tension is, of course, derived from the religious makeup of his parish. Many of the inhabitants were Methodist by persuasion, and most of the others paid at best a token lip service to the Anglican church. Thomas is enraged not so much at their religious heterodoxy as at their neglect of all spiritual values. While he can understand the materialism of a people that perforce lives barely above subsistence level, he finds it difficult to reconcile this understanding with what must at this time (though it is hardly a characteristic we normally associate with him) have been his religious idealism. In what is, in many respects, the most directly personal of his poems, "A Priest to his People," he offers a combination of testament and confession that gives vent to his impatience while at the same time it tries to acknowledge the potential heroism of their harsh lives. We can see his anger at their refusal to respond to his ardor—"I whose invective would spurt like a flame of fire/To be quenched always in the coldness of your stare." But he is also anxious to detect a different kind of spiritual satisfaction in their lives, and he tries desperately to recognize "The *artistry* of your dwelling on the bare hill" (italics added). The poem is moving for the personal urgency it communicates, but it is notable also as an example of an intensely local poem that gains universal applicability. Like J. M. Synge, like Shakespeare in *King Lear*, Thomas can present human life stripped to its basic elements and thereby offer a poignant portrait of "unaccommodated man."

Thomas may be said to pay his debt to these people who "affront, bewilder, yet compel [his] gaze" in one of his few long poems, "The Airy Tomb." Here he presents, sympathetically yet firmly, the day-to-day life of another ordinary man from the bare Welsh hills. Tomos is seen first as an unwilling schoolboy who at the end of his official education "could write and spell/No more than the clouds could"; he returns to help his father on the "gaunt wilderness" of his hill farm, and finds the work "play after the dull school." But his father dies, then his mother, and Tomos continues on the farm at the only labor he understands. He lives a hermit-like existence, alone, unmarried because he has learnt nothing of love:

> the one language he knew
> Was the shrill scream in the dark, the shadow
> within the shadow,
> The glimmer of flesh, deadly as mistletoe.

Not understood by his neighbors, and so disliked by them, he ekes out a hard existence and meets a hard death, as solitary as his life which, for all its deprivation, was in a strange sense free:

> and a fortnight gone
> Was the shy soul from the festering flesh and
> bone
> When they found him there, entombed in the
> lucid weather.

Tomos was entombed (the word makes one think fleetingly of Christ), but there are perhaps worse prisons than "the lucid weather." This eloquently moving poem ends, then, on a complex irony.

Thomas has been unsparingly critical of his early verse. He omitted almost half the poems in *The Stones of the Field* from *Song at the Year's Turning*, and only three survive in *Selected Poems 1946-1968* (1973). In "To a Young Poet" (in *The Bread of Truth*, 1963) the older Thomas observes:

> You will take seriously those first affairs
> With young poems, but no attachments
> Formed then but come to shame you.

This poem was written at a time when Thomas's poetry was in the process of changing course, and he may well have found the verbal richness of his previous verse increasingly inappropriate. Nonetheless, he displays a remarkable poetic technique in his early poems, upon which the spare effectiveness of his later work also depends. What one first notices is the characteristic intonations of a particular speaking voice manifest in an especially strong accentual beat. An early example is the opening of "Song":

> We, who are men, how shall we know
> Earth's ecstasy, who feels the plough
> Probing her womb,
> And after, the sweet gestation
> And the year's care for her condition?

The attractive jaggedness is caused by the way the

verse moves not from poetic foot to poetic foot, as in more conventional prosody, but from one emphatically stressed syllable to the next. The rhythmic balance within the opening line, the alliterating stresses (faintly suggesting the measures of Anglo-Saxon), the deliberate half-rhymes—all these, characteristic of Thomas—are secondary to the rhetorical force of the accents. So far as his early verse is concerned, these characteristics were to be his poetic trademark.

Another feature of the early poetry, to be severely qualified later, is what Calvin Bedient has described as his "magnificent talent for metaphor" in which Thomas "perhaps excels all English poets since Hopkins." This metaphorical display often manifests itself through adjectives, and it is worth noting at this point that Thomas pays considerable attention to the use of adjectives in English poetry in his W. D. Thomas Memorial Lecture, *Words and the Poet* (1964). There he observes: "I consider adjectives to be the mark of the poet as observer, and verbs of the poet as participator." In his early poetry Thomas is most often an observer, and it would not be difficult to add examples from his own verse ("the curious stars," "the night's unscaleable boughs," "the sun-dusted moor") to Thomas's list in that address. More specifically, a metaphorical identification is established between man and the land that he inhabits. Examples abound in the early verse. The human body in general is addressed as "Lean acre of ground that the years master/ Though fenced cunningly from wind and cold," and in the particular body of an old man he detects

> the bare boughs of bone,
> The trellised thicket, where the heart, that
> robin,
> Greets with a song the seasons of the blood.

The later Thomas has seemingly renounced this kind of linguistic exuberance, but we recognize it as a luxuriant celebration of language ("words and the poet"), the mastery of which makes the spare directness of subsequent work all the more impressive.

An Acre of Land, introduced by an epigraph in Welsh from the sixteenth-century poet Siôn Tudur, is noticeably more nationalistic in emphasis, with titles such as "The Welsh Hill Country," "Wales," "Song for Gwydion" (a Welsh mythological hero after whom Thomas named his son), "Cynddylan on a Tractor," "Welsh History," "Welsh Landscape." Nationalism is also manifest in erudite references to Welsh legend and story as well as in a dramatic monologue, "The Tree," put into the mouth of Owain Glyn Dŵr. The predominant tone in the volume is, however, complex. Traces of idealism still remain. "Memories" shows an immediate change of heart towards Prytherch, who is now addressed as "my friend," and Thomas continues:

> I will sing
> The land's praises, making articulate
> Your strong feelings, your thoughts of no
> date,
> Your secret learning, innocent of books.

But Thomas will later find little to praise in the state of the land. The Welsh references suggest a positive concentration on tradition and heritage; yet Thomas is at the same time aware of the contemporary erosion of that heritage. "Welsh History" embodies this uneasy tension:

> We were a people bred on legends,
> Warming our hands at the red past.
> . . . .
> We were a people, and are so yet.
> When we have finished quarrelling for
> crumbs
> Under the table, or gnawing the bones
> Of a dead culture, we will arise,
> Armed, but not in the old way.

This mixture of determination and distaste, of muted hopes and dour suggestions of despair, becomes characteristic. In "Welsh Landscape," Thomas argues that there is no present and no future in Wales, "There is only the past"; and the Welsh themselves are seen as "an impotent people,/Sick with inbreeding,/Worrying the carcase of an old song."

Thomas seems split between reverence for the old traditions and realization of the need for a new start. A similar tension is to be found in his attitude to the hill people themselves. He can see both the urgency for improvement in material conditions and at the same time the heavy price that will have to be paid for such improvement. The opening of "Cynddylan on a Tractor" is central:

> Ah, you should see Cynddylan on a tractor.
> Gone the old look that yoked him to the soil;
> He's a new man now, part of the machine.

The tone seems positive—indeed, this is the closest one is likely to come in Thomas's verse to the rhythms of approval. No one is likely to yearn nostalgically for the days when a peasant was "yoked . . . to the soil," and "a new man now" has religious as well as material connotations. But "part of the machine" sounds ominous, and "machine" is, in fact, a word that becomes increasingly important in Thomas's poetry, whether used in local, sociopolitical, or even cosmological contexts. The main lines of Thomas's position are by now clear. The relative merits of past and present, and the gloomy prospects for the future despite superficial (because merely technological) improvements are all debated and become focal concerns in later volumes.

It is curious to note how rare in these early books are unequivocally religious poems. What we do find, however (perhaps surprisingly in a poet otherwise so preoccupied with rural subjects), is an increasingly intellectual, even philosophical emphasis. As he notes in "Soil," the hedge defines/The mind's limits," and the comparison between physical and mental landscapes becomes a recurrent device hereafter. One of the features of Thomas's verse that readers gradually come to recognize is the way in which he establishes various key words and concepts at different stages in his poetic development and employs them again and again. As he notes in *Words and the Poet*, "there is probably something symptomatic in words that tend to recur in a poet's work." They come close, indeed, to fulfilling the function of leitmotivs. Like "machine," "mind" is certainly a key word in this volume; together they form the perimeters of his subject matter and express the dichotomies that generate much of his best poetry.

The Minister, which followed hard upon *An Acre of Land*, is an effective play for voices embodying the basic attitudes that Thomas had already expressed elsewhere. It is set in "The marginal land where flesh meets spirit/Only on Sundays," and we can see here the interchangeability of inner and outer landscapes with particular clarity. Furthermore, the insistence that, although the valley may be regarded as an open book, "the green tale/Told in its pages is not true" measures the extent to which Thomas's rural vision has transcended the limits of romantic Wordsworthianism. The central figure, Rev. Elias Morgan, B.A., is the minister of a dissenting chapel, but his physical and emotional situation is almost identical with Thomas's own. He is a pathetic, poignant figure, never accepted by his flock, never able to raise them from their harsh lives and often insensitive ways. An accepted truce un-

comfortably close to hypocritical acquiescence develops. In Morgan's words, "I knew and pretended I didn't/And they knew that I knew and pretended I didn't." And at the close, in sentiments that echo the earlier "A Priest to his People," Thomas under the cover of the narrator attacks

> Protestantism—the adroit castrator
> Of art; the bitter negation
> Of song and dance and the heart's innocent
> joy—
> You have botched our flesh and left us only
> the soul's
> Terrible impotence in a warm world.

As Roland Mathias has pointed out, the attack here (probably an unfair one) is not on Puritanism but on Protestantism, which makes the remark as much a reflection on Thomas's creed as on that of the Methodist minister. One detects here, and more generally just beneath the surface of Thomas's writings at this time, the evidence of a considerable inner crisis, which affects the tone of his earlier poetry and provides a starting point for the extraordinary intellectual and theological odyssey that manifests itself later.

The remaining poems in *Song at the Year's Turning*, first appearing in that volume, round off the collection and develop some earlier themes. There are more poems about Prytherch, allusions to the "bland philosophy of nature," and further confrontations between the natural world and the human mind. References to Plato, Coleridge, and Shelley emphasize Thomas's intellectual interests—and, perhaps, his intellectual loneliness. There are, too, a number of poems about God—often an aged, seemingly indifferent God—that anticipate later preoccupations.

At first sight *Poetry for Supper* (1958), following up the success of *Song at the Year's Turning* and dedicated to his publisher, Rupert Hart-Davis, and his sponsor, John Betjeman, seems to offer the same mixture as before. But the atmosphere is decidedly bleaker: Thomas is now especially concerned with the urbanization of Wales—stemming, of course, from England—and the flood of vulgarization that it has brought in its wake. Cynddylan on his tractor is here complemented by "Olwen in nylons." The other side of this particular coin is the depopulation of rural Wales (about which Thomas had written an early prose article) as the male work force is forced or cajoled into the industrialized cities. Thomas protests not merely the break in a traditional pattern of life but the acceptance of an imposed and alien English "culture" on the part of a Welsh population that has lost contact with its own roots. One of the speakers in "Border Blues," the opening poem, is placidly content with an excursion to the English pantomime at Shrewsbury ("It was 'The Babes' this year, all about nature") while another satisfies himself by whistling "tunes/From the world's dancehalls." Thomas as Jeremiah scourging his degraded contemporary countrymen is especially prominent here.

Also prominent is Thomas's increasing concern with the artistic role and problems of the poet—all part of a general turning inward. While there are more poems about Iago Prytherch, who continues to be treated sympathetically, Thomas is all the more aware of the fact that, as a poet, he is himself an intellectual among those who are conscious of no need for intellectualism. "Green Categories" begins: "You never heard of Kant, did you, Prytherch?" And the title poem, which takes the form of a dialogue between "two old poets" discussing their art over beer at an inn, ends not with any adjudication between their viewpoints (basically they represent the age-old rivalry between the respective claims of nature and artifice) but with the awareness that they are both out of place, outmoded, in a noisy environment "glib with prose." Other titles, "Temptation of a Poet," "Death of a Poet," are evidence of Thomas's discovery that his art can be its own subject, and this realization goes along with an uneasy suspicion that his previous material, with its emphasis on traditional ways of life and the values that are being lost, bound him to an excessively easy romanticism. In the first of the poems mentioned, the temptation in question is "to go back," and in the second a dying poet is imagined to have "preferred/The easier rhythms of the heart/To the mind's scansion." Despite the distanced effect ("a poet"), it is difficult not to believe that Thomas has his own poetry in mind; certainly, the direction indicated is that which his poetry was about to take.

In *Tares* (1961) the prevalent tone becomes darker still. The balance of the universe has shifted; Thomas can talk no more of "the old triumph/Of nature over the brief violence/Of man." Technology has now rendered such statements not only obsolete but untrue. He can see, even if Prytherch to whom he is speaking cannot, the "cold brain of the machine/That will destroy you and your race." While he never idealizes the harsh life that the traditional peasant was forced to live in the past, Thomas compares it unfavorably with his present lot as

> a servant hired to flog
> The life out of the slow soil
> Or come obediently as a dog
>
> To the pound's whistle.

And as the situation of the countryman has changed, so has the countryside itself. "I have seen land emptied of Godhead," he writes, implying not (it needs to be stressed) that God is dead—Thomas would have no patience with such clichés—but that he is displaced, unrecognized, denied.

While the same basic preoccupations established in the earlier volumes are here repeated, an interesting new formal development becomes noticeable. No less than ten of the thirty-six poems that compose this book may be classified as either regular or irregular sonnets. Although nowhere is its employment as conspicuous as in *Tares*, a survey of his whole canon reveals that Thomas has a particular and (in terms of the period in which he writes) an unusual interest in the form. It doubtless relates to the didactic preoccupations to which he has readily admitted on more than one occasion. As he notes in *Words and the Poet*, "there is always lurking at the back of my poetry a kind of moralistic or propagandist intention," and the sonnet form as a concise but convenient unit for the expression of a single thought appears well suited to his particular vision. Needless to say, there is no question of Thomas's slavishly imitating what has already been achieved within the sonnet convention. Occasionally, his poems follow the regular rules, but more often they are either unrhymed or half-rhymed, and in later books the lines may be basically tetrameter rather than pentameter. The division between octave and sestet, however, is generally maintained. Above all, the sense of unity of thought, of a meditation worked out comfortably and appropriately within the gentle confines of the form (Wordsworth's "scanty plot of ground"), makes these poems sonnetlike for all their superficial deviations from the strict rules.

His next three volumes, *The Bread of Truth* (1963), *Pietà* (1966), and *Not That He Brought Flowers* (1968), must be considered transitional. Although the verse is as accomplished and as eloquent as ever, *The Bread of Truth* shows little extension of range and only a limited development. For the most part, the same preoccupations recur. Wales is once again the subject for a kind of savage elegy, its green grass "not ours" because visitors are "buying us up" ("Looking at Sheep"). In "Strangers" Thomas speaks for an embittered, unfriendly native community addressing those who are intruding into their land: "We don't like your white cottage./We don't like the way you live." The old Wales seems to be passing once and for all into a now neglected history. But this is only a somewhat more sardonic version of an earlier strain. One cannot help wondering whether his determination, expressed as early as *An Acre of Land*, to "keep to the one furrow" has now become a liability rather than a virtue. Thomas's tendency to repeat himself in theme and approach (the recurring man/land analogy, for example) suggests that his distinctive style is in danger of degenerating into a forecastable mannerism. Although by contrast with *Song at the Year's Turning* these songs can be seen as starker, barer in language and thought, they also seem less impressive, less authoritative. The passionate directness of the earlier poems has given way to a mordant bitterness that, if encountered without the prior will to admire, may appear not far removed from a sour if stoical version of the stiff upper lip. Within the context of Thomas's development as a maturing poet, *The Bread of Truth* lacks—at least at first sight—the excitement of fresh growth.

Nonetheless, with the aid of hindsight it is possible to see evidence here of a significant shift in Thomas's technique that will eventually be found appropriate for the new concerns articulated in his later work. In poems such as the sonnet "This" we find all the stylistic qualities that had flowered in *Song at the Year's Turning*:

> I thought, you see, that on some still night,
> When stars were shrill over his farm,
> And he and I kept ourselves warm
> By an old fire, whose bars were bright
> With real heat, the truth might ripen
> Between us naturally as the fruit
> Of his wild hedges or as the roots,
> Swedes or mangels, he grew then.

That is the R. S. Thomas we have come to expect, and many—indeed most—of the poems here share the same accentual qualities. But a few achieve a very different effect, as the opening lines of "Becoming" illustrate:

> Not for long.
> After the dark
> The dawning.
> After the first light
> The sun.
> After the calm the wind,
> Creasing the water.

Here the spareness of diction that had been increasingly characteristic of Thomas's verse is taken to its extreme. Bedrock directness and simplicity replace verbal luxuriance and emphatic rhythms. And alongside this development we may discern the final stage of a related process. In *Song at the Year's Turning*, more than sixty percent of the poems employ rhyme. This percentage declines steadily through *Poetry for Supper* and *Tares* until in *The Bread of Truth* it is barely more than ten percent ("This" belongs to the small minority). Henceforward, rhyme in the strict sense of the word all but disappears, though he continues to employ the occasional internal or dissonantal rhyme within basically unrhymed poems, and retains an effect which Robert Duncan has called "rhymes of image" and might also be called conceptual rhyme ("out/in," "book/pages," "birds/flowers"). It is not unreasonable, then, to see *The Bread of Truth* as a pivotal volume between early and late Thomas.

Pietà also faces both ways. The opening poem, "Rhodri," is yet another critical portrait of the modern deracinated Welshman:

> He has six shirts
> For the week-end and a pocketful
> Of notes. Don't mention roots
> To Rhodri.

But "Because," which follows immediately, sounds a new note:

> The youth enters
> The brothel, and the girl enters
> The nunnery, and a bell tolls.
> Viruses invade the blood.

Moreover, the very title of *Pietà* anticipates the religious preoccupation of Thomas's later poems, even if it suggests a traditionalism that is the reverse of Thomas's spiritual attitude. Thomas has edited *The Penguin Book of Religious Verse* (1963) and *A Choice of George Herbert's Verse* (1967), and is clearly well acquainted with the meditational poetry of his predecessors, but his own religious poems face up to the realities of a secular world where faith is difficult and sanctioned conceptions of the holy and the divine no longer seem satisfactory. One of the finest poems in *Pietà* is entitled "In Church," where Thomas characteristically offers the unexpected. The poem is set not during but after a service. "Is this," Thomas asks, "where God hides/From my searching?" Thomas's God is most likely to be found in silence, solitude, and darkness. As priest, he is not a man with an impregnable and bracing faith but rather one who finds religious meaning in doubt, absence, and even betrayal. The poem ends on a note of dour splendor:

> There is no sound
> In the darkness but the sound of a man
> Breathing, testing his faith
> On emptiness, nailing his questions
> One by one to an untenanted cross.

In the last two lines we note a revival of Thomas's earlier metaphorical and adjectival gifts, but they are here subsumed into a new meditational eloquence.

The last of the transitional volumes is *Not That He Brought Flowers*. Here are more poems about Wales (though Prytherch is absent) and a few—not representing Thomas at his best—written as the result of trips to Spain and Scandinavia. And once again there is a series of often effective but at the same time troubling poems ("After the Lecture," "Kneeling") about religious observation and faith or the lack of it. "The meaning," we are told in "Kneeling," "is in the waiting," and we realize with something of a shock that Thomas has moved out of the orbit of Wordsworth and the romantics into that of Samuel Beckett. And "A Grave Unvisited" ("Søren's grave/In Copenhagen"), recalling a poem entitled simply "Kierkegaard" in *Pietà*, provides a clue to the special, brooding, daunting atmosphere of Thomas's personal Christianity.

His next book, the curiously titled *H'm* (1972), is to Thomas's later style what *Song at the Year's Turning* is to the earlier. It has a consistency of tone, style, content, and attitude that had not existed in the immediately preceding volumes. *H'm* is unified by a series of poems scattered artfully through the book that offer, as it were, alternative versions of Genesis. Half a dozen such poems, varied in approach and viewpoint—sometimes God is speaking, sometimes Adam—provide the dominant atmosphere, while others involve God, or Thomas's search for God, or present human experience within the context of a religious if often dour presentation of the universe. But the Genesis poems establish the peculiar distinction of the book. In "Once," the opening poem, Adam recalls his first coming to consciousness, his first awareness of Eve, and the manner in which (although no Fall is adumbrated within this particular version of the myth), they "went forth to meet the Machine." In "Cain" God anoints himself "In readiness for the

journey/To the doomed tree you were at work upon." And in "Soliloquy," in which God speaks to himself, a series of creations and destructions are remembered ("I have blundered/Before; the glaciers erased/My error") and we catch a fleeting glimpse, to be explored in later books, of a God who is not only totally misunderstood by his worshippers but who manifests himself through the "nature" not of romantic Wordsworthians but of twentieth-century scientists:

> Within the churches
> You built me you genuflected
> To the machine. Where will it
> Take you from the invisible
> Viruses, the personnel
> Of the darkness that do my will?

Whether the poems offer the narrative of original myth, or the somber meditations of Thomas or Thomas's God, they are unified stylistically or by a beautifully controlled language that is devoid of ornamentation, never rises above the most economical and basic statement, yet at the same time never falls into monotony. The renunciation of his earlier delight in the possibilities of language doubtless connects with his withdrawal from the materialist rat race of the twentieth century, his renunciation of human interchange (beyond his pastoral service to a small parish of simple folk forgotten by the world who understand neither his philosophy nor his anguish) in order to fulfill his lonely vigil, his personal and unimpeded quest for God. His language is as bleak as the countryside in which he lives, as gaunt as his own character, as uncompromising as the God he serves.

The main subsequent volumes, *Laboratories of the Spirit* (1975), *The Way of It* (on which he collaborated with the artist Barry Hirst, 1977), and *Frequencies* (1978), make further exploration of the material treated so consummately in *H'm*. They are not so rigorously focused as *H'm*, and there are occasional returns to the worlds of the Welshman and the countryman that seemed to have been left behind. Again we see the studied repetition of certain key words. "God" and "machine" here exist at the ends of Thomas's spectrum, and the extremes meet appropriately when reference is made in "Perhaps" (*Frequencies*) to "the machinery of God." In between, other significant words are "absence," "prayer" (and its cognates), "waiting," "darkness," "silence," and (the title of two poems, one in *Laboratories of the Spirit*, one in *Frequencies*) "emerging." The opening of the one in *Laboratories of the Spirit* provides an excellent example of the way Thomas can achieve originality while juggling his leitmotivs:

> Not as in the old days I pray,
> God. My life is not what it was.
> Yours, too, accepts the presence of
> the machine?

Moreover, the acknowledgment of change, whether for good or ill, at least relieves the burden of a deadening sameness. Although Thomas's private sentiments appear bleak ("The quality of life is deteriorating everywhere," he told Byron Rogers in an interview), his poetic self—which contains his intellectual, religious self—occasionally hints at redeeming positives. He has become increasingly fascinated with what he considers as the manifestations of God in science. As early as 1966, in "A Frame for Poetry," he had noted that science "has many branches, some of them perhaps poetic in themselves." In "Emerging" he speaks with a seemingly rejuvenated awe: "I begin to recognize/you anew, God of form and number." The "laboratory of the spirit" is the tall city of the scientific future rather than "that snake-haunted/garden" of the mythic past. And it is worth remembering that his continual searching for new ways to probe the problem of how to come to terms with God is itself positive. He differs from Hardy (whose poems about God—or It—are often brought to mind by Thomas's) in that the divine existence is never called into question; God's ways are acknowledged as inexplicable, given the state of the world, but he is never doubted. For Thomas, indeed, God is almost identifiable with "emerging."

The predominantly gray tone of his later verse is, however, regularly qualified by poems that seem, hardly affirmative perhaps, but at least not depressing. The title of one poem in *H'm* is "Via Negativa," but there are other ways possible. "The Bright Field" (*Laboratories of the Spirit*) is important because it suggests that Thomas's early Wordsworthianism, though tempered by hard experience, is never wholly renounced:

> I have seen the sun break through
> to illuminate a small field
> for a while, and gone my way
> and forgotten it. But that was the pearl
> of great price. . . .

The biblical allusion to Matthew 13:46 is used to describe a natural experience whose effect on Thomas was very like one of Wordsworth's "spots of time." Later in the poem (another unrhymed sonnet) Thomas insists that life is neither a hurrying into the future nor a retreat back into the past but "the turning/aside like Moses to the miracle/of the lit bush." The poem offers evidence of an eternal now, and thus connects with Thomas's statement quoted in the 1972 special issue of *Poetry Wales*: Eternity, he remarked, "is all around us and at any given moment we can pass into it." The simple, natural image of the sun shining upon a field reminds us that, although Thomas hardly ever celebrates natural beauty in his later poetry, it is always present, a revelation that can both satisfy and sustain.

It suggests also that the early and later phases of Thomas's poetic career may not, in fact, be radically different in emphasis. Recent commentators on Thomas have tended to underestimate the rural element in his work. Jeremy Hooker, for instance, in the course of a sensitive review of *H'm* in the same issue of *Poetry Wales*, wrote: "Of all the books so far this one offers the least excuse for encapsulating his work in the image still common in England and Wales, of the bleak nature poet taking his stand on the primal sanities of rural Wales. But perhaps that half-truth really is a straw man by now." The remark is valid enough for *H'm* itself, but the subsequent volumes qualify the qualification. In the same number, Thomas described himself as "a nature mystic" and went on to assert: "Poetry is religion, religion is poetry." Such remarks imply that his various roles as poet, priest, countryman, Welshman are all subordinate parts of a larger unity.

In *Words and the Poet*, written at a time when his earlier "nature poetry" was in the process of giving way (or blending into) his later religious meditations, Thomas offered a statement on the problem that remains crucial: "The common environment of the majority is an urban-industrial one. The political audience of a poet is one of town dwellers, who are mainly out of touch, if not of sympathy with nature. Their contact with it is modified by the machine. . . . And this is a problem which all poets must face. I don't believe for a moment the superiority of urban to country life. . . . But the fact remains that a very different kind of life is being lived by a majority of the people in this country now, and that most of the everyday objects of their world have new, often technical names. A vast amount of new knowledge is accumulating, with its accompanying vocabulary. One of the great questions facing the poet is: Can significant poetry be made with these new words and terms?" One can see how the later poems were in a sense written as a response to this same challenge. The imagery of nature is played down (not played out) because Thomas needs, like a clergyman preaching an effective sermon, to find an appropriate vocabulary for his contemporaries. God remains the god behind and within nature, but nature itself is offered as "a self-regulating machine/of blood and faeces" ("Rough," *Laboratories of the Spirit*). Yet God also writes "in invisible handwriting the instructions/the genes follow" ("At It," *Frequencies*) and is described as an unseen power "whose sphere is the cell/and the electron" ("Adjustments," *Frequencies*). The vocabulary has changed, but the basic conception of the relation of God to the things of this world has not. And Thomas continues to scatter poems within his books that illustrate the continuity. "The Moor," in *Pietà*, may be taken as a supreme instance. The moorland is "like a church" to him, but a church in which no prayers need be said. An account of another profoundly Wordsworthian experience, the poem shows an achieved unity between creature and creator, between personal and eternal, between the inner mind and the external world. Within the natural silence is revelation:

> What God was there made himself felt,
> Not listened to, in clean colours
> That brought a moistening of the eye,
> In movement of the wind over grass.

God, nature, and the enrapt poet are, for an eternal moment, one.

With the publication of *Frequencies*, it seemed as if the pattern of Thomas's poetic work were clear. But, like his God and the countryside he loves, he is full of surprises, and *Between Here and Now* (1981), while containing a section of "other poems" in which he continues searching the world, the universe, and his own mind for the God who may (or must) hide there, promises to initiate an exciting new phase. The first part, "Impressions," is made up of poems written as commentaries on a number of paintings in the Louvre, and they appear side by side with black-and-white reproductions of the paintings in question. Each poem accurately transposes the mood of a painting into words, and we can frequently hear the attitudes prominent in his earlier work. So "MONET: The Gare Saint-Lazure" begins:

> The engines
>   are ready to start

> but why travel
>   where they are aimed
> at?

And in "PISSARRO: Landscape at Chaponval" he observes:

> It would be good to live
> in this village with time
> stationary.

Many of the poems both discuss and evoke the beauty of the natural world as it is expressed within the paintings, but art becomes the prime subject for meditation: "Art is recuperation/from time" and "Art is a sacrament/in itself." These are, for Thomas, remarkably placid poems, revealing a poise and assurance that make this volume his most impressive since *H'm*. It reads as the harvest of his earlier collaborations with John Piper and Barry Hirst, but here poem and painting are fully integrated into a new artistic unity. It is also the harvest of the more positive hints and moments scattered in his later work. But in no way do these poems constitute a withdrawal. "I keep searching for meaning," he insists, and the search is renewed in his most recent volume, *Later Poems* (1983), which includes a selection from the books published since 1972 and forty-three new poems as crisp as anything he has written. His poetic debate with God and the universe continues in the same terms, and is even extended. "Our art is our meaning," he observes in "Sonata"; over the past forty years R. S. Thomas's art has persistently revealed its meaning and displayed a single-minded personal discipline unrivalled in contemporary British poetry.

References:

Sandra Anstey, ed., *Critical Writings on R. S. Thomas* (Bridgend, Mid Glamorgan: Poetry Wales Press, 1982);

Calvin Bedient, "R. S. Thomas," in his *Eight Contemporary Poets* (London: Oxford University Press, 1974), pp. 51-68;

W. J. Keith, "The Georgians and After," in his *The Poetry of Nature* (Toronto: University of Toronto Press, 1980), pp. 186-195;

James F. Knapp, "The Poetry of R. S. Thomas," *Twentieth Century Literature*, 17 (January 1971): 1-9;

Colin Meir, "The Poetry of R. S. Thomas," in *British Poetry Since 1970*, edited by Peter Jones and Michael Schmidt (Manchester: Carcanet Press, 1980), pp. 1-13;

W. Moelwyn Merchant, *R. S. Thomas* (Cardiff: University of Wales Press, 1979);

Merchant, "R. S. Thomas," *Critical Quarterly*, 2 (Winter 1960): 341-351;

Poetry Wales, special Thomas issue, 7 (Spring 1972);

Poetry Wales, special issue on Thomas's later poetry, 14 (Spring 1979);

Byron Rogers, "The Enigma of Aberdaron," *Daily Telegraph Magazine*, 7 November 1975, pp. 25-29;

H. J. Savill, "The Iago Prytherch Poems of R. S. Thomas," *Anglo-Welsh Review*, 20 (Autumn 1971): 143-154;

R. George Thomas, "The Poetry of R. S. Thomas," *Review of English Literature*, 3 (October 1962): 85-95;

Thomas, *R. S. Thomas*, with *Andrew Young*, by Leonard Clark, Writers and Their Work, no. 166 (London: Longmans, Green, 1964), pp. 27-43.

John Wain
(14 March 1925-   )

A. T. Tolley
Carleton University

See also the Wain entry in *DLB 15, British Novelists, 1930-1959.*

BOOKS: *Mixed Feelings* (Reading, Berkshire: Reading University School of Art, 1951);

Hurry on Down (London: Secker & Warburg, 1953); republished as *Born in Captivity* (New York: Knopf, 1954);

Living in the Present (London: Secker & Warburg, 1955; New York: Putnam's, 1960);

A Word Carved on a Sill (London: Routledge, 1956; New York: St. Martin's, 1956);

Preliminary Essays (London: Macmillan, 1957; New York: St. Martin's, 1957);

The Contenders (London: Macmillan, 1958; New York: St. Martin's, 1958);

A Travelling Woman (London: Macmillan, 1959; New York: St. Martin's, 1959);

Gerard Manley Hopkins: An Idiom of Desperation, British Academy Chatterton Lecture, 1959 (London: Oxford University Press, 1959; Folcroft, Pa.: Folcroft Editions, 1974);

Nuncle and Other Stories (London: Macmillan, 1960; New York: St. Martin's Press, 1961);

A Song about Major Eatherly (Iowa City: Quara Press, 1961);

Weep Before God: Poems (London: Macmillan, 1961; New York: St. Martin's, 1961);

Strike the Father Dead (London: Macmillan, 1962; New York: St. Martin's, 1962);

Sprightly Running: Part of an Autobiography (London: Macmillan, 1962; New York: St. Martin's, 1963);

Essays on Literature and Ideas (London: Macmillan, 1963; New York: St. Martin's, 1963);

The Living World of Shakespeare: A Playgoer's Guide (London: Macmillan, 1964; New York: St. Martin's Press, 1964);

Wildtrack: A Poem (London: Macmillan, 1965; New York: Viking, 1965);

The Young Visitors (London: Macmillan, 1965; New York: Viking, 1965);

Death of the Hind Legs and Other Stories (London: Macmillan, 1966; New York: Viking, 1966);

The Smaller Sky (London: Macmillan, 1967);

Arnold Bennett (New York: Columbia University Press, 1967);

Letters to Five Artists (London: Macmillan, 1969; New York: Viking, 1970);

A Winter in the Hills (London: Macmillan, 1970; New York: Viking, 1970);

The Life Guard (London: Macmillan, 1971);

The Shape of Feng (London: Covent Garden Press, 1972);

A House for the Truth: Critical Essays (London: Macmillan, 1972; New York: Viking, 1973);

Samuel Johnson (London: Macmillan, 1974; New York: Viking, 1975);

Feng (New York: Viking, 1975; London: Macmillan, 1975);

A John Wain Selection, edited by Geoffrey Halson (London: Longman, 1977);

Professing Poetry (London: Macmillan, 1977; , abridged edition, New York: Viking, 1978);

The Pardoner's Tale (London: Macmillan, 1978; New York: Viking, 1979);

King Caliban and Other Stories (London: Macmillan, 1978);

Poems: 1949-1979 (London: Macmillan, 1982);

Young Shoulders (London: Macmillan, 1982);

Mid-week Period Return: home thoughts of a native (Stratford-upon-Avon: Celandine Press, 1982).

OTHER: *Contemporary Reviews of Romantic Poetry*, edited by Wain (London: Harrap, 1953; New York: Barnes & Noble, 1953);

Interpretations: Essays on Twelve English Poems, edited by Wain (London: Routledge, 1955; New York: Hillary House, 1957);

Lives of the English Poets: A Selection, edited by Wain (London: Dent, 1975; New York: Dutton, 1975);

An Edmund Wilson Celebration, edited by Wain (Oxford: Phaidon Press, 1978);

The Seafarer, translated from the Anglo-Saxon by Wain (Warwick: Grenville Press, 1980);

Everyman's Book of English Verse, edited by Wain (London: Dent, 1981).

John Wain's first novel, *Hurry on Down* (1953), along with Kingsley Amis's *Lucky Jim* (1954), seemed in the early 1950s to present a new type of hero—educated and impoverished, dissatisfied with conventional roles, suspicious of culture and all forms of pretense—working out his destiny in the provinces. These books broke the hegemony of the "sensitive," upper-middle-class, metropolitan novel. Wain has written a large number of novels and collections of stories, among them *The Contenders* (1958), *Strike the Father Dead* (1962), *A Winter in the Hills* (1970), *The Pardoner's Tale* (1978), and *Young Shoulders* (1982). His literary essays have been brought together in several collections, and he is the author of a celebrated biography, *Samuel Johnson* (1974). He has been the recipient of the Somerset Maugham Award in 1958, the Heinemann Award in 1975, the James Tait Black Memorial Award in 1975, and the Whitbread Award for Fiction in 1983.

John Barrington Wain was born on 14 March 1925 at Stoke on Trent in Staffordshire, the son of Arnold A. Wain and Anne Wain. His father was a dentist, and Wain went to the high school in nearby Newcastle under Lyme. He early developed an interest in jazz, something he later shared with his friends Philip Larkin and Kingsley Amis. He was unfit for military service and in 1943 went directly

John Wain (© Jerry Bauer)

from school to St. John's College, Oxford. Though Wain was at St. John's, his tutor was the well-known renaissance scholar C. S. Lewis, at Magdalen College. Wain received his B.A. in English in 1946 and was Fereday Fellow at St. John's from 1946 to 1949. During this time he became a lecturer at Reading University, where he taught from 1947 to 1955, when, after the success of his first novel, he gave up teaching to devote all his time to writing. The years at Reading were the years of his first marriage (to Marianne Urmstrom), which was dissolved in 1956. His second novel, *Living in the Present* (1955), reflects the depressing effect of the breakdown of his marriage. In 1960 he married Eirian James.

Wain's first published works were poems that appeared in 1945 in the Oxford periodical *Mandrake*, of which he was earlier the founding editor. At Oxford he made the acquaintance of Kingsley Amis and Philip Larkin—the beginnings of important, lifelong friendships. (It was under the influence of Amis's example that Wain decided to try his hand at a novel in the early 1950s.)

The mid-1940s were not a propitious time for beginning poets, unless they could accept the "new

Romanticism" of the period. As Wain later wrote, introducing his contribution to D. J. Enright's *Poets of the Fifties* (1955): "Words were used imprecisely, structure was casual, logic was disregarded, and the two chief requirements, it often seemed, were a high emotional temperature and a heavy dramatisation of the poet's personality. . . ." Equally defeating to the young writer at that time were the achievements of the great modernists such as Eliot and Pound, who appeared to have preempted the major possibilities for innovation in poetry. A leader in poetic developments of this period, Wain later described the situation in his *Preliminary Essays* (1957): "After the war there was a great deal of reconstruction to be done in the arts. . . . It was rather like being confronted with a smashed-up tangle of railway lines and wondering which one to repair first. . . . The 'thirties were no use, at any rate as far as the main line was concerned, the Auden line; it was worn out even before it got smashed, and what smashed it decisively was not the war but Auden's renunciation of English nationality. . . . My own answer . . . was that the Empson track was the best one. . . ." His essay on William Empson, "Ambiguous Gifts," appeared in the last issue of *Penguin New Writing* (1950), one of the most influential periodicals of the 1940s. In 1953 Wain was asked by the BBC to take over from John Lehmann (the former editor of *New Writing* and *Penguin New Writing*) a radio program on new creative work. Under Wain's direction, *First Reading* featured the work of younger poets such as Kingsley Amis, Philip Larkin, and other "people whose view of what should be attempted was roughly the same" as Wain's. This program might be regarded as the public appearance of what came to be called The Movement, a group of poets who reacted against the vagueness and grandiosity they felt typified the poetry of the 1940s. Poems by a number of them, including Wain, were brought together in the influential anthology *New Lines* (1956), edited by Robert Conquest, who saw their poetry as submitting "to no great systems of theoretical constructs nor agglomerations of unconscious commands" but marked by a "refusal to abandon a rational structure and comprehensible language. . . ."

Wain's first book of poems, *Mixed Feelings*, published in 1951 in an edition of 120 copies by the School of Art at the University of Reading, was in many respects a prototypical Movement production, as was its successor, *A Word Carved on a Sill* (1956), into which the poems from the first book were incorporated. *A Word Carved on a Sill* includes poems of an aggressively deflationary stance such as

"Reasons for Not Writing Orthodox Nature Poetry" or "On Reading Love Poetry in the Dentist's Waiting Room." "Eighth Type of Ambiguity" makes an explicit bow to William Empson, whose *Seven Types of Ambiguity* (1930) was then his best-known and most influential critical work. Wain also uses the complex rhyming forms such as the villanelle or terza rima that Empson had employed in his work of the early 1930s. Empson, in poems such as "Missing Dates," had been the master of the sententious phrase, and Wain's "The Bad Thing" is almost a sequence of aphorisms:

> Sometimes just being alone seems the bad thing.
> Solitude can swell until it blocks the sun.
> It hurts so much, even fear, even worrying
> Over past and future, gets stifled. It has won
> You think; this is the bad thing, it is here.

Wain is affronting the expectations for poetry built up during the 1940s, and indeed affronting the whole modernist poetic, where the emphasis had been on the image, on the maximization of sensory impact, and where generalizations had been seen as the enemies of the poetic. Wain, like most of the poets whose work appeared in *New Lines*, is comfortable with a poetry of statement.

However, these poems are far from being doctrinaire literary stunts. Many stand out as simple and passionate statements on what have proved to be some of Wain's abiding themes: love, isolation, honesty, and sympathy for the deprived (as in "When It Comes," a poem about the atom bomb):

> I hope to feel some pity when the knife
> Plunges at last into the world's sick heart
> And stills its pounding and its seething strife:
>
> Mainly for those who never got a start;
> The painter with his colours in his head,
> The actor hoping for a speaking part.

The refusal to raise one's voice is more than a gesture against a certain kind of poetry: "it is a stand for honesty with one's feelings," as Wain shows in "Reasons for not Writing Orthodox Nature Poetry":

> How little beauty catches at the throat,
> Simply I love this mountain and this bay
> With love that I can never speak by rote.

Poems as seemingly artificial as "Gentleman Aged Five before the Mirror" or "Villanelle for Harpo Marx" survive as expressions of tenderness.

Weep Before God (1961) is a transitional volume. "Poem without a Main Verb" and "Apology for Understatement" continue the low-profile Empsonian manner. However, "Wise Men, All Questioning Done" clearly contains a submerged compliment to "Do not go gentle into that good night," one of the last poems by Dylan Thomas, the idol of the New Romantics of the 1940s, whose *Collected Poems* Wain had praised in a 1953 review in *Mandrake*. In 1958 and 1959, Wain was in America, first at the MacDowell Colony in New Hampshire and then in New York. This visit is commemorated in *Weep Before God* by "Brooklyn Heights" (where he lived in New York) and, above all, by "A Song About Major Eatherly," which was written slowly through a New England fall. Eatherly, the pilot who dropped the atom bomb on Nagasaki, later came to regard his pension "as a premium for murder" and took to petty theft. As Wain portrays it, the dropping of the bomb was for Eatherly a dehumanizing experience: "His orders told him he was not a man:/An instrument, fine-tempered, clear of stain." By refusing the pension "he fought to win his manhood back." Ironically, society was not concerned with Eatherly's feelings of guilt concerning the bomb, but only with his petty crimes:

> it is no outrage to our law that he wakes
> with cries of pity on his parching lips.
> We do not punish him for cries or nightmares.
> We punish him for stealing things from stores.

The poem marks a turning away from the lowered sights of Wain's earlier poetry toward the longer philosophical reach associated with modernist poetry. Its transitional nature is seen in the fact that two of its four sections are in fairly loose blank verse, while the other two are in rhyme and contain sententious, Empsonian utterances such as "Hell is a furnace, as the wise men taught." In comparing himself with Kingsley Amis at about this time, Wain wrote: "his work is based on a steadying common sense . . . mine, by comparison, is apocalyptic." This apocalyptic element begins to show itself decidedly in "A Song About Major Eatherly."

Wildtrack (1965) was a new departure for Wain—his first attempt at a long, philosophical poem that marks an acceptance of the modernist heritage of Eliot and Pound. Looking back on it, Wain wrote in a note to *Letters to Five Artists* (1969), "Every individual foreground has a racial and national background . . . a theme . . . dominant . . . in *Wildtrack*, with its inward-looking Night-self and outward-looking Day-self that together constitute the human personality." *Wildtrack* explores its themes of history and the individual, the will and the flux of time, creativity and homogeneity, through a series of images and incidents. In its opening, the snowflake is an image of the inescapable change that is the condition of existence; against it are set Henry Ford and Joseph Stalin, men of steel, who seek to impose their wills (an aspect of the "Day-self") on the living process—to "homogenise" the individual and to destroy history. Contrasted with them, in the adventures of the "Night-self," are incidents like the infant Samuel Johnson's cure of scrofula by the royal touch—examples of a benignity inherent in the human condition and to be discerned by those who accept that condition. A similar contrast is made later between the astronaut and the beggar. It is only the poet, as individual and dissenter, who can record history, as did the Russian poet Alexander Blok, called on in the opening to "Engrave the snowflake."

Wildtrack is a difficult poem, obscure in places, too explicit in others. Its mode is that of a suite of poems (or a continuous poem in a variety of metrical forms) rather than a narrative or an uninterrupted meditation. While there is some reprise of earlier imagery at its close, one feels that a more intense orchestration of imagery and tone might have brought individual sections into a clearer relationship with the poem as a whole.

Letters to Five Artists, Wain's next long poem, consists of an introductory poem and five separate epistles, to the jazz trumpeter Bill Coleman; Victor Neep, an English artist; the poet Elizabeth Jennings; Lee Lubbers, an American creator of junk sculpture; and Anthony Conran, an English poet living in Wales.

As Wain explains, the introductory poem is an "archway" to the rest (a constructional device that recalls Hart Crane's *The Bridge*, 1930), but, Wain says, "all these poems are intended to stand by themselves." However, "certain key-figures (Ovid, Villon) crop up." The loose structure is an attempt to solve one of the central problems of the modern long poem: that it should have unity, but that the unity should be discovered and in no way imposed. There is a strong concern with history—history seen as a product of individual lives and history seen as the past flowing into the future. The introductory poem which is full of images of water, liquid, flowing, contrasts Ovid with a fictional contemporary poet, "Dogrose": Ovid, exiled on the Danube, is seen as partaking of the milder Roman form of banishment known as "relegatio," which involved confinement to a particular area; while Dogrose, in the "aching gaps" of the present, partakes of "exsilium," which left the exile free to wander where he wished, but involved deprivation of citizenship and property—a condition representative of the contemporary situation.

In a 1982 letter Wain describes the way *Letters to Five Artists* operates, speaking specifically of the passages in "Music on the Water" (to Bill Coleman in Paris) in which he recalls the memorable recordings made in Paris during the 1930s by Bill Coleman with the gypsy Django Reinhardt, perhaps the greatest of all jazz guitarists: "Every individual and every society is in his/its present position because of a journey through time, and sometimes through space as well. In the Bill Coleman 'Letter' I deal with two minority peoples, the gipsies of Europe and the black American slaves, both of whom made journeys under conditions of persecution and ended up in their modern form and place. . . . Two exceptionally gifted individuals, one from each, got together in Paris . . . and made wonderful music." The image of the journey links with the images of flowing in the introductory poem.

As Wain points out, "the rhythm of these poems, while allowing of frequent departure and return, is basically the decasyllable or 'iambic pentameter.' This is the metre of English poetry when English poetry is in serious vein. . . ." Undoubtedly, the single basic meter, coupled with the repetition of the same basic epistolary form from poem to poem, gives *Letters to Five Artists* an unforced unity. However, given the letter form, a great deal of the writing is low key, and the final letter does not seem to constitute a climax or a rounding out for everything that has gone before.

Feng (1975) is a sequence of poems dealing with the Hamlet story, six of which, along with a seventh later excluded from the sequence, had appeared in 1972 as *The Shape of Feng*. Once again, there is a concern with the relation of past and present in this story of "the very early Middle Ages in Northern Europe as recorded by Saxo Grammaticus and subsequently refracted through the imagination of Shakespeare and Laforgue. . . ." As Wain explains in his introductory note, his "version is concerned with Feng [Shakespeare's Claudius], the sick and hallucinated person who seizes power and then has to live with it. Since I have lived through an age in which raving madmen have had control of great and powerful nations, the theme naturally seems to me an important one."

Horwendil (Hamlet's father) is seen as a mindless butcher among his mindless warrior

Front cover for the early poems in Wain's long sequence dealing with the Hamlet story. One of these seven poems, all completed by autumn 1971, was omitted from the final version of the sequence.

butchers, who worship power. Gerutha (Shakespeare's Gertrude) is a submissive chattel. The more intellectual and subtle Feng desires Amleth's girl (Shakespeare's Ophelia), in union with whom he sees the possibility of finding "truth somewhere among the lies." Feng's symbols are the tower (associated with isolation) and wings: "every man once in his life is the prey of the wings"; "When the wings came for me I became the murderer of my brother." Feng is encountered first feeding the deer: "Their compulsion is so graceful/and so simple, it makes our clutter of choices seem wasteful." Feng exhibits the characteristic twentieth-century longing to escape into their unhaunted world from "our abashed time-ridden existence," adding, "My prison is my life." Only through the pain of others can he "poultice the aching hole where my heart was." After he has finally assaulted Amleth's girl sexually, "the earth/rolled over on its side, and lay at peace." Retiring to the tower, he is changed to a stag and awaits Amleth's revenge.

Feng is Wain's most successful long poem to date, perhaps because the situation of the central character embodies the theme of isolation, one that Wain has always closely felt. It is central to his fable *The Smaller Sky* (1967) and is a submerged theme in *Hurry on Down*. In addition, because the poem has a story and a unifying central character, its symbols seem less willed than those of *Wildtrack*. A series of meditations by Feng, the poem accommodates, within the unity of his sensibility, the fact that, like so many modern poetic works, it is a sequence rather than a single poem.

As Wain has explained, "in my long and longish poems I have tried to build on the work of the great early modernists, notably Ezra Pound. He seems to me . . . insufferably silly in lots of ways . . . but nevertheless a man with an instinct of *how* to do it. He invented the long poem for our time. . . ." In developing the long poem as a continuation of the work of the early modernists, Wain made a break with the reaction against modernism that emerged in *New Lines* and that his friends Philip Larkin and Kingsley Amis have continued to espouse. Wain's devotion to the long poem—always full of pitfalls for the twentieth-century writer, to whom narrative seems unavailable—is at once courageous and surprising in view of his steady adherence to the realistic tradition in his novels. Whatever may be said about his attainment in his longer poems, he has not been content with the diminished ambitions that have often led to diminished poetry in Britain in the last quarter of a century.

Form has been a problem for the writer of the long poem in the twentieth century, and Wain has admitted, "I lack the power of sustaining large structures. . . ." In *Wildtrack*, although the themes of the "inward-looking Night-self and the outward-looking Day-self" and the relationship of the human personality to history bring into play some of Wain's continuing concerns, they do not seem to give rise to a related set of closely felt symbols. The exploration of his concerns through the figures of Alexander Blok, Dean Swift's "Little Woman," Rousseau, "the Beggar and the Astronaut," seems too deliberate, and the orchestration of the poem in a variety of forms (evidently intended to reflect a variety of perspectives) seems artificial. In *Letters to Five Artists*, the problem of form is in part solved by repeating the letter form, with the overall organization suggested by the introductory poem and by the juxtaposition of the poems. In *Feng*, the presence of the unifying, dramatized voice of Feng makes for a much more successful and compelling achievement.

"In recent years," Wain wrote in 1982, "I have become less interested in the very long poem, such

as I was trying to write in *Wildtrack*, and more interested in the poem of 75 to 150 lines . . . of which . . . Pound was a master in his early days." A few such poems are among the eight he included in *Professing Poetry* (1977), the Oxford lectures he delivered as Professor of Poetry, a position to which he was elected in 1973. Five of these appeared again in *Poems: 1949-1979* (1982), which includes selections from all his earlier books, except *Feng*, along with the first substantial printing of new shorter poems since *Weep Before God*: "Shorter Poems 1970-1978" and "New Poems 1978-1979" make up almost half the book.

"New Poems 1978-1979" consists of five "medium length" poems: "Visiting an Old Poet," "Thinking About Mr Person," "Enobarbus," "Poem for Kids," and a version of the Old English poem "Deor." These were followed, after the publication of *Poems 1949-1979*, by two further sequences, "Victor Neep: 1921-1979" (in the *Antigonish Review*) and the impressive and congenial "Twofold" (in the *Hudson Review*), which explores the relationship of a blind man and his dog. In these poems Wain aims at a more informal, discursive manner than that of his earlier shorter poems. "Visiting an Old Poet" invokes Walt Whitman: "Ah there, Walt! You invented this idiom,/this kind of talking and questioning in a poem," and many of his newer poems seem designed to give the feeling that the poet is engaged in finding his way rather than expressing already focused feelings. Whitman was the inventor of what might be called the "symphonic poem"— the suite of shorter poems like *Wildtrack*—and the new "medium length" poems deploy a variety of forms within the single poem. The informality is felt in the relaxed, conversational movement, particularly in the broken rhythm of the pentameter couplets that Wain frequently uses, as in these lines from "Victor Neep: 1921-1979": "I am not tempted to an elegy in sorrow./I shall see Victor when I wake tomorrow."

In Wain's recent shorter poems, there are echoes of the tighter Empsonian manner of his early poetry, and in a few brief lyrical pieces, such as "Blind Man Listening to Radio," he attains a tranquil clarity:

> Gold and silver carp
> nose to the surface
> of the flat pool. Lily stems
> trail through my fingers.
> The fish have cool, round
> invented voices.

These poems of the 1970s return frequently to one

of Wain's abiding themes, present already in *Hurry on Down*—that of the nature of the self, examined here in poems such as "To My Young Self," "My Name," "Visiting an Old Poet." "Thinking About Mr Person" is a meditation on Fernando Pessôa, the Portuguese poet who wrote "four highly differentiated bodies of poetry" under his own name and three pseudonyms; while Enobarbus, in the poem of that title, ends his meditation on Anthony "unable to call his name/or any name . . . my suchness/blown to a mist." Wain goes back to the Staffordshire of his boyhood, to which he always responds with directness and sincerity, in poems such as "Song of the Far Places"—"Before I saw any of the postcard places/I lived among Staffordshire names and faces"—and "Horses"—"your basic metaphor is the work-team:/the plodding alliance of man and horse/or man and wife. . . ." Some of these poems must be counted among the best he has written; they have an authenticity of movement and an individual voice.

Wain has said, "My medium is not the novel, or the poem, or the play, or the short story: it is the vocabulary," and he is unsympathetic to rigid distinctions between the novel, the poem, and other genres. For him, nonetheless, "poetry is not a way of saying over again things that I am already saying in prose; it is a different kind of writing, approached in a different spirit." Yet the abiding themes in his poetry also appear repeatedly in his prose: isolation, the relationship of the individual to history, the contrast of the repression by society with the liberation afforded by nature.

Wain's contribution to a particular genre must be valued in terms of his total achievement. Having begun as a teacher of literature and as a critic, he has remained committed to teaching and criticism, as he states in *Professing Poetry*. His most highly praised work is perhaps the prizewinning *Samuel Johnson*, while his edition of *Contemporary Reviews of Romantic Poetry* (1953) remains a book to which anyone interested in the poetry of the period can return with profit. *Interpretations: Essays on Twelve English Poems*, which he edited in 1955, remains a classic of its time. His novels and stories make up one of the more substantial bodies of contemporary fiction in English, despite the criticism some of them have received. His poetry stands as an important contribution to his total achievement and displays that concern with the life of literature in our day that has permeated his work. He may seem at his best in his earlier poems, where the Empsonian forms give a tightness that has sometimes eluded him in his more ambitious longer poems. Nonetheless, these longer works must stand as a powerful demonstration of his contention "that any poet who wants to work at the most effective level, to realize the power of his own imagination, and to communicate with the greatest number of people, will use the full resources of modern poetry as they have been developed, internationally, by experimentation and study." Indeed, what is most impressive about Wain's work as a poet may be summarized in his own words: "the incessant struggle to bring fresh territory within one's imaginative range, seems to me . . . the highest form of experimentation." Few contemporary British poets have been ready to take on so large and important a challenge.

Bibliography:
Dale Salwak, *John Braine and John Wain: A Reference Guide* (Boston: G. K. Hall, 1980).

Reference:
Dale Salwak, *John Wain* (Boston: Twayne, 1981).

Books for Further Reading

Abse, Dannie, and Howard Sergeant, eds. *Mavericks*. London: Editions Poetry & Poverty, 1957.

Allott, Kenneth, ed. *The Penguin Book of Contemporary Verse, 1918-60*, revised edition. Harmondsworth: Penguin, 1962.

Bedient, Calvin. *Eight Contemporary Poets*. London, New York & Toronto: Oxford University Press, 1974.

Berke, Roberta. *Bounds Out of Bounds: A Compass for Recent American and British Poetry*. New York: Oxford University Press, 1981.

Blackburn, Thomas, ed. *45 to 60: An Anthology of English Poetry 1945-60*. London: Putnam's, 1960.

Bradbury, Malcolm. *The Social Context of Modern English Literature*. Oxford: Blackwell, 1971.

Brown, Merle. *The Double Lyric: Divisiveness and Communal Creativity in Recent English Poetry*. New York: Columbia University Press, 1980.

Conquest, Robert, ed. *New Lines*. London: Macmillan/New York: St. Martin's, 1956.

Conquest, ed. *New Lines 2*. London: Macmillan, 1963; New York: Macmillan, 1963.

Davie, Donald. *Articulate Energy: An Enquiry into the Syntax of English Poetry*. London: Routledge & Kegan Paul, 1955.

Davie. *Purity of Diction in English Verse*. London: Chatto & Windus, 1952.

Davie. *These The Companions: Recollections*. Cambridge: Cambridge University Press, 1982.

Deutsch, Babette. *Poetry in Our Time*, revised and enlarged edition. Garden City: Doubleday, 1963.

Dodsworth, Martin, ed. *The Survival of Poetry*. London: Faber & Faber, 1970.

Ellmann, Richard, and Robert O'Clair, eds. *The Norton Anthology of Modern Poetry*. New York: Norton, 1973.

Engle, Paul, and Joseph Langland, eds. *Poet's Choice*. New York: Dial, 1962.

Enright, D. J. *The Apothecary's Shop: Essays on Literature*. London: Secker & Warburg, 1957.

Enright, ed. *The Oxford Book of Contemporary Verse, 1945-1980*. Oxford & Melbourne: Oxford University Press, 1980.

Enright, ed. *Poets of the 1950's*. Tokyo: Kenkyusha, 1955.

Finn, F. E. S. *Poets of Our Time*. London: Murray, 1965.

Finn. ed. *Here and Human: An Anthology of Contemporary Verse*. London: Murray, 1976.

Fraser, G. S. *Essays on Twentieth Century Poets*. Leicester: Leicester University Press, 1977.

Fraser. *The Modern Writer and His World*, second revised edition. London: Deutsch, 1964.

Fraser. *Vision and Rhetoric*. London: Faber & Faber, 1959.

Grigson, Geoffrey, ed. *Poetry of the Present: An Anthology of the Thirties and After*. London: Phoenix House, 1949.

Grubb, Frederick. *A Vision of Reality: A Study of Liberalism in Twentieth Century Verse*. London: Chatto & Windus, 1965.

Haffenden, John. *Viewpoints: Poets in Conversation*. London: Faber & Faber, 1981.

Hall, Donald, Robert Pack, and Louis Simpson, eds. *New Poets of England and America*. Cleveland & New York: Meridian, 1957.

Hall and Pack, eds. *New Poets of England and America, Second Selection*. Cleveland: Meridian, 1962.

Hamburger, Michael. *A Mug's Game—intermittent memoirs—1924-1954*. Cheadle: Carcanet Press, 1973.

Hamilton, Ian. *The Modern Poet: Essays from "The Review."* London: Macdonald, 1968.

Hamilton, ed. *A Poetry Chronicle: Essays and Reviews*. London: Faber & Faber, 1973.

Heath-Stubbs, John and David Wright, eds. *The Faber Book of Twentieth Century Verse*, second revised edition. London: Faber & Faber, 1975.

Hendry, G. F., and Henry Treece, eds. *The White Horseman: prose and verse of the new apocalypse*. London: Routledge, 1941.

Hollander, John, ed. *Poems of Our Moment*. New York: Pegasus, 1968.

Holloway, John. *The Chartered Mirror: Literary and Critical Essays*. London: Routledge & Kegan Paul, 1960.

Homberger, Eric. *The Art of the Real: Poetry in England and America Since 1939*. London: Dent/Totowa, N.J.: Rowman & Littlefield, 1977.

Jennings, Elizabeth. *Poetry To-Day, 1957-60*. London & New York: Longmans, Green, 1961.

King, P. R. *Nine Contemporary Poets: A Critical Introduction*. London: Methuen, 1979.

Larkin, Philip, ed. *The Oxford Book of Twentieth-Century English Verse*. Oxford: Clarendon Press, 1973.

Lucie-Smith, Edward, ed. *British Poetry Since 1945*. Harmondsworth: Penguin, 1970.

Maclaren-Ross, Julian. *Memoirs of the Forties*. London: Ross, 1965.

Mander, John. *The Writer and Commitment*. London: Secker & Warburg, 1961.

Maschler, Tom, ed. *Declaration*. London: MacGibbon & Kee, 1957.

Moore, Geoffrey. *Poetry To-Day*. London, New York & Toronto: Longmans, Green, 1961.

Moorish, Hilary, Peter Orr, John Press, and Jan Scott-Kilvert. *The Poet Speaks: Interviews with Contemporary Poets*. Edited by Orr. New York: Barnes & Noble, 1966.

Morrison, Blake. *The Movement: English Poetry and Fiction of the 1950's*. Oxford: Oxford University Press, 1980.

O'Connor, William Van. *The New University Wits and The End of Modernism*. Carbondale: Southern Illinois University Press, 1963.

Powell, Neil. *Carpenters of Light: Some Contemporary English Poets*. New York: Barnes & Noble, 1980.

Press, John. *A Map of Modern English Verse*. London: Oxford University Press, 1969.

Press. *Rule and Energy: Trends in British Poetry Since the Second World War*. London: Oxford University Press, 1963.

Ries, Lawrence. *Wolf Masks: Violence in Contemporary Poetry*. Port Washington, N.Y.: Kennikat Press, 1977.

Rosenthal, M. L. *The New Poets: American and British Poetry Since World War II*. New York: Oxford University Press, 1967.

Rosenthal, ed. *The New Modern Poetry: An Anthology of British and American Poetry since World War II*, revised edition. New York: Oxford University Press, 1969.

Rosenthal, ed. *100 Postwar Poems: British and American*. New York: Macmillan, 1968.

Ross, Alan. *The Forties: A Period Piece*. London: Weidenfeld & Nicolson, 1950.

Ross. *Poetry, 1945-1950*. London: Longmans, Green, 1951.

Schmidt, Michael. *A Reader's Guide to Fifty Modern British Poets*. New York: Barnes & Noble, 1979; London: Heinemann, 1979.

Schmidt, ed. *Eleven British Poets*. London: Methuen, 1980.

Sergeant, Howard, ed. *Poetry of the 1940's*. London: Longman, 1970.

Silkin, Jon, ed. *Poetry of the Committed Individual: A* Stand *Anthology*. London: Gollancz, 1973.

Skelton, Robin, ed. *Poetry of the Forties*. Harmondsworth: Penguin, 1968.

Spender, Stephen. *The Thirties and After: Poetry, Politics, People (1933-1970)*. New York: Random House, 1978.

Summerfield, Geoffrey, ed. *Worlds: Seven Modern Poets*. Harmondsworth: Penguin, 1974.

Thurley, Geoffrey. *The Ironic Harvest: English Poetry in the Twentieth Century*. London: Arnold, 1974.

Thwaite, Anthony. *Essays on Contemporary English Poetry: Hopkins to the Present Day*. Tokyo: Kenkyusha, 1957. Revised as *Contemporary English Poetry: An Introduction*. London: Heinemann, 1959.

Thwaite. *Twentieth Century English Poetry*. New York: Barnes & Noble, 1978; London: Heinemann, 1978.

Tolley, A. T. *The Poetry of the Forties*. Manchester: Manchester University Press, forthcoming 1984.

Treece, Henry. *How I See Apocalypse*. London: L. Drummond, 1946.

Wain, John. *Preliminary Essays*. London: Macmillan, 1957.

Walsh, Chad, ed. *Today's Poets: American and British Poetry Since the 1930's*, revised and enlarged edition. New York: Scribners, 1972.

Contributors

Jennifer Birkett ....*Dundee University*
William Blissett..*University of Toronto*
Neil Brennan ....*Villanova University*
Terence Brown...*Trinity College, Dublin*
Douglas Cleverdon ....*London, England*
Michael J. Collins...*Georgetown University*
William Cookson ....*London, England*
Peter Craven ....*University of Melbourne*
Thomas Emery..*DePauw University*
Joseph J. Feeney, S.J...*Saint Joseph's University*
John Ferns ....*McMaster University*
Roger Garfitt..*Hereford, England*
Dana Gioia ....*Hastings-on-Hudson, New York*
Desmond Graham ....*University of Newcastle upon Tyne*
Anthony John Harding..*University of Saskatchewan*
T. F. Healy...*University of Dundee*
Michael Heyward ....*University of Melbourne*
Daniel Hoffman ....*University of Pennsylvania*
Thomas H. Jackson ....*Bryn Mawr College*
W. J. Keith..*University of Toronto*
Stephen John Lane ....*Newcastle University*
Christopher Levenson..*Carleton University*
Douglas Loney...*University of Victoria*
Bruce K. Martin..*Drake University*
Margaret B. McDowell ....*University of Iowa*
Blake Morrison ....*London, England*
John Press...*Somerset, England*
Joseph Reino ....*Villanova University*
David S. Robb ....*Dundee University*
John Paul Russo..*University of Miami, Florida*
Paul Schlueter ....*Easton, Pennsylvania*
Peter Schmidt..*Swarthmore College*
John H. Schwarz ....*Villanova University*
Sibyl Severance ....*Pennsylvania State University, Delaware County Campus, Media*
Linda M. Shires..*Syracuse University*
Donald E. Stanford...*Louisiana State University*
Laurence Steven ....*Laurentian University*
A. T. Tolley...*Carleton University*
William B. Worthen ....*University of Texas at Austin*
Alan Young..*Cheshire, England*

Cumulative Index

Dictionary of Literary Biography, Volumes 1-27
Dictionary of Literary Biography Yearbook, 1980-1983
Dictionary of Literary Biography Documentary Series, Volumes 1-4

Cumulative Index

DLB before number: *Dictionary of Literary Biography*, Volumes 1-27
Y before number: *Dictionary of Literary Biography Yearbook*, 1980-1983
DS before number: *Dictionary of Literary Biography Documentary Series*, Volumes 1-4

A

Abbott, Jacob 1803-1879 ....DLB1

Abercrombie, Lascelles 1881-1938 ....DLB19

Abse, Dannie 1923- DLB27

Adamic, Louis 1898-1951 ....DLB9

Adams, Douglas 1952- Y83

Adams, Henry 1838-1918......................DLB12

Adams, James Truslow 1878-1949......................DLB17

Ade, George 1866-1944......................DLB11, 25

Adeler, Max (see Clark, Charles Heber)

AE 1869-1935......................DLB19

Agassiz, Jean Louis Rodolphe 1807-1873......................DLB1

Agee, James 1909-1955 ....DLB2, 26

Aiken, Conrad 1889-1973 ....DLB9

Ainsworth, William Harrison 1805-1882......................DLB21

Akins, Zoë 1886-1958 ....DLB26

Albee, Edward 1928- DLB7

Alcott, Amos Bronson 1799-1888 ....DLB1

Alcott, Louisa May 1832-1888......................DLB1

Alcott, William Andrus 1798-1859......................DLB1

Aldington, Richard 1892-1962......................DLB20

Aldis, Dorothy 1896-1966......................DLB22

Aldiss, Brian W. 1925- DLB14

Alexander, James 1691-1756......................DLB24

Algren, Nelson 1909-1981......................DLB9; Y81, 82

Alldritt, Keith 1935- DLB14

Allen, Hervey 1889-1949......................DLB9

Allen, Jay Presson 1922- DLB26

Josiah Allen's Wife (see Holly, Marietta)

Allott, Kenneth 1912-1973 ....DLB20

Allston, Washington 1779-1843 ....DLB1

Alsop, George 1636-post 1673......................DLB24

Alvarez, A. 1929- DLB14

Ames, Mary Clemmer 1831-1884 ....DLB23

Amis, Kingsley 1922- DLB15, 27

Amis, Martin 1949- DLB14

Ammons, A. R. 1926- DLB5

Anderson, Margaret 1886-1973 ....DLB4

Anderson, Maxwell 1888-1959......................DLB7

Anderson, Poul 1926- DLB8

Anderson, Robert 1917- DLB7

Anderson, Sherwood 1876-1941......................DLB4, 9; DS1

Andrews, Charles M. 1863-1943 ....DLB17

Anhalt, Edward 1914- DLB26

Anthony, Piers 1934- DLB8

Archer, William 1856-1924 ....DLB10

Arden, John 1930- DLB13

Arensberg, Ann 1937- Y82

Arnow, Harriette Simpson 1908- DLB6

Arp, Bill (see Smith, Charles Henry)

Arthur, Timothy Shay 1809-1885......................DLB3

Asch, Nathan 1902-1964 ....DLB4

Ashbery, John 1927- DLB5; Y81

Asher, Sandy 1942- Y83

Ashton, Winifred (see Dane, Clemence)

Asimov, Isaac 1920- DLB8

Atherton, Gertrude 1857-1948 ....DLB9

Auchincloss, Louis 1917- DLB2; Y80

Auden, W. H. 1907-1973 ....DLB10, 20

Austin, Mary 1868-1934 ....DLB9

Ayckbourn, Alan 1939- DLB13

B

Bacon, Delia 1811-1859......................DLB1

Bagnold, Enid 1889-1981......................DLB13

Bailey, Paul 1937- DLB14

Bailyn, Bernard 1922- DLB17

Bainbridge, Beryl 1933- DLB14

C

E

H

I

J

Cumulative Index

Y

Z